ZACHARY TAYLOR

Soldier in the White House

"OLD ROUGH AND READY" AS PRESIDENT

This rare print of a damaged and lost daguerreotype tells the story of the strain of office
on Taylor. Here we see the Twelfth President as he really was, and not as artists imagined
him to be. Reproduced by permission of Frederick Hill Meserve, of New York City.

Zachary Taylor

SOLDIER IN THE WHITE HOUSE

by *Holman Hamilton*

*Another pint thet influences the minds o'
 sober jedges
Is thet the Gin'ral hezn't gut tied hand an'
 foot with pledges;
He hezn't told ye wut he is, an' so there
 ain't no knowin'
But wut he may turn out to be the best
 there is agoin'.*

—THE BIGLOW PAPERS

ILLUSTRATED

THE BOBBS-MERRILL COMPANY, INC.

Publishers

INDIANAPOLIS   NEW YORK

First Edition

To

SUZANNE BOWERFIND HAMILTON

My Beloved Wife

CONTENTS

CONTENTS—*Continued*

ILLUSTRATIONS

CHRONOLOGY

1847 General Taylor returns in December from Mexican battlefields to his cottage at Baton Rouge, Louisiana, and his plantation in Jefferson County, Mississippi.

1848 Candidate Taylor's "First Allison Letter" is composed in Baton Rouge on April 21-22.
Taylor becomes the Whig Presidential Nominee on June 9, at a National Convention held in Philadelphia.
Nominee Taylor's "Second Allison Letter" is signed in East Pascagoula, Mississippi, on September 4.
On election day, November 7, Taylor defeats Lewis Cass and Martin Van Buren for the Presidency of the United States.

1849 Taylor's inauguration as Twelfth President takes place in Washington, D. C., on Monday, March 5.
President Taylor, in April, starts the California statehood ball rolling by sending Thomas Butler King to San Francisco.
President Taylor, in August, at Mercer, Pennsylvania, clearly opposes slavery's extension in the West.
President Taylor, in November, through George A. McCall, encourages New Mexico to apply for statehood.
In December, President Taylor's Annual Message concludes on a ringing Union note.

1850 From January to April, the pattern of the Great Debate is set by President Taylor and Senators Douglas, Foote, Clay, Benton, Houston, Berrien, Davis, Miller, Calhoun, Hamlin, Webster and Seward.
From April to July, the Great Debate continues. Texas threatens civil war over the New Mexican issue. The Nashville Convention meets. President Taylor, though acquiring another plantation and more slaves, solidifies his position in favor of freedom in the West. Supported by most Whigs in Congress and many Democrats, Taylor's Union stand is comparable to Andrew Jackson's in 1832 and Abraham Lincoln's in 1861. Taylor blocks the Compromise of 1850.
President Taylor, on July 5, proclaims the Clayton-Bulwer Treaty.
President Taylor dies on July 9, at the height of a domestic crisis. Millard Fillmore, succeeding him in the White House, favors the Compromise and assists its passage—with its fugitive-slave provision. One civil war threat recedes. Another perhaps becomes inevitable.

CHAPTER I

THE WORLD OF GENERAL TAYLOR

1

WHEN Zachary Taylor returned to the United States in December of 1847 from the blood and glory of the Mexican War, his role and his world were swiftly changing from the ones he knew before the conflict. Through his months of Army service in Texas and in Mexico, Taylor had already been translated from the obscurity of frontier outposts and the hard-earned lineal grade of colonel into acclaim as the nation's hero and a ranking major general. In the best American tradition, the man of laurels behaved with becoming modesty. Fame danced lightly on his epaulets. But fate was luring him to an eminence of which he scarcely could have dreamed, and toward which no Whig Warwick could have pointed him, in the first sixty years of his life.

Taylor had traveled a tortuous path from his boyhood in pioneer Kentucky. Yet now the youth who never went to college, the junior officer whose promotions were slow, the commandant of forts in Wisconsin and Minnesota who considered himself overlooked and bypassed, was praised and flattered and idolized. The soldier, who had won few honors in nearly four decades on active duty, became the recipient of honors galore. Medals of bronze, silver and gold—swords, scabbards, sashes, medallions—were showered on him by grateful compatriots. Popular songs were dedicated to him. Girls strewed flowers in his path. Even more than his victories, the unassuming manner of Zachary Taylor endeared him to American civilians, while enshrining him in his comrades' hearts. And, suddenly, the warrior who never voted became the masses' favorite candidate for the highest office in the land.

A triumph in the election of 1848 was eleven months in the offing when Old Rough and Ready, Old Zack, "de ole hoss," touched foot on Louisiana and Mississippi soil. The aura of Buena Vista stretched from crags and gullies of the Sierra Madres to the White House portico.

13

2

The world into which General Taylor moved, on short bowlegs and with unmilitary gait, was undergoing an alteration as amazing as that which had transfigured him. Europe teetered between crisis and crisis. While Irishmen agitated against Britain, Frenchmen chafed under Louis Philippe. Unrest infiltrated Italy, from Venice to Naples and from Milan to Palermo. Pope Pius IX would soon flee Rome, and Prince Metternich Vienna. Hungarians, led by Lajos Kossuth, prepared to strike a blow for freedom. Karl Marx was more than an interested onlooker when Bavaria's Ludwig tumbled from his throne, and Prussia's Prince Wilhelm scurried into exile.[1] Just as wishful thinkers began to project the chimera of perpetual peace, optimists' gauzy dreams were blasted—and rifles cracked at the barricades.

Meanwhile, in most of the twenty-nine states, from Maine to Missouri and from Florida to Texas, rapid expansion and mechanization shadowed forth the future's mightiest country. Especially in the North, hamlets and forests were becoming a succession of machines and farms. The American city began to emerge from infancy into gawky adolescence. Except in areas of the South and West, Thomas Jefferson's Arcadia was a vision of the past. Northern merchants and manufacturers, Northern lawyers and financiers strained to direct and dominate the economic life of a burgeoning nation. Railways extending toward the Mississippi, a network of canals and river highways, Eli Whitney's cotton gin, Cyrus McCormick's reaper and newfangled textile towns of Massachusetts bespoke a shrewd American inventiveness and the magnetism of industrial frontiers. Explorers, expansionists and exploiters sang sirens' songs of swollen borders—crying that Cuba, California[2] and Canada all should be annexed or conquered. Though the Mexican War was nearing its end, a youthful America went rampaging on.

Whither were sons of destiny trending? Old World diplomatists worried and wondered. As recently as 1844, the United States comprised less than 1,800,000 square miles. Soon it swelled to 2,400,000, and even now a treaty in the making would increase it to nearly 3,000,000. President James K. Polk himself was eager to acquire Cuba. Treasury Secretary Robert J. Walker wanted the whole of Mexico. With annexation sentiment spreading in Canada, and California under American troops, Hawaii also was examined with longing by ambitious barons of trade. John Tyler had dispatched a special emissary across the seas to distant China, and New York businessmen briskly insisted on penetrating isolationist Japan. Where would this thrust of commerce be halted? How far afield did the State Department look, with the gaze of American merchants glued to new and richer markets? "You Americans must be proud to see all Europe attempting to imitate you," a monarchic heir told George Bancroft. "The change in public opinion . . . is prodigious," Bancroft was to write Lewis Cass from London. "The world has entered on a new era, with America . . . in the lead . . . & the sovereigns know it."

Simultaneous with expansion beyond old borders was the germination of reforms at home. All the channels of the outside world were incapable of furnishing an adequate outlet for the pent-up energy of a virile people. Idealists and radicals of every tinge—economists, religionists, prohibitionists, abolitionists—convened and orated and passed resolutions, designed to speed some special millennium. Reformers sought to increase man's income, to limit the hours of his labor, to improve his working conditions, to strengthen his body, or to save his soul. Well-organized and frequently well-heeled groups—for prevention of war all over the world, for providing free homesteads in the West, for universal manhood suffrage or for extending civil rights to women— enlisted the hearts and brains of zealots, who embraced each new crusade with converts' fervor.

Communistic experiments dotted the land. Little utopias, spawned by idealists, often died but sometimes flourished. Every ism had its advocate: Fourierism, atheism, phrenology, clairvoyance, the cult of the Shakers and the cult of free love. Cheap postage, the right of petition and opposition to the flogging of American sailors were subjects of debate in Congress. On the lunatic fringe of American politics, the remnants of anti-Masonic bigotry dovetailed into anti-Catholic persecution. Immigrants from famine-stricken Ireland were assailed by the Native American party.[3] Such growths, bad and good alike, were typical of a turbulent surge in mansions of the rich and cabins of the poor. All reflected the drives of change, as evident in the New World as they were in the Old.

3

With something akin to inevitability, the antislavery phase of reform had a wider appeal than all the rest. Though other crusades were exclusively religious, economic or sociological, slavery was attacked on all these fronts and also in the political arena. Slavery, its opponents said, was morally wrong, economically unsound and sociologically indefensible. Thus ran the argument which, originally heeded by scattered idealists, now profoundly influenced congressmen and the public electing them.

Radical antislavery men, still less numerous than vocal, employed press, pulpit and lecture platform to forward their desiderata. Among friends of the slave were Philadelphia Quakers, as gentle and mild as Benjamin Lundy, yet as fearless in attacking slavery evils. Others were Southerners, like James G. Birney, who freed his blacks and moved to Michigan. There were also New England poets, like James Russell Lowell and John Greenleaf Whittier. Round, jolly lawyers like John P. Hale, genteel physicians like Gamaliel Bailey and eloquent patricians like Wendell Phillips forsook normal social environments to take up cudgels in the Negro's behalf. By odds the loudest and most dynamic was a Massachusetts printer-turned-editor. Where Bailey was urbane in combating the "slave power," William Lloyd Garrison was utterly venomous. He dipped his pen in vitriol. His manner, offensive to his enemies, often antagonized his closest friends. In the variety of their approach to Americans' love of mercy and justice, these radicals established a propaganda technique that has served as a model for generations. Never entirely agreed as to methods, some were intractable and humorless, others witty, resourceful and open to reason. And they acted as gadflies to politicians both in the South and in the North.

Garrisonian radicals, therefore, did not monopolize this cause. Nor were all officeholders of the period reluctant to acknowledge the horrors of slavery. It is true that many representatives and senators shunned the abolitionists. Also, like their Southern colleagues, Northern statesmen thought and talked in terms of the tariff, internal improvements, the banking system and foreign policy, as well as the issue of Negro slavery. But more than one Northern Democrat considered slavery an anachronism, out of place in a society quite ready to condemn lesser injustices of man to man. Northern Whigs, too, included in their number champions who made common cause with the more extreme Jacksonians. The Mexican War, which Taylor helped win despite the fact that he did not like it, had been opposed since its inception with varying degrees of consistency by Whigs on Capitol Hill and elsewhere. Now half a million miles of former Mexican territory would soon become an integral part of the American domain. What might be the fate of this vast acquisition? Was this expanse of Western land, won by the blood and treasure of both South and North, to be tilled by chattels in chains?

. On this issue, such Whigs as William H. Seward of New York, Thomas Corwin of Ohio and Abraham Lincoln of Illinois joined hands with such Democrats as David Wilmot of Pennsylvania, Preston King of New York and Hannibal Hamlin of Maine in opposing the slave states' claims. In 1847, one of these free-soilers tacked a momentous amendment onto a special appropriation bill—providing that Polk's peace negotiations would not receive needed financial backing unless slavery were prohibited in lands acquired from the enemy. This Wilmot Proviso never passed the Senate. But Representative Lincoln later declared that he voted for it in the House, in one form or another, "as good as forty times."[4] Defeated repeatedly by the South, and by conservative and middle-road Northerners, the proviso principle nevertheless dug deeply into the skein of partisan intrigue. As the presidential year of '48 approached, ideas implicit in the proviso clearly conditioned politicians' plans.

4

By no means all Northern politicians, however, or the moneybags who financed their campaigns, were aggressively antislavery. The upper economic classes were still fundamentally conservative. Rich men are traditionally opposed to radicalism, and the rich of that era were no exceptions. They lived in a land of vast resources and almost boundless opportunities—resources they had scarcely tapped, opportunities which beckoned to them.

In their iron mines and their clipper ships, their land speculations and stock subscriptions, they had interests enough to harness their imaginations without resorting to radical schemes. These lawyers, bankers, traders and investors considered reformers an alien breed. America, they felt, was sound without change. Why upset the economy, or tamper with the system, when profits flowed like freshets in the spring? Eastern manufacturers plumped for high tariffs. Westerners sought harbor subsidies. Business aims appealed to them more than disturbing notions hawked by fanatics, with a choke in the throat or a tear in the eye.

These men did not take kindly to Barnburner (or antiextension) Democrats—those who, their opponents said, resembled farmers burning their barns in order to drive out the rats. Nor did the conservatives relish being labeled "Locofocos." This term, now widely employed by Whigs as a synonym for all Democrats, originally designated anti-Tammany New Yorkers who used friction matches or "locofocos" when, at a Democratic meeting, Tammanyites turned off the gas lights. Most of the conservatives were Whigs, steadfast in adhering to Henry Clay's party. Many, however, were Hunker Democrats—their followers "hankering" or "hunkering" for jobs. Having supported James K. Polk, they were prepared to cast their ballots for Lewis Cass or James Buchanan.

Politically, Northern entrepreneurs had their counterparts in planters of the Southern states. Although fiery chieftains like Robert Barnwell Rhett, William L. Yancey and James H. Hammond were already flashing the beacon of secession across the valleys of the Lower South, the planter class on the whole remained as conservative as Northern bankers.[5] There were exceptions to prove the rule, notably in South Carolina. But, in the main, those responding affirmatively to extremists' demands for retaliation against the radical Northerners were not the big planters (of whom Taylor was one), but yeomen down the economic scale. If incendiary sparks of Northern abolitionists inflamed some of the South's best minds, calmer counsel still prevailed in circles of prestige and wealth. This applied especially to Southern Whigs, who saw the best insurance for their system in their community of interest with the "Cotton Whigs" of Boston.

In this connection it is important to tab Taylor as a planter to the manner born. It was a way of life he loved, and one with which he was long familiar. Brought up in the Kentucky countryside by a farming father who was also a slaveholder, Taylor acquired his first broad acres in the year of his marriage, 1810. A master of Negroes before he was thirty, of Louisiana land since 1823 and of Mississippi soil since 1831, he now possessed more than a hundred slaves and real estate in three Southern counties. His holdings had brought him a train of tribulations. A Kentucky title proved invalid, and a lawsuit was carried to the Court of Appeals. The disposal of part of a Kentucky farm caused complications when kinsmen died.[6] A sale of Louisiana land fell through when a would-be buyer ran short of cash. In the 1840s, the price of cotton dropped. There was bollworm and cutworm trouble, and, several years, General Taylor's plantation was flooded. Yet in 1847, Taylor was one of fewer than 1,800 planters who owned a hundred slaves. This placed him in an upper economic bracket, and led rich Southerners to look on him as one of themselves, as well as a hero.

The plantation segment of Taylor's environment, and the attitude of men identified with it, formed a striking contrast with the larger world of which he was a part. It is indeed essential to stress that Taylor's South was very different from the contemporary North. Entirely aside from their faddists and reformers, Northerners were the world's principal promoters of the steam, speed, and experimentation ushering in an industrial age. Humanity spun swiftly forward, powered by improvements on James Watt's singing kettle and George Stephenson's iron horse. In the midst of this quick transition from the stagecoach to the railroad, from an era of agriculture to one of machines, the South almost literally stood still. One invention, Eli Whitney's, at a single fateful stroke had hitched the pocketbooks of Southerners to the slavery system. Prior to widespread employment of Whitney's historic cotton gin, representative Southerners had come out for the gradual freeing of the Negro. Now slavery was too profitable to be abandoned. The institution, some Southerners insisted, was a positive blessing to the slave, giving him security unknown in the Northern factories. Such assertions as these satisfied most small farmers, as well as planters. But the North's way also had advantages, which it was not the South's luck to share.

5

The North's population was increasing almost twice as rapidly as the South's.[7] Northern income pyramided so fast that the Southland could not keep pace. If the North was nineteenth century, the South was eighteenth century. In a sense, the North could be described as mid-channel, buffeted by wave and wind, but heading toward the rocky harbors of the twentieth-century future. Meanwhile, the South—its farmers and planters pleased with the drift of their rural life—meandered up time's back bayous. Both sections' destinations were plain to a few discerning souls, as the South retreated farther and farther from the main current of what men call progress.

To many dwellers in the South this disparity was far from evident. Governmentally the South held her own in the White House, the Cabinet and the Senate. Business activity had increased in Louisville, Nashville, Savannah, Charleston, Augusta, Natchez and Mobile. On New

Orleans' teeming wharves, sight-seers might assume that here—where cotton bales were shipped and stevedores sweated in midday heat—was a city with as magic a future as any in the United States. If it was true that cotton was king, New Orleans was the crown's brightest jewel. Sixty per cent of American cotton cleared through the port with which Taylor was so familiar. And corn, wheat, sugar and livestock from the entire Mississippi Valley found their principal outlet there. To New Orleans river vessels plied. Bearded flatboatmen unloaded cargoes. Palatial packets discharged their passengers. And cabarets did a roaring business. It was still the day of the code duello. Cheats, pickpockets, pimps and whores descended on the city by battalions. The greater part of New Orleans, however, was devoted to legitimate pursuits. Commerce reigned. Factors thrived. Lawyers coined money. Religious folk worshiped. Balls and banquets, sumptuous dinners, entrancing women and gallant men made the Crescent City a social center rivaling the elegance of Paris and Vienna.[8]

All this belonged in Taylor's world, as did the mansions of the sugar planters. To the east were fashionable Gulf resorts—Pass Christian, Biloxi, Pascagoula—a region where Taylor had served in the Army a quarter century before. To the north, up the winding Mississippi, were other communities he knew so well—Baton Rouge, Natchez, Woodville, Rodney.[9] With this variegated region fellow Americans had come to associate the victor of Resaca de la Palma, Monterey and Buena Vista, pegging him not with forces of change or even with Andrew Jackson's nationalism—but with the agrarian slavocracy, so roundly condemned by Northern reformers.

Having jumped rather naturally to this assumption, they settled back to examine Taylor personally. Since the nation's birth, no public man had risen so rocketlike toward the White House.[10] And the longer his countrymen observed Rough and Ready, the more convinced many became that no other presidential possibility was more reluctant to seek the office, more deliberate in giving pledges, less thoroughly identified with Northern interests or more attached to the Southern system than this disarming professional soldier who never voted in his life.

CHAPTER II

TAYLOR AND HIS FAMILY: PEN PORTRAITS

1

IF VIRTUALLY all the contemporary writers emphasized his Southern background, the ingrained simplicity of Zachary Taylor was also stressed in their pen portraits. As husband, father, soldier, planter and idol of the multitudes, Taylor remained the modest individual he had been in Mexico. Whether leading combatants at Buena Vista, or chatting with field hands at Cypress Grove, or surrounded by friends at Baton Rouge, he was invariably true to type—one of the least ostentatious persons propelled to power in America.

Taylor's physique, talk, clothes and manners all contributed to this effect. Some of his relatives, including his father, had been tall, impressive-looking men. Taylor, however, was five feet eight—his stature more average than heroic. Muscular, big-boned, broad-shouldered, less fleshy than when he left for Texas, the General weighed approximately 170 pounds. His face, burned by Mexican suns, bordered on the color of mahogany. Taylor's most prominent feature, his brow, high and wide and somewhat slanting, stretched down to his hazel eyes from the graying hair of his full-shaped head.

The old soldier's face was less round than oval. His nose was long, with a suggestion of the Roman. His lips, neither weak nor sensual, now suggested the humorous and quizzical and again seemed firm and even obstinate. Taylor's cheeks were deeply lined. Cheekbones prominent. Chin determined. Journalists always mentioned his eyes. Expressive, now kindly, now searching, now sharp, they usually had an eaglelike look. Taylor's vision blurred when he read without his glasses, which he often misplaced when they were needed. At times his eyes appeared half closed, and he squinted more than most men.

Taylor's neck was rather thick, and as clean-shaven as his face. His chest was deep; pulmonary ailments apparently never bothered him. There is no record of a cardiac condition, despite the strains of an active career. Arms long, hands strong, legs disproportionately short, Zachary Taylor looked less commanding afoot than when astride his charger.[1]

21

2

The garb which the veteran habitually wore accentuated the impression of naturalness. Never a parade-ground dandy, in the heat of conflict he directed his regiments in nondescript civilian garments with a tatterdemalion hat on his head. His clothes were whatever came to hand. There was nothing of fuss or feathers about them. Now, in place of the brown overcoat shot up by Mexicans at Buena Vista or the dusty green one in which he was seen on the roads near Monterey, Taylor usually appeared in public in an "undress" military frock coat. This was blue. It had flat buttons. The material was shabby in places and the skirt was longer than the current mode. Instead of the gray trousers of wartime days, he felt comfortable in white ones, made of lightweight goods, often wrinkled, the bottoms tucked carelessly into long, old and flexible Army boots.

On his head, substituting for the flappy straw hat of his Corpus Christi period and the conventional oilskin cap in which artists liked to paint him, Taylor sported a fine drab beaver. This he "squelched" down on his neck at an angle of forty to fifty degrees, the back of the brim resting gently on his frayed coat collar. His entire outfit (excepting the hat) may have cost no more than his "uniform" back in 1845, when brother officers estimated its value at $7.50. It suited the character of an unaffected planter, who reminded a Hoosier volunteer of a market-bound farmer with eggs to sell. Together with his weather-beaten face, it documented an easygoing, sincere and unassuming man.

Should a stranger suspect that Zachary Taylor's appearance was other than genuine, a ten-minute dialogue would promptly dispel any such suspicion. In the most casual discussion he sometimes seemed embarrassed or shy. Then, as the conversation progressed, his hesitation fell away. Affable even with a chance acquaintance, he gradually grew more talkative about his Mexican campaign, Mississippi floods or crops or slaves, or even facets of politics. The General sometimes stuttered a bit and frequently paused for just the right word, but almost always he exuded good nature combined with conviction and common sense. Taylor enjoyed historical parallels, and some of his auditors, hearing him cite them, concluded he was well read in that field. One listener wrote that Rough and Ready had the moral courage of Andrew Jackson. And a little girl remembered years later that "Uncle Zack" was a lovable man, "good to children" and "fond of jokes."

Even more than his words and clothing, Taylor's manner revealed his nature. That he had a temper, there is no doubt; his private letters betray an animus toward Polk and other superiors. An officer who served with Taylor in Mexico never forgot how he reacted when an order from Winfield Scott foreshadowed the departure of seasoned soldiers, which led to the crisis of Buena Vista. Taylor read Scott's words without comment, prior to sitting down to supper. Then he furiously attacked his food, spreading mustard on meat and potatoes, bread and dessert, without seeming to see the victuals before him.[2] Nothing aroused his ire more than official military acts which he deemed irresponsible or vicious. And here the camera of history caught him in a moment when anger controlled his emotions.

Now that he was home on his long-deferred leave, Taylor appeared as docile as a kitten. An observer, who dined with him aboard one of the Mississippi river boats, noted that he conducted himself with the most unstudied ease. The strain of combat was now gone. And Taylor "set a fine example of modesty" in the Southwest, where "bragging is" a "besetting" sin. His manners were "frank, simple and kind." There was "not the slightest roughness in his address."

If most of these qualities were to his credit, others rounded out the Taylor portrait—making it three-dimensional instead of a solemn steel engraving. Neither a drinker nor a smoker, he continued to enjoy chewing tobacco; it is said that his aim was astonishingly accurate, whenever he shifted his quid and spat. Taylor liked to sit with his feet up on something—a desk, a box or a near-by chair. He habitually carried one arm behind him, when strolling alone or caught in a crowd. Through the years his favorite humor concerned the topic of matrimony. Happily married, a father and grandfather, he liked to josh his bachelor friends, recommending maiden ladies who might be induced to share their fortunes. He was not inclined to take himself seriously, except where principles were at stake. Taylor had been ignored too long, and had fought too hard for the laurels he gained, to imagine that he was something special—a little clay god or a mental giant. Humble and human he remained, and his virtues were simple ones.

Taylor's projection into politics was a source of delight to many, including some who esteemed him most. Among his close friends were Edward McGehee, Maunsel White and William Taylor. McGehee, who lived near Woodville, Mississippi, was one of the biggest planters in the South and possibly the state's most respected citizen. White, whom the General had known since boyhood, headed the firm that bore his name in Gravier Street, New Orleans; he was a cotton broker and banker of excellent repute throughout the country. William Taylor, Zachary's cousin, was a prominent planter near Pointe Coupée. The fact that such men were his intimates did the General's cause no harm.

There was at this time an instinctive revulsion, such as occurs periodically, against professional politicians, the wires they pull and the plots they hatch. James K. Polk, for all his intelligence and the relative success of his territorial program, typified the schemer to Whigs and independents who did not happen to agree with him. Buchanan, Clay and Daniel Webster had been before the public so long that voters were tiring of them, too, and sought a fresh face for the White House. During the war Taylor had written dozens of letters on political questions. Some were naïve. Others were graceless. But, thanks to the robustness of character which he exhibited from time to time, there was little diminution in the standing which his victories gave him before the country.[3] As his neighbors watched him go about his business at Baton Rouge and Cypress Grove, they concluded that the old-shoe fighter might be the person to fill the bill.

3

Those familiar with his family life knew that Taylor was above reproach. There is no breath of scandal here, no shady lady a step offstage. And the Peggy he loved as a young man was still his sweetheart in old age. Both he and Mrs. Taylor were well-born. If heredity counts, they were genteel. But each had absorbed Western ways and encountered pioneers' privations. Accompanying her husband to post after post from Fort Snelling to Tampa Bay, Mrs. Taylor had borne five daughters and a son and cared for them tenderly in primitive surroundings. She had seen two die as babies and lost still another of her children later. Thus life was harsh as well as rewarding, and no doubt she wept bitter tears. Now among her major interests were her grandsons and granddaughters, whom she helped their mother rear. Another source of consolation was the God to whom she prayed. The General was not a church member, but his wife adhered to the Episcopal faith. It was she who sponsored religious services at forts commanded by her husband, and Saint James parish at Baton Rouge had no more regular communicant.

Margaret Smith Taylor was of medium height. Slender, erect and with graying hair, she is described as "stately." Her manner, however, was pleasant enough—and her voice agreeable. For years her health had been below par. She now was a semi-invalid. The caricature of her, puffing smoke inhaled from a long-stemmed corncob pipe, is utterly without foundation. Nor was Mrs. Taylor crude, as she has sometimes been depicted. The second Mrs. Jefferson Davis, an aristocratic Natchez belle, liked the mother of her husband's first wife and found her "gentle" and "refined." To one of her grandsons, young Bob Wood, Mrs. Taylor seemed too strict. But Bob was a high-spirited rascal who may have needed a dressing-down, and his grandparent's tolerant, twinkling eyes behind her spectacles belied her sternness. Taylor was devoted to his wife. His words and actions proclaimed his love. After twenty-eight months of separation during and before the war, their reunion was the more poignant because of the delicate state of her health.

Mrs. Taylor had been in "a dreadful frame of mind," worrying that Zachary would be killed. She is said to have taken a vow that, if he ever returned from his battles, she would eschew all life of fashion and never go out in society again. As far as is known, she kept to this course, which did not surprise her friends at all and certainly accorded with the resolute will of the ailing woman of fifty-nine.[4] Now that the General was back, she had another source of concern. Taylor-for-President sentiment was spreading, and the White House glitter and glamour were without appeal for her. She herself stated that she prayed nightly that someone other than Zachary Taylor would succeed James K. Polk. The joys she valued were homey joys, not by-products of politics.

Husband, children, grandchildren, friends were all the company Mrs. Taylor needed. The Baton Rouge cottage, the broad Mississippi, helpful servants, her garden, her church composed the setting she preferred to any mansion in Washington.

4

At his wife's side during Taylor's absence, and with her to greet him when he came home, was his youngest daughter, Mary Elizabeth, a winsome miss of twenty-three. Lovely to look on, smart but unspoiled, Betty Taylor was the apple of her father's eye—not only because of her appealing grace, but also thanks to the filial care she lavished on her mother when he was away. Betty had written the General regularly, reporting on Mrs. Taylor's health, providing the cheer a soldier needs, discussing with him their domestic arrangements, and handling the funds for household expenses. No one who knew her had cause to doubt that she could prove equal to any occasion, social or otherwise, in a woman's sphere.

She had been given the best education money could buy for girls in that era. More consequential was the fact that Betty inherited the gift for detail, the resolution and moral resourcefulness that distinguished her father as an officer.

Somehow the weight of her responsibilities in no way detracted from Betty's charm. Her femininity was so refreshing, her nature so gay, her mood so lively, that she captivated young lieutenants who competed for her nods and glances. With sparkling eyes and rosy cheeks, glossy hair parted in the middle, she had the high cheekbones of her clan, a chin indicative of anything but weakness and a mouth that turned up at the corners in a beautifully winning smile. She was equally at home on horseback with gallants on cool afternoons, or leading the cotillion at military balls with a company commander as her partner. Despite (or perhaps because of) the competition for her hand, not until the war was over did a suitor win her heart. Betty chose wisely. Her fiancé was Brevet Lieutenant Colonel William Wallace Smith Bliss, one of the most skillful adjutants in the story of American arms.

Betty's senior by nearly nine years, Bliss was nicknamed "Perfect" by his friends. Considered a prodigy at West Point, with a gift for languages that bordered on genius, he enhanced his reputation as a master of staff work at every twist of the Mexican struggle. It was he who helped Betty's father write most of the official dispatches, which, after his victories, did so much to endear him to the American people. Taylor was as close to Bliss as to his brother or his son. And so it was that the General's cottage was something more than a candidate's home. It was the scene of a fluttering courtship, which—had "Perfect" Bliss survived to fulfill his promise in the Civil War—might be as immortal today as that of Sarah Knox Taylor Davis. With a presidential campaign in the offing, youth, beauty, brilliance and romance vied with politics for pre-eminence in the white frame building at Baton Rouge.

With his sister Betty, young Richard Taylor had sat out the greater portion of the war, a restless civilian, while his father fought. Born in 1826, Taylor's son was now twenty-one. Unlike his father, who lacked his advantages, Dick had received extensive schooling and was graduated from Yale at nineteen. Five feet eight and a half inches tall, with hazel eyes and a bronze complexion, he was a thinner man than his father, much less rugged as to build, but with his sire's oval face in a more finely etched edition.

Conversant with the classics, fluent in French, Dick Taylor was also a student of Spanish, a tireless reader, fond of history and master of a ready wit. Baton Rouge had seemed dull to him, especially with a war going on. Entirely on his own initiative and braving his father's possible displeasure, he had boarded a ship for the Rio Grande shortly after Resaca de la Palma. However, the inflammatory rheumatism from which he suffered much of the time forced him to leave within a month, and continuing sickness impelled him to search for a cure in Arkansas and Virginia. In the course of this health tour, men Dick met at White Sulphur Springs warmly admired his self-reliance and his conversation. In an early letter his father described him as being "warm and affectionate," albeit "a little hasty as to temper." In Mexico, Taylor characterized Dick as "talented" but "rather wild." It was with joy that the General now found his son in better health, and disposed to settle down and learn plantation management. "I want him to . . . have . . . supervision of the establishment" at Cypress Grove, "until he understands . . . principles of planting," Zachary Taylor wrote.[5]

The father was not disappointed. Richard rapidly took hold. Eventually he was to become a successful planter, general officer of distinction, author, politico and raconteur.[6]

5

From month to month others near and dear joined the household at Baton Rouge. The Taylors' firstborn, Ann Mackall Wood, had lived in the North during most of the war—prior to the return of her husband, Robert C. Wood, from Mexico. When Doctor Wood, an Army surgeon, was transferred to Louisiana, Ann had brought her younger children to Jackson Barracks where "the Doc" was stationed. Her oldest child, John Taylor Wood, at seventeen was a Navy midshipman with prospects his grandfather deemed "flattering." Her second son, Bob, still a harum-scarum lad, enjoyed playing the truant and delighted in pranks and boyish scrapes. Blandina, known as "Puss" or "Nina," was thirteen now and a Louisiana schoolgirl. Jefferson Davis' little goddaughter, Sarah Knox Wood, whom Zack called "Dumple," was nine years old and with her parents.

Off and on throughout this period, all the Woods visited the Taylors. On occasion, the boys' playmate was Edmund H. Taylor (later the distiller of Old Taylor whisky) who accompanied his uncle, William Taylor, from Pointe Coupée. Once, when Mrs. William Taylor was a guest in the cottage at Baton Rouge, a circus happened to come to town. John and Edmund were equally eager to follow the music and see the show.

The lads lacking cash, Edmund's Aunt Lucy told her nephew to help himself to whatever sum he needed from her purse. Mrs. Zachary Taylor, however, mildly reprimanding her cousin, insisted that fifty cents would be adequate. The decision was not one a youth should make, said she, handing her grandson a coin.

This vignette of the General's lady is remotely suggestive of her strength of character. Regardless of her husband's fame, Mrs. Taylor was more than his shadow. She commanded the respect of children and adults about her. In addition to the Woods and William Taylors, she and Zachary entertained many another relative and friend. Some were his kinsmen. Some were hers. The General's only surviving sister, Mrs. Sarah Gray, remained in Kentucky; blind for a number of years, she was not in the best of health. However, Zachary's younger brother, Joseph P. Taylor, came to Baton Rouge. So did his brother-in-law, John S. Allison. Mrs. Taylor's brother, Joseph Smith, was also an occasional guest. There was a steady flow of visitors—political acquaintances, Louisiana cronies and in-laws on both sides of the family. Where all these people slept is a matter for conjecture, since the Taylors' cottage was not commodious. Some of the men may have been bedded in apartments at the Baton Rouge Barracks. It is known that at least a few found rooms in an adjacent hotel.

Taylor's small but comfortable residence had been dilapidated when his family moved in just as the General was leaving for Texas. One story high, with only four rooms, it was built in the days of Spanish rule. The cottage was so tumble-down that Baton Rouge women wondered why Mrs. Taylor chose to live there, when trim brick quarters were available in the barracks quadrangle. Mother and daughter had lost no time in refurbishing the little house. With the aid of Negro servants, and soldiers recruited from the sick list, they made the necessary repairs. Furniture was installed, and a garden spaded. The fact that the quaint old Spanish cottage was a bit off the beaten path made it desirable to its occupants, and Taylor here spent all the time that he could spare from his planting interests.

On a bluff overlooking the Mississippi River, the cottage was "out of the way of the lawn and parade ground" of the military. Tall trees and a spacious yard surrounded it. There were flowers that could be cut, and vegetables for the Taylors' table. Mrs. Taylor had acquired a cow, and there was an abundance of milk and butter. The cottage itself was very plain. A far cry from the neo-Grecian mansions many men of wealth were then erecting, Taylor's abode resembled a houseboat drawn up on dry land after years on the river.[7] From a functional standpoint, its best feature lay in the fact that the parlor and bedrooms opened out upon old-fashioned galleries. These enclosed the dwelling on every side, with the result that even in the hottest weather there was always a cool and restful corner.

Here, in the shade of rose vines and honeysuckles, Zachary Taylor would play the host. Here, in the bosom of his family, the battlewise General could recline at ease. Now he relived his Mexican experience. Now he discussed party politics. His war horse, Old Whitey, was pastured near by. His loved ones and friends were all about him. With America well on the road to peace, the veteran's cottage was an ideal spot to revel in the leisure his valor had bought.

a week after returning from Mexico to Baton Rouge, Zachary Taylor
went to confer with Thomas Ringgold at Cypress Grove.

2

Situated in Jefferson County, near Rodney, Mississippi, Cypress Grove
—which Taylor described as his "unfortunate" plantation—contained
about 2,000 acres and fronted on America's most famous river. Here
Taylor had a modest wooden house, with a kitchen, bedrooms, a "capital" parlor and a "colonnaded verandah."

The best descriptions of the place are those of an Englishwoman and
her daughter who paid a visit to Cypress Grove during Taylor's ownership. Negro men and women were "mustered and marshaled" for the
foreigners to see. "Cotton was picked from the few plants" surviving
the "terrible" overflow, and the "interior of one of the slaves' houses
was exhibited to us." The latter was "extremely nice." Tastefully dec-
orated and excellently furnished, it was scrupulously neat and clean—
the walls covered with prints. As to the slaves, "they were well fed,
comfortably clothed, and kindly cared for." They seemed "happy and
contented." The colored men wore flannel trousers. Their wives' dresses
were made of white calico, "while almost all had woollen shawls."

Everyone was given milk to drink, and a pound of meat each day, as
much bread as was desired and an abundance of vegetables. On Sun-
days, every adult received coffee, butter and the flour needed for pastry
during the coming week. Taylor was especially insistent that the vege-
table supply be maintained. Sheep should be butchered regularly, he
wrote, and made into soup for the servants' meals. The General was
also outspokenly opposed to exacting toil from sick field hands. He
advised that they be allowed to rest until well and strong again.

In view of all this, it is hardly surprising that, when Taylor debarked
from his packet, the boat was met by some of his Negroes, who shook
hands with their master,[3] instead of groveling, and appeared delighted
to see him once more. If Lady Emmeline Stuart Wortley did not over-
draw her picture, and the deductions from Taylor's own writings are
faithful to the situation as it really was, slavery at Cypress Grove was
perhaps as idyllic as it ever became.

It was the antithesis of what would be printed on page after page of
Uncle Tom's Cabin. If all plantations had been like Cypress Grove, if
all slaveholders had shared Taylor's kindness, the Northern antislavery
forces would have had less cause for complaint. Jefferson Davis, whom

Taylor admired, has long enjoyed a reputation as one of the most humane of masters. Now Zachary Taylor himself can be portrayed in a similar role. His interest in his "hands," throughout his manhood, reveals the planter at his best. They were "servants" to him, rather than "slaves." Taylor's concern for them is documented by his letters to Ringgold, which, happily, have been preserved. It is instructive to witness Taylor, who later was to become so intent on opposing slavery's extension, exercising extreme benevolence where his own Negroes were involved. If Harriet Beecher Stowe had gone with Lady Emmeline to Cypress Grove, one wonders whether she would have written the volcanic tale that shook the world.

At Cypress Grove, Taylor had an opportunity to analyze his personal fortune, and to cast about for steps to augment it—even joining in the incorporation of the Taylor Cotton Mills at Cannelton, Indiana (which never passed the planning stage). Not long thereafter his worth in dollars was estimated by the press at between $60,000 and $80,000. Actually it was more than that. Taylor's slaves alone, if placed on the block, could have brought him $50,000. His three warehouses and small lot in Louisville, income from which was $600 a year, eventually were sold by his heirs for upward of $13,500. His bank and utility stocks in Kentucky were valued at more than $11,000. Taylor habitually kept at least $20,000 in the bank of Maunsel White & Company. His West Feliciana Parish plantation, now rented out, was worth $3,000. His annual Army pay and allowances came to $5,600, plus. All this was entirely aside from the value of Cypress Grove itself, which was assessed at $8,000 but ultimately sold for $20,000. This figure did not include farm implements, machinery, horses, mules and cattle—assessed at over $7,000. There was also the sum of $7,500, which Joseph Smith owed General Taylor, secured by a mortgage on Smith's plantation.

Depending on the amount of cash collected for Taylor in New Orleans by White or in Louisville by Allison, at various periods in the year, Taylor's estate had a round-number value of $135,000 to $140,000. This was a very substantial sum, considering the time and place. It should have led Zachary Taylor to feel he had invested well.

3

Taylor, however, was such a perfectionist where property matters were concerned that the recent history of cotton and floods was of a sort to give him pause. His fortune's foundation had been the farm presented to him by his father when he was a lieutenant of infantry. This, as a young man, he succeeded in selling at a profit of seventy-one per cent. Taylor then invested his enlarged principal in another tract of Kentucky land. The second farm, after many years (during which a tenant worked it), he sold for more than two and a half times the sum that he had paid for it.[4] Thereby, young Zachary Taylor's $3,500 had mushroomed into $16,200!

The goddess of chance, wisdom or skill had smiled on him, too, in other ventures. His income from cotton through the 1830s can only be estimated, but it must have been big. The fact that he purchased a cotton plantation at the very inception of a boom probably meant that he realized his principal over and over every six or seven years. Taylor's agent in Louisville, Allison, was on the lookout for sound buys there. Allison was partial to such securities as capital stock in the Bank of Louisville— which proved as good as gold to Taylor, who thus diversified his holdings. Taylor chronically complained of ill luck, which he said attended him in business. But, until the floods came, this stemmed in great measure from his foolish endorsement of friends' notes in the days of his inexperience—and from his commendable insistence in paying off his debts in specie, even in an era of wildcat banks.

Up to the hour he bought Cypress Grove, Taylor's investments had been remarkably successful. And so, as he studied debits and credits in December of '47, he must have been discouraged when he compared early rewards with recent disappointments. Except for a decline in the value of his land, his principal was solid as ever. But the dearth of non-military income, chiefly the result of inundations, made him consider abandoning cotton and putting his money into something else. This he later decided to do, when he bought a sugar estate near New Orleans. But, in 1847, Taylor was not yet willing to bow to Old Man River's whims.

4

Perhaps it was Taylor's past success, in the development of farm and plantation, that evoked a spirit of never-say-die with regard to Cypress Grove. "I do not despair" but "hope for better times," he had written as far back as '43. "We must take matters as they are, & not as we would wish them," the General counseled his overseer. "I must try & bear up . . . the best way I can," he told his brother on receiving bad news.

Hope springing eternal despite his reverses, Taylor went ahead with plans for Dick to take over as Cypress Grove's manager. Apparently the decision to give his son control was no reflection on Thomas Ringgold. Taylor's underlying purpose was to put his son to the test; if the youth could make a go of it here, under unfavorable circumstances, it seemed likely that he would excel as a cotton or sugar planter elsewhere. For years Taylor had been an advocate of soil conservation and crop rotation. At various stages of his life he had grown tobacco, wheat and corn—as well as cotton—and he was familiar with principles governing sugar culture. Now he raised cattle, sheep, hogs, poultry, Irish potatoes, sweet potatoes, peas and hay. He had turned his attention to a timber crop, back in the swampy part of his property. Before long, Taylor would invest in a steam sawmill and become a lumberman.

The General took infinite pains in guiding utilization of labor. The Negroes should pick the staple, he wrote, the moment that the white fluff opened. It should be handled neatly, he directed, and ginned efficiently. When the New Orleans cotton price was high, the bales must go to market promptly—as few as twenty at a time. If the market receded, however, Taylor advised that the crop be held after the first week in November; it could be ginned and baled in wet weather and sent down with a better price prospect in the spring. His manager was reminded to "take great care" to ship "first quality" cotton separately. An exception to this rule applied to rare seasons, when neither flood nor drought nor insect cut the size of Taylor's harvest. Then "you had better . . . go in for quantity" rather than let delay cause waste.

Taylor always hoped for a rich corn yield. The only time he came near chiding Ringgold, in any of the available letters, was when Cypress Grove ran out of corn and its manager bought a stopgap supply. Something close to self-sufficiency was one of the General's economic aims; money should not be squandered for things that could be raised on the plantation. "I wish to live within ourselves as much as possible," Taylor instructed. This maxim, he believed, should carry over to the handicrafts of Negro women. Ringgold was told not to "let spinning escape your vigilant eye, particularly as far as . . . Linsey is concerned, as well as anything else that you may find . . . convenient to manufacture, not forgetting the experiment of trying . . . comforts as a substitute for blankets." Taylor wrote that "whatever is saved is gained, in addition to which my motto is to save everything that is made." Yet Old Zack could be considerate, too. "Distribute . . . five hundred dollars . . . among the servants at Christmas," the manager was ordered one November. This should be done "in such a way as you think they deserve by their good conduct.''⁵ Thus the average Negro received a five-dollar Christmas gift from the master.

Taylor followed the cotton market's ups and downs, and compared notes on agriculture with other planters. This was not only in line of business, but was a source of pleasure for him. Rather than discourse on warfare or politics, he acknowledged to Jefferson Davis, "it would be much more congenial to my feelings to be sitting with you under your own vine & figtree . . . discussing the best mode of raising cotton." One of the most revealing aspects of the General's analysis of fundamentals was the emphasis he placed on timber, which for a while was his best-paying product. Wood sold for as much as three dollars a cord. And, when the cotton season was over, forty men could make thirty cords daily, which was "much more profitable" than cotton. It was at Dick's urging, and perhaps at James Thornton's, that Taylor agreed to invest in a sawmill. Thornton apparently was to have been a partner in the enterprise, the General sending him to Cincinnati with authority to contract for machinery there. When Thornton changed his mind, settling permanently in Kentucky, there was a delay in the mill's construction. But later, under Dick's supervision, the equipment he installed at Cypress Grove ran day and night in certain seasons and became the mainstay of the plantation's chief industry.

Not only cotton, timber and corn drew Zachary Taylor's attention, but he manifested an abiding interest in the levees and the ditching. If the levees were not strengthened, inundations were almost certain. The embankment along Black Creek depended on neighbors' co-operation; "if those who are interested will unite," Taylor and Ringgold "must not fail to do our part." As for the levee which "has given way" on the Mississippi, "you will have to repair it . . . as a matter of course." Taylor's front lands were worn and sandy. There the cotton opened too soon, and bad stands threw the field hands back in their picking. Heavy rains often curtailing logging operations, the importance of a floodgate on the bayou was stressed by Taylor. "But I would not sink" the frame too low, or it might carry away "everything connected with it in a great freshet."

Some of the income from the sale of wood should, wrote Taylor, be used to procure bagging and rope. Scaffolding and baskets must be in order, to secure "my cotton" when "it commenced opening." The General believed in husbanding resources, keeping his oven and cistern in repair and renewing "many buildings on the establishment," though "impossibilities ought not to be expected." The tone of Taylor's letters

5

At his Cypress Grove house, before a blazing log fire, General Taylor added up profits and losses and listened as Ringgold reported to him.

Early on December mornings he would saunter out to inspect the slave quarters. Then he would walk to the cotton fields and levees, examining truck patches on the way. Taylor lost a few acres as a result of a long-standing legal entanglement, adjudicated during a succeeding visit. He also continued to take a dim view of his planting operations, the "downward tendency" of which he did not "expect to arrest" for some time. "No one should attempt to plant, who cannot give it more of his personal attention than I am able to do," he wrote his brother. And yet he went ahead with his plans, testing fate in the shape of the Mississippi River. Taylor was to visit Cypress Grove four times in the course of thirteen months, spending a total of nine weeks there in December, March, June and January.

Here he had a hideout where politicians could not bother him. Here he could relax while destiny worked. On his piazza, Taylor could see the lights of river queens shimmering in the dusk. On those occasions when pilots were hailed to pick up a passenger or take on a cargo, Taylor would watch the side-wheeler's approach—while his servants fed "an immense fire in a curious apparatus, which resembled a huge saucepan stuck on the top of a magnified pitchfork." The Negroes energetically waved this to and fro, "making a picturesque red glare, vividly reflected on the river." Soon a "similar fiery saucepan was elevated on the signalled ship." And Taylor would see the prow of the vessel slowly turn to shore. When Old Rough and Ready himself was leaving, the planter-hero would hurry to the river bank—there to board the packet for Baton Rouge. Or, staying behind perhaps, he would see a friend off and wave a good-by—possibly exchanging a sentence or two with the skipper, whom Taylor was likely to know.

The routine was simple in rural Mississippi. Taylor often said that he preferred his planting duties to the Presidency, and there is no reason to suppose that he was insincere in disavowing ambition. More than nine years earlier Taylor had exclaimed: "I can assure you that my days, or dreams, of ambition, if they ever existed, are passed."[6] Now it is illuminating to trace his steps from planting and soldiering into politics.

CHAPTER IV

Political Overtones

1

GENERAL TAYLOR was well before the people as a presidential candidate many months prior to his landing at New Orleans. He had been at Matamoros, in Northern Mexico, when the presidential bee first buzzed about him. Almost overnight his Texas battles catapulted him into the national limelight. The memory of George Washington and Andrew Jackson was still fresh and vivid in American minds, and the nation knew what a military background had done for William Henry Harrison's candidacy. Resolutions were passed at scores of gatherings, in every corner of the United States, lauding the little-known General who had driven the Mexicans beyond the Rio Grande. Many of these meetings were nonpolitical, and were intended as a compliment to the commander and his troops. Others were distinctly partisan in tone, and local Whigs, Democrats or Native Americans sometimes went so far as to nominate him formally two years in advance of the election. Minor politicians of the wards and precincts were quick to capitalize on the victor's popularity, and not a few prominent statesmen of the land joined in the swelling chorus of prediction that here was a leader who might succeed Polk.

Taylor's admirers in 1846 and 1847 were an odd assortment of political allies. Whigs predominated on his band wagon, but almost every party was represented. There were Northern Whigs like Abraham Lincoln, Southern Democrats like Jefferson Davis, Southern Whigs like Alexander H. Stephens, Northern Democrats like Simon Cameron and Native Americans like Lewis C. Levin. There were Proviso Democrats and anti-Proviso Democrats, Polk Democrats and anti-Polk Democrats, old Clay Whigs like John J. Crittenden and anti-Clay Whigs like Thurlow Weed. Spoils-hungry Whigs, looking for a winner; dissident Democrats, on the outs with Polk; Calhounites, anxious for a Southerner in the White House—all eyed Zachary Taylor with interest.

Taylor corresponded with Senator Crittenden, whose son was Taylor's cousin and one of his aides. He communicated directly with others in politics and indirectly with Thurlow Weed. His most intimate remarks

were usually reserved for his son-in-law, Dr. Wood. Wood sent political gleanings to the General—as did his brother, Colonel Taylor; his
son-in-law, Colonel Davis; congressmen, neighbors and friends. As June
of 1846 stretched into July and July into August, Taylor was being
bombarded daily by letters from supporters of every stripe. Some of
these missives he did not answer. Others called for polite replies. But
the General, graciously returning thanks for the praise showered on his
achievements, was initially careful not to be enmeshed in the web of a
presidential candidacy.

2

Two of Taylor's earliest well-wishers were J. Trumbull Van Alen and
George Folsom of New York City. His reaction to their pleas to endorse political movements in his favor was couched in a courteous negative. To the former he wrote in July: "It becomes me frankly to assure
you that for the Presidency I have no aspirations. . . . Such a gift from
the hands of the people is eminently the ambition of the best *statesmen*
in the land." In August he informed Folsom: "The government has
assigned to me an arduous and responsible duty, in the prosecution of
the existing war; in conducting it with honor to the country, lie all my
real aspirations." So spoke the soldier, and from answers like these his
friends obtained not the slightest encouragement. Other letters were in
the same vein. William E. Russell, an Ohio editor, had written him
shortly after Resaca de la Palma, urging him to run in '48. For the
Executive Mansion, Taylor told Russell, he had no yearning. "Even if
the subject which you have . . . opened to me were acceptable at any
time, I have not the leisure to attend to it now. The vigorous prosecution of the War . . . demands every moment of my present time, and
it is my great desire to bring it to a speedy and honorable termination."
He also explained to Nathaniel Young of Delaware that he did not believe in military chieftains' elevation to civil eminence. "We must have
a statesman," Taylor insisted.

That the General's abnegation was no pose is borne out in his writings
to his family. As early as June 21, Old Rough and Ready informed
Wood that "I want nothing more than to see this campaign finished &
the war brought to a speedy and honorable close, & then to be permitted
to be quiet the balance of my days." On June 30, he repeated to his
son-in-law: "I shall not interfere with the election . . . in any way or
shape, nor shall I ever be a candidate for the presidency." On July 25

he stated categorically: "I would not be a candidate for the presidency if certain of reaching it."

Writing at Camargo the first of September, Taylor gave Crittenden the same assurance. "I have no political asperations," he advised the Kentuckian. "My . . . thoughts . . . are now occupied in bringing this war to a speedy and honorable close; let this be accomplished & I will be perfectly satisfied whether in a cottage or palace." Taylor had no cause to hide his true sentiments from Crittenden or Wood, who considered his remarks confidential. The fact that he said the same things to them and to individuals he had never met attests to the genuineness of his stand. Taylor was no coy near-candidate during the greater part of 1846. It is only after the Battle of Monterey that one detects a change in his position.

The first indication that Taylor was weakening is found in a private letter dated November 10, 1846, in which he rejoices at Whig control of the House of Representatives, and again discusses the presidential question. Now his language is somewhat less clear, but suggests a new direction in his thinking: "Even admitting I aspired to that high office . . . , which I have not the most distant intention of doing, this is no time for agitating that question, *it will be time enough to do so in 1848.*" "I will not say I would not serve," Taylor wrote, "if the good people were imprudent enough as to elect me." Still, "I would much prefer . . . to pass the few days or years which may be allotted me in quietness if not in retirement." Though not an active candidate, he was now receptive. He left the door open to a draft.

3

Meanwhile, the Taylor presidential picture took on a definitely Whiggish hue. Since the General had never voted,[1] there were those who considered him a Democrat and even an Administration stalking-horse, prior to November of '46. In that month, however, Taylor reacted violently to a reprimand meted out to him by Secretary of War William L. Marcy, following the capitulation of Monterey. In a private letter to Edmund P. Gaines, Old Rough and Ready expressed indignation at Marcy's attitude. He defended the liberal terms he had given the Mexicans at Monterey, on the ground that his column lacked supplies and reinforcements, which could be brought up during the armistice. Going further, he bitterly complained that he was being blamed for deficiencies of Quartermaster General Thomas S. Jesup. The letter was not intended

for publication, Taylor asking the recipient to "commit it to the flames."
But General Gaines, who had a bone to pick with the Administration
on his own account, inserted it in the New York *Morning Express*. Seiz-
ing the opportunity to discredit Taylor, Marcy characterized the communication as "mischievous" and "disgraceful," and accused him of
violating Army regulations in criticizing his superiors at Washington.

Taylor's reply was a masterpiece of rebuttal. He had written "only
for private perusal," and Gaines was "an old military friend." The
letter "was published without my knowledge and contrary to my wishes."
However:

I see nothing in it which, under the same circumstances, I would not
write again. . . . As to my . . . views in regard to the general policy to
be pursued toward Mexico, I perceive from the public journals that they
are shared by many distinguished statesmen. . . . It has given me pain
to be brought into the position in which I now find myself in regard to
the Department of War and the Government. It has not been of my
own seeking. To the extent of my ability, and the means placed at my
disposal, I have sought faithfully to serve the country by carrying out
the wishes and instructions of the Executive. But . . . the confidence of
the Department . . . has been gradually withdrawn, and my consideration and usefulness correspondingly diminished. . . . I ask no favor, and
I shrink from no responsibility. . . . I shall continue to devote all my
energies to the public good, looking for my reward to the consciousness
of pure motives and to the final verdict of impartial history.

This answer was a boomerang to Marcy, who had printed his reprimand in Democratic papers, and announced his intention of making public the entire correspondence. Soon Taylor was confiding his disgust to
his brother: "I regret the Secretary of War has given up the publication
of my correspondence. . . . Let them go through with it, & give the whole
to the country . . . be the consequences what they may." The General
had predicted that, when Marcy "gets my reply to his abusive . . . letter,
he will regret the course he has pursued." This, apparently, was what
occurred. Nothing further was heard of the episode from the Democratic
side of the fence.

4

Although Taylor's Monterey victory was widely celebrated in the
United States, his political prestige did not reach its apex until after
Buena Vista. "All parts and parties" called Taylor away "from the field

of battle to take upon himself the chief magistracy," Philip Hone recorded in his diary. "Webster and Clay, Scott and McLean, Calhoun
and Polk, are shoved aside to make way for the hero." Even the Quakers
wanted the warrior. "Gentlefolk in white kid gloves say, 'he must posi-
tively be the man,' fair ladies purse up their ruby lips and make his
support a passport to their favor, and the gentry with red flannel shirts
shout 'Rough and Ready' at the top of their voices." In New York, May
7 was a day of rejoicing. There was a grand military review. Hundred-
gun salvos boomed in celebration. Every ship in the harbor paraded its
flags. "In the evening occurred an illumination. . . . Public buildings,
hotels, and clubhouses were lighted up, and transparencies exhibited, in
which Scott and Taylor . . . were blazoned forth by 'inch of candle.' "

The year 1847 wore on. As spring advanced into summer and summer into fall, Taylor's popularity—which soared in March and April—
slowly slid down from its Buena Vista peak. This descent was due to
the ascending prominence of Winfield Scott; to certain inept remarks
vouchsafed by Taylor to ink and paper and to the fact that White House
rivals naturally combine against the man in first place. So gradual was
this trend that it would have been all but imperceptible to any save an
alert observer. Taylor was aware of what was going on, and three of
his letters to Wood trace his impressions. "Was the election to come
off this fall . . . ," he wrote in May, "I make no doubt . . . I would be
elected." "I would be elected by an overwhelming majority . . . tomorrow or even next Nov[embe]r," he declared in July, "but things may
greatly change." In October he surmised: It "may be" that "the excitement in my favor . . . is on the decline." This did not perturb him, for,
he said, "I do not care a fig about the office."

For a man who cared not a fig, Taylor showed an amazing proclivity
for political correspondence. Though his private letters were filled with
spleen against Marcy and others, nearly all the public mail he signed
was exceedingly circumspect.[2] The bulk of these letters to committees
and individuals followed a sure-fire formula. "My uniform reply is that
I have no wish for the office, that I have no time to attend to political
matters . . . ; but if the good people thought proper to elect me, I
would do all in my power to meet their wishes." If resolutions were
enclosed, Taylor expressed thanks. If nominations were offered, Taylor
accepted. He did not distinguish between Whigs and Democrats, or
between independents and Native Americans. Appreciating as he did
the intrinsic Whig weaknesses, the General's tactics were of such a
nature as to broaden the base of his popular support. Meanwhile, if

pressed, Old Zack avowed himself a Whig or a "democrat of the Jeffersonian school," and said he would have voted for Henry Clay, if he had voted at all in 1844. With scarcely an exception, he refrained from making pledges. Still, on occasion, his guard was down. On May 15, Taylor assured Crittenden that he would be exceedingly cautious. Yet, on May 18, he penned a letter to the Cincinnati *Morning Signal,* which exposed him to Southern attacks.

James W. Taylor, the *Signal's* editor and no relation to Rough and Ready, was a Democrat of the free-soil school whose fortunes were joined to Martin Van Buren's. Jim Taylor was young, his paper lively. To attract attention and boost his sales, he submitted an editorial to Old Zack, and asked him to comment at length on it. Four fifths of the General's answer was pleasantly evasive. But in it was a phrase indicating endorsement of the youthful journalist's views. Had Jim Taylor's article been innocuous or vague, nothing would have been thought of the matter. But the editorial in question happened to urge projection of the Ordinance of 1787, to keep slavery out of Southwestern lands. This was only one of several hot topics which the General embraced when he approved it. Did General Taylor design this as a bid for independent voters in the antislavery North? Or, by a thoughtless slash of the pen, had he alienated Southern Whigs? Taylor's stock fell because of the letter, which some of his friends charged was a forgery. He himself termed it "a seven day wonder," and glossed over the seriousness of his act. The Gaines correspondence had ended with a plume in Taylor's hat. But the *Signal* letter had no brighter side in the South; some loyal friends of its author could hardly comprehend it.

5

Other letters should never have been written. In one of these, which the General addressed to Edward Delony of Louisiana, he refused to reply to Delony's queries on the nation's banking and tariff needs. This, in itself, was not reprehensible in a soldier on active duty abroad, but Taylor's choice of words was poor. "I am *not prepared* to answer them," he admitted, referring to Delony's questions. Thus the candidate for Henry Clay's scepter airily disposed of Henry Clay's issues, and in the same breath drew the public's attention to his own presumed ignorance of political matters. Still another letter of interrogation, sent Taylor by Tennessee Democrats, failed to pin him down as to Democratic dogma— and he remained evasive, notwithstanding the pressure.

Critics have made much of Taylor's blunders, implying that his can-didacy would have been more robust had he taken an orthodox Whig position. Nothing is farther from the truth. Taylor's mistakes, almost exclusively, were mistakes in language and not in policy. The most glaring examples are contained in the *Signal* and Delony letters, errors which practical politicians probably would never have committed. But Taylor had something the politicos lacked. Consciously or unconsciously he developed an over-all strategy superior to Henry Clay's and other Whigs'. From November 1846 to November 1848, Taylor's appeal was primarily made neither to disciplined Clay Whigs nor to standpat Ad-ministration Democrats. Most of the former would give him their bal-lots against any Democrat who might oppose him; the latter would *never* vote for him, regardless of his rival's identity. Taylor's reluctance to take a stand, to debate the issues or to bind himself to pledges, was the essence of the tactics he employed to woo lukewarm Whigs, border-line Democrats, Native Americans, professional Southerners and the in-dependents who decide elections. "I am gratified I took the position I did, which was not to be the exclusive candidate of any party," the Gen-eral wrote Wood before leaving Mexico. If "I am elected at all, it will be by a union of a portion of Whigs, Democrats & native votes."

That this was logical is almost self-evident; master politicians, before Taylor and since, have followed a nearly identical pattern. The best proof of its soundness, in the General's case, is that his stature in the eyes of the public did not shrink farther than it did when on bad days he spelled out his careless phrases. Taylor's position was still a strong one. He remained a hero to the people. As Seward observed to Weed, letters like Taylor's would ruin any other candidate. Their effect was slight on Zachary Taylor. Though he did not stay on the pinnacle of adoration built up in the weeks following Buena Vista, he towered above rival Whig aspirants, notwithstanding slips of the quill.

6

That Taylor was not so naïf as some of his enemies preferred to think is shown in his private correspondence. To Davis he made it clear that he welcomed Democratic support, but, when Davis advised that Whigs were "haling off from" him and that he ought to court Democratic lead-ers, the General wrote Wood: "I think he is mistaken" though "I know he is my . . . devoted friend." Taylor promised Crittenden to appoint a

Whig Cabinet, if and when he should be elected. At the same time he launched an ingenious appeal to Crittenden's self-esteem by prodding the Senator to run in his place. Both to Crittenden and to Joseph Taylor, Old Zack praised old Henry Clay; these tributes, however, were modified by reminders of Clay's unavailability. Taylor soft-pedaled his hatred of Scott in his letters to Crittenden, who admired Scott, and, writing to Joseph, he rarely neglected to express admiration for Judge John Mc-Lean, whose daughter was Taylor's brother's wife. Thus the General kept the home fires burning, and the fences in good repair.

What General Taylor really thought about measures and men in 1847 was revealed to his closest advisers. The United States Bank "is dead," Taylor wrote, "& will not be revived in my time." The tariff "will be increased" but "only for revenue."[3] "Nor will there be" surplus funds from the "sales of public lands." Internal improvements "will go on in spite of presidential vetoes, & the Wilmot proviso, which was brought into congress to array the South" against the North, "ought to be left to congress." The President "has nothing to do with making laws"; he must merely "approve or veto them." Thus, Taylor to Wood. But to Davis he added: "No man of ordinary capacity can believe" that, if the whole or any part of Mexico were annexed, Congress "will ever permit a state made from it to enter our Union with the features of slavery connected with it." Again: "So far as slavery is concerned, we of the south must throw ourselves on the constitution & defend our rights under it to the last, & when arguments will no longer suffice, we will appeal to the sword, if necessary." Taylor would "be the last to yield one inch." And yet: "I will not make myself unhappy at what I cannot prevent; nor give up the Constitution or abandon it because a rent has been made in it, but will stick by & repair it, & nurse it as long as it will hang together."

Relying on the friendship and sagacity of Davis, Taylor granted in August that the *Signal* letter "may not have been worded as carefully as it might have been," but "how the people of the South" could infer "that I was unfriendly to . . . Southern interests is hard to see." Taylor's "feelings and associations, independent of pecuniary considerations, should allay any apprehension. . . . I look on the question of slavery as the [most] important one . . . since the organization of the government." The subject "will no longer admit of . . . calm discussion . . . in the pulpit or Congress, in the newspapers or . . . primary assemblies." The moment Northern radicals "go beyond that point where resistence becomes right and proper, let the South act promptly, boldly and decisively;

with arms in their hands if necessary, as the Union in that case will be blown to atoms, or will be no longer worth preserving."

Taylor thus dismissed at one swoop four Whig issues of past campaigns: Bank, tariff, internal improvements and the use of income from the public lands. He expressed his determination to uphold the South's constitutional right to maintain and protect its slavery. But he also implied a fervent hope for conciliation, even in the face of his accurate prediction that no slave states would be carved out of the territory taken from Mexico. This is a point which historians have a tendency to overlook, so interested have they been in Taylor's threat to "appeal to the sword." Taylor's strong words, plucked from their context, have occasionally been quoted in an effort to prove that the man who uttered them was a proextension zealot, his actions in the White House violating his earlier views. As a matter of fact, Zachary Taylor *was* proslavery then *and* later—insofar as slavery appertained to the region where it already existed. He was against abolition *and* slavery extension.

In his August letter, both fists flying, Taylor did not hesitate to attack the "intemperate zeal" of "fanatics" both in the South and in the North. "Let justice be done to and in every part of the country," he insisted, "North, East, South and West." To Wood he wrote: "I hope some compromise will be entered into between the two parties[,] slavery & anti slavery[,] which will have the effect of allaying violent passions on both sides . . . [and perpetuate] instead of wrecking . . . the Union." Again: "I observe your friend . . . alludes to my being from a slave state as a principal bar to my reaching the presidency; I would not do so if I could by advocating either the propriety of slavery, or abolition; let this vexed question remain where the constitution placed it." Surely, these were not the words of a firebrand or a fire-eater.

The correspondence with Davis included one final feature which rounds out Taylor's confidential platform. This involved the General's concept of the checks and balances of the Constitution, and, especially, his opposition to unwarranted use of the veto power. "No president should hesitate . . . to veto any law . . . which conflicted with the provisions of the constitution," he wrote, "but on matters of expediency great forebearance should be used and only after the most mature consideration" ought the power to be invoked. Taylor assailed centralization of authority in the hands of the President: "We are considering the office of chief magistrate . . . of too much importance, instead of its being what it was intended to be, a co-ordinate branch of the government. It is rapidly swallowing the other two." Let "the three great

POLITICAL GAME OF BRAG, SHOW OF HANDS

Brag was a popular card game of Taylor's time, and the predecessor of poker. In the cartoon, Taylor (fourth from left) has three aces or "bullets," and is therefore the winner. The other men, left to right, are John C. Calhoun, Lewis Cass, Henry Clay, James Buchanan and James K. Polk. From the Library of Congress Collection.

departments revolve within their proper circle and all will go right."
Regarding this issue, if not those of the Bank, the tariff and internal
improvements, Taylor planted his feet squarely on traditionally Whig
soil. "Executive tyranny!" was a Whig rallying cry that harked back to
the reign of Jackson, and Polk's vault into war with Mexico made it a
timely talking point.

"It is this party spirit," said the no-party candidate, "which has the
effect of strengthening the . . . president in such a way if he is not
looked to . . . [to] legislate for the country, he will be . . . the source
from which all honors are to flow, the hand which is to confer them."
How Davis the Democrat reacted to such talk, the biographers do not
record. But Taylor thought well enough of the criticism to bring it out
into the open later in the preconvention campaign.

7

Taylor's acid comments on prominent Democrats and Whigs are even
more readable than his strictures on issues. When he mentions Marcy,
Scott or Jesup, Lewis Cass or Thomas Ritchie, one can visualize Taylor's
flashing eye, and his deep resentment even as his stubby pen point bit
into the paper.

Of Democrats in executive power, only President Polk himself, Secretary of State Buchanan and Secretary of the Navy John Y. Mason were
spared the rolling thunder of Taylor's stormy adjectives. Mason he
considered the best of the Cabinet. Buchanan he held in fairly high
regard.[4] Polk, of course, by virtue of his office, was the titular head of
the armed forces, and, even in his angriest moments when he castigated
the entire Administration and accused the "powers that be" of intriguing
to weaken him before the enemy, the General was careful to bend over
backward so as not to criticize his commander in chief.[5] Nevertheless,
on one occasion, when Polk was reported dead, Taylor exposed his innermost feelings to the trustworthy Dr. Wood. "While I regret to hear
of the death of any one," he wrote, "I would as soon have heard of his
death if true, as that of any other individual." As for Marcy, it was
Taylor's opinion that he "disgraced" his department. Taylor had "not
the slightest respect" for "the veracity of the War Minister," and believed Marcy "would not hesitate to state the grossest falsehood" or
commit any "act equally criminal."

Scott's treatment of Taylor, before Buena Vista, was "unmilitary &
outrageous." He was guilty of "the grossest flattery while . . . doing all

in his power to cut my throat." Jesup, according to Taylor, was nothing more or less than "demented." If Scott charged Gaines "with being crazy," the latter could "with great propriety return the compliment." Polk's law partner, Gideon J. Pillow, was put down as "that contemptable fellow"; Senator Cass as "one of the most unprincipled demagogues in our country," and Thomas Ritchie, the Administration's Washington editor, as a "rabid" flunky who trafficked in "vituperation" and "slander" and "has assailed me without regard to truth." Cass was one of Polk's "tools." Jesup "has been a great courtier & time server his whole life," and "Cass and Jesup are pretty much on a par. . . . One will make the most glaring misstatements, & the other will" back him up. When Thomas Hart Benton had a falling out with Polk, Taylor sat back delighted in the expectation that the fur would fly. "He has my full permission to annihilate Marcy, Walker[,] Cass & the whole pack, himself among the number," was Rough and Ready's gleeful remark. Benton "could not render the State a more acceptable service," he added. Zachary Taylor's Whig sympathies were never more apparent than when he exclaimed to Wood: "The 'lord deliver me' from all locofocoes may I ever pray!"

Democrats, however, had no monopoly on the blistering barbs of the outraged General. One Whig, in particular, was not immune to the wrath of the man who was convinced that his troops had been placed in jeopardy by the low connivings of the Administration and its willing accomplice, Winfield Scott. Taylor's estimate of Scott had been relatively high when the war began. To Wood he wrote on at least three occasions—June 3, 12 and 21, 1846—that he wished Scott might come to Mexico and supersede him on the Rio Grande. In the June 12 letter Taylor also stated: "I consider this command properly his, & I have no wish to prevent his exercising it, but much rather he would do so than otherwis[e]." Later in the summer of 1846, when Old Zack was being bombarded with pledges of support for the White House race, he expressed the hope that Scott "will be selected as the Whig candidate for the next presidential term." Scott and Taylor had been acquainted for years and were cordial and mutually respectful. Yet, almost overnight, Zachary Taylor reversed his attitude toward the general in chief. Halfway between his victories at Monterey and Buena Vista, Taylor had been "stripped" of his veteran troops in a manner he considered underhanded. For this he blamed "Scott, Marcy & Co." who were "more anxious to break me down, than they have been to break down . . . the Mexicans."

Straightway Scott was singled out for even more searing epithets than

the scorchers Taylor fired at Marcy. Scott had made "untrue" remarks.
"His duplicity . . . has been rarely equalled." He would "stoop to any
thing . . . low & contemptable." He "played me false" with his "sugared
letter," but what more could a man expect of a "complete sycophant" of
the Administration? "Scott will be used by certain designing politicians
who are wolves in sheeps clothing," Taylor wrote. Scott "sold himself
to Marcy for the command in Mexico." He had bartered "body & soul."
"I look on him as h[e]artless & insincere an individual as exists." "The
White House has set the whole pack . . . to barking & snapping at my
heels." "Old Harry . . . take the hindmost. . . . They are all of a piece."

General Scott came in for more attention as the preconvention jockeying seesawed in earnest. For Scott was a Whig, a presidential rival, and
one who might wrest the prize from Taylor. "Genl Scott . . . will be a
candidate," Taylor opined. He "may prove a very formidable one."
Many Whigs would vote for him "in the great state of New York," and
Taylor was sold on the notion that Polk and his clique, if unable to elect
one of their own cabal, would shift their weight to Scott—"he giving
certain pledges, which he will not hesitate to do." "Cass will no doubt
be the Loco[foco] candidate. . . . Polk will be thrown overboard, or
discarded as was Tyler." What an outlook! Scott *versus* Cass! Taylor
shuddered at the prospect. "I would rather undergo political martyrdom
than see . . . Scott or Cass" in the White House. Thus we see the
extent of his feeling toward "Old Fuss and Feathers" and "Old Dough-
face."

8

Taylor treated Clay more gently. He spoke of Clay with respect and
even reverence. For years the soldier from Kentucky had admired the
idol of the Bluegrass, and there was no doubt in Taylor's mind that Clay
ought to have defeated Polk. As far as 1848 was concerned, Old Rough
and Ready was for Clay, he said, provided the venerable leader could
win. "I would at once . . . retire from the contest," if certain that Clay
could carry the election. But this, thought Taylor, was most unlikely.
And he took alarm from the fact that Clay's sharpest critics, during the
last campaign, were trying to procure Clay's renomination. This simply
did not add up. The object of these creatures was to "divide & sow
dissentions among the whig party, which if they can succeed in doing,
will insure the election of one of their own thinking."[6] Publicly Taylor
continued to praise Clay, but privately he laid great emphasis on the

assumption that the Millboy of the Slashes had retired from politics. This idea governed his references to Clay before the autumn of '47, when Zachary Taylor began to suspect that the old political war horse smelled powder, and was out of the stables and running again.

With this suspicion, Taylor's view of Clay changed. He wrote Wood that Henry Clay appeared to be secretly encouraging the talk in his favor, notwithstanding the alleged retirement. In October the General dis-cussed the presence of Clay's "bitterest defamers" in his camp, and their probable motives for the scheme. "How far Mr. Clay . . . will coun-tenance such a movement, I am unable to say," he added, "& am not so certain but what he has given it his countenance. . . . He has been un-usually reserved on this subject, which satisfies me he is holding aloof . . . to take advantage of circumstances; evidently still desiring the office." When a correspondent "thought I would aid in bringing Mr C before the country for the office in question; in reply I informed him that altho I would much prefer seeing Mr Clay in the chair of state than myself, & would not be in his way if I knew he could be elected, yet I would not loan myself to elevate Mr C."

By February 1848, Taylor concluded that "a portion of the Whigs would rather be defeated with Mr Clay . . . than . . . succeed with any one else," and that "if the present party in power is saddled on the country the responsibility will be with Mr Clay and his Whig friends." This was adverse criticism, but certainly not harsh, and had little in common with the attacks on Scott. It was only on a rare occasion, and very confidentially, that Zachary Taylor would charge Clay with being "more anxious for office than for the interest of the country, or the success of the whig party." Even this accusation was comparatively mild. Henry Clay came off remarkably well when Taylor tossed his epithets around.

Aside from Clay and Scott, no Whig aspirant for the Presidency re-ceived more than passing notice from Taylor. Though on friendly terms with McLean, and confidential with Crittenden, he was convinced that they, like Clay, could not be elected—and what the Whigs needed was a winner. Taylor also quickly passed over Senators John M. Clayton of Delaware and Thomas Corwin of Ohio. Daniel Webster is not men-tioned by Taylor in the *Letters . . . from the Battle-fields*. The General understood, fairly early, that Clay and Scott and he himself were the leading Whigs on the White House track. Barring a deadlock, it ap-peared certain that one of the trio would be nominated by the 1848 Whig National Convention; and, estimating the strength of the candidates, Taylor's thinking was straight and to the point. He did not clutter up his mind with improbabilities, insofar as his rivals were concerned.

9

Meanwhile he continued to look on politics not as a highroad to power and glory, but rather as a path to be followed reluctantly to the place where a citizen could perform a service. "I want quiet, & should have it at my time of life," Taylor had written in mid-1846. The Presidency "will neither lengthen my days," nor "add to my happiness." "Why then should I wish it?" he asked Dr. Wood. "I do not care a flint whether I am elected or not." Still, "I suppose I must serve if elected." The General hoped that the members of his family would not adopt too serious an attitude toward the presidential fanfare; he counseled them to avoid conversing on the subject "except in a jocular way among themselves."

Nevertheless, in Taylor's eyes, America was ailing. The nation needed a physician.

As to political matters I am free to say that I take but little interest in them personally, but the deepest as regards our country; & look upon our political affairs, in a worse condition than they have been since the adoption of the Federal constitution[,] growing out of . . . the Mexican War & the slave question, which if not speedily arrested will lead to great confusion, if not to disunion.

This gloomy sentence was penned at Baton Rouge, a month after Taylor returned to the United States. It represents the seriousness of his views on national affairs, both in his wartime days and in the months to come. The General was not at all optimistic regarding the solution of sectional difficulties. He was certain no Democrat could allay the strife. Scott, in his judgment, was out of the question. And no Whig statesman could be elected. Therefore, by the process of elimination, Taylor felt duty-bound to run. "I cannot withdraw from the Canvass," he wrote. "I am in the hands of the people."[7]

CHAPTER V

THE WHIG HIGH COMMAND

1

THE people accepted Taylor as they found him—a military hero, uncommitted, unpledged. They were charmed by the rustic exterior of the man, his bluntness, his courage, the cut of his jib. They asked some questions, but got few answers and seemed glad the politicians did not often trip him. Taylor had ideas, fundamental ideas, concerning agitation, slavery and the Union. But the people were not primarily interested in the theorizing of the brave old man. He was a folk hero, and had become available—as Harrison and Jackson and Washington became available—by fighting battles and winning victories.

But Harrison and Jackson, like Washington before them, possessed civil prerequisites which Rough and Ready lacked. Harrison gave a dozen years of his life to the governorship of Indiana Territory; he served in both houses of Congress and also on a diplomatic mission. Jackson was a territorial governor, a senator, representative and judge. Washington was active in the Constitutional Convention, and could point to his years in the Virginia House of Burgesses and to his tactful handling of the Continental Congress as suitable preparation for civil leadership. Zachary Taylor had no such record. For months the electorate stood in doubt as to the party he belonged to. Never a senator, representative or governor, he was closely identified with no major issue. Taylor's active military service was longer than Jackson's and Harrison's combined. But, for the first time in American history, the man looming largest on the presidential horizon was a grizzled soldier from the Western frontier who had never occupied a civil office.

There are, manifestly, explanations for so unprecedented an occurrence. These are found not only in Taylor's victories and personality, but also in weaknesses of parties and leaders, and in the political *impasse* produced by the Mexican War. From the day of John Quincy Adams' defeat up to 1845, the majority element of the Democratic party had been the lengthened shadow of one man—Andrew Jackson of Tennessee. It has been characterized as "an organic party whose dominant note was equality . . . and whose common tendency was westward expansion."

52

Like Old Hickory himself, it "caught the imagination or catered to the appetite of Southern yeomen and petty planters, of pioneer farmers in the Northwest, German and Irish immigrants in the Northern states, and plain country folk in New England and New York." When Jackson left the White House, the party he led failed to find a champion who proved his equal. An economic depression jettisoned Martin Van Buren. Northern and Southern factions developed, and only an odd combination of circumstances eked out a narrow victory for Polk.

Polk attempted to reconcile conflicting Democratic elements. He succeeded to a marked degree in carrying forward the party's expansionist tradition. But, whereas Democrats had promised to extend American sovereignty to Oregon and Texas, Polk compromised the Oregon issue, and his expansion took only a southwesterly tack. Being a Southerner, he was assailed in the North for allegedly favoring Southern interests. The hobgoblin of slavery veered to the fore. The conflict with Mexico grew unpopular in the North. And the Democratic Party lost control of the House in the off-year congressional elections.

2

As early as 1846, when Taylor was first injected into politics, both major parties cast about for presidential candidates. Of the two, the Democrats were the more cohesive. Despite some divisionist sentiment, especially in New York and South Carolina, there remained a factor of mutual confidence in most of the Democratic high command. Polk persisted in his promise not to seek re-election, but many prominent party leaders reached out eagerly for the honor. Lewis Cass, the portly senator from Michigan, became the favorite candidate. Also in the race were Secretary Buchanan, Vice President George M. Dallas, New York's Silas Wright, South Carolina's John C. Calhoun, Senator William Allen of Ohio and Judge Levi Woodbury of New Hampshire. Allen, Buchanan, Cass, Dallas and Woodbury were all in or near Polk's intimate circle, and Wright (had he not died suddenly in August 1847) might have bridged the widening chasm between the dissident Van Burenites and Polk.

A fair degree of unity was still evident in the national Democratic Party, notwithstanding the sectional troubles which Calhoun and Van Buren personified. Democrats controlled the federal patronage and could boast a record of positive achievement, with all pledges but one redeemed by Polk. This was more than could be claimed for Whigs, who, hungry for the spoils of office, turned rather desperately to Taylor—hoping his luster might lend prestige to their strange political group.

With the exception of the Native Americans, who of course were out of the question, the Whig party presented the only alternative to the incumbent Democrats. But Whigs, too, were weighted with liabilities. Theirs was primarily the party of property. The rich, the well-born, bankers and commercial men were generally Whigs. In the North, with Webster, "they carried on the nationalist and paternal tradition" of Alexander Hamilton. Many Westerners were attracted by Clay's personality and by "the hope of getting something done about the public lands. . . . Sugar planters of Louisiana, who wanted protection against Cuba; big cotton planters who regretted the [veto of the] United States Bank . . . , and antique Republicans of Virginia and North Carolina, who disliked Jackson's agressive nationalism and 'executive tyranny'— all went Whig" at one time or another. Having fought for the Bank and internal improvements and against the annexation of both Texas and Oregon, they now found their old issues unpopular. The Whigs, in short, were an aggregation of regionalists and "antis"—vehemently opposed to Democratic proposals, but with no broad platform of their own. "Nowhere but in America," say Morison and Commager, "could a political party have been formed from such heterogeneous elements."

3

The statesman who held these elements together until his 1844 defeat was the colorful, impetuous, masterly, suave, tough, resilient Henry Clay. A Kentucky lawyer, orator, hemp grower and fancier of Bluegrass thoroughbreds, Clay was a political cock of the walk even in his Madisonian days, when, slender and ingratiating, he was elected Speaker of the House on his first day as a member.

Clay could be the soul of courtesy, in the drawing room or in debate. He was usually genial, cordial and gracious, and his personal magnetism was proverbial. In his heyday, even those who opposed him felt drawn to him in spite of themselves. When a certain Georgia Democrat entered Congress, a mutual friend asked: "May I introduce you to Henry Clay?" "No, sir!" was the stern response. "I am his adversary, and choose not to subject myself to his fascination." Clay still exuded his fabulous charm at three score years and ten, when so many of his old associates lay moldering in their graves.

Another quality of Clay's aided him even more, politically. This was his parliamentary knack, his genius for guiding legislative assemblies. Active in politics since attaining his majority, he served as Speaker more than ten years—nor was this merely a statistical achievement. The War of 1812 was the military baby of young legislators whom Speaker Clay led. The Treaty of Ghent, in 1814, was a triumph of Clay and J. Q. Adams. The Tariff of 1816, the Missouri Compromise and the Compromise Tariff of 1833 stemmed largely from Henry Clay's acumen in the House and later in the Senate.

Long a demigod to his lieutenants, elegant, imperious and resourceful in debate, Clay also accumulated frailties which kept him from reaching his loftiest goal. From the time he joined forces with the erudite Adams in the election of '25, he was identified increasingly with propertied interests, which did little to endear him to the masses. His internal improvements program was widely popular. But he chose to combat Jackson on the issue of the Bank, and herein lay a major error of judgment—Jackson defeating Clay resoundingly in the campaign of '32. When 1839 came along, and the hour was ripe for a smashing Whig victory, Clay's very brilliance told against him; rival managers within the Whig party nominated the more pliable Harrison. In '44 Clay won the nomination, and his second great mistake ensued. Texas' annexation was then the chief issue, and Harry of the West (instead of facing it manfully) vacillated weakly and antagonized both sections, first the South and then the North. He rang his political knell when he declared, shortly after his defeat by Polk, that never again would he aspire to the White House unless the whole American people should call him to the Presidency by acclamation. Thus, for three years, many Whigs assumed that under no ordinary circumstances would the thrice-vanquished candidate consent to accept another nomination.

Even when Clay in a Lexington speech—delivered in November 1847—threw out a hint that he still was interested in becoming President, there were those who remembered his glorious utterance that "I had rather be right than be President," and also his reference to his happiness in "the retirement which henceforward best becomes me."[1] Had the Old Chief been sincere, men wondered, when he renounced his life's ambition? Or was his heart gnawed by the hope that he might yet sit in the President's chair? There was an undertone of incredulity in speculations of the rank and file, for Clay had not stated in so many words his intention to seek the nomination. Perhaps, after all, he did not propose to reconsider his abdication. Perhaps he was merely exercising the prerogative of an elder statesman to criticize the party in power and point out a path for successors to follow. It seems to have been the impression of Crittenden, and others who had followed Clay, that such was the elderly Clay's design. For, surely, there had been no cry of acclamation, no unanimous, country-wide insistence for him to emerge from his self-imposed retirement and cross blades with the Democrats again.

Aside from their doubts regarding Clay's wishes, many Whigs who cheered him loyally in the past raised three objections to his running in the future. First, he was an old man now and would be nearing seventy-two at the time of the next inauguration. No President ever reached that mark; Harrison, the eldest of all, died after thirty-one days of pressure. Harrison's quick removal from the scene, followed by the Tyler troubles, discouraged Whigs from taking a chance on another oldster's heading the ticket.

The second objection to Clay concerned his reported querulousness. No longer was he as gay as formerly. Not that anyone objected to his giving up gambling or joining the church, but rumor made him out to be surly, and—true or false—some admirers were offended. Always burdened by an ugly temper, Clay had controlled it with marked success. Now he appeared crotchety at times. Having slipped from his place of power in the party, he may have resented what he thought was the base ingratitude of mortals. With the coming of 1848, there appeared indications that—despite all he had said to the contrary—the septuagenarian was again in the lists with his eye on renomination. This angered numbers of faithful Whigs, of whom William Burnet was typical. "Mr. Clay is bending all his energies . . . to secure the nomination," Burnet wrote McLean. "[He] will trample over every thing and every body that . . . thwarts his purposes, just as he always has done."

This brings us to the final objection to Henry Clay as nominee—the fact that he had lost so often, carrying his party to defeat. The other arguments might have been nullified by the prospect of victory, but the words "Clay" and "victory" were far from synonymous. "I am tired of being beaten," another Whig partisan exclaimed. "I am in favor of Mr Clay," but, "if we persist in his nomination, defeat is certain." "With the administration of Genl Taylor[,] many of Mr Clays friends who have grown old in his service would be brought up" to their merited rewards, an up-and-coming Kentuckian confided to Crittenden. "I prefer Mr. Clay to all men," but "my . . . involuntary conviction . . . is that he cannot be elected," Crittenden himself admitted.

4

If Clay was considered a foredoomed leader, who then was eligible for the succession? Many a Whig, long in Clay's shadow, lanced forward to secure his mantle. Prominent among these was Daniel Webster, eloquent orator, old voice of New England. Before the public as long as Clay, pre-eminently the champion of the national state, Webster had adorned the House or Senate periodically since 1813. Like Clay, Webster was a party elder. He was now in his middle sixties, but for all the brandy he sniffed, the rich foods and liquors he swallowed and grief expended in presidential quests, he remained a figure of vitality—proud of his capacity for work.

At no other juncture of American history has a single individual so symbolized the Senate. Somewhat above medium height, immaculate in buff and blue, his body well-proportioned and his gestures effective as he addressed the chair, Webster could not steer legislation like Clay— but in clinching the debate he had few rivals. Colder, sterner, graver than Clay, Webster on occasion could be sunny and blithe. But, except in Massachusetts, his intellectual intimates were few—and he seemed to look down on lesser men. Impressing foreigners as well as Americans, compared to Mars and Jupiter Olympus, he enjoyed the nickname of "the Godlike Daniel." And an English wit exclaimed: "That man is a fraud, for it is impossible for anyone to be as great as he looks."

Fraud or no fraud, Webster had his handicaps. John Quincy Adams had cruelly referred to "the gigantic intellect, the envious temper, the ravenous ambition, and the rotten heart of Daniel Webster." Adams was bitter and unfair. But if Clay was inconsistent on the issue of the Bank (having opposed its rechartering in 1816 and reversed his stand in 1832), Webster's position on the tariff and the Union made his rival appear consistent by contrast. Webster had followed the interests of his section, and, as they changed, he changed with them. Here was no real independence, no high motivation of an abstract right, no yearning to benefit the underdog. Webster was on record as a seeker of "refreshments"—and the coin of the realm was bestowed on him often by Nicholas Biddle and others of the grateful. If Clay had supporters throughout the country, Webster's backing was largely localized. Commercial men adored him in New York and Philadelphia, as did conservative New England Whigs. But now it was clear to nearly everyone, save Webster, that his presidential candidacy was only a form. In the sunset of his life, Webster had many of Clay's liabilities. And he possessed hardly one of Clay's assets, as a prospective nominee.

5

In view of Webster's disqualifications, some Whigs turned to Winfield Scott. This was anathema to Taylor, but there were those who considered Scott the strongest candidate the Whigs could offer. Six feet five, erect and dignified, Scott had entered the Army the same day as Taylor, and, like Taylor, was born in Virginia. His rise in the Army had been swift, his projection into politics by no means slow. A captain when only twenty-four, a lieutenant colonel at twenty-seven, he distinguished himself in the War of 1812 as a brevet major general before he was thirty. Having harbored presidential ambitions as early as the 1830s, Scott was no political novice as the calendar turned into '48.

As far back as 1839, when the Whigs nominated Harrison at Harrisburg, Scott figured in convention maneuvers and was backed by many anti-Clay people. Disappointed when Harrison was picked that year, and when Clay was selected in '44, Scott looked forward hopefully to '48; he almost certainly would have been named, if the early battles of the Mexican War had thrust him—instead of Taylor—into popular esteem. The fact that Old Zack commanded the troops on the Rio Grande was due largely to Polk's jealousy of Scott, his knowledge of the latter's political affiliations and his hunch that Scott was more likely to capitalize on prestige stemming from victories. Thanks to Palo Alto and Resaca de la Palma, Taylor benefited from a running head start which "Old Fuss and Feathers" never overcame. There was more to Taylor's edge, however, than the advantage of being first in the field. For Scott's personality was not the sort to endear him to the masses, who loved Taylor. His very nickname suggests the fuss-budget, the stickler-for-terms, the insister on technicalities. Scott had a fatal tendency to write long letters at the wrong time to the wrong people on the wrong subjects. Taylor may have hurt his cause when he composed his communication to the Cincinnati *Signal*. But, compared to his rival's inept epistles, Taylor's letters were well phrased.

In analyzing Scott as a correspondent, the conclusion must be reached that he appears ridiculous. Whereas Taylor's reply to Marcy was masterful, Scott came off second-best in his correspondence with the Secretary of War. He had been interrupted by official dispatches while "taking a hasty plate of soup." And he charged the Polk Administration with di-

recting a "fire on my rear." Scott had cause for stressing his devotion
to his duties in Washington, and no doubt Marcy and Polk were guilty
of attacking him unfairly through the press. But the language in which
he couched his objections injured him—instead of his targets.

These phrases, "fire on my rear" and "a hasty plate of soup," were
forever after used to Scott's disadvantage. And his subsequent run-in
with Taylor, when the latter accused Scott of filching his troops prior
to the crisis at Buena Vista, more than counterbalanced politically Scott's
splendid record on the march from Vera Cruz to the City of Mexico.
Scott was vulnerable on two other counts. First, he had sent an anonymous letter to the Washington *National Intelligencer* in 1844, thrusting
at immigrants arriving from Europe.[2] This was resented, in particular,
by communicants of the Catholic Church, who saw in Scott a front and
symbol for forces of intolerance. Secondly, though a native of Virginia,
Scott now resided in New Jersey—disassociating himself from the South.
Southerners accordingly looked on him, Webster, and even Kentucky's
Clay, primarily as candidates of Northern Whigs, while Taylor alone
was bracketed with Southern interests and Southern economy. Taylor
thereby profited from divisions in Northern Whig support.

6

At least one Northwestern Whig refused to be downhearted by Taylor's favored position in the presidential derby. This was Ohio's John
McLean, who today is almost forgotten, but in his own age was widely
known as a perennial candidate. Originally a Jeffersonian Democrat
and later a member of James Monroe's Cabinet, McLean has been accused
of trimming his sails to suit the breeze of the moment and shifting or
drifting from party to party. Postmaster General under three Presidents,
and efficient in instituting postal reforms, he backed Adams when Monroe retired; subsequently, "Old Man Eloquent" charged him with throw-
ing his support to Jackson while retaining his seat in Adams' Cabinet. It
was Old Hickory who kicked McLean upstairs to the Supreme Court.

The bench, to McLean, was no ivory tower but a springboard for
plunging into politics again. In '31 he had a chance to run for President
on the Anti-Masons' ticket. This dubious honor he sensibly declined, but
never again was he immune to the presidential fever. In '36 and '39, he
had admirers among the Whigs but always appeared in a compromise
role, never as the leader of a clamoring horde. Since Clay's defeat, Mc-
Lean and his friends considered the Ohioan Clay's logical successor.

But even in the Buckeye State there was no unanimity for him. Ohio's Whig Senator Thomas Corwin was the fair-haired boy of the Western Reserve; opposing Polk's war with thrilling words, he commanded the free-soilers' fervor. Compared to Corwin, "the Wagon Boy," the black-robed judge seemed cold and distant. It was not so easy for average men to warm up to the stately jurist as to Corwin of the silver tongue, whose smile was warm and handshake hearty. Gradually Corwin withdrew from the canvass, and by '48 was no longer in the picture. But, even then, there was little enthusiasm for Associate Justice McLean.

One further point about McLean in connection with Zachary Taylor: He was Joseph P. Taylor's father-in-law, and "Colonel Joe" was Zachary's brother. There was, however, no hidden understanding between the General and the judge, with Joseph a go-between. The evidence suggests that McLean, like Clay and Webster and General Scott, regarded Taylor as an interloper muddying the party waters. McLean's advisers tended to lose heart when Taylor's popularity swept the nation. Long before 1847 ended it was obvious that McLean's slim chance to be nominated lay in a deadlock of the national convention. Indeed, neither he nor his coterie turned a finger in '48 to sign up delegates for the opening ballot. They hoped against hope that the leading candidates would cancel one another out of the running, in which case horse traders could do worse than trot out the ubiquitous judge.

7

Two dark horses on the presidential track, who at times were taken more seriously than McLean, were the senior Senators from Kentucky and Delaware, John J. Crittenden and John M. Clayton. Crittenden was one of his party's ablest men, eloquent, dynamic and a brilliant organizer. His Taylor-like cheekbones, "quick, piercing" eyes, and firmly set mouth (dour in repose) made noteworthy a florid face which otherwise would have been ordinary enough. Of medium height and rather spare build, the Kentuckian was a gregarious soul, an easy mixer in Washington and Frankfort, a "keen blade" and a shrewd performer.

Since his soldiering days in the War of 1812, Crittenden had never been out of law and politics. He first sat in the Senate at thirty, and repeatedly was returned to that body. When not in Washington, he was a state legislator—elected twelve times, and Speaker six. He also held appointive jobs, filling each post with distinction, serving as Harrison's Attorney General and then resigning when Tyler was President. Ingratiating, resourceful and urbane, Crittenden might have gone farther than he did—had it not been for Henry Clay. But Clay was his senior, mentor and friend. And Crittenden, for a quarter century, played second fiddle to the Old Prince. Not till Clay "retired" in 1844 did the younger statesman come into his own.

With Clay apparently out of the running, Crittenden was urged to strike out for himself. Before the Mexican War he was considered a presidential contender. Then Taylor's sudden emergence pushed Crittenden back into a secondary role, as Rough and Ready's Washington manager in fact if not in name. Crittenden advised Taylor, warned him, promoted him, sponsored him as enthusiastically as he had sponsored Clay. Still there were Whigs who were eager for Crittenden to become a candidate. Even when huzzahs for Taylor echoed across the United States, some saw in Crittenden a possible compromise, capable of making a strong race.

Clayton was an ally of Crittenden's in the national councils of the Whigs. Younger than the leading candidates and Crittenden's junior by seven years, he was only fifty-one and capable of grueling if uneven work. Clayton was an orator, and on occasion electrified the Senate galleries, having shared Whig honors with Webster and Clay in debates on the Bank and internal improvements.[3] His chief weakness in the national field lay in the fact that his state was small. Still he was popular in Pennsylvania, Maryland and New Jersey, in addition to Delaware, which he tightly controlled. More than one Whig in the populous East, alarmed by Taylor's Southern connections and disinclined to push Clay or Scott, looked on Clayton as a Crittenden-like compromise. Among those toying with the possibility was Thurlow Weed, the boss of New York.

8

Weed himself was never a candidate. He fled suggestions that he should seek office. But, a power in the Empire State, he was a force on the national scene. A newspaper publisher with his hands on the purse strings, and intimate with New York merchants, Weed had his finger in every Whig pie. Through his Albany *Evening Journal,* he had influenced legislation twenty years and dominated state and national conventions. This Albany Warwick was a giant of a man. Six feet three in height, his towering frame was familiar in lobbies and smoke-filled rooms. His countenance bland, his manner agreeable, Weed's appearance belied his reputation as a crafty political schemer—the man who, more than anyone else, had secured the nomination for Harrison. Editor Weed was the first Whig of influence to promote Taylor publicly as a White House prospect, and, as the contest developed, he rang the changes with the clang of praise. But Weed's boosts for Taylor were not always consistent. His motives were ulterior or at best expedient, not personal like those of Crittenden. Whenever Taylor's stock was high, Weed was there with a pat on the back; when it fell, Weed had a word to say in favor of some other candidate. It was hard to pin Weed to a position. Clay and Scott had tried it and failed. Now it was the Taylorites' turn to learn that the journalist played his cards with precision and a poker face.

One important politician who captured Weed's lasting devotion was William H. Seward of Auburn, New York, the former governor and state senator, who began his career as Weed's protégé—eventually becoming an equal partner. An upstate New Yorker born and bred, gifted in the law, a classical scholar, with a love of gossip and political intrigue, Seward had a social charm and, affable and generous, entranced the ladies. Shrewd, ambitious, energetic, convivial, Seward split his time between politics and law—and gave to each the best that was in him. Elected governor at thirty-seven and re-elected at thirty-nine, for five years he had nominally been out of politics, working hard at his profession. Seward never really forsook politics, however; he took part in the campaigns and cemented support for future contests. He was frequently mentioned for the Vice Presidency in '47 and '48, and was considered a presidential prospect by the antislavery men.

On the slavery question, and other reforms, Seward usually stood midway between Weed and Horace Greeley. Greeley, a baby-faced, nearsighted man with spectacles perched on the tip of his nose and a fringe of whiskers surmounting his collar, seemed the perfect picture of abstraction, of absent-mindedness and whimsicality. There was more than whimsy, however, in an editor who in seven years built up his paper, the widely read New York *Tribune,* into a most influential daily. Like Seward, Greeley started out under the guiding hand of Weed, and there were those who still considered "the firm of Weed, Seward, & Greeley" a political triumvirate. But Greeley's peculiar qualities already placed him in a niche apart. Although Weed took kindly to mild reforms, he was at heart a party boss and secondarily a newspaper publisher bent on obtaining favors for his friends and printing contracts for himself. Seward was bold, occasionally impulsive and radical on the slavery issue,

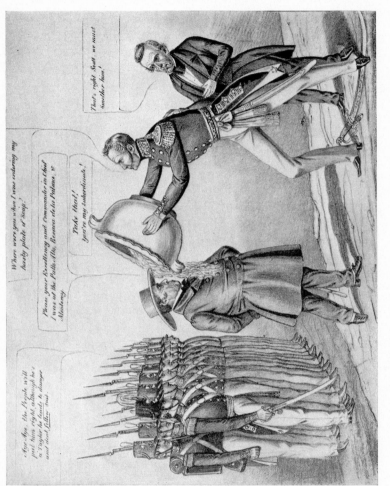

DISTINGUISHED MILITARY OPERATIONS WITH A HASTY BOWL OF SOUP

The foreground figures are Taylor, Winfield Scott and President Polk. The soup reference is to a phrase in one of Scott's inept letters. Polk and Scott are represented as wanting to smother Old Zack because of his wartime popularity. From the Library of Congress Collection.

but aspired to higher honors and was affected by the quest. Greeley, though a Whig and faithful to the party, grew increasingly independent. No man could rule him. No faction could own him. A born idealist with the zeal of the breed, postage reformer, tariff reformer, land reformer and slavery reformer, Greeley was convinced that Zachary Taylor was not the man for the times and issues. While Seward and Weed flirted with the General, Greeley remained adamantly opposed.[4]

As Weed and Seward lost their grip on Greeley, they found a stout ally in Truman Smith. Smith, now forgotten, contributed more to Whig unity in '48 than anyone else in the councils of the party. An able attorney from Litchfield, Connecticut, currently serving his fourth term in Congress, the porcine Smith wore half-moon glasses not unlike those of Horace Greeley. Neither handsome nor commanding nor especially attractive, Smith excelled in political management. More than anyone else, he understood that the Whigs needed a tightly controlled, amply financed and unified national organization. Mainly on his own initiative, but with the backing of Weed and Crittenden, Representative Smith raised funds and formed a Whig executive committee, capable of channeling the party's energies. This was valuable to the Whigs, most of whose champions were prima donnas. As early as the spring of 1847, Smith laid the groundwork for the coming campaign.

9

The organization perfected by Smith was designed to benefit the Whig nominee, whether the lucky man happened to be Taylor, Clay, Webster, Scott or McLean. Smith himself was in the Taylor camp. He made no secret of his preference. Though Smith's section in the main was unfriendly to Taylor, he wanted a winner—and Old Zack was available. With Crittenden's approval, Truman Smith was prominent in the formation of a pro-Taylor congressional group, composed principally of Southern Whigs but including in its number a tall, muscular man, clean-shaven, fun-loving, deeply thoughtful—Abraham Lincoln of Illinois. In addition to Lincoln and Smith, the original "Young Indians" of Capitol Hill comprised two Georgia members and a trio of Virginians. The Georgia Representatives were child-faced, girl-voiced Alexander H. Stephens and big, booming Robert Toombs. The Virginia group was composed exclusively of first-termers—John S. Pendleton, Thomas S. Flournoy, and William Ballard Preston. Alabama's Henry W. Hilliard and Florida's E. Carrington Cabell later swelled the Taylor contingent, and other congressmen—notably Kentuckians—hovered on the Young Indians' periphery.

Thanks to Lincoln's subsequent prominence, and the ever-expanding Lincoln cult, the Young Indians have been accorded their rightful place in the Taylor story. History, however, has dealt less kindly with two other groups which promoted his claims. Both of these were dominated by Crittenden. One had its impact in the Bluegrass State, where Robert P. Letcher, Orlando Brown and Charles S. Todd worked in Taylor's behalf. Letcher was a former governor of Kentucky and Crittenden's right-hand man in Frankfort. Lighthearted and irrepressible, "Black Bob" Letcher had a host of friends; he kept contact with Clay while campaigning for Taylor. At his side was the scholarly Brown, who organized Taylor strength over the state. In Shelby County, Colonel Todd (who had figured prominently in the Harrison canvass) arranged to travel through New England and New York, lining up delegates for Taylor.[5] What hurt Clay's candidacy most was that so many members of his party in his own home state supported his principal rival. Had it not been for Crittenden and his lieutenants, Taylor's boom might have died aborning.

Equally important to Taylor's success were advisers he found in Louisiana. Here again Crittenden's influence was felt. Albert T. Burnley, formerly of Frankfort, was a personal friend of Crittenden and Brown. Temporarily a Texan, admired by Sam Houston and at the Alamo a week before its fall, Burnley was entrusted with delicate missions to Britain and France by the Texas Republic. "Strikingly handsome and with a grace of manner and distinction of appearance which lasted him through life," he was now in business in New Orleans, and acted as a liaison agent between Crittenden and Taylor. Burnley was the sort of man whom Taylor instinctively admired. He had a place in Old Zack's circle both before and after the nomination.

Nor was Burnley the only ex-Kentuckian who boosted Taylor's stock in the South. Alexander C. Bullitt was at least of equal value to the Taylor cause. Originally a lawyer and Clay adherent, Bullitt helped edit the New Orleans *Picayune* as a partner of George Wilkins Kendall. On good terms with Burnley and other friends of Crittenden, he wrote editorials advancing Taylor's claims at a time when Kendall seemed inclined to back Scott. The *Picayune* was to Whigs of the South what the New York *Tribune* was to Whigs of the North—a paper frequently quoted and clipped by dailies and weeklies throughout the Southwest.

Supplementing Bullitt and Burnley was James Y. Love, who—like

Bullitt—was a native of Kentucky. Another stalwart, Logan Hunton, had grown up in the Bluegrass State. Both were essentially citizens of the Southwest more than of any given locality, Hunton having come to Louisiana after practicing law in Saint Louis, and Love being interested in Texas lands. Still another New Orleans associate of Zachary Taylor, Balie Peyton, had been district attorney there. A veteran of the Mexican War, this former Tennessean was representative of the numerous ex-Democrats who found their way to Taylor's support.[6]

If Taylor's candidacy had failed to take hold, not one of this Frankfort and New Orleans group would have had a place in the Whig high command. In their stead, history would properly record the names of Edward Curtis and George Ashmun (special friends of Daniel Webster), or Leslie Combs, John M. Berrien and John M. Morehead (who supported Clay), or Robert C. Schenck (of the Scott camp), or James E. Harvey (close to McLean). But, as Taylor's name captured the imagination of delegates to the Whig National Convention, relatively obscure personalities who early found seats on the Taylor band wagon became increasingly identified with the national leadership. These individuals played their parts effectively in helping make Taylor available. With them at his side, his prospects prospered. Contrary to the traditional view, Taylor's military victories *alone* did not gain the Presidency for him. The groundwork laid by Crittenden and Smith, the maneuverings of Seward, Greeley and Weed, and the contributions of Burnley, Bullitt, Letcher, Brown, Love, Hunton and Peyton all have a part in the Taylor story. Now let us move on with the actors in the drama, to see how each influenced the outcome in his locale and in the nation.

CHAPTER VI

BARKIS IS WILLIN'

1

As THE year 1848 opened, Taylor stock still was high. "Every thing seems to be going well for Taylor," Peyton wrote Crittenden from New Orleans. In New York City "there is a decided proclivity to Taylorism, and a great demonstration is in progress," an Indiana Whig advised his congressman. In Washington, Seward noted Taylor's popularity. Attending a dinner party given by Speaker Robert C. Winthrop, he found other Whigs around the board, including McLean and Joseph Taylor. "It was amusing to mark the respect shown to Colonel Taylor," Seward informed his wife. The deference paid Old Rough and Ready's brother "was ominous to Judge McLean." Four fifths of the Kentucky Legislature "are decidedly for Genl Taylor," Crittenden learned from a Frankfort lieutenant. If Clay would only make up his mind and withdraw his name, wrote a friend of McLean's, "we might yet fix upon" a compromise nominee. "But if this is not done very soon[,] Genl. Taylor will . . . be the candidate—I do not like it—but it is inevitable."

There were those who were not prepared to agree as to the assumed inevitability, and among the dissenters was Clay himself. While Taylor remained in the Southwest, declining invitations to visit the North, Clay traveled leisurely to Washington, arriving a month after Congress convened.[1] By the end of January the "Great Rejected" was holding court daily in the capital. Old friends flocked to greet him, and associates denied that Clay would consider withdrawing from the race. Washington society was captivated by him. Matrons saved as relics the gloves he pressed, and young ladies kissed him in public. "Did ever the fashionable . . . of America obtain such a triumph," Seward asked, "as they would have in his election?"

Not only did Clay gain strength, but Taylor lost a little. "Taylor cannot run with the least prospect of success in the North," observed Representative Caleb B. Smith, should he adhere "to his present position of declining to give his opinions." Reporting on a "Taylor Mass Meeting," a Cincinnatian declared that "the Taylor fever" lost "contagious qualities in a Northern atmosphere." Politicians, however, were far from

66

unanimous as to the rapidity of Taylor's decline. "The strength of Genl Taylor in Cincinnati . . . may be considered powerful, although by no means preponderant," another McLean man told the judge.

Opposition to Taylor was strident in Ohio, due to his slaves and no-party stand. The Whig State Convention reflected the "bitterness between the forces of Corwin and McLean," but these Ohio rivals and Scott and Clay had more of a following there than Taylor. Corwin said Old Zack's qualifications consisted of "sleeping forty years in the woods, and cultivating moss on the calves of his legs." At the convention's close, cheers were given for Corwin, Clay, other "distinguished" statesmen "and for General Zachary Taylor." But editors added a warning that, to secure Whig support in Ohio, the man presented for the next Presidency must be "a whole Whig and nothing but a Whig."

2

South of the Ohio River, the situation was reversed. In Kentucky Taylor seemed popular as ever, and the Taylor managers' problem was to give no needless offense to Clay. Washington's Birthday was the date set for the meeting of two Whig groups in Frankfort. One was the regular Whig State Convention, the other a gathering of Taylor men. Since Taylorites composed a majority of those assembling to select a state ticket and national delegates, enthusiasts like Richard Hawes and Humphrey Marshall favored committing the entire Whig party of Kentucky formally to Taylor. Letcher and Brown, however, were answerable to Crittenden. And Crittenden bent over backward to avoid a rupture with Clay, whose candidacy was not in the open.

"Things are in . . . terrible confusion," Letcher admitted. With Hawes insisting on a formal nomination, and Taylor's "wisest friends" opposed, "the fat is in the fire certain." Letcher was satisfied that Clay would run. "But great G-d if he could have foreseen the predicament" in which he placed his party, he "could not have hesitated a moment about declining."

There was a second source of friction at a lower level. Archibald Dixon and William J. Graves, candidates for the governorship, split Kentucky Whigs into warring camps. The party was in the greatest distraction. Letcher had never seen it so alarmed. The upshot was that Dixon and Graves withdrew their names, and Crittenden emerged as the choice for governor. Letcher and Brown prevented the outright pledging of Kentucky to Taylor, which Crittenden warned would offend

Clay. Nevertheless, all but one of the delegates to the National Convention were "either original friends of Taylor preferring him above all others, or who believe that Clay has no chance . . . & that our only hope is for Taylor."[2] After the regular state convention adjourned, the Taylor men met and enthusiastically proclaimed Old Zack's virtues.

The only unhappy feature of the outcome, from the standpoint of Taylor and Crittenden, was the latter's prospective removal to Frankfort in the capacity of governor. This would deprive Taylor, as President, of a counselor he rated above all others. Although Crittenden's running for governor was likened to "loading a cannon to shoot a pig," its immediate effect was to instill confidence in the Whigs. Washington took note that Clay was no longer the dictator of Kentucky. Virginia and North Carolina—where Clay had been strong in other campaigns—named Taylorites to the National Convention, and in other states of the South the Crittenden impact was felt. Only the North appeared impervious to the Kentucky outcome.

3

Above the Mason-Dixon line, Greeley loomed as the most articulate leader in opposition to Taylor. As Clay's principal Eastern spokesman, he tended to offset Crittenden. Who has "so good a Heart" as Greeley? asked a McLean follower. What other man was so absolved of self-interest? That the Whigs should adhere to time-tested Whig principles, and eschew military glamour, was an oft-repeated argument with which Greeley bombarded his readers.

Still there were Northerners, as well as Southerners, who questioned Greeley's reasoning. The Philadelphia *North American* and Albany *Evening Journal* were among the numerous Whig organs refusing to follow Greeley's lead. James Gordon Bennett's New York *Herald* was in Taylor's column more often than not, and James Watson Webb's *Morning Courier and New York Enquirer* backed Old Zack against all comers. Even the *Tribune,* by some accounts, remained a political question mark. Judged by what he admitted privately, its editor was less pro-Clay than anti-Taylor. Although he eulogized Clay in his paper, Greeley acknowledged that his second choice was Corwin, and his third, McLean.

A case could be made for the supposition that both Greeley and Weed were actually working for Seward's nomination. The "little ex-governor" lost no chance to make himself available. Seward had much to offer the North. Opposed to the extension of slavery, on intimate terms with Corwin and Clayton, he could be counted on to break the Democrats' stranglehold on the immigrant vote; Seward's position was peculiarly strong in view of Scott's anti-immigrant record. At least one student of the period has suggested that Weed's hemming and hawing, as well as that of Greeley and the *Tribune,* can be interpreted only in the light of a *sub rosa* Seward campaign. It is possible that they hoped to do for Seward what Pillow and Bancroft had achieved for Polk in '44. The final evidence, to date, is lacking. Suffice it to say, until other facts are presented, that Greeley wanted anyone but Scott and Taylor. Weed would have been happy to see Seward as the vice-presidential nominee, in the event that Clay headed the Whig ticket.[3] Other than that, it is difficult to determine the strings on which his speculation played.

The single discernible effect of the Greeley-Weed-Seward maneuvers is the impression created by them that Northern Whigs were divided when Southern Whigs were unified. While Southerners joined in promoting Zachary Taylor's candidacy, Northerners squabbled and bickered like the factionalists they were.

4

In contrast to Clay (who spent two months in Washington in 1848) and Webster (who exhausted himself on an electioneering tour the year before), Taylor figuratively hugged his hearth. He was at Cypress Grove in December and again in March. Visiting New Orleans once during the winter, he received official welcomes at Natchez and Woodville. With these exceptions, Taylor declined invitations—including bids from the legislatures of Mississippi, Kentucky, Indiana and New York. Taylor could appear in Natchez, Woodville and New Orleans with perfect propriety, since legitimate business took him there. To stray afield in order to be honored, however, did not appeal to the hero. His leave of absence from the Army had been granted to enable him to be with his loved ones, and to attend to his private affairs; it did not appear seemly to take advantage of it to campaign actively for President. Taylor had also informed the War Department that he was ready to return to Mexico whenever his services might be needed—even before his leave was up. This necessitated his remaining near Baton Rouge.

Physical necessity had a part in keeping the General at home. Around January 20, he suffered an attack of rheumatism—the first in his life—and this confined him to his house five weeks. The illness postponed

his trip to Woodville. Not until the last of February was he well enough
to keep the appointment. The sight of old friends, whom he had known
in his Wilkinson County days, apparently acted as a spur to his recovery.
He was in good health by the end of March.

Wherever he went, Zachary Taylor was greeted with enthusiasm that
nearly overwhelmed him. Local military companies were drawn up in
his honor. Parades were staged, and cannon roared. In Woodville, as
previously at Natchez and New Orleans, veterans of the Mexican War
stood conspicuous among the citizens. Homage paid him by the gallant
volunteers was almost too much for Old Zack's sensibilities. He acknowledged their tributes under deep emotion. Of course the Whig press
took appropriate notice of each detail bracketed with Taylor's appearances. Reports of the receptions achieved wide regional circulation. Even
in the North the picture was appealing—more so than the accounts of
Clay in the role of a lobbyist for himself on Capitol Hill in Washington.

As Taylor did what came naturally, he devoted much of his thought
to his plantation—which accorded with Southerners' ideas as to what
was logical and fitting. Cypress Grove was in sorry shape, and its owner
gave top priority to setting matters right. Wherever Zachary Taylor
traveled, up or down the broad brown river, he turned the conversation
to planting problems and seemed eager to profit from fellow travelers'
experience. Here, again, was the sort of individual whom the South
could readily appreciate.

Concurrently, Taylor maintained his negative attitude toward the
Presidency. To be sure, he accepted local nominations—whether Democratic or Whig in origin. But Taylor was purely receptive. He courteously answered letters as they came, but was careful not to commit himself on issues. It would be a mistake, however, to assume that he took
no notice of political trends. In private letters he favored acquisition
of part of California—including San Francisco—and enough of New
Mexico to cancel claims. This moderate commitment was opposed by
his Southern Whig advisers, who urged Crittenden to call Old Zack's
attention to political perils in the project.[4] Crittenden never released
Taylor's program. And so, for the record, he was silent on this issue.

5

Men, being mortal, took divergent views of the relative chances of
Taylor and Clay. In February, Alexander H. H. Stuart thought Clay
unequal to carrying Virginia, while "Taylor would be certain of it."

Thomas Metcalfe found Taylor sentiment "growing in strength," and another Kentuckian doubted Clay's ability to win his own state. Burnley wrote Crittenden that Clay "can't be elected—even if Genl Taylor were dead—What reason is there to suppose he can get more votes than he did before. . . . Is he not indulging his vanity at too high a price?" A Maine Whig pressed Greeley to use McLean's name to "prevent the spreading of the 'Taylor fever.'" Truman Smith was fervid in Old Zack's behalf, and Smith's influence in New England was great. Abraham Lincoln expressed his settled conviction that "we can elect nobody but General Taylor." Robert Toombs of Georgia said: "I am a Taylor man without a second choice."

Representative Washington Hunt, on the other hand, wrote Weed: "I feel Taylor cannot be nominated. . . . Clayton and Corwin are now ardent for Scott." Caleb B. Smith agreed that Clay and Taylor prospects were receding: "The public mind is fast coming to the conclusion that some third man will be taken." "Taylor cannot . . . be the Whig candidate," Salmon P. Chase prophesied. The New York editor, Henry J. Raymond, was conversant with "Washington . . . this winter" and said that he "could not see, or hear, any serious talk . . . for Genl. Taylor."[5]

If not Taylor, who then? Henry Clay? Increasingly, observers were convinced that the Clay movement lacked spontaneity. Hone recorded that four professed friends of Clay—all prominent in Whig circles— were secretly for Taylor, and admitted it. Burnley saw no Clay enthusiasm, save on the part of his "peculiar friends—*his enemies*—& all those opposed, from selfish motives, to Genl. Taylors elevation." Clay failed to take hold in Ohio, where Scott benefited from the Corwin-McLean split. If Clay had come out powerfully against extension of slave territory, "he might have obtained the support of Ohio." But the Kentuckian, fearful of offending the Cotton South, deprived himself of backing in a state which he carried in '44.

"The Whig Members of Congress say . . . Clay cannot be nominated," Weed reported in April. McLean was told that "the East is forming against . . . Clay." The imprudence of Clay's and Taylor's "too anxious friends" hurt both men, wrote another of the judge's correspondents, who considered Clay "shamefully deceived" by "the most unblushing scoundrels . . . that ever lived."

As early as January 1848, when Clay's New York promoters were "zealous and active," they seemed in a Whig minority. By April, Greeley admitted privately that Clay could not be nominated, and, if nominated, would lose in November. The Whig majority in the New York Legis-

lature passed a resolution complimentary to the "Old Chief." Yet the
commendation had no more ignition than a bonfire of wet sponges.
Former Clay admirers felt that his Eastern visit did him no good. And
many said he would decline to run.[6]

6

It was April 10 when Clay finally announced his candidacy. "Mr.
Clay's card produced a marked sensation," observed McLean's friend,
Harvey, who found but one Whig approving it. The *Indiana State
Journal's* able editor saw nothing but failure in Clay's effort: It would
be "infatuation to run him again." The "fourth defeat" would certainly
result! "To my . . . amazement I met the Address of Mr Clay," wrote
a McLean man from Wheeling, Virginia. The "response," he predicted,
would make "Clay's cheeks tingle." Contrary to the traditional view
that Clay was long an active candidate, his belated decision created
astonishment.

Clay's letter "has done him much injury," Joseph Taylor wrote Thurlow Weed. "It is the opinion of many . . . Whigs in Kentucky that he
would not carry that state. . . . Scott, I consider, stronger than Mr Clay
tho' he is greatly deficient in common sense. . . . He would make a
better race than . . . Clay." Old Rough and Ready's brother concluded
that "the masses of the people are decidedly in favour of General Taylor," and politicians "opposed to him." If it was necessary for "Brother
Joe" to write Weed, this was a sensible psychological approach to so
subtle an operator.

Meanwhile, as Clay fervor cooled and jelled, more than one Whig
manager smiled in Scott's direction. "Scott has risen rapidly," Harvey
granted in April. "There is a . . . growing feeling for Scott [in] the
last two weeks," Hunt agreed—but revelation of the old *Intelligencer*
letter was "embarrassing & may prove fatal." People "take more pleasure in looking at Scott's foibles than in contemplating his great qualities," Hunt observed. Not only did Scott offend immigrants and come
off second-best with Marcy, but 1848 found him enmeshed in a court-
martial and a feud with three generals—when he should have kept his
coattails clean.

Despite Scott's plight, there were those who supported him. Skeptical
of Taylor's no-party stand, Godlove S. Orth of Indiana guessed that
Scott would attract more votes than Taylor in the Western country.
"Shall this party disband," Orth asked, and follow one unwilling to

pledge himself to principles? "Never, never!" exclaimed the Hoosier—whose candidate was Winfield Scott.

To such a crest did the Scott wave roll that Greeley, who opposed both Scott and Taylor, became "somewhat alarmed." William F. Johnston and other Pennsylvania Whigs were "strong for Scott" in April. Hugh White, an old Clay man, called attention to Scott's rise. Pennsylvania had a large Scott majority, White reported, and New Jersey and New York "would easily be persuaded to unite with Pa." Congressman Robert Schenck now formulated plans to promote Scott in Ohio. Though no great enthusiasm was felt for either soldier there, Ohioans preferred a Northern general to a Southern one and decided to give Scott their twenty-four votes in a last-minute attempt to block Taylor. Scott's bud blossomed too late. Not enough Clay men turned to him. Weed withheld the prestige of his name. And Greeley seemed as eager as ever to discredit all soldiers, Scott included.[7]

7

If Scott's aspirations had hard sledding, the same could be said for John McLean's. McLean himself, in whose opinion Taylor could not be elected—and no military man ought to be—remained half hopeful despite rebuffs. But few people supported McLean. Even in the late winter, when some correspondents submitted optimistic reports, others were strikingly pessimistic. "The great majority of the thinking men in the West and North look to you," William Burnet advised, but "thinking" people were not active enough. Caleb B. Smith confided that McLean could be nominated only if Ohio Whigs united on him, while Corwin men preferred an outsider to their factional enemy.

Unrealistic as McLean's hopes were, they contrasted favorably with Webster's. "Godlike Dan" was a rank outsider. A careful study of the writings of men involved in convention preliminaries reveals that Webster was barely mentioned in discussions of available Whigs. The few votes pledged to him were more in the nature of a tribute to what he had been in bygone times than an indication of current strength. Webster seemed bitter as the campaign progressed. He had been "very glum" one winter day when some Massachusetts people called on him. Laudatory remarks being made, he "waked up and his eyes flashed and sparkled." He was definitely against Taylor, he stated. He opposed his old rival, Clay, also. Indeed, there was not an entry in the field who elicited Webster's wholehearted approbation. Weed made an attempt, he said, to interest the Senator in the Vice Presidency. But the tail of the ticket lacked appeal.[8] And so Daniel Webster, sulking in his tent, missed the second chance in his career to follow a hearse into the White House.

Corwin was counted out of the race. As early as January, Seward wrote that Corwin "seems to forego all hope of the Presidency, just now at least." "The friends of Mr Corwin give up pretty generally all hope before a National Convention, and are beginning to beg for the vote of *Ohio* on the *first ballot* as a compliment," one of the McLean clique noted. In February, Horace Greeley stated categorically that Corwin "will not be a candidate."

8

Up to April 22 there was an opportunity for a very dark horse to be touted by the Whigs. Clay's candidacy was fading. Webster and Corwin were eliminated. McLean lacked fire. Scott's handicaps were heavy. And Taylor, who was still out in front, continued to embarrass some partisans by insisting over and over that he was opposed to national conventions, to strict party ties and to making commitments. As a result he lost prestige in the first four months of 1848. Congressional sentiment began to form in behalf of Clayton, Crittenden, or another compromise. "I think . . . Taylor cannot get a Whig nomination unless [he] promises to be a Whig President—, and it seems too late for that," Weed wrote on April 9. "Perhaps it may go off on Scott, though I think Clayton would be the better man!" Apparently, Weed made a similar proposal to Representative Hunt, for on April 17 Hunt acquiesced—perhaps after taking a poll on the Hill—"Either of the two you suggest would be judicious. Probably a majority would say Crittenden: We'd prefer Clayton on some accounts." Hugh White wrote that, through the month of April, "there . . . has been . . . a sort of private, secret intrigue in the Senate, by and through which some choice spirits are to be placed at the head of affairs."

Was the "intrigue" to which White referred the same as the intraparty plot never mentioned by Weed in his *Autobiography* but revealed in correspondence? The answer, it appears, is yes. There is no evidence to show that Crittenden was a full-fledged partner in the scheme. But Weed, Hunt and Clayton were certainly active, and it is probable that— had Taylor made no gesture to improve his standing with Whig leaders—Clayton or Crittenden might have emerged as the Whig standard-bearer when the smoke cleared away.

What hits the student between the eyes is how pitifully eager most of these men were to annex the highest prize. Following the example of Webster and Clay, the younger Whigs clung to the notion that destiny would tap them lightly on the shoulder and waft them to the Executive Mansion. Like Dickens' Micawber, each was "ready . . . in case of anything turning up." Though in some cases words belied ambition, usually attitudes did not. The symptoms of the disease were in all, perhaps excepting Crittenden. Whenever availability was broached, their unspoken answer was "Barkis is willin'." Pathetic were their twists and turns, tin-soldier tactics, deals and deceptions after April 22. On that day the die was cast. Until it dawned they had a chance. But the next-to-last Saturday in April found Taylor signing the First Allison Letter, which insured his victory and their defeat.[9]

CHAPTER VII

The First Allison Letter

1

JOHN STADLER ALLISON, to whom the letter was addressed, might never have figured in history if he had not won the heart of Miss Emily Taylor, a Kentucky belle. His marriage to Zachary's sister took place in 1822, and almost at once the bridegroom became one of his brother-in-law's closest friends. The fact that Allison was a tobacco middleman, wholesale grocer and commission merchant in Louisville, familiar with crop prices and investment trends, made him a valued counselor.

After his wife's death, Allison went on working in Kentucky. As a partner in Hewitt, Allison & Company with offices on Third Street between Main and Water, he acted as Taylor's local agent. Later he traveled in the Lower South, spending part of his time in New Orleans, where he was in business on Madison Street. Allison believed in putting money in stocks, whereas Taylor preferred plantations and slaves. Notwithstanding this difference of opinion, the two men continued to respect each other. The General thought so well of Allison that he gave him his power of attorney, was willing to entrust him with his daughter's education, and in an early wartime will named Allison an executor of his estate.

There was nothing spectacular in this. On the basis of his business career, Allison would remain a shadowy figure. Fortunately, however, he can be re-created from records of his Army service and accounts of people who knew him well. He wore old-fashioned clothes, these tell us, and was eccentric in manners and dress. He had served in the War of 1812 and his military reputation clung to him. A third of a century after Pakenham's defeat, he was still "Captain Allison"—addressed by the title of his soldiering days. Yet Allison's unique distinction was the comb he sported from morning till night—for his hair arrangement was in a class by itself, and he came to be known as "the Captain with the Comb." In circles where Allison was a stranger, this adornment gave rise to mirth. But when he called on friends, Negro butlers announced him formally as "Captain Allison with the Comb." Here there was no attempt at facetiousness, so accustomed were his intimates to his peculiar taste. Captain Allison was visiting Taylor on April 21, 1848, when three of the General's political friends arrived at Baton Rouge on the boat from New Orleans, armed with the draft of a letter which they hoped to persuade the candidate to sign.[1]

2

Much has been written, in biographies and memoirs, on the subject of the letter in question. Every book reference printed to date has its quota of errors, which historians have repeated for want of fresh evidence. Long attributed to Crittenden or Stephens, the letter should at last be credited to its actual author, Logan Hunton, with corrections and additions by Taylor himself. To be sure, many Whig politicians prepared statements they thought Taylor should issue. Abraham Lincoln was one of these. Stephens, probably, was another. John Bell of Tennessee was a third, Meredith P. Gentry a fourth. Crittenden, certainly, submitted a proposal. Weed may have done the same. There is a manuscript in Seward's hand, which could have been copied for a similar purpose. Another correspondent, who perhaps thought he inspired the Allison Letter, was Representative Truman Smith.

About April 10, certain Southern Whigs in Congress "became alarmed at the manifestations of public opinion in reference to Taylors no party attitude." Colonel Bliss arrived in Washington that day. On April 11, after "a conference with several members among whom was a locofoco Senator" (possibly Jefferson Davis), Bliss departed for Baton Rouge with the "united entreaty of these gentlemen" that Taylor would "declare himself a Whig." "It is supposed the letter will reach Washington on the 1st to 5th of May," James Bowen predicted to Weed. "Those with whom I consulted," Bowen continued, "are confident the letter will be forthcoming & that it will be all that is desired."

If the modern historian had nothing to go by aside from Bowen's communication, and if Weed's interest in promoting Clayton were not apparent from his correspondence, the supposition might be reached that Weed and his friends were primarily responsible for Taylor's letter to Allison.[2] However, Crittenden's Southern lieutenants, far removed from the halls of Congress, brought pressure to bear on Zachary Taylor while Bliss was still en route. Logan Hunton was one of these, James Love a second member of the group. And Balie Peyton joined Love and Hunton in urging Taylor to follow their suggestions.

These men had met some days before at the Saint Charles Hotel, New

Orleans, with Hunton as the guiding spirit. Like the congressmen many miles to the north, they felt uneasy because of Taylor's "refusal to write his political . . . opinions . . . as a platform for his nomination at Phil[adelphia], the only chance he had to secure it." They took under consideration the letters which the General "had been induced to write by injudicious friends," accepting random nominations and failing to bind himself to the Whigs. Hunton, Love and Peyton all admired Taylor. In their opinion, "he had the simplicity of an honest heart untainted with a thought of self—where his country or his honor were concerned."

But was an honest heart enough? Love, Hunton and Peyton were aware that many a Taylor backer "wished him to be an independent candidate," and avoid a convention altogether. Experienced at the polls and on the hustings the three well-wishers realized that a no-party stand would only guarantee Taylor's defeat. As to the autumn they had no doubt; Taylor's fame would bring to his side "sufficient . . . supporters" in November. But in the spring, the trio concluded, his "only chance for success . . . was a distinct avowal of Whig doctrine"—so as to "satisfy and unite" delegates to the Whig National Convention. Before separating they decided to consult some of Taylor's "most reliable friends," and not long afterward a larger gathering assembled in a Saint Charles parlor. Alexander Bullitt was now of the number. "We made our proposition and it was agreed to," Love recorded for posterity. Bullitt, Peyton, Hunton and Love were appointed members of a committee to compose a letter, and to go to Baton Rouge for its submission to Rough and Ready. "Bullitt declined, and did not accompany us." But Hunton, Love and Peyton went. Hunton drew up the draft—"every word of it." "It was submitted & approved," and "we took our way."

Hunton, Love and Peyton reached Baton Rouge on Friday morning, April 21. Taylor met them at the landing, conducted them to their lodgings and thence to his quarters where they were to dine. "We had told him our business, and when we reached his residence . . . we assembled around a table," and there the draft was presented by Hunton. As Hunton read aloud, Zachary Taylor made those "pithy remarks" for which he was noted. Love jotted down what Taylor said, while Hunton intoned and Peyton listened. The General then "showed us . . . letters he had received from many leading men"—"some of them asking him to write that which would have ruined his chances." He also carefully explained that such had been the press to write, and not to write, that he did not think he would write.

After dinner, Taylor and Love took seats at the end of the gallery overlooking the river. There Love warned his host that the only chance for success lay in the Whig nomination, and to secure it "he had only to say in writing what he . . . said today to us, and [I] read over to him what he had said." When Love and Taylor rejoined their friends, Hunton's draft was considered a second time. Finally the General agreed to sign a letter incorporating "what he had said & no more." Peyton had another engagement, but Hunton and Love returned to their rooms to rewrite and condense the candidate's words. The labor of composition, Love has testified, was entrusted entirely to Hunton, who pruned and polished the manuscript far into the night.

"It was a very short letter," Love later wrote Hunton. "We criticised every word, sentence & paragraph. It was every word written by you, from Genl. Taylors remarks. Its grammar, punctuation, and all is yours."

When Love and Peyton had approved the statement, the three breakfasted at Taylor's cottage. Hunton read aloud what he had composed. Taylor assented and prepared to sign, but Hunton insisted the letter must be in Taylor's handwriting. The General copied and addressed it to Allison, who had no factional connections. Thus the most important document of the preconvention campaign came to be known as the "Allison Letter."

Hunton, Love and Peyton were anxious to board the ten o'clock boat that Saturday morning, so as to be in New Orleans quickly and give Bullitt the letter for publication. By the merest chance the boat which was to take them landed Bliss on the lawn above Taylor's quarters. "We went out and met him," Love recorded. "He brought voluminous dispatches. . . . Some few were read. Genl Taylor said he had written all he intended," and invited Hunton to read the letter to the group. When Love asked Bliss what he thought of it, he replied he was no politician but considered it "better than any he had seen."

Peyton, Hunton and Love departed. And on Tuesday the Allison Letter was printed in the *Picayune*. It is reproduced here from the original manuscript, with dots substituted for punctuation incongruities:

Baton Rouge April 22d, 1848

Capt. J. S. Allison
Dear Sir,

My opinions have recently been so often misconceived & misrepresented I deem it due to myself if not to my friends to make a brief exposition of them upon the topics to which you have called my attention. I have consented to the use of my name as a candidate for the presidency. I have frankly avowed my own distrust of my fitness for

that high station; but having at the earnest solicitation of many countrymen taken my position as . . . a candidate, I do not feel at liberty to
surrender that position until my friends manifest a wish that I should
retire from it—— Then I will most gladly do so—I have no private
purposes to accomplish—no party projects to build up—no enemies to
punish—nothing to serve but my country; and the station would bring
with it cares and responsibilities as well as honors——

I have been very often addressed by letter & my opinions have been
asked upon almost every question that may occur to the writers as affecting the interests of the country or their party for the past[,] the
present or the future—I have not responded to these enquiries for various reasons—— I confess whil[e] I have great Cardinal principles
which will regulate my political life, I am not sufficiently familiar with
all the minute details of political legislation to give solemn pledges to
exert my influence if I were President to carry out this or defeat that
measure. I have no concealments. I hold no opinion which I would not
readily proclaim to my assembled countrymen; but crude impressions
upon matters of policy which may be right today & wrong tomorrow
are perhaps not the best test of fitness for office; & one who cannot be
trusted without pledges, ought not to be confided in merely on account of them—— I will now however proceed to respond to your
inquiries——

First, I reiterate what I have often said . . . I am a Whig but not
ultra Whig. . . . If elected I would not be the mere president of a
party—I would endeavor to act independent of party domination, &
should feel bound to administer the Government untrammelled by party
schemes——

Second—The veto power—The power given by the Constitution to
the Executive to interpose his veto is a high conservative power; but in
my opinion it should never be exercised except in cases of clear violation
of the Constitution, or manifest haste and want of due consideration by
Congress—— Indeed I have thought that for many years past, the
known opinions & wishes of the Executive have exercised undue & in-
jurious influence upon the Legislative Department of the government,
& from this cause I have thought our system was in danger of undergoing a great change from its true theory——

*The personal opinion of the individual who may happen to occupy
the executive chair ought not to control the action of Congress upon
questions of Domestic policy; nor ought his opinion & objections to be
interposed when questions of Constitutional power* have been settled by
the *various* Departments of government *and acquiesced in by the people*——

Third. Upon the subject of the Tariff, the Currency, the improvements of the great Highways, Rivers, Lakes & Harbours the will of the
people as expressed through their Representatives in Congress ought to
be . . . carried out and respected by the Executive——

Fourth. The Mexican War. I sincerely rejoice at the prospect of peace—— My life has been devoted to arms, yet I look upon war at all times & under any circumstances as a national calamity to be avoided if compatible with National Honor; the *principles* of our Government as well as its true *policy* are opposed to the subj[ug]ation of other nations & the dismemberment of other Countries by Conquest—— In the language of . . . the immortal Washington 'Why shoul[d] we quit our own to stand on foreign ground'.

In the Mexican War our National honor has been vindicated[,] amply vindicated, and in dictating terms of peace we may well afford to be forbearing & even magnanimous to our fallen foe[.]

These are my opinions upon the subjects referred to by you, & any reports or publications written or verbal from any source differing in any essential particulars are unauthorized & untrue——

I do not know that I shall again write upon the subject of National politics—I will engage in no schemes—no combinations, no intrigues. If the American people have not confidence in me[,] they ought not to give me their suffrages—— If they do not, you know me well enough to believe me when I declare that I shall be content—I am too old a soldier to murmur against such high authority——

                                                    Z. TAYLOR.[3]

3

The reaction to the Allison Letter was extremely favorable. "If Gen. Taylor's letter of [the] 22d could be presented alone and all the others forgotten, it would . . . turn the scale in his favor," wrote Washington Hunt, who was pro-Scott. "The friends of Gen Taylor have rallied with . . . increased vigour" since the publication, Hugh White noted. Many agreed and Greeley feared "that Zachary Taylor is getting strong." Harvey was of the opinion that "Taylor stock has gone up very much," and "the Taylor fever" in Washington was described as "burning."

Still there were complicating factors. The day before Hunton's arrival, Taylor had penned another letter—addressed to the editors of the Richmond *Republican*—in which he reaffirmed his no-party position, in an effort to hold independents in line. "During a recent visit to Philadelphia, I found a decided hostility to Taylor for his letter of the 20th," Harvey reported to McLean. The *Republican* document, however, had an immediate purpose to serve. Harvey said that Clay had shown him a communication from Taylor, promising to "stand aside" in the event of Clay's being a candidate. The letter of April 20 denied such a pledge.

If Taylor had a real rival now, Scott—not Clay—was the man. Schenck made a hurried trip west, returning with the news that Ohio was "in a blaze for Scott" and would cast her votes for him. Schenck also saw

Scott portents in upstate New York, but Washington Hunt was not so sure. "No man can doubt . . . Scott's election if nominated," Hunt predicted, "but will he be nominated? That probably depends on New York——" Seward and Greeley opposed Scott. The "blaze" was notably lacking in New York City, when Fuss and Feathers arrived from Mexico in May. Scott's reception "showed no enthusiasm on the part of the people." To Caleb Smith "the great danger" was Taylor or Scott "would be the nominee." Elisha Whittlesey was more realistic: "Taylors friends . . . are more confident of success, and are better organized than the friends of any other candidate." This summed up the situation in a nutshell.

Taylor's letter to Allison served as a banner to rally wavering Taylor men. It provided a broad platform on which Whigs could stand, and was—in Love's opinion—"the most effective" paper of its kind "ever written[,] all the circumstances considered."[4] But the letter was not wholly responsible for his swelling support. Taylor had organization strength. He was the beneficiary of backing at the grass roots. Before Hunton grasped his hand at Baton Rouge, Old Rough and Ready had been nominated locally by independent state conventions in Louisiana and Kentucky; by a Whig state convention in Virginia; by Whig legislators of Iowa and Georgia, Alabama and Arkansas; by independents in Pennsylvania; by Whigs of Tennessee; by Whigs and others in Illinois, and by independents in Mississippi. Town, city and county meetings had advanced his name for the Presidency. Rough and Ready Clubs were formed in nearly all the large cities, and rank-and-filers responded emotionally to the neophyte in politics.

Taylor lost favor here and there. The Syracuse *Journal* hauled down his flag, at its masthead nearly two years. The Boston *Courier* could not bring itself to endorse him under any conditions. The leading Whig newspaper in Indiana, for Old Zack in the preliminary heats, now plumped for Judge McLean. Greeley continued in opposition. Weed was reported clinging to Clayton. An effort was made to combine Scott's following with Clay's, Clay heading the ticket with Scott as the tail. Someone assured an anti-Taylor New Yorker that "our Ticket would be Clay & Scott." "Glorious this," exclaimed one of Weed's henchmen, who feared the rumor was "too good to be true."[5]

Still Taylor's candidacy prospered. Truman Smith "is a strong friend," wrote Todd, who was touring the East in the General's behalf. "We think half of N—— England will go with the South if the South will stand by Gen Taylor." Todd was heartened when Maine "fulfilled my anticipations by electing Taylor Delegates, & 3 out of 7 have been chosen in N. Jersey." Meanwhile, there was also good news from Georgia, where men friendly to Taylor were picked. And Florida followed suit.

4

Taylor's powerhouse was Kentucky. While Hunton wrote Taylor's Allison Letter, and Todd journeyed through the East, Crittenden continued to give direction to the Taylor forces in Washington. And Crittenden's *alter ego,* Brown, tightened the party reins in Frankfort.

As if by prearrangement Brown swung into action at the Kentucky capital the same day Hunton set foot in Baton Rouge. No longer concerned with the possibility of hurting Taylor by offending Clay, Brown and four associates addressed a printed circular letter "to the Friends of General Taylor in Kentucky." Pointing out that they had been named to constitute a "Central Committee," the five asserted that Clay's decision "is different from what was anticipated by the Whig Conventions in Frankfort." Taylor "occupies the same position now that he has always done." With this as a premise, they urged Kentucky delegates to the National Convention to "bear in mind the circumstances under which they were appointed," and not to forget that "Taylor is an available candidate in Kentucky." If "an occasion should arise," they should "proclaim this truth and . . . act upon it."

Brown's circular contained no condemnation of Clay. Its moderation made it the more effective. Taylor enthusiasts took their cue from it. Of the twelve delegates, only James Harlan was counted out of Taylor's camp. The fact that Kentuckians favored Taylor constituted a political asset which Brown and Crittenden labored to protect. The nation's Whigs took notice of the product of Brown's pen, which was second only to the Allison Letter in solidifying Taylor's strength.

5

There is one more episode of the preconvention story that bears retelling. This was the famous "Battle of the Chalk-backs," which Alexander Stephens described. During the winter of '47-'48 the Taylor stalwarts in New York City had been unable to cope successfully with bands of hoodlums who insulted their speakers and broke up their meetings. Humphrey Marshall had been howled down. His fellow orators were hissed and heckled. Sponsors were at a loss to know how to handle the intruders, most of whom they could not identify. Cries and catcalls, jibes and yells, became standard practice at Taylor gatherings. Not until two of Crittenden's "Young Indians" hit on a solution in Washington could Taylor's cause be fairly presented at a public assembly in the city.

Stephens takes most of the credit for getting in touch with Isaiah Rhynders (a leader among New York toughs), who was "sore at the manner in which he had been treated by the Polk administration and . . . in sympathy with the Taylor movement." Rhynders and a crew of his "boyhoys" met Robert Toombs in a Manhattan saloon on Wednesday evening, April 26. Here, enjoying a round of drinks, they reached an understanding that the next night would find them in the hall where Toombs would speak. On parting Rhynders told Toombs not to retire to his seat even if outbursts should occur. Toombs was to continue his oration as if nothing unusual were happening. Rhynders and his confederates then could be counted on to do the rest.

On April 27, at Lafayette Hall, an enthusiastic crowd assembled. But no sooner had Toombs stepped forward and said, "Fellow citizens of New York——" than a yell went up: "Slaveholder!" "Slaveholder!" Toombs remained composed. He started over, only to hear: "Hurrah for Clay!"

Toombs, in imperturbable temper, not seeming . . . excited in the least, again commenced; again yells arose. [Then] there was the greatest row you ever saw. "Put him out!" rang from one side of the hall to the other, and everywhere a stalwart arm was seen pitching some fellow out. Rhynders's men were at work. Some who were being pitched out exclaimed: "I made no noise!" "You have chalk on your back!" was the reply; "and you've got to go."

In two minutes the hall was cleared of some forty "chalk-backs." Rhynders's plan, as he afterward told Toombs, had been to scatter his men through the audience; they were quietly to mark the backs of all who made interruptions; on the order, "Put them out!" they were to seize and put out by force all chalk-backs. He and they knew pretty well beforehand who were the brawlers sent to break up the meeting; but, to make certain, his plan was first to spot them. The hall was soon cleared of rowdies. The audience was quiet and orderly while Toombs gave them one of his masterly popular harangues. Before the conclusion, the wildest enthusiasm prevailed; loud shouts of applause went up; and then came "three cheers for old Zach!" given with . . . vim as Toombs took his seat. Our victory was complete; we had a foothold in New York; our battery in that stronghold of the enemy was well served afterward and did most effective work. Great events often turn on small ones.[6]

Stephens may have exaggerated the importance of what Rhynders did in Lafayette Hall, but not the color of the incident or the virility of the men involved. The significance of the "Battle of the Chalk-backs," however, really lies in the Georgians' strategy more than in the Rhynders tactics. Like the Allison Letter and Orlando Brown's circular, it indicates the skill of Taylor's supporters in coping with problems as they came to them. With Hunton's composition as their keynote they now approached the Whig National Convention resourceful, alert and unafraid.

CHAPTER VIII

HORACE GREELEY'S SLAUGHTERHOUSE

1

IN ANALYZING the Philadelphia convention, it is well to recall Taylor's long opposition to submitting his name to such a gathering. Taylor discerned Whig weaknesses more acutely than the professionals themselves. He knew the Whigs were a minority party, and that his own strength lay in his following of Democrats and independents plus Whigs. It was vital to victory that he retain every portion of his political appeal, rather than appear as the exclusive nominee of a party accustomed to run second best.

The Allison Letter did not reverse Taylor's attitude. Stressing his relative independence of pledges and party platforms, the General's language reminded Whig waverers of his attractiveness as a candidate. He still believed that "a Whig national convention . . . will result in no good," because it would aid the "bringing about" of "a strict party vote." In February, Taylor had written: "Should I be nominated by a Whig or Democratic convention . . . exclusively on party grounds, I would . . . decline." But, should "either or both" leave "me free to act on the grounds I have taken, I should have no hesitation in accepting." This remained Taylor's stand. Since it had been decided to hold a Whig convention despite the General's preference, he had to slant his candidacy Whigward, while doing as little as possible to antagonize his non-Whig friends. Reluctantly he concluded that he must be nominated at Philadelphia first, in order to be elected later.

One facet of the Allison Letter's success is seen in the disinclination of Taylor's non-Whig supporters to disown him the moment it was published. Ultimately this was of great importance—for without keeping part of his independent backing his prospects for the Presidency were doomed. Neither the pro-Taylor Democrats nor the Native American party, which had "recommended" him to the franchise of its members in a national convention held in November, backtracked from Taylor in the spring. These were in a position to bid for the balance of power, and their leaning toward Taylor influenced many Whigs. Meanwhile, not only was Joseph Taylor "persuaded of the Success of his brother in the Convention," but Corwin predicted in May that "Taylor would be the nominee," and Greeley "almost despairs of being able to defeat the nomination of Taylor." When reports arrived from New England that half the Maine delegation would vote for the General, even C. B. Smith admitted "that the nomination of Taylor is inevitable."[1]

2

Delegates began trending toward Philadelphia as early as the second week in May. They rattled and bumped in archaic stagecoaches, lurched aboard their primitive trains, or sat serenely on the decks of luxurious river packets. Nearly all had been chosen in state or district conventions, where their presidential preferences were known or suspected. A few were obscure creatures of political caprice, Philadelphia-bound because their betters had defaulted. South Carolina was represented by but two men, Arkansas by one, Texas by none. New York, on the other hand, had thirty-six delegates—and Ohio twenty-three. Indiana sent forty Whigs, though entitled only to a dozen votes.

Most of the Western and Eastern delegates did not pass through Washington on their journey, but many of the Southerners did. The Palo Alto Club met them at the station. Overwhelmingly for Taylor before they reached Washington, they found their ardor reinforced by Truman Smith and Crittenden. Now and then a Whig or two looked in at Baltimore, where the Democrats nominated Cass. But most went directly through to Philadelphia, and it was there that Henry White of Pennsylvania pounded the gavel on the second floor of the Chinese Museum at the northeast corner of Ninth and George streets, shortly after noon on Wednesday, June 7.

As early as Monday, Philadelphia was excited. "Nothing but the Whig Convention," said the *Public Ledger,* "and the names of . . . Taylor and . . . Clay fill the mouths of debaters at the hotels. . . . Men never . . . remarkable for their penetration in the ordinary affairs of life have grown suddenly sagacious in political matters. The delegates themselves are beset with arguments, influences, and all sorts of . . . canvassing."

3

Individual delegates were less interesting personally than the ballots they cast. The *North American* counted 314 of them altogether, including the supers from Indiana, but the total vote to which they were entitled was only 290. Most belonged to the second order of politicians (state legislators, county officials, district bosses). Only one United States senator, three ex-members of that body, fourteen men currently serving in the House, and twenty-four ex-representatives sat among the accredited. There were, however, nine former governors, two future Vice Presidents of the United States, lawyers, planters, journalists, poets, a shoemaker, a shovelmaker, merchants and judges.

It is true that the Massachusetts delegation included Rufus Choate, then possibly the brightest star of New England's legal firmament. Connecticut had sent Truman Smith. The abilities of Rhode Island's James F. Simmons, Virginia's William S. Archer, Alabama's Henry W. Hilliard and Ohio's John A. Bingham were well above average. Still, the conclusion is inescapable that the delegates as a whole were rather mediocre. The strongest delegations were those of Massachusetts (with Charles Allen, Henry Wilson, George Ashmun and Choate); Tennessee (headed by Senator John Bell) and Ohio (which included John Sloane and Joseph Vance, together with young John Sherman). Georgia, Virginia and North Carolina were ably represented. Attention was centered on the six Louisianians, whose spokesman, Lafayette Saunders, had known Taylor many years, while Cuthbert Bullitt, another member, was Maunsel White's son-in-law. Friendly relations obtained between them and Louisiana's most famous citizen. And Saunders had stopped off to see the hero on his way to Philadelphia.[2]

A list of influential wirepullers reads like a roll call of prominent Americans who dominated the middle of the century. Crittenden, Weed, Greeley, Clayton, Lincoln, Colfax, Leslie Combs, Millard Fillmore—all these were present, but not as delegates. It is hard to imagine Weed casting his vote individually, in preference to recording it through twenty or thirty mouthpieces. Establishing headquarters in a hotel room, he was often seen at Josiah Randall's house (where Joseph Taylor was ensconced as a result of Weed's influence). Weed's attitude is no easier to analyze during the convention than before it, and he appears not to have abandoned hope of Clayton's or Seward's chances to the very end. He thought well enough of Taylor's prospects, however, to see Zack's brother handsomely entertained.

Another mystery involving Weed concerns his attitude toward the Vice Presidency. In his *Autobiography* Weed tells of his trip to discuss the second place with Webster, but he does not integrate the Weed-Webster interview with the ambitions of Seward, Abbott Lawrence and Fillmore. The Seward angle is peculiarly baffling. That Seward had not entirely discarded the vice-presidential possibility as late as May 27 is shown in a letter to Weed. "I leave the whole matter to your discretion," Seward wrote.

4

With Weed engrossed in his fathomless game, Crittenden and Smith worked tirelessly for Taylor. Smith personally took part in the crucial third-ballot shift. Crittenden kept out of sight as far as the written record is concerned, but was equally efficient in promoting Taylor's fortunes. They had powerful tools to work with. Still they had much to contend with, too. Antislavery Northerners, inveighing against Taylor's "noncommittalism," whispered the warning that his nomination—unless fortified by pledges against slavery extension—would signal revolt in Northern states.

This was a real threat. Taylor's men had the votes for his nomination—perhaps on the first ballot, assuredly on the fourth. The South was nearly solid for him—Pennsylvania split—Clay's own Kentucky predominately pro-Taylor. Ohio, on which Clay counted heavily, had been persuaded by Ex-Governor Vance to throw its weight to Scott, thus dividing the opposition. And from twenty states or more came one, two or three delegates receptive to the argument that Taylor was available. The problem of the Taylorites was to secure Taylor's nomination while giving least offense. They could have bludgeoned Taylor's enemies with sledgehammer strokes, but only at the risk of inviting reprisals.

The Taylor strategy resolved itself into winning major floor contests and forfeiting minor ones. On Wednesday noon, when White rapped for order, John A. Collier of New York was made president *pro tempore,* and James Harlan of Kentucky secretary *pro tem.* There was no objection, though both were Clay men. Later, a Taylorite—Charles M. Conrad—announced that Louisiana was authorized to represent Texas, which had failed to send its own citizens to the convention. This involved four Taylor votes, and was therefore of greater consequence. But even here Conrad did not force events. The subject was diplomatically passed over, and Thomas Butler King moved the naming of one delegate from each of the states to a committee empowered to recommend a permanent convention organization. Included in this group, as the Texas member, was Joseph M. Wray of Louisiana. A Clay delegate insisted this was improper, since Wray was no Texan. But when he submitted a motion that Wray be removed from the committee, Collier—though for Clay—

ruled the motion out of order. This was the initial test of Taylor power.

During the second Wednesday session the nominating committee brought in the name of John M. Morehead, former governor of North Carolina, as the convention's presiding officer. Morehead was a conservative Clay Whig, whose presence in the chair gave assurance of fair play. Tall and portly, fifty-one, Morehead delivered an ornate speech to which few Whigs could take exception. No sooner had he finished than the right of Samuel J. Peters (Louisiana) to sit as Texas' vice chairman was abruptly questioned. After some discussion Peters was seated, the permanent organization was concurred in and the convention granted authority to King's nominating committee to pass on the credentials of all delegates. Thus the second skirmish was won for Taylor, and the convention adjourned till the next morning.

5

There were fifteen Taylor men on King's committee, eleven planning to support Clay on the first ballot, two for Webster, one for Scott, and one for Clayton. In reality several of Clay's backers were favorably disposed toward Rough and Ready. Hence it was no surprise when on Thursday King presented three resolutions which, if adopted, would aid Taylor's cause.

The first of these was the most controversial. In full convention the slave states would have had 123 votes, and the free states 167. However, seven South Carolina and three Alabama districts being unrepresented, the South's total went down to 113. Seven of the nine delegates present from these two states were for Taylor. The North had only one missing district. Accordingly, when King submitted a resolution "that the majority of delegates from States not fully represented . . . vote for the districts from which there are no delegates . . . and . . . fill vacancies," it was clear that its adoption would give Taylor a substantial increase. This resolution produced a spirited debate, and some of the Taylor men spoke in its favor. They were by no means united in its support, however, and a Taylorite from South Carolina stood in the forefront of those who assailed it as a matter of principle. The convention's rejection of the resolution, by a majority of thirty, was indicative of moderation.

The second resolution concerned the Louisiana men at Philadelphia. A Louisiana Whig convention had approved eighteen delegates, of whom fifteen were for Taylor and three for Clay. Though the state was limited to six votes, ten Whigs had come. Which six should be selected? In this case the Taylor master minds acted with more slickness than honesty. They argued that those casting Louisiana ballots should be divided proportionately to the original eighteen—five for Taylor and one for Clay. This was well enough, but they also insisted that the lone Clay delegate be G. B. Duncan, not William Brashear. The lukewarm Duncan might be expected to switch to Taylor on an early ballot, while Brashear was a *bona fide* Clay man whose faith in his idol never wavered. Eighty-three years old, he pathetically protested before a majority cut him down.

The third critical resolution dealt with the Texan anomaly: *"Resolved, That . . . the delegation from Louisiana be empowered"* to vote for the Lone Star State. Strangely enough, in view of the objections twice voiced on a like issue the previous day, there was little disposition on the part of non-Taylor men to object. The Texas resolution quickly passed, Taylor obtaining four additional votes. Incidentally, instead of including Brashear in the Texas contingent, Bullitt was named with three others, and thus was a delegate from two states!

6

At this point, on a Clay man's motion, the delegates adjourned to reassemble at four o'clock—behind closed doors and with spectators barred. Even reporters were kept out. It was rumored that the doors were locked to enable the delegates to discuss, privately and without interruption, the merits of the various candidates. It was also said that a delegate had in his possession a letter from Taylor, in which the General took "a decided stand in favor of Whig principles."[3] This was probably the statement Taylor wrote May 20 and addressed to Balie Peyton. Representative Garnett Duncan had a copy, but no other has ever come to light. Supplementing the Allison Letter, it was somewhat more Whiggish—the sort of communication which, had it been turned over to the press, might have hurt Taylor in the autumn. Here in the National Convention, however, it was the first of two pieces of evidence offered to forestall anti-Taylor attacks. It was doubtless the primary reason for the mysterious hush-hush. Meanwhile, Saunders, King and others probably spoke. And, judging by nearly all events taking place Thursday night and Friday morning, enmities were mollified and friendships promoted.

When the public was readmitted, some signs of friction still remained. But the lone delegate from Arkansas, who was for Taylor, was authorized to cast three ballots. Maine's Edward Kent, ardent for Taylor and eager to get the voting under way, moved that at half past five o'clock the convention should take a first ballot. This was subsequently postponed to a quarter past six, on a Webster supporter's motion. Now some angry language was exchanged, and much good accomplished by the secret session was undone, Ohio's Lewis D. Campbell introducing a resolution studiedly offensive to the Taylor side.

Campbell presented it in the form of an amendment to a routine procedural motion. He wished no man to be considered eligible for the nomination unless pledged to abide by the decision of the convention and promote the measures of the Whig party. This was a stiff backhand slap at Taylor, but Morehead in the chair ruled it out of order— not on merits or demerits, but because it was not germane to the parent resolution. Campbell appealed. His appeal was tabled. There was much confusion, and only after further delay did the convention proceed to its principal business.

7

Scott was the first claimant to be nominated, his sponsor being the persistent Campbell. The Ohioan described his man as "a thorough Whig," who "would stand by the principles of the Whig party." Asahel Huntington said simply: "I nominate as a candidate for President, Daniel Webster, of Massachusetts." Taylor's spokesman, Edward Kent, followed with the declaration that "on behalf of the *people* of the Union, I nominate General Zachary Taylor." Here the most enthusiastic applause broke out on the convention floor and in the galleries. The cheers "lasted many minutes," and there could be no doubt of Taylor's popularity as the rafters rang after Kent sat down. There was applause, equally loud, when N. Bowditch Blunt of New York named Henry Clay. These were the two big demonstrations. John M. Clayton was also nominated, and an Ohio delegate said he was authorized to withdraw McLean's name if presented, but it was not until Morehead recognized Judge Saunders that more excitement was felt throughout the hall. Explaining that much misunderstanding existed in relation to Taylor's principles, Saunders presented a statement from the Louisiana delegates that Taylor's friends would be bound by the convention's decision, and would withdraw him in the fall if not now nominated. This declaration may have influenced the voting, which now got under way.

On the first ballot, Taylor did not have a majority. He polled 111 votes; Clay, ninety-seven; Scott, forty-three; Webster, twenty-two and the rest were scattered. Clayton had Delaware's three. Nearly all of Webster's tallies came from New England. Twenty of Scott's delegates were from Ohio, nine from Indiana, five from New York and six from Pennsylvania. Clay's following was more widely distributed, but his power stemmed chiefly from New York, where twenty-nine delegates were for him. His weakness revealed itself in four ways. His following in the Cotton South was negligible; Kentucky divided against him, seven to five; Ohio accommodated with only one vote and the New England states with only sixteen. Clay had been led to count heavily on Ohio. If three fourths of Ohio's delegates had plumped for him, Clay would have nosed out Taylor for the lead. Taylor polled fifteen votes from Virginia, six from North Carolina, one from South Carolina, ten from Georgia, six from Alabama, six from Mississippi, five from Louisiana, four from Texas, thirteen from Tennessee, seven from Kentucky, six from Missouri and three apiece from Arkansas and Florida. These accounted for eighty-five of his total, the remainder being given him by Maine, Vermont, New Jersey, Pennsylvania, Ohio, Indiana, Illinois, Wisconsin and Iowa.

On the second ballot, Taylor advanced but slightly. Charles Jackson of Rhode Island, John C. Clark of New York, David Taggart of Pennsylvania, Joseph Warner and Daniel Sigler of Indiana, J. W. Grimes of Iowa and Duncan of Louisiana backed the General for the first time, his total advancing to 118. At the same time, Clay's strength slumped from ninety-seven to eighty-six. Scott, who rose slightly from forty-three to forty-nine, still was nowhere as a challenger. As the hour grew late, over fifty Whigs sprang to their feet to move adjournment. Crowds still congregated on the streets as delegates strolled off toward their hotels, and, when it was learned that Taylor led on the first tests, there was loud shouting all around the town. The popular reaction was pro-Taylor.[4]

8

An analysis of the shifts of Friday morning suggests that whatever finagling was done in Taylor's behalf late Thursday night was engineered largely by Truman Smith and Maryland's Reverdy Johnson.

Maine voted first, Scott gaining a recruit—Louis O. Cowan, who had been for Webster. New Hampshire and Vermont stood pat. Rhode Island also repeated—one vote for Taylor, three for Clay. But when "Connecticut!" reverberated through the hall, there was evidence where Smith's true sympathies lay. The six delegates of the state had been instructed to vote for Clay. Now, however, Smith led the way—and two colleagues followed—into the Taylor camp. This was the first break in the dam.

Clay picked up a Webster vote in New York, but lost one of his own to Taylor and two to Scott. This meant little—likewise Pennsylvania's showing, and that of Massachusetts, New Jersey and Delaware. It was not until three Clay votes from Maryland landed in Taylor's column that everyone realized the extent to which Clay's prospects had declined. Taylor advanced elsewhere (North Carolina, Indiana), but the real damage to Clay's cause was done by Connecticut and Maryland. Taylor had a gain of fifteen on the third ballot, Scott a gain of five and Clay a loss of twelve. The totals now ran: Taylor, 133; Clay, seventy-four; Scott, fifty-four; Webster, seventeen; Clayton, one. Taylor had moved within seven points of winning the nomination.

What happened on the fourth ballot was almost an anticlimax in the light of the trend revealed on the third. New Hampshire and Vermont cast larger votes for Zack, and three Rhode Islanders—who had never deviated from Clay—joined Ex-Governor Jackson in making their state unanimous for Taylor. Victory was in sight—the long contest nearly over. New York delivered the finishing stroke to Clay and Scott when Taylor gained four delegates there. The voting continued. Eleven other states swelled Taylor's triumph. Big shifts were in Maryland, North Carolina, Kentucky, Wisconsin and Illinois. Then came the totals—171 for Taylor; sixty for Scott; thirty-five for Clay; fourteen for Webster. It was a clean-cut victory. The crowds gathered outside the hall broke into "a roar of huzzas." This thunder echoed in the Chinese Museum, where the cheers of the galleries also showed the emotional preference of the people for Taylor. "Many members of the Convention joined in the shout," and "for five full minutes" there was "irrepressible" enthusiasm everywhere.

Viewing the vote objectively, it is obvious that Weed had less to do with the outcome than Crittenden, King, Bell, Johnson, Smith and the Rhode Islanders. On the last ballot, when Taylor was given six votes by the New York delegation, Scott got fourteen—which certainly is not indicative of fervor there for Taylor.

9

Once nominated, Taylor stood to benefit or suffer from the convention's aftermath. There were appeals for recognition from the chair, cries of "No! No!" "Sit down!" and motions for adjournment. In

The Juggler in Trouble

General Taylor, in the role of a Chinese juggler, says: "I berry much 'fraid dat some of dese d——n knives tumble down an' cut my finger. I can't keep um up much longer." From *The John-Donkey,* a humorous magazine of 1848. Reproduced through the courtesy of Ohio State University, Columbus.

the midst of the cacophony, New York's Collier was recognized by Morehead. An anti-Weed Whig, Collier pleaded for harmony. He also put in a well-timed plug for the vice-presidential candidacy of Fillmore, then comptroller of the Empire State.

Less harmonious remarks were made by Allen of Massachusetts. In a "quiet voice" and without gesticulation, Allen objected to the proposal that Taylor's nomination be made unanimous. "We have" a man who "will continue the rule of slavery for another four years. . . . We spurn the nominee," he said. Then, referring obliquely to Lawrence's vice-presidential prospects, Allen continued: "Massachusetts will spurn the bribe. . . . I say that the Whig party of the United States is . . . dissolved." Here came "tremendous hisses and confusion," some cheers too. "Order must be preserved!" cried Morehead. But the determined Campbell followed Allen with a resolution that was dynamite: "Resolved, That the Whig party . . . pledges itself to abide by the nomination" of General Taylor, "if he shall agree . . . to its great principle—no extension of slavery over territory now free, and . . . protection of American industry." (Shouts of "No! No!"—"Withdraw it!")

"I must decide the motion out of order," Morehead ruled. "The order of the day is the nomination of Vice-President."

Campbell: "Am I to be gagged?"

Johnston of Pennsylvania attempted to conciliate Campbell, explaining that he, like the Ohioan, had been uncompromising in his support of Scott. The chairman, however, cut him short.

Wilson of Massachusetts: "I have never scratched a ticket . . . but I will go home, and so help me God, I will do all I can to defeat that nomination."

Great confusion, excitement, cheers, hisses. A Pennsylvania Taylor man moved to adjourn until half past three.

Cries of "No! No!" and "The ballot. The ballot!"

Morehead: "We must proceed to the order of the day."

10

Even the Vice Presidency called forth some color. Fourteen individuals were placed in nomination, including the inscrutable Weed. Others were Thomas Ewing of Ohio, William Woodbridge of Michigan, George Evans of Maine, King of Georgia, Abbott Lawrence and Robert C. Winthrop of Massachusetts, John Sergeant and Thomas M. T. McKennan of Pennsylvania, and five New Yorkers—Fillmore, Seward, Governor John Young, Hamilton Fish, and James Watson Webb. (Tradition persists that Kenneth Rayner of North Carolina also was under consideration in caucus.)[5] Actually only four were taken seriously—Lawrence, the millionaire, who had entered the convention a heavy favorite; Seward, who was not interested; Ewing, an ambitious and receptive leader, and Fillmore, who has come down in the histories as an instrument of accident, a sop to the Clay men, or purely a product of Collier's speech.

In fact Fillmore was all three of these—but he was something else beside. Prominent in the politics of western New York for nearly half of his forty-eight years, he had become a national figure of the second magnitude as chairman of the House Ways and Means Committee in Washington, where he was partly responsible for the passage of the Tariff of 1842. It is not widely known that as early as that year he enjoyed a small boom for the vice-presidential nomination, and in '44 he was disappointed when Theodore Frelinghuysen was picked to run with Clay. In 1848, rivals stood in Fillmore's path, but with destiny's aid he outdistanced them. His natural opponent was Seward, who might have been nominated with Weed's blessing, had he desired the place.[6] Fillmore's next obstacle was Lawrence, who made no secret of his eagerness. Here Massachusetts factionalism entered the picture. The mood of the Wilmot Proviso Whigs was dangerous. How to placate them? Why, one way was to sacrifice the manufacturer, who continued to be an active candidate—but was impotent after Allen spoke.

It may seem astonishing that Ewing did not defeat both Fillmore and Lawrence. In many ways he would have strengthened the ticket. But, after a New Yorker withdrew Seward's name—apparently with the latter's approval—Campbell of Ohio addressed the chair for a similar purpose regarding Ewing. Ohio wished "no sugar plums," he cried. When a Pennsylvanian inquired by what authority Campbell withdrew Ewing's name, Campbell replied that he did it in behalf of the Ohio delegation. According to Governor William Bebb, this was untrue. Nevertheless, Campbell's remarks eliminated Ewing, who might have given Fillmore a spirited run.

On paper, the contest became one between Fillmore and Lawrence, but soon it was no contest at all. The first ballot was close, Fillmore polling 115 votes to Lawrence's 109. Really, however, there was not the slightest doubt about Fillmore's triumph once Seward and Ewing were scratched. On the second ballot most of the favorite sons were eliminated. Pennsylvania plumped unanimously for Fillmore and he drew votes from every state but three. His total was but one point short of doubling Lawrence's. There was "long continued cheering" when Morehead proclaimed him the vice-presidential nominee.

11

This was the ticket then—Taylor and Fillmore—and a typical compromise it proved to be. The major parties were closely divided. No candidate for either office could please both sections. When the Democrats had nominated Lewis Cass and William O. Butler at Baltimore, important minorities had been alienated among Northern and Southern delegates there. The same was true at Philadelphia, but Southerners at the Chinese Museum swallowed Fillmore with better grace than Northerners accepted Taylor.

Taylor's candidacy was not unanimously confirmed, and the delegates adopted no platform. Reconciled to the sentiment that extremists of North and South could never agree on the extension issue, they did not even bother to indorse planks on banking, improvements or the tariff. It was enough to cheer Taylor's heroism, to enumerate his victories, to smell again the gunpowder of Monterey and Buena Vista.

That night in Philadelphia newsmen reported "an immense Ratification Meeting" in progress. "Speaking is going on from the principal stands and from a dozen stumps. . . . Bengola lights, illuminated lanterns, are . . . hanging from the . . . trees. Fireworks, squibs and crackers are in full operation." Correspondents described the "tremendous enthusiasm" of the crowds gathered around the orators, cheering their pronouncements to the echo. There was considerably less enthusiasm in one of the rooms of the Chinese Museum where men from Massachusetts and Ohio condemned Taylor's nomination. Greeley, too, was "mad clear through." Accosted by a reporter as he hurried down Chestnut Street, the *Tribune* editor was asked how he liked the outcome of the convention. "Can't say that I admire it" was Greeley's curt response. And it was not long before the *Tribune* broke out with an impassioned anti-Taylor editorial entitled "The Philadelphia Slaughterhouse."[7] The convention was "a slaughterhouse of Whig principles," Greeley insisted. **And, in fact, it was.**

CHAPTER IX

CAMPAIGN IN THE SOUTH

1

THE most dramatic political episode following the Taylor-Cass nominations stemmed from the readiness of many Northern Democrats to break with their party's nominee. Barnburners of the New York Democracy had bolted the Baltimore convention, and their antipathy to Cass increased during June and July. Their objections to the rotund Senator from Michigan went far beneath the political surface. In contrast to their Hunker rivals, these Barnburners were Wilmot Proviso men. They were also practical politicians, who resented the fact that Hunkers received top favors in Washington. Nor were they forgetful of the treatment meted out to Martin Van Buren four years before, when, paced by Cass, the dark horse Polk secured the Democratic nomination.

A young friend of George Bancroft's outlined the situation in prophetic vein. Opposition to the Cass ticket was of a sort not to be adjusted, he wrote. "Before the proceedings at Baltimore it would have been . . . difficult to produce . . . harmony in this State; but after them, perfectly impracticable." The third ticket which "we talk of nominating at Utica," together with the enthusiasm for Taylor, "leaves the Cass chances at the minimum point." When the Barnburners met at Utica, Van Buren's faction nominated him for President. The Barnburners also arranged with Conscience Whigs and some abolitionists for a great national convention of free-soil advocates at Buffalo on August 9.

Grumbling in the Democratic ranks was not confined to the Northeast. It spread south to the Gulf of Mexico, and indeed the largest proportionate Whig gains of 1848 were in Southern states. Of the thirteen states where slavery was legal in '44, Clay had carried only five. Florida and Texas had entered the Union during the interval between campaigns, and now fifteen slave states had 121 electoral votes. The fact that this was no landslide year, like '28 and '40, necessitates a scrutiny of local situations and individuals. The shift of voters in Alabama, for example, was more extensive than in Virginia. State triumphs hinged on state conditions as well as on national issues and men.[1]

2

Alabama was Exhibit A where local angles were important. In '44 it had given Polk a larger popular majority than any other slave state. Only South Carolina, which voted through its legislature, had been more Democratic. Alabama was too much like Mississippi and Georgia to rationalize on economic grounds a Democratic margin nearly twice the size of theirs. The discrepancy can best be accounted for in terms of men—not lands or money. From early times in Alabama, its Whig leadership had been spotty. The people were normally Democratic, except in some central and southern counties and notably in cities like Montgomery and Mobile. Even the wealthier planters were less inclined toward Whiggery than in adjacent states. Most of Alabama's hard-fought battles were waged between Democratic factions rather than between Democrats and Whigs.

In 1844 the party of Polk enjoyed relative unity in Alabama; this was responsible for his big majority. In 1848 the Democracy was split. Governor Reuben Chapman was losing his following. Although most Democrats remained loyal to Cass, the eloquent Yancey objected to the nomination at Baltimore. When Yancey said Cass was not to be trusted, a minority of Democrats nodded assent. The beneficiary was Taylor, who, as a Southern man, also had converts among Democratic planters. Thus, despite a weak Whig machine, Taylor acquired votes on the fringes. The popular Whig Henry W. Hilliard meanwhile stumped in Taylor's behalf. Many Whigs doubted that Old Zack could capture the state's electoral vote, but observers rubbed their eyes at the Alabama Whigs' intense activity.

Whig portents were also seen, at the outset, in South Carolina. There was more nationalism there than is generally understood. But aristocratic low-country interests used an ancient "parish representation" system to control the only state still voting through its legislature. Disregarding the Unionist views of Joel R. Poinsett, Benjamin F. Perry and James L. Petigru, Senator Calhoun's tight little clique dictated South Carolina's course. Calhoun did not look with favor on Cass. True, he was a Democrat—but, by Calhoun's standards, parties were secondary to the South's welfare. The preceding December, Calhoun had referred to "the impossibility of finding a candidate at the North, and the hazard of looking . . . to that quarter." Calhoun's *presumed* attitude was reflected in the press. And the fact that the nullifier Isaac E. Holmes was running for Congress as a Taylor advocate bracketed Taylor with the extremists. There was thus a temporary tendency to list South Carolina as "probably" Whig, despite its history.

3

Alone in the South, Louisiana had a special interest in high tariffs. Sugar was one of its principal products, and sugar planters wanted protection. Louisiana's vote for Clay had been large; he would have carried the state, except for a mammoth fraud in Plaquemines Parish. Now Whigs were especially careful that the '44 steal should not be repeated. There was also considerable pride in a favorite son's ambitions. Taylor's New Orleans friends were numerous. President Samuel J. Peters of the Chamber of Commerce and Maunsel White (a Democratic legislator) were equally strong for Taylor. Like South Carolina and Alabama, Louisiana seemed to favor Taylor in the early summer.

Mississippi's political position lay between Alabama's and Louisiana's. Its Polk majority was more typical of the entire South than any other state's except Virginia's.[2] Supporting the victorious candidate from 1828 to 1844, Mississippi seemed a perfect barometer. Numerous Democrats strung along with their Jefferson County neighbor. But whether Taylor's planting interests could swing a majority into the Whig column, few Mississippians could say.

Georgia deserves particular attention. It elected Whig and Democratic governors and senators, congressional districts dividing four and four. Georgia was a fiercely contested battleground. Taylor's chief supporters—Stephens, Toombs and T. B. King—had to contend with transplanted Calhounites as well as Democratic highlanders. In this campaign, however, the state's Whig partisans—whether hailing from hills or bottoms—trusted Taylor as Stephens and Toombs did. Taylor men in Georgia were organized to an extent which their Alabama brethren never approached.

One other Southern state, Taylor's native Virginia, presented peculiar local problems. Delaware, Maryland, North Carolina, Kentucky and Tennessee were Whig in '44 and expected to repeat. Missouri and Arkansas were Democratic; it was the consensus they would remain so. Texas and Florida, new and sparsely populated, did not come in for much attention. In Virginia, however, parties underwent frequent and drastic revisions. Many prominent Whigs, like William C. Rives, were old Democrats who had broken with Jackson or Van Buren. Ranged against them were former Whigs, such as Ex-President John Tyler. Virginia had given Polk a majority almost equal to Mississippi's, but in '47 there was a revulsion in the western counties and six Whig congressmen were chosen. Still, the Virginians sent to the Senate that year were Calhoun protégés. Complicating the picture was the attitude of Clay men. Some reacted bitterly to Taylor's nomination. Most cooled off, but John M. Botts of the Richmond district kept the embers glowing.

4

As the campaign interest heightened, attention centered on the August vote. North Carolina, Tennessee, Kentucky, Missouri and Alabama were to ballot for various candidates on August 3. Though local personalities and absorptions twisted issues out of shape, prophets sought a sign in Whig North Carolina and Democratic Missouri (where the trend seemed to be Democratic), and in Whig Tennessee and Democratic Alabama (where the opposite was true). More glances turned to Kentucky's gubernatorial campaign. Since Kentucky was a banner Whig state, few believed that young Lazarus Powell, the Democratic nominee, had an outside chance to beat Crittenden. But a small margin for Crittenden might furnish proof that the difference between victory and defeat for Taylor reposed in the hands of Henry Clay.

Powell and Crittenden made spirited speaking tours, and at first the latter seemed a victim of Clay's retaliation. But as Crittenden's battalions went into action, Brown, Letcher, Metcalfe, Todd, Hawes and Duncan proved effective in winning back recalcitrants. More than anyone else in Kentucky, Crittenden sold himself to the people. His national prestige was tremendous. Before leaving Washington, he was honored at a dinner which nearly every Whig in Congress attended. En route to Kentucky, he had been feted—and during the journey responded readily to requests for partisan orations. At Pittsburgh, Crittenden hit the campaign's keynote. His emphasis was all on Taylor. Touching on the causes of the war, Democratic culpability and the veto power, Old Zack's chief sponsor stressed the soldier's personal qualities rather than specific issues. Friendly and lighthearted, injecting humor into sallies at the Democrats, Crittenden appeared at his best on the familiar Kentucky stump. At Russellville he regaled his audience with the homespun tale of a young Kentuckian who found people "much split up" regarding the Presidency: "*Rough and Ready* had . . . many friends, but he believed *General Taylor* would beat him; but . . . one they called '*Old Zack*' would beat both!"

Hardly sidesplitting humor, this, by sophisticated standards. But on the hustings most effective!

Linking his own candidacy to Taylor's, Crittenden in August won the governorship with an 8,500 majority. The Whig press publicized it widely, and the fact that a weak Whig candidate barely came through in North Carolina appeared less significant by Whig interpretation than the Kentucky returns. Such was the *official* Whig reaction. *Unofficially* Whig partisans were less confident. John S. Pendleton wrote Crittenden of his disappointment when the totals were revealed, and Burnley also had hoped for a more sweeping majority.[3]

5

Zachary Taylor did not campaign personally. By modern standards he was inactive. Though he took brief trips and appeared in public several times, he never ventured outside Louisiana and Mississippi. Taylor was at his plantation when word of his nomination reached him. The telegraph had flashed the message as far south as Memphis, in time for the steamboat *General Taylor* to pick it up before speeding downriver. When the packet came churning up to the Cypress Grove landing, her captain told Taylor the news, which he heard with no apparent emotion while excited passengers cheered. Taylor's casualness was not deceptive. As he walked off in the direction of his house, he gave the impression that such an event was only an incident to him.

Taylor's letters also mirrored his modesty: "The nomination was to me a matter of no exultation. . . . Even should I be the successful candidate I shall not rejoice, or mourn if defeated." The Philadelphia accolade was "an honor of which I may be justly proud . . . coming as it does from one of the purest, most talented & patriotic" bodies ever formed "for a similar object." Taylor approved Judge Saunders' assertions in the convention: "I am satisfied there was nothing improper or even inconsistent in them." And yet "I do not conceive I have departed from the position I assumed ever since my humble name was brought before the country for the high office in question."

Despite this, a report circulated that Taylor repudiated Saunders' pledges. Peyton, Hunton and Bullitt moved to correct this impression: "We are authorized by Gen. Taylor to say that the course of the Louisiana Delegation . . . meets with his . . . unequivocal approbation." This was on June 23. Six days later, writing a Baltimore committee of independent Taylor men who had questioned him, the General again expressed his approval of what Saunders had done. Taylor explained that, before the convention met, he had informed Saunders that as delegates "my friends . . . were . . . bound, if I were not nominated, to sustain and support the nominee." "I was a candidate," the old soldier continued, "only so far as my friends had chosen to make me one. . . . I did not feel myself at liberty . . . to withdraw myself . . . [but] my friends . . . could do so whenever they should see fit." Finally he had pointed out that if they could elect "any one better qualified . . . than I," it was "their duty to go for him; and . . . I should hail the result with joy."

Taylor saw no inconsistency between this position and "the language which I have uniformly held on this subject." Under "the general authority . . . given these gentlemen, I . . . deem whatever statements they may have made to be right. . . . Confident in their integrity, and in the sincerity of their friendship for me, I shall sustain them without qualification. I, therefore, now take . . . the responsibility of the acts of the . . . delegation . . . and am prepared to stand by the consequences." Taylor voiced regret that the Maryland independents had "misunderstood" Saunders' course and "imagined that I . . . abandoned the position which I have . . . held. . . . I cannot expect . . . that any of my friends . . . should do violence to their own sense of right . . . by supporting my election, while they believe I have changed my political views. . . . I take every American citizen's interest in his country to be as pure and deep as my own; and I have . . . no right, and . . . no desire, to influence his action in the . . . important duty of voting."

Taylor specifically asked that the letter be kept out of type, "though I have no objection to your circulating" the original among "your friends." Aversion to the "appearance of my name in the public prints, in connexion with such subjects, is my apology for the request." Taylor must have been motivated by something other than this. Perhaps Peyton, Hunton or Bullitt emphasized the risk of offending non-Whigs among the General's followers. If so, their strategy was mistaken. Either the letter should never have been written, or it should have been published at once. If it lost Old Zack a corporal's guard of independent supporters, its determined tone could have commended him to other waverers and dispelled confusion regarding Taylor and Saunders.

6

A Georgia Democrat left perhaps the best contemporary description of Whig campaigning in the Lower South. Whigs' speeches consisted

Of "abuse of Cass and the Democrats, comments on the danger to slavery, and the impossibility of trusting any Northern man, exemplified by the course of Van Buren—and lastly a glorification of Old Taylor's battles. I have never heard . . . them advance a principle—save . . . that Congress ought to decide all questions, as per Allison letter." They "refuse to acknowledge that they are for any of the old Whig measures . . . and go it blind for Taylor as a slaveholder and a hero." One advantage was that Whigs had no common platform. In the South they took "ultra Southern ground and abuse us as traitors . . . for not going so far as they do, and in the North vice versa. They don't care a fig what you prove on them about their Northern allies. They don't profess to think alike— and . . . will give up . . . Northern Whigs freely (except Fillmore) if they can involve . . . Northern Democrats in the same odium."

Southern Democrats' "hardest work" was to meet "the prejudice against . . . Northern men," which the Whigs "foment so artfully by taunting us with Van Buren." Was not Cass Van Buren's former associate in Washington? After supporting "Van" in '36, had he not been minister to France when the Red Fox was President? Now the former Chief Executive deserted the regular Democrats to spearhead the Free-Soil movement! What was there to prevent Cass from ultimately doing the same thing? Cass's record on extension was open to attack in both sections. As recently as '46 he intimated approval of the Proviso principle, yet in '47 he reversed his stand, enunciating the doctrine of Popular Sovereignty. Congress, Cass argued, possessed no constitutional power to pass on the extension of slavery. Residents of the several territories should determine slavery's fate in the West. "Leave to the people who will be affected by this question, to adjust it . . . in their own manner," Cass wrote a Tennessean, Alfred O. P. Nicholson. But was this Cass's last word? Why take a chance with Cass, when Taylor was available?

This theme ran through Whig sectional tactics. Together with lavish praise of Taylor, it was a thread in the political skein which bound enough Democrats to Rough and Ready to give him majorities in some Southern states. Nearly everywhere Taylor rallies were well attended— with a sprinkling of Democrats usually present. Leadership of the cause, however, almost invariably lodged in Whig hands. This was true from Wheeling, Virginia, where "the Mayor of the city presided" and "spirit-stirring songs were sung,"[4] down to New Orleans and the Louisiana bayous. In Kentucky "bonfires gleamed" when news of Taylor's nomination penetrated to remote hill settlements. People "bored augur holes in . . . forest trees, and filled them with powder" in celebration. When

Taylor's nomination was announced, New Orleans Whigs' "anxiety . . . gave way to wild joy"—S. S. Prentiss, Judah P. Benjamin and Peyton lauding Taylor and predicting his election. Peyton and Prentiss attended also "a large and enthusiastic meeting" at Mobile, where resolutions hailed the Taylor-Fillmore ticket as a "harbinger of incalculable good to our country."

Not only at the outposts of the South but also in the states between, Whig politicians swung into stride behind their leader's banner. Georgia associates of Stephens and Toombs, Tennessee friends of Bell and North Carolinians like Rayner set a fast and faster pace. Whigs took heart when the Charleston *Mercury* lashed at Cass's nomination. A meeting of Charleston Democrats denounced the Baltimore proceedings as "unsatisfactory." Archer of Virginia, an ancient Clay foe, exclaimed, "Thank Providence! We have got rid of the old tyrant at last"—and he put his heart into the struggle. Mississippi's local pride in Taylor resembled Louisiana's; the intimate Taylor-Davis friendship meant much to the borderline voters, and the Natchez *Courier* carried at its masthead: "For President, Zachary Taylor, of *Mississippi*."

7

Thus Whig optimism boomed in the South. The Democrats, however, were not marking time. Their managers were busy, their speakers forceful. Stephen A. Douglas orated in New Orleans on behalf of Cass, but most of their phrasemakers were Southerners, imbued with devotion to Southern rights. The governors of every state south and west of Tennessee, and the bulk of the congressmen, were members of Cass's party. Armed with patronage and organizing potential, there was nothing halfhearted in the Democrats' efforts. Such figures as Pierre Soulé of Louisiana, William Trousdale of Tennessee and John A. Quitman of Mississippi took to the stump. Whigs quoted Cass as saying: "We are no slaveholders. We never have been. We never shall be. We . . . pray for" slavery's "obliteration . . . when it can be effected justly, peaceably, and easily." Democrats countered by asserting that Whigs could not be trusted to defend the South—Taylor's silence being interpreted as a "mask for antislavery opinions."

As the charges flew thick and thicker, songs were written, marches composed, slogans adopted by the faithful. On the Whig side there were Rough and Ready Clubs, Rough and Ready airs and *Rough and Ready* propaganda sheets. Because their nominee was less colorful than

Taylor, Democrats seemed less flamboyant than their opponents. Both parties appealed to racial minorities in New Orleans—where Spanish, Italian and German organizations mobilized for Cass or Taylor. Boatmen, draymen, butchers, coopers, river pilots, even hatters were represented in the marching. Politicians duplicated this program in other communities, and attention was paid concurrently to residents of upland areas—where Whigs traditionally polled a light vote with the exception of 1840's. More than one attempt has been made to show that the big-plantation counties voted Whig with the greatest regularity.[5] But in '48 the Southern Whigs made substantial gains in cities, and in rural areas where slaves were comparatively few. This was an anomalous feature—anomalous, that is, if the appeal of Taylor's personality is not appreciated.

Van Buren, of course, had few backers in the South. When the telegraph brought word of his nomination as the Buffalo Free-Soil standard-bearer, Southerners accepted it as further proof of Yankee hostility. There was talk of placing a fourth party in the field. This would have been a Southern Rights party, created for the purpose of rallying extremists to the banner of such exhorters as Yancey. It never became an actuality. Old alignments were still binding. Although some of the chivalry looked askance at Taylor and Cass, prevailing opinion induced most voters to conclude that one or the other could be trusted. Had a fourth party been formed, it is more than likely that (except in South Carolina) it would have sapped Taylor's strength—for his supporters were less homogeneous than the Democratic nominee's. Probably the Whigs would have split wide open in many of the cotton states, since it was Taylor's presumed Southernism that attracted his sectionalistic neighbors. The desertion from Taylor never took place; plans for the new party faded in talk, and the contest in the South continued to be a two-way affair.

8

There was a time in the late summer when a swing to Cass seemed in the making. This trend had begun in North Carolina, where the Whig Charles Manly nearly lost the governorship. As recently as July 20, Taylor Democrats in South Carolina had nominated a Taylor-Butler ticket, and the Charleston *Mercury,* organ of the hotspurs, withheld its endorsement of Senator Cass. Thirty-odd days later the political climate underwent a change. Democrats, including Calhoun men, expressed their preference for the Baltimore candidate "because he was a Democrat and also because he . . . denied the constitutionality of congressional legislation" on slavery. It is hard to understand why Cass's position, so unsatisfactory elsewhere in the South, seemed convincing in Calhoun's state. Possibly Cass had given private assurances on policy to Calhoun. Though Calhoun himself made no pronouncement for either Cass or Taylor, and is said to have advised against the pro-Cass meeting, Calhoun's friends boarded Cass's band wagon. And Rhett's *Mercury,* no longer hesitating, likewise came out for Cass.

Gideon Welles, a Connecticut Democrat and none too intimate with Cass, inscribed in his diary the importance he attached to the Carolinas. "All who know any thing of the views of Mr Calhoun and his friends," Welles wrote, "are aware of their . . . dislike of Cass. . . . Yet they have come into the organization." This "re-invigorates" Democrats "through the whole South." Should the "movement unite the . . . South, and the N Carolina election indicates a tendency that way, then there is . . . a probability that Cass will succeed, which until those indications seemed an . . . impossibility."[6]

How mistaken Welles was is quite clear when his jottings are studied with advantages of hindsight. Manly's near-defeat in North Carolina was unrelated to Calhoun's decision. Manly simply was not a popular figure. His Democratic opponent, David Settle Reid, was militant and attractive to the people. The issue of this gubernatorial race was "the abolition of the requirement that a voter for state senator must possess a freehold of fifty acres of land." It had nothing whatever to do with Calhoun. Furthermore, Welles's complementary opinion—that South Carolina would reinvigorate the Democracy all over the section—was rooted almost as deeply in error. The sweep of events in other cotton commonwealths ran counter to that in South Carolina, where Cass electors were finally chosen by 129 votes to twenty-seven. But the trend in other states actually was away from Cass.

In Louisiana, Peyton predicted on August 29 that "we will carry the State if our party keep[s] up the fire hot . . . and heavy . . . but the majority will be small." In Alabama, such prominent Democrats as James E. Belser and Samuel F. Rice led their followers to the Taylor reservation, and Yancey, though he would not vote for Taylor, refused to the last to support Cass. Some of the best work for Taylor was performed in Mississippi, where Alexander K. McClung of Monterey fame recovered from his wounds sufficiently to join A. B. Bradford, William R. Miles and William A. Lake in beating the bushes as Taylor electors. In Georgia the vote given the eight Democratic candidates for the House exceeded the Whig total by only 260. This spurred the Whig managers, who capitalized on a vicious physical attack and knifing of "Little Alec" Stephens by a Democratic orator on a railway platform. Stephens became a Georgia hero, and General Taylor would reap the reward.

Thus the campaign progressed in a region where Whig Chairman Truman Smith had hopes of picking up thirty-four electoral votes (those of Alabama, Florida, Georgia, Louisiana and Mississippi) in addition to the faithful Whig nucleus of Delaware, Maryland, North Carolina, Tennessee and Kentucky. Smith placed South Carolina in the doubtful column until August, and kept Virginia there till November. Only in the extreme Southwest—Texas, Arkansas and Missouri—did Southern men seem entirely unreconciled to Zachary Taylor's candidacy.[7]

CHAPTER X

CAMPAIGN IN THE NORTH

1

THE three most populous states in the Union held the key to Northern votes. These were New York, Pennsylvania and Ohio—of which only Ohio had supported Clay. Still pivotal, New York had thirty-six electoral votes: Pennsylvania, twenty-six; Ohio, twenty-three. These added up to eighty-five, more than a quarter of the nation's total and enough to decide the race.

In New York, Taylor was far from popular—not so much on his own account but because of esteem felt there for Clay. Though he had never carried the state, nowhere were the Kentuckian's friends so devoted as in New York City. Clay had been the first and only choice of sixteen New Yorkers in Philadelphia. Of their twenty fellow delegates, thirteen were for him on one or more ballots. In New York, too, were Horace Greeley, Willis Hall and Luther Bradish, who refused to ratify Taylor's nomination. Due to the fact that without New York the Whig ticket could not win, the dour response of Clay's thick-and-thin advocates upset Whig regulars after Philadelphia. Growls were heard where there should have been harmony, and only the more raucous quarrels of the Democrats drowned out the dissonance of the Whigs. If at Buffalo a Whig had been made the third-party candidate, many New York Whigs would have abandoned Taylor for Free-Soil. This, however, never eventualized. McLean was turned down[1] in favor of Van Buren, so the Whigs were cemented and the Democrats split.

From August on, the Democratic rift made Clayites' murmurs of little consequence. No matter how flagrant were Whig errors made by factional managers, the Whigs enjoyed the unusual advantage of not having to worry about New York. Weed, Seward, Fillmore and their colleagues were confident by the middle of the summer that New York was in the bag.

2

If the Whigs had been equally confident of retaining the eleven states carried in '44, the campaign would have been far less exciting. Their

105 electoral votes plus New York's thirty-six left only five needed for victory. With the Cotton South veering toward the General, Taylor's statisticians could then have counted on Louisiana or Georgia to slide him over the top. The professionals, however, were leery of presumptions. And Truman Smith's Whig organization doubled and redoubled its efforts.

Ohio, especially, was a hard nut. Clay had cracked it, but General Taylor never was strong in the Buckeye State. After his nomination, Governor William Bebb, Senator Corwin, Thomas Ewing and Joseph Vance urged Taylor's election. But the Cleveland *True Democrat, Western Reserve Chronicle,* Lebanon *Star,* Lorain *Courier,* Medina *Whig,* Marietta *Intelligencer,* Greenfield *Patriot,* Piqua *Register,* Tiffin *Standard* and other journals renounced him.

Particularly in the Western Reserve, the campaign was off to a sizzling start. Even before the Buffalo convention, Free-Soil meetings were held in Geauga, Lake, Butler, Columbiana, Madison, Mahoning, Cuyahoga, Trumbull and Knox counties.[2] If some antiextension Democrats fell away from Cass, a majority of Ohio's Free-Soilers were Whigs—and it was small satisfaction to know that Democrats also had troubles. Whig leaders did not abandon Ohio, but arranged for intensified stumping from the river to the lake. They were far from sanguine—and Corwin was especially glum.

3

Pennsylvania, with twenty-six votes, was the natural offset to Ohio. Antislavery sentiment there was most prevalent in normally Democratic sections, like David Wilmot's Towanda district. In Pennsylvania, Van Burenitis seemed fatal to Democrats rather than Whigs.

There was more to the Pennsylvania scene, however, than Wilmot's adherence to Van Buren. Residents of Pittsburgh thought in terms of coal and iron, not cotton or Negroes. Other communities—Lancaster, for instance—blended antislavery with business conservatism in the person of Thaddeus Stevens. Some quarters expected Stevens to switch to Van Buren and Free-Soil. But the brilliant, fanatical, clubfooted Stevens delivered a Fourth of July speech for Taylor and ran for Congress as a Whig. The reason lay in the preoccupation of his neighbors with the Tariff of '46. A slump in the price of iron products—followed by a manufacturing decline—was blamed by Whigs on Dallas, Buchanan

OLD ZACK TAYLOR IS THE MAN!

THURLOW WEED   JOHN J. CRITTENDEN

In the cartoon, Taylor (at the right) holds his White House lease. A beardless Uncle Sam directs Lewis Cass (one leg over fence) to stay out, and Polk and other spoilsmen evacuate the Mansion. The author is indebted to the New York Public Library and the Filson Club, Louisville, for the Weed and Crittenden likenesses.

and the whole Polk crowd. Since Stevens had lost money in the Caledonia Iron Works, defeating Democrats naturally was the first order of business with him.

At least as important as Wilmot and Stevens was a gifted adventurer named Lewis C. Levin, who was chiefly responsible for the growth of the Native American movement. Under him it had been a force in Pennsylvania politics since vicious anti-Catholic rioting sullied the City of Brotherly Love. Reckless, unscrupulous but withal a spellbinder, the devious Levin with devilish skill welded anti-immigrant groups into a majority, which sent him to Congress in '44 and '46. His had been a guiding hand in the Native American National Convention which in '47 "recommended" Taylor for the Presidency—without, however, committing him to Native "principles." Taylor formally acknowledged the overtures, as he did those of every party. But Levin's decision to back him in the summer of '48 was premised primarily on a deal made with the Pennsylvania Whigs. This consisted of a coalition slate: Taylor for President, Levin for Congress, each supported by Whigs and Natives. Not only in Levin's First District but throughout Philadelphia and its environs, the Natives were to swing the balance of power in Taylor's favor. Clay had carried Philadelphia—city and county—by only 4,438 votes. So now the promise of a plurality twice that size heartened Taylor's sponsors.

Pennsylvania, thus, was atypical. It resembled neither Ohio nor New York. Such old conservatives as Andrew Stewart of Uniontown, Walter Forward of Pittsburgh, Sergeant of Philadelphia, and McKennan of Reading added their zeal to that of younger Whigs like James Cooper, William M. Meredith, Alexander Ramsey, Randall and Johnston. But essentially, it was the unbeatable combination of Wilmot's Democrats, Stevens' Whigs and Levin's Natives that brought smiles to the faces and hope to the hearts of Taylor's friends.[3]

4

There was no Levin in Massachusetts, where most of the noise (if not the skill) originated with Free-Soilers. Samuel Hoar guided a minority Whig faction, which repudiated Cass and Taylor and made C. F. Adams Van Buren's running mate. Waving the Buffalo banner of "Free Soil—Free Speech—Free Labor—and Free Men," young Massachusetts enthusiasts headed by Charles Sumner were heard on political platforms from Boston to the Berkshires. Despite their reputations current and subsequent, they were less effective than Albert J. Beveridge and other writers have indicated; Taylor men were far from being "well-nigh para-lyzed" by the neophytes. Such redoubtable Whigs as Rufus Choate, Nathan Appleton, "Honest John" Davis, Charles Hudson and Robert C. Winthrop remained loyal and useful to the General. Eventually, Webster also gave qualified adherence to Taylor and the Whigs.

"I am an anti-slavery man," Webster wrote E. Rockwood Hoar, but ". . . I have no confidence in Mr. Van Buren. . . . I would much rather trust General Taylor on this very question of slavery, for I believe . . . Taylor is an honest man. . . . I am sure he is not so much committed on the wrong side, as I know . . . Van Buren to have been for fifteen years."

Beveridge claims that Webster, on the hustings, rescued victory from near-defeat. It was no singlehanded achievement, and Black Dan's role may have been exaggerated. Webster's voice did not go unheeded, but the available evidence reduces the god to human size. Millowners, mer-chants, lawyers, bankers—with Abbott Lawrence as their prototype—called the tune for the majority, just as they had called it in Jackson's day. It was not Webster alone, but Webster plus Lawrence plus Choate plus the rest, who put Massachusetts out of danger for Zachary Taylor in '48. They had the dollars, prestige and votes. When Sumner chided the elderly Appleton for failing to enroll in freedom's ranks, and charged that an "unhallowed union" joined "the lords of the lash and the lords of the loom," Appleton was prompt in declaring that slavery was a local question "with which . . . New England was no longer cursed." Winthrop thought Taylor would be elected; since Van Buren could not, the alternative was Cass. Whigs who chose to aid Cass's for-tunes, directly or indirectly, "may denounce whom they please as being no true Whigs; they will convict nobody but themselves," he said.

This was a telling argument, and as early as September 8 a Whig poli-tician could write with assurance: "We . . . shall carry . . . the Old Bay State . . . for Taylor *beyond all question.*" Such calmness seems strange in the face of the storm howled up by third-party orators. But, although ex-Whigs dominated the Free-Soil cause in Massachusetts, many of its rank and file were ex-Democrats. The Democratic party had never been well-disciplined in this Whig stronghold. Polk lost,[4] and Cass could not ignite enthusiasm where Polk had failed. In Worcester, Free-Soil strength was greatest—but mild compared to the Western Reserve. Su-perior organization kept ninety per cent of the Whigs in line.

5

Of the remaining Northern states, five were traditionally Democratic, four Whig and two new. Both new states—Iowa and Wisconsin—seemed inclined to go Democratic; the recent arrival of Mormons in Iowa confused predictions there. Settlement of upstate New York Barnburners in Wisconsin and northern Illinois raised Whig and Free-Soil hopes. In Indiana and Michigan, sectional pride in the career of Lewis Cass offset the eagerness of young Free-Soilers—notably George W. Julian—to repudiate the traditional parties. The region as a whole continued to be swayed by Jacksonian expansionist theories, exemplified by Cass—the "Father of the West." Beyond Ohio there was no Whig governor, no Whig senator and only an occasional Whig congressman. Since the Democrats had an advantage in their state organizations, many Whigs conceded the entire Northwestern bloc.

New Jersey resembled Pennsylvania in the emphasis it attached to tariff protection; having voted for Clay in '44, it was even more Whiggish in '48. As an aftermath of the Dorr Rebellion, Rhode Island was especially conservative. Whigs were gaining in Connecticut, perhaps because of John M. Niles, who steered more Democrats than Whigs to Van Buren. Maine and New Hampshire present problems for historians. Maine's position on the country's periphery, and the West-like pioneer conditions there, may account in part for the Democrats' edge. Next door, thanks chiefly to Levi Woodbury and a Concord lawyer named Franklin Pierce, Democrats could rely on their best-oiled machine anywhere north of South Carolina. Cheshire was the only New Hampshire county where Clay had beaten Polk, and only in South Carolina and Michigan was Taylor's showing in '48 as sorry as in Pierce's state.

In September Taylor's supporters looked to Vermont for victory omens. As results came trickling in to national headquarters in Washington, the Whig choice for governor was well out in front, Whig nominees for Congress triumphed and Senator William Upham seemed assured of re-election. This was nationally important, Vermont's citizens being the first to vote where Free-Soilers were militant. Gideon Welles thought Democrats espousing the Free-Soil cause "act in better faith than . . . Whigs. . . . Vermont Democrats are in a minority . . . and therefore had less to lose in disregarding their old organization." Taylor men were delighted, and far and wide Vermont was cited as an election index.

Abraham Lincoln, speaking in Massachusetts, directed his auditors' attention to what Vermont had done. Roger S. Baldwin, in Connecticut, referred with "great satisfaction" to the "cheering intelligence" from Vermont.[5]

6

Maine Whigs also cheered when Democratic officeholders received reduced pluralities. Pennsylvania's sick Democratic governor resigned—placing the Whig, Johnston, in his chair; Johnston used patronage wisely to consolidate pro-Taylor forces and ran as a candidate to succeed himself. Meanwhile, Patterson of Chautauqua County, New York, advised Weed on August 24: "The nomination of any other man than Van Buren would have made a large hole in our ranks, but I think with *work* we will bring in nearly all the Whigs." Seward wrote in the same vein: "I perceive a feeling of distrust about Taylor's success in other states," but New York "Whigs . . . have . . . the strongest motive to action—Hatred of Van Buren. . . . They will vote for Taylor to save themselves" or else "will not vote."

Back in June, John Botts offered to bet a thousand dollars that "neither . . . Taylor nor . . . Cass will be elected President by the people, and that the election must come into the House." "They hope" to take it "to the House," James A. Hamilton told Weed; "it is suggested that as there will be no election there," the Democratic vice-presidential candidate, Butler, "will be chosen" for second place by the Senate and "will under the Constitution *be the P[resident]*."[6] Thus Butler's succession was premised on Van Buren's presumed ability to carry New York, thereby preventing Taylor or Cass from obtaining an electoral majority.

There was no danger of this, except briefly in late summer. Instead of ignoring the announcement of a Taylor-Butler ticket in South Carolina, Taylor in August thanked William B. Pringle for calling the ticket to his attention. "Concluding that this nomination, like . . . others . . . in various parts of the union, has been . . . offered me . . . without pledges or conditions it is thankfully accepted," he wrote.

Comparable to the *Signal* Letter and one or two others of the previous year, it was possibly more damaging because of the election's proximity. Taylor insulted Fillmore by running in South Carolina with Butler. Flagrant consorting with Southern Democrats was offensive to Northern independents, as well as rank-and-file Northern Whigs. By implication Taylor denied the restraints of Saunders' pledge. Finally the General gained nothing whatever to compensate for his mistakes. About the time he put ink on paper, Calhoun decided to help Cass.

Nowhere were retributions more ominous than in presumably "safe" New York. Saturday afternoon, August 26, a telegram reached Albany "stating that Taylor . . . accepted the nomination of the . . . nullifiers, with Butler for Vice President." It was followed by a copy of Taylor's words lifted from Horace Greeley's *Tribune*. "The excitement of the whigs . . . was intense. Albany's streets were alive with angry politicians." Fillmore, indignant, joined Weed at the *Journal*. In half an hour handbills were circulated announcing a "Whig rally" at eight that night "for the purpose of considering . . . Taylor's letter." Weed's staff officers were in evidence when the meeting opened at the Capitol. An Albany alderman, urging prompt action, favored a state or national convention, and was for the nomination of "Harry of the West and Fillmore of the North." Amid "an uproar" Lewis Benedict declared he could not support Taylor until the General defined his position on the free-soil question. Although the words were Benedict's, the sentiments presumably were those of Weed. Oddly it remained for Collier—Millard Fillmore's special friend—to calm irascible Weed lieutenants, and exhort them to deliberate delay. "We must do nothing," said John A. Collier, "which might lead to the election of Cass." In line with Collier's plea, the chairman appointed a resolution committee "to report to a meeting on Monday." "Excitement continued great throughout the night. . . . A large crowd gathered in front of the *Journal* office, and a procession with drums, trumpets, &c., paraded the streets . . . till nearly midnight, breathing the most violent animosity to Taylor."

7

Over the nation attention was focused on the Albany fireworks. Taylor's loose remarks had long upset his discriminating friends: "Why does not the old Genl stop writing letters. . . . They want explaining, & that is always unfortunate." Much as Northern Whigs had murmured, Clay's admirers louder than the rest, there was thus far no explosion such as the Albany fuse might set off. Now, lo and behold, here was Weed— the smooth dictator, the resourceful fixer—apparently toiling behind the scenes to encourage anti-Taylor revolts. Whigs and Democrats gawked in fascination, while Free-Soilers underscored the "split," and Clay's friends discussed a Clay-Fillmore ticket.

The zealots cooled off over the week end. Monday evening "Collier was called for" and said "there was evidently some mistake. . . . The nul[l]ifiers had not dropped Fillmore but Cass, and although he was . . . indignant on Saturday . . . , he was . . . disposed to be . . . well pleased now. . . . The cause of the . . . excitement was not even alluded to, and, under the skilful management of Mr Collier, 'those who came to scoff, remained to pray,' the meeting agreeing to support . . . Taylor . . . 'letter or no letter.' Thus evaporated all the indignation . . . of the mighty whigs of Albany. Mr. Collier, the Touchstone of the play, managed the whole matter." Weed, Benedict, and their associates went home, "cursing themselves for not sooner perceiving that it was Cass who was dropped instead of Fillmore . . . and that Gen. Taylor . . . had done a very clever thing."[7]

For all the discernment and sarcasm of the editor quoted above, he did not penetrate to the cause of the Albany poof-and-fizzle. In accepting Collier as the Touchstone of the play, he failed to peer into the prompter's box to identify the instigator of the drama. There, bland as ever, smilingly assured, was the genial physiognomy of Thurlow Weed. With talent tested on a hundred stages Weed grasped the implications of the Pringle letter. Directing Benedict to saunter out on the boards on Saturday, he had him make a declamation sounding like an anti-Taylor diatribe. Then Fillmore's Collier became a conciliator, creating the impression that Fillmore's friends were less anti-Taylor than the General's champion. This excellent theater, too subtle for most, achieved the effect which Weed desired. What argument, indeed, could the Clay men make when Fillmore himself was reconciled? The mock heroics were perfectly gorgeous, though few had the sense to appreciate them. With Benedict in Collier's natural role, Collier in Benedict's, Weed in the box and Fillmore in the wings, every actor acquitted himself like a seasoned trouper. Judged by high critical standards, no other act of '48 was quite so professional as this August comedy.

CHAPTER XI

THE SECOND ALLISON LETTER—AND VICTORY

1

FROM the day of his nomination by the Whigs until the campaign ran its course, General Taylor performed peacetime Army duties and tended to his cotton planting. Visiting his neighbors or visited by them, he went on no electioneering tours and delivered no political speeches. Except for a jaunt in July to New Orleans for the purpose of receiving a medal, he spent most of the summer at his Baton Rouge headquarters. Returning from his plantation about June 18, he was probably at Baton Rouge when Morehead's letter of notification arrived at the local post office. As time wore on, politicians wondered why Taylor sent Morehead no reply. Didn't the General want the nomination? "The delay . . . is ominous," Seth Hawley wrote Weed. And Hawley's view was widely shared.

Finally, on July 15, Taylor acknowledged Morehead's letter. "Grateful," he wrote, "for . . . the confidence implied in my nomination . . . , I cordially accept . . . but in the sincere distrust of my fitness to fulfil the duties of an office . . . which has been rendered illustrious by the greatest names in our history. . . . Should the selection of the Whig Convention be confirmed by the people, I shall endeavor to discharge the new duties . . . so as to meet the expectations of my fellow citizens, and preserve undiminished the prosperity and reputation of our common country."

Taylor's language had the negative merit of containing no harmful phrases. Its errors, if any, were those of omission. A Weed follower felt "sadly disappointed. . . . Taylor's acceptance is as . . . non-committal as he could . . . have made it had he thought it . . . unnecessary to secure the vote of a single Free State. I cannot avoid the conclusion that he is . . . under Southern influence." Southerners criticized it, too, but in both sections comment usually concerned the delay rather than the contents. Democrats seized on a humorous angle. Finding his mail expenses burdensome, sometime in the winter or spring Taylor had informed the Baton Rouge postmaster that he was unwilling to foot the bill for non-prepaid communications. In June the postmaster forwarded forty-eight letters to the dead-letter office. Most of these were for Taylor—one the missing Morehead message. Surmising its fate, Taylor asked for the package's return, paid what was due, and sent off his acceptance. Nothing like this had ever happened before. While Whigs praised their candidate's frugality, "economical, comical Old Zack" evoked many a Democratic snicker.

2

Taylor wrote some good letters that summer, but the most adroit was not widely circulated. Thanking Edward Kent "for the . . . active part which you have taken in my nomination," the General was confident that "the people of Maine understand the . . . just policy to all sections . . . which would govern me in the event of my election." "I shall be most happy," Taylor continued, ". . . if my course . . . should tend . . . to moderate the bitterness of party spirit or . . . unite the great interests of all . . . our country." The nominee concluded in a manner worthy of a practiced politician. "I honor no part of our country," he wrote, "for substantial qualities & patriotism, more than the N. England states, and should deem myself greatly complimented to receive the vote of any portion of her citizens." "To the state of Maine," he reminded this original Taylor man, "I feel grateful for the first movement in N. England in my favor."

To John Churchill Hedges of Virginia, Taylor wrote felicitously. Hedges had asked if the General considered the Madison, Monroe, Jackson, Van Buren, Tyler and Polk administrations "to have been conducted upon the principles of the Jeffersonian school." Taylor replied: "I hardly deem it proper . . . in my present position before the . . . people . . . to comment upon . . . our former Presidents. . . . Touching this subject, my opinions . . . are embraced in the . . . letter to . . . Captain Allison." This was a soft answer, but as aptly put as the Taylor denial of prejudice against immigrants or opposition "to the exercise of the . . . franchise by them." "In reply to these charges I have only to say that *they are absolutely false,*" he informed another correspondent. "I have ever considered that adopted citizens are entitled to all the rights and privileges of native citizens. . . . I have . . . always treated them with equal respect. . . . They deserve the honor of the country for the courage . . . and fidelity with which they have defended her interests and honor."[1] So spoke the candidate "recommended" by the Native Americans.

While charges flew misrepresenting Zachary Taylor's investments and income, the General addressed a tongue-in-cheek note to Alexander M. Mitchell, a wartime comrade. "In reply to your inquiries," Taylor told him, ". . . I have no land on the Rio Grande, or slaves in Washington. Among . . . accusations brought . . . by my opponents, I should be . . . gratified to learn . . . they . . . succeeded in substantiating the charge that I have . . . so large a sum for any purpose as the one . . . mentioned. I beg that you will not put yourself to . . . trouble to meet the objections urged against me, by those opposed to me." When they "disregard . . . truth, it is useless to contend with them."

Taken together, Taylor's letters to Kent, Hedges, H. B. Miller and Mitchell suggest that the old Indian fighter was less naïf than legend has made him. Kent's was warm and appreciative, Mitchell's light-hearted, Miller's righteously indignant, Hedges' a diplomatic brush-off. Again comes the question: Who actually authored the many missives Taylor signed? Democrats attributed the best of them to Bliss, and the worst to Taylor himself. This explanation is unsatisfactory; on days when some effective ones were composed, the brilliant Bliss was nowhere near. Robert S. Garnett and Joseph H. Eaton, two young officers, helped with the correspondence. Hunton, Peyton and Bullitt could be called whenever their assistance was needed. But nearly every Taylor statement bears the imprint of his personality. His favorite expressions, adjectives and verbs reflected his views of issues and men. The presumption that Taylor had little to do with political communications has no root in reality. He deserves credit for well-turned sentences as well as blame for mistakes when guilty. In both cases he alone assumed the responsibility.

3

A number of other documents point to Taylor's campaign resourcefulness. One went to his oddly named biographer, J. H. Clay Mudd. A second, containing a denial of statements made by J. Pinckney Henderson of Texas, was at once discreet and forthright—reminiscent of Taylor's scorcher to Marcy. The nominee regretfully declined Indiana Whigs' invitation to celebrate with them the anniversary of his defense of Fort Harrison. He extended thanks to one William Holdredge for approving his political position. "Among the greatest objections . . . to . . . the presidential chair," Taylor wrote, "is the responsibility connected with the appointing power. . . . There will not be an office for one applicant in twenty." Those disappointed "will . . . be my . . . implacable enemies

for life." Yet Taylor was willing to enter the White House, hoping
Holdredge and others would "attribute my errors to the head & not . . .
the heart." "To the head & not . . . the heart," was a phrase Taylor
used long before meeting "Perfect" Bliss.

Exactly what was in Taylor's mind during the summer of '48 is revealed in a letter to his brother. "The manner in which I was nominated," he told Joseph, ". . . adds to its value far beyond what I can
express." That "so many sages & fathers of the land . . . should have . . .
selected me[,] an humble individual, unknown personally to most of
them . . . is an honor I ought not to have expected, & much fear did not
deserve." That they did this "without asking pledges" evinced "a confidence in my . . . integrity . . . without . . . parallel since the days of
the Father of his Country."

Zachary had much to tell his brother. The Baltimore convention was
"not over harmonious." Still, the Democrats made "as judicious selections as they could well have done." Cass, "vulnerable in many respects"
and "the greatest demagogue among them," was "a man of as respectable
talents as any of the party." Taylor characterized Butler as "an individual
of very ordinary . . . acquirements," but "nothing can be said against"
him even "during such corrupt times." "I do not believe they can be
elected," Taylor confidently stated, "unless . . . difficulties between . . .
Barnburners & . . . Hunkers can be healed before the election." This
"I presume cannot now be done." It was possible, the General added,
that enough Northerners would vote for Van Buren to "carry the election
into the House"; this "I cannot believe will be the case." Reasonably
certain of a Whig victory, Taylor also discussed his assignment to command the Western Division. With private letters as criteria, it is reasonable to assume that Taylor's printed remarks were largely his own
and not a ghost writer's.

Further proof of this point is found in the General's least inspired
utterances. His words to Pringle were no erudite craftsman's, but a self-
schooled frontier veteran's. His adopting the same stand in relation to
South Carolina Democrats as to less explosive elements underscored a
consistency which expediency-minded strategy boards would never have
devised on the spur of the moment. Taylor likewise wrote to George
Lippard, who, trained for the law and the ministry, was now a sensational
novelist. There was nothing stable or passably respectable about this
freakish dilettante. Yet Taylor told Lippard in July: "I am not a party
candidate, and if elected cannot be President of a party, but the President
of the whole people." The fact that Taylor took notice of Lippard con-

demned him in conservative eyes, and the nominee's dilution of a Whig candidacy mortified many of the faithful. "I hope Genl. Taylor has got done writing letters," a Weed associate complained. "The last I've seen . . . is . . . to . . . Lippard. . . . He says 'I am not a party candidate.' This is . . . annoying."[2]

4

Thus two of Taylor's midsummer declarations hurt his prospects, while most unquestionably helped them. What he should or should not say was a favorite topic of the Whigs. The time had arrived for one last definitive expression. Peyton, Hunton and Bullitt probably met in New Orleans toward the end of August, their purpose being a repetition of the success of the Allison Letter. By removing all doubt of the General's Whiggery, they could assist him in reaching the goal toward which destiny headed him. There may have been a Taylor-Bullitt interview in New Orleans around September 1. Then Bullitt wrote (perhaps at Taylor's dictation) a letter which the General signed at East Pascagoula, Mississippi, on Monday, September 4.

Known as the Second Allison Letter, this product of Taylor's pen was his only significant stroke during the first three weeks of September. Taylor spent the hiatus with his family at East Pascagoula and Pass Christian, where skies were bright and breezes bracing. Sometimes he was seen sitting sideways in a split-bottomed chair in the lobby of Pascagoula's luxury hotel, reading newspapers which he held quarter-folded in his right hand. Visitors, meeting him on the hotel grounds, noted the military cap and loose-fitting clothes Taylor liked so much. There were receptions in the hero's honor, casual meetings with old associates and also military reviews—for thousands of soldiers came there from Mexico to be demobilized and paid. Most of the time Taylor stayed at his small cottage on the water front. Here, on the edge of a tree-shaded knoll near the Gulf and the Singing River, he probably wrote out the important document which is incorrectly said to have been composed by Crittenden. Extremely effective in the campaign, it is presented here *in toto:*

East Pascagoula, Sept. 4, 1848.

Dear Sir:

On the 22d day of April last, I addressed you a letter explaining my views in regard to various matters of public policy, lest my fellow-citizens might be misled by the many contradictory and conflicting statements in respect to them which appeared in the journals of the day and were circulated throughout the country. I now find myself misrepresented and misunderstood upon another point, of such importance to myself personally, if not to the country at large, as to claim from me a candid and connected exposition of my relations to the public in regard to the pending Presidential canvass.

The utmost ingenuity has been expended upon several letters and detached sentences of letters, which have recently appeared over my signature, to show that I occupy an equivocal attitude towards the various parties into which the people are divided, and especially towards the Whig party as represented by the National Convention which assembled in Philadelphia in June last. Had these letters or scraps of letters been published or construed in connection with what I have heretofore said upon this subject, I should not now have to complain of the speed with which my answers to isolated questions have been given up to the captious criticism of those who have been made my enemies by a nomination which has been tendered to me without solicitation or arrangement of mine, or of the manner in which selected passages in some of my letters, written in the freedom and carelessness of a confidential correspondence, have been communicated to the public press. But riven from the context, and separated from a series of explanatory facts and circumstances which are, in so far as this canvass is concerned, historical, they are as deceptive as though they were positive fabrications. I address you this letter to correct the injustice that has been done me, and the public to the extent that I am an object of interest to them, by this illiberal process.

I shall not weary you by an elaborate recital of every incident connected with the first presentation of my name as a candidate for the Presidency. I was then at the head of the American army in the Valley of the Rio Grande. I was surrounded by Whigs and Democrats who had stood by me in the trying hours of my life, and whom it was my destiny to conduct through scenes of still greater trial. My duty to that army, and to the Republic whose battles we were waging, forbade me assuming a position of seeming hostility to any portion of the brave men under my command—all of whom knew I was a Whig in principle, for I made no concealment of my political sentiments or predilections.

Such has been the violence of party struggles during our late Presidential elections, that the acceptance of a nomination under the rigorous interpretations given to the obligations of a candidate presented to the public with a formulary of political principles, was equivalent almost to a declaration of uncompromising enmity to all who did not subscribe to its tenets. I was unwilling to hazard the effect of such relationship towards any of the soldiers under my command when in front of an enemy common to us all. It would have been unjust in itself, and it was as repugnant to my own feelings as it was to my duty. I wanted unity in the army, and forebore any act that might sow the seeds of distrust and discord in its ranks. I have not my letters written at the time before me, but they are all of one import, and in conformity with the views herein expressed.

Meanwhile I was solicited by my personal friends and by strangers, by Whigs and Democrats, to consent to become a candidate. I was nominated by the people in primary assemblies—by Whigs, Democrats and Natives, in separate and mixed meetings. I resisted them all, and continued to do so till led to believe that my opposition was assuming the aspect of a defiance of the popular wishes. I yielded only when it looked like presumption to resist longer, and even then I should not have done so had not the nomination been presented to me in a form unlikely to awaken acrimony or reproduce the bitterness of feeling which attends popular elections. I say it in sincerity and truth that a part of the inducement to my consent was the hope that by going into the canvass it would be conducted with candor if not with kindness. It has been no fault of mine that this anticipation has proved a vain one.

After I permitted myself to be announced for the Presidency, under the circumstances above noticed, I accepted nomination after nomination in the spirit in which they were tendered. They were made irrespective of parties, and so acknowledged. No one who joined in those nominations could have been deceived as to my political views. From the beginning till now I have declared myself to be a Whig on all proper occasions. With this distinct avowal published to the world, I did not think that I had a right to repel nominations from political opponents any more than I had a right to refuse the vote of a democrat at the polls; and I proclaimed it abroad that I should not reject the proffered support of any body of my fellow citizens. This was my position when in November last I returned to the United States; long before either of the great divisions of the people had held a National Convention, and when it was thought doubtful if one of them would hold any.

Matters stood in this attitude till spring, when there were so many statements in circulation concerning my views upon questions of national policy, that I felt constrained to correct the errors into which the public mind was falling by a more explicit enunciation of principles, which I did in my letter to you in April last. That letter, and the facts which I have detailed as briefly as a proper understanding of them would permit, developed my whole position in relation to the Presidency at the time.

The Democratic Convention met in May, and composed their ticket to suit them. This they had a right to do. The National Whig Convention met in June, and selected me as their candidate. I accepted the nomination with gratitude and with pride. I was proud of the confidence of such a body of men representing such a constituency as the Whig party of the United States—a manifestation the more grateful because it was not cumbered with exactions incompatible with the dignity of the Presidential office, and the responsibilities of its incumbent to the whole people of the nation. And I may add, that these emotions were increased by associating my name with that of the distinguished citizen of New York, whose acknowledged abilities and sound conservative opinions might have justly entitled him to the first place on the ticket.

The Convention adopted me as it found me—a Whig—decided but

not ultra in my opinions; and I should be without excuse if I were to shift the relationships which subsisted at the time. They took me with the declaration of principles I had published to the world, and I should be without defence if I were to say or do any thing to impair the force of that declaration.

I have said I would accept a nomination from Democrats; but in so doing I would not abate one jot or tittle of my opinions as written down. Such a nomination, as indicating a coincidence of opinion on the part of those making it, should not be regarded with disfavor by those who think with me; as a compliment personal to myself, it should not be expected that I would repulse them with insult. I shall not modify my views to entice them to my side; I shall not reject their aid when they join my friends voluntarily.

I have said I was not a party candidate, nor am I in that straightened and sectarian sense which would prevent my being the President of the whole people, in case of my election. I did not regard myself as one before the Convention met, and that body did not seek to make me different from what I was. They did not fetter me down to a series of pledges which were to be an iron rule of action in all, and in despite of all, the contingencies that might arise in the course of a Presidential term. I am not engaged to lay violent hands indiscriminately upon public officers, good or bad, who may differ in opinion with me. I am not expected to force Congress, by the coercion of the veto, to pass laws to suit me, or pass none. This is what I mean by not being a party candidate. And I understand this is good Whig doctrine—I would not be a *partisan* President; and hence should not be a party candidate, in the sense that would make one. This is the sum and substance of my meaning, and this is the purport of the facts and circumstances attending my nomination, when considered in their connection with, and dependence upon, one another.

I refer all persons, who are anxious on the subject to this statement for the proper understanding of my position towards the Presidency and the people. If it is not intelligible, I cannot make it so, and shall cease to attempt it.

In taking leave of the subject I have only to add that my two letters to you embrace all the topics I design to speak of pending this canvass. If I am elected, I shall do all that an honest zeal may effect to cement the bonds of our Union and establish the happiness of my countrymen upon an enduring basis.

Z. TAYLOR.

To Capt. J. S. Allison.

5

Strong and affirmative, the Second Allison Letter combined justification and defense with a smashing counterblow. It struck straight to its target, yet exemplified dignity. It explained away weaknesses in Taylor's position and still was no weak-kneed apology—insincere, crawling or unseemly. Though the candidate steered clear of the slavery issue, he upheld the consistency of his attitude toward parties and reaffirmed his Whig allegiance. He primarily sought to please Northern Whigs, and these reacted favorably. From the embattled North came approbation. Truman Smith's only regret was that the letter was not composed earlier. Weed observed that Taylor, like good metal, "rings clearest when . . . severely tested"; his "frank, manly, independent" communication would lead "thousands of alienated Whigs" to "warm back to General Taylor." "He is all truth and . . . patriotism," the Albany *Journal* editorialized. "The country and the crisis demand such a man."

Praise like this was more than perfunctory. Although Taylor might have held his own, even without the Second Allison Letter, its appearance bolstered his chances. Desperate Democrats would have welcomed a clumsily contrived Taylor statement. Instead, they found themselves contending with unanswerable assertions. Cass, meanwhile, silent in Detroit, did nothing of a positive nature to augment his dwindling prospects. Van Buren, remote at Lindenwald, campaigned only vicariously through his personable son, "Prince John." Taylor alone, of the presidential aspirants, made a distinct individual effort to retain or regain the allegiance of voters.

Due to the Second Allison Letter and also to the drift of events, Whig politicians were buoyed up from early September on. In October, several states elected Whig governors. In Pennsylvania, Johnston won; in Ohio, Seabury Ford.[3] Though each race was long in doubt, both were Whig victories. Johnston's success in a normally Democratic constituency was especially pleasing to the Whigs. Ohio's result, unlike Pennsylvania's, showed a Whig decline from previous years—yet the propagandists crowed there, too.

The pace, indeed, was speeding up. Speaking in Massachusetts, Abraham Lincoln—bringing prairie wit to bear on the gentry of New England—joined forces with New York's Seward in undermining the Free-Soilers. What would be the outcome, Lincoln asked, of a Van Buren plurality there? Instead of electing a Free-Soil President, it could only benefit Cass. Was this the great desideratum—the hope and aim of Conscience Whigs? While Sumner and Adams, Whittier and Lowell lauded the Free-Soil ticket, Lincoln ridiculed their platform—comparing its promises to pantaloons a Yankee peddler once offered for sale, "large enough for any man, small enough for any boy." Seward, likewise, attacked Van Buren. And Webster, Davis, Winthrop, Choate and half a hundred of the stalwarts appeared in Faneuil Hall or elsewhere to keep their followers in line. When Sumner asserted that the Harvard faculty would not go for Taylor, Lawrence replied he was more interested in where the truckmen went. In the Massachusetts of '48, the old Whig party was still transcendent.

6

In Pennsylvania, events were trending precisely as Whig strategists planned. Spring Garden and Southwark, the Natives' strongholds, were pillars of power for Johnston and Taylor. Out-of-state speakers like Seward and Clayton joined local orators in thumping the war drums. Lewis Levin and Thad Stevens whipped up the cry for Rough and Ready. In contrast to relative apathy elsewhere (reported by Gideon Welles in Connecticut, by Calvin Fletcher in Indiana), "excitement in Philadelphia . . . exceeds anything of the sort since 1840." Some Whig politicians were worried.[4] Even after their October triumph, doubts remained and appeals went out to New York and Boston for campaign funds. Abbott Lawrence, Simeon Draper and their friends contributed thousands of dollars. Wilmot's district caused concern when a Michigan Democrat was reported coming to lure Wilmot back to the fold. "I get . . . good advices from Pennsylvania except from Wilmot's district," Greeley wrote, but "I hear . . . he is doing right."

Greeley scrawled this report on October 28. About a month before, he tacked Taylor's flag to the *Tribune* masthead—appealing to New York recalcitrants. On September 22, Greeley spoke in the past tense of the "movement to bring out Mr. Clay as a Whig candidate . . . at the eleventh hour." Botts of Virginia also plumped for Taylor at a Clay meeting in New York City. Clay might have reduced the Taylor vote had he not forbidden the use of his name. Botts "swallowed the Taylor pill" with "a wry face." And Greeley wrote Weed: "I will do all that my judgment approves to promote Taylor's election, though I expect to be driven into opposition before he has been a year in power."

From the tone of Greeley's belated acquiescence, it may seem surprising that Weed, Seward and Smith looked to Greeley to help in Ohio. The *Tribune* was shipped wholesale to the Western Reserve, but Greeley refused to go there because of his wife's delicate health. Seward's extensive canvass of Ohio may have improved Taylor's prospects slightly,[5] but the die was cast against him there. Though Thomas Metcalfe of

Kentucky, Francis Granger of New York, Corwin and Ewing declaimed on the hustings, the Proviso was "stronger in Ohio than Whiggery, democracy and military glory." This was corroborated by rough-and-tumble A. B. Dickinson, who advised that "Whigs looks and acts bad"; and by Seward, who found things worse than expected. Though Corwin said he *knew* General Taylor would not veto the Proviso, Clay's torpor and Joshua R. Giddings' work for Van Buren damaged the Ohio Whigs. "We are wasting strength on Ohio that is needful elsewhere," Greeley concluded.

7

As rumors flew from state to state and prophets searched for signs,[6] Taylor returned to Baton Rouge and was there for the bad news from South Carolina. There Calhoun-dominated voters picked a legislature sure to name Cass electors. Mississippi, Virginia and Alabama being toss-ups—Texas and Arkansas securely Democratic—Taylor's late prospects in the South did not appear encouraging. Indeed, the only Southern states where Whigs seemed likely to gain were Florida, Georgia and Louisiana.

Despite urgings to appear more often at local Louisiana gatherings, Taylor kept out of sight, except at occasional barbecues. When he did mingle with the public, emphasis was on his military triumphs. Taylor's letters now were likewise few. The contest, he felt, was virtually decided. Frantic, last-minute maneuverings would be undignified and ineffectual. Writing a little to close associates, he also sent off a final denial of prejudice against foreign-born citizens. More indicative of his frame of mind is the fact that on October 30, when the campaign had only a week to go, Taylor dictated a ten-page biography of his father, requested by Lyman C. Draper. The General remained at his Baton Rouge cottage until after election day. There is no evidence that he voted. The knowledge that thousands of fellow Americans were promoting the Taylor-Fillmore ticket could not change the habits of a lifetime. Taylor was never eager to shoulder the burdens of the White House. Nor was this passivity a pose. It was ingrained in his personality.

If Taylor was passive, resigned and relaxed, his well-wishers were eager and active. Even the skeptical Gideon Welles found the public's "indifference or sluggishness" roused to vitality toward the end. In mid-October, the diarist predicted that the close gubernatorial results in Pennsylvania and Ohio "will . . . stimulate the parties to greater exertions." Every tactic was resorted to—the singing of catchy campaign tunes, distribution of cartoons and circulation of anecdotes. The streets of American cities rang with such infectious verses as:

> Come fall in, boys, eyes right and steady,
> And raise the shout for Rough and Ready,
> He licked Old Peg-leg with his Pass
> And now he'll use up Lewis Cass,
> Chorus: Then go it, boys, strong and steady
> And raise the shout for Rough and Ready.

A favorite Free-Soil song was:

> Come, ye hardy sons of toil,
> And cast your ballots for Free Soil;
> He who'd vote for Zacky Taylor,
> Needs a keeper or a jailor.
> And he who still for Cass can be
> He is a Cass without the C;
> The man on whom we love to look
> Is Martin Van of Kinderhook.

Or, again, the Taylorites chorused:

> Rough and Ready is the man
> That all good Whigs delight in;
> He's just the sort for President,
> And 'a' the man for fightin'.
>   Then raise the song, the States along,
>   From Maine to Louisiana.
>   We've got "the coon" that sealed the doom,
>   Of Polk and Santa Anna.

Two campaign "lives" of Cass were issued—the first sent South, the second North. "In one he appeared as a slavery-extensionist, and in the other as a 'Wilmot Provisoist;' each proving its case by quotations from his speeches." Ben: Perley Poore wrote a Taylor biography, "large editions" being published at Boston and Albany. Nathaniel P. Willis' quill helped the Whig cause, James Fenimore Cooper's that of the Democrats, and Lowell's and Whittier's the Free-Soilers'.[7] Books on the candidates in the German language were ordered by the thousands, and every device was used to depict Cass, Taylor or Van Buren as the champion of this or that minority group. Most amusing, perhaps, were caricatures displayed in shop windows in major cities. "One of a fine cow with . . . Cass pulling at the horns and Taylor at the tail . . . while . . . Van Buren is milking her dry" told its own story. "Another represents Genl Taylor . . . smoking a segar with his feet elevated . . . and displaying . . . his broad posterior; and sundry politicians propounding . . . questions as to his principles. The Genl tells these . . . gentlemen to ask the part of his person so prominently exposed."

"A . . . boisterous friend of the Generals," the Democrat Welles related, "was . . . making known his opinion that the Genl had returned a right answer, when a queer fellow remarked that he thought so too, for . . . it was of . . . little importance which end was applied to for information. This was such a sudden transfer of the joke, as . . . to change the countenances of the dozen spectators—long faces growing . . . short, and . . . short ones . . . elongated." Thus the crude byplay and witticisms!

8

As election day neared, the torchlight processions, parading and shouting multiplied. Even Welles admitted that "the popular pulse is . . . at more than fever heat." Disturbances and riots marred parades. A Democratic procession was moving through New Orleans, when a "disgraceful affray" occurred in front of the Rough and Ready Club. A man on the sidewalk taunted the Democrats, shouting "Hurray for Taylor and Fillmore!" When a marcher thrust a torch in his face, he drew a pistol and fired. "He continued . . . until all the shots . . . were discharged," whereupon the Democrats moved in—and burned the clubhouse to the ground. Such intensity of partisan feeling was by no means confined to Louisiana. Through the nation, excesses shocked law-abiding Americans.

This was one facet of the excitement which the campaign evoked across the land. In a savage fight a man's arm was broken; another had a kettledrum jammed on his head. Celebrating the anniversary of the Battle of Monterey, torchbearers were blinded by smoke and dust, yet they stuck to their posts "like heroes." Marchers were jostled by exuberant roughnecks. Lovely ladies, in gay attire, fluttered handkerchiefs on balconies festooned with flags. Betting was prevalent. Wagers "as high as $5,000 and $10,000 have been made in Cincinnati." Baltimoreans "bet without stint." A newspaper reported fantastic odds—"$100 that . . . Taylor will not get 6 states; $100 on 8 states; $100 on 10 states; $100 on 12 states; $100 on 14 states; and $500 that he will not be elected." Bribing and drinking went along with the gambling. Here and there women drunks were arrested. In Philadelphia an intoxicated girl told police she was "Rough and Ready"; under that name they locked her up. In New Orleans there was evidence of corruption. Five hundred laborers were suddenly employed to "work" on the new customhouse, committing themselves (so said the Whigs) to vote Democratic on November 7. Whigs muttered and grimaced at the sight of loafers shoveling "each other . . . out of each other's way."[8] In Pennsylvania, there was fear of floaters. Philadelphia Democrats were reportedly relying on "colonizing voters" from New York, and on *tricks and bribery*." Recriminations flew both ways, as ward heelers scrambled for loose change.

At the campaign's close the candidates became targets of foul assaults. Desperate politicians pulled no punches. Even earlier "bitterness and blackguardism" had been thought "unparalleled." But now old charges were raked over. Both Cass and Taylor, their opponents claimed, had drawn extra pay illegally, bilking the Treasury of thousands of dollars. A man in Holly Springs, Mississippi, described Taylor as an "ignorant hireling." Cass was a "monarchist"; moreover, he was fat, and Fillmore's law partner in deplorable taste dwelt on Cass's avoirdupois. Van Buren, described as a traitor and a hypocrite, was Judas Iscariot to the Cass men. No abuse was too vengeful or too vile, but often epithets ricocheted. An ex-soldier, charging Taylor with blasphemy, was said to have been rebuked in Mexico "by Old Zack for *robbing a hen roost*," and indicted in Ohio "for *stealing a hog*."

As the political cannon thundered and the partisan rifles cracked, false allegations collided in mid-air, while transparencies fluttered above the streets. Sometimes orators declaimed like gentlemen, but coarse levity intruded, and character assassination muddied the rallies. These heavy-handed thrusts were typical of what passed in the guise of humor: "The Whigs . . . have taken . . . Taylor as a connubial partner. . . . It is clear the . . . party is not very particular. . . . First he courted the Democrats . . . then the Natives. . . . Next he married the Whigs. . . . His indiscretions before marriage might have been lost sight of, but even after . . . he is caught wantoning with the nullifiers of Charleston, and has got their nomination too." In New Orleans "a Democrat in the crowd" thought Peyton was "sugaring Old Zack . . . too much, and shouted 'Cass is as good a man.' 'Yes,' answered Peyton, 'he is good—good for nothing but extra pay.' 'They say he broke his sword on a stump [in the War of 1812], and I shouldn't be surprised if he swallowed it too, he's so fond of rations.' . . . Peyton gave a 'glowing account' of the prospects of . . . Taylor in Tennessee. . . . 'Everybody,' he says, 'black and white, are in favor of the old man.' "

9

As the campaign double-timed to its climax, vituperation canceled some of the blandishments. Ritchie termed the Second Allison Letter "fatal" to Taylor; his Washington *Union* said Whigs were "whistling to keep their courage up." Nevertheless, the Taylorites' optimism was premised on something more substantial than hope. Whigs in Washington claimed as "certain" 163 votes for Taylor, out of a total of 290. Safe states, according to the General's publicists, were Massachusetts, Rhode Island, Vermont, Connecticut, New York, New Jersey, Pennsylvania, Florida, Georgia, Louisiana, North Carolina, Tennessee, Kentucky, Maryland and Delaware. Greeley's *Tribune* agreed substantially. Ritchie, on the other hand, gave Pennsylvania, Georgia, and Louisiana to Cass, together with states most Whigs conceded.[9]

Election day bore out the Whig prediction. After all the sweat and furor, Whig strategists were exactly right in their mid-October forecast. Reports from Pennsylvania showed Lewis Levin keeping his part of the bargain. Stevens, too, was faithful to Taylor. Allegheny County gave the Whigs a good margin. In the counties where Wilmot was running, Taylor's total exceeded Johnston's, while Van Buren cut sharply into Cass. Cass abandoned hope when it was clear that Taylor had carried Pennsylvania.

In most Northern states a mere plurality gave electoral votes to Taylor or Cass. In New York and Massachusetts combined Cass-Van Buren supporters were more numerous than Taylor's. This was true also in Vermont and Connecticut. Only Rhode Island and New Jersey joined Pennsylvania in the North in giving Taylor a popular majority. In the South the situation was less complex; Van Buren being no factor there, popular margins were clear-cut.

In the Northwest pluralities were important. There Cass benefited from Free-Soil diversion to an appreciable degree. Although Taylor nearly nosed out his chief rival in Illinois, Iowa, and Wisconsin, the third-party feature aided Cass in the West, while in the critical states of the East it worked to Zachary Taylor's advantage. Nine contiguous Western states voted for Cass on November 7. Nine contiguous Eastern states cast their ballots for Taylor and Fillmore. While Texas and New Hampshire were giving Cass majorities, Vermont and Florida were safe in Taylor's column. General Taylor received the vote of ten of the original thirteen states; Cass carried twelve of the seventeen newer ones, pointing up the chronic Whig weakness in the West. That Taylor's victory was national in character is shown by the fact that, of his fifteen-state total, eight were Southern and seven Northern. With his popular plurality in the North and clear majority in the South, his margin in the electoral college was twenty-five in free states and eleven in slave. Taylor's grand total was 1,360,099—Cass's 1,220,544, Van Buren's, 291,263.

The following table gives the breakdown, both for 1848 and for 1844:

	POPULAR VOTE, 1848			ELECTORS, 1848		POPULAR VOTE, 1844			ELECTORS, 1844	
STATES	TAYLOR, WHIG	CASS, DEM.	VAN BUREN, F.S.	TAYLOR	CASS	CLAY, WHIG	POLK, DEM.	BIRNEY, LIBERTY	CLAY	POLK
Alabama	30,482	31,363	......	..	9	26,084	37,740	......	..	9
Arkansas	7,588	9,300	......	..	3	5,504	9,546	......	..	3
Connecticut	30,314	27,046	5,005	6	..	32,832	29,841	1,943	6	..
Delaware	6,421	5,898	80	3	..	6,278	5,996	.....	3	..
Florida*	3,116	1,847	......	3	..	......	......			
Georgia	47,544	44,802	......	10	..	42,100	44,177	......	..	10
Illinois	53,047	56,300	15,774	..	9	45,528	57,920	3,570	..	9
Indiana	69,907	74,745	8,100	..	12	67,867	70,181	2,106	..	12
Iowa*	11,084	12,093	1,126	..	4	......	......			
Kentucky	67,141	49,720	......	12	..	61,255	51,988	.....	12	..
Louisiana	18,217	15,370	......	6	..	13,083	13,782	......	..	6
Maine	35,125	39,880	12,096	..	9	34,378	45,719	4,836	..	9
Maryland	37,702	34,528	125	8	..	35,984	32,676	......	8	..
Massachusetts	61,070	35,281	38,058	12	..	67,418	52,846	10,860	12	..
Michigan	23,940	30,687	10,389	..	5	24,337	27,759	3,632	..	5
Mississippi	25,922	26,537	......	..	6	19,206	25,126	......	..	6
Missouri	32,671	40,077	....	..	7	31,251	41,369	.....	..	7
N. Hampshire	14,781	27,763	7,560	..	6	17,866	27,160	4,836	..	6
New Jersey	40,015	36,901	829	7	..	38,318	37,495	131	7	..
New York	218,603	114,318	120,510	36	..	232,482	237,588	15,812	..	36
North Carolina	43,550	34,869	......	11	..	43,232	39,287	.....	11	..
Ohio	138,360	154,775	35,354	..	23	155,057	149,117	8,050	23	..
Pennsylvania	185,513	171,176	11,263	26	..	161,203	167,535	3,138	..	26
Rhode Island	6,779	3,646	730	4	..	7,322	4,867	107	4	..
S. Carolina†	......	......	......	..	9	......	......	......	..	9
Tennessee	64,705	58,419	......	13	..	60,030	59,917	.....	13	..
Texas*	4,509	10,668	......	..	4	......	......			
Vermont	23,122	10,948	13,837	6	..	26,770	18,041	3,954	6	..
Virginia	45,124	46,586	9	..	17	43,677	49,570	......	..	17
Wisconsin*	13,747	15,001	10,418	..	4	......	......			
TOTAL	1,360,099	1,220,544	291,263	163 127		1,299,062	1,337,243	62,300	105 170	

* Admitted to the Union after 1844.
† Presidential electors appointed by the legislature.

10

From this table it is evident that Taylor ran well as compared to Clay's showing four years before. Winning all Clay's states except Ohio, he brought New York and Pennsylvania, Georgia and Louisiana from

Democratic to Whig control. If he was aided by outside influences (notably Van Buren in the Empire State), the Free-Soilers hurt him in Ohio—and Taylor's success in Pennsylvania was comparable to Polk's in '44. The returns, state by state, show an over-all change complimentary to the General. Almost everywhere Taylor benefited from the backing of independent Democrats. This was especially true in the South, where a comparison of the totals in Kentucky, Tennessee, North Carolina and Arkansas provides an index of his popularity. The electoral switch of Louisiana and Georgia would have been duplicated in Mississippi and Virginia with just a little more impetus from their creaking Whig machines. In Alabama the big Whig gain almost threw the state into Taylor's camp. Equally gratifying was Illinois' showing. There the voters had always been Democratic, even in '40 when New Hampshire was the only other Northern state to cling to Van Buren. In '48 its Whigs had not bothered to nominate a candidate for governor. Yet Cass retained Illinois by a tiny plurality—and Taylor might have nosed him out with indirect aid from "Long John" Wentworth.

Thus local traditions and men had their impact on the results. Birthplaces of all three candidates—Orange County, Virginia; Exeter, New Hampshire; and Kinderhook, Columbia County, New York—voted for Old Rough and Ready. Taylor carried Jefferson County, Kentucky, where he had spent the years of his youth, and Jefferson County, Mississippi, where his plantation was situated. He came within six votes of defeating Cass in his home parish of East Baton Rouge, which Polk had carried by seventy-four. In Orleans Parish (with which he was identified) Taylor more than doubled the old Whig majority. These figures must have been a source of peculiar gratification to Taylor; they showed the personal esteem in which his friends and neighbors held him.

New York has received its share of credit in every account of this campaign. That Old Zack could never have vanquished Cass without the Barnburner rift is certain. But even with New York for him, Taylor would have lost to Cass without the backing of Pennsylvania. It was to Pennsylvania, not New York, that politicians looked for portents. "I am satisfied that Penn. is to be the great battle ground," a Massachusetts Whig wrote Weed. "The locos turn . . . their attention in that quarter" and "you must do likewise," Weed was warned. The outcome hinged on Philadelphia (city and county), where Taylor obtained nearly 10,000 more votes than Cass. This differential was greater than what was needed by either party to win the state's plurality.[10] It was the Quaker City that gave Taylor the margin that made him President.

CHAPTER XII

PRELUDE TO GLORY

1

ZACHARY TAYLOR did not swell up with self-adulation as the returns came in. "When . . . news of the result in Pennsylvania reached him . . . he . . . heard it with . . . composure and dignity which are so essentially parts of his character." Once the polls had closed the outcome was not long in doubt. Even in remote sections travelers brought word that Taylor was victorious. In metropolitan centers—and smaller communities—journalistic patrons of the "magnetic telegraph" paid extra for the prompt reports. As early as eleven o'clock on the night of the election New Orleans Whigs were satisfied that the General would carry the state. Similarly in Kentucky, Georgia and Connecticut the trend was evident at an early hour. Easterners kept their ears attuned to the vote from Philadelphia; when Taylor carried Pennsylvania all was over but the shouting.

On November 8, Gideon Welles was "satisfied . . . Taylor is elected." In the White House President Polk noted that "information . . . published in the morning papers . . . indicate[s] the election of Gen'l Taylor." Polk was disconsolate, and Welles disappointed. "While I do not mourn the defeat of Cass," wrote Welles, "I do not rejoice in Taylor's triumph." Polk considered the victor "wholly unqualified." Elected "by the Federal party and . . . factions of dissatisfied persons . . . broken off from the Democratic party," Taylor—in the President's opinion—"must be . . . under their absolute control." He "will . . . rely upon . . . designing men . . . and will . . . reverse, so far as the Executive can reverse, the whole policy of my administration."

Other Democrats reacted comparably, Buchanan attributing Pennsylvania's loss to the coal and iron interests. In Philadelphia credit was correctly given to Levin. Taylor's admirers were lavish with encomiums. Thomas Dabney, the Mississippi planter who had entertained Taylor at Pass Christian, was informed by his aged mother that her faith in the Republic was restored. "I congratulate . . . my country on General Taylor's election," she wrote. ". . . General Taylor is a great man, and I hope he will honor the Presidency. It will not honor him . . . after the

134

scoundrels that preceded him." Welles opined that "all in regard to him is mere speculation. Even those . . . acquainted with him, seem not to know his . . . capability." William Ballard Preston had no such qualms: "The glorious victory . . . has . . . revolutionized all things. . . . It fills me not only with joy, but with thankfulness and praise to God for the . . . blessings with which he crowns our people."

As Democrats resigned themselves to the outcome, and Whigs exultantly crowed, the object of the praise and criticism boarded a steamboat for his plantation. A few days later newspapers regaled their readers with accounts of an incident aboard the *Rowena*. "A passenger, not knowing the General, accosted him . . . and introduced the subject of politics, stating that he . . . voted for Cass. . . . He thought very well of . . . Taylor as a man, but . . . always stuck to the party, and besides, did not think Gen. T. was qualified. . . . He then asked the General if *he* was a Taylor man, to which the General replied, 'Not much of a one—that is, he did not vote for him—partly because of family reasons, and partly because his wife was . . . opposed to sending "Old Zack" . . . to Washington, where she would be obliged to go with him!' At this moment, another passenger . . . accosted the General, calling him by name! The other party looked a little wild . . . and . . . slipped off, before the General" could relieve "him from . . . embarrassment." Taylor "was in fine health and spirits." He "talked . . . little about politics and less about the elections, but was otherwise . . . quite sociable. He had on that same . . . blue coat and white hat."[1]

2

Taylor spent barely a week at Cypress Grove. He composed no important letters. His thoughts must have been varied, however, for he now had the responsibility of selecting members of his Cabinet; there was Army business to be wound up, and personal affairs demanded attention. The price of cotton remaining low, Taylor's income was disappointing. It is probable that he seriously considered transferring his investment to sugar lands. But he and his son made no specific plans—and Taylor went away satisfied with Dick's work as manager.

Military business took him to New Orleans, where he received happy Whigs with "courtesy, and simplicity of manner." Taylor had a severe cold but otherwise was "in the enjoyment of good health." His arrival created "lively enthusiasm," and artillery companies fired salutes. "Wearing his . . . military coat and cap, he quietly took his way on foot to his quarters; but the moment . . . word went round, 'There's Old Zack,' he had such an escort that he found it almost impossible to put one foot before the other. The old General was obliged to carry his cap in his hand, bowing and smiling all the way. . . . The President elect is a little above the middle stature, with compact frame, and rather stout. . . . His ruddy countenance and almost wonderful activity, bespeak him in the enjoyment of . . . perfect health. As he sits in the . . . hotel, chatting with all, his appearance is that of a downright honest man, of sound sense and great frankness, good humor, and urbanity. . . . Gen. Taylor is one of the most sociable men in the world. . . . His off hand speeches . . . show unusual intelligence and concentration of thought, clothed in simple and beautiful language."

Taylor did not have long to wait for opportunities to demonstrate the presence or absence of "unusual intelligence." On December 5 at Baton Rouge he gave his daughter Betty in marriage to Bliss, but no sooner had the newlyweds departed on their honeymoon than the General bore down on his correspondence, which—for the most part—he had been neglecting. There were certain exceptions to the neglect. (Taylor had written Clay on November 17, and also defined his attitude toward Webster in a letter to his Massachusetts backer, George Lunt.) But stacks of mail awaited his attention, and he answered the trivial along with the important. An offer of free passage to Washington elicited Taylor's polite refusal. Requests for his signature or a lock of hair found the General complying. Each imposition was small compared to his principal problem—the formation of the Cabinet—but together they added to the burden. Like many another President-elect, Taylor was a badgered man as he approached what were in some respects the most important decisions of his career.

3

Would he choose Webster for the Cabinet? Crittenden, Clay, Evans, Truman Smith, Lawrence, Ashmun, Hudson, Choate, Jacob Collamer of Vermont? Other possibilities included Frederick Whittlesey of New York; Clayton of Delaware; Johnson of Maryland; the Pennsylvanians— Stewart, McKennan, Randall, Meredith, Joseph R. Ingersoll, Horace Binney; Rives and Preston of Virginia; Todd and Letcher of Kentucky; William A. Graham and Edward Stanly of North Carolina; and Waddy Thompson of South Carolina. Georgia offered Toombs, King and George W. Crawford; Mississippi McGehee and William L. Sharkey. There

were also Peyton, Peters, Meredith P. Gentry, Ohio's Ewing and Samuel
F. Vinton, Caleb B. Smith of Indiana and Edward D. Baker of Illinois.[2]

Henry Clay had rather strong claims; Taylor might have dealt his
prospective opposition a smashing blow by picking Clay. Webster, who
badly wanted a berth, would have brought the regime prestige. And a
third Whig statesman whose presence in the Cabinet could have been
of inestimable value was the able, diplomatic Crittenden.

Taylor really wanted Crittenden, who had proved his tireless loyalty
while Webster sputtered and Clay sulked. Whether Clay would have
accepted the State Department remains conjectural; Taylor never offered
it, and Clay did not expect it. Already the public assumed that Clay
would soon return to the Senate, and Taylor's friends believed his motive
was to "play hell" with the Administration. The General was the soul
of cordiality in the November letter to Clay. He also told Lunt that he
nursed no anti-Webster grudge. However, he could not trust either
man. And very early he decided to give Crittenden his choice of portfolios.

4

Crittenden's inclusion in the Cabinet would have been of tremendous
value to Taylor. Either as Secretary of State, or in his old post as Attorney General or back in the Senate as Taylor's floor leader, Crittenden
was needed in Washington. On the basis of past relationships as well
as future promise the Kentuckian was Taylor's ideal adviser. But when
Old Zack urged him to sit at his right hand in the White House, Crittenden declined the honor. Having been elected governor, he felt he
should not leave Kentucky. For this and possibly other reasons, he forced
Taylor to look elsewhere.

Taylor at first was disinclined to accept the refusal at face value. Urging his friend to reconsider, he held the State Department open until
he could visit Crittenden in Frankfort. Meanwhile, the General turned
his attention to other Cabinet prospects. He wanted Binney for Secretary of the Treasury, and on the surface this choice was odd. Binney was
neither an active candidate nor notably prominent in politics. Now
sixty-eight and semiretired, Binney was surprised to be Cabinet timber.
Taylor's regard for Binney, however, is very easy to explain. The General had long admired successful lawyers and businessmen. He was
closer to them in spirit than to professional politicians. Taylor considered
the Treasury a business office—one in which Pennsylvanians were pe-

culiarly interested. What, therefore, could be more logical than naming this famous attorney, particularly if (as was later supposed) Taylor had been present in the courtroom when Binney argued his Girard Will brief prior to the Mexican War?[3]

No Taylor-Binney correspondence is available; the probability is that Old Zack's advisers dissuaded him from issuing a formal invitation. Not entirely giving up Binney, the General weighed other pros and cons. Evans, qualified for the Treasury, hailed from a Democratic state. More consideration was given Lawrence; however, he had factional troubles at home—and the South disliked his tariff ideas, as well as McKennan's, Stewart's and Randall's. Of Meredith comparatively little was known. Widespread opinion pointed to Taylor's naming Clayton to the Treasury.

If Taylor had been sure that Crittenden would accept the State portfolio, he could hardly have done better than to back him up with Clayton. The two were stanch friends, old Senate associates, moderate Whigs and revolters against Clay. With Crittenden present in the Cabinet to give direction to his comrade's talents, there is no telling how much good Clayton might have done. When Crittenden declined the State Department, the President-elect began to see in Clayton a possible substitute. As early as December Clayton's presence in the official family was regarded as certain.

5

By no means all the prominent Whigs, however, looked with favor on Clayton's qualifications. As in Evans' case men whispered that he was too convivial. Having undergone a series of family bereavements, climaxed by the fatal illness of his son, Clayton's stability was open to question—and Truman Smith thought Rives a better choice. Seward and Weed preferred Whittlesey for the Treasury, while some Southerners promoted Peters; if Taylor had picked someone from that section, McGehee might have been the man. King was a candidate for the Navy Department,[4] Todd for the War Department, Johnson for Attorney General, Caleb Smith for Postmaster General. Preston and Crawford had important backing. Toombs could have had a berth if he wished to leave the House. Crittenden wanted Letcher to be Postmaster General. And Truman Smith was half inclined to enter the Cabinet instead of the Senate.

While Taylor and the nation studied the aspirants, Welles noted a "perceptible difference . . . in the tone . . . of many . . . papers on both sides." Before the election his supporters declared that Taylor's "would not be a party administration." Yet these same editors, Welles continued, "are now . . . forming a cabinet of ultra partizans and urging the extreme of . . . malignity. On the other hand many democrats . . . are now claiming" for Taylor "great independence and denying that his course will be one of extreme party." "I have not doubted," the diarist concluded, "that he would . . . associate with those who elected him."[5] Taylor himself stated, long before, that none but Whigs should enter his Cabinet. Regardless of Democrats' wishful thinking that one of their party might head a department, the President-elect adhered to his decision and premised his Cabinet plans on it.

In letters sent Fillmore and Truman Smith, Taylor wrote that "with one exception" he would invite no one to join his Cabinet until he reached Washington. He also voiced "determination not to be a proscriptive President." "I do not propose," he advised Smith, "to remove . . . subordinate officers of the Government who have faithfully and capably executed their duties, merely for opinions sake." Advancing the same idea to Fillmore, Taylor assured the Vice President-elect that he would be considered ex officio a member of the Cabinet. Such notions disturbed Seward and Weed. "We have no clue to the *One* exception," Seward wrote. "It is not the Kentucky friend. . . . I think it is a gentleman from Delaware." In another communication Seward reported: "Public opinion seems to indicate J.M.C. for State. T.S. of Connecticut does not like this. . . . T.S. inclines to Ashmun for Attorney General and is willing to go South . . . and take Peters."

While Weed, Seward and Smith tasted discouragement, Binney gained the impression that Taylor thought of him for the State, not Treasury, Department. Two Bostonians saw "a strong probability" that Lawrence would get the Treasury. "It seems to be conceded," wrote a Washington man in December, "that . . . Crittenden will come as Attorney General." William Campbell Preston advocated Calhoun for Taylor's Cabinet, but William Ballard Preston dissented: "The public heart and eye are turned to other men, Crittenden, Lawrence, Truman Smith, Meredith of Philadelphia, Rives, Clayton and *yourself*." A Massachusetts Whig reported: "Our 'God like' [Webster] is moveing quietly . . . to take the office of Secretary of State. . . . Uncle Dan . . . I think is not the Man for the Occasion. . . . There are strong objections."[6]

Ethan Allen Hitchcock, who encountered Taylor in late December, found he "has not named a single member of his Cabinet." A New Orleans hotel man corroborated Hitchcock's testimony. "The General has

not made up his mind as to the persons who shall compose his Cabinet,''
a Weed henchman was informed. Thus Seward was mistaken when he
assumed that Clayton was the ''one exception''; the President-elect still
thought Crittenden might reconsider.

Burnley told Crittenden that, based on Taylor's comments to him and
Peyton, ''I gathered . . . his cabinet will consist of one member each
from New England, Pennsylvania, Delaware, Georgia, Kentucky or
Tennessee, and Virginia or North Carolina.'' Burnley's was an exceedingly accurate prediction, but his guess that Winthrop or John Davis
would be the New England minister was poor. Taylor considered
Lawrence ''too much identified with Manufactures'' and lacking ''requisite ability.'' ''He would prefer Binney in the Treasury. . . . If he can't
get him, then he is bothered by a host, none of whom he knows sufficiently. From Delaware Clayton—who it has been intimated would
decline, & I believe the old man would be very willing to see him remain
in the senate. From Ky, you are his first choice, & the only one he has
written to—— He fears you will decline, but still has some hope.'' Regarding Letcher, ''I was . . . sorry to hear the Genl. say—no, after I have
offered one appointment to Ky, if it is declined, I must go to Tennessee—— In which event, Gentry is pretty certainly his man. . . . In
Georgia Crawford is his favorite—— In Va—Ballard Preston.''

Burnley found Taylor ''very much bothered . . . because he does not
know all these men, & will *therefore* have to . . . consult with his
friends—*which he would rather not do*—for I tell you *he* means to be
president of these United States *himself*. . . . His Cabinet must, in his
opinion at least, be harmonious[,] honorable, patriotic, talented, & *hard
working*—— They must . . . be of irrepro[a]chable private character
& he rather inclines to young men, because he thinks they can work
harder than old ones. . . . He is . . . impressed with the idea, that if he
can get hard workers, he can get along with . . . *very little counsel.''*
Burnley's words to Crittenden on patronage would have relieved the
realistic Weed: ''Taylor is opposed to proscription—but says all must
go who have interfered in elections, or are incompetent . . . & that . . .
the offices may . . . [be] equalized, if . . . now filled by democrats. . . .
These rules will not leave many representatives of democracy alive.''

To Dr. Wood, Taylor complained: ''My troubles and trials have commenced.'' Every mail ''was filled with applications.'' Taylor's relatives
''are particularly anxious.'' His nephew wanted to be consul at Havana;
a nephew-in-law, postmaster at Louisville. Others begged because ''they
are connected with some member of my family. . . . I cannot entertain

such applications. . . . Was I to do so, I would break myself down in less than 6 months."

6

While the Cabinet and nepotism beset Old Zack, he came face to face with Clay. Taylor was at the Baton Rouge landing when Clay, New Orleans bound, tarried there aboard the *Princess*. Peyton and Burnley were taking the same boat, and Taylor accompanied his guests aboard. As the General passed the dinner table, he recognized Clay and bowed. Clay not appearing to recognize him, a gentleman remarked: "Mr. Clay, that is General Taylor."

"Is it!" ejaculated Clay with surprise and pleasure on his countenance. He then walked into the social hall and earnestly extended his hand to the General, who grasped it warmly and shook it energetically.

"Why, General," pleasantly remarked Mr. Clay, "you have grown out of my recollection!"

"You can never grow out of mine" was the ready response of the General, whose face beamed with warm regard, and whose good-natured wrinkles almost obscured his bright and benevolent eyes.

Twisted versions of the meeting might be accepted today, were it not for the *Picayune's* detailed commentary. The historian Poage has assumed a "coldness" in Taylor's demeanor. However, the words "warm" and "benevolent" appear in the journalistic accounts. There was a "most agreeable conversation," and the captain of the *Princess*, "not wishing to interrupt so pleasant a reunion of . . . old friends, detained the boat. . . . Finally . . . the General and Mr. Clay parted, with expressions of mutual esteem, and a hope that they might soon meet again."[7]

Clay's disappointment, if it existed, was traceable to no social chill. Taylor did not fail to recognize him; it was Clay who, but for a timely reminder, would have permitted the General to pass unnoticed. Clay's dissatisfaction had bitter roots in the soil of repeated political defeats. For twenty years he was discontented. His treatment of Harrison had been unkind. He broke quickly with Tyler, and his attitude toward Taylor's election was unbecoming. Stephens and Toombs looked with horror on Clay's prospective reappearance in the Senate. John P. Gaines of Kentucky wrote: "The disinclination to see Mr Clay return . . . is . . . universal." Peyton was sure that, "impelled by a morbid state of feeling, he will play hell, and break things . . . and unless the old general obeyed his orders . . . he would make war upon him too." Burnley believed "Mr Clay's election can be productive of nothing but harm—— He will try to rule or ruin—& his rule would be ruin." Crittenden told Clayton: "I shall, for reasons personal to him, as well as for public considerations, regret that he should desire to return to his seat." All the fretting developed from dread that, instead of co-operating with Taylor, Clay would utilize his prestige to hamstring the Administration.

That such a possibility was not lost on Taylor is evident from Burnley's correspondence with Crittenden. The General "says he . . . knows . . . Mr Clay . . . better than you do—that the only objection to you . . . is that you are too good & . . . forgiving . . . & can't say *no* . . . when you ought." Proof of Taylor's accuracy is found in Crittenden's acceptance of the notion that Clay intended to aid Taylor, if sent to Congress. Although believing it "beyond question" that Clay's "feelings were for a time . . . perverted in respect to the . . . nomination and election," Crittenden was disposed to be charitable. "When . . . told by a friend . . . it was . . . suspected that if [he] should . . . go to the Senate, it would be to oppose the Administration," Clay replied that he would give the General "a cordial support." Crittenden confided this to Clayton, and with the backing of the Kentucky Whig caucus Clay was named for a six-year term.[8] Socially, Taylor was affable to Clay. Politically, he remained skeptical. Clay's antipathy was altogether too evident to warrant unlimited confidence.

7

In the meantime Taylor was not unaware of events in the West and Washington. Discovery of gold in California and renewed congressional debates on slavery were inextricably connected. Reports of riches in the Sacramento Valley had trickled, flowed, poured into the East, until they came with torrential velocity. Around Cape Horn, by way of Mexico, or via Panama, the Forty-niners fared forth for fabled El Dorado. Even before the news arrived, the Thirtieth Congress wrestled with California's quasi-military status and the problem of slavery's westward projection. Several solutions were proposed. Clayton's compromise provided for excluding slavery from Oregon Territory, forbidding California and New Mexico from acting on slavery in any manner and appealing slavery cases from local judges to the Supreme Court.

Though Clayton thought this an "excellent plan" to "steer clear" of the Wilmot Proviso, the bill was tabled in the House. This was "a great mistake," Clayton wrote Crittenden, but "I have another project." Pointing out that "the people of New Mexico . . . are probably 50,000 or

ZACHARY TAYLOR, NOMINEE

The admirable line engraver, Joseph Andrews, based this unfinished picture on a daguerreotype made in the early summer of 1848. Taylor's horses and his Baton Rouge house are
shown in the background. For the presidential stress and strain, compare this engraving
with the daguerreotype taken less than two years later, and used as the frontispiece of this
book. From the author's collection.

60,000," while California residents were more numerous, Clayton believed that "on a hint" from Washington they would "form state constitutions & present them to Congress at the next session." Then, in the summer of 1850, Congress would "admit them into the Union." Avoiding territorial interludes, the people themselves "will exclude slavery & . . . relieve us from the trouble forever."

Following up this Clayton plan, Ballard Preston spoke in the House for a measure of his own. Advocating state government for California, Preston argued that his "remedy" would give "finality to the question" and "come over this nation like the sweet breath of spring . . . healing, strengthening, renovating all of us." The significance of Preston's bill was twofold. First, for a time, there seemed a fair chance that it would become law during the short session—relieving Taylor of a thorny inheritance. Secondly, not many weeks would elapse before Taylor made the plan the cornerstone of his own domestic policy. The identity of Whigs and Democrats who supported Preston's principle leads one to wonder why his bill did not pass. Clayton was for it. Crittenden thought the "project . . . quite practicable." "Southern Whigs are now nearly unanimous in favor of it," wrote Toombs, "& will be wholly so before the vote is taken."

Democrats also liked the statehood remedy. When Calhoun called on Polk, the President expressed "my hope that Governments might be provided for California & New Mexico, and especially the former, by admitting it into the Union as a State without having the Bill . . . embarrassed by the . . . Proviso." Polk also "conversed with . . . members of Congress . . . and urged . . . the great importance of passing a law to admit California . . . as a State." Senator Douglas of Illinois was convinced of statehood's desirability—even sponsoring a bill in the Senate, comparable to Preston's in the House. When Butler of South Carolina blocked it, the Douglas effort died aborning. Preston's measure hung fire till February 27, but then, amended beyond recognition, was rejected with its amendments. There ended a valiant but futile fight. And the session's sole pro-Union accomplishment was that of Howell Cobb, Stephens and Toombs, who in January defied Calhoun's ambition to form a sectionalistic party.[9]

8

Taylor now completed arrangements for the journey to Washington. Before departing from Baton Rouge he took leave of Mrs. Taylor and the Blisses, who were to proceed to Baltimore by an unpublicized south-easterly route. The General's last military act was to relinquish command of the Western Division on January 23 to his distant relative, Edmund P. Gaines. The same day his neighbors gathered at the Spanish Cottage to bid him adieu. Thomas B. Thorpe, the writer-artist who had been with Taylor in Mexico, was their spokesman.

"Believe me, General," Thorpe said, ". . . you will leave behind you . . . a united community of personal friends" who join "in a heart-felt prayer that you and your family may . . . be blessed with long life, continued health and unbounded prosperity."

"It is with feelings of no ordinary character," Taylor responded, "that I meet with my fellow-citizens on this occasion, many of whom I have been associated with . . . more than a quarter of a century. . . . I should have much preferred to retain the office I am now about to vacate, and have remained among you; but the people have, without my solicitation, seen fit to elevate me to another, and although I fear I am not qualified to discharge the . . . duties imposed upon me, yet . . . I shall endeavor to fulfil them. . . . Permit me . . . to invoke God's blessing upon you all! May he grant that you and your families may enjoy long life and pros-perity—— Farewell." The old soldier spoke "with unusual feeling." Gray-haired residents of the town—"who have for so many years been his friends"—seemed moved as much as he was. Taylor left Baton Rouge for his plantation, where he spent nearly a week, and then con-tinued on a succession of packets to Vicksburg, Memphis, Nashville and Louisville. Large and enthusiastic crowds greeted the President-elect and entertained him royally, the loudest cheering and most lavish ban-quet awaiting him at Louisville.[10] Later, leaving Madison, Indiana, the General suffered his first mishap when a trunk in the gangway rolled over on him and bruised his left arm and side. Notwithstanding the in-jury he went ahead with his schedule—ascending the Kentucky River to Frankfort, where Crittenden stood by smiling as Kean O'Hara (Taylor's old teacher) joined younger people in welcoming him.

To an appreciable degree the make-up of the Cabinet hinged on Tay-lor's discussions with Crittenden. Jefferson Davis had urged the gov-ernor to "talk fully with General Taylor; he knows . . . little of our public men personally." "We want you here, above all things, and *you must come*," Stephens had insisted in December. "Don't think of *not* coming into the administration," Toombs had added. In Frankfort, Taylor renewed his plea to Crittenden. Despite the pressure the gov-ernor declined. Taylor thereupon decided to offer the State Department to Clayton.[11] Other portfolios were discussed, Crittenden advising the President-elect to consult Stephens and Toombs in Washington.

9

Taylor left Frankfort Thursday on the *Blue Ridge*. That evening at Carrollton, he transferred to the *Ben Franklin* and traveled now on it, now on the *Telegraph No. 2* (the boats lashed together), to Cincinnati. Despite the Queen City's high winds and low temperature men, women and children packed the levee and the streets to an extent "witnessed on no former occasion." As the parade moved up Broadway, "house-tops, windows, balconies . . . were thronged with ladies, waving scarfs to the man of the people." At Masonic Hall, "the crowd being so great, the Mayor's speech was interrupted, and, owing to an accident which Gen. Taylor met with on the boat, the formality of a reply was dispensed with. After exchanging . . . congratulations with the ladies, the General retired to the Pearl Street House, where rooms had been prepared for him."

On his arrival Cincinnatians had pushed Taylor against the guard of the boat with such force as to injure his right hand. His left arm and side still smarting, he also contracted a cold. Begging to be excused from a banquet in his honor, he still extended himself to receive a group of wartime volunteers. He also wired Clayton, inviting him to become Secretary of State.

The *Telegraph*, with Taylor aboard, passed Pomeroy, Ohio, and Parkersburg, Virginia, without unusual difficulty. The river was full of floating ice, and five miles above Marietta the steamboat ran aground. After an hour's detention the boat was freed, but it later yielded to gorged ice and low water at Captina Island, seven miles below Mounds-ville. A messenger having procured sleighs and coaches, the passengers abandoned the vessel, and went to Moundsville and on to Wheeling on February 20. At Wheeling a "grand and imposing" parade led Taylor to the United States Hotel. Ladies waved from every window. "Snowy white banners and hearty cheers given by 10,000 citizens . . . formed a picture which we acknowledge our inability to portray." A formal ad-dress of welcome was delivered on the steps of the hotel. After the General responded, a "pure . . . democratic shout . . . went up." Taylor, escorted to his chamber, at a later hour was "introduced . . . to . . . his fellow citizens."

10

Originally Taylor hoped to include Pittsburgh in his itinerary. The frozen Ohio changed his plans. Wednesday morning, February 21, he set out by coach for Cumberland. At the Old Globe Inn in Washington, Pennsylvania, a reception was held and luncheon served. Taylor spent Wednesday night in Uniontown and Thursday night in Cumberland, where he planned to take a train Friday. During the two-day journey from the Ohio to Western Maryland, the General was conveyed over the old pike by one of Cumberland's most indefatigable Whigs, Thomas Shriver, who had gone to Wheeling to meet the party.

"The road was a perfect glare of ice, and every-thing . . . plated with sleeted frost. The scenery was beautiful; to . . . mountaineers too common to be of much interest, but to a Southerner like General Taylor . . . it was a phenomenon." Descending a spur of Meadow Mountain, the presidential coach danced on the polished road with every sign of capsizing. "Shriver was in the rear, and in the greatest trepidation" for Taylor's safety. "Down each hill and mountain his bare head could be seen protruding through the window of his coach to discover if the President's coach was still upon wheels. The iron gray head of the General" frequently appeared outside his window, "not to see after anybody's safety, but to look upon what seemed to him an arctic panorama." At length the last long slope was passed. "At twilight the narrows were reached, two miles west of Cumberland, one of the boldest and most sublime views on the Atlantic slope. General Taylor . . . ordered a halt. . . . Out he got in the storm and snow and looked . . . until he had taken in the grandeur. . . . The President-elect was tendered a reception . . . at Cumberland, and the next morning he and his party left on the cars for Washington."

Friday February 23 was the final day of what had been intended as a triumphal prelude to glory, but was actually a rather tedious and sometimes painful journey. Despite the lameness of his hand, his other injuries and his cold, Taylor appeared to hold up well. When he entrained at Cumberland on Friday morning, his car was "waylaid by a party of miners . . . who determined to have a . . . sight at the General. In a few remarks . . . he said they were the men who developed the wealth of the country, and added that good roads and good laws were all that we wanted, for the American people knew how to take care of themselves." Taylor displayed a lively interest in the country through which the railway led him. Ellicott's Mills made a particular impression, and he ventured the prediction that the place might become "the Lowell of Maryland."

Reaching the Relay House at four o'clock, the General was met by committees from Washington, by Baltimore admirers and by Colonel Taylor, Bliss and Wood. Altogether, 3,000 people gathered at the Relay House. Taylor was his usual modest self. "He . . . said that the battles attributed to his valor were won by the bravery of the soldiers. . . . He intended to do all in his power to benefit the American People; but if he should commit errors, as he necessarily must, he would depend upon the magnanimity of those who had placed him in office." He called out to a poorly dressed lad: "Come here, my little fellow, you may be a general yourself some of these days." He kissed a little girl, and, singling out an elderly member of the crowd, said: "It does my heart good to see you, sir, for you are, like myself, an old man. . . . It seems to me this immense throng . . . is chiefly composed of young men, all in the prime of life." To those who pressed around him, he extended his hand, remarking: "If it were not for this lame hand, my good friends, I could make my way among you as well as the best of you." There can be no understanding of Taylor by those who fail to appreciate that simple greetings were, in his case, not chicanery but the natural expressions of a humble soul.

After tarrying briefly in Baltimore, the General's train hastened on to Washington, where elaborate preparations had been made to herald his arrival. Bonfires blazed. Cannon boomed. The flight of rockets in the night added man-made brilliance to the star-swept sky. The *National Intelligencer* reported that spectators, blocking the route from the station to Willard's Hotel, were more numerous than any previously witnessed. When Taylor stepped out on the balcony and returned thanks for the enthusiasm, he was welcomed by "deafening huzzas."

There is a story, familiar to Washingtonians, that Taylor's appearance on the balcony was not immediately impressive. John Boyle, an Irishman who long had served as a Navy Department clerk, bore a striking resemblance to the President. Mrs. Wilhelmina Easby-Smith has written that, when Taylor went outdoors to thank his well-wishers, they mistook him for Boyle and "would have none of him, breaking out in howls and jeers: 'Ah! Get out, Johnny Boyle, you can't fool us!' " Discovering their error, however, they heartily cheered the General's remarks.[12] Aside from its humorous implications the Boyle incident serves to show a later generation that, more than any of his predecessors, Taylor was an unknown quantity—physically as well as politically—to residents of the capital. He was equally unknown to the men and women of other communities, except for his Louisiana, Mississippi and Kentucky neighbors and the friends of his Army days. It was to this stranger on Pennsylvania Avenue that the nation turned for guidance, and the politicians for juicy plums, at the onset of a domestic crisis—already confused and grave—which was to grow in confusion and gravity during days that stretched ahead.

CHAPTER XIII

INAUGURATION

1

WHEN Taylor reached Willard's that Friday night he was obviously weary. His wrinkled face was patched with pallor. His injured arm hung limp at his side. With characteristic common sense, he refused to see callers on Saturday and Sunday, devoting the week end to recuperation. On Monday he felt well enough to call on Polk. "Between 12 and 1 O'Clock," his predecessor noted, "my messenger announced . . . that Gen'l Taylor . . . was in the parlour below. I immediately repaired to the parlour and was introduced to him, for I had never . . . seen him. He was accompanied by a number of friends"—among them Clayton and Jefferson Davis. Shortly after Polk and Taylor met, Mrs. Polk, her nieces and two other young ladies joined the President and his guests. "I received Gen'l Taylor with courtesy and cordiality," Polk observed. "He remained some 20 or 30 minutes. I invited him to dine with me on thursday next. He replied that he would do so if his health would permit it."

The General shook hands with many visitors—women as well as men—at his hotel. Included were Secretary Buchanan, Alexander H. Stephens, Daniel Webster and Philip Hone. Seekers of Cabinet portfolios and their sponsors were among those conferring with Taylor, but others—political enemies and friends—entered his presence out of politeness or to conform with the social code. "We have reason to believe," said the *National Intelligencer,* "that the impression made on the numerous persons . . . who called on the General yesterday, scarcely one of whom had ever seen him before, was highly favorable. The blended urbanity and dignity of his demeanor, his kindness . . . and . . . benevolence . . . are . . . calculated to win . . . esteem. We . . . were pleased to observe the alertness and vigor which mark his movements, after . . . many years of hard . . . and wearing service."

On Tuesday the calls continued, with members of the Polk Cabinet prominent. Tuesday evening the President-elect was the guest of honor at a dinner given by Winthrop. Wednesday dawned, and Seward was one of Taylor's conferees. Seward wrote:

All the world is in Washington, and the rest are coming. There is every thing to be done, nothing can be done, and there is no time to do any thing. I have seen the lions—General Taylor, his daughter Betty, and the Secretary of State that is to be. If you had ever seen Colonel [Joseph P.] Taylor, I could make you understand . . . the President. He is the most gentle-looking and amiable of men. Every word and look indicate sincerity of heart, even to guilelessness. He was kind to me, recognized me, and inquired without art about my son. . . . His daughter is pretty, unaffected, and sensible. . . . We go to Mrs. Polk's last levee tonight.

Zachary Taylor did not attend the levee. Perhaps he was tired from his exertions Wednesday afternoon when he delivered a short address in Georgetown in recognition of ceremonies held in his honor. Thursday afternoon found him greeting the corporate authorities of Washington, and Cass was a caller at Willard's Thursday morning. Taylor was seated when Cass appeared, but, noticing his erstwhile rival, rose and went to meet him.

"Good morning, General, how do you do?" Taylor said, holding out his hand.

"Very well indeed, General Taylor. This is the second time I follow your route, but you got twice ahead of me."

"The race," answered Rough and Ready, "is not always to the swift, nor the battle to the strong."

A few hours later Taylor and Cass met again—this time at the White House where the former sat at Mrs. Polk's right, and the latter at her left. Also present were the Blisses, Mrs. Dallas, Fillmore, cabinet members and their wives, the John Bells, Jefferson Davis, James A. Pearce and Mayor W. W. Seaton of Washington. "The whole number consisted of about 40 persons," the diary-keeping host recorded. ". . . Genl Taylor . . . waited on Mrs. Polk to the table. . . . I waited on Mrs. Dallas. . . . The Dinner was finely gotten up. . . . It passed off well. Not the slightest allusion was made to any political subject. The whole company seemed to enjoy themselves." Friday and Saturday found Taylor's personality continuing to please those who sought him out. "He is besieged by an army of his countrymen," wrote Hone, "numerous as the . . . forces of Santa Anna and not so easily dispersed. I went to see him this morning, and was graciously received. 'Mr. Hone of New York,' said . . . the gentleman who introduced me. The hero-President took my hand and said: 'I know Mr. *Philip* Hone well, although we have never met before.' People are delighted with his kind, plain manners and self-possession, and I do not wonder at it."[1]

2

Notwithstanding Polk's emphasis on social niceties the greater part
of Taylor's time was taken up with more important matters. From the
hour of his arrival at the Washington station he had little more than a
week in which to select his official advisers. Only Clayton had been
chosen, and pressure was on the President-elect, with rival Whig factions
from various states appealing for recognition of their favorites' claims.

During his brief visit in Frankfort Taylor had listened to Crittenden's
plea that he name Letcher to the Postmaster Generalship. No other politician was better suited for this patronage-dispensing assignment. Intimate with Crittenden, Letcher was still on friendly terms with Clay, who
favored his appointment and half expected it. With "Black Bob" in
his Cabinet, Taylor would have had a link with his chief supporter and
also with the proud and self-willed Clay. This might have been a ten-
strike, but the President-elect seemed to think that, having offered a place
to one Kentuckian, other Kentuckians were automatically excluded until
Ohio and Tennessee were given the refusal of a Cabinet berth.

With Kentucky eliminated from consideration (as were Louisiana and
New York because Taylor and Fillmore came from them), Taylor turned
his attention to Pennsylvania. Binney had been his first choice for the
Treasury, but that gentleman evinced no interest in it. Andrew Stewart,
long a Whig wheel horse in the House, was trotted out by Pennsylvanians
in Congress. His views on the tariff and subtreasury questions, however,
were unpopular in the South. Either as a result of this or because he was
in poor health, Stewart was rejected. And Clayton was quick to recommend Meredith, a Philadelphian of legal note who had never served in
Congress and was politically obscure. "It gives me the sincerest pleasure," Clayton advised Meredith on February 28, "to announce to you that
Genl Taylor has selected you to preside over the Treasury."[2] Meredith's
appointment was approved by insiders, but to Americans as a whole the
announcement came as a surprise.

Other Cabinet problems were nearly as acute. King's claims for
the Navy portfolio demanded Taylor's attention, but eventually he
shunted King aside and offered the War Department to Crawford, whom
Stephens and Toombs put forward. This left the Navy open; Abbott
Lawrence was tentatively slated for it, and Preston for Attorney General.
When Gentry displayed no interest in leaving the House to manage the
postal service, Taylor designated Ewing for the place that Crittenden

desired for Letcher. He asked Truman Smith to head the new Home Department—subsequently the Department of the Interior—in the probable event of its creation. Near the end of the preinaugural week it seemed likely that Taylor's official family would comprise Clayton, Meredith, Crawford, Preston, Ewing, Lawrence and Smith.

Lawrence, however, disappointed in being passed over for the Treasury, told Taylor he would not consider the Navy. Smith declined the Home Department. Ex-Senator Archer of Virginia, who did not admire Preston, asked the General "if . . . he intended to make Preston the law officer of his Administration. 'Yes, I have determined to appoint him,' said Taylor. 'Are you aware that an attorney-general must represent the government in the Supreme Court?' continued Archer. 'Of course,' answered the [incoming] President. 'But do you know that he must there meet . . . leading lawyers as opposing counsel?' persisted the President's caller. 'Certainly. What of that?' inquired Taylor. 'Nothing,' said Archer, 'except that they will make an infernal fool of your Attorney-General.' "

Taylor met the objections to Preston's legal qualifications by appointing him Secretary of the Navy, simultaneously naming Reverdy Johnson as Attorney General. He shifted Ewing to the Home Department, and for Postmaster General picked Collamer of Vermont. Thus the President-elect completed his Cabinet, Johnson's appointment being made Saturday, and Collamer's on Sunday or Monday. "There had never been a cabinet organized," James G. Blaine wrote long afterward, "in which so deep an interest was felt,—an interest which did not attach so much to the persons who might compose it as to the side—pro-slavery or anti-slavery—to which the balance might incline."[3] Clayton, Crawford, Preston and Johnson hailed from states where slavery was legal. However, Clayton had voted in favor of the Wilmot Proviso; neither Preston nor Johnson was a fire-eater, and Crawford alone came from the cotton belt.

3

Throughout the week of Cabinet construction Taylor kept in touch with Capitol Hill. Developments there were rather discouraging. Preston's bill was amended to death. Bell met with no better success, and Douglas also fared poorly. Notwithstanding the attitude of both Polk and Taylor some Southerners apparently believed that a territorial bill might yet be passed without the Proviso.

In the Senate, amid verbal swordplay, Webster and Wisconsin's Isaac

P. Walker championed conflicting views. Walker tried to alter the civil appropriation bill, which passed the Senate and—if approved in the House—would have abrogated antislavery Mexican statutes in New Mexico and California. Taylor, opposed to the Walker plan, but eager to substitute order for knives and revolvers in the West, realized California's need of civil government. Clayton, Ewing and Senator-elect Seward saw eye to eye with Taylor in this regard. Seward and Ewing lobbied at the Capitol in behalf of a plan similar to Webster's, designed to retain Mexican laws in California and New Mexico, and also to set up a civil regime—albeit on a temporary basis—pending permanent establishments.

"I . . . prepared what I contemplated as an amendment of . . . Walker's amendment, or . . . a substitute for it," Seward wrote. Afterwards, discovering that Webster's proposal contained everything he had contemplated, Seward urged its adoption on members of the House. Successful there, "I . . . exerted myself to procure the assent of the Senate . . . and . . . insisted . . . no different provision ought to pass. I continued my efforts until the Senate decided to disagree. . . . The whole design of a government for California failed by reason of that disagreement."

Seward may not have realized that Polk was prepared to veto Webster's proposal, which Polk thought bore the Wilmot taint. Considering the mood of Congress, it is remarkable that anything constructive was accomplished. Many members were drunk. More were disorderly. A fist fight occurred in the Senate, and blood was spilled on the floor of the House. Nevertheless, some important business was transacted, including provision for the establishment of Minnesota Territory and the Home Department. The night of March 3 the general appropriation act finally went to the President. And, at the last minute, Congress applied the revenue laws to California. Still, New Mexico and California remained without civil government when at seven o'clock, Sunday morning, March 4, Speaker Winthrop and Senate President *Pro Tempore* David R. Atchison adjourned their houses *sine die*.

4

The question has been raised whether Atchison, by virtue of his Senate position, was President of the United States from noon of March 4 to noon of March 5. The Fourth of March happening to fall on Sunday, an interesting case can be made for the Missourian's brief presidential incumbency. The issue is academic, however, as no public business was transacted. Experts are of the opinion that Taylor was the Chief Executive during this period[4]—in fact, if not in accordance with ceremony.

At daybreak March 5, clusters of the American people began to congregate at the Capitol, eventually forming the largest crowd that Washington had ever seen. In railway cars, on steamboats, in carriages, on horseback and afoot, residents of every corner of the country had poured into the District of Columbia days and sometimes weeks in advance of Taylor's inauguration. Modish New Yorkers, the last word in fashion, rubbed elbows with hardy frontiersmen of the West. Wealthy planters mingled with abolitionists. Soldiers were there in profusion: battle-scarred regulars of Mexican service; gray-bald veterans of the War of 1812; dashing officers of the militia, whose prancing steeds, epaulets and plumes belied the fact that they had never gone to war. The Navy and Marine Corps were represented. Volunteer fire companies turned out in force. Bands blared martial music. Church bells rang incessantly. "And hundreds of star-spangled banners . . . were unfolded to the breeze."

Neither clouds that hung ominously in the overcast sky nor unsolved problems tasking the nation could mar the gay holiday humor of this unprecedented crowd. Spectators lining Pennsylvania Avenue, lads perched on the roofs of houses, men and women peering out of windows—all were there to see the sights, and no mood could be too festive. The enthusiasm of Whig partisans was mirrored in the expectancy of those awaiting the start of the parade. Silenced were growls and grumbles over exorbitant prices in Washington hotels and sectionalists threatening the Union's integrity. The Day of Days in Washington was a quadrennial event. And the multitudes made the most of it.

In contrast to the spirit of the throng was the setting of the scene. A medium-sized Southern community of 40,000 inhabitants, with slave pen and auction block, open gutters and nondescript architecture, Washington was still the City of Magnificent Distances.

Little else about it was magnificent. . . . There was a maze of broad, unpaved streets, dusty in summer, muddy in winter, along which were scattered detached houses or straggling rows of buildings. Lamps were few. Houses were not numbered, and the visitor who wanted to find a residence had to depend upon the hack-drivers; whose method of memory seemed to be, that each person lived "just a little way from" somewhere else.

Whig politicians, hungry for patronage, adopted the Democrats' partisan cry—"To the victors belong the spoils!" Office seekers of every

description were on hand to pluck the plums. Conferences in hotel bedrooms were heated and interminable, lobbies and corridors jammed to
the walls, ambitions unrestrained, and introductions now empty, now
fulsome. The only fly in the ointment was that applicants outnumbered
jobs.

5

As the hands of the clock at Willard's passed the hour of eleven the
restlessness of the crowd grew more apparent. Several minutes after the
hour Zachary Taylor appeared on the steps and was greeted by rounds of
applause. Accompanied by Winthrop and Seaton, he walked from Willard's to the open carriage waiting for him on Pennsylvania Avenue.
Drawn by four handsome gray horses, Taylor's vehicle proceeded to the
Irving Hotel where Polk was escorted to the right rear seat, with Old
Rough and Ready on his left. Onlookers broke into cheers of approbation when the President-elect extended his hand in the friendliest manner
to his partisan foe. And all along the line of march, deafening shouts
from thousands of throats soared above the trumpets and the guns. In
spite of the attempts of a hundred mounted marshals to keep the crowd
in check and off the street, so surging was the pressure and so slow the
paraders' pace that an hour elapsed before Taylor and Polk gained the
summit of the Hill.

While Taylor drove along the Avenue, removing his hat from minute
to minute to acknowledge the people's plaudits, the small semicircular
Senate chamber was already packed with dignity and glamour. The rotund Russian minister's American wife, whose grace and beauty were
proverbial, had flounced herself into a chair in the section reserved for
legislators. But most of the celebrities' female relatives, dressed in the
height of fashion, crammed into the narrow gallery, where the irrepressible buzz of voices was punctuated by rustling silks and the endless flut-
ter of fans. Three women fainted. Their survivors strained to catch a
glimpse of Vice President Fillmore as he took the oath of office and delivered his brief inaugural address. At the left of the dais, masters of
protocol had lined up the members of the Diplomatic Corps,—their glittering orders and military erectness making them stand out in contra-
distinction to the "dark robes and grave law faces" of Supreme Court
justices seated opposite.

The stage was now set for the arrival of the principals. The eager
audience, tense and hushed, awaited the two Presidents. On the Senate

floor, where even Sam Houston had been shocked by violence and intemperate talk on the closing nights of the Thirtieth Congress, bigwigs
on their best behavior refrained from visiting the "Hole in the Wall,"
where whisky, gin and brandy so often relieved the tedium of dreary
speeches and dull debate. Molders of opinion eyed the clock. Congressional flunkies, momentarily important, hastened back and forth with
messages. Then, band music echoing louder until it filled the marble-
pillared room, the great door of the Senate opened wide. Down the
aisle, side by side, came the man of the past and the man of the future.
On the right strode James K. Polk, aged beyond his fifty-three years, his
emaciated features and solemn mien indicative of the White House toll.
On the left was Zachary Taylor, seemingly recovered from illness and
injuries, his appearance so unassuming that men nudged their neighbors
to ask if this could really be Rough and Ready. Taking the place of
honor assigned him, the hero saluted those near by with an air of frankness and good will, then conversed with Chief Justice Roger B. Taney
anent the forthcoming ceremony.[5]

6

Soon the orders of the day were solemnly announced. The chief actors
led the way, like infantrymen at drill, marching to the Capitol's eastern
portico. Here Taylor took his post on the improvised wooden platform
and rose to address an audience estimated at 20,000. "Elected by the
American people to the highest office known to our laws," he began, "I
appear here to take the oath prescribed by the Constitution, and, in com-
pliance with a time-honored custom, to address those who are now
assembled."

Ill at ease on less challenging occasions, Taylor was now no orator.
But he continued:

The confidence and respect shown by my countrymen in calling me
to be the Chief Magistrate of a Republic holding a high rank among the
nations of the earth have inspired me with feelings of the most profound
gratitude; but when I reflect that the acceptance of the office which their
partiality has bestowed imposes the discharge of the most arduous duties
and involves the weightiest obligations, I am conscious that the position
which I have been called to fill, though sufficient to satisfy the loftiest
ambition, is surrounded by fearful responsibilities. Happily, however,
in the performance of my new duties I shall not be without able co-operation. The legislative and judicial branches of the Government present
prominent examples of distinguished civil attainments and matured ex-

perience, and it shall be my endeavor to call to my assistance in the Executive Departments individuals whose talents, integrity, and purity of character will furnish ample guaranties for the faithful and honorable performance of the trusts to be committed to their charge. With such aids and an honest purpose to do whatever is right, I hope to execute diligently, impartially, and for the best interests of the country the manifold duties devolved upon me.

In the discharge of these duties my guide will be the Constitution, which I this day swear to "preserve, protect, and defend." For the interpretation of that instrument I shall look to the decisions of the judicial tribunals established by its authority and to the practice of the Government under the earlier Presidents, who had so large a share in its formation. To the example of those illustrious patriots I shall always defer with reverence, and especially to his example who was by so many titles "the Father of his Country."

To command the Army and Navy of the United States; with the advice and consent of the Senate, to make treaties and to appoint ambassadors and other officers; to give to Congress information of the state of the Union and recommend such measures as he shall judge to be necessary; and to take care that the laws shall be faithfully executed—these are the most important functions intrusted to the President by the Constitution, and it may be expected that I shall briefly indicate the principles which will control me in their execution.

Chosen by the body of the people under the assurance that my Administration would be devoted to the welfare of the whole country, and not to the support of any particular section or merely local interest, I this day renew the declarations I have heretofore made and proclaim my fixed determination to maintain to the extent of my ability the Government in its original purity and to adopt as the basis of my public policy those great republican doctrines which constitute the strength of our national existence.

In reference to the Army and Navy, lately employed with so much distinction on active service, care shall be taken to insure the highest condition of efficiency, and in furtherance of that object the military and naval schools, sustained by the liberality of Congress, shall receive the special attention of the Executive.

As American freemen we can not but sympathize in all efforts to extend the blessings of civil and political liberty, but at the same time we are warned by the admonitions of history and the voice of our own beloved Washington to abstain from entangling alliances with foreign nations. In all disputes between conflicting governments it is our interest not less than our duty to remain strictly neutral, while our geographical position, the genius of our institutions and our people, the advancing spirit of civilization, and, above all, the dictates of religion direct us to the cultivation of peaceful and friendly relations with all other powers. It is to be hoped that no international question can now arise which a government confident of its own strength and resolved to protect its own just rights may not settle by wise negotiation; and it eminently becomes a government like our own, founded on the morality and intelligence of its citizens and upheld by their affections, to exhaust every resort of honorable diplomacy before appealing to arms. In the conduct of our foreign affairs I shall conform to these views, as I believe them essential to the best interests and true honor of the country.

The appointing power vested in the President imposes delicate and onerous duties. So far as it is possible to be informed, I shall make honesty, capacity, and fidelity indispensable prerequisites to the bestowal of office, and the absence of either of these qualities shall be deemed sufficient cause for removal.

It shall be my study to recommend such constitutional measures to Congress as may be necessary and proper to secure encouragement and protection to the great interests of agriculture, commerce, and manufactures, to improve our rivers and harbors, to provide for the speedy extinguishment of the public debt, to enforce a strict accountability on the part of all officers of the Government and the utmost economy in all public expenditures; but it is for the wisdom of Congress itself, in which all legislative powers are vested by the Constitution, to regulate these and other matters of domestic policy. I shall look with confidence to the enlightened patriotism of that body to adopt such measures of conciliation as may harmonize conflicting interests and tend to perpetuate that Union which should be the paramount object of our hopes and affections. In any action calculated to promote an object so near the heart of everyone who truly loves his country I will zealously unite with the co-ordinate branches of the Government.

In conclusion I congratulate you, my fellow-citizens, upon the high state of prosperity to which the goodness of Divine Providence has conducted our common country. Let us invoke a continuance of the same protecting care which has led us from small beginnings to the eminence we this day occupy, and let us seek to deserve that continuance by prudence and moderation in our councils, by well-directed attempts to assuage the bitterness which too often marks unavoidable differences of opinion, by the promulgation and practice of just and liberal principles, and by an enlarged patriotism, which shall acknowledge no limits but those of our own widespread Republic.

Taylor's address cannot be ranked among the most eloquent presidential papers. It did possess the merit of brevity, being one of the shortest inaugurals in history. As Seward pointed out to Weed, it was "negative and general," by which Seward probably meant that it failed to specify the President's position respecting slavery extension. Foreign-policy references were equally vague, and Taylor's negativistic approach to many functions of the executive branch (which had grown more powerful under Jackson and Polk) accorded with Whig fundamentals.

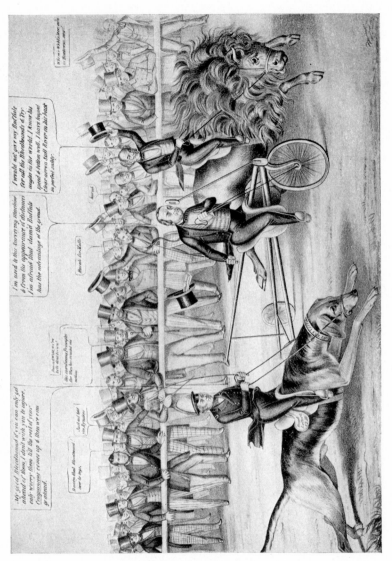

GRAND PRESIDENTIAL SWEEPSTAKES FOR 1849

Slanted in favor of Martin Van Buren and the Free-Soil Party, the above lithograph depicts Van Buren as the probable winner over Taylor and Cass, the Whig and Democratic nominees. Taylor is mounted on a bloodhound, reminiscent of his employment of dogs in the Second Seminole War. Cass sits astride a "try-angle." Van Buren's buffalo is a reminder of the Free-Soil convention, held at Buffalo, New York. From the Library of Congress Collection.

Moreover, his attitude toward the Union—though it did not go as far as Seward might have liked—was nationalistic at its core. In view of the peculiar complexion of the Whig party, and the troubled conditions which Taylor faced, a more concrete stand would hardly have been politic. Taylor's delivery was poor; Polk, who was in a position to hear him if anyone could, noted that he read "in a very low voice and very badly as to his pronunciation and manner." Nevertheless, the crowd cheered him as lustily as if he had been Demosthenes or Prentiss. And Taylor was gratified at the acclaim.

On concluding the inaugural, Taylor turned to face Taney. With hand upraised, he took the oath. Taney congratulated him. Polk shook his hand and said: "I hope, sir, the country may be prosperous under your administration." Salvos of artillery terminated the ceremony. While guns still smoked, Polk and Taylor re-entered their carriage. The former got out at the Irving Hotel, the latter continued to the White House. "Followed by a vast concourse of people," the *National Intelligencer* reported, "the President entered the Mansion . . . and there received . . . the salutes of some thousands of persons, passing in a long array in front of him."

7

It was snowing in Washington at nine that night, when Taylor and Fillmore drove from the White House through rutted thoroughfares to three inaugural balls. Their first stop was Carusi's Saloon, on the northeast corner of Eleventh and C Streets, where visiting soldiers were being entertained. Thence they made their way to the Washington Assembly Rooms in Jackson Hall, on Pennsylvania Avenue, where the Democrats danced away the disappointments of defeat. Finally, an hour before midnight, the guests of honor reached the City Hall. Here the inauguration's outstanding social event was sponsored by 230 managers, including Abraham Lincoln and Robert E. Lee. Army duties had called Lee to Florida, far from the amenities of capital society, but the tall, angular, good-natured Lincoln was on hand with political friends. Horace Greeley, too, was there, eccentric in appearance, forceful in speech. Philip Hone, the diarist, had brought his daughter Catherine to "the largest ballroom, the largest company, the most painful and dangerous pressure . . . I ever witnessed; from four to five thousand persons were present, each one of whom seemed to think that he or she was alone entitled to be there; but it was nevertheless a grand affair."

The ballroom proper adjoined the west side of the municipal building. It was a temporary wooden structure, 160 feet long and fifty feet wide. Flags draped the cotton-covered walls. Illumination was supplied by candles in huge chandeliers, from which tallow dripped on dancers executing the polka and the waltz. When the President appeared, the entire company stood at attention while Gungl's celebrated band struck up "Hail Columbia!" Taylor descended the twenty steps of the staircase and walked the length of the room, bowing on each side as the ladies waved their handkerchiefs in welcome.[6] Pausing at the far end of the hall, Taylor talked to foreign diplomats, rural politicians, social paragons, senators, governors and generals. Now, as partners swung into the dance, the jewels of America's capital sparkled. Expensive women competed for the courtesies of outnumbered, though dashing, gallants. Wallflowers and their ambitious mammas envied the grace of those few girls whose escorts avoided the push and shove. The most glamorous young matron was the Baroness Bodisco, crimson satin sheathing her charms and a diamond tiara crowning her beauty. More admired, however, was the President's daughter—the bride of three months, Betty Bliss. Vivacious, and her taste perfection, she had chosen a simple white gown for the ball. A single flower adorned her hair. (It was Betty who was to act as her father's official hostess, Mrs. Taylor being not well enough to undertake the responsibility.)

When an attendant announced supper, the company scrambled up the stairs and into the City Hall's corridors. Here President Taylor first joined the ladies, who tried to take nourishment in a room intended to accommodate half their number. An observant Englishman left a picture of the feasting and drinking of the men, some of whom "doubtless had . . . [had] nothing to keep soul and body together" for days. "I saw knots of men like so many vultures, pulling and hauling" at skeletons of turkeys, on which no meat remained. The British guest then bribed a waiter to fetch a bottle of champagne. He descended the stars to "witness the spectacle of a lady being carried out fainting." This was repeated as the evening wore on, and, the Britisher added ironically, appeared "to be getting contagious . . . for it was not confined to the weaker sex." Even Rhynders, the New York tough, "was disgusted with the want of order."

As night rolled on the cloakrooms were chaotic. Fine ladies nudged and bumped one another, attempting futilely to ferret out their wraps. Men's cloaks, coats and hats, pitched into one common pile, were at least breast-high. And the only thing to do was to "try on till you got a coat to fit. Of hats there was but little choice; they had all become of one style." Ex-Congressman Lincoln couldn't find his hat. At four in the morning, he walked out into Judiciary Square and started off to his lodgings. "It would be hard," wrote an eyewitness, "to forget the sight of that tall and slim man, with his short cloak thrown over his shoulders" and no hat on his head, setting out on the long walk home. Zachary Taylor, whom Lincoln supported so loyally and so zealously, left the party three hours earlier. After shaking hands until nearly one o'clock, he departed for the White House and a strange bed.

Lincoln would soon be leaving Washington to join his family in Illinois. Buchanan would forsake the capital for a country place in Pennsylvania. As Taylor went from dance to dance, James K. Polk embarked for Nashville. These men could relax—but not the old soldier. Already his Cabinet had met informally, and most of the members would be sworn Thursday. Taylor had consulted with Fillmore and Seward and other rivals for power and glory. But, essentially, it remained true that he knew "little of our public men personally."[7]

CHAPTER XIV

Cabinet and Confidants

1

INITIALLY the man in Taylor's Cabinet to whom the President deferred most often was Delaware's John Middleton Clayton. Over six feet tall, inclining to portliness, with white hair, black brows and twinkling gray eyes, Clayton was known as a *bon-vivant* with a taste for terrapin, old Madeira, canvasbacks and fine rye whisky. He was also a Yale alumnus, a gifted lawyer, and brilliant in the Senate where he performed so masterfully that John Q. Adams described a speech as "one of the most . . . eloquent orations ever delivered in . . . the halls of congress." Orthodox on the Bank and tariff, Clayton became a leader early. Briefly, in 1848, his supporters boomed him for the White House.

For years, however, a series of tragedies dragged him down and sapped his spirit. Clayton had lost his beloved wife and nearly all his close relations. Now the death of a favorite son was almost more than his heart could bear. He seemed less affable and approachable than otherwise would have been the case. Clayton's political history, too, shared sorrow's responsibility for defects which soon grew evident. His forte was oratory, not administration—and his executive background was slight. Bereavements, unfamiliar duties, or a combination of them, produced irregular office hours, unkept promises and a tendency to ignore influential Whigs. Clayton's burden was exceedingly heavy. Formulating foreign policy, aiding Taylor on California, grappling with patronage demands, he often labored sixteen hours and sometimes twenty of the twenty-four. Clayton had two able assistants in William Hunter and George P. Fisher. But, considering its program's scope, his State Department was understaffed.

Zachary Taylor would have done well to confine Clayton's activities within the sphere of foreign affairs. Clayton's load could then have been lightened and his restless energy channeled. As it was, he spread his talents thin. Not only Toombs and Truman Smith but men more charitably inclined undercut and sniped at him. In 1848 Seward had written: "Clayton is impulsive and forgetful." Others had warned of Clayton's ambition. It was also charged that he imbibed too freely, and his drink-

ing may have impelled Smith to say to Gideon Welles: "If . . . Taylor . . .
knew what I know of that rascal, he would . . . kick his backsides out, and
tell him to be gone forever." Nevertheless, the handsome Clayton attacked his work with confidence. Friendly journalists referred to him
as the Administration's "Atlas." And no mere tippler, "fast using himself up," could have functioned as well as he did.[1]

2

In personal appearance and political prestige William M. Meredith
was Clayton's antithesis. If Meredith's face had a bulldog cast, part of
his pugnacious look was due to the shortness of his neck—his head
cocked owllike on half-hunched shoulders. Now fifty years old, he had
been precocious and, as a lad barely in his teens, delivered his college
valedictory. Later, the boy wonder of the Philadelphia bar, he prepared
his briefs with care to rank with the best in his profession. State assem-
blyman, district attorney and president of his city council, he had achieved
a measure of prominence, but it was largely legal and local. From the
standpoint of most Americans, the black-haired, bulky, hulking Meredith was still a political question mark.

Meredith believed in the protective tariff, in specific—as against ad
valorem—duties, and that the Law of '46 "involved insult" and "injury" to Pennsylvania. It was as a symbol of iron interests and manufacturers generally that Meredith drew the Treasury assignment. When
factional rivals attacked his appointment for patronage and kindred reasons, few guessed the Philadelphia aristocrat would become the Cabinet's
most popular member. Unacquainted with the ways of Washington,
Meredith at first gave the impression of being John M. Clayton's yes-
man. But little by little he made himself felt, and not his least asset was
Mrs. Meredith, "a noble woman," as Letcher said.[2] As the weeks and
months advanced Meredith grew ever closer to Taylor.

A third important member of the Cabinet was the doughty Thomas
Ewing. The oldest and most experienced minister, Ewing was a massive
man with features that were crude and strong—a huge bald head, powerful shoulders, ham hands and a big round belly. Coming to the Senate
in the 1830s, he was a Whig at the party's creation, and his forcefulness
on the Hill brought him the title of "Logician of the West." Second-
ranking man in Harrison's Cabinet, he and four colleagues deserted Tyler
despite the fact that Webster stayed. The Ohio lawyer's clients were
numerous, retainers large, and cases varied. Also, Ewing's private life

was a source of profound satisfaction to him. His Maria presented him with two daughters and four sons; in addition, they reared William T. Sherman, who was to marry their daughter Ellen. An ardent Catholic, Mrs. Ewing endowed her children with the same deep faith that filled her days with religious fervor. There was no more devout Catholic family anywhere in the United States than that of the Protestant, Thomas Ewing.

In the Interior Department Ewing faced an administrative challenge. His job included supervision of patents, pensions, public lands and Indian affairs—responsibilities for the first time unified in a single office. He believed in the spoils system. In his eyes the substitution of deserving Whigs for Democrats was no casual order of business, but a transcendent preoccupation. In contrast to Meredith and Preston he insisted on wholesale removals from the start; this made him popular with favored Whigs and a prime target of Democrats. Though he gave an impression of roughness—so much so that Harriet Martineau had described him as "primitive-looking"—Ewing was a personage of intellect, a scholar as well as a man of action. If his enemies criticized Ewing's proscription, Taylor needed just such a man—especially when John Clayton wobbled, and before Meredith asserted himself.[3]

3

Alongside the Big Three of Taylor's Cabinet, their colleagues were either small-caliber men or (notably in Johnson's case) hedged about by routine duties. Secretary of War George Crawford owed his position to Toombs-Stephens influence. Toombs, in recommending him, said: "There are . . . few abler and no purer men . . . and he has administrative qualities of an unusually high order." Since 1832, however, the sharp-eyed, canny, crafty Crawford had been counsel for the Galphin family, whose members sought payment on a claim in which he was financially interested. This Galphin Claim was fated to cause Zachary Taylor untold anguish, possibly contributing to his death. Since no presentiment of scandal warned the incoming President now, he appointed Crawford on Toombs's word. Fifty years old, Crawford looked younger. Brown hair parted on the side, features regular, expression pert, he was an immaculate dresser whose reputation for political skill hinged on two terms as Georgia's governor. With little influence respecting policy, not much patronage at his disposal and few Army tangles to unsnarl, Crawford seemed harmless enough at first—but later proved to be dynamite.

Redheaded Naval Secretary Preston knew little or nothing of skippers and ships. He brought to Taylor's councils, however, something unusual in a Virginian—a burning desire to reach a settlement of the crucial slavery issue, on terms acceptable to the North. Tall, straight, slim, with the air of a dandy, Taylor's youngest official adviser had been a legislator in Richmond at intervals for seven years. The length of his service was less significant than the fact that, in '32, Preston supported Thomas Jefferson's postnatal plan of abolition. Recently his speech for California statehood, in the House, had attracted attention. The knowledge that Southerners like Stephens and Toombs endorsed Ballard Preston's bill, and backed its author for the Cabinet, led Taylor and Clayton to assume that herein lay a hope of peace. Forty-three years old, close to Clayton and Crittenden, Preston became Taylor's loyal lieutenant. As Southern opposition developed and he was lauded in the North,[4] Preston was branded in his own section as a Southern man with Northern principles.

Postmaster General Jacob Collamer was described by a Democratic critic as "plodding" and "narrow minded," and by his law partner as possessing a mind of "perception" and "commonsense." Collamer's career was a series of successes, and he became Vermont's favorite politician. After years of elective offices he was now—nominally, at least—chief dispenser of federal patronage. With 17,000 post offices at stake, his influence might have been immense, had not realists like Weed frequently by-passed him to deal with his associate, Fitz Henry Warren. It was neither his steady eyes, lofty forehead, prominent nose, frizzled sideburns nor hidden humor—but, rather, the combination of all—that gave him the look of a fashionable preacher. If he failed to rank high "in the scale of great men," Collamer was "stern in principle" and (albeit less vigorous) as proscriptive as Ewing. Many acquaintances would have nodded agreement when Taylor later termed him stiff and blunt.

Unlike other Cabinet members the Attorney General had almost no help from executive assistants or clerks. There being no Department of Justice, Reverdy Johnson wrote his own briefs and appeared before the Supreme Court in person. Of medium height and "solidly . . . built," Johnson had lost the sight of one eye. But his most notable physical feature was the back of his head, which "was shaped like a barrel and seemed to bulge out all around." The same age as Clayton, four years in the Senate and by no means obscure politically, he was primarily a first-rate lawyer—rich and a leader of the Baltimore bar. Shortly after Johnson's appointment a Mississippi paper assailed him as a Bank man, rabid Whig and "plunderer of . . . widows and orphans." His biographer, however, directs attention to quickness of mind, "uniform courtesy," "resistless" arguments and inspired tact. Mrs. Johnson's kinship to Mrs. Taylor[5] also may have had something to do with Old Zack's regard for his chief law officer.

4

Zachary Taylor's Cabinet was, in the opinion of the *New Hampshire Patriot,* "the weakest one in . . . twenty years." "The cabinet will be far inferior . . . to that which retired with President Polk," predicted the *Kentucky Yeoman.* According to the Cincinnati *Enquirer,* "the Cabinet . . . with but three exceptions . . . is composed of men without political note. . . . Wildest guessers could scarcely have hit upon them in surmising who they would be." Said the Memphis *Appeal:* "We cannot . . . congratulate . . . Taylor upon the strength . . . of his cabinet. . . . The leaning of several of its members is to abolition and free-soilism." The opinions of these four influential journals were typical of the Democratic press.

Whig editors, as a whole, were no more objective. In New York Webb's *Courier & Enquirer* found the Cabinet "well received in all political circles" and "able and influential." "It is made up of the most moderate spirits among the Whigs of the nation," said the Richmond *Republican,* and the Baltimore *Patriot* believed that "better men could not have been called." "The country has . . . a guaranty for . . . ability . . . as well as . . . patriotism," opined the Nashville *Republican Banner.* The Philadelphia *North American,* close to Clayton, became lyric: "It is a noble vessel, and nobly may it . . . pursue its . . . course of patriotism through winds and waves." Bennett's independent New York *Herald* was more realistic, asserting merely that the Cabinet was "well organized" and "composed of . . . intelligent and respectable men." Greeley's *Tribune* damned the ministers with faint praise: "Most of them are other than those we . . . desired . . . but . . . all . . . are . . . steadfast Whigs, men of unblemished character." A more representative Whig reaction appeared in the Louisville *Courier:* "We have never seen a happier comminglement of . . . usefulness and greatness . . . than . . . in Taylor's Cabinet."[6]

Actually, the official family in the aggregate was mediocre—weaker than Harrison's and Polk's, less puny than Tyler's and about on a par with the first Jackson group. It may seem surprising that men so able formed a no more effectual team. All were college graduates, leading lawyers, and four really eminent professionally. Three had served in the Senate, three in the House, one in Harrison's Cabinet and one as a governor. New England, the Middle Atlantic states, the South and West were all represented, as were freedom, slavery and the border commonwealths. Taylor's critics, however, were far from satisfied. Schuyler Colfax considered Ewing Eastern in spirit. Johnson, Clayton and Meredith lived within a sixty-mile radius. The Cabinet was too "huddled" geographically. Fourteen westernmost states had no representation.

More telling criticism developed from the fact that no Clay or Webster intimate was included. Democrats also caviled because the Cabinet was exclusively Whig. In view of his early promise to Crittenden, it is hard to see how Taylor could have named a Democrat. But he would have done well to pick Letcher for Collamer's place, and someone acceptable to Webster (Ashmun, for instance) as Attorney General. There was too much "sameness" in the Cabinet, too great emphasis on legal ability, too little connection with Capitol Hill. The New Orleans *Picayune* described the secretaries as "more intellectually vigorous than politically strong." And soon an avalanche of abuse descended.

Clayton was compared, in Welles's diary, to "a . . . libertine" who "debauched" Preston—"a simple minded girl of sixteen." Ewing was "violent and unscrupulous"; Meredith, "training in a bad school"; Crawford, "narrow minded and proscriptive"; Johnson, selfish; Collamer, hypocritical. Burnley (a zealous Taylor supporter) became as vehement as the Democrats, convinced that the "cabinet is *incompetent,* or *incapacitated*" from fulfilling "high duties which the . . . situation . . . demands." Above all, the Secretary of State "is selfish . . . & will not stick to the truth."

Other criticisms of Taylor's appointees mirrored different schools of thought. To Edmund Burke, a Democrat, Ewing was a "reckless Butcher" and Jacob Collamer "insignificant." Clay's friend, Botts, was as bitter as Burke, theorizing that the entire Cabinet was chosen on the principle of hostility to Clay. That antique Republican, Ex-President Tyler, shot a glance at the capital from Sherwood Forest, concluding that "the cast of the cabinet . . . is decidedly federal." Truman Smith, once ambitious for the Treasury, considered himself double-crossed by Clayton—a "corrupt and vicious man." As to Taylor himself, Smith exclaimed: "He is a good old man . . . but . . . has been deceived." Crittenden was responsible. "He did wrong."[7]

Since most of the criticism came from Democrats or personal enemies of the men assailed, a grain of salt should be swallowed with it. President Taylor's strategic dilemma lay in his minority position, with specific reference to the party division in the two chambers of Congress. Had he commanded healthy majorities in both the Senate and the House, many attacks on his appointees would have been tamed down or withheld. The second they entered Taylor's Cabinet the seven secretaries joined him in becoming the prime target of vituperation. Since their personal popularity had never equaled the General's own, his armor was thick where theirs was thin—and more violence was hurled at them than at him.

5

The President and ministers were sometimes joined at the Cabinet meetings by Seward, who lost no time in gaining Taylor's confidence. Seward's success was the more remarkable since he and Fillmore were factional rivals. In Louisiana Taylor had spoken of Fillmore "in the highest terms," and it was widely assumed that the Vice President would sit with the Cabinet ex officio. The idea appalled Seward and Weed. And in November and December they had sent agents and exhorters to spread pro-Seward, anti-Fillmore gospel in Zachary Taylor's Southern camp.

While this was going on in Louisiana, Seward scored a ten-strike in Maryland. No sooner had Taylor defeated Cass than Seward completed plans to take part in a patent suit. The case was tried at Baltimore, the Army station of Joseph P. Taylor. During the preconvention canvass Seward had hobnobbed with the colonel and made a hit with the colonel's wife. Now in November they were delighted to see the engaging New Yorker again. Dr. and Mrs. Wood also were living in Baltimore, so Seward enjoyed the company not only of General Taylor's sister-in-law, only living brother, nieces and nephews, but also his son-in-law, daughter and grandchildren. While "my Patent cause hangs on," he wrote Weed, ". . . I am having a very pleasant time." There was a "proprietory feeling . . . towards us. . . . Col. Taylor is cordial and disposed to be confidential. But I avoid all conversations that might seem to tread on the delicacy of his position." So Seward became a family friend before he met the President-elect. Small wonder that Millard Fillmore made little headway against such a rival!

Fillmore possessed engaging qualities, which might have prevailed against average competition. Handsome and virile at forty-nine, he had white hair, kindly blue eyes, a sturdy frame and a ruddy complexion. Not every feint or spar of Fillmore and Seward is discernible a century later. But enough can be made out to justify the view that, compared to Seward, Fillmore was a plodder whose every move was anticipated by the sleepless Senator.

Before going to Washington, Fillmore and Seward met under Weed's roof, where they agreed to an even distribution of New York spoils. According to Weed's version Fillmore broke his word and, gaining the upper hand over Seward, was dominant in party councils and a sort of patronage arbiter until Weed visited Washington. Weed says he called on Fillmore, Seward, Johnson and Collamer. The Vice President was "more courteous than cordial." Johnson "received me so coldly that I did not even sit down." And Collamer "informed me . . . he could make no New York appointment" without Fillmore's approval. What a colorful account! The Albany Warwick cooling his heels, Seward mortified, the secretaries glacial and Fillmore crowing like a barnyard rooster!

But things did not happen that way. The *Autobiography,* in which Weed's story appears, was written when he was elderly and published long after the "events." True, Seward and Fillmore were at loggerheads during the month of March, and some of Fillmore's allies were nominated for jobs. Nevertheless, *in the first fortnight,* Seward blocked many of Fillmore's favorites—his prestige *at least* on a par with his rival's. The principal bone of contention between them was whether both factions had agreed on John Collier as New York's naval officer. When Fillmore advanced this argument to Meredith Seward denied it. So the battle raged, but Seward won it with a series of rapierlike thrusts. Even before the inauguration he had lobbied for the Taylor-favored California amendment. He defended Collamer's appointment to the Cabinet when Senate approval was somewhat in doubt. He performed necessary chores for Taylor and Clayton in the press and elsewhere. Finally, with Taylor's hearty assent, he daringly proposed that New York's patronage be taken out of his and Fillmore's hands and given over to the state administration. Since a recommendation from Hamilton Fish was tantamount to one from Weed, Fillmore was edged into the cold, though at first he may not have known it.

As early as March 25 Seward confidently told Weed: "Let Governor Fish now write to me when you have any advice to give the Cabinet. . . . This saves the necessity of deciding between the V.P. and the Senator." "This seasonable step has removed all difficulties," he wrote Lieutenant Governor Patterson. "Every member of the Cabinet breathes more freely. . . . You need have no fears." The Fish solution cast the die, but this might well have happened even if Seward had not paved the way socially.

Seward had written: "There is as yet no ascertained way upstairs through the kitchen of the White House." Possibly not, but William H. Seward within a month became a power.

6

Taylor's Administration was barely three weeks old when Senator Seward appealed to his partner: "We must have an *organ* here[.] Cant you come on and shew us how to get it going."[8] (He referred to the need of a Washington newspaper, handing down the party line to Whig dailies and weeklies across the land.) As matters eventuated neither Weed nor any other Northerner became the driving force behind such a journal. Before Taylor left Louisiana Burnley had outlined to Crittenden his hope of establishing a paper at the capital. Precedents for a parent press were numerous. Such journalistic giants as Duff Green, Francis P. Blair and Thomas Ritchie had exerted a tremendous influence in the capacity of "organ-grinders." Some reaped fortunes from the public printing—their prestige equal to Cabinet members'. The assignment was not to be given haphazardly to the weak Washington *Whig* or even to the *National Intelligencer* (friendlier to Clay and Webster than to Taylor). Just as Andrew Jackson and his congressional partisans made Blair rich and powerful, Taylor bestowed his blessing on Burnley.

If Burnley had not acted as a sort of Lepidus between Taylor and Crittenden, the President might never have made him proprietor of his gazette. Burnley's loyalty being unquestioned, his business capacity also qualified him for what was a sizable financial venture. As publisher of the Washington *Republic* Burnley symbolized Crittenden's circle of moderate Southerners. Predicting a large *Republic* circulation, Burnley thought the Administration would have been ruined if left to the *Intelligencer's* "masterly inactivity."

Working with Burnley on the *Republic,* and responsible for the editorial page, was another Southern friend of Taylor's. Alexander C. Bullitt, formerly of the *Picayune,* was devoted to Old Zack personally. As author of the Second Allison Letter, his part in the campaign had been consequential. Forty-two years old, of medium height and bearing some resemblance to Taylor, Bullitt could compose ringing leaders and seemed the ideal editor. His associate in the sanctum, John O. Sargent, had written for the Boston *Atlas,* New York *Courier* and Harrison and Taylor campaign sheets. Still in his thirties, Sargent in later life would be better known as a classical scholar.[9] Though in theory Sargent the

Northerner balanced Bullitt the Southerner, the latter with Burnley dominated the *Republic*—now turning to Taylor for inspiration, now striding
forward on their own.

7

Aside from his political associates, the people closest to Taylor in
Washington were relatives and Army friends. The President's primary
consideration was reserved for Mrs. Taylor. But the traditional picture—
of Betty Bliss furnishing all the gaiety and sparkle in the White House
of Taylor's time—is unfaithful to the facts. Nor was Mrs. Taylor, week
in and week out, quite the invalid of tradition. She was frail and the
state of her health continued to concern her husband, but there were
keys to her personality which have been insufficiently stressed. The first
was her piety; no preceding First Lady was more religious than she. She
worshiped regularly at Saint John's, and, in her eyes, church attendance
was not merely for Sunday mornings but for every day in the month.
Exceedingly devout, and at least as concerned with the hereafter as with
life on earth, Mrs. Taylor was little interested in White House pomp
and ceremony. She shunned dinners and receptions, which Mrs. Polk
graced in previous years. On this account writers have presumed that
the social climate in Taylor's day was a rather chilly one, warmed on rare
occasions only by Betty Bliss's vivacity.

It is true that Mary Elizabeth Bliss was a capable—almost an ideal—
hostess, taking her mother's place at her father's side downstairs throughout his Administration. Upstairs in Mrs. Taylor's sitting room, however,
the "old lady" (as Mrs. Ewing called her) was the center of attention.
She loved having her family around her. In-laws came from near and
far. Ann Wood and the Doctor brought "Puss" and "Dumple" over
from near-by Baltimore. Rebecca Taylor, Colonel Joe's teen-age daughter, lived at the Mansion much of the time when not attending school in
Georgetown. From Louisville came nieces and nephews, children of the
late Mrs. John Gibson Taylor. Toddlers, infants and babes-in-arms arrived with mamas, papas and nursemaids—and with all the baggage of
babyhood—for those lengthy, old-fashioned, Southern visits which the
President enjoyed. There were dances and young people's parties, as
well as stately presidential dinners, and many a uniformed gallant called
to squire Miss Becky about the capital. Far from forbidding in Taylor's
regime, White House corridors rang with laughter and echoed the patter
of little feet.

Nor was the White House circle limited to blood relations of its master. During the congressional session Varina Davis often was welcomed to Mrs. Taylor's cheery room on the second floor overlooking the garden. This lovely Mississippi brunette was Jefferson Davis' second wife, and, while no one could take the place of "the sainted Sarah" in her parents' hearts, Varina was accepted gladly into the bosom of the Taylor family. Davis, too, was welcomed by the President who had frowned upon him in his youth, when, a slender subaltern, he courted and flirted with Sarah Knox Taylor.

President Taylor's esteem for Davis was a feature of his later years. However, their relationship was purely personal and without effect on Taylor's policies. If Seward's social blandishments (rather than Taylor's own ideas, so often expressed in his past letters) had really been responsible for Taylor's Union stand, one might wonder why Davis' near-filial status did not influence the President as much as Seward's friendship. It would then be easy to attribute this to ice water in Davis' veins, which, many thought, lessened his arguments' attractiveness. But Jeff Davis was far from frigid when Taylor first knew him, and the General had also seen him in battle—an impetuous knight of a man, hell-for-leather, impulsive, daring. That Taylor's position was nearer Seward's does not imply it was due primarily to Davis' failure—or Seward's success—in the role of courtier. No flaw in the Taylor-Davis friendship was responsible for the trend of the President's thinking. It was *in spite of* their intimacy—sorrow, dangers and triumphs shared— that Zachary Taylor and Jefferson Davis went separate ways in politics.

8

Just as Davis was disappointed in Taylor's domestic policies, Bullitt and Burnley grew dissatisfied with Cabinet, program, patronage—all three. Southerners generally were taking note that Taylor's advisers, or at least most of them, were a very different set from those who directed his '48 campaign. Crittenden and Brown were over the mountains. Hunton chose to remain in New Orleans. Letcher and Peyton went abroad. Taylor's personal friends, McGehee and White, stayed in Mississippi and Louisiana. Of the Cabinet, only Crawford spoke up occasionally for Southern interests. Clayton and Johnson were anti-extension— Preston and Seward hand in glove. Taylor himself, who had been considered a Southern candidate by Southerners, seemed opposed to extension, too. How dangerous—disquieting—topsy-turvy!

In the late spring Crittenden made arrangements for Brown to go to Washington. He became Commissioner of Indian Affairs. But Crittenden wanted Brown to act as his Washington liaison agent, and the President was a frequent visitor at Brown's F Street house. Close to Taylor, of course, were Bliss, his son-in-law and private secretary, and the youthful Joseph Eaton, who acted as military aide. Both resided at the White House,[10] enjoying Taylor's confidence. But Eaton's connection with politics was negligible. And so many routine demands were made on Bliss's time that he was no policy maker despite Taylor's high opinion of him.

The Zachary Taylor of 1849 was the same individual he had been the year before, but the Taylor some of his friends thought he was—the myth they imagined him to be—vanished almost overnight and never was seen in this world again. When Taylor became President statesmen and political theorists had long been debating various concepts of the basic nature of American government. Ideological followers of Alexander Hamilton, Edward Livingston and Joseph Story believed in (and provided intellectual and activist support for) the consolidated or "national" state—not importantly different from what is taken for granted as "republican nationalism" a century later. Northern Whigs generally applied Hamilton-Livingston-Story arguments to buttress their opposition to slavery's expansion and establish their power to resist it, stressing their devotion to a Union where slavery would be rigidly contained. State-Rights Southerners, on the contrary, defined the Constitution as a compact among sovereign states; they, too, repeatedly emphasized *their* devotion to the Union—but it was to *the Union as they interpreted it,* not in line with Northern Whigs' definitions. Between Northern Whigs and Free-Soilers on the one hand and Calhoun Democrats on the other, many shades of opinion could be found—but it was all pro-Union opinion, according to each man's version of his views. Though the Calhounites made frequent minority demands on the Northern majority with secession as a threat and/or alternative, the term "disunionists" or "secessionists" should not carelessly be applied to them all as of '49—since they had not quite reached the point where their own logic must inevitably lead them. The only out-and-out disunionist groups remained the Rhett-Yancey extremists of the South and the Garrison abolitionists of the North—both still small but very vocal.

How did Taylor fit into this verbal bombardment where combatants used finespun legalisms as grapeshot and economic and moral ammunition as canister? Zachary Taylor was no Judge Story and he was no John Calhoun. It is doubtful that either Taylor or Andrew Jackson before him could have attacked or defended successfully *on his own,* in the sphere of sophistries and syllogisms, disquisitions and legalistic discourses. What Taylor brought to the Presidency was the military mind, with all the bluntness, directness, practicality and absence of theory that the term implies. Schooled for thirty-nine years in "chains of command," Taylor was a soldier before he was a cotton planter—a Westerner before he was a Southerner—a great admirer of businessmen and business practices—a Unionist somewhat in the Jackson tradition, somewhat in the sense of Northern Whigs, certainly *not* in the sense of Calhoun and his Democratic faction.

First and foremost, Taylor was a soldier. His approach to the Union was a soldier's approach. If this caused him to march in the direction of what many Southerners described as the consolidated state, Old Rough and Ready did so for no cloudy theoretical reasons but because he wished to do what he believed was best for the country—what was patriotic— what was national, according to his soldierly standards.

CHAPTER XV

FORMULATION OF DOMESTIC POLICY

1

IN 1849's lush spring the future of California presented President Taylor and the country with their knottiest problem. When Polk broached the subject to Taylor during their March 5 drive to the Capitol he understood his successor to say the region was so distant that it might as well be independent. This shocked Polk, who concluded that Old Rough and Ready was "exceedingly ignorant of public affairs, and . . . of very ordinary capacity." Taylor had limitations, surely, but it is doubtful that his predecessor heard him aright that blustery morning. If he did make the remark, it was wholly inconsistent with action he had taken through Seward and Ewing two days before. It was out of line also with the program he adopted in the next five weeks. Unfortunately Taylor kept no diary, but circumstantial evidence strongly suggests that Taylor's words were not clear to Polk or (less likely) misrepresented by him. It is not only improbable but out of character that Taylor would have sandwiched between strenuous statehood efforts such an observation as Polk reported.

True, Taylor was not explicit on California in his inaugural address, which—the Boston *Post* observed—foreshadowed his views but hardly did more. The New London *Democrat* complained: "It . . . shapes no definite policy," and the people "are . . . as much in the dark" as to Taylor's course as "a month ago." Some Southerners suspected that Taylor's failure to take an anti-Proviso stand might mean he was secretly pro-Proviso. It was charged in April that a Cabinet majority favored Proviso principles. The Washington *Whig* denied the *Intelligencer's* assertion that free-soil sentiment in the Administration did not amount to much. As the discerning Elias Kingman informed the Charleston *Courier,* the *Whig* refused to believe "the President 'will not interfere with . . . the legislative power.' 'President Taylor,' it says, 'does not . . . talk about things before hand.' " The *Whig's* words may have been inspired. Kingman probably thought they were, and the question he placed before his readers transfixed public men everywhere.

Zachary Taylor's chief concern was not what South or North might think, but how the nation could best be served. California was fast becoming a criminal and anarchic land, peopled by roughhewn men who sought vast riches in El Dorado. In normal circumstances the region might not have become a critical issue for a dozen years. In '48 its population was generally considered insufficient to warrant statehood. Then, as if by magic, the land was transformed from one of padres and tolling bells into raw and bustling communities of ambitious, active men armed with pans, "cradles" and baskets—not above riot and murder—living in tents, and often sleeping out under the stars.

This transformation had come about because, in January '48, James W. Marshall found loose flakes of gold in the American River. The discovery was kept quiet for a time, but by May the word had spread. Nearly every male Californian who could go to the placers went. Lawyers, physicians, storekeepers, clerks joined rancheros, Indians, farmers. Sailors left their ships. Soldiers deserted. Brevet Brigadier General Richard B. Mason, who was California's governor, learned that "upwards of four thousand men were working in the gold district" in August—and "from $30,000 to $50,000 worth of gold, if not more, was daily obtained." Mason wrote of two miners who, in a week, made $10,000 in a gutter a hundred yards long.[1] Never before had average men found it so easy to get rich quick.

Mason's accurate and vivid report received national circulation when, in December, Polk's Annual Message accredited the New Golconda. Adventurous spirits no sooner heard of fabulous returns from pick and pan than they headed toward the Pacific. The rash became an epidemic. Polk referred to it as a "rage." Within a month the memorable "gold rush" of 1849 was on.

2

"Every city, large or small, from . . . Missouri to the Atlantic seaboard, was affected by the California fever." Emigrants in covered wagons set out from Saint Joseph and Independence. Parties traveled through northern Mexico. Some boarded ocean-going ships. Between December 14 and January 18, sixty-one sailing vessels "left New York, Boston, Salem, Norfolk, Philadelphia and Baltimore for the Pacific coast." Many more departed from New Orleans, Charleston and other ports. On January 30 the New York *Herald* listed ninety-nine craft, carrying 5,700 persons, as having weighed anchor since January 1. Nine days later the *Tribune* named 131. Seward wrote, in New York in February: "The world seems almost divided into two classes . . . moving in the same direction . . . to California in search of gold, and . . . to Washington in quest of office." By the end of 1849 California's population would reach 95,000. Since this enormous increase was predictable when Taylor entered the White House, he was aware that concrete moves must be made to provide a civil structure, under which Californians could live in safety and peace.

California's governmental status quo was inadequate for meeting new demands—limited, makeshift, quasi-military, a hangover from Mexican days. Mason, finding himself in charge at the close of the Mexican War, wrote Washington in mid-1848 that "no civil officers exist" save the alcaldes. To throw civil management off on them would "probably lead to endless confusion, if not to . . . anarchy," he added. "And yet what . . . authority have I to exercise civil control in time of peace? . . . If sedition or rebellion should arise[,] where is my force to meet it?" Two companies of regulars, every day diminishing by desertions, "will soon be the only military force in California." And they must remain at San Francisco and Monterey, to guard powder and munitions. Unsustained by troops or positive instructions, "I feel compelled" to control the alcaldes and maintain order if possible, "until a civil governor arrive, armed with . . . laws to guide his footsteps." Neither Polk nor Congress gave the general any substantial satisfaction, except to transfer additional soldiers to California during the winter. Thus Mason was left governing American soil, in circumstances so extraordinary that "it is doubtful if anything like it is known in history."

Since Mason's superiors did nothing constructive, some of the more forward residents took matters into their own hands. At the end of '48 and the start of '49, mass meetings were held at San José, San Francisco, Sacramento, Santa Cruz and Monterey. Resolutions were passed that "frequent murders and other . . . outrages committed" without "legal protection for . . . lives and property . . . forced the people to conclude that Congress had been trifling with them." There was "no more time to wait." Instant "steps should be taken to establish a . . . government for themselves." Delegates were named to a general convention—where they would frame a constitution—first planned for March, postponed to May, then scheduled for the first Monday in August.

The convention was still embryonic when two new figures appeared on the scene. In February Brevet Major General P. F. Smith assumed command of the military district of the Pacific; in April Brevet Major General Bennet Riley succeeded Mason as commanding general of Military District Number 10, and ex officio, provisional governor.[2] Riley has been given a lion's share of credit for moves subsequently made to bring California into the Union. Smith, however, was a factor, too. As Riley's superior and Taylor's intimate friend Smith lent a magnetic personality and conciliatory influence to the functioning of Riley's machinery.

Though in contact with Smith, Taylor's main contribution to stable government in California was embodied not in a military man but in the person of T. Butler King, whom he sent to the region as his special agent. King, a Georgia representative in Congress, was in certain ways an ideal choice. As Secretary Clayton indicated, King—"fully possessed of the President's views"—was to inform the Californians of the "sincere desire of the Executive" to protect them "in the formation of any government, republican in its character, hereafter to be submitted to Congress, which shall be the result of their . . . deliberate choice." Clayton was quick to add that "the plan of such a government [state or territorial, free or slave] must originate with themselves, and without the interference of the Executive." What Taylor and Clayton told King in confidence may never be known, but correspondence between Clayton and Crittenden leaves no doubt as to Taylor's aims.

"The slavery question is the only . . . formidable obstacle in the way of the Administration," Crittenden advised. It could "be effectually removed by admission of California" as a state. This "ought to be regarded as the *great object* of the Administration, and its accomplishment sought with all . . . policy & energy." "Not only the safety of the Administration, but the safety of the country," Crittenden continued, "may depend upon it." All government agents and officers in California "ought to have . . . discretion enough to see the importance of the object, & to act upon it, *without any formal Instructions*. Their influence might be great for good or evil." Taylor and Clayton were in solid agreement. On April 18 the Secretary of State gave this assurance to his Kentucky friend: "As to California . . . every thing is done as you would wish." The state "will be admitted—free and Whig!"

3

King reached San Francisco June 4. The previous day Riley had issued a proclamation designating September 1 as the date—and Monterey the place—for holding a constitutional convention. Many a Californian questioned Riley's right to initiate the call, a minority preferring territorial status to immediate statehood. King, Smith and Riley went to work selling statehood to the people. "I had the opportunity of becoming acquainted with most of the principal inhabitants," King reported to Clayton, ". . . and explaining to them, as far as was proper, the views of the President." The feeling "in favour of forming a State Government soon became so universal" that the factious "found successful resistance impossible." A meeting at which King spoke passed off well. General Smith "united most cordially in promoting the object we have in view. . . . We are now on the high road to success."

Smith also was optimistic. "The convention to form a State Constitution is meeting under favorable promise of a good conclusion," he wrote Taylor in September. "I do not approve of all Gen. Riley's measures in relation to the civil government," Smith added. Some "are adverse to my advice," but "I have let" little vexatious things "go by without notice, so as not to create . . . jealousy . . . until the State government is organized. I have made this the great object of all efforts. . . . I will leave nothing undone to insure it." Smith reminded the President "how anxious I am to do every thing in conformity with your wishes & to have things take such a position as will remove" that "terrible" Wilmot Proviso. "Wherever you think I can aid . . . in or out of the regular discharge of my duties[,] I beg you will only let me understand your wishes."

At Colton Hall in Monterey the delegates met on September 3. Although roughly a third were Southerners, slavery never became an issue. On a Southerner's motion the territorial alternative was shelved, and the state constitution they adopted unanimously prohibited slavery for all time.

In the story of California's convention the most arresting phase concerns the lengths to which Southern men went to bring about a free state's creation. The historian Goodwin wrote, years ago, that it is "hardly correct . . . to say" with Hubert Howe Bancroft that the gathering at Monterey "was understood to be under the management" of individuals from Southern states. Goodwin's statement is accurate if applied only to delegates, but inaccurate when related to prominent leaders who appreciably influenced the decisions. T. Butler King, rich in cotton fields, rich in Negroes, was a king in fact as well as name on the golden isles of Georgia. Smith, a resident of Louisiana, was a lawyer with business interests there long before he became a soldier. Riley had been in the Army for years, but a Southerner at the start, born in Maryland. William M. Gwin, the most prominent delegate, hailed from Tennessee and Mississippi.[3] Crittenden, who favored a free state, was governor of a slave commonwealth. Clayton, who instructed King, dominated a state where slavery was legal. Above all, Zachary Taylor, who set the California ball in motion, owned more than a hundred slaves. If a majority of Monterey delegates came from the freedom-loving North, Southerners in posts of power were equally opposed to slavery's extension and worked against it in California.

4

Though California was Taylor's principal problem in 1849, New Mexico also clamored for attention. Just as California's fate was made acute by the discovery of gold, New Mexico's was dramatized by Texan claims. The New Mexico of '49, like California and Texas itself, was an enormous, thinly populated region—its government semimilitary, comparable to California's under Riley. Control of New Mexico was entrusted to Brevet Lieutenant Colonel John M. Washington, son of the First President's cousin and an artilleryman who played a hero's part under Taylor at Buena Vista.

Colonel Washington's instructions from Secretary of War Marcy, and later from Crawford, called for maintenance of order under military rule. Ranged against him was the aggressive government of Texas at Austin, which insisted that a major part of New Mexico was property of the Lone Star State. There was much in favor of the Texans' contention. New Mexico's legal limits had never been definitively established when it was a Spanish or Mexican province. Before American annexation of Texas, Sam Houston's fledgling republic declared its own boundary to be the Rio Grande from mouth to source—territory containing a wide expanse, including Santa Fe. Texas, as a state of the Union, through successive governors and legislatures, reasserted the republic's title. Moreover, Polk declared that though the boundary was a question on which Congress should pass he believed in Texas' right to the whole region east of the Rio Grande. This was an important pro-Texas acknowledgment. But at the time Polk took his stand the Mexican War was still being fought. Texas, having no reason to extend control to the claim at once, patiently waited for the end of the war in the belief that the military would then give way.

Before the conflict ceased, however, some New Mexico residents rebelled against absorption by Texas soon or ever. They felt the Treaty of Guadalupe Hidalgo gave them the right to become a territory and eventually a state. In October 1848 a convention at Santa Fe asked Congress for territorial government, stating its members were antislavery, and protesting New Mexico's dismemberment "in favor of Texas, or for any other cause." Texas anticipated this move by providing for enforcement of her own jurisdiction: Santa Fe County was created, and Spruce M. Baird sent there as judge with instructions to formalize Texas' authority.

Baird arrived in Santa Fe November 10. Twelve days later he had his first brush with Governor Washington. Expressing astonishment that soldiers still controlled New Mexico, Baird said flatly that Texas "must" regard as void all judicial and civil proceedings "inconsistent with her laws." Colonel Washington was equally outspoken. Pending congressional action, Polk had said, the military should continue on—even with the advent of peace. The colonel intended to act accordingly, "at every peril," until ordered by his government to desist. When Washington on November 23 returned Baird's documents, hinting he would not be permitted to "publish a proclamation announcing the purpose of his mission," Baird "felt . . . further progress was blocked." He reported that nothing could be accomplished until Congress settled the jurisdiction issue unless further instructions came from Austin or "Washington received new orders from the President."

5

All this occurred three months before Taylor reached the nation's capital. Before the inauguration Marcy had advised Colonel Washington to respect any civil authority which Texas might establish in New Mexico. Now, however, Crawford qualified his repetition of Marcy's instructions by writing that Texas was not expected to extend her jurisdiction. This has been interpreted by a leading scholar as indicating Crawford's lack of knowledge of the situation in the Southwest. But one wonders if Taylor and his Cabinet were not already anticipating a basic change of national policy—providing Washington with a loophole for continuing opposition to Baird. If his superiors did not *expect* Texas to become aggressive, was it not logical for the colonel to look askance at the Texas claims! There was considerable jockeying for position between Washington and Baird from March to July. Washington, maintaining his advantage, balked Baird's every move and kept him from breaking into print. As a result Baird left Santa Fe convinced he could do nothing without more power—or unless Governor George T. Wood won Taylor over to Texas' side.

Meanwhile, during Washington's absence from Santa Fe in pursuit of Indians, Brevet Lieutenant Colonel Benjamin L. Beall issued a call

for another convention to draw up a new petition to Congress.[4] When
the delegates met on September 24 many of them favored statehood, just
as the Californians had done. They may have been influenced by the
counsel of James S. Calhoun, who had been dispatched as an Indian agent
by President Taylor and Secretary Ewing. But Crawford's instructions
were not such as to encourage statehood at this time, and the convention
advocated a territorial form. Texan politicians were equally busy. There
being considerable anti-Wood sentiment on the theory that he lacked
aggressiveness, Wood lost his race for re-election to the militant Peter
Hansborough Bell. Bell trounced his opponent on the issue of expediting
New Mexico's incorporation, under the flag of the single star.

Bell succeeded Wood in December. But even before he came into
power rumblings from the White House indicated that Taylor was prepared to match the dynamics of Texas with some of his own. Bell and
the legislature were working overtime to formulate new plans for New
Mexico. The *Texas State Gazette* breathed secession: The "banner of
the Lone Star shall again be unfurled; not for *offence,* but for *defence,*
and those who were foremost to cry aloud for annexation, will be foremost to sever the country [i.e., Texas] from a *Union* that embraces but
to crush and destroy." This was fire-eating of an extreme kind, comparable to the Bluffton utterances in South Carolina, and representative
of views beginning to dominate Texan thought.

Weeks before he received news of these fulminations Zachary Taylor
came out in favor of statehood for *both* California and New Mexico.
When Brevet Lieutenant Colonel George A. McCall left the East to
join his regiment at Santa Fe, he was informed by Crawford that "if the
people of New Mexico desired to take . . . steps toward securing admission as a state, it would be his duty . . . 'not to thwart but to advance their
wishes,' since it was their right to ask for admission." Thus the gauntlet,
flung by Texas, was caught in mid-air by Old Zack. In the state of "Colts
and Bowies, hard-riding cowboys and swaggering planters, two-cent beef
and twenty-five-cent whiskey," the extremists had their answer from the
soldier in the White House. The situation was probably not altogether
to the liking of a moderate individual like Taylor, whose tendencies in
normal times were conservative. The President, after all, was a Whig
by conviction. Committed in his campaign to co-ordination of executive
and legislative power, Taylor waited eight months before deciding that
duty led him to such forthrightness. This was the Texas-New Mexico
situation in the late autumn of '49 when Taylor contemplated presenting
his two-way statehood plan to Congress.

6

California and New Mexico—states or territories, free soil or slave soil, admission into Union partnership now or at some vague future date? These were the only internal questions on which Taylor took an advanced position, implemented by executive action, during 1849. On no other phase of domestic business, save the matter of appointments and removals, did the President stride forward with similar boldness. In view of his generation's widespread faith in the desirability of a weak central government, it is doubtful that he could have effected more. If Taylor had called a special session of Congress to alter the Tariff of 1846, to authorize routing of railroads in the West, to create a bureau of agriculture or to enact a homestead law, it is unlikely that the Senate or House would have been able to disentangle constructive legislation from the slavery snarl.

In addition to New Mexicans and Californians, Brigham Young's Mormons in Deseret (Utah) were yearning for authorized government.[5] Whigs sought river and harbor improvements. Coal and iron interests appealed for more protection than the Walker Tariff gave them. Still, fear of "executive tyranny"—a Whig bugaboo since the Jackson days— was so strong that it is surprising to find Taylor daring to go as far as he did. Because of slavery agitation American society was trending toward confusion, chaos, civil war. It was in the hope of preventing strife that President Taylor asserted his leadership out in the land of the setting sun. His aim was to short-circuit sectional antipathies by presenting South and North with the *fait accompli* of Western statehood. So he departed from weak-government theories in the region where the need was urgent for swift and unconditional relief.

Aside from his efforts to obtain a solution of the statehood-territorial issue, Taylor's main domestic contribution involved the Florida Indians. In July wild rumors reached Washington that Seminole braves were killing whites. Alarmists depicted the situation as similar to those of '18 and '37 when Andrew Jackson and Zachary Taylor led American troops into hammock and swamp. There was sentiment in Florida for the President to call out volunteer armies, and a full-scale Indian war was desired by certain elements. The panic was "complete" among south Floridians. "All industrial pursuits . . . ceased," settlers were "forted as far north as Fort King," and there was a determination "not to return until the Indians are removed." "The opinion is . . . general that the outrages were perpetrated by the Indian nation," not by a few outlaws, wrote Brevet Major General David E. Twiggs. "I am disposed," Twiggs added, to "coincide in this opinion." On what evidence did Twiggs base his conclusion? Why, the Seminoles had "purchased 120 rifles" since 1842, and "have largely supplied themselves with . . . everything necessary for hostilities. . . . Three hundred warriors may be stated as an approximation of their force."

Fortunately for Indians and whites, Taylor and Crawford analyzed the disturbance more accurately than some people on the spot. At Taylor's direction Crawford ordered troops from Jefferson Barracks, New Orleans and elsewhere to report to Twiggs at Fort Brooke. But the President refused to call Florida militiamen into federal service, Crawford writing Twiggs: "A hostile purpose seems not to be general. . . . It would be cruel to involve the whole tribe in the guilt of a few, and punish accordingly." What were the facts? On July 12 one white had been killed by five young Seminoles—their leader an outlaw—who, several days later, committed two more murders. This was the total score to be settled with aborigines who for seven years had given the paleface no cause for complaint, and even now were trying to apprehend the murderers. It is to Taylor's and Crawford's credit that, instead of plunging the peninsula into combat, they relied on conciliation and reason.

There happened to be a junior officer who sized up the facts much as Taylor did. Captain John C. Casey, disagreeing with Twiggs, thought the Seminoles as a whole were guiltless, and, acting on this assumption, courageously sought out representatives of the chief, Billy Bowlegs. From these emissaries he learned that Billy and another chief, Sam Jones, disavowed and regretted the outrages, and that "all the Indians" were opposed to war. "They are satisfied with their country, and with the treaty under which they are living," Casey reported to Twiggs's adjutant. The upshot of the Casey mission was that Billy Bowlegs conferred personally with Twiggs at Charlotte Harbor. He agreed to hand over the culprits to the Army, and, though two escaped, three were delivered. Meanwhile Taylor, Crawford and Orlando Brown were instrumental in bringing to Tampa Bay a delegation of Western Seminoles, sent to persuade their Florida relatives to follow their example and emigrate. The delegation, headed by the famous Wild Cat, reached Fort Brooke early in November. Some of the red men did emigrate, and those remaining made no further trouble during the Taylor Administration.

"It is a simple act of justice," Twiggs wrote, "to acknowledge the important service" Casey rendered in "probably averting . . . war." To Taylor tribute should also be paid for the policy he sponsored. His achievement deserves a shining page in the notoriously sordid annals of America's Indian relations. Curiously, prevention of strife has never been deemed as glamorous—by spectators at a distance—as the flash of sword or boom of cannon. Hence Rough and Ready's solid sense in postponing a tragic Third Seminole War[6] remains a dim, forgotten footnote.

7

Concurrent with the Florida disturbance was Indian trouble in the Southwest. Americans and Mexicans were murdered in April between Mier and Corpus Christi. Others were slaughtered in May and June. In July and August the attacks continued. On August 25 Henry L. Kinney, Taylor's old associate, wrote the President that conditions were "horrible"—with upward of two hundred slain, $40,000 stolen and women carried into captivity. In September Kinney listed thirty-nine people killed, wounded or taken prisoners in the Corpus Christi area within five months. There was a sizable discrepancy between thirty-nine and two hundred! But the exaggeration was less striking than the error of Brevet Brigadier General George M. Brooke who, charged with defending the frontier, wrote Crawford in mid-July that "no Indian depredations have occurred for some time." Crawford naturally paid more attention to this ranking subordinate than to private citizens. Small wonder that Kinney, in desperation, dashed off a frantic plea to Old Zack, insisting that Crawford's reliance on Brooke was mistaken and "not right." Assailants were hard-riding Comanches, who—together with Apaches and Caddoes—presented a far more serious problem than Billy Bowlegs and his Seminoles.

Crawford had previously directed Brooke to accept Texas Rangers for federal service should the Indians prove unruly. Brooke finally did this in mid-August after tidings from Colonel Kinney reached him at San Antonio. No sooner had three mounted companies been federalized than Corpus Christi depredations ceased—teamsters, herdsmen, laborers and travelers moving freely through the countryside again. Now, however, the Navajos made trouble. Caddo Indians stole pioneers' property in the vicinity of Georgetown, Texas. There were forays near Laredo, and Second Lieutenant Egbert L. Viele reported on August 18 that "every rancho" on the Rio Grande "has been attacked within the last month."

People worked in the fields with guns on their backs. "With but nine men for duty, I can do nothing."

This young shavetail and his comrades faced four liabilities in the outposts. The first was Brooke's inexcusable misinformation in the early summer. Then, too, the Army's nine camps, with two exceptions, were undermanned. Thirdly, few Regulars having horses, they could hardly catch hit-and-run Indians. Finally, the Rangers, equipped with fleet ponies, were often more interested in ruthless warfare than in control and pacification. No land having been set aside for the Indians' exclusive use, repeated brushes were almost inevitable. Brooke finally ordered a partial remount. More important was the backing he gave Brevet Captain William Steele, who received assurances from Chief Buffalo Hump that henceforth the Comanches would be peaceful. Temporarily, at least, Steele's accomplishment was comparable to Casey's in Florida. Encouraged, Brooke declared in October: "I feel very little apprehension . . . since the report" of Captain Steele.

Meanwhile there were bloody skirmishes between Apaches and American patrols in New Mexico. The Indians came off second-best, leaving their dead and wounded on the field. Colonel Washington, more aggressive than Brooke, pushed out from Santa Fe to Jemez and beyond. In the Navajo stronghold, at the head of 320 troops, he engaged the redoubtable Chief Narbona—whom one of his sharpshooters killed. Washington and Calhoun signed a treaty, which they were assured by Narbona's successor was binding on all the Navajos. This was one of several substantial accomplishments of Colonel Washington, whose skeptical, wait-and-see attitude was aptly summarized in his June 4 report: Latest accounts represented "the Eutaws . . . as being inclined for peace." They "express a willingness to surrender" murderers. "Should they act in good faith, which is by no means certain, the war with them will cease."

Colonel Washington and Captain Steele in the West, like Captain Casey in Florida, acted with the courage and seasoned judgment on which President Taylor placed a high premium. It would have been comparatively easy for Indian conflagrations to spread, which some civilians were ready to welcome. But Zachary Taylor kept his good sense, and (except for George Brooke's blunder) his old Army friends were most efficient in carrying out the President's wishes. The Washington Union, quick to criticize Whigs, accused Taylor of waging two Indian wars[7]—which was precisely what he did not do. Far from fomenting hostilities, Taylor placed the full power of his government behind the cause of frontier peace.

CHAPTER XVI

A TYRO IN DIPLOMACY

1

IN A VERY different sphere Taylor was as inexperienced as any President has ever been. This was the whirlpool of international affairs, which challenged the White House and State Department with a succession of churning problems. Foreign ministers and Washington envoys with whom more than routine business was transacted represented France, Portugal, Germany, Denmark, Austria, Spain, Great Britain and Nicaragua—in addition to agents of Kossuth's Hungary and Narciso López' revolutionary Cubans. The negotiations with Nicaragua and England were the most consequential. But none was more fantastic than the tempest brewed in a Potomac teapot by a Frenchman named Poussin.

Guillaume Tell Lavallée Poussin had a strange background for diplomacy. Engineer by training, rebel by instinct and for years an American Army officer, the French minister acted as if his merest bagatelle of business deserved Clayton's exclusive attention. Even if Clayton had been blessed with more aid than fourteen clerks could give him, he should not have dropped every other problem to oblige Poussin on a minor matter. With thousands of petitions to be read and applicants clamoring at his door, Clayton was overwhelmed by patronage. Poussin, therefore, could have bided his time until Clayton was free to listen.

Notwithstanding this, on March 17 Poussin pressed a trifling thousand-dollar claim of a Frenchman—Alexis Port—on Clayton for settlement. The claim's history began with confiscation of tobacco in Mexico by American troops during the war. Port had purchased 500 bales at auction for $12,000 with the military governor's approval. Later it was discovered that the bales had previously been bought by D. B. Juan Domerey. Before the governor learned he and Port had been in error, Port resold the tobacco for $16,500 to Juan Abadie, who disposed of it to Manuel de Murquiro for $17,500. Striving for fairness, an American court consigned the tobacco to Domerey and awarded $12,000 with interest to Port. Port returned $16,500 to Abadie, who paid back $17,500 to Murquiro but demanded that Port make good the difference. It was this figure which Port now sought from Washington as indemnification.

Clayton found no opportunity to answer Poussin's inquiry until after the French minister followed up his interview with two badgering notes at six and five-day intervals. When the Secretary replied on March 28 he flatly turned down the claim and approved the Army court's decision. This angered Poussin. Reasserting the claim, he intimated that the military governor lied as a witness before the court. Now Clayton, questioning Poussin's veracity, charged Port with conspiring to defraud. Since Port knew the tobacco was "private property," why should the United States guarantee "speculations" made in such circumstances? As matters tumbled from bad to worse, Poussin lost his self-control. Surely, he announced, "it is more honorable" to acquit a debt than to "avoid its payment" by branding "the character of an honest man." Clayton hit the ceiling when he read that sentence and took his troubles to the White House.

Taylor was as incensed as Clayton over Poussin's disrespect. With the President's approval Clayton warned the Frenchman that his language would not be admitted into the record unless a vigorous protest were lodged with Foreign Minister Alexis de Tocqueville. This seemed to frighten Poussin, who deleted his rudest words. Thus Poussin rang the curtain down on the first of two feverish acts.[1]

2

Port's claim was pressed no further. But before long Poussin and Clayton were hammering at each other over Commander E. W. Carpender's rescue of the French barque *Eugénie* from a reef off the Mexican coast. Poussin charged Carpender with detaining the *Eugénie* contrary to international law, asking Secretary Clayton to disavow the American's conduct. Instead of complying Clayton submitted a copy of Carpender's report, together with his own opinion that it should remove all misunderstanding. The trigger-tempered Poussin prepared a blistering rejoinder: Carpender's "explanations" could not "dispel the discontent which his proceedings have caused . . . my Government." Carpender considered the case "one of salvage," entitling him to keep the vessel until his "extravagant pretensions" were satisfied! Condemning the commander's conduct, Poussin said he was now "induced to believe" that "your Government subscribes" to Carpender's "strange" doctrines. "And I have . . . to protest, in the name of my Government."

As another piddling incident stretched to exceptionable proportions Clayton again consulted the President. Poussin's arbitrary tone might have justified his dismissal. But Taylor shifted responsibility, Clayton instructing Richard Rush (American minister in Paris) to deliver a protest to Tocqueville and leave action in French hands. Tocqueville replied unofficially that Poussin would be replaced. However, he later told Rush that Clayton—as well as Poussin—had used undiplomatic language, the context of Tocqueville's note suggesting that Poussin would be retained. The bland manner in which the French seemed inclined to dispose of the issue provoked Taylor and Clayton anew.

Rush being recalled and his successor (William C. Rives) not having reached Paris, Clayton wrote directly to Tocqueville that Taylor was dissatisfied with the French course. The same day (September 14), Clayton added, the hapless Poussin had been dismissed. The ouster may have been just, but its timing was bad, for, prior to hearing from Clayton, Tocqueville not only appointed Poussin's successor but considered the Carpender matter closed. When Clayton's sharp note came he let it be known that Rives's presentation to Louis Napoleon must now "be adjourned & the whole subject submitted to the . . . Council of Ministers."

Rives at once set out to re-establish friendly relations, prevailing on the Foreign Minister to discuss the affair informally and plainly. Tocqueville conversed cordially, Rives reported to Clayton, but considered Clayton's note "wounding" to French dignity. Though Rives assured him of Taylor's and Clayton's "sincere friendship for France," Tocqueville wrote Clayton that France had not received "satisfactory explanations" as to Poussin's ouster: Did the dismissal spring from "a misunderstanding" or from "an intention to wound the French Government"? The word "misunderstanding" gave the Americans a chance to effect a graceful withdrawal, and Clayton was half inclined to seize it. Taylor, however, remained unyielding and directed Clayton to reaffirm his stand: "Studious" to observe "high courtesy," the United States expected "functionaries of other Governments" to comply with usages of "civilized nations." It asserted the right to decline correspondence with any minister guilty of "intentional discourtesy," maintaining that "the exercise of that right affords no just ground of complaint."

Thus the comic opera lost itself in a maze of mutual misconceptions, and in the press there was dark talk of the possibility of war. On his side Taylor was intransigent, and a similar attitude prevailed in France until Louis Napoleon's imperial dreams made Franco-American friendship expedient. In early November the President of the Second Republic (later to become Napoleon III) made overtures to Rives and assured him of Paris' high consideration for Washington. This ended the incident. Taylor, in his turn, reciprocated by speaking well of France in his Annual Message. When a career diplomat took over the discredited Poussin's legation, tranquillity marked diplomatic exchanges between the Potomac and the Seine.[2]

3

While Taylor and Clayton were wrestling with Poussin, dispatches from George W. Hopkins, chargé d'affaires at Lisbon, diverted part of their attention to American claims on Portugal. In the War of 1812 the American privateer *General Armstrong* had been destroyed by the British in a Portuguese harbor under guns of a Portuguese fortress. Claims against Britain were abandoned under stipulations of the Treaty of Ghent, but successive United States diplomats sought damages from Portugal for neglecting her neutral duty. Portugal had also taken money from the ship *Shepherd* in '28 on the assumption that Americans removed the sum illegally from Portuguese soil. Since the vessel's captain was exonerated in low and high Portuguese courts the funds ought to have been returned and the incident terminated. This was not done, however, and the property was confiscated by the despotic Dom Miguel.

Miguel had long been supplanted by Queen Maria da Gloria when Zachary Taylor took office as President. It seemed reasonable to him that, under her aegis, just claims would be given fair treatment. In addition to the *Shepherd* and *General Armstrong,* the *Bolton's* boats had been seized, cargo of the *Miles* taken, passengers and crew of the *Magoun* imprisoned and the *Colonel Blum* wrecked. There were also smaller claims for damages to the *Ganges* and *Long Island.* "The patience of the claimants and . . . their Government has become exhausted," Clayton wrote Hopkins in April. Responsibility must rest with Lisbon if Washington should resort to "ulterior measures to enforce its demands." Taylor contemplated laying "before Congress the result of this final appeal." And Hopkins was told that, in presenting the "frank avowal of a fixed determination," he should stress the President's anxiety to avoid suspending diplomatic relations. "Recourse to that measure would, most probably, prove . . . the antecedent to Reprisals." "Enforce," "Reprisals," "final appeal" and "ulterior measures" were fists of steel in an international warning. And Hopkins gave the Conde do Tojal, Portugal's foreign minister, until October 1 to submit a reply on the oldest claims.

Although Tojal released his answer before the deadline, it proved unsatisfactory. Rejecting the *General Armstrong* claim, Portugal promised

The Presidential Fishing Party of 1848

Taylor, at the right, finds the fishing good. Van Buren, at the left, has had a strike but his line is broken. John P. Hale gives up, and Lewis Cass fails to get a nibble. This cartoon is in the collection of the American Antiquarian Society, Worcester, Massachusetts.

to make good only on damages she might find justified after subsequent investigation. Taylor, displeased with Tojal's airiness, stated in his Annual Message: "It is a matter of profound regret that these claims have not yet been settled. The omission of Portugal to do justice . . . has now assumed a character so grave . . . that I shall . . . make it the subject of a special message."[3] The next year the President continued to regard Portugal's attitude as inexcusable. Eventually he would take drastic action—comparable to his dismissal of Poussin.

4

Taylor's resolute Portuguese policy was matched by the vigor with which he prevented German violation of an American law. During Polk's regime Germany had begun refitting a commercial steamship as a war vessel in an American port—an act unobjectionable at the time because the Germans were at peace. Shortly after Taylor's inauguration, however, they resumed hostilities with Denmark, causing the Danish chargé to protest emphatically. Continued work on the ship, complained Steen Bille, infringed on American neutrality.

Bille's protest reached the State Department when the President and Clayton were extremely busy with patronage and Poussin. Clayton, however, lost no time in telling the German minister, Baron Friedrich Ludwig von Roenne, he had "irrefragable proof . . . that this war-vessel was really designed to be employed" in war. There must, he added, be no "infringement of the laws of the United States." The Neutrality Act of 1818 required "forcible detention" of warships, "intended to commit hostilities against a friendly power." Fines and imprisonment could legally be imposed on "persons engaged in such enterprises"—and their ship forfeited. But if "solemn assurance" were given that the vessel would not be sent against "any power with which the United States are now at peace," the President would feel justified in allowing the steamer to proceed.

After considerable correspondence, in which Clayton had the better of the argument, Roenne capitulated. In May he gave bond. In June the steamer sailed. Taylor, Clayton and Bille were satisfied—and American neutrality had been upheld.

Neutrality also was Taylor's watchword in what might have become a serious incident affecting American-Canadian relations. To some Americans annexation of the British province appeared desirable. John F. Crampton, Britain's chargé in Washington, admitted to the Foreign Office that the "uneasy" feeling in Canada produced inflammatory articles in American newspapers. However, the excitement did not manifest itself in "more substantial form." Taylor's moral force was important in the event of a showdown. The President expressed his "determination"—should proceedings be attempted, such as once had jeopardized friendly relations—to prevent execution of schemes of violence. "General Taylor's character inclines me to attach a great deal of importance to a declaration of this nature. . . . Extremely slow to pronounce a decided opinion upon . . . questions admitting of discussion, he has been remarkable for the fearless and determined manner in which he follows up a . . . course when he has . . . made up his mind that it is his duty to pursue it." There had been few Presidents whose "personal influence would give greater effect to a measure of the sort than would that of General Taylor."

Perhaps Crampton was thinking also of the President's words to him at a reception. "Nothing could be more cordial than his manner to myself," or more "affectionate" than his allusions to Anglo-American relations. "We," Taylor exclaimed, shaking hands warmly, "are of the same bone and sinew, and there is, I thank God, now no reason why we should not also be of one heart and one mind."[4] Canadian annexation never materialized, and private citizens as well as chargés took note of Taylor's attitude.

5

Taylor-Clayton policies regarding Canada, Germany, Portugal and France pale into insignificance through the vista of the years alongside Administration hopes for a trans-isthmian canal. Whig and Democratic leaders had long preached the need of a waterway from the Pacific, through Lake Nicaragua and the San Juan River, to the town of San Juan on the Caribbean. Interest had been neither deep nor sustained, but now acquisition of California and mass immigration into the gold fields made practical men enthusiastic. The Atlantic and Pacific Ship-Canal Company wished to do the dredging and then operate the canal, on the basis of a long lease and joint American-Nicaraguan protection. Nicaragua's government was favorably disposed, and Taylor and Clayton thought in terms of an artery open to commerce of all nations.

There were stumbling blocks, however. Although the United States and Nicaragua considered San Juan a Nicaraguan community and the coast north to British Honduras Nicaraguan territory, England recognized the claim of the degraded Mosquito Indians and exercised a protectorate over them. In 1845 British officials had picked an Indian boy, made him their instrument and given him the imposing Hanoverian name of George Augustus Frederick. They carried him to Belize in a British man-of-war and crowned him "King of the Mosquitos." The episode has been interpreted as a stroke aimed at the United States, but modern scholarship classifies it as a genuine measure for protecting natives from unscrupulous British speculators. In the background was a tangled story of land grants and crazy colonizing schemes, plus New Granada's claim to the coast and some Englishmen's hopes of organizing a federation under British influence. Probably with a federation in mind a British consul general in '48 took forcible possession of San Juan. He tore down Nicaragua's flag, substituted the Mosquito banner and ruled the region's residents as the agent of "His Mosquito Majesty."

This coup was carried off much in the manner of Gilbert and Sullivan. Nevertheless, it had its serious side—and Secretary Buchanan commissioned Elijah Hise chargé to Guatemala with instructions to report on the entire isthmus and particularly San Juan. A high-strung, second-rate Kentucky lawyer, Hise in December '48 composed his first detailed dispatch, which arrived in Washington on March 16. Nicaragua, Honduras and El Salvador, he wrote, published protests against British occupation. "It is clear" that Britain "designs" to occupy Atlantic and Pacific ports, which "will be" the canal's "points of termination."

6

Taylor and Clayton originally intended to pick no new diplomats till June. But British aggression in San Juan, coupled with Buchanan's instruction to Hise not to treat with Nicaragua, impelled the Administration to send a chargé to the critical area. In April Taylor appointed E. George Squier to succeed Hise in the Central American states; to conclude treaties with Nicaragua, Costa Rica and Honduras and to secure a contract for the Ship-Canal Company. Successively a teacher, prison reformer, newspaperman and legislative clerk, Squier hankered for archaeological work—writing a treatise for the Smithsonian that "became authoritative in its field." It may have been to the desire of the historian William H. Prescott for data on Nicaraguan antiquities that Squier primarily owed his assignment. The chargé, only twenty-seven, had never been abroad and knew little of diplomacy—his inexperience as glaring as Hise's.

The treaty with Nicaragua, Clayton told Squier, should secure to

American citizens a free transit between the oceans on terms enjoyed by Nicaraguans. In view of "conflicting claims respecting the Mosquito shore and . . . San Juan, it is not deemed expedient" to guarantee "the independence of the country through which the canal . . . might pass." Squier should not involve the United States in entangling alliances or unnecessary controversies. "We only ask an equal right of passage for all nations." And to this end Washington and Managua would protect the proprietors opening the water communication.

On May 2, the day after this was written, Clayton sent word to Bancroft in London that Nicaragua requested "interposition" with reference to Britain's San Juan seizure. The British claim, "nominally in behalf of His Mosquito Majesty," had "no reasonable foundation." President Taylor could never allow such a "pretension" to stand in the way of American rights or interests. Induce Britain to desist, Clayton urged. If unsuccessful in his oral approach, Bancroft was directed to address a formal written protest to Foreign Secretary Viscount Palmerston.

When Bancroft appeared at the Foreign Office Palmerston postponed the scheduled interview. Bancroft called later, but the Englishman was busy—and again and again put him off.[5] Finally, on July 13, before word arrived from Bancroft or Squier, Clayton received a dispatch from Hise announcing his intention "to conclude a Special Convention with Nicaragua." Hise, unaware of his recall, admitted he lacked instructions. But "matters . . . cannot be procrastinated." Although the British had not yet seized Nicaragua "and *all* her ports," they "design" to do so. When Hise signed this treaty he pledged protection to Nicaragua in return for the right of way—acting without authorization and disobeying Buchanan's instructions. Thus, at a critical hour, while Bancroft attacked the Mosquito protectorate, Hise promised Nicaragua comparable aid from the United States. As Taylor waited in the hot Washington summer for reports from Bancroft and Squier, he was given fresh cause for concern by Hise's ill-advised treaty.

Little was accomplished in London. Lord Palmerston "is in no haste to converse about Nicaragua," Bancroft wrote, "partly because he is at work night and day, preparing for publication an immense mass of papers" on Italy. In August Bancroft managed to closet himself with Palmerston, after Nicaragua's envoy pleaded vainly for restoration of the San Juan area to his country. Asked whether England intended to appropriate San Juan, Palmerston answered in the negative. Then in whose hands was it? "For the present in those of the British commissioners." Did that not add up to occupation? "Yes"—but only temporarily. Bancroft gave

Palmerston reasons for the opinion that there was "no such body politic as the Kingdom of the Mosquitos." Even if there were, its jurisdiction "does not reach to the river San Juan, and even if it did . . . no right of exercising a protectorate belongs to Great Britain." Indicating a "strong disinclination to restore the Port," Palmerston insisted the canal "would be better promoted" by his policy "than in any other way." "You and we can have but one interest," he added. Nevertheless, the interview "was very short, and came to an end abruptly." The Foreign Secretary showed "no desire to renew it," but for one reason or another Bancroft failed to submit the formal protest.

Before this rather negative outcome was made known to Taylor and Clayton, they feared Hise's treaty might be considered a reflection on Administration policy. If this were so, London could logically charge Washington with a breach of faith. How to drive home to Palmerston the fact that Hise violated his instructions? Although Bancroft had been recalled, Abbott Lawrence was not ready to sail. Therefore, Clayton's instructions to Rives directed him to "pass through London on your way to Paris" and "call upon Lord Palmerston." This the Virginian did in September. He and Palmerston did not see the Mosquito title in the same light. But Palmerston assured him that Britain would work to patch up differences between Nicaragua and the Indians, after which she would aim at international guarantees to protect the canal's freedom and "secure it's benefits alike to all." Though no signed agreement was proposed, Palmerston received Rives's suggestions in "the most favorable manner." His conversation "left me under the impression that he was sincerely desirous of acting in friendly concert," Rives wrote home. Rives left immediately for France, with the diplomatic soil prepared for seeds to be sowed by Lawrence in October.

Meanwhile, Squier advised Clayton that he had obtained a ninety-seven-year contract from Nicaragua for the Atlantic and Pacific Company, and would soon secure a ship-canal treaty. Extending Washington's "protection over the proposed canal," he continued, the convention would recognize Nicaraguan sovereignty over the route and would guarantee its neutrality. Both treaty and contract were "awaiting . . . action of the Legislative Chambers" at Managua on September 15.

7

Lawrence was unaware of what Squier had done when Palmerston received him on October 11. Indeed, not until the following week did

Clayton send off instructions including news of Squier's treaty. Clayton's comprehensive communication reviewed Britain's premise that Mosquito never belonged to Spain—and therefore could not be part of Nicaragua, branding it a "bold" assumption "negatived by . . . history." Could Britain imagine that "the world can allow her by means so insidious to obtain . . . control over the right of way" to the San Juan port and river? The United States would never acquiesce! Taylor and Clayton believed the canal might, with strict regard for dictates of philanthropy, be kept free from obstruction by Mosquito pretensions. How was this to be achieved? By signing an Anglo-American treaty guaranteeing independence to Nicaragua, Honduras and Costa Rica; the Mosquitos' right to "pursue their . . . occupations" within limits; extinction of their title to territory essential to the canal's construction, and Nicaragua's compensating the Indians for land given up. Lawrence was not only to recommend such a convention to Palmerston, but was to show him a copy of Squier's treaty. "Say to him" that Washington hoped Britain would sign a similar treaty. "Place the . . . negotiation on the broad basis of a great highway," dedicated to the equal advantage of all!

The United States would "gladly" join in binding both nations "never to colonize, annex, settle, or fortify" Nicaragua, Costa Rica, Honduras or "the whole Mosquito coast." But if Britain "shall reject" these overtures "we shall" protect "our interests" despite opposition. Taylor would not support Hise's treaty, if Anglo-American interests were placed on a satisfactory foundation. "But if our efforts . . . should be abortive, the President will . . . submit" Hise's or Squier's treaty to the Senate. "We do not court a collision with Great Britain," Clayton proceeded. ". . . We desire no exclusive right." If "you find his Lordship" willing to cooperate, but still tenacious about the Indians, "say to him" that Nicaragua would give them "a proper annuity" to extinguish their title. "Should Lord Palmerston refuse all our propositions," Lawrence was to "enter the protest" which Bancroft had not presented. "Bring" the negotiation to a "speedy close," one way or the other!

"We are ready for either alternative," Clayton concluded. The President would never consent to Britain's enjoying "any exclusive possession" within Nicaragua. "If we adopt" the Hise treaty and Britain perseveres in the Mosquito title, "I know not how we can avoid a collision." However, if "Britain should . . . meet our proposition in the spirit in which it is made, the two greatest commercial nations" would accomplish "an object which may redound more to the . . . glory of each . . . than the most successful war in which either could engage."

Lawrence immediately set to work, explaining to Palmerston that his objective was "a declaration in writing" of British views on occupation, colonization and the "neutrality of a . . . canal or other communication across the Isthmus." Palmerston responded he would reply after conferring with the Prime Minister, Lord John Russell. Lawrence also said he hoped it was unnecessary to discuss the rights of the Mosquitos, but he was prepared to show that neither the Indians nor Britain "had the slightest claim." Following the conversation, the American diplomat addressed a formal inquiry, asking "whether Great Britain intends to occupy or colonise any part of Central America"—and if she "would join . . . in guarantying the neutrality of a ship canal, railway, or other communication."[6] Palmerston answered that his country did not intend to occupy or colonize any part of Central America—and, though a close political connection existed between the British and Mosquitos, the former did not claim dominion. Regarding San Juan he would "undertake to obtain the consent of Mosquito" to arrangements rendering that port "applicable" to the purposes of a canal. Britain "received with great satisfaction your assurance that the United States have no ulterior purposes," and Her Majesty's Government stood "ready" to enter "a mutual agreement."

To this extent the negotiations progressed satisfactorily. Then conditions exerted a retarding influence. Palmerston soon expressed the fear that one object of Squier's treaty was to compel Britain to "deliver up" San Juan to Nicaragua. This "would involve the United States in an unprovoked aggression," the Foreign Secretary insisted, showing no disposition to alter the protectorate. Palmerston then was away from London, and Lawrence was too sick to transact business. More consequential was the spirited Yankee reaction to the report that Tigre Island (commanding the proposed canal's Pacific terminus) had been seized by British sailors under orders from their consul. Since Tigre was Honduran soil the consul used the financial indebtedness of Honduras to England as a pretext for his strong-arm action. The real reason for this tactic was not lost on Washington, especially after Squier induced Honduras to cede Tigre to the United States for eighteen months—and the British tars still stayed. With Britain controlling both ends of the canal route, Sir Henry Lytton Bulwer left London as the new British minister to Washington—and negotiations shifted to the American side of the Atlantic.

The question arises as to how personal a part Taylor took in canal matters. The earliest evidence that his views were considered especially significant is contained in Crampton's report on a meeting held in September '49. Crampton, in charge of Britain's legation pending Bulwer's arrival, was conferring with Clayton when the President came "into Mr Clayton's room." Taylor "waived all ceremony, and joined in our conversation with great frankness, and every appearance of a wish to make proof of the most friendly feelings," Crampton noted. The chargé was "the more anxious to report accurately" Clayton's remarks because Taylor was present and concurred wholeheartedly.

During this three-way discussion Clayton held over Britain the Hise treaty threat. "The United States Government," he declared, "would entirely disapprove" of Hise's treaty—unless "driven to adopt it" to "counteract the exclusive claim of some other country." Such a claim might be that of the Mosquito Kingdom or Costa Rica over part of the canal route. "You affirm the Mosquito title," he continued. "We deny it." If the "controversy be not arranged amicably, the canal will probably never be made." How to resolve this disagreement? Cession of the disputed land to Nicaragua for a reasonable indemnity and Indian removal to another section "might be easily effected without . . . injury to the Mosquitos" or "abandonment of their interests." Reverting to Hise's convention, Clayton ascribed its popularity to Americans' conviction that it "might defeat" a British "monopoly" of the passage. To avoid this denouement, "let us both abandon . . . claim" to Nicaragua and construct a canal. "If you refuse this offer," Clayton concluded, "we are driven in self defence" to adopt Hise's treaty.

In these observations, Crampton wrote Palmerston, "General Taylor cordially concurred." Attempts, the President remarked, to produce a misunderstanding or collision could be met by "frankness and fair dealing." It was Taylor's earnest desire "that the matter . . . be laid in this spirit before Your Lordship," and arranged "to the honour and advantage of both Countries."[7] Taylor's later role in the canal negotiations was no more passive than in the case of France and Canada. But at the outset Clayton—not Taylor—took the lead in policy expression.

8

Explosive Hungary also came in for the President's consideration. For years a group of Hungarian liberals, guided by Lajos Kossuth, had been struggling for reforms under Habsburg Austria. In '48 their agitation helped force Metternich out of Vienna, and Emperor Ferdinand reluctantly gave in to demands for an independent Hungarian ministry and abolition of feudal practices. The cabinet at Vienna, however, continued

intriguing against the Hungarians—Austrian agents fomenting insur-
rections among southern Slavic tribes and in Transylvania.

In August '48 Kossuth threw off the yoke. Their fervor kindled, Hungarian nationals joined patriots of Poland in bloody battles against the
Imperial Austrian Army. Autumn, winter and spring, they fought—and
in April '49 the Hungarian Diet at Debrecen proclaimed its independence and appointed Kossuth governor of the land he sought to free.
Already Americans, sympathizing with the revolutionists, were forming
pro-Hungarian societies—Kossuth, the Magyar nobleman, becoming a
hero to democrats. Politicians generally rushed to acclaim him, and
Taylor and Clayton hoped their government might be the first to acknowledge Hungarian independence in the event of Kossuth's success.

On June 18 Clayton entrusted a secret mission to A. Dudley Mann,
who was to proceed to Hungary and determine whether Kossuth's regime
was strong enough to stand. Mann, a Virginian, was an attaché of the
Paris legation and familiar with European intrigue. His commission
reaching him July 12, by month's end he was in Vienna—where he
learned the Hungarian forces had suffered critical reverses. In mid-
August the revolutionary armies surrendered. Kossuth sought sanctuary
in Turkey, and by September 27 the conquest was complete. "The
Austrian flag is suspended over Komorn," Mann wrote Clayton. "There
is no longer a Magyar arm raised against autocratic rule."

Recognition of the Hungarians was now an impossibility, but Taylor
was on record as having favored it. "If Hungary sustains herself in this
unequal contest," Clayton had written in June, "there is no reason why
we should not recognise her independence." This attitude was not soon
forgotten by young Emperor Franz Josef, who remonstrated against it
through his chargé, the Chevalier Johann von Hülsemann. As late as
1852, and after, the names of Kossuth and Hülsemann remained on
American lips.[8]

9

Just as Hungarian recognition appealed to American emotions, the
Cuban situation also struck a responsive chord. This was especially true
in the South where adventuresome spirits dreamed of liberating Cubans
from Spanish oppression—at the same time extending slavery through
southern expansion of America's domain. Some Northerners agreed.
"We must have Cuba," Buchanan wrote Clayton. ". . . and above all we
must not suffer its transfer to Great Britain. We shall acquire it by a
coup d'etat at some propitious moment, which . . . may not be far dis-

tant." Other Northern Democrats felt likewise, including former Vice President Dallas. In South Carolina Calhoun hungered for Cuba. In Kentucky Clay came to consider annexation inevitable. In Louisiana and Mississippi fire-eaters were aflame. James D. B. De Bow, perhaps the leading Southern editor, predicted: "North Americans *will* spread out. . . . They *will* encroach again and again upon their neighbors. New territories will . . . be annexed! . . . The isthmus cannot arrest—nor even the Saint Lawrence!! Time has all this in her womb."

The yearning for Cuba was dramatized by the fact that some Cubans themselves agitated for intervention. Exiles in New York and New Orleans, young Cubans studying in the United States, and, above all, Narciso López fortified the hope that the islanders would revolt against Spain with American encouragement. Cubans in New York organized a junta for propaganda and financial purposes. The sum of $30,000 was sent from Havana to promote the cause. *La Verdad* in New York, *La Patria* in New Orleans and the English-language New Orleans *Delta* attacked Spanish institutions. And many a Southern politician spread the gospel with religious fervor.

López, the liberators' dynamo, was no typical revolutionary but a former senator in the Cortes, field marshal under Maria Christina and governor of Trinidad in central Cuba. When eventually superseded as governor he continued to hold his commission as general but intrigued for Cuban separation as early as 1842. After embarking in private business in Cuba, López lost heavily in mining, planting and gambling—and this experience may have exerted a corrosive influence on his loyalty. Regardless of his pecuniary troubles López was a liberal at heart. And his personality was appealing. Five feet eight and of military mien, he was stocky and swarthy, with bright black eyes and snow-white hair. If the general possessed less caution than zeal, he was rich in qualities needed to ignite the spark of Manifest Destiny, but he wisely offered the liberation command to Jefferson Davis and Robert E. Lee. When both turned it down López decided to head the filibustering expedition himself, securing the co-operation of Colonel G. W. White, a Mexican War veteran, who gathered recruits while López obtained steamers and made promises to volunteers.

Taylor had no tolerance for López' scheme. It was as repulsive to him as the unsubstantiated rumor that Spain contemplated ceding Cuba to Britain. Clayton anticipated the latter possibility on August 2—instructing Daniel M. Barringer, his new envoy, to inform Madrid that cession would be "the instant signal for war." Taylor was equally forthright when he learned from Twiggs that several hundred men under White were encamped on Round Island in the Gulf. More specific intelligence came from the Mobile district attorney, who reported nearly two hundred thousand dollars at White's disposal in Mobile—and said White was offering eight dollars a month to private soldiers, and $1,000 outright to each man after twelve months' service. On August 7 Logan Hunton, now district attorney at New Orleans, forwarded a letter from a Mississippi friend of the President's who personally investigated Round Island activities. "I doubt not" that the White group's object "is unholy and illegal," Hunton commented.

The Administration at once enunciated a clear policy toward the filibusters. Convinced that White and 800 followers intended to embark for Cuba at some point near New Orleans between August 20 and 25, Clayton instructed Hunton on August 8 to enforce the law. The next day he advised the Spanish minister, Angel Calderón de la Barca, who was summering on Long Island, that "business of great importance . . . requires your presence" in Washington. He also wrote the New York district attorney to take action similar to Hunton's if there were evidence of filibustering in New York City—where López was active. Meanwhile Preston ordered Commodore Foxhall A. Parker to the mouth of the Mississippi River. There Parker was to ascertain if "any hostile military . . . enterprise is begun" against "territory or dominions," with which "the United States are at peace." Should "you discover" an attempt to invade Cuba, "you will employ" force "to prevent it." Thus, unequivocally, Taylor met the challenge of Manifest Destiny.

10

The serial story of the López freebooters will be continued later on, as will the gradually unfolding tale of Nicaragua and the canal. Already, however, Taylor's foreign policy was of a strong and affirmative nature. When other countries trespassed on American rights—or what were deemed American rights—the President protested infringements, demanded indemnities and threatened reprisals. The might of Britain never awed him. Nor did the posturing of Guillaume Poussin. Satisfaction was demanded of Portuguese debtors as long as Taylor remained in the White House. And before her vessel sailed for Europe Germany was induced to give bond that the ship would not be used against Denmark. On the international front the Administration developed as positive a program as it did in California and New Mexico.

There was a difference, however, between Taylor's moves and Polk's. The Tennessean had favored territorial extension, whereas Taylor sternly opposed it. He and Clayton refused to let proponents of Manifest Destiny (of whom Weed was one in regard to Canada) run roughshod over adjacent soil, the property of friendly nations. This stand was deprecated, especially in the South. Nevertheless, he adhered to it rigidly, refusing to be budged from devotion to principle. Taylor regarded Kossuth and his compatriots as a different breed from the López adventurers. Concerning the Hungarians he agreed with Crittenden that "the great conflict" in Europe was one between "popular rights" and "despotic powers." Recognition would surely have been granted had the Magyars been successful.

Most historians have assumed that Clayton was chiefly responsible for Taylor's international record. Indeed, the Secretary wrote in April: "Congress must settle . . . questions of *domestic* policy. I will settle . . . questions of *foreign* policy." Actually the triumphs and rebuffs—both abroad and at home—had their roots in measures for which Taylor was responsible, if he did not always originate them. We have seen that he had his own ideas on the subject of slavery in the West; his taking Preston's plan as a model for his proposals does not prove that Preston, rather than Taylor, was the principal sponsor of immediate statehood for California and New Mexico. Likewise Clayton's off-the-cuff remark should not be accepted as evidence that Taylor was a rubber stamp, inked and used whenever it suited the Secretary of State's convenience.

Old Zack was no bold projector of foreign policy in the manner of Polk. But the anti-López procedure, for example, was in line with sentiments expressed by Taylor—with regard to Polk's belligerency in Mexico—back in 1845. His upholding of the 1818 law in connection with German attacks on Denmark echoed his remarks on neutrality more than two decades before.[9] The Portuguese claims probably were brought to Taylor's attention by Clayton, who, with his staff, usually composed the official notes and instructions. But the impress of Taylor's character—his bluntness, honesty, love of fair play and "don't-tread-on-me" nationalism—is found on documents which Clayton issued. On two important foreign-policy facets affecting Cuba and the canal Taylor's influence is unmistakable.

Forsaking diplomacy, the camera now turns to suppliants for the loaves and fishes—Whigs, Democrats, Free-Soilers, Natives—scheming for political power or dreaming of spots on the federal pay roll.

CHAPTER XVII

"THE LOAVES AND FISHES"

1

WHEN Taylor and his Cabinet first gathered around the council table several important patronage questions confronted them. The most fundamental was whether they would adhere to the Spoils System, instituted by Andrew Jackson and followed by Van Buren, Harrison, Tyler and Polk. The alternative was to take honesty and capacity as the only criteria for retaining or ejecting officeholders. Since most incumbents were honest and capable, the vast majority of offices would then have been left in Democrats' hands; they had controlled the patronage, with one brief interruption, for twenty years.

If Taylor had reinstituted the merit system, he and his advisers could have concentrated on matters of policy—instead of being badgered by place hunters' importunities. However, a blood-curdling howl would have risen full-throated from thousands of disappointed Taylor men. Holdover Democrats also would have been loyal to their first love, the Democratic Party. Thus Taylor would be twice impaled, on Whig and Democratic stakes. Ewing, Weed and other seasoned politicians argued that only by rebuilding the Whig party on a patronage foundation could Taylor obtain support for measures in the country's best interests. This argument sold Taylor on reversing his announced position, and the replacement trend was on before the Administration was a month old. All observers wondered about was the frequency with which the guillotine would fall. Critics noted that Taylor's counselors were not agreed on the rate of execution. Ewing cried out for blood and allied with him was Collamer. Meredith believed in the efficacy of slow removals. Preston, too, proved conservative. It is not certain where Crawford stood; he probably felt much as Preston did, although on occasion his attitude satisfied Seward. Johnson wavered. And Clayton, though at first as restrained as Meredith, later came over to Ewing. Ultimately the extremists converted the moderates.

So much for the seven secretaries' opinions. But where stood Zachary Taylor, their chief? Initially he usually sided with Clayton and Meredith

against Ewing and Collamer. But, at first, the President was no patronage arbiter. Before long Democrats charged that appointees were picked
on a secret ballot—Taylor's own vote being one in eight. This may have
been true in some cases; if so, the office of President rarely has been more
impotent. It certainly was *not true* throughout, and Taylor asserted himself increasingly to insist on his personal choices. On occasion the President overruled the entire Cabinet in effecting patronage decisions. He
often turned down Ewing's favorites—picking Ignatius Mudd, for example, and Orlando Brown for responsible posts though the Ohioan
opposed them.

2

There can be no understanding of Taylor's gradual shift to active
leadership without analyzing the patronage ordeal's peculiar relationship to him and the Whigs. Although the civil service was nearly 18,000
strong, third and fourth-class postmasters composed the bulk of the
federal pay roll.

Only 929 offices were classified as "presidential"—filled directly by
Taylor with the Senate's "advice and consent." These included members
of the Cabinet; federal jurists (appointed for life); diplomats and con-
suls; district attorneys and marshals; collectors, surveyors and naval officers of ports; employees of the General Land Office and Office of Indian
Affairs; territorial governors, judges and secretaries; first and second-class
postmasters; miscellaneous Treasury personnel and a few District of
Columbia officials. (Some of these appointees, notably the collectors, had
large staffs classed as nonpresidential.) The number of "presidential"
incumbents was barely twice as large as in Jefferson's day, and only fifty
per cent greater than when Jackson succeeded Adams.

Jefferson made only sixty-nine "presidential" removals; Madison,
twenty-seven; Monroe, twenty-seven; Adams, twelve, and Jackson, 252.
Van Buren ousted eighty officeholders, Harrison and Tyler made 458
changes—116 above the number supplanted by Polk. Such figures, small
by modern standards, were large proportionately and show that the rota-
tion-in-office principle was well entrenched when Taylor came in.

Democratic dominance of patronage from Jackson's time to Polk's was
as important as the removal precedent in influencing Taylor. Save for
Harrison's month in the White House, every President for two decades
was a Democrat at heart if not in name. True, Tyler commissioned some
of Harrison's friends, but they were in a minority. Thus, in this period,

Democrats had been given an overwhelming majority of jobs, although Whig workers were equally numerous and as interested in rewards. Taylor, who had recommended Whigs for preferment in '41, concluded his party should now emulate its foe.

Whigs' need of a smooth organization was easier to affirm than fill. No party was ever less united—Clay, Webster, Crittenden, Bell, Berrien and Mangum all having their sergeants and corporals. Many Whigs followed Truman Smith. Some looked to Thomas Corwin for guidance. In Massachusetts Webster, Lawrence, Davis and Governor George N. Briggs expected pap for their followers. The New York competition involved Seward, Weed, Fillmore, radicals from the western counties and influential Manhattan merchants. Pennsylvania supporters of Cooper, Meredith, Randall and Johnston fell furiously with Native Americans into a battle royal. In Ohio Corwin expected rewards. In Indiana Caleb B. Smith, E. W. McGaughey, Joseph G. Marshall and Richard W. Thompson were leaders to be reckoned with. Illinois aspirants for the Land Office commissionership would include Lincoln and Justin Butterfield. Rivalries flared in Georgia between Stephens-Toombs and King forces; in Tennessee, between Bell and anti-Bell men; in Louisiana, between original Taylorites and those remaining close to Clay. Across the nation most Whigs were factionalists first and partisans later. This was Whiggery's heritage.[1]

Under masterful patronage dispensers the handicap might have been surmounted. Had Taylor laid out a comprehensive plan, promising patronage on an integrated system (departmental and geographical), factionalists *might* have toed the mark—at least during the first few months. His procedure was not wholly haphazard, but too much of the haphazard marred it. Some jobs were earmarked for certain states— the Land Office for Illinois, for example. Other distribution was broken down along factional *and* geographical lines. Clay and Crittenden, Webster and Lawrence, Toombs and King, Fillmore and Seward, Butterfield and Lincoln, proslavery and antislavery men were recognized. Still a specific formula was lacking. No authoritative voice went out from Washington, saying: "To this extent and not beyond it will patronage favors go, unless you deliver votes in Congress supporting the Administration!"

3

Instead of sponsoring a procedure like this, the Administration dallied here, dallied there and never insisted on a *modus vivendi*. Attempts were made to appease components. Clay's son, Webster's brother-in-law, Webster's son, Truman Smith's nephew, Crittenden's son and John Collier's brother obtained appointments. Taylor gave jobs to Clay protégés and to Webster satellites. Lewis Cass, Jr., was kept on in Italy, and Calhoun's son-in-law in Belgium, despite the Casses' and Calhouns' undeniably proscriptive bent. Possibly the least defensible appointment was that of Edward A. Hannegan to the Berlin mission. A lame-duck Democratic senator, the intemperate Hannegan was nominated by Polk shortly before his term expired. Taylor could have canceled the assignment. Instead, Hannegan sailed for Europe—where he made an ass of himself.

Two practical considerations affected the distribution of plums. Congressional elections were held in the spring in several states, notably Virginia. Also, the Senate remained in executive session for a few March days, and its Democratic majority was inclined to reject certain Whigs for office. Taylor, therefore, bided his time before submitting many replacements. After the Senate's adjournment he could fall back on recess appointments—postponing the hazard of that body's disapproval. (This was logical, but he would have done better to obviate the knifing of McGaughey, who was rejected for Minnesota's governorship.) Equally curtailing were advices from Virginia where April was election month. Taylor was led to hope that some Democrats would support Whig congressional candidates provided he embarked on no strenuous removal program in Virginia. Thus the Richmond postmaster and Norfolk navy agent were reappointed. Appeasement's ineffectiveness was borne out when Virginians sent Democrats instead of Whigs to Congress. But not till the counting of official tallies were Taylor's advisers convinced of their folly.

Of Taylor's other early appointments, perhaps the best were those of Maine's Evans and Indiana's Smith, two of the Mexican claims commissioners. William Pennington of New Jersey, whom Taylor picked for Governor of Minnesota after the rejection of McGaughey, was a genial six-foot-two Whig partisan who had served five one-year terms as governor of his state. For chief justice of Minnesota Territory the President gave the nod to Aaron Goodrich of Tennessee, who ably filled the position and was more of a power—personally and politically—than his associate judges, David Cooper and Bradley B. Meeker. Commendable, too, was the naming of John Gayle as Alabama district judge; James Collier as collector of customs at San Francisco; Charles Hudson as naval officer at Boston; and Archibald Williams and Jesse K. Dubois, who received minor Illinois offices. It is interesting to note that Williams

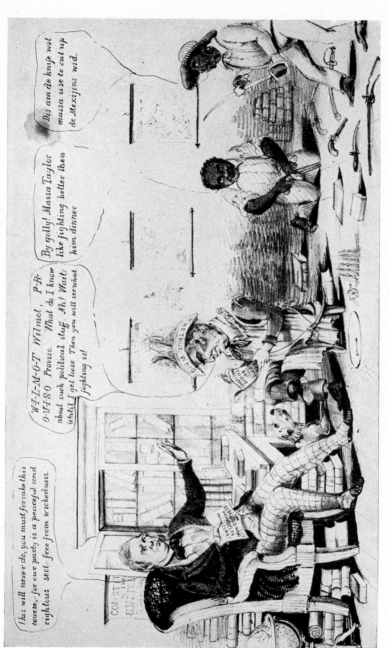

STUDYING POLITICAL ECONOMY

In this Democratic version of 1848 politics, Pupil Taylor fails to learn his lesson at the feet of Teacher Millard Fillmore, Whig candidate for the Vice Presidency. From the American Antiquarian Society's Collection.

and Dubois were Abraham Lincoln's friends. One final point ought to be made regarding the preadjournment selections. William Carey Jones, secretary to the Mexican Claims Commission, was Senator Benton's son-in-law. Gales Seaton, youthful son of the Washington publisher, reaped the reward of his father's influence as legation secretary at Berlin. Thomas Ewing, junior, aged nineteen, became assistant secretary to Taylor to sign land patents.[2] Thus nepotism flourished under Taylor, just as under his predecessor.

4

Among the President's first recess appointees were John Wilson and James S. Calhoun as Indian agents at Salt Lake and Santa Fe. Calhoun and Wilson exerted a more decisive influence on execution of basic policies than many men whose assignments made a bigger splash in the press. Charles B. Penrose of Pennsylvania (appointed assistant secretary of the Treasury) and Samuel J. Anderson of Georgia (chief clerk of the War Department) were experienced and nationally known. Samuel J. Peters and Nathaniel Young, new collectors at New Orleans and Wilmington, were Taylor's personal friends. Philip Greely, Jr., collector at Boston, was backed by Lawrence and Weed. Taylor picked J. Prescott Hall, a leading Manhattan lawyer, for the district attorneyship there—after the fur flew long and furiously over Hall's campaign for collector of the port.

Some exceedingly well-qualified men were given office on a merit basis—notably Thomas Ewbank, the inventor, who supplanted a politician as patent commissioner. Other positions went to stanch partisans like George Lunt, who switched from Webster to Taylor at Philadelphia and became Boston's district attorney. Philadelphia's collectorship was a Native American sop. Weed's ascendency was dramatized when one protégé became Albany's postmaster and another first auditor of the Treasury. A Clay man won the Washington post office, but the new district marshal's selection was correctly attributed to Truman Smith.

Taylor relied on his own judgment in Louisiana and Kentucky appointments, honoring personal friends, often without their knowledge or assent. He surprised Maunsel White and Thomas B. Thorpe with assignments; both declined, but Logan Hunton accepted the New Orleans district attorneyship. The President made a nephew-by-marriage postmaster at Louisville, and an old friend pension agent there; his nephew,

Dick Allison, a purser in the Navy; and his grandson, Bob Wood, a West Point cadet.[3]

5

Taylor's first group of diplomats was widely publicized in June—one of the best being George P. Marsh—the worst, Alexander K. McClung. Sent to Constantinople, Marsh was a linguist of almost unsurpassed ability who later served twenty-one years in Italy under six Presidents. McClung, a Monterey veteran and Mississippi stump speaker, had no diplomatic bent. He gambled away his funds before sailing for South America, and it was well that he went to Bolivia, where he could do little harm. Taylor's soft spot for heroes who had bled in Mexico is exemplified by his giving a sinecure to his old subordinate, Colonel McClung.

Two other mid-June appointees were Taylor's personal selections: Thomas W. Chinn and J. Trumbull Van Alen, preconvention Taylorites who went to the Two Sicilies and Ecuador. Rives of Virginia was an excellent choice for the Paris post he knew so well, and North Carolina's Daniel M. Barringer proved a suitable selection for Madrid. Taylor's offer of the British mission to Abbott Lawrence attracted criticism. Yet the textile prince conducted himself most satisfactorily at Saint James's— a fact generally overlooked, since Anglo-American negotiations were transferred from London to Washington.

For the time being Democratic incumbents continued at Moscow, Buenos Aires and Rio de Janeiro. Peyton and Letcher received their assignments to Chile and Mexico later in the year. George Folsom, author, Native American and early Taylor adherent, subsequently sailed for the Netherlands. Other chargés d'affaires were run-of-the-mill Whig politicians whom Taylor sent to Bogota, Copenhagen and Stockholm. Thomas L. Crittenden and Edward Kent drew lucrative consulates at Liverpool and Rio, while less desirable ones were allocated to members of various Whig factions.

A study of *all* successful contenders for places on the federal pay roll reveals that Taylor did not exclude any Whig group from consideration. The President divided the spoils among supporters of Webster, Clay, Crittenden, Smith, Lawrence and the Natives as well as other elements. The cases of Hugh Maxwell and John Young illustrate Taylor's basic control. Young, like Prescott Hall, hoped to become collector of the port of New York. Young had split with Weed. Fillmore backed him for collector. But, instead of acceding to Fillmore-Young pressure or naming

Hall or the man Weed wanted, the President worked out his own solution. He made Young subtreasurer, nominated Hall for district attorney, completely ignored the Weed-Seward candidate and settled on Maxwell for collector—an officer wielding tremendous power, with a horde of subordinates answerable to him. Maxwell, independent of the bosses, could be reached by Weed only indirectly. Thus the lie is given to the allegation that Seward and Weed ran the whole show.

Only one other Whig in '49 doled out more minor offices than Maxwell. This was Second Assistant Postmaster General Fitz Henry Warren of Iowa. Warren, ex-editor of the Burlington *Hawkeye,* brandished the ax over small-town postmasters as ruthlessly as Democrats had done. He consulted Weed and Seward frequently and played along with Ewing, Collamer and Smith. But he was in no sense exclusively a Weed man, Seward man, Collamer, Smith or Ewing puppet. Warren worked for Taylor in a job demanding finesse as well as toughness. Though more responsive to Seward and Weed than was Maxwell (who kept them at a distance), Warren knew he was ultimately answerable to Zachary Taylor and none other.

How did Taylor's appointees stack up against his predecessors'? On the basis of ability there was little over-all difference. From the standpoint of total removals Taylor was more of a spoilsman than Jackson, Polk or Tyler. But when party affiliations of Presidents from '29 to '49 are analyzed objectively the change-over seems justified. After twenty years of Democratic domination it was fair to give Whigs their portion of the preferment—the "presidential" offices involved amounting to 540 in '49 and '50. In Taylor's first year, when the civil service added up to 17,780, some 3,400 were removed and 2,800 resigned. Democratic squawks were heard on high. Taylor, however, had made up his mind. Whenever he determined on a policy it took more than bleatings of outraged Democrats to budge him or his advisers from it.

6

A tragicomic sidelight on Taylor's patronage program concerns two of his greatest contemporaries—Abraham Lincoln and Nathaniel Hawthorne. Taylor's connection with Lincoln has been misinterpreted by Albert J. Beveridge, who rated Lincoln "a failure" because Taylor chose Justin Butterfield for commissioner of the General Land Office. Lincoln applied for the job, traveled from Illinois to Washington in the hope of getting it and then lost out. "Lincoln . . . failed," says Beveridge, jumping to conclusions, and implying that he was unsuccessful not only in this specific quest but also in the sense that Taylor refused to clothe him with power Lincoln thought his due. Beveridge also points out that Taylor offered Lincoln the secretaryship of Oregon Territory, concluding that this berth was "the measure of the . . . Administration's estimate of Lincoln's . . . importance."[4]

The fact is that Lincoln had the refusal of two responsible and lucrative posts. One was the Land Office commissionership, which he later sought and did not obtain. The other was Oregon's *governorship,* Beveridge to the contrary notwithstanding. Lincoln declined to be considered for the former honor in March before he left Washington and turned down the latter in September. His early attitude toward the Land Office is documented by Lincoln's correspondence; proof of the second declination is found in a letter and telegram to Ewing. Beveridge mistakenly wrote: "Lincoln did want to be Governor of Oregon, but the place was never offered to him." Moreover, though not erring so obviously concerning the Land Office, Beveridge said "it would appear" that Lincoln *"never* had a chance" for the appointment. Lincoln had little chance for it in June—and this may be what Beveridge meant. However, his book is seriously misleading in regard to the Land Office and wholly in error with respect to Oregon.

On February 20 Lincoln wrote: "I believe that, so far as the Whigs in Congress . . . are concerned, I could have the Genl. Land Office almost by common consent. . . . While I think I could easily take it myself, I fear I shall have trouble to get it for any other man in Illinois." On July 13 he confirmed this: "At a word I could have had the office any time before the Department was committed to Mr. Butterfield,—at least Mr. Ewing and the President say as much. That word I forbore to speak." Why did Lincoln not grasp the prize when it was within his reach? He was committed to support Cyrus Edwards, Mrs. Lincoln's brother-in-law's uncle and Lincoln's "cherished" friend and ally. Lincoln felt obliged to say as late as April 7: "Give it to Mr. Edwards or, if so agreed by them, to Colonel [J.L.D.] Morrison, and I decline it; if not, I accept." Subsequently Lincoln learned that Edwards and Morrison were looked on in Washington as mere outsiders, whereas Butterfield was gaining strength. This was a source of concern to Lincoln, who was reminded that Butterfield "fought for . . . Clay and against . . . Taylor" in the '48 preconvention contest. One of Butterfield's backers was Lisle Smith, who opposed Taylor on three ballots at Philadelphia. "It will mortify me deeply," Lincoln wrote, "if General Taylor's administration shall trample all my wishes in the dust merely to gratify these men."

Finally, convinced that the "old drone" Butterfield was favored by Ewing, Lincoln reluctantly pressed his own claims. "Try to defeat Butterfield," he advised Duff Green. ". . . Use . . . Edwards . . . Morrison . . . or myself, whichever you can to best advantage." In May he flooded the White House and Interior Department with letters of recommendation. But when he journeyed to Washington in June and pleaded in person with the authorities it was too late. Lincoln's magnanimity early in the year caused his own defeat three and a half months later. To Lincoln's sorrow Butterfield triumphed in mid-June when both men were in Washington.

Illinois Democrats had gleefully watched the literal, as well as figurative, Lincoln-Butterfield race. "On Sunday evening last," observed a Springfield editor on June 14, "Lincoln and Butterfield 'went off handsomely' " to Washington—"it being a 'steeple chase,' " and "the goal . . . the federal capital. . . . Bets run high. . . . Backers of Lincoln give slight odds." The journalist also celebrated Lincoln's and Butterfield's departure with doggerel captioned "Cowper improved for the 'Heroic Age' ":

> Away went *Justin,* neck or naught;
> Away went hat and wig;
> He little dreamed when he set out
> Of running such a rig.

> Away went *Lincoln,* who but he;
> His fame soon spread around;
> He carries weight! he rides a race;
> *He's for an* OFFICE *bound!*

The thing was humorous but it was also tragic. Lincoln temporarily lost the friendship of Edwards, who misinterpreted Lincoln's course, complaining that Lincoln tried to use him "as a cats-paw" to promote his own success. Lincoln grieved over the rift. "The better part of one's life consists of . . . friendships," he wrote; "and . . . mine with Mr. Edwards was one of the most cherished." Disappointment over losing to the Chicagoan, however, rankled less than might be expected. "I am not greatly dissatisfied," he said.

Lincoln lost not only because he did not take the job when he could have had it, but also because Butterfield was an able man and an active applicant. Had Butterfield been less prominent, Lincoln might have won, notwithstanding the time element. But, as Judge McLean expressed it, Butterfield was "a gentleman of high character" who would fill "any office" with "advantage to the public." Clay, Webster, McLean, Weed and Ewing supported him, as did many of the older Whigs and Caleb B. Smith of Indiana. "All the members of the . . . Chicago . . . bar . . . and of Galena and Joliet and Ottawa . . . signed recommendations" in his behalf. He was also a Clay man—and by June Clay papers were objecting to original Taylorites' preponderance in the patronage lists; here was a chance to please the Kentuckian as well as northern Illinois.

Did Taylor and his Cabinet underrate Lincoln's service or withhold his share of the victors' spoils? On the contrary they made the Land Office available, which Lincoln twice acknowledged. Then, with "the question . . . narrowed down to Mr. B——— and myself . . . , the Cabinet . . . postponed the appointment, three weeks, for my benefit."[5] Before this they had given offices to numerous individuals sponsored by Lincoln. Finally, following Butterfield's selection, Taylor offered Lincoln the Oregon governorship with the chance of returning to Washington a senator when Oregon became a state. Fortunately for Lincoln's future he took neither of the plums. Instead of risking his popularity as the Land Office's patronage distributor or moving into semiexile in Oregon, Lincoln practiced law and tended his political garden in Springfield. Fame would come in eleven years, but as early as '49 Taylor and his advisers recognized in Lincoln at least some elements of his political prowess.

7

Nathaniel Hawthorne was another American immortal affected importantly by the patronage. A Democrat, Hawthorne had been made customs surveyor at Salem, Massachusetts, by President Polk. Never a politician in the usual sense, he owed his position to Franklin Pierce's friendship and recognition of his literary worth. In the customhouse the author vegetated three years, performing routine duties which failed to challenge his fertile mind or mystical nature. He was reasonably satisfied with his post, since attainment of financial security had been his motive in seeking it. Still neither leisure nor a steady income aided Hawthorne in composition. He did his best work as a writer under pressure of economic necessity. This had been true in his earlier years when his short stories developed from foot-loose wanderings through New England. Hawthorne's months in Boston, as weigher and measurer in the customhouse, had contributed little to his literary output. To this experience his surveyorship period was similar in nearly every respect.

Thus Hawthorne remained an author of promise rather than one whose promise was fulfilled. At forty-four he could point to only three volumes of reprinted stories as yardsticks of his productive genius. True, while he was surveyor he penned "Ethan Brand" and "The Great Stone Face," considered classics of their kind. But there must have been something about the customhouse that made him incapable of sustained effort. Though a man of ideas, conveyor of moods and interpreter of the preternatural before he accepted preferment from Polk, he published no *Scarlet Letter* at this time, no *House of the Seven Gables*, no *Blithedale Romance.*

In 1849 Charles Wentworth Upham and other Salem Whigs charged that the surveyor wrote partisan articles for the *Democratic Review,* utilized his position to proscribe Whigs and thus was ineligible for retention. Taylor and the Cabinet, believing the reports, removed Hawthorne in June. Some months before he had written a friend protesting that it would be cruel and senseless to dismiss from "a pitiful little office" an "inoffensive man of letters," who never "acted as a politician" despite what Whig petitioners might say. "I am informed," the author had admitted, "that there is to be a strong effort . . . to remove me. . . . I do not think this ought to be done. . . . I . . . gained my position . . . by my literary character and have done nothing to forfeit that tenure."

When word reached Salem that the dismissal actually had been effected Hawthorne exclaimed: "I am turned out . . . !"—but "there is no use in lamentation." If "you could" procure "me . . . literary employment," it "could not come at a better time." Proofreading, a newspaper job or something "connected with the Boston Athenaeum" would be appreciated. "Do not think anything too humble. . . . I shall not stand upon my dignity."

Hawthorne did not stand on his dignity when he read the Salem Whigs' allegations that he meddled in politics. Branding their statements in securing his removal slanderous and ugly, he declared them founded on fabrications. Fighting back, denying the charges, Hawthorne brought pressure to bear. So many of the author's admirers—George Ticknor, Rufus Choate, John L. O'Sullivan, Horace Mann—protested against his removal that the Administration wondered if it had done the right thing. Meredith informed Webster that the President and Cabinet "have learnt particulars which . . . may . . . prevent a . . . change. . . . I wish it may be so. . . . Many . . . Whigs . . . do not see . . . good grounds for the removal." Webster replied: "It will be best to leave Mr. Hawthorne where he is." Edward Everett, friendly to Upham, wrote that Hawthorne had been "the agent of . . . objectionable . . . party measures" and destroyed "all claim to . . . neutrality." A century later Hawthorne biographers considered his position somewhat equivocal. Though claiming immunity from political interference, during his incumbency he had given at least lip service to the Salem Democracy. Hawthorne stayed fired, and on the day of his dismissal he went to work in earnest on *The Scarlet Letter.*

Would the author have produced this book had he continued as surveyor? Hawthorne himself said he would not. Why? Literature was then "of little moment in my regard. I cared not . . . for books; they were apart from me." Again: "My imagination was a tarnished mirror. It would not reflect, or only with miserable dimness, the figures with which I did my best to people it." After his ousting by Taylor, *The Scarlet Letter, The House of the Seven Gables,* and *The Blithedale Romance* poured forth from Hawthorne in "a serene flood." These were his three most important books, and of them *The Scarlet Letter* was the greatest. It placed Hawthorne in the first rank of American novelists of all time. Thus Taylor, without realizing it, contributed indirectly but vitally to the enrichment of literature. By making Hawthorne dependent on literary output for bread and butter the President helped him fulfill the promise of his Bowdoin days.

8

Hawthorne's was one of many removals criticized in public and private. In Hawthorne's case the Washington *Union* grieved that "an eminent . . . writer . . . has been compelled to surrender" a "humble office." The Philadelphia *Bulletin* agreed. The "worthy man" ought to be "saved from the pinch of poverty, and enabled to devote his leisure to literature." The New York *Mirror,* an original Taylor paper, also censured the dismissal. The Boston *Transcript* joined in the cry. What happened at Salem "was what Talleyrand would have called 'something worse than a crime—a blunder.' . . . Washington should make amends . . . by giving Hawthorne a better berth."[6]

Hawthorne's admirers were not the only critics of policies supposed to govern the patronage. To an Indiana Whig Caleb Smith's exclusion from the Cabinet, McGaughey's rejection and Hannegan's appointment were incomprehensible. Another Hoosier considered McGaughey's ill-treatment an indignity to the Whig party—but blamed it on Indiana's Democratic senators. The naming of Meeker to the Minnesota bench brought forth caterwauling from Kentucky, Crittenden leading the choir of anguish. Letcher assailed (while Crittenden approved) the assignment of Henry Clay's son to Lisbon—insisting that Clay solicited the appointment despite Clay zealots' angry denials. Crittenden was disturbed by the rumor that Taylor gave young Clay the mission so as to shut the old man's mouth; too much had been said on the subject, he counseled Clayton, and factional differences should be reconciled. Meanwhile one of Meredith's correspondents wrote that Virginia Whigs "generally complain" of reappointments of Democrats "after their commissions . . . expired." And prominent Tennessee Whigs found successful office seekers unsatisfactory.

Typical of Weed's mail was a letter complaining because a new postmaster had not voted for Taylor. A Weed lieutenant thought the Poughkeepsie-Troy appointments calculated to drive Whigs to distraction. Though Clayton was told the New York City replacements were highly popular, Seward and Hunt denounced the selection for a minor job of an "old harlot" who had voted for Van Buren![7] The chorus of criticism swelled in Massachusetts, where an ambitious resident of Groton had "himself appointed postmaster," and (according to a Democratic paper) four fifths of the local Whigs "signed . . . a petition for his removal." The Washington *Union* quickly explained that "vultures and turkeybuzzards" seemed favored. Nor was all the carping of Democratic origin. There were objections to the Marsh and Lawrence missions. Clayton's prominence piqued Truman Smith, whose satellite Warren was a natural target. Ritchie assailed Taylor's assistant treasurer at Boston because he was a bank president. And George Lunt's appointment upset Webster and Choate.

In Kentucky and Maryland disappointed place hunters wept in one another's mailboxes. In Illinois a friend of Lincoln's blamed the "odious" Ewing for Butterfield's triumph and pilloried him as a "rough" man who "stinks in the nostrils of the nation." A Virginian who aspired to a foreign mission complained when Rives went to France. A South Carolinian deplored the tendency to overlook Taylor Democrats. Democratic editors counted fifty-four removals one day in the Postoffice Department; 132 in one week! The New York *Globe* reviled the President, the *Express* defending. A "strictly neutral paper" in New York said that "the process of removal thus far has gone on with . . . celerity *unex-*

ampled in the annals of the nation." "What a commentary on no-party pledges!" Ritchie's *Union* croaked.

9

Criticism hit Taylor, Cabinet members, Fitz Henry Warren and indeed anybody in the line of fire. Perhaps Taylor recalled a February warning: "The General will . . . find cares . . . among his honors"—"his heels bayed by office-hunters, and . . . his . . . energy . . . unable to keep them aloof." The President was too afraid of making mistakes, one Van Buren Democrat wrote. He was "humbugged" by enemies and lukewarm supporters. Friends urged Crittenden to go to Washington and give the "Administration . . . your counsel." Crittenden, however, surmised a visit would be the "theme of a thousand lies." Limiting himself to long-distance advice, he encouraged Secretary Clayton: "Rouse yourself & go ahead."[8]

Ritchie harped on the allegation that appointees were chosen by Cabinet ballot, charging that "Taylor has not power enough . . . to save his best friends." Selection of one man for a place was bound to offend from two to six rivals. The Baltimore *Sun* made an apt analysis: Whigs set aside leading candidates when in sharp conflict, taking "a third person, though much less prominent." This course could never "gain the confidence of its own friends" or "the country." Thus big guns of the Opposition boomed, and cap pistols were fingered by trigger-happy Democrats. In the Portland *Argus'* opinion the President did not earn his salary: "He . . . passes away his life in . . . semi-stupefaction, and makes his understrappers do . . . the work. The contract . . . binds us to keep him during his term; but . . . he will have no re-engagement." Democrats, said the *Republic,* "adopted, systematically, a style of scoffing . . . when speaking of General Taylor, which . . . will scarcely command the sympathies of the American people. They allude to him as an imbecile" and "the tool of his Secretaries." And the *Republic* rushed to his defense.

Nathan Sargent, a trained observer, feared the Democratic strategy's effectiveness. People suppose Taylor is an automaton, he reported to Crittenden; this "erroneous" impression could do harm. Enough removals were made to "exasperate" enemies, but not enough to satisfy friends. Things, Sargent insisted, should be done decisively. His own admiration of the President increased every time he saw him—but the people should see him, too! Sargent, like Clayton, appealed to Crittenden to come on to Washington.

Sargent's candor resembled that of Abraham Lincoln, who admonished his friends for treating Ewing harshly. Ewing's position was difficult, Lincoln pointed out; "a more intimate acquaintance . . . would probably change the views of most of those who have complained of him." Lincoln, in July, wrote constructively to Clayton: "It is understood that the President" made "a general rule . . . to throw the responsibility of . . . appointments" on the departments. "I am disappointed" with its "effect on the public mind. It is fixing for the President the unjust and ruinous character of being a . . . man of straw. This must be arrested, or it will damn us all. . . . The appointments need be no better . . . but the public must . . . understand . . . they are the President's appointments. He must occasionally say, or seem to say, 'by the Eternal,' 'I take the responsibility.' Those phrases were the 'Samson's locks' of Gen. Jackson, and we dare not disregard . . . lessons of experience."

10

All this time Taylor's position on foreign policy, California statehood and Indian affairs was firm and bold. But the people hearing little of these matters, their first estimate of Taylor as President was premised on his allocation of plums. If he neglected a segment of the party faithful, or if wails rose more rapidly than cheers, each error coursed home to the rank and file. Superficially Taylor's chief defect lay in delegating too much of the load. At root, however, the trouble was one not of delegation but of public relations. Individually selecting a substantial number of officials, Taylor often overrode his Cabinet—but the people knew little of this. The truth was not properly projected—with repeated, repeated, repeated emphasis. Abraham Lincoln was dead right. By midsummer, however, Ritchie's pungent references to the "heptarchy" were widely accepted.[9]

If Taylor was politically sound in starting a removal program, he had to delegate authority to a considerable degree. Had he himself tried to review backgrounds, aptitudes and alignments of every applicant for office, he would have found it physically impossible. With a secretariat of a dozen Blisses Taylor might have made some headway, but necessity dictated delegation outside the White House whenever possible. He signally failed to stress the fact that *he* controlled *major* appointments, to the end that not even Ritchie could make criticism stick. The Opposition would then have been limited to less telling attacks on patronage strategy. What made Ritchie's assault so devastating was its undermining of Whigs, who began to believe Taylor was confused, delegating too frequently.

The President himself did not seem worried by attacks in the Democratic press. For a man who lacked political experience he conducted himself with surprising serenity, accepting partisan mud as part of a President's lot. His health appeared good, and he adjusted easily to social as well as business obligations. Because he had been a border captain, there were many who thought that frontier crudity might mar his tenure of the Mansion. This, however, was not the case. Taylor made frequent spelling errors, especially when writing at high speed. He sometimes produced unhappy combinations of plural subjects and singular verbs. But he was also a gentleman, inherently gracious, even gallant where women were concerned, and an affable and agreeable host.

There was no mistaking Taylor's fund of good will, his cordiality to his guests or his disarming conversation when colleagues partook of the bounty of his table. If he chewed tobacco in his office and spat into a sawdust-filled box, this was the habit of the times—and one he shared with cultivated statesmen. He sometimes lost his spectacles and talked about the weather. But in the courtesies he dispensed to Nelly Custis Lewis and other women, in the hospitality he extended, in the dignified simplicity of his manner, he was true to the Virginia-Kentucky tradition of unstudied gentlemanliness. After all, his relatives included James Madison, Robert E. Lee, John Taylor of Caroline, the Barbours, the Pendletons, the Strothers and Dabneys. During his Presidency George Washington Parke Custis—General Washington's adopted son, and master of Arlington—was one of Taylor's admiring intimates. Rough Taylor might be on the battlefield, but the Custises, Madisons and Lees did not hobnob with boors or oafs. So it is that, to re-create his likeness in the "Residence of Presidents"—and out on a tour among the people— attention should be given the social side of Zachary Taylor's life in the White House, and in the course of a summer journey.

CHAPTER XVIII

Taylor in the White House—and Among the People

1

UNTIL August 9, 1849, when he left to visit New York and Pennsylvania, President Taylor never ventured far from his Washington base. There were too many duties to perform, too many callers to receive, to warrant Taylor's loafing at the Rip Raps, Piney Point or Old Point Comfort. Peacetime functions of nineteenth-century Presidents may seem rudimentary today. But in the succession of White House levees, and elbow rubbing with office seekers, the President's lot was not one of seclusion. A steady stream of job hunters, dignitaries, Taylor's friends and the merely curious flowed through the Mansion at levee time and also during evening receptions. White House doors swung open to all. Strangers marched unannounced to the East Room, breezily presenting themselves to the President. Taylor "mingles with the crowd in the most familiar manner," commented the admiring Washington *Whig*. "He has no personal attendants . . . to stand between him and the people."

Gideon Welles has left a description—perhaps the best—of the ordeal. Arriving at half past twelve, Welles found sixty or seventy persons, some on the White House portico, "some in the Hall, and some in the . . . oval room, the room east and the East room. About . . . half were females. . . . The Cabinet was still in session. . . . Waited more than an hour, and amused myself with observing the company. . . . A majority . . . called as a matter of ceremony . . . but many were expectants, and anxiously so. . . . Then there were agents . . . intriguing for others than themselves. Knots gathered in corners . . . some conversing freely on . . . current news, but more . . . in earnest whispers. It was nearly two when the President . . . entered the oval room. . . . He bowed to . . . right and left and . . . looked as if searching for some one." Taylor immediately came up to Welles and his companion, "shook hands," and "exchanged a few words." The crowd "getting round him, we, in a few moments, withdrew from the circle." Welles lingered at the edge "to witness proceedings." "It was a matter of ceremony, and so considered by him." Taylor "came to show himself, not . . . because he desired to . . . but as one of his duties." His manner was "kind & friendly."

Taylor's amiability was remarked by all. "Our good President [is] very pleasing in appearance—hale, hearty and sensible," thought a Cabinet minister's daughter. When a visitor complimented him on his judgment in public affairs Taylor shot back: "I hope you will say that four years hence, sir." A Southern Democratic paper depicted Old Zack as a victim of pressures: "Does the President . . . seat himself to write on some matter of importance . . . the door-keeper presents him with a card" from someone, begging an interview to ask an office for himself or friends. "The interview is granted. In walks the office seeker, who, seeing the President . . . has Col. Bliss . . . at hand, says, 'Sir, can I have a . . . private conversation?' " " 'Certainly, sir,' replies the President with one of his Buena Vista looks, and an awkward attempt at politeness. . . . 'Walk to this corner of the room,—it is cold in the hall.' They . . . sit down together." Minutes run on. Meanwhile "a dozen others have reached the outside of the door . . . each anxious . . . to see" Taylor on similar business. "The President . . . desires to be rid" of such annoyances. "But how is he to refuse an interview" to editors or congressmen?

"This is his daytime besiegement. At eight o'clock P.M. . . . office seekers go . . . to his room, where himself and lady, and Col. Bliss and lady receive company. . . . They 'sit it out' till the ladies retire, then open their battery upon the President. . . . Last night he was unable to . . . go to bed, till from 12 to 2 o'clock. Such treatment is more than flesh . . . can bear." If they "knew the President, they would . . . desist. . . . He has determined that those who . . . perseveringly annoy him shall not be selected for office." He gave a job to a New Yorker who never approached him "on the subject in person," in preference to a rival who "greatly bored the President." When a job holder sent him "an extra fine umbrella" by a man who was to have made a speech, Taylor would neither receive the umbrella nor hear the speech. "He ordered Col. Bliss to . . . have the man removed."

2

The place where Taylor worked can be re-created through the eyes of Salmon P. Chase. Old Zack was bending over a plain flat-topped table, reminiscent of the rude trunk on which he had written his wartime dispatches, when Chase called not long after the inauguration. "Bliss . . . took me up to see the President" in the southeast section of the Mansion's second floor. "I found the old gentleman . . . the very counterpart of Col. Jo Taylor, with the same person, countenance, & manners. . . . He was very kind and sociable . . . and when I left invited me to come again." Taylor had "some papers—apparently charts—spread out before him—in what he called his office, sitting at a table drawn tolerably close to an indifferent wood fire burning in a very ordinary Franklin Stove. Leaving him I descended . . . to the parlor, where I found Mrs Bliss and Mrs Wood . . . who seem . . . rather pleasing women. Becky Taylor is also at the White House," but "had not made her toilet."

Adjoining Taylor's study was Bliss's office. Across the hall and also to the west were the bedrooms of the President, Mrs. Taylor, the Blisses, the Woods and Wood children (when visiting), Becky Taylor and the Eatons. Mrs. Taylor's sitting room was near the head of the stairs; there the ladies of the family gathered, and friends joined the feminine circle. Since Mrs. Davis described the sitting room as "pretty" and "bright," other second-floor chambers presumably were livable enough. But much of the first floor was stiff and cheerless. Moreover, gutters and pumps and water pipes were out of order. The house needed paint. The roof leaked. The furnaces were faulty. The Mansion's situation near the marshes of the Potomac was unhealthy—the kitchens being so moist that their walls were actually wet—and "the upper stories partake . . . of the humidity." Humid in March, the downstairs was damp in May and unbearably hot in July. Members of the household were sick from time to time. But Taylor himself seemed strong and well.

The most famous part of the White House was the East Room, where half a century before Abigail Adams hung her washing up to dry. Forty feet by eighty, it contained ornate decorations and simpler ones in better taste. Here were four marble mantelpieces, two at either end of the room, above open grates and surmounted by handsome French mirrors. Other mirrors, flanking the fireplaces, at night reflected the eighty-one candles in three chandeliers. Beneath these chandeliers stood bronze tables set in mahogany. Mahogany chairs and sofas, covered with flowered worsted, dotted the room. Along the wall, between windows curtained with crimson damask, pier tables rested on feet of bronze. Here the mob had stormed and women fainted in the crush when Andrew Jackson began his first term, men in muddy boots jumping on the furniture "to get a better view of the hero." Here Harrison's body had lain in state, and Tyler, the Virginia cavalier, captured the fancy of the young and lovely Julia Gardiner. In this historic atmosphere Taylor greeted celebrated beauties, Indian chiefs and titled envoys, while Betty Bliss entertained "with the artlessness of a rustic belle and the grace of a duchess."

Next to the East Room was the East Parlor. Rectangular, furnished in green, it connected the East Room with the elliptical Reception Room, later known as the Blue Room. The Reception Room's imitation Brussels carpet was fawn-colored, its wallpaper pearl-white with a small gilt figure. Blue and white damask covered the chairs; curtains of the same material framed the windows. A chandelier, a table and two tall mirrors completed the *décor*.

Adjoining the Reception Room, the red-appointed West Parlor led into the State Dining Room, where Taylor gained a reputation for gracious and bountiful hospitality. Official dinners would be held twice weekly throughout the congressional season, usually on Wednesdays and Saturdays at six o'clock. But Taylor apparently preferred the coziness of a smaller room, beyond the east-west corridor, where he took most of his meals informally and *en famille*.[1]

3

From the demands of his office Taylor escaped for occasional walks when pressures eased. He did not customarily shop for the White House food, as Harrison had done, but enjoyed visiting the markets and engaging farmers in conversation. Wearing a black broadcloth suit tailored for comfort rather than style, and a silk hat perched on the back of his heard, the President became a familiar figure on the streets of Washington. There was much of the sight-seer in him, and he took pleasure in the scenes—strolling around Lafayette Square (where the Jackson statue would soon stand), and sauntering down Fifteenth Street past the two-story State Department building, and the unfinished Treasury, to the Washington Monument. If time permitted, he would retrace his steps part way on Fifteenth, turning east at Pennsylvania Avenue and following its brick sidewalk that stretched toward the Capitol. Or he would walk west from the Mansion toward Seventeenth Street, perhaps stopping in at the War Department.

The Washington of 1849 was an "ill-contrived, ill-arranged, rambling, scrambling" town, a "jumble of magnificence and squalor." Taylor probably saw less of the squalor and more of the magnificence. Though he passed privies, pigsties and scattered garbage, the White House was in a fashionable section, and some neighboring buildings also were superb. Across the Avenue from the War Department a high board fence and a hawthorne and crab-apple hedge bounded the garden of Blair's mansion, which Secretary Ewing rented. Near by stood the three-story Decatur house, erected shortly before the gallant seaman's fatal duel; the Madison house, where the Widow Dolley lived for years; the "haunted" Octagon House, a fine example of the late Georgian, and Saint John's Episcopal Church ("the Church of the Presidents"), where Taylor and his family worshiped. From downtown Washington Taylor could see the great portico of Arlington, the Custis residence. And now and again he drove through Georgetown, past reticent Colonial dwellings and their spring and summer flowers, riotous in bloom.

Ceremonies—academic, religious, civic, military—occupied much of the President's time. Postmasters, mail agents, even justices of the peace appeared at the White House for little functions, singly or in groups of five or fifty. Senator Calhoun, whom Taylor had once admired extravagantly, called and "received . . . the most . . . friendly notice." War of 1812 veterans were gratified by their comrade's graciousness. Cabinet members introduced friends and delegations. Taylor's second week in the Mansion opened with the call of the new Brazilian minister. Later Taylor received the Diplomatic Corps headed by the Argentine envoy. Wednesday, Scott saluted his recent rival. And Taylor terminated his first fortnight by visiting Mrs. Madison, Mrs. Alexander Hamilton, and Mrs. John Quincy Adams, venerable ladies whose Washington parlors held memories of sprightlier days.

On March 19 the Russian minister, Baron Alexandre de Bodisco, made an official call on Taylor. Two days later, at the Capitol, the President attended a congressman's funeral. March 26 Taylor received officials of the Washington Monument Association. On April 4 Collamer appeared with mail contractors in tow, and the fourteenth found Taylor conferring with Crampton, the British chargé. On April 19 the President dined with Clayton at his C Street house. On the twenty-first he inspected the Marine Barracks, and on the twenty-fourth accepted a handsome $1,400 gold sword from the Commonwealth of Virginia. That evening the Baker Family, then celebrated as vocalists, sang at the White House. The following night the Virginia sword committee was entertained in the State Dining Room.

There were special days when Taylor was honored or honored others. On the Fourth of July, with Mrs. Taylor at his side, he listened to Baptist Sunday-school children treble a patriotic hymn; afterward he drove to Capitol Hill for ceremonies sponsored by the Monument Association. James K. Polk having died in June, on July 9 his successor heard Senator Henry S. Foote eulogize him at the E Street Baptist Church. Death came to Dolley Madison on a hot night that same week. Taylor attended the funeral with his family, and Clayton and Meredith acted as pall-bearers. In July, too, Taylor was present at commencement exercises of Georgetown College, Columbian College and the Convent of the Visitation, as well as the Washington Seminary's "annual exhibition." He made a short excursion to Laurel, Maryland, tarrying a night with Horace Capron, a scientific farmer and a personal friend.[2] By the time August rolled around his plans were completed for a much longer trip into Pennsylvania and New York.

4

From several standpoints this journey was unfortunate. During May and June the nation and the President had become increasingly concerned over Asiatic cholera, which had taken many lives in Southern states and was spreading in the North. Early in July Taylor issued a proclamation suggesting that the first Friday in August be set aside as a day of fasting and prayer. But six days later he set out on his scheduled tour, despite the certainty of attracting crowds and the possibility of increasing contagion. Taylor's announced purpose was to augment his knowledge of the North's economy and needs and wishes of citizens there. He and his advisers must also have been mindful of the prospect of enhancing his popularity through direct contact with the people. Setting out by train on August 9, Taylor was accorded enthusiastic receptions at Baltimore, Maryland, and at York, Columbia, Lancaster, Mount Joy and Harrisburg, Pennsylvania. At Harrisburg he signed a proclamation destined to exert an appreciable effect on his standing as a statesman.

The '49 Cuban crisis was then at its peak. The Cabinet moved earlier in the week to halt the López-White filibusters, and the President's drastic state paper may have been prepared in Washington before he left. There being "reason to believe" that "an armed expedition" would invade Cuba, Taylor considered it a matter of duty to "prevent . . . aggression . . . upon . . . territories of friendly nations." He "thought it necessary" to warn Americans connected with "an enterprise . . . in violation of our laws and treaty obligations" not to "subject themselves to . . . heavy penalties denounced against them by . . . acts of Congress." Forfeiting their claim to their country's protection, they could not expect the United States to interfere in their behalf, "no matter to what extremities they may be reduced." Taylor exhorted "good citizens" to prevent the enterprise. He called on government officers to arrest every offender.

To Southern expansionists this seemed extreme, Taylor favoring strict interpretation of the 1818 Neutrality Law. Due to his action and his subordinates' corollary moves, the Round Islanders were blockaded, supplies cut off, two vessels in New York harbor seized and White and López checkmated. The Northern Whig press heaped praise on Taylor, but Southern Democrats censured his "ill-timed" and "impolitic" doctrine, with support from some Southern Whigs and Northern Democrats. The President stood his ground. Aside from rumors regarding California, his Cuban stand was the first clear indication of his sectional independence.

A very different source of trouble aggravated Taylor at this time. Midday heat exhausted him. Even nights brought little relief. Though he rested Sunday at Harrisburg, he was weak and tired when he left on Monday, and he had diarrhea when he reached Carlisle. "Owing to a change of water, the heat . . . or some other cause, my bowels became slightly affected, & continued so at intervals for 12 or 15 days." At first the impairment did not seem serious. Wood prescribed for him, and Tuesday morning when the President arrived in Chambersburg, he appeared to have recovered.

From Chambersburg, Taylor went on through McConnellsburg, Bedford, Somerset and Greensburg to Pittsburgh[3]—and thence through Economy, Beaver and New Castle to Mercer. At Lancaster, in Thaddeus Stevens' presence, he had launched into a tariff discussion which Clayton was quick to commend. In Pittsburgh, informed that "four-fifths" of the country's iron houses had recently failed, the President repeated his Lancaster remarks in favor of specific duties. Mercer, where he stopped on the twenty-third, was the setting for his most significant speech. "The people of the North," he boldly asserted, "need have no apprehension of the further extension of slavery"; and "the necessity of a third party . . . would soon be obviated." Taylor's implication was that, under him, the Whigs would constitute a major antiextension party. Convinced since long before the election that slavery's expansion was undesirable, he may have felt also that Whig prestige (after suffering setbacks in Virginia and Kentucky congressional contests) could be regained in Pennsylvania and Ohio. Thus political expediency paralleled the President's desire to contain slavery.

Somewhere north of Mercer, probably near Meadville where he spent Friday night, Taylor experienced an acute recurrence of his Carlisle illness, and he was seriously sick by the time he reached Erie. Now he had a fever as well as diarrhea. On Wood's advice the patient was taken at once to the Reed House, where he went to bed, with his physician in attendance. Since Taylor could not review the torchlight procession, Governor Johnston divided the honors with Vice President Fillmore, who had driven over to urge his chief to visit Buffalo en route to the Syracuse fair. Saturday night passed disagreeably for Taylor. He could not sleep. Restless and haggard, he was worse on Sunday. His son-in-law called into consultation Dr. W. M. Wood of the Navy, who was stationed in Erie harbor. On Tuesday, following three nights and two days of complete prostration, the President was moved to the naval surgeon's residence on Eighth Street, where it was hoped he could recuperate more speedily. Tuesday morning Robert Wood informed Fillmore that Taylor "is better to-day, but feeble." That afternoon he was still "very weak." Wednesday he "continues better." Thursday he was "very much better," but not out of danger. His doctors feared a relapse. He slept but fitfully, and "painful anxiety" was felt throughout the country.[4]

How near President Taylor came to dying in Erie cannot be accurately ascertained. He was pale and debilitated Saturday when he boarded the small steamer *Diamond* for the lake trip to Niagara Falls. Reaching Schlosser (the Niagara Falls landing) after dark, he was "barely able to walk" to the carriage which took him, Fillmore and the physicians to Hollis White's Eagle House at the resort. "I saw him now for the first time," wrote an eyewitness. ". . . He looked feeble and worn, and . . . older . . . than I had imagined."

5

At the Eagle House the sick President mended. After spending Sunday September 2 in his room, he felt well enough Monday to visit Goat Island and drive across the suspension bridge linking the United States with Canada. He enjoyed the company of such friends as Letcher, Peyton and Bullitt, and felt so encouraged by his improvement that he considered adhering to his original schedule—with many stopovers in New York State. His doctors ruled otherwise. Deferring to them, he reluctantly decided to skip the fair and return to the White House without delay. Wednesday he was on Lake Ontario, bound for Oswego—whence he would continue by train and boat to Albany, New York City and Washington.

Nothing of moment occurred during the remainder of Taylor's journey, except for the fact that Weed's lieutenants were prominent in the entourage, to the exclusion of the Fillmore faction. As the *Bay State* glided past Fort Niagara after leaving Lewiston, the President stepped out on the promenade deck, doffed his hat, and bowed to the garrison. Modesty characterized the veteran. The *Republic* correspondent had observed many great personages, but no one whose conversation was so devoid of "I-am-a-great-man-ishness." No wonder he gave his idolizing troops "a power of self-possession" which made them invincible!

Retiring early, Taylor was in his stateroom before the *Bay State* chuffed into the Genesee River and nosed up the channel to Rochester. At Oswego he drove through the town to the cars of the Oswego & Syracuse Railroad. At Syracuse he again voiced regret at being unable to remain and referred to his own plantation in connection with New York farmers' interests. "I have had to neglect my own affairs," Taylor said, "but I believe I never did those of my country." Continuing by train, he breakfasted at Oneida and then went through Schenectady to Albany, where the station was "densely thronged." Governor Fish received the "Old Hero," and "our citizens . . . gave him a right good . . . welcome." After calling on Mrs. Charles E. Dudley, a relative of Doctor Wood's, he proceeded to Fish's mansion, where he dined in state. When the "multitude" outside demanded a speech, "Old 'Rough and Ready' appeared at an open window . : . but was not as 'ready' in speech as with his sword. He made a brave attempt . . . but . . . seemed . . . feeble and his voice was . . . weak."

That night Taylor left Albany on the steamer *Isaac Newton,* and Friday found him in New York City breakfasting at Simeon Draper's house. Meredith and Reverdy Johnson joined him for the boat trip from Philadelphia to Baltimore, where Colonel Joe Taylor was on hand. "The President appeared very feeble and suffering," a newspaperman noted, "seeming to walk with difficulty from the boat to the hack in which he was conveyed to his brother's residence." The journey was concluded Saturday at Washington.[5] In the bosom of his family Taylor gradually regained his strength—and, by the time Congress convened in December, he gave the impression of being robust.

6

In addition to taxing Taylor physically the northern tour was a political failure. Democrats, of course, labeled it ludicrous.

Whig and Democratic writers differed as to the contents of Taylor's speeches. Ritchie charged that "the federal press" put "imaginary" phrases into his mouth. Democrats issued a parody of his Cuban proclamation: "Whereas . . . an armed expedition of Dutchmen is about to be fitted out, and . . . it points to Holland. . . ." They poked fun at Old Zack's inability to orate, jumped all over his Mercer speech and made sport of the President's ailment. A threatened libel suit spiced up the scrivenings, and here assailants rocked with glee. When the Pittsburgh *Gazette* reported Taylor's remarks, the rival *Post* branded its version a forgery. When libel action was "commenced" against the *Post's* editor, Democrats predicted that the President himself—"as a matter of course"—would be subpoenaed. "It will, indeed, be a rich affair," the Opposition writers chuckled. Whig organs were not silent during these assaults. The *Republic* stressed differences between Democrats who "have seen the President" and others as yet "deprived of that privilege." At New Castle "an individual of the Democratic species" clapped his hands, "saying 'I've seen him! I've seen him! Joe'll testify to that!' 'S'pose'n you hev seen him; he ain't nobody,' said a gruff-looking individual. . . . 'We'll lose half our votes if Old Zeke Taylor goes through here again, shakin' everybody by the hand, and . . . kissin' the babies and old women. . . .' And the fellow pulled his hat down with a petulant jerk, and walked off."

This venture into dialect may have been as apocryphal as Democrats liked to think Taylor's speeches were. It is difficult to tell where truth stopped and imagination soared. Whigs as a whole, however, commended the presidential journey less eagerly than the Democrats satirized it. Draper wrote Weed, "All is well," on escorting Old Zack to Philadelphia. Congressman E. G. Spaulding agreed: "Every thing is all right now. We cannot afford" to lose the "old Chief. . . . May he live at least 8 years longer." Abbott Lawrence assured Taylor that his trip was a success. Various papers underscored the argument that Taylor proved himself no worse than Jackson as a speaker.[6] This was praising with faint damns, since Old Hickory was no standout forensically. To Taylor's credit, in Northern Whig eyes, he spoke out boldly respecting Cuba, slavery extension and the tariff—critical issues before the nation. Still he had been no Webster or Prentiss. As inarticulate as any President, not excluding Harrison, Taylor attracted few new supporters during his midsummer excursion.

CHAPTER XIX

THE GATHERING STORM

1

WITH the Pennsylvania-New York experience behind him, Taylor did little in the early autumn to elaborate on his Mercer speech, Harrisburg proclamation or California action. It was the public's turn to respond, Americans of both sections and all parties redefining their views on slavery expansion with the President's avowals in mind. Congress was scheduled to convene in December, but, long before that, discontent seethed south of the Mason-Dixon Line. Now that they knew Taylor's position, congressional leaders prepared their followers for support of the Administration, concerted opposition or limited assent.

More than ever before, John C. Calhoun stood forth as the prophet and exemplar of Southerners who sought drastic means of strengthening their "peculiar institution." Calhoun's "Southern Address" of the preceding January, though opposed by all the Whigs save two, provided a rallying point for those who believed that the Southern way of life was jeopardized by fanatics in the North. During spring and summer, this document was made a test of loyalty in contests for the House. Incumbents who had refused to underwrite it found themselves handicapped by their failure to sign. Many went down to defeat. Such a popular Whig as Hilliard of Alabama experienced difficulty in winning re-election. In Kentucky John P. Gaines—Taylor's friend—lost to a Democrat. And in Virginia the sole Whig victor was one who shot the moon on Southern rights. Patronage played its part in the trend, Taylor's appeasement in Virginia being unrewarding there, and the Tennessee appointments helping Whiggery not at all. Clay factionalists' defection also was important. But the South harkened chiefly to the tocsin of Calhoun and his fellow sponsors of the "Southern Address."

This trend was evident even before Taylor made his remarks at Mercer. As summer months rolled by, Whigs who had ardently backed him read portents in Southern skies. Worried, then alarmed, finally incensed, such leaders as Toombs and Stephens would sever their connections with Taylor in December and join forces with the Opposition. This was high drama, for the Georgia representatives originally opposed the "Southern

Address." However, they saw and heard what the President was doing and saying. For a time, they strung along with Taylor, hoping the reports were erroneous, or that his "blunders" could be rectified by Crittenden or by themselves. At length they became convinced that Taylor was in bad hands, and that they had no choice but to abandon him. Before resuming their seats in the Capitol, Stephens and Toombs decided to act independently of the Administration.

This was a portentous break, but almost as meaningful was the attitude of North Carolina's Thomas L. Clingman, the independent and conscientious congressman from Buncombe County. Representing a mountain district which had little in common with the plantation belt, this Whig had frequently denounced Southern extremists and all their works. However, traveling extensively in Northern states during the summer of '49, Clingman concluded the North as a whole was antipathetic toward the South. Straightway, this once-moderate man signaled his intent to work in conjunction with aristocrats of the Palmetto seaboard.[1] Clingman's attitude was ominous, for many others felt as he did. Together with the Stephens-Toombs shift and the Southern election trend, it pointed up sentiment prevailing in virtually every Southern state.

2

Still another index was Mississippi, where Calhoun's techniques came into evidence. Believing the time had arrived for "arresting" Northern "aggression," Calhoun had written in April that the South must present "an unbroken front to the North" in a convention of Southern states. The function of this "front" was to give Northerners "the alternative" of "dissolving" the Union or "ceasing . . . to violate our rights." The "great object . . . is" preparing " the way for a Convention," Calhoun advised. "We must force the issue on the North. . . . The sooner it is done, the better," he wrote Abraham W. Venable. Addressing a Mississippian, Calhoun urged "a Southern convention" as the "one thing" holding "the promise of saving both ourselves and the Union." He reiterated this advice to Senator Foote on August 2, meanwhile expressing the hope that Alabama or Mississippi might issue the call for the "indispensable" sectional convention. South Carolina was always prepared, but the official initiative should originate elsewhere. The essential machinery existed in Mississippi, where politicians already were perfecting plans for a nonpartisan state-wide gathering at Jackson in early

October. Calhoun doubled his efforts in that state. How effective he was, Anderson Hutchinson reported on October 5.

"Your letters to Gen Foote were enclosed to me," Hutchinson wrote Calhoun, "to be used" at "my discretion. . . . That suggesting a Southern Convention was shown . . . to . . . mutual friends . . . who, altho Whigs[,] are well up to Southern rights. We adopted the idea with ardor, but all" felt that "if we should [merely] proceed on a course recommended from S. Carolina, we should fail. . . . A Southern Convention had previously" been projected "here—but . . . your opinion . . . confirmed and animated us." Hutchinson wrote Foote that "it had occurred *in Mississippi* that a Southern Convention was . . . required. You will understand this." Hutchinson's gathering appointed twelve delegates to "a Convention of the Fifteen Southern States." A leading Whig "and myself thought Washington . . . the best place. . . . But the majority preferred Nashville as more *central!* All agreed that February or March was the time, but . . . the majority believed . . . the . . . States" could not "act" before June 1. If the South "shall . . . support . . . Mississippi . . . the Constitution and the Union will be rescued from . . . hands of madmen and traitors."

Thus the author of Mississippi's "Address to the Southern States" told Calhoun his offensive was moving as planned. The Jackson resolutions and Hutchinson's "Address" could scarcely fail to elicit Calhoun's endorsement. The "Address" itself "expressed the determination of the South to preserve the Union, if . . . possible, clearly set forth . . . dangers threatening the slaveholding states, resolutely maintained their right to resist those dangers, and . . . faced the fact that those states might, in the last resort, be driven to . . . form . . . a separate union to protect their liberties and rights."

In this tone and with this fire Mississippi responded to Calhoun's bid. The roles of Whigs who had supported Taylor underscore the backing given the "Address." Here was a document transcending partisanship. Calhoun's movement grew nearly South-wide, expansive but intense, popular, resilient. The Democratic party more entrenched than ever (with Calhoun's philosophy gaining new recruits), the Southern wing of Whiggery suffered serious setbacks as a result of what Taylor said and did. Foote noted: "The . . . Administration . . . policy . . . is to settle the . . . Proviso question by admitting California and N. Mexico . . . as states." Herschel V. Johnson of Georgia observed: "It is said . . . Taylor has sent . . . a Commissioner to California to urge . . . the people to make a Constitution preliminary to admission into the Union. . . ."

This is . . . a circuitous mode of cheating the South . . . and gaining the object of the Provisoists." Governor Reuben Chapman of Alabama was equally concerned. Calhoun himself wrote: "The appearance is . . . that Taylor's administration will prove a failure" from the Southern viewpoint. "I fear he is . . . in . . . Northern Whig . . . hands."[2]

3

The North, which Calhoun considered the aggressor, was far from passive in '49, countering the South's every step with moves against slavery and its extension. This was especially true in New England, New York, Ohio and Illinois. In Massachusetts Garrison's *Liberator* cried as stridently as ever for abolition. In the District of Columbia Bailey's *National Era* provided a second mouthpiece. Gerrit Smith of New York, Hale of New Hampshire, Chase of Ohio, Giddings and fellow converts of Theodore Dwight Weld, Preston King and David Wilmot represented segments of radical opinion. In and near Boston the Sumners and Wilsons stormed away for the Free-Soil cause. No less resolute was Seward, who with Greeley and Weed labored to transform the Whig party of New York into a predominantly antislavery vehicle. Outside New York the Northern Democracy generally stole a march on the Whigs by joining forces with the '48 Free-Soilers. This was the case in Massachusetts, where the pro-Sumner coalition began to crystallize; in Connecticut, where Democratic gains in the '49 elections were appreciable; in Ohio, where already Chase had vanquished Ewing, and in Indiana, whence George W. Julian rocketed into the House.

Nowhere was antiextension feeling more positive than in the old Northwest Territory. "Rather than see slavery extended one inch . . . we would see this Union rent asunder!" the Cleveland *Plain Dealer* exclaimed. The Norwalk *Experiment* took the same view. "The great principle of Human Freedom" transcended all others, delegates to a Western Reserve convention asserted in the spring; "questions of a . . . partisan or temporary nature . . . ought not to be . . . tests of fidelity." The Indiana Democratic State Convention resolved that "it is the duty of Congress to prevent the introduction of slavery" in California and New Mexico. "Our . . . campaign . . . cannot be closed," the *Tippecanoe Journal* served notice, "until Freedom and Right . . . have finally triumphed." Similar opinions were expressed in Illinois, Michigan, Wisconsin and Iowa by individuals, newspapers and party assemblies. Nor were Democrats and Free-Soilers alone in advocating a stand diametrically opposite Calhoun's. The Chicago *Journal* reported "every Whig in both houses" of the Illinois Legislature in favor of instructing Sucker congressmen to vote for the Proviso. The Indiana Whig State Convention "expressed the conviction" that slavery's extension "ought to be prohibited."

One by-product of this pent-up energy was a Cleveland convention, nominally called to commemorate the Northwest Ordinance, which marshaled the Proviso's friends in a solid phalanx in advance of Congress. With Giddings the chief sponsor, delegates from as far away as Maine cheered messages from Clay, Adams, Sumner and Martin Van Buren. Since the previous year's position seemed adequate, there was no dramatic new one to take. But the Cleveland zealots gave rounds of applause to their orators, including "Prince John" Van Buren, whose presence suggested Barnburners' intent to continue active in free-soil battles. Held nearly a year before the Nashville Convention, this gathering may have had some influence on the mobilized Southern hotspurs. If so, the evidence is inconclusive. Calhoun and his lieutenants went their way, convinced that Northerners were hostile, without waiting for the Cleveland spur in the shape of the Buffalo platform's endorsement.

From the Taylor Administration's standpoint a discouraging Northwestern development was the relative ease with which Democrats aligned themselves with the Free-Soilers. Many Ohio cities and counties saw both groups "unite on a common ticket." Indiana witnessed much the same trend, as did parts of Illinois and Wisconsin. The picture reversed itself in Michigan, where Free-Soilers combined with Whigs. But there, as elsewhere in the Northwest, the Democracy emerged victorious at the polls. Whereas Ohio and Illinois sent nineteen non-Whigs as against nine Whigs to the House in '48, Indiana chose eight Democrats, one Free-Soiler, and only one Whig in the '49 election.[3] Never had the Whigs been weaker in the Northwest in the party's history. This fact was of enormous importance to politicians planning for the Thirty-first Congress, and one that reflected Free-Soil gains, registered directly or indirectly.

4

While the Giddingses warred on slavery and the Calhouns rushed to its defense, the Taylor regime suffered not only from the squeeze of those extremists, but also from Whig criticism directed at patronage distribution. The Cabinet was miserable, Taylor a cipher and New York appointments were bad, one of McLean's friends complained. Henry Clay felt his followers had not been sufficiently recognized. Webster waxed harsh in condemnation, although his son, brother-in-law and close associates came in for plums. In New York a Fillmore circular symbolized opposition to Weed-Seward influence. Weed and the Senator voiced dissatisfaction with Collector Hugh Maxwell, who resented their dictation. In Pennsylvania Josiah Randall (early alienated when excluded from the Cabinet) was only one malcontent. Cooper grew increasingly hostile as Meredith's supporters won berths. Moreover, Meredith had a falling-out with Charles B. Penrose, who resigned as Assistant Secretary of the Treasury. The breakup of this Damon-and-Pythias relationship reverberated, as did the neglect of Peter Sken Smith's Native faction. Ohio criticism mounted against Ewing, who was said to be too kind to his confederates while overlooking other Whigs.

If Taylor's appointments caused resentment in the North, the reaction in the South was worse. Southerners raised their loudest wail because of their feeling that Northerners were using the patronage to rebuild the Whig edifice along antiextension lines. Few, however, were interested exclusively in over-all trends or ultimate aims. To many, jobs for themselves or their associates held transcendent and immediate import. One politician attributed the Democrats' resurgence in New Orleans to recognition of *"White kid glove Whigs,"* in lieu of harder-working elements. In Kentucky Clay charged that "appointments . . . have been pretty much confined to . . . Taylor men to the exclusion of . . . friends of other candidates." Such a course was "unwise and unjust." A bitter Baltimorean described the Administration as "a bastard without a head." Old Zack's "individuality is . . . lost in the new sphere of action to which he has been *hurried* up like a half-cooked mutton chop. . . . We were mistaken in his character . . . and I regret that a fine *imaginary personage* has been lost to . . . history." Caleb Atwater, writing Senator Mangum from Ohio, was an equally irate critic: "This state is . . . far less friendly to . . . Taylor . . . *now* than . . . last autumn. . . . Taylor might have been popular, but . . . it is . . . perhaps . . . too late to retrieve" prestige "lost by appointments so disastrous."

Taylor did what he could to reconcile Clay. In a very friendly letter he commented on a remark (attributed to the old Whig leader) that "you could not recommend anyone for office, as you was not aware of my feelings toward you." Taylor's feelings were as warm as ever, he asserted, and in that spirit he took "much pleasure" in sending Jim Clay to Portugal. Thomas B. Stevenson was encouraged by this. A Clay lieutenant, he opined to his mentor: "The administration will be wise enough to avoid a conflict with you. . . . I shall even yet . . . not be surprised if . . . the President . . . will be gratified to see you . . . head . . . the party in the Senate." Nevertheless, Stevenson sniped at Ewing. And Clay himself complained in June that "many . . . appointments have given much dissatisfaction." "The Cabinet . . . has no unity . . . no identity of character," exclaimed Tom Corwin. Later, in his fun-poking vein, Corwin referred to the secretaries as "High Priests," against whom "loud complaints . . . are rife."[4]

The suggestion that Taylor should dismiss Cabinet members emanated from both sections. Seward found signs of Clayton's unpopularity in Philadelphia in October. Crawford was attacked unfairly because of his chief's sane Florida program. Southerners, repudiating Preston, assailed Collamer as well as Ewing. Missions to Moscow and Berlin were mentioned as suitable for ex-secretaries—and soft enough to cushion the blow. Though gossip linked Crittenden with the State Department, he refused to be considered. However, he thought Letcher should supplant Collamer, with the latter relegated to Mexico.

Another disagreeable reality resulted from the congressional elections. The Whig party was to be in a minority in the House as well as the Senate. It was the first time that a new President, elected by the people, lacked at least a nominal majority in one chamber or the other. For some time the Democracy had been assured a Senate margin of at least nine votes. Now it was certain that there would be also more House Democrats than Whigs, with Free-Soilers holding the balance of power. The President could not even be confident that the Whig Senate leadership would champion Administration proposals. Much depended on Henry Clay. It had been Letcher's and Crittenden's understanding that Clay would lend Taylor the weight of his influence; on this premise Taylor's Kentucky friends supported the aged statesman for the Senate. Rumor, however, now had it that Clay would branch out on his own, independent of the Executive Mansion.

Subsequent Clay-Webster eloquence was such that President Taylor's own pulling power during the debates has been minimized. Decisions made and action taken by Senators Roger S. Baldwin and Truman Smith of Connecticut, John Wales and Presley Spruance of Delaware, "Honest John" Davis of Massachusetts, William L. Dayton and Jacob W. Miller of New Jersey, Thomas Corwin of Ohio, Albert C. Greene and John H. Clarke of Rhode Island and Samuel S. Phelps and William Upham of Vermont have almost disappeared from the histories. These Whigs, together with Seward, Chase and Hale, were destined to play a significant part in the several showdowns of 1850. Whigs first, individualists second and prima donnas not at all, they gave Taylorites cause to surmise that, if not numerous enough to put across a White House program, they could muster sufficient Senate strength to block compromises or appeasement appearing feasible to Clay and the Democrats. Due to this backing Taylor wielded far more influence than is generally realized. If he did not dominate, he affected profoundly the Thirty-first Congress and its members.

5

Meanwhile, as the battle lines formed, Taylor gradually won back his health. On September 10 he was still "very feeble," and Monday morning's Cabinet meeting broke up ahead of time to permit the President to rest. Tuesday, Taylor wrote Jefferson Davis that he considered himself "entirely relieved from everything connected with the disease. . . . I have gained some strength since my return" and—"with proper care" and "quiet"—"will soon be restored to my usual health." On September 13 Taylor was better. On the fifteenth the correspondent of the Charleston *Courier* reported that he "continues to recover." Journalists' references to Taylor's sickness grew less frequent, until in October he was described as "in excellent health and spirits." Nevertheless, it took Taylor over a month to recuperate. Though there is no evidence that this signaled the disorder that was to kill him, his digestive apparatus was no less vulnerable to faulty diet or climatic change than in his younger days.

For a man in his sixties Taylor came through the Mexican War in splendid shape. But all his life he had been exposed to the elements— sleeping on the ground, living in malarial regions, undergoing his share of physical suffering. Sick before and during Fort Harrison's defense, and again before the Black Hawk War, he had been frequently indisposed in Florida. Fond of raw fruits and vegetables, Taylor ate freely and relished what he ate; he also drank whatever water happened to be available. Small wonder that he had lain prostrate in the Reed House at Erie, or that care and quiet were prescribed in Washington.

Physical worries were by no means Taylor's only source of concern. Though in public he leveled no retaliatory remarks at those who lashed out against him, in private the President had much to say. Writing Davis

on September 11, the Whig President declared to the Southern Democrat: "Notwithstanding . . . statements in the Union & . . . kindred
prints, the utmost harmony has prevailed in the Cabinet." The ministers
never "exercised . . . anything like" an undue "influence towards the
Chief Magistrate. . . . They are aware had it been done it would have
been promptly & properly rebuked." As for comment that he ought to
include Democrats in his official family, "I distinctly stated before the
contest . . . [that] my Cabinet . . . would be composed of Whigs. . . . In
selecting them my object was to be surrounded by men of pure morals . . . , undoubted talents & integrity . . . who were neither proscriptive
nor ultra. . . . I may hereafter change my opinion" but "am now satisfied
my selections . . . were as good as could have been made under the circumstances. . . . I sincerely believe they have only in view the success of
my administration." Taylor also assured Davis: "Depend on it that none
of them . . . have attempted any game for the succession. . . . Nor do I
apprehend they will. . . . There is not one among them who stands so
conspicuous above the others as even to aspire to the presidency." Collamer "is unfortunate[ly] too stiff & blunt . . . to make many warm
friends," Taylor said. "But I think he is honest . . . & will administer
faithfully . . . the laws."

"I admit with sorrow that there has [sic] been some unfortunate appointments," Taylor continued. ". . . There is no portion of . . . my . . .
duty . . . that I have been more solicitous about than making proper &
judicious appointments . . . & have . . . when it was possible to do so . . .
looked myself closely into those matters." Taylor entertained the opinion
that

a large portion . . . of my fellow Citizens will be satisfied with . . . my
Administration. . . . Without . . . being . . . brilliant . . . so far as adding
foreign territor[y] is concerned, which I am opposed to, I hope it will . . .
prove beneficial to the whole country & . . . will bear favorably the
strictest scrutiny of investigation & of time. . . . That I will commit many
blunders there can be no doubt. . . . But I flatter myself they will . . . be
attributed to the head & not to the heart—— I shall make no declaration as regards my serving or not a Second term until the proper moment
arrives . . . leaving that matter in the hands of the people. . . . If they . . .
prefer an other[,] it will neither be a source of mortification or disappointment . . . & I will retire from the White House with much more
pleasure than I entered it, & will occupy myself . . . in superintending a
small cotton establishment or wheat farm. . . . I can make . . . a few
bales . . . or . . . bushels. . . . A small number of either will . . . be
sufficient to meet all my real wants the balance of my days.

Before closing Taylor referred to his and Davis' political differences: "I wish you to pursue that course . . . which your good sense, interest" and "honor . . . prompt you to do. . . . Even if not in accordance with my views . . . it will" not "interrupt our personal intercourse, or my esteem & friendship for you." The President's plantation outlook was dim. Dick Taylor, who passed through Washington in July, "informed me of . . . the entire loss of my . . . crop, in addition to other serious injury from the effects of the great flood of . . . last winter & spring." The river continued "so high during the summer," and precipitation was so great, that "my people" were prevented "from doing anything"— even chopping wood or sawing lumber. However, "we . . . ought to be thankful that matters were no worse," Taylor philosophized in a fatalistic vein. The President made big money in the Mansion. Still his resigned attitude toward Cypress Grove was unusual in a man of property.

This heretofore-unpublished letter presents with maximum fidelity Taylor's state of mind in the White House. It reveals how he reacted to members of his Cabinet—their weaknesses and strengths; the premise on which their appointments were made and their limitations as presidential rivals. Students, who have read how incensed he was by secession threats the following year, may be surprised to find the President so fair. Taylor also indicated how his loved ones felt about the future President of the Confederacy: "The family[,] including Dr. Wood & Ann who is with us, join me in kindest regards to your better self, your worthy brother & his most excellent lady as well as yourself. . . . Wishing you all continued health and prosperity[,] I remain truly Your Friend Z. TAYLOR[.]"[5]

6

Recovering his energy, appetite and color, Taylor seriously considered resuming his broken journey to Philadelphia, New York City and New England. Eventually he gave up the idea, setting out by rail again but traveling only to Baltimore. Arriving Wednesday, October 10, he took the Marylanders "somewhat by surprise," and proceeded to Barnum's City Hotel "without any one being aware of his coming." "He was expected to-morrow," the *Republic's* correspondent reported, "and would have been . . . welcomed by thousands of citizens." The President went out to Carroll's Woods to see the State Agricultural Fair and Cattle Show. Here he seemed in the best of spirits. Francis Preston Blair, who had ridden over from the capital with Taylor, characterized him as "very gracious both on the way & at the fair."

Blair wrote that Taylor "gave evident symptoms that he was out for re[-e]lection." What these symptoms were Blair did not specify, but John Branch "told me . . . Taylor made it clear, he intended" to be "an 8 years president." Blair, who had no love for the Whigs, said "the President begins to complain bitterly of . . . desertion of . . . Democrats in the late elections." However, he based this on secondhand evidence. ("I *hear* . . . he speaks quite vehemently of their . . . ingratitude and . . . resolved upon a clean sweep of . . . democratic Office-holders.") Despite Blair's version of Taylor's innermost thoughts, there were no signs of anything but the most unruffled demeanor, as Rough and Ready seemed gentle and kind in shaking hands and exchanging compliments there at the fairground in Maryland.

More friends and admirers greeted the President the following fore-noon at his hotel. At noon he returned to the fair, where a plowing match was the featured event. The Baltimore *Sun* pictured him watch-ing the "ploughs as they threw up the broad furrow," moving "rapidly from one to another," and regarding the teams with an expert's eye. "He was received at all parts of the ground with . . . enthusiastic demon-strations of respect." Seeing him astride "a white horse," spectators "imagined" they saw "the veritable 'Old Whitey' and his gallant master though the scenes of their exploits were . . . the reverse of those in which they will figure in . . . history." Friday found Taylor rising early and visiting the Lexington Market, where he "had a hearty welcome" from people "delighted to see the President . . . mixing with his fellow citizens." At ten o'clock he looked in on a second fair, staged by the Maryland Institute. Later he drove in a barouche back to Carroll's Woods, where the erudite Senator James A. Pearce delivered the agriculturists' annual address.

Taylor also came in for praise premised on remarks prompted by recol-lections of camp and field. One evening when he was feted in Baltimore, an Army captain—who had shared the General's bivouac in the Seminole campaign—spoke from the fullness of his heart. "In a voice almost choked by emotion" the captain alluded to Taylor's kindness "when he was borne from the field, crippled by disease." The President, after a pause, "replied, without rising, in a chaste, appropriate, terse and feeling speech, that brought every man to his feet." The words came without hesitation, easily and smoothly, the *National Intelligencer's* correspond-ent wrote. It has been my pride, said Taylor, to foster merit among young officers and those under them. "When disease . . . crept into our ranks," it was "my . . . duty to show the sufferer that he was cared for by his brethren in arms, and conveyed where softer . . . sympathies awaited him. . . . It would be a great mistake to suppose that soldiers are strangers to . . . kindly feelings. . . . Cultivation of those feelings . . . is not only the . . . pleasurable . . . duty of a general officer" but one "he will not fail to attend to, even if . . . selfish or ambitious"—for "upon the affections of the army he must depend in the day of trial. If I have been successful in any military action of importance, it is to this I am indebted." Unpracticed in framing sentences for a lengthy speech in a crowd, Taylor's diffidence disabled him from appearing to advantage there. But, surrounded by a few friends at table, and on an occasion when his feelings were aroused, "he holds such language as few men can command." It was of no use to indulge in toasts and speeches after this. "The company adjourned . . . to talk over their surprise and admiration somewhere else."

Since the *Intelligencer* was a Whig newspaper, part of its "admiration" may be discounted. The word "surprise," however, suggests that the account was truthful. Without reactions of this kind, rationalizing Taylor's dynamic qualities and his least effective public appearances would be difficult indeed. In the Army, with the gauntlet down, Taylor was spirited, resourceful, bold. What a contrast between this leadership and portrayals of the weakling, stooge, or mumbler credited by most Democrats! Such contrasts would be incomprehensible, if Taylor's deficiency as a formal speaker were sloughed over in this discussion. The modesty of Taylor's nature and his inexperience on the hustings made him at least as inadequate an orator as Andrew Jackson had been. Old Hickory's defect was less glaring because Democrats focused attention on their President's strong points, which the Whigs seldom managed to do.

Old Zack should have been spared, insofar as possible, appearances of the sort he made in Pennsylvania. If he had been advised to speak only when the spirit moved him, the effect might have been as favorable as his Baltimore performance. Had Taylor relied more on his superior instinct, and less on conforming to political convention, his first half-year as President might have revealed him to the multitude not only as a strong-minded leader but also as the sympathetic gentleman, who inspired affection and enthusiasm in the friends that really knew him. Had Taylor enjoyed the inspired publicity of a Kendall, Ritchie or Blair, the masses might have understood him earlier than they actually did. As stanch an upholder of the Federal Union as Jackson had been, and as Lincoln was to be, Taylor should have been proclaimed from the outset as the Union champion he was. Unfortunately for him this did not happen. He did what he could regarding California, New Mexico and Cuba. But it remained for the Twelfth President to project his ideas and his individuality more emphatically, the hard way, after Congress convened.

7

Taylor left Baltimore Friday evening, October 12, terminating what was probably his most pleasant sojourn outside Washington. That night he wrote Representative Joseph Grinnell from the capital expressing regret that circumstances prevented his visiting New England. Tuesday he advised Mayor C. S. Woodhull of New York City that "duties incident to the approach of a session of Congress . . . compel . . . me reluctantly to defer my tour." He also signed routine letters on trivial subjects, like one thanking the Astor House proprietors for the "delicious pears which you had the kindness to send me." However, the Chief Executive's thoughts turned into more serious channels. There were instructions to be given McCall, affecting Texas and Santa Fe; conferences with Meredith regarding the tariff; curtailment of Indian difficulties, and reports from King, Smith and Riley. The British negotiations weighed heavily on Taylor's mind. French, Portuguese and Cuban episodes hung fire. Trouble brewed in Vienna, where Mann's mission was a failure because of the Hungarians' defeat, and there were treaties in the making with Brazil and the Sandwich Islands.[6]

In the weeks that followed, spacing one of Washington's loveliest falls, the Poussin affair drew to an end. The Cuban furor simmered down. Taylor declined to issue a Thanksgiving Proclamation lest it interfere with state rights, and played host to European notables, Osage Indians, and miscellaneous callers. General and Mrs. Taylor became life members of the American Sunday School Union, and the President accepted honorary membership on the American Board of Commissioners for Foreign Missions. The White House had been repainted. Visitors who called Tuesday and Friday afternoons, or were received by the President on Friday evenings, not only met with a cordial welcome but found the historic Mansion spick and span. Marine Band concerts had been resumed in the White House grounds on Saturday afternoons, and Taylor again gave elegant dinners twice a week. As late as October "the surpassing splendor of the President's garden . . . elicits high admiration from every visitor. Dahlias, roses in many varieties, and indeed every description of flower and shrubbery, appears in gayest attire." Auctions, theatricals, dancing assemblies and private parties in Cabinet members' dwellings attracted the fashionable and frivolous. Yet over the festivities hung the pall of the gathering political storm.

The convening of Congress was the event toward which politicians pointed. In late November, the newspapers noted, senators and representatives were arriving.[7] Hotels and boardinghouses met their quotas. Messes formed, most of the members arranging to take their meals near the Capitol. Though observers felt the sectional showdown would come in the Senate, rather than the House, they initially concentrated on the lower chamber's composition. On the agenda the first event was the House's organization, with the speakership election testing partisan and sectional strength.

CHAPTER XX

HOWELL COBB AND THE SPEAKERSHIP STRUGGLE

1

AMONG the Whigs who gathered in the House that first Monday in December, Robert C. Winthrop was the key figure. Only forty, but with eight congressional years behind him, he represented conservative Bostonians who still preferred his middle-road policies to Charles Sumner's radicalism. Erect and spare, with a long, thin face and spectacled eyes, Winthrop suggested the professorial type rather than the career politician. If less eloquent than Webster, his oratorical ability was conceded, and he appeared to excellent advantage in a parliamentary body. Winthrop gave the impression of being cold and analytical, relying on facts in appealing to his auditors. Personally opposing slavery's extension, he understood the attitude of moderate Southerners and tried to reconcile their views with his own. There was nothing uniquely compelling about Winthrop that grappled associates with hoops of steel, but, Southern and Northern Whigs electing him Speaker in '47, he presided with a fairness that became him. Though not unusually ambitious, Winthrop was again a speakership candidate at this first session of the Thirty-first Congress.

None of Winthrop's rivals on the Whig side commanded so substantial a backing, just as none quite equaled him in the combination of talent, energy, experience, moderation and party regularity. The tall, robust, booming Toombs or the dyspeptic, cadaverous Stephens might have succeeded Winthrop in the chair, had they not broken with the Whig organization, absenting themselves from the party caucus and refusing to support its candidate. Followed by other ex-Taylorites like Henry Hilliard and E. Carrington Cabell, they promoted a small rump faction, thereby weakening Winthrop's position and making themselves ineligible. Such Northerners as Ashmun and Horace Mann of Massachusetts, William Duer of New York and McGaughey of Indiana held too pronounced antislavery opinions to be acceptable to the Southern wing. The same was true of a newcomer, Pennsylvania's Thaddeus Stevens, the most dynamic of them all. On the score of seniority no other Whig could approach Ohio's Samuel F. Vinton, a seasoned parliamentarian and Ewing's confidant. Southerners, however, tarred Vinton with the anti-

slavery brush and looked with displeasure on his Cabinet intimacies. Of
the sixty-nine Northern Whigs Winthrop alone appealed to considerable
numbers of his fellow partisans from both sections.

Southern voters had elected only twenty-eight Whigs to the House,
more than half hailing from Kentucky, North Carolina and Tennessee—
states where, in bygone days, Whigs of New York and New England
often found allies for middle-road programs. With Stephens and Toombs
no longer interested in party harmony, Northerners desperately scanned
the delegations from these three states, in the hope of picking a Southern
Whig whom they could conscientiously support. Clingman, of course,
was definitely out. Meredith P. Gentry did not return to Washington
until January, and the fact that the Georgians favored him for speaker
may have motivated others in edging away from him. The likeliest Southern possibility, and one that conceivably might have succeeded, was
Charles S. Morehead of Kentucky. Thrice speaker of the Kentucky
House and a former state attorney general, Morehead enjoyed a fine legal
reputation and was—like Winthrop—of a scholarly bent. Presiding over
the Whig caucus (certainly a mark of esteem), Morehead thought he had
a chance to recruit enough Democrats to form a majority in his favor.
Ultimately he got nowhere, which he attributed to the Georgians' decision
to switch their corporal's guard to him from Gentry on the thirty-fifth
ballot. Since this was a kiss of death, Morehead's candidacy never materialized.

In addition to Morehead North Carolina's Edward Stanly was a prospect of sorts. Disinclined to rank sectional bias ahead of Whig and
national loyalties, Stanly was the combative type and engaged in personal
encounters during earlier congressional service. Passionate, sarcastic and
sometimes unrestrained, Stanly's tongue spared neither enemy nor friend.
He had held positions of honor, comparable to Morehead's, in his state,
and now came back for his fourth House term, still a young man and
full of fire. Notwithstanding his strength of character, Stanly would
have made a strange speaker on account of his personal idiosyncrasies.
The fact that sensible men turned to "the terror of the . . . party" as a
possible compromise on the fortieth ballot underscores the plight of the
Whigs.

2

In the Democratic caucus there was a larger array of talent, although
(as in the Whig camp) one candidate towered over the rest. Howell

Cobb, now generally bracketed with events of '60 and '61, was then a statesman of Unionist concepts. A lifetime resident of Georgia, Cobb had been on the Hill as long as Stephens and longer than Morehead, Duer or Toombs. Despite this congressional seniority he was only thirty-four. A mountain of a man, large, round and jolly, he had proved effective and popular as minority leader in the previous House. Familiarity with the rules, skill as a debater and the knack of inspiring confidence in older men made Cobb a natural choice of the Democrats for the speakership. In contrast to a later reputation for evasiveness, ambiguity and skin-deep friendships, he displayed a marked degree of integrity in personal relations and regarding principle. When Calhoun projected the "Southern Address," Cobb was one of four Southern Democrats who joined the Whigs in refusing to sign. This was an act of courage in a Georgian who believed in slavery, but the fat boy then saw no incompatibility between national patriotism and proslavery views.[1] Because of this some Southerners would have preferred another candidate. Conversely, Northerners were attracted. Refusing to enter shady deals, Cobb amassed the largest number of votes on the first ballot and the last, yet it was always a mere plurality, never a majority, of the members. This was due to the balance held by others than Whig or Democratic regulars—which led, at various times in the voting, to the dropping of Cobb and to substitutions.

No fewer than fifty-three Democrats were given one or more votes on one or more ballots in the course of the next three weeks. James S. Green, a Missouri lawyer, was one of the promising younger men whom Southern extremists were willing to support. William J. Brown, an Indiana journalist, also was acceptable to the fire-eaters—as was John K. Miller, one of Ohio's few Democrats not aligned with the Free-Soilers. Among the able Southerners were Albert G. Brown, the animated former Mississippi governor; Ex-Governor James McDowell of Virginia, Benton's brother-in-law, now in his third term; Robert Ward Johnson, of the famous family that dominated Arkansas twenty-five years; Frederick P. Stanton of Tennessee, who represented the Memphis district; and western Kentucky's seven-term idol, Linn Boyd of Cadiz, whose ambition matched his virile vigor. The North offered William Strong of Pennsylvania, forceful, sociable and a legal scholar; Emery D. Potter of Toledo, Ohio, the first Democrat from his section to poll over seventy votes; the aforementioned Brown, who came nearest to attaining a majority, and William A. Richardson and John A. McClernand—Illinois lieutenants of Senator Douglas.

Significantly, excepting Boyd, every Cobb rival on the Democratic side
resided in a Northern state, just as Southern conservatives were the most
powerful Whig contenders for Winthrop's mantle. Thus the principal
parties' strategy became perfectly clear as ballot followed ballot. The
Whigs initially ran the Northerner who, they hoped, might appeal to
the South, and Democrats parried with the Southerner who had friends
in both sections. When Winthrop and Cobb fell short of a majority,
Whigs switched to Southerners, and Democrats to Northerners, in experiments testing reverse procedures. No secondary Northern Whig
approached Winthrop's total at any time. Nor did another Southern
Democrat equal Cobb's maximum strength. These two (with Brown
briefly sharing the spotlight) were the key figures throughout. And, had
it not been for Brown's double talk, it is doubtful that the tubercular
Hoosier could ever have threatened their dominating position.

Before the voting is reviewed in detail, the Free-Soilers' role in this
unprecedented drama should be considered. Nine and sometimes ten in
number, out-and-out Free-Soilers were forerunners of the radical Republicans of a later day. Not only did they hold the House balance of power
in 1849, but they influenced such Whigs and Democrats as Ohio's Lewis
D. Campbell and Connecticut's Chauncey F. Cleveland. James Duane
Doty of Wisconsin, Lucius D. Peck of Vermont and Horace Mann of
Massachusetts were others whose opposition to slavery pulled them away
from traditional anchors. The Free-Soil nucleus, however, comprised
only Allen of Massachusetts, Walter Booth of Connecticut, Charles
Durkee of Wisconsin, Giddings and Joseph M. Root of Ohio, John W.
Howe and Wilmot of Pennsylvania, Preston King of New York and
Amos Tuck of New Hampshire. To this group were added, at various
times, William Sprague of Michigan (irregular) and Indiana's Julian
(late in arriving). On occasion most of them voted for Root, Tuck,
Julian, Strong or Stevens, but usually their candidate was Wilmot. They
were not a bloc in the sense of unitedly favoring this or that contender.
But, invariably, they *were* a bloc in opposition to Winthrop and Cobb.[2]
Their discipline helped them achieve resilience in expressing individual
preferences, and still come back to the fold when expediency dictated
that they form a front. Whether ex-Whigs or ex-Democrats, all believed
in the Wilmot Proviso. Had they and the Stephens-Toombs rump faction
joined in support of Winthrop, the Bostonian would have won re-election. Had they collaborated with the Democrats, Cobb's triumph would
have been assured. Instead, they refused to compromise. And a memorable battle resulted.

3

On the first ballot Cobb set the pace, with Winthrop in second place. Cobb polled 103 votes; Winthrop, ninety-six; Wilmot, eight; Gentry, six, and Horace Mann, two. Wilmot cast his vote for Root, and the remaining five were scattered. The next six ballots were similar. On the eighth Cobb descended to ninety-nine, Winthrop stood at ninety-seven and the count never strayed far until Wednesday December 5. Then, on the thirteenth roll call, Winthrop led as Cobb fell back—Richardson receiving six votes, Root seven, and Potter nine, to Cobb's ninety-three and Winthrop's ninety-eight. At this point an erstwhile Tennessee tailor, Representative Andrew Johnson, proposed scrapping the majority rule and letting a plurality suffice for election. Had Johnson's resolution passed, Cobb would have won, for such Democrats as Kingsley S. Bingham of Michigan, Armistead Burt and young James L. Orr of South Carolina, David K. Cartter of Ohio, Andrew J. Harlan and Joseph E. McDonald of Indiana, Samuel W. Inge of Alabama, Johnson of Arkansas and Loren P. Waldo of Connecticut (all in Potter's or Richardson's column) would have hastened back to the Georgian's standard.

Opposition, however, stemmed not only from Ashmun and Venable (Northern Whig and Southern Democrat) but also from South Carolina's flamboyantly independent Isaac E. Holmes. Holmes had run for re-election in '48 as a "Taylor Democrat," but now opposed Old Zack and all his works. A veteran on the Hill, he displayed his contempt for the Cobb regulars by voting for thirteen different Democrats (twelve of them Southerners, but never Cobb) on the first thirteen ballots. This was less an erratic stunt than a protest against Cobb's failure to sign the "Southern Address." Keeping the House in turmoil was also grist for Holmes's mill. He and Venable, too, may have feared a Free-Soil combination with either Whigs or Democrats, helping to form the desired plurality in return for committee chairmanships. Thus Holmes protested: "We should never intrust . . . so far as legislation . . . [is] concerned . . . anything to pluralities." Ashmun agreed, and Venable implied that the Free-Soilers ought to take the initiative for electing a speaker on a majority basis: "Let the responsibility of the disorganization . . . rest upon those who disorganized." This was also the view of other members, and so the resolution was tabled.

Another tactic was tried to eliminate delays inherent in the voting. The House being speakerless, the retiring clerk (who was powerless to

rule on disputed issues) presided in lieu of an elected officer. McClernand and Hilliard then placed in a hat the names of Boyd and Vinton
(senior Democrat and senior Whig), agreeing between them that the
one pulled out would be presented for "temporary" chairman, until a
speaker should be chosen. The lottery luck chanced to be with Boyd. On
December 6 McClernand advocated granting Boyd permission to go to
the dais, arguing that the Kentuckian "would be responsible . . . to the
House and . . . the people, whereas the Clerk had no . . . responsibility"
except what "attached to him as Clerk." Duer of New York suspected
there was more to the proposal than met the eye. Its effect must be "that
the temporary Chairman would . . . [remain as] Speaker for the session.
Once there, he would continue there." Duer countered by recommending
"that the last Speaker . . . be invited to preside . . . until the election of
a Speaker." When a Maryland Whig hit on a plan for Vinton and Boyd
to take turns as chairman on alternate days, Root reminded his colleagues
that Giddings—as the senior Free-Soiler—ought to be included with the
Whig and Democratic choices. Amid laughter Root joked that this
"precious company of chairmen . . . would stand together, or lie down
together, and look well anywhere."

Thus, while Root poked fun at the predicament, McClernand's plan
went by the board—as Johnson's had before it—and the tabulation
dragged painfully on through the first week and into the second. Winthrop hit a new high on the twentieth ballot, his total being 102 out of
225. This he maintained, with one exception, from the twenty-first
through the thirtieth tally. Meanwhile Cobb gradually slipped down to
five paltry votes on December 8 and 10. Potter had his chance, but
seventy-eight was as high as the Ohioan could rise, while Richardson's
maximum was twenty-nine and Green's a meager twelve. Boyd went up
to twenty-two, but tapered off and vanished for a time. These diversions
accomplished nothing, and Whigs held grimly on to Winthrop more
out of habit than hope. The stalemate might have become permanent,
had not Potter—then in second place—retired from the fight, encouraging his fellow Democrats to launch another aspirant.

4

The newcomer, it turned out, was William J. Brown, ex-hatchetman
of the Polk Administration. Of the fifty-three votes given him on the
first count following Potter's withdrawal, nearly half were from the
North. As Brown's following expanded, however, Southern influence

was unmistakable. To eighty, to eighty-four, to eighty-eight, his backers steadily swelled. Then the band-wagon surge began. Nine more were added on the thirty-sixth ballot, prominent among them three South Carolinians. On the thirty-seventh Brown went beyond Winthrop, with 107 to 101. Nine of the latest converts were Southern extremists, suggesting that Calhoun or Burt (Calhoun's relative) was sprinkling incense from Fort Hill on Brown's sudden popularity. The Hoosier was now in striking distance—needing only six or seven to go booming over the top. Alabama provided one; Tennessee another. Still Brown's strength eased off toward the climax, with 109 tantalizing votes on the thirty-eighth and thirty-ninth ballots.

Exactly what transpired on Wednesday December 12 has unfortunately been lost to history. Enough of the facts remain, however, to highlight trends and point a moral. That afternoon Brown polled the largest aggregate registered in favor of any candidate at any time. But (and this is of paramount significance) five of his adherents were Allen, Durkee, Giddings, Wilmot and Preston King. As these Free-Soilers voted for Brown, three Southerners transferred their support to Boyd. (The vote of George W. Jones of Tennessee was lost in the shuffle.) The official total credited to Brown was 112 votes, though only 110 names appear in the breakdown—slightly below a majority, despite its exceeding the Cobb and Winthrop highs. But this sizable figure interested Congress less than the five Free-Soilers' motives. As early as Tuesday, whispers went the rounds that Brown promised Wilmot, if successful in the speakership quest, to form the committees on the District of Columbia, territories and judiciary in a manner satisfactory to the Free-Soil clique.

This rumor carried the implication that the heads of the vital committees would be men of Wilmot's stamp—which would have exasperated nine tenths of the House, and especially Calhoun's friends. Was it true? Following the fortieth ballot, Stanly made a move to find out. Something was "rotten in Denmark," he said. He surveyed the Whigs of the House "without blushing," but "blushed when he looked at the other side." What did Stanly's insinuation mean? Virginia's Thomas H. Bayly shot back. Did he attach "importance to an imputation . . . circulated . . . in whispers . . . through this Hall?" Had something "improper" occurred? "I am rejoiced . . . that the gentleman made the remark. . . . It enables us to brand the rumor, in the outset" as having "no foundation in truth."

Answering Bayly's categorical denial, Ashmun took up the torch for the Whigs.

ASHMUN: "Will the gentleman from Virginia allow me to put a question to him?"

BAYLY: "Certainly."

ASHMUN: "Has not a correspondence taken place between the member from Indiana and some member of the Free Soil party, in which he . . . pledged himself to constitute the committees in a manner satisfactory to them?"

BAYLY: "I know of no such correspondence. Is the gentleman authorized to say that there has been such a one? If so, what is his authority?"

ASHMUN: "Common rumor."

BAYLY: "And does the gentleman know that common rumor is a common liar?"

Turning to Brown, the Virginian asked: "Has any such correspondence taken place?"

The Hoosier, still seated, shook his head.

"I am authorized to say," Bayly continued, "that no such correspondence has taken place"—the shake of the head by William J. Brown adding up to "authorization."

The House was on pins and needles now. It was the most theatrical moment in a week and a half of declamation and suspense. Rapt, the members listened. Bayly spoke. Then Root. Then Bayly again. He had conversed with Brown, and now admitted he erred in denying the Ashmun-Stanly charge. Communications had indeed been exchanged between Brown and a Free-Soiler. All was admitted. The debate grew torrid, Brown seeking to explain away his "bargain," Burt demanding to "see that correspondence," and David Wilmot joining in. Soon after, the Brown-Wilmot letters were read, for Wilmot in fact *was* the other party. Stanly's imputation was wholly sustained: Brown *had* traded with Wilmot, the committees *were* involved, and Brown's near-victory vote hinged directly on the deal![3]

The debate continued that day and the next. "Great confusion prevailed." Southern members became irate. Brown's fellow Democrats sprang to the defense of their cornered colleague. On Thursday came another clash, when Duer branded the Virginia Democrat, Richard K. Meade, a "disunionist."

"It is false," cried Meade.

"You are a liar, sir," Duer exclaimed.

Quick as thought Meade rushed toward Duer, his blood boiling at the charge. Northerner and Southerner were surrounded by comrades. "Indescribable confusion followed." "Threats, violent gesticulations . . . and demands for adjournment were mingled together. The House was like a heaving billow." Came the sergeant at arms of the Thirtieth Con-

gress, Nathan Sargent, with the symbol of his office. There were yells
of "Take away the mace!" and "It has no authority here!" The clerk
attempted a call to order, but "there were none to heed him" in a crisis
with the lie direct bandied about.

5

Eventually, relative calm was restored. But eight more December days
went by before more than half the representatives assented to a plan for
resolving the deadlock. Meanwhile the fiftieth ballot was reached. The
fifty-third. And the fifty-fifth. Many panaceas were sponsored, including ten major resolutions proposing various compromises. All were
knocked into cocked hats by members who did not relish the prospect of
a speaker whose political faith differed from their own.

Boyd led the aspirants on ten ballots. Stanly had his hour in the spotlight, as did McClernand, Stevens and Strong. On the fifty-second count,
Winthrop revived, with ninety-five followers to Boyd's sixty-six. Winthrop then dipped down, Cobb started to come up, but the fifty-ninth
time that the roll was taken—on Thursday, December 20—Stanly had
seventy-five votes; McClernand, fifty; Boyd, twenty-eight; Strong, fifteen;
Winthrop, thirteen; Wilmot, seven; Miller and Cabell, six apiece; Robert
C. Schenck, two; Cobb, two; McDowell, two; Stevens, two, and the
remnant divided among more also-rans. Christmas drew near, and with
it an adjournment. The House was trending nowhere fast. What was
to be done? Would the House have no speaker? As the result of a
Whig-Democratic conference, held December 21, Stanton of Tennessee
presented a "proposition," said to be of Whig origin: *"Resolved,* That
the House will proceed immediately to the election of a Speaker, *viva
voce;* and if . . . after the roll" is "called three times" no member obtains
a majority, "the roll shall again be called, and the member who shall
then receive the largest number of votes . . . shall be declared to be
chosen Speaker."

Even now dissension arose from pugnacious bitter-enders. Rival resolutions were squelched, however, and at long last Stanton's proposal carried by a margin of seven votes. Members clambered over party fences
time and again to reach the verdict, numerous Democrats and Whigs
combining against comrades who had previously sided with them but
now, oddly, were opposed. Ashmun and Vinton, for example, favored
the Stanton Resolution, as did Andrew Johnson, William J. Brown,
Thaddeus Stevens and Robert C. Winthrop. Cobb voted against it, to-

gether with Giddings and Holmes, Wilmot, Toombs and Stephens. When tellers announced the outcome, McClernand and Stanly withdrew their names, Cobb and Winthrop resuming their places as standard-bearers for the *dénouement*.

Cobb led on the sixtieth and sixty-first ballots, with ninety-five votes to Winthrop's ninety, and ninety-six to his ninety-two. On the sixty-second Winthrop tied the score. But on the momentous sixty-third, Cobb breasted the tape with 102 against Winthrop's ninety-nine. The standing of Wilmot and others did not matter. Cobb was the new Speaker of the House.

The harassing struggle finally was over, three weeks after it began![4]

6

For all the shifts of strategy, Cobb's total at the end was one less (Winthrop's, three greater) than at the inception of the voting. Sixty-three trials demonstrated that no single party or section could qualify for majority control of the House. Even this fact of high importance, however, was now overshadowed by the certainty that the machinery in *both* chambers would be controlled by the Democrats. All Washington had watched with fascination as factions within parties and schisms within factions asserted themselves, some for the first time. To a degree, this marked a dividing line between party sovereignties of the past and sectional sovereignties of the future. To the extent that Southern and Northern interests now overlapped on partisanship, frontiers of bygone times no longer had meaning this fateful winter.

Conceivably the pattern would have changed without Taylor in the picture. This historians can hardly prove. But we know the alteration did come with him, and that he had an effect on it. The Toombs-Stephens element forsook the Whigs because of what Taylor had done. Free-Soilers, however, were not yet willing to accept his leadership in December. Clingman, despite his growing convictions, still clung to Whiggery and voted for Winthrop. The flux in the House mirrored uncertainties and waverings through the entire country. The events of 1850 also would be a reflection not only of individuals' convictions but of partisan sentiments and sectional views.

Because of the diverse considerations inspiring members of Congress a careful analysis of motives must be made. Nuances are important in any analysis of House and Senate votes in '50. The instant Cobb became Speaker attention of observers and actors shifted precipitately from

House to Senate, from Senate to President, and back and forth along the Avenue—with Zachary Taylor and Henry Clay eventually the focal points. This was drama of the highest order. As a symbol of confusion and change permeating the nation at this juncture, only the Taylor-Clay fight-to-the-finish surpassed the stormy displays in the House prior to Cobb's limited triumph.

CHAPTER XXI

Taylor's Plan to Uphold the Union

1

DURING the prolonged speakership contest the House at times seemed ready to disperse in "a general row." After the "agitation and unparalleled excitement" there was "every foreboding of a stormy session." The "extravagant" expressions, "great" commotion and "intense" feeling augured trouble. Threats of the Union's dissolution had been heard on the floor and elsewhere in the Capitol. If Free-Soil tactics repelled most Southerners, the strategy of Toombs and Stephens was a thorn in the flesh of Northern Whigs.

"With some gentlemen of the South there is a hypocritical profession of attachment to the Union," Orlando Brown advised Crittenden, " . . . & ardent hope . . . that the North will pass the proviso to give them a popular reason for the most violent measures." Calhoun informed his son-in-law: "The South is more united . . . and . . . bold and decided . . . than I ever knew it. . . . The North must give away, or there will be a rupture. . . . There is no telling what will be the end." "The Southern members are more determined . . . than I ever saw them," the Carolinian wrote. "Many avow themselves . . . disunionists," and still more "admit . . . there is little hope of any remedy short of it." Meanwhile Northerners "show no disposition to desist from aggression. . . . The Session will be stormy, but I hope . . . a final and decisive issue will be made up with the North. There is no time to [lose]."

If sectional antipathies had been confined to the House, the President might have appealed initially with brighter prospects of immediate success—over the representatives' heads—to the upper chamber and the nation. In preceding months, however, and also after Congress convened, state legislatures passed resolutions so strongly worded that grass-roots conciliation seemed impossible. Northern governers' annual messages resoundingly approved the Proviso principle. Southern governors defended their institutions, and the coming Nashville Convention cast a shadow over efforts to compromise.

It was an involved state of affairs, the more so because the man in the White House adhered to his soldierly concept of nationalism. Certain

TAYLOR AND HIS CABINET

ABRAHAM LINCOLN   NATHANIEL HAWTHORNE

From left to right in Mathew B. Brady's Cabinet group are: Attorney General Johnson, Secretary of the Treasury Meredith, Secretary of the Navy Preston, President Taylor, Secretary of War Crawford, Postmaster General Collamer, Secretary of the Interior Ewing, and Secretary of State Clayton. Lincoln and Hawthorne were the two most notable Americans whose careers were importantly affected by the Taylor Administration's patronage policies.

Southerners yet believed that "Genl. Taylor . . . would be glad" if territorial bills "can be passed without the proviso, and would prefer such a settlement" to a *"non-action* policy." Among those still adhering to the impression that Taylor would veto the Proviso was Jefferson Davis. Not so Toombs. "When I came to Washington," Toombs wrote, "I found the whole Whig party expecting to pass the proviso, and that Taylor would *not veto it.* . . . I . . . talked fully with . . . General Taylor. . . . While he stated he . . . *would give* no pledges either way . . . , he gave me *clearly* to understand that if it was passed he would sign it." "My course became instantly fixed," explained the Whig whose oratory helped Taylor become President. "I would . . . oppose the proviso, even to the extent of a dissolution of the Union. . . . My whole subsequent course has been governed by this . . . policy."

2

Taylor remained calm and firm, notwithstanding congressional turmoil. In November Seward wrote Weed: "The malcontents of the South mean to be factious and . . . expect to compel 'a compromise.' I think the [President] as willing to try conclusions with them as . . . Jackson was with the Nullifiers." "The President . . . will not flinch from any duty," Seward predicted December 3.[1] "I understand . . . the President is in excellent spirits, and treats . . . lightly the difficulties under which the House labors," the Charleston *Courier's* reporter commented.

Taylor's health, during this "national and legislative crisis," was excellent. He seemed to have recovered completely. "The old chief is looking very well indeed," Letcher had observed in November. "He is very cool, very deliberate, and . . . *determined* to go along regardless of censure or praise." Taylor "looks well" and "acts well," the bluff Kentuckian added in another letter. "The President talks freely, and shows no anxiety," a newsman noted December 7. A new Kentucky congressman, calling at the White House, was "perfectly charmed" and opined that "all Hell cant beat" Taylor "in the next race." Others disagreed anent Rough and Ready's political strength. Calhoun called the Administration "prostrated" and "feeble." Fillmore's law partner thought "the President . . . inclined to be a cipher . . . at the left hand of . . . his Cabinet (the sum . . . being . . . expressed by a decimal as .07)." There also were rumors of "a difficulty in the Cabinet," and Clayton threatened to resign.

Whatever friend or foe might think, Taylor remained "entirely satisfied" with his official advisers—Meredith holding first place in his affections. Taylor's attractiveness led William Tecumseh Sherman to comment: "I had never seen him before . . . and was most agreeably surprised at his fine personal appearance, and . . . pleasant, easy manners." As to the trouble beating about him, "the General feels no apprehensions—standing unshaken in the lowering sky." This attitude was perhaps best exemplified in the annual message Taylor sent to both houses on Christmas Eve.

3

The message had been written in November, its authorship variously ascribed to Clayton, Meredith and Bullitt. All of these, plus the President and Ewing, had a finger in the pie, Clayton probably composing the first draft. Taylor and his ministers read copy, with Letcher joining in the "pruning." Perhaps there were too many authors. The message—in its first published form—contained a malapropism as incredible as ever appeared in a state paper. Part of the third paragraph, "We are at peace with all the nations of the world, and seek to maintain our cherished relations with the rest of mankind," sent congressmen into peals of laughter. Merriment reverberated in private letters and the press.[2] Although the offending phrase was culled, no belated official change could erase the first impression. For the duration of Taylor's regime, Democrats would jeer, scoff, and chant *"With the rest of mankind!"* whenever they thought the Whigs were growing cocky or needed trimming down to size. The refrain was too gorgeously mirth-provoking for Taylor's opponents to resist.

Nine tenths of the message added up to a competent, if pedestrian, recital of Taylor's policy—with somewhat over half devoted to international affairs. Almost at the outset, the President emphasized friendly relations with Great Britain. Stressing "strongest ties of amity" with France, he passed lightly over the Poussin friction. Regarding the German-Danish episode, and in a résumé of his Cuban policy, Taylor underscored neutrality and his pride in upholding it. The revolutionary movements abroad? "I have scrupulously avoided . . . interference" in European "wars and contentions." However, the Magyars had Taylor's sympathy; he would have gladly been "the first to welcome independent Hungary into the family of nations." Portuguese claims, minor treaties and suppressing the "barbarous" African slave trade came in for a share of attention. Because of their delicate nature, the canal negotiations went unmentioned. But Taylor warned against any great maritime state's commanding the Isthmian "commmunication."

Devoting brief paragraphs to the Treasury's receipts and expenditures, to the tariff and subtreasury system, and recommending a bureau of agriculture, the President's message included sections on the coast survey, Indian agencies, rivers and harbors, Army and Navy affairs, postal business, the Seventh Census and a California branch mint. None of this was heady stuff. But near the middle of the message, which the clerks intoned that Monday afternoon, a passage of electric interest contained one of Taylor's two references to the slavery issue. Terribly important to the whole country, this was the first formal announcement of what came to be called "the President's Plan." Pensive people scrutinized Taylor's ideas on the subject—so adjacent to the nitroglycerin of sectional wrath—but expressed in language remarkably statesmanlike if judged by standards of that dramatic period.

Sketching the background, Taylor recalled that the Thirtieth Congress failed to provide civil rule for California. Therefore, the "people of that Territory, impelled by . . . their political condition," met "in convention for the purpose of forming a . . . State government." The result? "Latest advices give me reason to suppose" that this "has been accomplished"—and "it is believed they will shortly apply for . . . admission" into the Union. "Should such be the case," said the slave-owning Taylor (perfectly aware of Monterey sentiment), "and should their constitution be conformable to . . . requisitions of the Constitution of the United States, I recommend their application to the favorable consideration of Congress." This was Point Number One of the President's Plan. New Mexico's "people . . . will also, it is believed, at no very distant period present themselves for admission into the Union." This was the broaching of Point Number Two, although Taylor did not now specifically sponsor New Mexican statehood. He was content for the present to hint broadly at it, leaving implementation for a later date.

"Preparatory to the admission of California and New Mexico," Taylor continued, "the people of each will have instituted . . . a republican form of government, 'laying its foundation in such principles and organizing its powers in such form as to them shall seem most likely to effect their safety and happiness.' By awaiting their action [philosophically,] all causes of uneasiness may be avoided and confidence and kind feeling preserved." "With a view of maintaining the . . . tranquillity so dear to all," the President declared in the most quoted lines of the historic message, *we should abstain from the introduction of those exciting topics of a sectional character which have hitherto produced painful apprehensions in the public mind;* and I repeat the solemn warning of the first and most illustrious of my predecessors *against furnishing 'any ground for characterizing parties by geographical discriminations.'* "

4

Concluding, Taylor expanded on his conception of the executive branch's place in the presidential-legislative picture, as set forth in his inaugural. "Our Government is one of limited powers," he asserted. ". . . Its successful administration . . . depends on . . . confinement of . . . coordinate branches" within "appropriate" spheres. "The Executive has authority to recommend (not to dictate) measures to Congress. . . . The . . . veto will never be exercised by me except" as "contemplated by the fathers of the Republic. *I view it as an extreme measure, to be resorted to only in extraordinary cases,*" as when "necessary to defend the executive against . . . legislative . . . encroachments . . . *or to prevent hasty . . . or unconstitutional legislation.* By cautiously confining this remedy . . . the will of the people . . . will have . . . full effect."

The italicized words gave Congress and impatient people pause. One phrase—"an extreme measure, to be resorted to only in extraordinary cases"—appeared to spell out Taylor's disinclination to veto the Proviso. Yet was not the Proviso, according to many Southerners, "inconsiderate" and "unconstitutional"? Some sage heads concluded that definitions of proper employment of the veto power remained academic, since Taylor would by-pass the Proviso by admitting California and New Mexico as states. Others attached significance to his dwelling on this topic; as we have seen, Senator Davis held that the veto separated the passage of anti-extension bills from their enactment into law.

A final all-important feature, however, could have prevented misreading of Taylor's intent. "Attachment to the Union . . . should be habitually fostered in every American heart," he insisted. "For more than half a century . . . this Union has stood unshaken. The patriots who formed it have . . . descended to the grave; yet . . . it remains, the proudest monument to their memory. . . . Its dissolution would be the *greatest of calamities.* . . . Upon its preservation must depend our own happiness and that of countless generations to come. *Whatever dangers may threaten it, I shall stand by it* and maintain it in its integrity to the full extent of the obligations imposed and the powers conferred upon me by the Constitution."[3]

This peroration was Jacksonian in its essence, and made the whole a ringing Union message. Designed to shatter doubt wherever doubt remained, it assured nationalists of Taylor's stamp that the hero in the White House could be relied on. Had men of Taylor's breed been in control of Congress, friendly leaders in each chamber might have carried on from there. Instead, his partisan opponents controlled the House and Senate machinery. Worse from the President's standpoint was the fact that sectional antipathies were growing rather than diminishing, with a Southern demand for a reinforced fugitive slave law only one of the involvements. Since his cherished two-point program could not be shepherded safely through Congress, the best Taylor could do was to defeat drifts or drives he considered harmful, meanwhile keeping before the nation the plan he had so carefully projected.

Reactions to the message were keen and swift, and more or less what had been expected. Division of opinion still ran primarily along party— rather than sectional—lines.

Possibly the fairest estimate came from the *National Era.* Albeit extreme in his views, Gamaliel Bailey neither used fanatical language like Garrison's and Rhett's nor groped in blind partisanship like Webb and Ritchie. "There is nothing in it to justify extreme praise or censure," Bailey wrote of the message. "It is . . . respectable in style, manner, spirit, and dimension," and the advice to Congress to abstain from introducing questions relating to slavery "is the first authoritative intimation" of the President's policy. To this dispassionate appraisal there should be linked the singular objectivity of the Boston *Post,* which indulged in the conventional sniping of "outs" against "ins," but concluded by lauding the President's Unionism. "Should . . . the patriotism of the nation . . . be . . . tested on this point," said the *Post,* "we hope . . . Taylor will . . . imitate the Hero of the Hermitage, and put . . . the leaders of DISUNION . . . down."[4]

The Charleston *Mercury's* accusation of cloudiness with regard to Nicaragua was true, though silence here may have been justified by the delicate state of negotiations. The document certainly was not "disgraceful"—nor was all of it "noble" and "beautiful"—the truth lying somewhere between the extremes. But Taylor's Unionism and antiextensionism should not have been mistaken, even by partisans, snide remarks of the *Indiana State Sentinel* and *Liberator* notwithstanding. It is noteworthy that most of the well-edited newspapers, on both sides of the line, quickly comprehended the President's nationalism, though some objected strenuously to the handwriting on the wall.

5

Delivery of Taylor's annual message was the final act in the drama of statesmanship and politics preceding the nation's holiday respite. Christmas came on a Tuesday, and congressmen took off Tuesday and Wednesday to celebrate the season—as best they could—in their boardinghouses and hotels. Most of the senators and representatives did not have their families with them in Washington. Some paid calls or exchanged informal visits, but the "bitter cold spell" kept many in their rooms where they gathered around available stoves, venturing out only for a meal or a toddy. In the residences of Cabinet ministers and such fortunate senators as Benton, a normal Christmas environment prevailed, with motherly souls like Mrs. Meredith, Mrs. Ewing and Mrs. Benton presiding over festive tables. Frances Seward was with her husband on F Street, but Lucretia Clay had remained behind at Ashland, and Floride Calhoun in South Carolina. Calhoun had his niece Martha Burt and her husband for company in Washington. Although friends surrounded Clay when he descended for dinner at the National Hotel, no doubt he missed the familiar Kentucky faces. Abigail Fillmore was in Buffalo, her husband alone in bachelor quarters at Willard's on the Avenue. But a true Christmas atmosphere was nowhere more in evidence than at the Executive Mansion itself, where the Taylor circle was almost complete, with grandchildren the guests of honor. Family man that he was, Old Zack's heart must have swelled with gratification as he surveyed the near and dear ones, especially his granddaughters and their cousin "Little Belle." There is no record of the entertainment provided to amuse the younger generation. But if the Taylor party-giving tradition was maintained, host and company had a happy time.

This was, of course, but a brief interlude amid White House formalities. Before and after Christmas President Taylor was busy as usual in welcoming dignitaries to the Mansion. Sir Henry Lytton Bulwer, the new British minister, was among those he received; Bulwer and his wife, the Duke of Wellington's niece, would soon become leaders of the diplomatic set, and Bulwer's attaché was his bantering nephew, later "Owen Meredith," the poet. Other arrivals from abroad included Baron Friedrich von Gerolt, minister resident of Prussia, and Señor Don Eduardo Carcache, the Nicaraguan chargé. Subsequently Poussin's successor would appear, and Hungarian refugees headed by Ladislade Ujhazy. Most famous at the time was the Reverend Theobald Mathew—Father Mathew, the celebrated Irish Catholic priest and temperance reformer, who found Rough and Ready ingratiating and hospitable at "a grand dinner . . . served in sumptuous style" on the evening of December 20.

Taylor did the honors at numerous dinner parties, "frequently" entertaining "strangers of distinction," as well as old friends, Army officers and members of the House and Senate. With Betty Bliss acting as hostess when the ladies were invited, guests regarded Taylor's table as "unexceptionable," and his excellent taste in food and wine was praised as "free from ostentatious display." "Remarkably hospitable" was a phrase often used in characterizing Taylor, and this meant much since cuisine standards in Washington then were high—Corcoran the banker, Seaton, Gales, Blair, Ewing and Meredith being among the favorite hosts. Clayton's evening parties, smaller and more intimate, sustained the *bon vivant's* reputation as a connoisseur of viands and vintages. Meredith and his charming Catharine delighted such gourmets as Letcher and Brown with their gustatory treats. Winthrop's suppers were "the decided thing" and described by a contemporary as "not slow"—his meat and drink as "good as could be commanded"—and, like the President, he invited every congressman to come in for refreshment at least once.

The capital, therefore, was far from dull as statesmen and their ladies made the rounds. After December 26 the cold weather eased, but not for long. On New Year's Day it was six above zero shortly before seven in the morning. Although a sheet of snow covered the ground, and the January air was brisk, officialdom ushered in the crisis year of 1850 with the amenities of tradition. And a "bright and unclouded sky" smiled on the fashionables' New Year's visits.

Seward's social activities on January 1 were typical of many congressmen's. With Mrs. Seward he called at the Bentons' on C Street—where Old Bullion "was very agreeable"—and "we took a cup of chocolate" with Mrs. Benton. "From there we drove" to Mrs. John Quincy Adams', but the Sixth President's widow was not receiving. And so "we went" to Mrs. Alexander Hamilton's. "Here," wrote Mrs. Seward, "I was much interested, not only by the lady herself, but by the ancient furniture and pictures." Gilbert Stuart's Washington, "a bust of Hamilton, a picture of . . . Mr. and Mrs. Hamilton . . . [and] a cake-basket of silver filigree work one hundred years old . . . were examined with an interest . . . you will easily conceive." Following these calls Mrs. Seward went back to F Street, where she was "at home" to "numerous . . . ladies and gentlemen," while Seward took the children to the White House to present them to Zachary Taylor.

"The great centre of attraction" that first of January "was . . . the President's Mansion," where Taylor "with his frank cordiality . . . returned the salutations of thousands." Plain everyday Americans, "the Heads of Departments, the Representatives of Foreign Powers, Judges of the Supreme Court, Senators and Representatives, and . . . Military, Naval, and Civil Officers . . . poured into the building without intermission" from noon until well after two o'clock. "The company were enlivened from time to time with admirable music from the Marine Band." The "light-fingered gentry" were at work. "Several gentlemen lost their pocket-books" and a lady missed her valuable gold watch. But the *Republic* and *Intelligencer* insisted that good order generally prevailed, pickpockets being no novelty in that era whenever large crowds gathered.

The "immense throng" not only noted the President's fit appearance and affable personality, but also admired extensive improvements within the White House and out on the grounds. The roof was "now deemed . . . free from leaks. . . . The house has been thoroughly painted, inside and outside, except the basement rooms. . . . The south external wall and the walls and ceilings of the various passages, halls and apartments, and . . . wood-work and fixtures . . . were in excellent order. The furnaces have also been . . . repaired . . . the stables . . . improved. . . . A portion of the fences dividing the parks and that which encloses the President's garden have been reconstructed, and iron gates at the east entrance . . . repaired." Other changes preserved "pavements, gutters, gravelled ways, pumps, water-pipes, and hot-houses." All was not perfect, however. The "lower courses of stone around the main building, and at the base of the terraces and colonnades" were "mouldered and crumbling." Much, too, needed to be done to "apartments in the basement" and "pavements, drains, and sewers contiguous." But few visitors noticed such oversights, since the East Room was the focal point. And new paint, new rugs, new draperies, new china, new glass commanded their attention and drew their compliments.[5]

6

The politicians did not wait for the dawning of the new year to agitate pet schemes or sectional arguments. Although Root introduced a resolution providing for slavery's exclusion from the West, most of the aggressive steps at this time were Democratic, with Southerners usually setting the pace.

Senator Foote of Mississippi moved on December 27 that "it is the duty of Congress, . . . to establish suitable *territorial* governments for California, for Deseret, and for New Mexico"—a motion running counter to Taylor's statehood recommendation. Jeremiah Clemens of Alabama and Sam Houston of Texas called on the President to supply the Senate with all the correspondence bearing on Monterey and Santa Fe. Venable, in the House, took a similar step. Senator James W. Bradbury, a Northern Democrat, further embarrassed the Administration by requesting that "charges . . . preferred . . . against individuals . . . removed from office" be "laid before the Senate." This was an oblique partisan assault on Taylor's patronage policy; though it had no bearing on slavery's extension, Bradbury attacked at a spot where Democrats considered Old Zack vulnerable. Thus, whether on the sectional issue or not, Taylor was speedily made the target of militant Democratic leadership, armed with the numerical might of a plurality in the House and a majority in the Senate.

Moreover, after the turn of the year, as the congressional debate grew hotter, Democratic aspersions and Southern passions electrified the Capitol atmosphere. To be sure, Free-Soilers and Northern Whigs contributed to the heightened tempo, and an effective Union utterance was enunciated by Missouri's Benton. But Southerners like Foote and Clemens, James Murray Mason of Virginia, Solon Borland of Arkansas, Atchison of Missouri, and Andrew P. Butler of South Carolina took the floor more often in defense of Southern interests than Northerners did in retaliation.

Some, like Clemens, were caustic and violent; others matter-of-fact and restrained. Calhoun, the old lion of the South, spoke briefly but gloomily of the Union's future. Davis grappled with the Free-Soiler Hale in a furious bout of conflicting charges. Atchison placed proslavery resolutions of the Missouri General Assembly on record. William Upham of Vermont, a Whig, countered with another set of resolutions— denouncing slavery in vituperative terms—which his state's legislature had passed. Language used by provincial politicians in Jefferson City and Montpelier provided a sounding board for the Senate. Thus Benton, denying that most Missourians concurred in their lawmakers' decisions, seized the occasion to dramatize the danger of civil war. Calhoun despaired of seeing "the encroachment of the North . . . arrested in Congress. . . . What the South will do is not for me to say . . . [but Southerners] will meet it . . . as it ought to be met." Mason and Borland took umbrage at the Vermonters' assertion that "slavery is a crime against humanity."

Clemens accused the North of libeling Southern citizens, advocating the murder of slaveholders and appealing to "the worst passions of the slave." John P. Hale then replied with a characteristic melange of stern denials and homey humor. Butler supported the militant Clemens. And Jefferson Davis announced: "I know the temper of those I represent, and they require no promptings to resist aggression."

Similar speeches followed in the Senate. Meanwhile the valuable time of the House was consumed by incredibly long and involved maneuvers to choose a clerk, a sergeant-at-arms, and (unsuccessfully, after fourteen ballots) a doorkeeper! If the Senate made little progress toward a solution of the sectional issue, the House had even less to show for all the energy expended. As Davis pointed out, it was "a melancholy fact . . . that morning after morning"—when congressmen came to transact business—"our feelings should be . . . harrowed" in various ways "by . . . this . . . profitless subject" of slavery. Leadership was sorely needed. In the circumstance of both houses' organization by a party vehemently opposed to the man in the White House, it was inconceivable that effective legislative guidance could emanate at once from him. Despite the heavy handicap, and no doubt certain that his proposals would run into a wall of partisan and factional disapproval, Taylor on January 21 sent a special message to the Hill which developed and implemented somewhat "the President's Plan," as previously broached.

7

The *raison d'être* of this special message was contained in requests for an accounting of the President's action in California and New Mexico. Since the men most eager to probe the record were not supporters of Taylor's regime, they probably wished to embarrass him, for they knew he favored direct statehood as the cornerstone of Western development and this they diametrically opposed. Had the resolutions been fathered by Smith, Seward, Winthrop, Stanly or any other pro-Administration Whig, they might be regarded as friendly "plants." But with Venable, Clemens and Houston the initiators, the motivation was fairly obvious.

Taylor rose to the occasion, not in the role of a cringing apologist but in the spirit of direct responsibility for what had been done—and *all* that had been done. "On coming into office I found the military commandant of . . . California exercising the functions of civil governor," a forceful President reported. ". . . I thought it best not to disturb that arrangement . . . until Congress should take . . . action." However, "I did not hesitate

to express" to the Californians "my desire" that they should, if prepared
to comply with requisitions of the nation's Constitution, form "a plan of
a State constitution and submit the same to Congress with a prayer for
admission . . . as a State."

Was this not logical, even essential, in view of the chaos in the gold
fields? Would not Taylor have been delinquent in the exercise of executive functions, had he twiddled his thumbs during Congress' adjournment? At the same time, he had ever been at pains not to swing outside
his constitutional limits. "I did not anticipate, suggest, or authorize the
establishment of any such government" in California "without the assent
of Congress." To be sure, he had sent King to the Coast. But Taylor
had not empowered any "agent . . . to . . . exercise . . . influence or control over the election of delegates or over any convention." On the contrary, "my . . . instructions . . . were that . . . measures of domestic policy
adopted by the people of California must originate . . . with themselves."
Yes, the Californians distinctly understood that any governmental plan—
proslavery or antislavery—would be "the result of their . . . deliberate
choice . . . without the interference of the Executive." Taylor still lacked
official intelligence regarding the Monterey decision. This would soon
arrive, he felt, and thus not much time would elapse before Congress
received California's statehood application. Such a course, Taylor explained in peculiarly interesting language, "though in accordance with
. . . my wishes," would not be adopted "exclusively in consequence of"
them. If the "proposed constitution" satisfied federal requisitions, "I
earnestly recommend that it may" be given "the sanction of Congress."

With regard to New Mexico the President was reminded that "a claim
has been advanced by . . . Texas to a very large portion" of its most
populous district. "If . . . New Mexico . . . had been admitted . . . as a
State, the Texas boundary question could have been resolved by a judicial
decision. Since no court possessed power to pass on an issue between a
state and the United States, Congress must "devise some . . . adjustment." Taylor questioned the expediency of establishing a territorial
government, "which by including the district . . . claimed would practically decide the question adversely to . . . Texas, or by excluding it
would decide it in her favor." It was Taylor's belief that "New Mexico
will at no very distant period ask for admission into the Union" as a
state. On that occasion the residents of the region would "settle all questions of domestic policy to suit themselves."

When Taylor used the expressions "domestic policy" and "domestic
institutions," it was manifest that he referred to slavery. However, he

did not mention the word "slavery" in his special message, falling back only once on "involuntary servitude." As in the annual message, the President still did everything within his power linguistically to avoid references magnifying "exciting topics of a sectional character." "Every new acquisition of territory," he said, "has led to discussions" as to whether "involuntary servitude . . . should or should not be prohibited." Previous "periods of excitement . . . have been safely passed," he was glad to note but—without removing the cause of agitation by adopting his direct statehood plan—it appeared "probable that similar excitement" would "prevail to an undue extent." Yes, he believed that the issue now arousing "painful sensations . . . will in the end certainly be settled by the silent effect of causes independent of the action of Congress." Therefore, "I again submit to your wisdom the policy recommended in my annual message of awaiting the salutary operation of those causes. . . . Every dictate of wisdom, every feeling of duty, and every emotion of patriotism tend to inspire fidelity and devotion" to the Union—and "admonish us cautiously to avoid any unnecessary controversy which can either endanger or impair its strength, the chief element of which is to be found in the regard and affection of the people for each other."[6]

8

Criticism of Taylor's special message was tart on one hand and sugary on the other. Now, however, some newspapermen took a different position than in December. Again the *Pennsylvanian, New Hampshire Patriot,* Richmond *Enquirer* and *Indiana State Sentinel* initiated all-out attacks. Again the New York *Courier & Enquirer,* Washington *Republic, National Intelligencer* and papers like the Saint Louis *Republican* extolled the President and his program. But something new had been added to the critical motif. No longer did partisanship pure and simple all but monopolize the editors' thinking. Threadbare generalities of approbation and traditional patterns of abuse meshed with novel lines and angles. Differences between South and North and individualistic slants were more subtle and creeping than galloping or grand. They were present none the less, and they claim a moment of the historian's attention.

Thus Northern critics tended to harp on Taylor's "theft" of Cass's plan, while some Southerners capitalized on the idea that the President sought to circumvent Southern interests by achieving the Proviso's goal indirectly. Strong cases could be built for both these theories, but it is indicative of the flux of the hour that editors took widely varying tacks. In

Concord the *Patriot* underscored "the . . . monstrous fraud practised upon the people by Taylor." Taylor's had "stolen the 'non-intervention doctrine' of Gen. Cass . . . which two years ago" the Northern Whig press "declared to be . . . dangerous, and *certain,* if acted upon, *to ensure the extension of slavery to the new territories."* The *Patriot* gingerly side-stepped the question whether what Cass "favored" in '48—and Taylor in '50—was right for the country. Instead of meeting this issue head-on, Franklin Pierce's sharpshooters emphasized only the "inconsistency" of Whigs. "Having been elected upon . . . representations" favoring "both sides" of the slavery question, Taylor "now begs . . . Congress to save him from the disgrace . . . of confessing himself a . . . falsifier." What could result from the President's Plan but extension of slavery's "curse" to the West? "A more disgraceful . . . recommendation . . . never emanated from a Chief Magistrate. . . . Yet the whole federal press . . . is out in full endorsement . . . of this doctrine and course." Any convenient conclusion could be reached from the *Patriot's* position. An antislavery zealot might assume that Taylor's Plan was designed to extend slavery to the Pacific, while a Southerner—overlooking one reference to "the curse of slavery"—could concentrate on Taylor's alleged duplicity. Paradoxical as were these twists of the truth, they appealed to many partisans.

The *Pennsylvanian* reflected the views of James Buchanan's coadjutor in Philadelphia. Finding Taylor's message "a strange tissue of contradictions and evasions," the editor saw "guilt . . . stamped" on every reference to "the mission of certain politicians" sent west to "demoralize California . . . by making it a Whig State." Though the "guilt" had been "detected," the Administration lacked "the courage to avow its shame." However, "it is . . . confessed that . . . King was the paid agent of Taylorism . . . and that 'other officers' . . . united with him in an errand which the people of the Pacific region . . . indignantly rebuked." At the same time "we can approve" Taylor's stand "against Congressional action on the subject of slavery" and his unfurling "the flag of Non-Intervention in regard to the new territories. . . . His . . . manly . . . offer to sustain California· in her application for admission . . . speaks the sentiments of a vast majority . . . North and South. We may expect an exciting debate, and some rare developments arising out of this strange production." Since this editorial was widely quoted (by the Nashville *Union,* among other dailies), the juxtaposition of adverse criticism and muted praise merits more than passing notice. In their first reactions to the President's Plan numerous Democratic papers joined it in approving Taylor's California statehood principle, supposing they could not consistently castigate Taylor without condemning Cass. Although the *Penn-sylvanian* all but branded Taylor a liar, it attached the adjective "manly" to him and did not suggest that he tried to extend "the curse of slavery," as the *Patriot* had. Indeed, a comparison between *Pennsylvanian* comments of January 22 and December 27 points up the tendency toward editorial independence, which Taylor's special message evoked.

As well as any journal William Cullen Bryant's New York *Post* symbolized gradual shifts in opinion regarding slavery and Zachary Taylor. Friendly to Van Buren, the *Post* declared that "General Taylor expresses himself in a firm and manly [again that word] manner" concerning California's admission. The voters there "have decided upon the institutions . . . they prefer. . . . If they are . . . repulsed in their application . . . because they . . . favor . . . freedom, they will have, says the message, the mass of the . . . people on their side"—resisting "this violation of their rights." But the *Post* was not wholly eulogistic. "The policy . . . of leaving" New Mexico and Utah "without a territorial government"—until sufficiently populous to form states—"is . . . feeble and temporizing." Interestingly enough the *Post* completely misjudged Taylor's motive in dispatching King to California and in leaving the slavery question in the hands of Monterey delegates. The result "is likely to disappoint . . . Taylor, as it would have disappointed his predecessor"—since Taylor, like Polk, would rather incur "the feeble . . . discontent of the north . . . than the displeasure of the fiery South." This must have been news to the Charleston *Mercury* and Richmond *Enquirer,* each of which berated the President for his sectional apostasy!

Most Whig comments were less involved and more conventional than Democratic overtones. According to the Saint Louis *Republican* the special message "played the very deuce with . . . Locofoco . . . calculations." The Clemens-Venable resolutions put "searching inquiries to the President"—which were expected to "overwhelm" him with charges of treason and usurpation. Bending back his opponents' aims, the "straightforward" Taylor had released "a clear, unsophisticated, manly document—frankly stating all . . . he has done and taking the responsibility of it." If ever "a Document . . . was . . . entitled to the praise of honesty . . . and devotion to the Republic," the *National Intelligencer* agreed, "it is the Message transmitted . . . by the President on Monday." Northern Whig editors generally approved. More striking was the virtual unanimity of Whig papers in the South, despite the "yes-butting" of a few. Even the *Southron* in Jackson, Mississippi, which found fault with the annual message, assented to the January declaration. Hear this from the Magnolia State: "No message since the . . . proclamation" of Old Hickory "against nullification has excited . . . such a sensation of joy in all patriotic bosoms. . . . Everyone feels . . . danger is past. The poisonous fangs of faction are extracted and though it may still hiss and foam, no one will longer heed it."[7]

9

Thus, if the press represented the people, Taylor's friends had much on their side in assuming his plan contained hope of success, even *assurance* of harmony. The situation, however, was far from static. Public opinion had not jelled. Already Ritchie was sharpening his stiletto. And eventually the *Patriot* and *Pennsylvanian* would swing into the *Union's* song and dance that Cass's plan was opposed to Taylor's, despite their initial view to the contrary.

Southern extremists, paced by Rhett's *Mercury,* surprised few Americans by seeking to show—with Calhoun and Clemens—that Taylor was faithless to the South. But the man who held the key to more uncommitted newspaper support or nonsupport of Taylor than any orator we have considered was Henry Clay, the venerable Whig. The Kentuckian grasped in the palm of his hand the opportunity to steer congressional debate—that debate which the *Pennsylvanian* predicted would prove "exciting." If Clay chose to champion the Whig Administration, he might attract enough Democrats and Free-Soilers to Taylor's standard to marshal a majority in the President's favor. Conversely, with the Democratic leadership anti-Taylor, with some Southern Whigs blowing hot and cold, and with Free-Soilers still antipathetic, there was an equal opportunity for Clay to direct the Opposition. In that case, he might gain prestige comparable to that of his younger days when he captained the forces for the Compromise Tariff and the Missouri Compromise in '33 and '20.

If Clay were a small man, narrow in outlook, he might wreak political vengeance on the hero who had defeated him for the presidential nomination—by masterfully sponsoring his own pet solution for the sectional puzzles confronting the country. If Clay were a big man, primarily statesmanlike, with the vision of a Jefferson and the vigor of a Jackson, should he not do what his conscience said was right, regardless of Taylor or incidental consequences?

Thoughts like these must have coursed through his mind, and through the mind of President Taylor, on those summerlike days[8] in January of '50 when the "Old Prince" prepared to take the floor.

CHAPTER XXII

The "Yawning Abyss" of Henry Clay

1

BEFORE Clay rose to the challenge of the crisis, other colorful figures—long since forgotten—responded to the Taylor Plan with threats and fulminations. In the House Clingman eased deceptively into an impassioned oration by briefly and paradoxically praising Taylor. "I have great confidence in the judgment, integrity, and patriotism of the President," the gentleman from Buncombe County admitted with a flourish. But this bow in Old Zack's direction was a gesture misleading few who sensed the ardor of Clingman's feeling.

The very suggestion that the South, a section furnishing "two-thirds" of America's troops in the Mexican War, should be excluded from the new lands astonished Clingman and shocked him. The proposition was downright *"impudent."* What would be the result? "California, Oregon, New Mexico, Deseret, and Minnesota . . . will come into the Union"—all as free states. The North would then have "a . . . majority of ten or fifteen votes in the Senate," while the House division would be "nearly two to one." With the South as powerless as a shorn Samson, would not the dominant North "at once . . . abolish slavery in the States?"

"These facts are staring us in the face," said Clingman, "as distinctly as the sun . . . at noonday." Surely, Northerners must agree that "the evils already inflicted on us . . . greatly exceed . . . any injury that Great Britain attempted when she drove the colonies into resistance." If Southern spokesmen consented to be "degraded and enslaved," they should be "whipped through their fields by their own negroes."

"Give us . . . fair settlement!" Clingman cried. But do not "cheat us by a mere empty form!"

What might be reasonable? Clingman was willing to give up "the whole of California," provided the South "could have all on this side of it, up to about . . . 40°"—including the whole of what was then New Mexico. In addition he looked forward to the acquisition of foreign soil bordering on the Gulf, "well suited to be occupied by our slave population." An extreme demand? Not to his mind. The idea of the North's giving nothing to the South, falling back on "senseless" cries

Two Dramatic Moments in the Great Debate

In Peter Frederick Rothermel's painting (top), Henry Clay in the Senate addresses his remarks to Vice President Fillmore. At the far left sits Benton; near him (head in hand), Webster; at the far right, Seward; next to Seward, Cass. Calhoun stands, third from right. In the bottom picture, Webster delivers his Seventh of March Speech. In the right corner is Douglas; next to Douglas, Albert C. Greene (with glasses); in the left corner, Benton (long, dark sideburns), Hamlin, Downs and Mason; behind Mason, Jefferson Davis; next to Davis, Calhoun. The Clay setting is idealized, the Webster setting reasonably realistic. The Rothermel painting by courtesy of the New-York Historical Society.

of "Union, union!" disgusted the Carolinian. If Northerners "will do us *justice,* we do not need their lectures. . . . Their declarations seem . . . hypocritical cant." And "when these things come from southern men, I have even less respect for them." Clingman discussed secession openly. The South's splitting off from the North would benefit the former and damage the latter. If under the "form" of the Constitution *"gross injustice"* is done to states, "then the Union ought not to stand . . . as an instrument of . . . oppression."

As to the course that could immediately be taken by those who felt as Clingman did, it was always possible to filibuster. They could refuse to pass an appropriation bill. They could "stop the wheels of . . . Government." No idle threat this, in view of the composition—sectional and partisan—of the Congress! There might even be "a collision," yes, "a bloody revolution." Sooner than submit, "I would rather see the South, like Poland, under the iron heel of the conqueror." Then "let the future traveler, as he passes over a blackened . . . waste, at least exclaim, 'Here lived and died as noble a race as the sun ever shone upon.' " But was so drastic an alternative necessary? Surely now was the hour to repel aggression. Succeeding in this, "we shall have peace."

"Do us justice," Clingman concluded, "and we continue to stand with you; attempt to trample on us, and we part company."

2

Clingman (later a Confederate general) was not the sole Southerner who in 1850 seethed and breathed fire and fury into defense of Southern interests. Following him, two Democratic representatives swung forward into the feverish war dance and beat the tomtoms of state rights. For all the vigor of his speech, Clingman spared the President personally, attacking Taylor only by implication. This was not true of Volney E. Howard. Being a Democrat, the irascible Texan felt none of the compunctions of old Whig ties. He was especially wrathy regarding Taylor's New Mexico policy. Reasserting the Lone Star claim, Howard denied "the power of this government" to change historic facts. Guarantees, "resting on solemn compact," could not be altered by the President or the Supreme Court.

What had happened in California was a "dangerous" precedent—"an excess of power . . . which ought to be resisted." But, concerning New Mexico, not only opinion but law and treaty showed Taylor acting in violation of the views of Polk and other statesmen. Moreover, Clayton's

instructions to King spelled underhandedness to Howard. Taylor's real
policy had been entrusted to King by word of mouth because it was "not
quite safe to place upon paper." Nevertheless, King imposed it "upon
the people of California, with all the force and authority of his relation
to the President."

Not long afterward "the impression was made" that California could
not become a state without adopting "the free-soil principle. . . . Her convention acted under the coercion of that belief, to the exclusion of the
South. . . . Such . . . was the intervention of the *non-intervention* of the
President." Yes, Howard asserted, if Taylor "is allowed . . . to promote
his wishes as to . . . domestic institutions in . . . States about to be
formed," he could "dictate their principles" and "practically reduce . . .
new States to petty corporations." Howard, of course, made this point
in an effort to broaden the base of opposition by harping on the hoary
"executive tyranny" theme, which might attract some Northerners. From
the Southern standpoint there was a more serious charge. "The President
admits that his object in bringing in California and New Mexico as
States was 'to remove all occasion for unnecessary agitation of the public
mind.' Did he not know that this could be affected only by adopting the
Wilmot Proviso . . . ?" Could he have any other purpose? No, the
South had been "prostrated . . . by a southern candidate . . . elected
through the instrumentality of southern votes." But "the South is aroused
and will act as one man."

3

For all Howard's thunder and Clingman's lightning it remained for
James A. Seddon of Virginia to lay down a barrage which for force and
effectiveness was unsurpassed in the House this session. Action taken
through King, Seddon warned, was "to my mind so . . . dangerous, as
to demand . . . examination and exposure." The Taylor-Clayton-King
arrangement involved "grave violations of the Constitution" and "gross
usurpation of powers." It was "insidious and fatal to the rights and interests of my section." It was "wrong" and prejudicial. The future Confederate Secretary of War was outraged that the Taylor regime cast its
"whole weight against the . . . slaveholder" to settle a "purely judicial
controversy" bound up in the "relation of master and slave." The Administration had "assumed high legislative powers," attempting to by-
pass Congress' discretion. This "seems like the crude fantasy of a crazed
brain, rather than . . . reflection and wisdom."

Though he predicted that "this shirking, shuffling policy will fail of its promised end," Seddon stepped out of his way to withhold blame from Taylor. Like many another Southerner the young representative found it hard to believe that a Louisiana slaveowner would harness the South's extension dreams. "For General Taylor," Seddon said, ". . . I have respect and confidence." But his "unsuspecting honesty has been practised on—his generous confidence abused." The Cabinet ministers were villains who pulled the wool over Taylor's eyes. There should be a new Cabinet, and Taylor's policy should change. It would be an "insult" for the South to be excluded from the West by "a northern majority." But how much more grievous for the "injury" to be "insidiously perpetrated" through a Southern President! "His interests . . . sentiments . . . associations . . . forbid it. Thank God, we have no traitors at the South."

The implication here was that Taylor would betray his class and section by championing the plan he enunciated and signed. The fact that Seddon sought to drive a spike between President and Cabinet was of particular moment. Furthermore, his sketch of Taylor as a well-intentioned but misguided man became one of the favorite modes—adopted by partisan and sectional foes—of maligning the "brave old soldier."

Between them, Seddon and Clingman—aided by Howard and, briefly, by Venable—did their share in arousing the capital to fever heat that January. This was "gasconade," the Northerners insisted. If so, it was inspired gasconade. In the future there would be similar orations in both chambers on the Hill. Could the issue be compromised, by Taylor or by anyone else? This question was uppermost in Whig and Democratic councils, as the wintry blasts of February neared.

4

While Clingman, Howard and Seddon held forth in the House, the Senate was neither idle nor quiet. Even before Taylor's special message jarred his fellow Southerners, another slaveholder—and a Democrat to boot—introduced a bill for chopping up Texas.

Thomas Hart Benton's service in the Senate was of greater duration than that of any of his colleagues. Beginning in 1821, it had continued twenty-nine years, so constant was Missouri's confidence in her senior statesman. For nearly half the Senate's history, while Presidents came and Presidents went, Benton remained a Washington fixture. Aristocratic in appearance and bearing, fairly tall, his forehead high, nose long and pointed and strong jaw the mark of a determined leader, Benton at the age of sixty-seven was still the man he long had been—tireless, high-principled, impervious to pressure. If his egotism was towering, and if enemies complained of Benton's long-windedness, he also possessed the will and courage to do what he thought right. Grandson of a Midas-touch land speculator, son of a bookish traditionalist, his invalid wife a Virginia lady, and himself kin to Lucretia Clay, it might have been natural for one of Benton's relationships to kowtow to the conservatives. Yet, in Jackson's time, Benton proved himself one of Old Hickory's ablest lieutenants in the war on Biddle and the Bank. And now, though he owned slaves, he opposed extension. Despite his enemies' success in capturing positions of control in Missouri, Benton jeopardized his re-election prospects in order to fight for a matter of principle.

With all the energy at his command, on January 16 Benton stole a march on his archantagonist, Foote of Mississippi. Knowing that Foote intended to introduce legislation creating two slave states in Texas, Benton initiated a rival proposal. Superficially similar to Foote's, it contained the contrary provision that large sections of Texas' land should revert to the federal government in return for $15,000,000, earmarked for retiring the Texas debt.

The area of Texas was too great, Benton argued. It "ought . . . to be reduced to a reasonable size." Texas should be made "a State of about 150,000 square miles" and, eventually, "two States of . . . 75,000." Neither the present white population nor even the unorganized counties would be affected; only "wild lands" need be ceded, totaling some 200,000 square miles. Stretching from the Rio Grande to the Arkansas, the proposal covered "the whole country which lies at the head of our rivers in front of the New Mexican mountains." Moreover, the need of protecting settlers justified such a relinquishment. "We cannot [now] protect New Mexico—we cannot go to her, or to California, upon any direct line . . . without going through . . . Texas." Yet Texas had shown herself incapable of providing the soldiers and roads whereon security depended. Assuredly, the United States could do better in that regard!

Not only that, Benton continued, but "Texas and New Mexico are about coming into collision" and "the United States . . . must be a party to that collision." It was Washington's duty to "stop it . . . amicably and paternally" by extinguishing Texas' claim to territory in dispute. "This bill . . . will have that effect"—giving Texas "a defined western boundary four degrees east of Santa Fé" and removing "all cause of collision."

Benton thus mentioned but did not underscore the point that his bill would expand the area from which Northern Free-Soilers and President Taylor wished to exclude domestic slavery. His implied approval of creating two slave states in Texas being vague in the extreme, it was inevitable that Foote would lock horns with the old Jacksonian and charge him with treason to the South. Benton, Foote believed, had meanly cribbed the two-state notion from Foote's own compromise solution, previously shadowed forth in the Senate and the press. No sooner was Benton seated than the short, bald, eccentric but eloquent Mississippian rose to reply. Sponsoring territorial (rather than state) governments for California and New Mexico, Foote favored a comparable arrangement for Mormon holdings in Deseret and division of Texas into states of Texas and Jacinto—the latter to "embrace . . . what is now Texas lying . . . east of the river Brasos." Foote agreed "that Texas, with . . . boundaries that of right appertain to her, is too large for a single State." But Foote did not "perceive the wisdom of excluding from . . . Texas . . . the territory" which Benton hoped to buy. Every acre, once purchased, would "be claimed infallibly as subject to the Wilmot proviso." Must any of Texas' "sacred" soil be "given to her . . . worst enemies?"

The mettlesome Foote was not through with Benton, but indulged in bitter personalities. Essentially passionate by nature, a four-time duelist, forcible and fluent, possessing a temper that pounded at his temples, and a tongue that slashed and invective that stung, Foote set out full-tilt after the Missourian, caught him and whipped him with abuse.

"Never did it enter my head," Foote said, sneering, that "a human being . . . representing . . . one of the slave States . . . would . . . bring forward a bill like that which . . . made its ghastly apparition . . . this morning." This "offensive conduct," he continued savagely, ". . . has been practised by an individual more responsible . . . than any man . . . for the unhappy condition in which the country is involved. . . . This . . . person . . . has presumed . . . to lend . . . encouragement . . . to . . . enemies of our institutions. . . . This, too, sir, is the indiscreet rhetorician whose inflammatory addresses . . . in Missouri . . . produced a most startling effect among the slave population." Foote compared Benton to a "degenerate Roman senator"—Cataline, no less. And when Benton, having stomached enough, stalked from the Senate chamber, his antagonist gleefully cried to Fillmore, "See, Mr. President, he flies!" Mixing the language of Cicero with florid Latin of his own, the Mississippian wound up in a fervid peroration, flailing the absentee, throat and thigh.

5

Foote spoke no more that January day. But the Ciceronian periods with Southern overtones uttered by the little man from Jackson accentuated combat-to-come as surely as Benton's antiextensionism. Melodramatic as it may seem, the episode has a much deeper meaning than appears on the surface. Its significance lay in the fact that, for all the fur that flew, neither Foote nor Benton represented radical doctrines in the Calhounite or abolitionist sense. Both were Southerners. Despite their antipathies, each had been elected as a Union man, and each remained a Unionist by his own standard. The difference between their ruling ideas lay in Benton's opposition to slavery's advance and Foote's readiness to back a compromise, acceptable to most Southerners, and leaving up to Congress the problem of the West with slavery legal in part of it. Foote also would have brought to Washington a brace of pro-slavery senators from the romantically named Jacinto. Less comprehensive than the scheme subsequently devised by Clay, Foote's bill anticipated it, while Benton's position was close to Taylor's.

Just as Taylor and Clay would become rival leaders later in the year, Benton and Foote earlier symbolized irreconcilable views. Party lines meant little here. Benton and Foote were Democrats; Taylor and Clay, Whigs; all four, Southern men, all owners of human property, all opposed to abolition. Individual convictions, not partisan alignments or economic interests, formed the premise for their actions, with each man sold on his integrity, each certain of his rectitude. So cocky was Benton, so combative was Foote, that in delineating them it is dangerously easy to let personalities obscure principles. If emotions were involved, so were intellects. If prejudice was appealed to, so were ideals.

6

Senate speeches, immediately following the Foote-Benton pyrotechnics, were drab and humdrum in comparison. Connecticut's Smith and Georgia's Dawson defended Taylor when Douglas assailed the President's instructions to King. Cass charged that the Wilmot Proviso was inexpedient and unconstitutional. Samuel S. Phelps of Vermont suggested that, if the Proviso were a purely constitutional issue, it ought to be submitted to the Supreme Court. Butler held forth in support of Mason's proposition for recovering fugitive slaves. Mason, after a week-end adjournment, presented a brief in his bill's behalf.[1] But Mason's language, like Phelps's and Butler's, was as dull as a poem by Joel Barlow. And not even Cass raised the debate above a mediocre level.

Perhaps the most disappointing figure in the story is Lewis Cass. Here was a man who, had he risen to the challenge of the occasion, might logically have been the Democracy's protagonist. Having read of his exploits in Michigan Territory, familiar with his record in Washington and Paris, aware of his narrow loss of the Presidency, one might expect dynamic qualities to stamp him as a leader now. However, Cass had become a plodder. At sixty-seven he showed his years. Fat and ponderous, he had lost much of his former zeal and zest. To be sure, Cass was "regular" by Democratic standards. And he was "safe"—eternally safe. But age and obesity were crawling up on the brain and body of the portly Detroiter, whose dewlap, jowls, dark-circled eyes and moplike wig were hardly inspirational assets. So the long Cass speech was dismal droning. And a potentially great Democratic exemplar permitted others to scale the heights of drama and of oratory.

It is surprising, too—unless one reads the record with the thoroughness it deserves—to find the brash Stephen A. Douglas away from the center of the Senate spotlight. The political vaulting of this young Vermonter who charmed and conquered Illinois is a thrilling and all-but-incredible chapter in the yarns of Yankee careerism. A cabinetmaker in boyhood, living in New York and moving to Ohio before venturing farther west, he held office after office in the state of his adoption, and bossed it with inspired precocity. Legislative and judicial honors seemed to come the easy way. It was as if Douglas held a magnet to attract shavings of political steel. Elected to Congress when he was thirty, and to the Senate at thirty-three, he was only thirty-six when Taylor was President— already starred as a child of destiny.

One of the shortest senators in history, Douglas was barely five feet four. Chubby and chunky, he was impressive none the less—his torso not below the average; his well-formed head set on strong, square shoulders. Only legs, hands, neck and nose edged an otherwise herculean frame toward the diminutive if not the dwarflike. First impressions were redeemed by a broad forehead, more full than high; by a mass of thick hair, a mouth that meant business, a combative chin and the arresting depth in his eyes—large, steady and dark-blue, verging on the violet and even the black. Friends found "peculiar fascination" in Douglas' voice, in tones distinguished by "vibrant energy," in words "round, deep and sonorous." A "steam engine in britches" he had been called, and the title of "the Little Giant" became him. But what was the Little Giant doing in this historic hour? (As chairman of the Committee on Territories, he could influence critical measures.) By choice rather than force of circumstance Douglas avoided forensics now. Ostensibly he even opposed some sentiments of the Websters and Clays. Later, contemporaries and also historians would understand his true importance. But, for the time being, it seemed logical to him for a Whig like Clay to perform before the footlights—while Douglas labored effectively off-stage. Before long, we shall see him hard at work, declaiming as well as marshaling his troops. But now we are glad to stop and observe the masterful strokes of Clay himself.

7

We have met Clay before—as a presidential candidate. Close-up, he is more appealing. For all his congressional tragedies and comedies, Clay never appeared to better advantage—at least emotionally—than now in the Senate. Outside the Capitol the January weather had been unseasonably warm. Inside, the courtly Kentuckian, nearing his seventy-third birthday, seemed almost equally impervious to the frosts of advancing years.

A tall, thin, rangy willow of a man, Clay had never been handsome in the classic sense. "His nose was too long, his ears were too big, his mouth was too wide" to be called good-looking. His forehead was too high, its loftiness accentuated by a fringe of stringy hair, which, graying now and thin on top, draped down nearly to his collar. Beauty of feature had never been among the adornments of Henry Clay, and the "Sage of Ashland" seemed downright ugly. Yet so penetrating was the glance of his eyes, so winning his smile, so compelling his manner, that his very homeliness was attractive. Harriet Martineau, years before, with admiration not typical of her characterized Clay's voice and manner as "deliciously winning" and "irresistibly persuasive." Now added to old appreciations was the public's curiosity in Clay's return to the Senate floor from his self-sought "retirement." It was virtually as if an American immortal had risen from the dead to deliver an address, as if Jefferson or Jackson had burst open the coffin and appeared again in living flesh.

On Tuesday January 29 Clay submitted eight resolutions seriatim to the Upper House. Only one was in line with the President's Plan—

admission of California as a state "without imposition by Congress of . . . restriction in respect to . . . exclusion or introduction of slavery." The second sponsored *territorial* governments for New Mexico and Deseret. Three and four curtailed Texas' boundaries (leaving that state, nevertheless, decidedly the country's largest) and provided for payment of Texas' debt. The fifth and sixth declared, despite the *inexpediency* of abolishing slavery in the District of Columbia, that the *slave trade* there should be prohibited. The seventh favored "more effectual provision" for "restitution and delivery" of fugitive slaves. The final one affirmed the principle that Congress lacked power to "obstruct" the slave trade between slaveholding states. Clay's first resolution favored the North. The second was more pro-South than otherwise. The third and fourth accorded with the ideas of many Southerners, especially in regard to the generous cash settlement. Though the fifth and eighth gave the South nothing tangible, they supported two "rights" on which her statesmen volubly declaimed. The sixth, pro-North, affected only the District. The seventh was definitely pro-South; more than any other provision, it came to be violently resented by Northerners. Clay's most interesting assertion involved his projection of territorial governments, which he premised on the "fact" that slavery was not "likely to be introduced" in New Mexico or Deseret, whether specifically outlawed or not.[2] The New York *Express* had this in mind when it referred to an "ordinance of nature," and Webster later employed the same phrase to more telling effect. "Why legislate one way or the other, when nature automatically keeps slavery out?" This, in substance, was what Clay asked.

Clay's voice was still "clear and distinct." His language was more earnest than eloquent. Aside from introducing his resolutions, Clay limited the nucleus of this speech to explaining and defending them. He ended by appealing for "mutual forbearance" and "an amicable arrangement" between the sections. His chief plea, Clay readily admitted, was directed to the "free States of the North," since his compromise called for more "extensive concession" there than he "asked from the slave States." Why this imbalance? Clay quickly rationalized. "You are numerically more powerful," he advised the Northern senators. Should not "greatness and magnanimity" go together? Yes, and there was another reason. The Northern viewpoint toward slavery, he insisted, was based on "sentiment of humanity and philanthropy" but nothing more than sentiment. No "sacrifice," no "danger," no "loss" was involved on the Northern side! "How is it on the other side . . . ?" Not only was an "incalculable amount of property to be sacrificed," but "social intercourse, habit, safety, property, life, everything, is at hazard in a greater or less degree in the slave States."

"Behold, Mr. President," Clay cried, the "dwelling-house" of the South "now wrapped in flames." Listen! Rafters and beams are falling! "Behold . . . women and children . . . flying from the . . . scene. . . . Whose house is that? . . . Yours in the free States? No. You are looking on in . . . security, whilst the conflagration" rages in the South, "produced from the inevitable tendency of . . . measures which you . . . adopted," and which abolitionists "have carried far beyond what you . . . wished."

"In one scale, then, we behold sentiment, sentiment, sentiment alone," Clay concluded. "In the other[,] property, the social fabric, life, and all that makes life desirable." Dramatically holding aloft a fragment of George Washington's coffin, Clay said that the First President's voice came from the grave, warning congressmen to "beware" and "reflect" before lending themselves to purposes destructive of the "Union . . . cemented by his exertions and example."

8

Before Clay left the Senate floor, his resolutions drew comment from nine fellow legislators. More important, they were made the special order for Tuesday February 5, which was to mark the formal start of a full-dress debate famous in American annals. Clay's initial outline and defense occupy less than three pages of the *Congressional Globe*. His set speech in February was four times as long, and into it he packed nearly every argument that could be mustered. The Kentuckian labored on his draft for days in rather close seclusion, taking no part in social activities, going to bed at ten o'clock, and conferring with but few of his colleagues.

While Clay put the finishing touches on his address, word spread through and beyond Washington that the delivery would be historic; so visitors flocked into the capital. The day finally came—a "brilliant and sparkling winter's morning." People of eminence, power, and fashion packed the Senate galleries and floor. Arrayed in their freshest and finest dresses, lovely ladies flounced up the Capitol steps with congressmen, diplomats and dandies for escorts. Marylanders, Philadelphians and New Yorkers climbed the Hill in high anticipation. The House of Representatives, adjourning, let its members swell the Senate audience. Newspaper correspondents bustled and whispered. Senators had trouble finding seats, some gallantly bowing wives and daughters of their associates into their chairs. A number clustered around the dais, to obtain the best view of all.

Clay had seemed in rather poor health that morning. Now, as he walked up the Hill from the National, he leaned on the arm of a friend, often pausing for breath or stopping to cough. Annoyed by a bad cold in December, he had not fully recovered. But, once he entered the Senate Chamber, Clay appeared remarkably fit for a man of his age and once-gay habits. After some preliminary business the graceful figure of the master rose. Exciting the crowd which craned forward eagerly for an unforgettable glimpse, he nervously but distinctly addressed the chair.[3]

"Never, on any former occasion," Clay opened, "have I risen under feelings of such deep solicitude. I have witnessed . . . periods of great anxiety . . . but I have never before" addressed an "assembly so oppressed, so appalled, so anxious." To what were the "dangers and difficulties" due? To "violence and intemperance of party spirit." It was to help "restore peace . . . quiet . . . harmony . . . happiness" that Clay had returned to Washington despite "private . . . inclinations." He had cut himself off from "social life" in order to find "some mode of accommodation" for dispelling the "menace to the . . . Union." Several general purposes seemed "to me most desirable." One was to "settle all . . . controverted questions" connected with slavery, rather than to solve *one* problem and leave others unadjusted. Another was to frame a scheme whereby neither South nor North "should . . . sacrifice . . . any great principle." Then, too, both sections should make "some concession, not of principle . . . but of feeling." Finally (and this Clay phrased none too clearly), the North should give in to the South on certain issues "without any compensation."

Regarding California's admission, Clay spoke with comparative brevity. "If slavery be interdicted by California, is it done by Congress, by this Government? No, sir; the interdiction is imposed by California herself." A state about to enter the Union "has a right to decide for itself whether it will or will not have . . . slavery." Here was "a case where neither party concedes." If Clay's argument was oversimplified, and one to which such Southerners as Davis would object, he chose not to elaborate—but passed to Resolution Number Two.

Here Clay was involved in a detailed exposition. For more than two hours he reviewed the issue as to whether "by law slavery no longer exists in . . . the acquisition . . . from . . . Mexico"—and whether "slavery never will be introduced" into it. "I have heard it said," Clay declared "that this . . . is equivalent to the . . . proviso." However, what Wilmot sought was a "positive enactment" by Congress, whereas all Clay desired was recognition of a *de jure* and *de facto* condition. Slavery had been abolished there by Mexico many years before, and the situation "remains unchanged until . . . altered by the . . . acquiring power." Moreover in California "slavery has been excluded by the . . . unanimous vote . . . of the convention." Many Monterey delegates originally hailed from slave-holding states. But all "concurred" in the decision, later confirmed by California voters "from all parts of the United States." Was it not logical that, if barred from California, slavery would be kept out of unproductive New Mexico?

Texas' boundary presented a "difficult and troublesome" problem. New Mexico's military government was "temporary . . . and inefficient." Embarking on this compromise phase, Clay gave way to adjournment late Tuesday—his conclusion to come the following day. Before the interruption, however, he stressed that, in reducing Texas' soil, he proposed to recognize her sovereignty from the Sabine to the mouth of the Rio Grande, thence to southernmost New Mexico and on "to the boundary between the United States and Spain" marked out in 1819. This vast terrain, nearly equal to what Texas "indisputably possessed before," was "sufficiently large . . . to carve . . . two or three additional States" when the population warranted this step. Was it not also fair to "pay a certain amount of the debt of Texas"—perhaps $3,000,000, perhaps more? "I should be greatly surprised if the people of Texas . . . hesitate . . . to accede" to such a proposition!

9

Resuming on the morrow, Clay tarried momentarily on the Texas debt before passing on to slavery and the slave trade in the District of Columbia. Attempting to satisfy Southern senators, he discussed the point—raised earlier by Foote—as to the constitutionality and expediency of abolishing slavery in the District. Congress *did* possess the power, Clay replied to the Mississippian, but it ought not to be exercised so long as slavery existed in near-by Maryland. Since Maryland had generously contributed soil to formation of the District, slavery's elimination would be tantamount to lifting "the sword" from Marylanders' bosoms to "strike at their own hearts." The resolution "neither affirms nor disaffirms . . . constitutionality." It "asks . . . both parties to forbear urging their respective opinions"—conceding "all that the South" should demand, "security for . . . property in slaves within the District." As to abolishing the *slave trade,* that was both constitutional and "acceptable" to slaveholders and nonslaveholders. "Why should the feelings of those . . . outraged . . . by . . . *corteges* . . . of manacled human beings" be aggravated by "the continuance of a trade . . . so repugnant"? Both sections should "rejoice to adopt" a concession lessening "the irritation and discontent."

In supporting his fugitive-slave resolution Clay took extreme Southern ground. The Supreme Court's decision in a recent case involving Maryland and Pennsylvania had been misrepresented, he was convinced. State legislation, "by which obstructions . . . have been thrown in the way of recovery of . . . slaves," was unconstitutional and "originated in a spirit which I trust will correct itself." The South had "just and serious cause of complaint against the free States," who failed to fulfill "a great obligation"—being "unneighborly" instead of "fraternal"—even seducing family servants away from masters who indulged them. Since existing laws for rendition of Negroes were "inadequate and ineffective," Congress should "assist in allaying this subject" and "make the laws more effective." Clay would "go with the farthest Senator from the South . . . to impose . . . heaviest sanctions upon . . . recovery of fugitive slaves and . . . restoration of them to their owners."

After a one-paragraph analysis of his eighth resolution Clay discussed the leading Southern alternative to the greater portion of his plan—extension of the Missouri Compromise line to the Pacific—sponsored by Davis among others. Davis said he wanted "positive recognition of slavery south of the line of 36° 30'." But did anyone suppose "you can get twenty votes" in favor of this? All Southerners could "expect to get" was action north of the line and "non-action, as regards slavery" south of it. Such an outcome would be "illusory." Nonaction in both sections would be "better for the South," Clay continued, "than . . . interdiction" in one without "action for admission" in the other. "I know it has been said . . . that non-legislation upon the part of Congress implies . . . exclusion of slavery. That we cannot help. . . . If nature has pronounced the doom of slavery in these territories . . . , who can you reproach but nature and nature's God?"

Like Taylor, Clay in conclusion appealed for the strengthening of the Federal Union—a Union now "threatened" with destruction. "I am . . . opposed to . . . secession" and separation, the venerable Compromiser cried. ". . . I am for . . . fighting for my rights . . . under the safeguard

of the Union." Dissolution and war "are identical and inseparable."
And what "an exterminating war would follow," the end product of
which would be the crushing of liberty in both sections! "I conjure gentlemen . . . by all they hold dear in this world—by . . . love of liberty—
by . . . veneration for their ancestors—by . . . regard for posterity—by
. . . the duties they owe . . . themselves—by all these considerations I
implore them . . . solemnly to pause—at the edge of the precipice, before
the . . . disastrous leap is taken into the yawning abyss below, which will
inevitably lead to . . . irretrievable destruction. . . . Finally . . . I implore,
as the best blessing" of Heaven, that "if the . . . dissolution of the Union
shall happen, I may not survive to behold the sad and heart-rending
spectacle."

10

So ended Clay's eventful argument—quoted here, at some length, because of the importance of so seasoned a politician's opinions. It and
Taylor's special message were the two springboards from which nearly
all Whigs—and most Democrats—leaped into the debate featuring
the final five months of the Taylor Administration. The right or wrong,
logic or illogic, and possible motivations behind Clay's position will be
treated in a later chapter. Other aspects, however, bear earlier discussion.

Oratorically Clay's speech was no masterpiece if judged by standards
prevailing in his era; with very occasional exceptions it lacked the rounded
periods and arresting phrases of a Webster or a Prentiss. The ingenious
philosophizing of a Calhoun or Jefferson were wanting. Repetitious as
to language (at times designed and effective), the address was hampered
by a monotony which only Clay's attractive personality could minimize
in delivery. Historians have frequently observed that Clay was not a
widely read man, and this limitation affected his style. He was, however,
richly experienced in the politics of compromise. And there is no question that his Unionism touched the heartstrings of many hearers, including some who could not accept the mode of compromise he blueprinted.
Clay's personal friends and political idolaters (who were numerous yet
never numerous enough to elect him to the White House) immediately
lauded his speech and plan, supported them at public meetings, and because of their fervor have led chroniclers to magnify Clay's influence on
the Senate. As the old man sinks into his seat and hears the plaudits of
the galleries, so sweet to the ears of a sensitive spirit, may not we too
settle down to appraise the effect of his effort on the Senate?

Precisely what senators had he influenced? Whom would he captain in the weeks to come? So supercharged with melodrama was the atmosphere that few interpreters have stopped to take a tally on the line-up of votes on Capitol Hill. We, like they, shall follow in detail the head-turning sentences, figures of speech, and philosophical niceties of the orators. But first it behooves the critically minded to grasp essentials in clear-cut terms of parties, factions, sections and individual preferences. The most significant and (to some) most astonishing fact is that Clay led no more than two Northern Whig senators during Taylor's Presidency. The exceptions to a total lack of such followers were Daniel Webster and James Cooper. (It might be added that Webster probably arrived at his conclusions more independently than otherwise, and that Cooper may have been influenced by Pennsylvania factionalism.)[4]

If we attribute the position of Webster and Cooper to Clay's effectiveness, it is utterly impossible to find any other Whig north of Delaware and Kentucky who sided with Clay in the Senate lists as long as Zachary Taylor lived. Davis of Massachusetts, Smith and Baldwin of Connecticut, Greene and Clarke of Rhode Island, Phelps and Upham of Vermont, Seward of New York, Miller and Dayton of New Jersey and Corwin of Ohio all followed Taylor—none followed Clay. Add to these, Spruance (who wavered) and Wales of Delaware and thirteen are found in Taylor's camp. Clay's only unconditional Southern Whig supporters were Kentucky's Joseph R. Underwood, Maryland's Thomas G. Pratt, North Carolina's Willie P. Mangum and George E. Badger,[5] and possibly Georgia's William C. Dawson. Berrien was veering away from Clay in the direction of Calhoun.[6] Jackson Morton of Florida, nominally a Whig, had been elected largely by Democratic votes and was aligned more with the Democrats than Whigs in Washington. Tennessee's Bell inclined toward Taylor's standard, while Pearce of Maryland seemed to swing toward Clay's.[7] Such is the true story of positions assumed by Whig senators in 1850. It shows—no doubt to the amazement of those who have heretofore accepted the oft-repeated tale of Clay's influence at face value—how *un*influential the Kentuckian was, insofar as the Whig position affected over-all Senate sentiment.

If Clay packed no punch where Senate Whigs were concerned, to what extent did he carry the guidon for "rival" Democrats? As we shall soon see, four fifths of his support came from such Democrats as Cass, Douglas, Foote, and Alabama's William R. King. Although many remarks we are about to study appear self-contradictory, it will become clear that a majority of Democrats backed Clay to the hilt. Some Democrats, to be sure, parted company toward the end.[8] Others, like Missouri's Benton and Maine's Hannibal Hamlin, announced their adherence to Taylor's Plan early, eloquently and with ardor. Still others, either following Calhoun or falling barely short of his stand, went along with Davis on the Missouri Compromise extension. Most Senate Democrats, however, trumpeted the Clay proposals when Whigs were silent or opposed.

Was this Clay's doing? Does he deserve credit for Democratic votes that came his way? Unfortunately for his fame there is little evidence that Democratic regulars would not have supported some such compromise, regardless of whether Clay sided with them. One discerning critic reached the formerly unorthodox opinion that Douglas was the real author of the Compromise of 1850, in the form it assumed later that same year. Should scholars not go farther and conclude that, with an exception here and there (perhaps as many as eight Whig votes), Clay brought no Senate strength to the compromise widely attributed to him? It was essentially a Democratic measure if its backers' identities provide a true yardstick. Aside from the Calhoun-Davis factionalists, its chief opponents were old-line, Eastern, long-conservative Whigs—the Baldwins, Phelpses, Millers, Uphams—whom historians have underplayed, just as newspapermen usually lose sight of Administration supporters in Congress.[9]

In the pages that follow attention will be given such dissident Democrats as Benton and Hamlin and such militant Free-Soilers as Chase and Hale. But Whig influence in championing Taylor's plan (and, conversely, in opposing Clay's) should constantly be borne in mind. Harkening to Houston, Hamlin and Berrien, let us remember that Taylor and his followers possessed the power Clay could not shake. Had they seen eye to eye with the Kentuckian and his new-found Democratic friends, there would have been no need whatever for a long-drawn-out debate. Convinced that the compromise was inadequate, Rough and Ready meant to fight along Jacksonian lines for the Union as he understood it—regardless of the consequences.

CHAPTER XXIII

President Taylor and the Senate Drama

1

Swinging into support of Clay was that Paul Bunyan of the Southwest, the robust, picturesque, courageous Sam Houston of Huntsville, Texas. A hero in the War of 1812 and a brilliant commander at San Jacinto, Houston had been wounded by Indians and Mexicans, tangled in a web of marital mystery, and worshiped by the people whose destiny he carved. He had lived with admiring Cherokees, who gave him the name of Co-lon-neh (The Raven). In his thirties he governed Tennessee, and twice he presided over Texas. One of his state's original senators, he cut an arresting figure on the floor, appealing to gawkers and hangers-on. Clad in outlandish clothes, his giant's bulk slouched in his chair, his gray eyes seemingly oblivious to tall talk going on about him, he liked to whittle on chunks of wood in the rear of the chamber while others spoke. Houston was a Jacksonian Democrat, a Unionist but also a Texan. Now he parted company with his old friend Benton, to string along with Jackson's enemy Clay and to oppose President Taylor.

Houston launched no frontal attack on Taylor. His backing of Clay was more implied than explicit. However, his words were the sort Clay applauded—especially those touching on fugitive slaves. When he rose to his majestic six feet two, and the fluttering womenfolk were admitted to hear him, Houston denied the power of Congress "to legislate upon the subject of slavery . . . in the Territories or . . . any other section." If majorities south of 36° 30′ (extended) "shall establish . . . or prohibit . . . slavery," their decision should "be deemed no objection to . . . admission of such . . . States." He regretted that Clay "questioned" Texas' "right to the . . . only . . . boundary . . . she ever asserted." But Houston was equally outspoken against Clemens' "extreme" remarks, opposing secession threats as vehemently as he assailed the Wilmot Proviso.

"No one feels a more sincere desire . . . to see . . . agitation . . . calmed," said Houston. Violent emotions, influencing Congress, should be "put to rest" immediately. And he himself was a Southerner—a Southerner but a Unionist, too! Had he not enlisted as "a private soldier," spilling his blood "in the centre of the South?" Houston's "southern heart" was "large enough . . . to embrace the whole Union, if not the whole world."[1] Then Houston enunciated a principle, which Abraham Lincoln would reiterate with a single variation years later: "A nation divided against itself cannot stand!" (The Gospel According to Saint Matthew was as familiar to Houston in '50 as to Lincoln in '58.)[2] The Senate applauded when Houston declared: "I wish, if this Union must be dissolved, that its ruins may be the monument of my grave. . . . I wish no epitaph . . . to tell . . . I survived the ruin of this Glorious Union."

2

The speaker following Houston, Georgia's John M. Berrien, keyed his remarks to a different pitch. A former judge and attorney general with a suggestion of Calhoun's approach to state rights, this Whig was cut off a conservative bolt—his manner cold, his method legalistic. In his youth, Berrien had been dubbed "the American Cicero." John Marshall described him as "honey-tongued," and Lucian Lamar Knight refers to his using "the court language of the Augustan age." However, Berrien at sixty-eight was less the spellbinder, less the stylist, more the courtroom technician. As a constitutional lawyer, he ranked with Webster, Calhoun and Choate. But, dry and dogmatic, he rarely allowed bright tones to tint his Southern slant.

Arguing that Georgians and Southerners generally were "a wronged and insulted people," Berrien depicted Northern aggression as "systematized and extended." The South, "aroused" by the "calculating . . . spirit" and "madness" of the Northerners, should appeal to the Supreme Court. The question was not slavery extension, but "whether a *slaveholder* . . . because *he was a slaveholder* . . . should be *excluded*" from the West. If a citizen's right "to remove with . . . slave property to a territory was ascertained," and obstructions appeared to exist there, anyone refusing to exercise constitutional power to eliminate "such obstructions," must "choose between . . . fealty to that Constitution, and . . . indulgence of his own speculative opinions." Such involved language was typically Berrienian, and he set out to document the "right" whereof he spoke.

Citing constitutional sources (and the international law expert, Emmerich von Vattel), Berrien insisted that slavery, once existing, "exists everywhere" until inhibited by a sovereignty within whose limits it comes. The Constitution conferred "no such power." No judicial decision or legislative precedent sustained it. *"If the Constitution . . . recognizes my title to the slave within my State, beyond my State, and within a sovereign State that inhibits slavery,* does it deny that title *within a territory that is the common property of the United States?"* Certainly not, and "Mexican laws" never could "extinguish it." Even if Congress possessed power to shut slaveowners out of the West, "would it be . . . consistent with good faith . . . to exercise that power?" Since Clay did not seek slavery's elimination from the District, "similar forbearance" seemed "at least equally . . . imperative" in a "more extended theatre." Northerners' promise to let the institution alone in fifteen states "is good" only "as far as it goes"; they should also cultivate tolerance toward the Southern concept of slavery in the West. "My best efforts," Berrien promised, "shall be employed to avert" disunion. Still, he owed allegiance to Georgia. "In weal or wo," he concluded, "the lot of her people shall be mine." Thus a Whig, long considered conservative and loyal to Clay in '48, stood up to be counted in a position far on the road toward John C. Calhoun's.

3

The day after Berrien finished, Jefferson Davis addressed the Senate. It is the fashion to think of Davis as a man of a merely "legal mind, autocratic and of little humor, who could dictate but . . . could not argue or listen." Scrutiny of his life reveals that, despite the manacles of self-discipline, he could be intensely human. The former Army lieutenant who wrote impassioned love letters sprinkled with wit and gaiety had developed his intellect for eight sad years on his plantation, until he had become one of the ablest and most scholarly of Southerners. No one understood slavery in its rosier aspects more clearly than this Mississippian, who worked out a patriarchal system of caring for the toilers on his land. *If* slavery could be ideal (which Northerners doubted), then it *was* ideal at Brierfield.

Thinking no doubt of his own Negroes, Davis described the transplanted Africans as "comfortable and happy" in the South. "Provided for in age and sickness," engaged in "useful employment," restrained from "vicious indulgences," they not only were "advancing in intelligence" but enjoyed "kindest relations" with their masters. What a contrast in the North, where colored men and women filled "penitentiaries and poor-houses"—"objects of scorn"—their children "excluded, in some places, from the schools." Yet Northerners urged that "beneficial"

slavery be supplanted by "evils" to the very race for which they claimed
to be solicitous. Slavery was less cruel than "any other relation of labor
to capital," Davis asserted with assurance and dignity.

Though Andy Johnson branded Davis a swaggering scrub-aristocrat,
the lean and graceful Mississippian seemed a Southern avatar. His military bearing, high cheekbones, symmetrical features and lofty, intellectual
brow distinguished him even in august company. If he shifted his stance
from time to time, it was to rest his wounded foot, for only recently had
he discarded the Buena Vista crutch and cane. His voice had a musical
tone. Black hair parted at the side, light-blue eyes shining with emotion,
he surveyed "the gathering storm." Against the "settled, selfish" attitude
of "revolutionary" Northern aggressors, Southerners claimed for their
institution only the protection accorded "every other species of property."
Neither section should have "power in Congress" to "trample" on the
other's rights. Northern control of the House should be balanced by a
Southern majority in the Senate. With legislation thus "restricted," no
encroachments could jeopardize either portion of the Union. "The reverse being the case, who knows how soon the time may come when men
will rise in arms to oppose the laws . . . ?"

The federal government was one of "limited" powers, Davis, like
Berrien, insisted. As a mere "agent" of the states, it could not prohibit
slavery in the West. "Sovereignty rests in the States," and no other
power "can exclude . . . property" from "Territories . . . held by the
States in common." Here was the fundamental state-rights principle, as
applied to the Mexican acquisitions, reduced to its least common denomi-
nator. The young and virile Davis' lucidity contrasting with Berrien's
lumbering approach, the Mississippian drove home his points with ham-
mer blows of precision logic.

Having done its part toward organizing the Western lands, the South
also had tried unsuccessfully to transfer the problem from Congress to
the Supreme Court. Yet "we are now told" that in California's case "we
ought not to object" to terms dictated by a "conglomerated mass of gold-
hunters, foreign and native." This so-called "decree of nature" was
worse than the Wilmot Proviso—the former denying the "existence . . .
of my rights," while the latter only tried "to rob me" of them. Davis
scorned congressional provision for "recovery of fugitive slaves," which
would "be a dead letter" wherever public opinion opposed it. Clay's
reference to the North's yielding "to the South far more than she re-
ceives" failed to convert the skeptical Davis. Concessions to the South
were conspicuous by their absence. Only a "substantial" proposition

was acceptable to one who said of his section: "Give her justice, sheer justice"—and "reliance" on her "will never fail you." "I dissent" from the "opinion," Davis continued, that "Nature . . . excluded . . . slavery . . . from . . . California and New Mexico"; slave economy was "adaptable" to "gold-washing," mining, and farming dependent on irrigation. Moreover he was convinced that the slave trade "was a blessing" to "the African." Brought "from a benighted region," sold "into a Christian land," the "descendant of the graceless son of Noah" . . . "entered the temple" of religion and culture "through the portal of slavery alone." Slavery was "established by decree of Almighty God"— is "sanctioned in the Bible . . . from Genesis to Revelations"—and "has been found among . . . people of the highest civilization." As for the Nashville Convention, it stemmed from "doctrines of Madison and Jefferson," which went back to the American Revolution and thence to green Runnymede. "If . . . necessary, we will claim from this Government, as the barons . . . claimed from John, the grant of another *magna charta* for our protection."

Davis' speech was exceedingly strong—perhaps the strongest he ever delivered. One cannot avoid the temptation to speculate on Taylor's reactions as the younger man rode up and down the line of declamation, forming his batteries to uphold the Southland Taylor loved only less than the Union itself. Davis, at one point, eloquently pledged his own devotion to the Union. But the Union's integrity through the years depended on the South's obtaining "justice." "If . . . seeds of disunion have been sown broadcast . . . , they have . . . not . . . been scattered . . . by . . . the South."[3] Guilty Northerners should bear in mind what a separate Southern nation would mean! Davis' words now anticipated those of William J. Bryan in '96 and Herbert C. Hoover in '32 (anent Free Silver and a high tariff).[4] "Grass will grow on . . . [your] pavements," he predicted, ". . . and . . . shipping will abandon your ports. . . . We who produce the great staple upon which your commerce and manufacturing rests, we will produce . . . staples still. . . . Shipping will fill our harbors," and the "ruins of Carthage"—"mouldering palaces of Venice"—"faded purple of Tyre" furnished precedents for Northern blights. Prevention depended on the Northern majority. The Southern minority could pass no measure; "therefore I have none to suggest." The South desired "permanent . . . security." California's "irregular" admission as a state definitely could *not* be accepted. Beyond this Davis would not specify. But he hinted several times that extension of 36° 30′ might do.

4

The next two orators in the Senate, Louisiana's Solomon W. Downs and New Jersey's Jacob W. Miller, could well have spoken from opposite poles. Had Downs lived till '61, he probably would have figured prominently in the epic story of the Stars and Bars. A native of Tennessee and (like Davis) an alumnus of Transylvania, he had been a state legislator, presidential elector, and United States district attorney, before entering the Senate as a Democrat from Taylor's adopted state. Downs's height, blue eyes, black curly hair, olive complexion and scarred left cheek gave him a bizarre and romantic appearance, which his illegitimate origin did nothing to offset.

If part of what Downs believed and said accorded with the principles of Davis and Berrien, the cotton planter from Ouachita Parish differed with them in seriously questioning Taylor's motives and methods respecting California. The Walker Amendment, Downs alleged, would have been passed in early '49 if Taylor's friends had not blocked and killed it. Walker's proposal might have set up a suffrage system "by competent authority" on California's disputed soil. Instead, an "ambassador," no less, had been dispatched "to exercise powers far more extraordinary than . . . could have been" granted by Congress. Wasn't this "ambassador," King, responsible for California's constitution? Surely, said Downs, it did not spring from "spontaneous" Western movements, but had been "concocted" elsewhere. "Extraordinary . . . and monstrous intrusions" had been made. As proof of the Taylorites' sinister intent he cited (in Clayton's instructions to King) "three disclaimers" of interference "in one short sentence." Aside from this, Downs's most intriguing point concerned his conviction that Pennsylvania would side with the South should war occur, and New England would not fight at all. Although Downs was a skilled debater, his presentation lost force because Davis and Berrien had covered much of the same ground. His California-Taylor remarks, however, were so explosive that clearly the President needed an out-and-out defender.

This first friend of the White House to make a set speech for the President's Plan is now as thoroughly forgotten as Downs. A Whig lawyer and former state lawmaker, with more than a local reputation at the bar and on the stump, Jacob Miller was about halfway through his second Senate term. Though still in middle life, he could count himself more familiar with congressional procedures than many an older colleague. He had displayed his talents to advantage in a debate with Cass, which influenced the Democrat to write the Nicholson Letter. Still it would be an error of judgment to claim too much for Miller's abilities. He was no Clay, no Davis, no Houston. The historian is permitted to wonder, however, whether such contributions as Miller's have been illogically obscured by the blazing reputations of better-known figures. It is likewise noteworthy that no oration truly reflecting Taylor's position has been given proper emphasis in general histories old or new.

Almost at once Miller denied that the North had committed "acts of aggression upon the . . . rights of the people of the slave States." The North had *not* violated the Constitution. Nor was it the North's object to overthrow slavery in the states, emancipate the slaves, or indulge in "usurpation . . . and oppression"—though this cry (raised by the South) daily "is . . . ringing in our ears." Quite candidly Miller acknowledged that he favored abolishing slavery in the District, but only *if* slaveholders there desired it. There was nothing new in the belief that Congress possessed "constitutional power to prohibit slavery in the territories." Back when "the Union was formed, the slave States . . . understood . . . they could not carry . . . slaves into . . . the then territories. . . . By a subsequent act of Congress, this exclusion was confirmed." No "inequality" lay hidden here. Southerners' slavery rights were "local"—"founded upon State institutions." But perhaps the question was academic, since "California has . . . taken the . . . proviso in her own hands, and relieved Congress from the difficulty which prevented action during the last two sessions." California should be admitted forthwith *as a state,* Miller of Morristown contended.

Miller then answered Downs's accusations regarding Taylor, Clayton and King. "It is gravely charged that the Executive coerced . . . or . . . persuaded the people of California to put in their constitution the prohibition of slavery. . . . No one who knows . . . the distinguished patriot . . . at the head of the Executive Department . . . would ever believe . . . he would . . . do" this. "In all his administration . . . there is no trick, no intrigue, no concealment." True, Miller granted, Zachary Taylor had sent a commissioner to California. But King was instructed "simply to recommend to the people of California to form a constitution for themselves." Thus Taylor carried out "the idea of Gentlemen of the South," as proposed in previous sessions. King's arrival in San Francisco postdated Riley's Monterey proclamation, and there was no "communication" between them. Indeed no "secret instructions" reached Riley from any source! Miller then trained his guns on Downs, who "said he had no

positive evidence" of his charges' truth, but "formed his judgment from
. . . circumstances." Because Clayton "directed the commissioner not to
interfere" in California politics, "the Senator infers . . . that he really
was directed to interfere!" "I never before heard it assumed," Miller
shot back, ". . . that if a man denies a charge three times . . . he therefore
admits it to be true." Would "a southern President" send "a slaveholder
from Georgia" to induce the Californians to keep slavery out? "How
preposterous!" Miller exclaimed.

Having replied to Taylor's critics and to Southerners accusing the
North of aggression, Miller went all-out for Taylor's Plan. The South
had long declared "that non-action is all she asked of the North—hands
off—let us alone; say nothing about slavery in the territories, and we are
satisfied." The Chief Magistrate "recommends that very policy," leaving
the issue of slavery with the people affected—to be "prohibited or admitted by them when they come into the Union as States." If the South
looked calmly at the President's proposition, Miller thought she would
accept it "as the true mode of settling this vexed question." Still there
was talk of resistance and disunion. What could the South gain thereby?
"Can you form a constitution in . . . the nineteenth century, which will
secure the . . . property . . . you wish to protect . . . more faithfully than
your present Constitution? No, sir! . . . Our ship of State . . . with such
a pilot . . . as we have now . . . will sail on and onward, through many a
stormy sea." As for Miller's own state of New Jersey, "her people will
stand by the Union, as they would stand by their . . . hearthstones, and
die in its defence."[5]

5

Miller's effort in Taylor's behalf, begun Thursday February 21, was
not completed till the following Monday. During the intervening period,
while Southerners gathered ammunition for their return to the attack, the
President himself drew his share of attention at a public appearance in
Virginia.

The occasion for Taylor's trip was the dedication of the cornerstone
for the Richmond monument to George Washington. Thursday morning, accompanied by George Washington Parke Custis and other friends,
Old Zack cruised down the Potomac on the steamer *Baltimore* to Aquia
Creek. Here he was met by a committee from the Virginia Legislature,
and with them he partook of a "fine collation" before boarding a special
train of the Richmond, Fredericksburg and Potomac Railroad. Passing

through Fredericksburg, Guiney's Depot, Mattapony, North Anna and Chickahominy, he reached Richmond at four in the afternoon. After alighting from his car "amidst enthusiastic cheers," the President took his seat in an open barouche drawn by four beautiful bays. With Virginia Military Institute cadets preceding him along the route, Taylor was driven past applauding throngs to the Capitol where Speaker Henry L. Hopkins formally addressed him.

"Mr. President," said Hopkins, ". . . to your person . . . is developed" an "advantage derived from our free institutions . . . in value, beyond *all price*. It is . . . that personal merit and a pure patriotism may elevate an unpretending man . . . to the most exalted post . . . known to the civilized world. For forty years you served your country in . . . camp and . . . field . . . and . . . we now behold the citizen President receiving the enthusiastic honors of his countrymen in the Capitol of his native State. In the name . . . of the House of Delegates, I salute you, and tender to you . . . a hearty welcome." Taylor modestly replied: "It cannot be expected that one whose time has been occupied in camps and in the field should be able, without reflection, to address such a . . . wise assembly. . . . But I . . . do, from the bottom of my heart, return to this . . . renowned Commonwealth . . . my sincere thanks for the high honor done me." The initial ceremony over, the President was escorted to his quarters at the Exchange Hotel. That evening he was feted at a "sumptuous" dinner, and toasted by the admiring company. Later, after "a large and brilliant party" at Governor John B. Floyd's "elegant mansion," Taylor retired early enough to rise the next day with the dawn.

The anniversary of Washington's birth found his eleventh presidential successor mingling early—as he loved to do—with farmers and shoppers at the market house. There he demonstrated anew that "highest honors have not turned his head. . . . He is the same man now . . . as when . . . a Lieutenant." At the market Taylor "entered into familiar conversation with the persons about," none of whom at first recognized him. But when someone whispered his identity, the whisper—"gaining ground"— induced "the old gentleman to move off without taking leave." Whereupon the planter President strolled back to his hotel.

Zachary Taylor's presence in Richmond drew thousands of people from the countryside and necessitated elaborate arrangements. While the parade was being formed, Masons, Odd Fellows and Sons of Temperance took their posts near the military units on Main Street, and Ex-President John Tyler joined Taylor to honor Washington's memory. According to a newspaperman, "it was the greatest crowd ever seen in this city." The *Times* reported that the line of march was the longest in the seven hills' history. Before the procession arrived at the Square, all the seats set up for spectators had been filled. "A . . . mass of human beings pressed closely to the spot, whilst a vast number occupied the grounds near the Capitol and . . . City Hall." A space having been cleared around a big circular pit dug to hold the cornerstone, Governor Floyd, with Taylor on one arm and Tyler on the other, advanced to the designated spot. Here Floyd halted, while Taylor and Tyler ascended a high platform "erected in the centre of the great walk." There followed the rites traditionally performed by Freemasons on such occasions. Records were placed in a "large nether stone," upon which the granite capstone was lowered, Floyd helping to adjust it. Robert G. Scott, Masonic orator of the day, was followed to the rostrum by the Governor, who made "appropriate allusions" to Taylor and Tyler, sitting near him. "The reference to General Taylor elicited the most enthusiastic cheers." When the President was introduced, he "spoke a few unpretending sentences," received "in the spirit of . . . sincerity with which he uttered them." Unassumingly Old Zack voiced "the pride" he felt in looking upon Virginia as his native heath. In his long absence, the Old Dominion "never caused him to forget that she was his mother." Taylor then reviewed the V.M.I. students in a march-past at the Capitol's northern front. He also attended gatherings at Military Hall and Stuart's Factory, witnessed the fireworks touched off at Gamble's Hill and in the Capitol Square and finally lent his presence to a "splendid Masonic Ball" at the Union Hotel.

Complimentary remarks were made publicly and privately during Taylor's Virginia stay. "There was so much plainness . . . simplicity . . . kindness . . . about him, that one person remarked . . . he had seen nothing like it . . . since the days of John Marshall. . . . Others . . . expressed a fervent wish that every man in Virginia could . . . converse with him. . . . He evidently felt much pleased at the reception . . . , and his good humor communicated itself to all." (Thus the leading organ of Taylor's party.) Democrats were considerably less enthusiastic, and John Tyler dryly observed to his son: "Gen. Taylor . . . mistook all the demonstrations of popular feeling as evidences of his popularity, in . . . which he was in great error."

Tyler and the Democratic journalists were perfectly entitled to their opinions, but the fact that Virginians differed as to Taylor's popularity suggested his program was less widely detested than some Southern rhetoricians supposed. Although the President carefully said nothing that might offend his Richmond hosts, Tyler found him "quite communicative" in private conversations, and it is presumed that—if approached on the subject—he probably reaffirmed his attitude toward the integrity of the Union. It was not until Saturday, however, that Taylor again gave strong public utterance to the major conviction of his life. At Fredericksburg which he reached shortly after noon he again acknowledged compliments showered by Virginians on his patriotic services. "As to the Constitution and the Union," Taylor said, "I have taken an oath to support the one and I cannot do so without preserving the other, unless I commit perjury, which I certainly don't intend to do. We must cherish the Constitution to the last. There . . . will be local questions to disturb our peace; but, after all, we must fall back upon" Washington's "farewell advice, and . . . preserve the Union at all hazards." Taylor returned at nightfall to Aquia Creek and the *Baltimore*. The run up the Potomac took two hours and a half of a bright and pleasant evening. As the vessel tied up at the Washington wharf, guests paid "their parting respects to the President"—who then drove off to the White House and a distraught nation's business. Among those accompanying him on the brief excursion were Edward D. Baker and Robert S. Garnett, both destined to die in action in Virginia—one a Union, the other a Confederate, commander—in the first half year of the Civil War.

Though evidence is lacking as to Taylor's manner in delivering his important Fredericksburg sentiments, it was unstrained enough to invoke "laughter" when he said he did not "intend to . . . commit perjury." There is no record of smiles or nudgings, however, when he exhorted his fellow Southerners to *"preserve the Union at all hazards."* This, the keynote of Taylor's philosophy, was more consequential than any part of the Richmond ceremonial. The cornerstone of Miller's remarks in the Senate, it was part and parcel of the policy enunciated by Taylor at Mercer and also in his messages. Albert J. Beveridge once concluded: "Taylor might as well not have spoken. Nobody paid the slightest attention to what he said."[6] But from letters penned in Washington throughout this period, as well as from the Great Debate, it is clear that Whigs and Democrats paid attention aplenty to the Unionist convictions of Zachary Taylor.

6

The New Orleans *Picayune's* Washington correspondent stressed the importance of Taylor's position. Northern congressmen, he observed, "do not seem inclined to go further than . . . embrace Gen. Taylor's proposition." The South "will not assent to that." "I am . . . delighted to hear that 'Old Zack' talks with . . . Jacksonian emphasis of his inflexible purpose to maintain the Union, at all hazards, against all foes," Clay's friend, Stevenson, exclaimed to Orlando Brown; ". . . I want you to book me in Old Rough's roll, as a volunteer in any fight he may have on that question." Seward wrote Weed on February 2: "I saw the P. on Friday. . . . I told him that . . . faction would run into sedition" but "that he would be re-elected the Savior of the Union—He understands himself and us." One of Fillmore's cronies criticized the Albany Journal's "fulsome laudation of . . . Taylor & his platform." But another Fillmoreite admitted: "I much prefer the course pointed out by Gen Taylor," and "regret . . . to see" that Clay "has taken a different cou[r]se." Minnesota's delegate advised Governor Ramsey: "Mr. Clay's speech has done no good towards quieting the public feeling. It is denounced by the South, and does not satisfy the North." A Weed henchman thought "Clays compromise . . . as dead as herrings that are red. He has offended the South without appeasing the North—He should retire from that kind of business." Brown wrote Crittenden that, "while threats . . . are the order of the day & unfeigned apprehension for the most disastrous conclusion is on the increase, the President . . . is as calm . . . and determined as a great & good & brave man alone can be on the eve of momentous events in which he may be . . . the most conspicuous actor."

How widely Clay and Taylor differed was not crystal-clear to all observers. The Washington *Republic,* under Bullitt's editorship, complimented Clay in such a way as to confuse many readers: "While . . . the plan recommended by President TAYLOR is the most practicable . . . and . . . meets with most general favor . . . , the speech of Mr. CLAY cannot fail to exercise a most salutary influence upon public sentiment." The Baltimore *American* discerned "no essential discrepancy" between "views expressed in Mr. Clay's resolutions and those set forth in President Taylor's message." The New York *Post* asserted, however, that Clay's proposals "differ wholly from those . . . announced in General Taylor's message." The Washington *Union* approved Clay's idea of "saying grace over the whole barrel" in contrast to "Taylor's dilatory, temporizing, timorous policy." Most of the "regular" Democratic papers lined up behind Ritchie in praise of Clay, while a majority of Whig journalists in the North—and some in the South—opposed Clay and backed Taylor. This development, similar to the course of Whig and Democratic senators, has likewise received inadequate notice in most of the history texts.

With Clay looming as the champion of a Democratic-supported compromise, and Taylor carrying the standard of Union-at-all-hazards men, Capitol tempers grew more frayed. "Any one present in the House last night would have seen in the spectacle . . . the beginning of the end," a conservative Southerner wrote in mid-February. ". . . About fifty Southern members" made motions "with a view to prevent the main question. . . . Neither party would give way. The geographical line was strictly drawn. . . . Thus the struggle between . . . North and South has commenced in earnest. . . . It is not intended by the South . . . that any appropriation bill shall . . . pass. . . . I have no idea that the House will transact . . . business until the territorial question be settled. . . . Next June or July . . . the House will become . . . jaded and maddened, and will break up in a row, perhaps with violence."

"The breach is widening," a Minnesotan feared. The "apprehension . . . that a separation of the Union would take place . . . is now universal." Yes, blood might be "spilt in the Halls of Congress before the end of the Session." Clemens and Foote "produced quite a panic . . . by declaring that, unless something was very soon done, events . . . would render a dissolution of the Union certain."[7] With Clingman declaring the South ready for disunion, and James Buchanan advising the South that "the Eastern people" would "back out" of "the crisis" despite "long continued agitation," a Mississippi representative predicted his section would grasp its rights by armed occupation—if not granted them by nonintervention. Southerners, meanwhile, appointed delegates to the Nashville Convention. Edward Everett of Massachusetts wrote: "There never was a period when the continuance of the Union seemed to me so precarious." Seward referred to the "national and legislative crisis." Soon after Taylor's return to Washington a "difficulty" took place between Senators Borland and Foote in front of the *Intelligencer* office. Foote baited his fellow Democrat with "a few words" about "servile" followers of Calhoun, which Borland felt reflected on himself. A scuffle ensued, Borland hitting Foote in the face. Finally Borland apologized. But the incident was "to be regretted," the more so because the two men were "friends."

Another quarrel, with serious implications, involved Jefferson Davis and William H. Bissell. Bissell offended Davis by asserting in the House that the Mississippi regiment was a mile away from the Mexicans at a critical hour in the Battle of Buena Vista. When Davis (ever proud of his military record) demanded a retraction from the Illinois veteran,

Bissell refused. Davis challenged him to a duel, and the hostile parties were preparing for bloodshed when President Taylor stepped into the controversy. According to Taylor each antagonist referred to a different phase of the battle and no cause for disagreement existed. Satisfactory explanations were then exchanged, and lethal weapons at dawn avoided.[8] *Opera bouffe?* By hindsight, surely. Yet, in the climate of vituperation, sensible men felt hot blood surging and hearts pounding in anger.

7

In this crisis period, Stephens, Toombs and Clingman went to the White House for a stormy interview. Urging Taylor to favor California's admission on Clay's terms, they succeeded only in convincing him that their alternative was disunion. Hannibal Hamlin entered the President's office upon the Southerners' departure. He found Taylor pacing the floor, agitated and "indignant." According to Hamlin the President told him the three Whigs intimated that, unless their demand was met, the South would not "submit." Taylor then declared that, if Southern leaders and people carried out treasonable demonstrations, he would exert the whole power of the government to snuff out rebellion in any form, even if obliged to head the Army himself. Taylor was still walking briskly to and fro when Thurlow Weed, the next caller, arrived. "Did you," the President asked with an oath, "did you meet those traitors?" In strong language Taylor related what had taken place. The Southerners "came, he said, to talk . . . about his policy upon pending slavery questions. . . . Informed that he would approve any constitutional bill that Congress might pass, and execute the laws of the country, they threatened a dissolution of the Union." Taylor replied that, if necessary, "he would take command of the army"—and "if they were taken in rebellion against the Union, he would hang them with less reluctance than he had hung deserters and spies in Mexico!"

Clingman, Toombs and Stephens were less typical of the over-all Whig reaction to the Taylor-Clay division than Whigs of the Senate or Whigs of the press. A contemporary who stumbled near a comprehension of the true Senate alignment was a Democrat with a funny name, L. Q. C. Elmer of New Jersey. In his book of reminiscences Elmer tells of his visit to Washington in the early spring of '50: "I saw, with . . . amazement, Miller and Dayton, and most of the other Whig members, following the lead of Mr. Benton . . . while most of the Democrats were just as implicitly following the lead of Mr. Clay. I could not help . . . congratulating Mr. Miller on his very remarkable choice of a leader. . . . He replied with very good humor, that it certainly was an unlooked for change, but circumstances had rendered it necessary."

Elmer failed to discern that the real leadership lay not in the hands of Benton and Clay, but in Taylor's and the Democratic chieftains'. Superficially it did seem incongruous for Clay to side with the Democrats, and for Benton to act with the Whigs. In fact, this was as natural as nature— in view of the "circumstances" to which Miller referred. The first session of the Thirty-first Congress marked a historic switch in political fealties, when ideas and ideals related to slavery were beginning to overlap partisanship. Taylor, however, was unaffected by sectional ties prominent in the positions so many men took. Elmer grasped this when, accompanying Miller, he was introduced to Old Zack at the White House. "After a polite reception the President commenced talking to Mr. Miller very rapidly, and with considerable excitement in reference to the proceedings in the senate, and declared himself in favor of admitting California without terms, and opposed to Mr. Clay's propositions."[9] As long as Taylor lived, the President and Clay remained thus diametrically opposed—and the President and most Democrats likewise.

CHAPTER XXIV

THE GREAT DEBATE; THE SEVENTH OF MARCH

1

THUS, with sectional loyalties hardening, the debate in the U. S. Senate continued—usually echoing the vehemence outside, and sometimes concentrated on a single issue. Sixty-seven-year-old John C. Calhoun had hoped to present his views to the chamber a day or two after Miller finished. However, Calhoun felt unequal to the effort. Tuberculosis racked his frame. A cruel cough lacerated his lungs. Remaining in his quarters, the dying lion attempted to recruit his strength, while his friend, Texas' Thomas J. Rusk, held the floor for two days running.

On March 4 a hush enveloped the Senate as Calhoun painfully teetered to his feet. The Carolinian had been handsome. When Rusk first knew him, his bushy hair was brown, and he walked with a long, loose-jointed stride. Though he still was tall, now shoulders sagged, and faltering steps betrayed debility. Gray hair falling in profusion over his wrinkled forehead, eye sockets cavernous, face pinched by disease, Calhoun's dour mien was reminiscent of Andrew Jackson's in those grim moments when Rachel's honor was impugned.

Once Calhoun had been a nationalist, sponsoring internal improvements, rationalizing high tariffs, his name linked in voters' minds with the Websters and the Clays. Deprecating "refined arguments on the Constitution," which "was not intended as a thesis for the logician to exercise his ingenuity on," he had thought "the instrument . . . ought to be construed with plain good sense."[1] Yet, beginning in the late 1820s, no other political philosopher interpreted the Constitution more ingeniously or interminably, no other rhetorician spun more syllogisms on it, than this erstwhile pragmatist. Nearly as fanatical in defense of state rights as Garrison was in opposing slavery, Calhoun was the intellect, conscience, inspiration behind some of the most brilliant Southern thought and theory. Humorless, severe, disciplined, opinionated, he had been termed "cast-iron" by Harriet Martineau, and Mrs. Jefferson Davis described him as "a moral and mental abstraction." Now this "incarnation of the wrath of God" looked burned out, like the ash of a man, as,

302

swathed in flannels, he said that illness forced him to ask a friend to read his speech.

With Calhoun sitting directly in front of him, and Calhoun's manuscript before his eyes, the round-faced, fiftyish Mason of Virginia intoned his plain, incisive sentences. "The Union is in danger," the sick man began. ". . . How can the Union be preserved?" The answer hinged on the "character of the cause"—the *"immediate* cause" being the South's "almost universal discontent." The *roots* of this unrest lay in "the belief of the people of the southern States . . . that they cannot remain, as things now are, consistently with honor and safety, in the Union." Long-continued agitation on the part of the North had much to do with this conviction. But destruction of the sectional "equilibrium" was the "great and primary" reason for it. In the republic's early days, this equilibrium—"nearly . . . perfect"—afforded each section "ample means" to protect itself against "aggression." Now, however, one could "control . . . the Government"—while the other was unable to prevent "encroachment." Yes, and the '50 census would add to this "decided preponderance." If Western lands were brought in free, ten more years would see forty Northerners in the Senate as against twenty-four men from the South.

Legislation, not natural change, produced the imbalance, Calhoun charged. First the Ordinance of 1787, then the Missouri Compromise and recently the formation of Oregon Territory excluded the South from almost 1,125,000 square miles of the states' "common territory." The system of revenue and disbursements was also unfair to Southerners. Duties from imports fell on exporting states, and the North got a "greater portion of the revenue . . . than its due share." The added capital increased the North's population by "attracting emigrants." Thus the strength of one section swelled through its "disproportionate" growth. Worst of all, in Calhoun's eyes, was Washington's assumed "right" to determine the extent of its own authority. With the North dominating political machinery, how could "separate . . . States . . . protect the powers reserved to them"? Was there no constitutional means? If not, "the character of the Government has been changed . . . from a Federal Republic . . . into a great national consolidated Democracy."

Disunion could not be effected by a single blow, Calhoun's manuscript continued. Only a "long process" could sever spiritual, political and social cords. But some already had been broken by the "slavery agitation." The Methodists and Baptists had each divided along sectional lines into "hostile bodies." The Presbyterians were parting company, and now the Whigs and Democrats fared no better than the churches. If Northern "agitation goes on, the same force . . . will . . . snap every cord." Then "nothing will be left to hold the States together except force." But such an arrangement was no Union. *Subjugation* was the name for it! If ancient bonds could not save the Union, eulogies must prove inadequate. The cry of "Union, Union, the glorious Union!" could no more prevent disunion than the cry of "Health, health, glorious health!" by a physician could save a patient. Nor was Union salvation to be gained from invoking the name of George Washington. He was "one of us—a slaveholder and a planter," who grew to manhood under another "Union." When the colonies were oppressed, however, "he did not hesitate to draw his sword"—and this was Washington's "crowning glory."

Calhoun barely mentioned Clay's resolutions, but Taylor's Plan drew his prolonged attention. "The Executive proviso," as Calhoun called it, was "unconstitutional, unjust," and calculated to "destroy irretrievably the equilibrium between the . . . sections." Making California and New Mexico states was more "objectionable" than what Wilmot desired. The latter acted "directly and openly," whereas Taylor's crowd schemed "indirectly and covertly." Calhoun questioned the assumption that California residents possessed the inherent right of self-government. "The United States . . . conquered California, and finally acquired it by treaty." Therefore, the power of legislation was vested in Congress, not in the Californians, who were led into a "rebellious" act by Taylor's "Executive branch." Through Mason, Calhoun asked: "Can you believe that there is such a State . . . as the State of California? No; there is no such State. It has no legal or constitutional existence." If California was not to be admitted, what might be done with her? "Remand her back to the territorial condition," Calhoun recommended, "as was done in the case of Tennessee, in the early stage of the Government."

As Mason read, Calhoun sat motionless as stone. The iron Ulster will held sway over physical infirmities. "Not a change passed over his face," the observant Charles A. Dana reported. ". . . With eyes partly closed and head never wavering," Calhoun waited for "the last word before he exchanged a glance with . . . friends around."

Now Mason neared the end of the discourse, reading Calhoun's demands on the North. First, he said, the South should be given "an equal right in the acquired territory." Fugitive-slave stipulations must be "faithfully fulfilled," and the North should "cease . . . agitation of the slave question"—a large order in itself. Finally Calhoun called for a constitutional amendment, restoring to the South "the power she possessed of protecting herself, before the equilibrium . . . was destroyed." Though he failed to define his amendment's terms, he did insist that it be adopted—and this amounted to an ultimatum. "We, as the representatives of the States of this Union," Calhoun concluded, ". . . should come to a distinct understanding . . . in order to ascertain whether the great questions . . . can be settled." If the North will not "settle them on the broad principle of justice and duty, say so; and let the States . . . separate. . . . If you are unwilling we should part in peace, tell us so, *and we shall know what to do.* . . . If you remain silent, you will compel us to infer by your acts what you intend. In that case, *California will become the test question.* If you admit her . . . you compel us to infer that you intend to exclude us from the whole of the . . . territories, with the intention of destroying irretrievably the equilibrium. . . . *We would be blind not to perceive, in that case, that your real objects are power and aggrandizement, and infatuated not to act accordingly."*

2

In the initial reply to Calhoun, Hannibal Hamlin served notice that some Democrats—as well as Whigs—refused to play the game according to Calhoun's rules, or even Clay's. On March 5 the Maine man became the first New Englander to join in the full-dress Senate debate. Like Miller he enthusiastically supported Taylor. Tall and muscular, the swarthy Hamlin might have passed for a mulatto or an outsize son of the dark but shorter Daniel Webster. He was not exactly handsome but commanding in appearance in a rough-and-tumble, big-fisted, big-featured, manly sort of way. His struggle up from obscurity as surveyor, journalist, teacher and lawyer had led him to two terms in the House— and in '48 to his Senate entrance. And how the stand taken by the forty-year-old from Penobscot County must have gratified the Administration!

Hamlin lost no time in wading waist-deep into the debate. California, he said, ought to enter the Union without delay. Irrelevant subjects somehow had found their way into the oratory; territorial governments, the Texas boundary and restoration of fugitives complicated the discussion, which should be limited to essentials. There was one issue properly before the Senate: California's admission. Hamlin accused Calhoun and Berrien of advocating, in the previous Congress, the very methods used at Monterey. Yes, Berrien had asserted: "The power conferred . . . on

Congress is to admit new States, not to create them. . . . Creation of a
State is an act of popular sovereignty. . . . It is by the will of the people
. . . assembled in convention . . . that it is created." And Calhoun had
said: "I hold it to be . . . fundamental . . . that the people have a right
to establish what government they may think proper. . . . Every State,
about to become a member of this Union, has a right to form its own
government. . . . There is but one qualification, and that is the government shall be republican."

What changed the minds of these elder statesmen who now deplored
what they formerly approved? In '48 and '49 the South had tried to
insert a proslavery clause in California's constitution. Now the situation
was altered, and neither Calhoun nor Berrien enjoyed the irony of events.
They were apologists, Hamlin implied, evolving doctrines to meet immediate needs and abandoning them when it suited their purposes. He
also tore into Calhoun's testimony regarding Tennessee. Calhoun failed
to look closely into the record; Tennessee had never been remanded. But
even more pertinent than the Tennessee precedent was Hamlin's praise
of California's people. Worthy and intelligent men "have come here
asking us to admit them into this Union." "That, sir, is the question for
our decision," he trumpeted with the confidence of a Marine Band
bugler. "I have no doubt" that California's star "is to stud with other
stars our national flag."

If perhaps it is understandable that students have ignored Miller's
position, the overlooking of Hamlin's speech is almost beyond comprehension. Not only did Hamlin go on to new prominence as Lincoln's
running mate in 1860, but throughout the intervening decade he loomed
as an antislavery stalwart in New England and Washington. Hamlin's
performance as a verbal archer was of championship quality. The barbs
he let fly at Calhoun's brief found their mark more than once. If Calhoun's words are reported in detail, is it fair or balanced to by-pass
Hamlin? Should this Democrat's decision to follow Taylor receive the
briefest (if any) mention? The meeting of Clay, Calhoun and Webster
in the Senate Chamber for the final time has so captured Americans' imaginations that only a few are aware that other actors were not pygmies.
Vital insight can also be gained from differences in opinion and language
expressed by the Hamlins, Rusks and Davises. Calhoun, Clay and Webster should continue to be stressed, but nothing can be allowed to interfere with restoring the entire scene's perspective. Let this be borne
constantly in mind, as the basic pattern of debate is rounded out by
Webster, Seward and Douglas.

3

As a superfine oratorical gem, no other address of 1850 excelled Webster's silvery sentences. Like Clay's speech Webster's was resoundingly
heralded up and down the Atlantic Seaboard and out along the National
Road. Isaac P. Walker of Wisconsin held the Senate floor on Wednesday March 6, and was scheduled to conclude Thursday afternoon. However, he graciously gave way to Webster.[2] Thus, due to the courtesy of
this Milwaukee lawyer (whose own florid remarks were of doubtful
significance), the Great Debate's most memorable oration is known as
the Seventh—not Eighth—of March Speech.

We have seen Webster in '48 as a would-be and disappointed presidential candidate. Then he appeared bereft and pathetic. Now, however, he was utterly different—and he felt as thoroughly at home in
Washington as on his seaside acres at Marshfield. Sixty-eight years old
that winter, Webster was perhaps the supreme parliamentary orator in
the history of the United States. Webster's health was poor in '50. Suffering from insomnia, he lived under the influence of drugs. Yet his
personality remained powerful and winning. And the crowds, cramming
the corridors, and clamoring for admittance to the galleries, remembered
that Webster's "air of Imperial strength" had been compared to Julius
Caesar's, his eyes to great "anthracite furnaces," his mouth to a mastiff's
and his cadences to thunder. And so he spoke "not as a Massachusetts
man, nor as a northern man, but as an American. . . . I speak to-day for
the preservation of the Union. 'Hear me for my cause.' "

With the attention of his audience riveted on him Webster pictured
"imprisoned winds" as "loose"—endangering "our institutions" of government. "The East, the West, the North, and the stormy South . . .
throw the whole ocean into commotion . . . and . . . disclose its pro-
foundest depths. I do not . . . regard myself . . . as fit to hold . . . the
helm in this combat of . . . political elements; but . . . I speak to-day,
out of a solicitous . . . heart," for restoring quiet and harmony. In a
rapid review of recent history, including the Mexican War and gold's
discovery, Webster reached the California constitution—the antislavery
provision in which had been passed unanimously. Thus Southerners like
Gwin had approved of the Monterey prohibition, which was part of the
cause of the whole vexatious question's coming "upon us for a fresh
discussion."

Launching into an analysis of slavery's status ancient and modern,

Webster was reminded that the Hebrews, Greeks and Romans justified it. There was "no injunction" against it in "the teachings of Jesus Christ." Northerners now believed, however, that it was not "kindly affectioned." It did not let "the oppressed go free." Thoughts like these had taken hold of Northern religious sentiment. But many Southerners, who could not "see the unlawfulness of slavery," were "just as conscientious" as Northerners holding different opinions. Condemning emotionalists and referring to rifts in the church denominations, Webster said such cleavages were developed by persons to whom slavery seemed absolute—absolutely wrong or absolutely right. Such men thought right could be distinguished from wrong "with the precision of an algebraic equation." They dealt with morals as with mathematics—too impatient to wait for "the slow progress of moral causes in the improvement of mankind." They were the sort who forgot that "the doctrines and miracles of Jesus . . . have, in eighteen hundred years, converted only a small portion of the human race."

The Senator from Massachusetts also recalled that earlier Americans considered slavery less a moral than a political evil. This was as true in the South as in the North. Blight, blast, mildew, scourge and curse were words Southerners selected to describe the institution. Back in 1787 the congress set up by the Articles of Confederation did its utmost to curtail slavery's spread. The Northwest Ordinance bore the "hand and seal" not of a mere majority but "of every southern member." Since then opinions "changed North and changed South," said Webster—his manner deceptively calm and his facts deployed before him like riflemen on patrol. He imputed to the South "no particularly selfish view." Through prosperity based on cotton, there had come "a new desire to promote slavery, to spread it and to use its labor." Had not measures contributing to this result been brought about by Southern men, who took "the general lead in the politics of the country"? Louisiana, Florida and Texas were annexed—and slavery planted in most of the land included in these annexations. Moreover, in the case of Texas, more slave states could be carved from it if the Texans so desired.

"As to California and New Mexico, I hold slavery to be excluded" there "by a law even superior to that which . . . sustains it in Texas—I mean the law of nature," Webster declaimed. Yes, "the law . . . of the formation of the earth" decreed "with a strength beyond all terms of human enactment that slavery cannot exist in California and New Mexico." These storied regions were "composed of vast . . . mountains, of enormous height, with broken ridges and deep valleys. The sides of these mountains are . . . entirely barren—their tops capped by perennial snow." Webster backtracked a little when he admitted that "no doubt there are . . . in California . . . some tracts of valuable land." But "it is not so in New Mexico." If "a resolution . . . were now before us, to provide a territorial government for New Mexico, I would not vote to put any prohibition into it whatever." The use of such an antislavery clause would be "idle." There followed a classic example of Webster's ability to restate in rhythmic prose the ideas and expressions of others: "I would not take pains to reaffirm an ordinance of nature, nor to re-enact the will of God." No such wound as the Wilmot Proviso should be inflicted on anybody "unless something essential . . . to the country, and efficient to the preservation of . . . freedom, is to be effected," he said.

Webster now detailed the grievances which each section held against the other, excepting only Calhoun's charge that "the North has grown upon the South in consequence of the manner of administering this Government, in the collecting of its revenue, and so forth." This topic was so "disputed" and intricate that he had "no inclination" to enter into it. The one really justifiable complaint was that of the South regarding fugitives. "In that respect, it is my judgment that the South is right, and the North is wrong." As to other disputed matters, each side was at fault in some degree. To the extent that they were founded "in matters of opinion, in sentiment, in mutual crimination and recrimination, all we can do is . . . endeavor to allay the agitation, and cultivate . . . more fraternal sentiments."

Moving into his peroration, and with the gaunt Calhoun now present to hear him, Webster said he heard the word "secession" with pain. "Secession! Peaceable secession! . . . Who is so foolish . . . as to expect . . . any such thing?" Webster ridiculed the very notion. "Where is the line to be drawn?" he asked. "What States are to secede? What is to remain American? What am I to be?—an American no longer?" Webster was ashamed to pursue this line of comment. "I would rather hear of . . . war, pestilence, and famine, than . . . hear gentlemen talk of secession. . . . To break up this great Government! to dismember this great country! to astonish Europe with . . . such . . . an act of folly . . . ! No, sir! no, sir!" There was no such thing as peaceable secession. "I see it as plainly as I see the sun in heaven . . . that disruption must produce . . . war"—and it would be "such a war as I will not describe."

Instead of speaking of the possibility or utility of secession [Webster closed], instead of . . . groping with . . . ideas so full of all that is horrid and terrible, let us . . . enjoy the fresh air of liberty and union; let us . . . devote ourselves to . . . great objects . . . fit for our consideration and . . . action; let us raise our conception to the magnitude . . . of the duties that devolve upon us; let our comprehension be as broad as the country for which we act, our aspirations as high as its certain destiny. . . . Let us make our generation . . . the brightest link, in the golden chain . . . destined . . . to grapple the people of all the States to this Constitution, for ages to come. . . . This Republic now extends . . . across the . . . continent. The two great seas of the world wash the one and the other shore. We realize on a mighty scale . . . the beautiful description of the ornamental edging of the buckler of Achilles—

> "Now the broad shield complete the artist crowned,
> With his last hand, and poured the ocean round;
> In living silver seemed the waves to roll,
> And beat the buckler's verge, and bound the whole."[3]

If any element aside from pessimism and outright support of Taylor or Calhoun was notably absent from the Seventh of March Speech, it was the quality of specification as to *means* to be employed. Webster praised the Union and warned against tampering with the "golden chain." But only rarely and then vaguely did he say *how* the Union might best be buttressed along legislative lines. Many a Whig and not a few Democrats had anticipated something more concrete. Some assumed that Clay's program was foredoomed to failure; hence Webster might fashion a *better* compromise. Glittering as they were, his recommendations consisted mainly of generalities. To change the figure, he diagnosed the ailment, warned against poisons and panaceas but hesitated to prescribe the cure.

Why did Webster not go into detail, regarding proposals, as Clay had done? The reason is evident. No doubt he acted as Clay and he had agreed he should act. Since the old Whig leaders were allied on fundamentals, what could be more logical than for Webster to give abstract support to Clay's plan, instead of inaugurating one of his own? The two had conferred in private. What each told the other has not been revealed. But the upshot was that Webster lent tone, a conciliatory air and ringing affirmations to Clay's less flashy arguments. Webster thus supplemented Clay, and together they contributed to the compromise cause qualities which the Democrats lacked. Therefore, the address of "Black Dan" was more than a vehicle for aphorisms. It packed an oratorical wallop, though it changed few—if any—votes in the Senate.

4

The nation's reaction to Webster's words has been variously interpreted. One school is awed by antislavery attacks. The other stresses
conservatives' approval.[4] In Webster's time there could be no question
as to the fury of cannonading from abolition guns. William Lloyd Garrison led the barrage. Gamaliel Bailey's battery responded. Sumner
declared that "Webster . . . placed himself in the dark list of apostates."
Theodore Parker knew of "no deed . . . done by a son of New England
to which I can compare this, but the act of Benedict Arnold." Edmund
Quincy referred to the "meanness of the lion turned spaniel in his fawn-
ings on . . . masters whose hands he was licking for the sake of . . . dirty
puddings they might . . . toss . . . him." Ralph Waldo Emerson said:
"Every drop of blood in this man's veins has eyes that look downward."
Henry Wadsworth Longfellow noted that " 'Fallen, fallen, fallen from
his high estate!' is the universal cry, in various phraseology." John Greenleaf Whittier lamented that "Ichabod" was "fallen" and "lost"—"the
light withdrawn which once he wore!" The emotional appeal of Whittier's verse was reminiscent of Browning's treatment of Wordsworth:

> Of all we loved and honored naught
>   Save power remains;
> A fallen angel's pride of thought,
>   Still strong in chains.[5]

In contrast to these denunciations, based chiefly on Webster's fugitive-
slave attitude, we find the Senator dubbed Sir Knight by admiring correspondents. From South and North encomiums poured into Webster's
mailbox. In Alabama a preacher lauded his "enlarged . . . and self-for-
getting spirit of *patriotism.*" A New Yorker wrote: "The Union has
been again threatened and you have come with undiminished power to
the rescue. . . . Lovers of that Union must rally round you." "Your
speech has saved the Union," said a Pennsylvania Democrat. A Charles-
tonian felt that on Webster "now depends . . . the tranquillity of our
common country." "The tendency of your speech," a Philadelphia admirer added, "is to bring about a right spirit & to mitigate that feeling
at the South which[,] in retort for . . . attacks on their sensibilities &
interest[,] would strike down . . . great interests of the North." Among
Webster's well-wishers were Joel R. Poinsett, the Palmetto Unionist;

Robert B. Minturn, the New York merchant; the scholar, Francis Lieber, and the lawyer, Daniel Lord. The number of eulogistic letters from Southerners was rather disproportionate, but Northerners also joined in the chorus. From Pittsfield, Massachusetts, came this word: "Your . . . fame is in the keeping of . . . honourable hands." From Newburyport: "The speech I . . . perused . . . with . . . delight." From Boston: "You will never have cause to regret a speech which will ever remain a monument of your fame." In Cincinnati and Saint Louis, there was further praise for the famous Whig. Two major collections of Websteriana reveal some support from every quarter.[6]

Herbert D. Foster performed a valuable service in 1922, when he quoted a portion of these pro-Webster citations. Foster left the picture unfinished, however, failing to state that the letters received by anti-Webster senators were usually as harsh as the mail kept by Webster was flattering. The John P. Hale Collection, in the New Hampshire Historical Society, goes far toward restoring the balance of reality. Webster "has betrayed the interests & done violence to the religious feelings of the free states," a Dover man wrote Hale. He was a "traitor" who "has been bought by certain of the South," in another constituent's opinion. "His speech falls upon N.E. like a cold northeast wind from the iceburgs," was the impression of a Sullivan County Whig. A former governor said: "I trust . . . our northern representatives will not be induced, even by Webster, to abandon the proviso." From Connecticut came the prophecy: "If the Course of Clay & Webster is to be the Course of Whig action[,] then they are doomed." From Boston: "Our Governor, Lieut. Gov.[,] all but one of the members of his council, and all but one of the Whig State Central Committee are strongly opposed to Mr Webster." From an unschooled Granite Stater: "Mr Calhouns overbearing . . . and falts [sic] charges . . . together with Mr Websters confirmation of the same . . . caused a dark . . . clould [sic] to hang over our hopes for freedom." From Tioga County, New York: "What . . . disgrace attaches to . . . N. York, Massachusetts & Michigan for the course of . . . Dickinson, Webster & Cass! . . . In the integrity, fidelity, sagacity & ability of yourself and our . . . beloved . . . Seward, I . . . cherish . . . unbounded . . . confidence."[7]

5

The Seventh of March Speech surprised no one more than President Taylor and his friends. On March 3, referring to Webster's address,

Winthrop wrote Everett: "I have every reason to think that it will look to the President's plan." The Boston *Advertiser's* Washington correspondent also predicted that Webster would "advocate a straightforward course of legislation essentially such as the President has recommended. . . . To this point public sentiment has been gradually converging." Giddings understood that Webster would sustain free-soil doctrine. Horace Mann believed he would not compromise the great question. There was reason aplenty for erroneous prophecies. Winthrop advised Everett, one month afterward, that Webster "told me" he favored "Taylor's plan . . . before . . . his speech." According to Winthrop, Stanly of North Carolina had said: "I am very anxious Webster should know" that if he endorsed the President's position, "Taylor's Southern supporters are prepared to do their best to make him the next President." Webster assured his fellow Bay Stater that "he had not pledged himself to sustain Clay's resolutions." "I am substantially with the President," he added, "and you can tell Mr. Stanly so." Since Winthrop passed the word along to the White House, Taylor anticipated contents in Webster's effort that were not there.

A curious side light lies in Webster's statement that he favored Taylor's Plan *after,* as well as *before,* his oration. "Yet in the speech . . . he said not a word about it, and is now declaring his readiness for *Territorial Bills.*" Winthrop left a full account of his discussion with Webster on March 8:

He said . . . he had omitted . . . allusion to . . . the President's plan . . . for want of time, and with a view of making it the subject of a distinct speech hereafter; that he . . . thought of writing . . . the President to explain this. "Why not go . . . and tell him so," I replied; "it is his reception night and I will call for you with my carriage." He said he was too tired, but would take it as a great favor if I would say . . . to the President . . . that, in order to finish his speech in one day, he had omitted . . . a tribute he would gladly have paid to the President's patriotic policy . . . which it was his purpose to . . . advocate in the Senate. . . . He repeated, "I am in favor of supporting General Taylor's plan, unless he himself should . . . recommend . . . a Territorial Government for New Mexico." . . . I told all this to the President, who said he was a little surprised . . . not to find in . . . the speech . . . a word about the Administration or its policy, but that he should be very glad of Mr. Webster's support whenever he saw fit to give it.

Reconciling the contradiction between Webster's private assurances and his public statements would be difficult, had not many Whigs encour-

aged the delusion that no essential difference separated Taylor's stand
from Clay's. Webster no doubt deemed it advisable to do as little as
possible toward widening the breach. If one scans political realities,
however, the element of candor certainly seems to be absent from the
declarations Webster gave Winthrop. As early as January 21 the Massachusetts Senator encouraged Clay to think that the Kentuckian could
count on his support. Hence his assertions to Winthrop take on the character of flimflam. It was as impossible for Webster to support Taylor
and Clay at the same time as for a horseman, however skilled, to ride two
steeds racing in opposite directions. If Winthrop told the truth, Webster
appears at less than his best in the Winthrop conversations.

In the spring of 1850 numerous individuals outside Congress—initially dubious about Webster's address—switched and sided with him
and Clay. Others took a stand with Taylor. Webster's speech calmed
passions and soothed feelings, particularly in the Southern states. Coming so soon after Calhoun's speech was read by Mason, it was accorded
applause in the South that contrasted with the unfavorable reception
given Calhoun by conservatives there. Beyond this, in gauging Webster's
effectiveness, no responsible historian should go. One must view with
misgivings a pro-Webster man's conclusion that "the tremendous influence of his personality and 'unanswerable' arguments eventually swung
the North for the Compromise." No Northern Whig senator changed
his position because of Webster's speech. Of the Northern Whig representatives, Ashmun might qualify, but his case is questionable. Godfrey
T. Anderson, in his splendid study (unfortunately still unpublished),
quoted a source stating that only six New England papers outside Boston
cheered Webster while more than ten times that number disapproved.
To too great a degree credit has been accorded his oration as a molder
of congressional and editorial sentiment. For all the glamour surrounding his appearance, he had little to do with directing majority opinion in
his party, his section, Congress, or the press.

With Webster busily engaged in franking his speech, with Taylor
looking forward to Seward's effort, with Calhoun dying at Hill's, and
Clay admitting that there "is . . . yet discernible . . . no specific mode of
settling . . . matters in controversy," the time has come for the last two
speeches forming the pattern of the Great Debate. To this hour, as Clay
himself indicated, nothing definite had been decided[8]—with the Senate
divided along and across sectional and party lines. Though Hamlin and
Miller had spoken for Taylor, and Webster and Houston for Henry
Clay, there had been more extremist Southern oratory than anything else

in the historic chamber. Berrien was moving away from Clay. Rusk, a nonsigner of the "Southern Address," now was ranged on Calhoun's side. Davis already demonstrated qualities commending him as Calhoun's successor. Most of Clay's Democratic adherents and Taylor's Whig friends had not been heard when Seward on Monday March 11 shocked his colleagues by speaking grimly of "a higher law than the Constitution."

CHAPTER XXV

SEWARD PILLORIED; CALHOUN DEAD

1

IN 1850 William H. Seward already loomed as a political titan. Considered the number-one extremist among Whig senators of the Northeast, he also was Taylor's intimate adviser, powerful in the patronage sphere. Seward's appearance was unforgettable. With his tousled, straw-colored, red-tinged hair, his gray-blue eyes, now keen, now dreamy, his great bony beak of a nose and receding pin point of a chin, he held his head like a wise macaw and cocked it birdlike in conversation. Seward's slight and boyish figure, sloping shoulders, gangling arms, silver snuff-box, and unlighted cigar were now as familiar sights in Washington as for many a year in New York.

Seward had been listened to with attention during the Taylor-Cass campaign, but his delivery was sermonic-somber, and certainly he was no born spellbinder. The forty-eight-year-old lawyer from Auburn had a husky voice, incapable of free intonation. On March 11 he read from a manuscript, contrary to the prevailing fashion. Some senators stayed away from the chamber, and Seward could attribute their absence as much to his lack of forensic talent as to radicalism they resented. Whatever the cause, their shabby treatment was a matter of indifference to him. Seward appealed to a larger audience than that contained by the Senate's walls—coolly preparing his paragraphs to reach the country's tiniest hamlets, for repetition at the grass roots. A realist and ahead of his time, he valued content more than manner.

Still, much of the address was far from dull. So striking, even memorable, were some Seward passages that Webster scarcely took "his eye off him." Calhoun, "restless at first, soon sat still"—his chair "turned toward the speaker, his head leaning on his hand." Hale "listened . . . delighted." Foote "rose up spasmodically now and then . . . exchanging whispers" with Douglas. Corwin gave Seward "his whole attention." And Benton "closed the quarto he had been poring over, to wonder at" the "new novelty."[1]

Summarizing California's status, Seward saw no valid objection to her entry into the Union. When he came to Downs's assertion that the Taylorites unduly influenced the Californians, he recalled that the charge "is peremptorily denied, and the denial . . . not controverted by proofs." True, the President had declared that the "adoption of a constitution, subject to the approval of Congress, would be regarded favorably." And why not? The complaint used to be that military power was a fearful innovation for maintaining order in California. Now the direction of attack had changed. Storming with ferocity from an opposite quarter, the assault had victimized Zachary Taylor. With gusto Seward mounted the ramparts to uphold the Chief Executive, who had merely induced legislative authority to establish civil institutions. He thought "this Republic" would be well off, if no future President committed "a more serious . . . usurpation." Following his effective defense of Taylor, Seward shifted from the White House line. A natural leader, he stretched his thesis into a more exposed position than the one covered by Miller and Hamlin.

Seward's most dubious deviationist remark was that he would have voted for California's admission, "even if she had come in as a slave state." He also asserted that, if California's star were not added to the flag, Oregon and perhaps the rest of the West would join in forming a separate country. There had been speculation on this, but Seward proclaimed it to be a *fact*. Braving the lairs of Calhoun, Clay and Webster, the New Yorker advanced on surer ground. Clay was his first target: "I AM OPPOSED TO . . . COMPROMISE, IN ANY AND ALL THE FORMS . . . PROPOSED." Seward thought "legislative compromises radically wrong and essentially vicious." If this was anathema to Clay, what must Calhoun have thought when Seward condemned him for seeking to change "a national democracy, operating by a constitutional majority . . . into a Federal alliance, in which the minority shall have a veto against the majority"? Calhoun had talked about sectional balance under the Constitution. Yet, Seward continued, this very balance was not in existence after 1787—"that is, it began to be lost two years before it began to exist!" Again, "the principle of the law for the recapture of fugitives" was "unjust, unconstitutional, and immoral." The suggested compromise of the Texas-New Mexico boundary was "a judicial question" or, at least, one of "legal right and title." Kept separate from other matters, it should be "settled by itself."

Seward disagreed with Webster regarding "the alleged obligation of Congress to admit four new slave states" from Texas land. Nor was this the only point at issue. "The article of the annexation of Texas" was itself unconstitutional, Seward declared. Turning now to Calhoun's

premises and now to Webster's, he insisted that "the States are not
parties to the Constitution *as States.*" The Constitution belonged not to
states, but to the people of America. Compromise notions gave "complete ascendency . . . to the subordinate, accidental, and incongruous
[slavery] institution over its paramount antagonist." These likewise reduced the national domain to "a possession . . . enjoyed" exclusively
by "citizens of the old States." Soil acquired "by the valor and . . . wealth
of the whole nation" should be held by no "arbitrary power." The Constitution required "stewardship" and dedication of the "domain to union
. . . and to liberty."

Thereupon Seward uttered a revolutionary sentence. "There is a higher
law than the Constitution," he declared, "which regulates our authority
over the domain, and devotes it to the same noble purposes." Revolutionary? The adjective is no latter-day addendum. The expression "higher
law" and the concept underlying it immediately met with adverse criticism of a sensational variety. Objections sprang full-throated from
widely known constitutional interpreters, from the Berriens of the South
and Websters of the North, and from hundreds of lesser Berriens and
Websters. Despite fuss, furor and harsh opinions, Seward's reference
to the "higher law" was vague in the extreme. He did not advocate, as
some critics implied, the flouting of constitutional precedents. He traced
the Constitution's relation to slavery (as he, an antiextensionist, conceived it), advancing to the high moral ground that he and his contemporaries were "stewards" of the "Creator of the universe." What alarmed
conservatives was the assumed need of considering something beside the
Constitution. This, rather than any definite recommendation, convinced
them that the phrase was revolutionary. It is, however, instructive to
note that, having spoken thus, Senator Seward returned to constitutional
arguments and issues.

The remainder of Seward's address was less original. Praising the
Union, and defending Northern legislatures, he predicted "no disunion
and no secession," but "I do not say . . . there may not be disturbance."
Meanwhile, the idea of divided allegiance—"to States severally and to
the Union"—ought to be dispelled. "I know of only one country and
one sovereign—the United States of America and the American people."
Compromises seemed unnecessary, Seward repeated. "Let . . . those who
distrust the Union . . . make compromises to save it. . . . I shall vote for
the admission of California . . . without conditions . . . and without
compromise." For the vindication of that vote the New York Whig
exclaimed: "I look not to the verdict of the passing hour . . . but to that

SCENE IN UNCLE SAM'S SENATE

ALBERT T. BURNLEY   ALEXANDER C. BULLITT

Edward Williams Clay, who graphically depicted the Foote-Benton fracas, was perhaps the ablest caricaturist of Taylor's time. Here Foote points his loaded weapon at chesty Benton, while Senators Badger, Dickinson, Mason and Henry Dodge seek to restrain them. Clay tut-tuts, and Webster (far right) looks on. (Library of Congress Collection.) The Burnley and Bullitt portraits represent them as they appeared some years prior to the election of President Taylor. (Courtesy of Frick Art Reference Library, Mrs. William I. Wymond and Miss Lucy Powell.)

period, happily not far distant," when these "vast regions . . . shall have received their destined inhabitants." Countless generations rose up to say: "Waste your treasures and your armies, if you will; raze your fortifications" and "sink your navies . . . but the soil you hold in trust for us, give it to us free. . . . Let your broad domain descend to us unincumbered, and free from . . . calamities . . . of human bondage."

2

Although six more senators made major speeches in March, and two others in April, none varied the pattern of the Great Debate. Stephen A. Douglas' remarks alone are entitled to special analysis. Hopkins P. Turney, Tennessee Democrat, backed Davis in most particulars. George E. Badger, North Carolina Whig, was compromise-minded and supported Clay. Dayton was just as pro-Taylor as Miller. Virginia's Robert M. T. Hunter, one of the South's most eloquent sons, walked in Calhoun's footsteps. Chase, Ohio's free-soil Democrat, delivered a strong and scholarly oration somewhat less significant than Seward's. Joseph R. Underwood of Kentucky went down the line for his comrade, Clay. Benton enraged the South more than ever by continuing to speak for the President's Plan.

From these brief summations the fact should be luminous that nothing said by Calhoun or Webster—or the recent maneuverings of Clay—changed the trend of conviction and oratory in the Senate well into April. If we single out Douglas' performance as worthy of detailed treatment, it is not because Douglas disproved the rule but for further evidence of the "regular" Democrats' tie-in with Clay.

At first, Douglas made a point of seeming to disagree with Webster, replying with apparent ardor to "taunts . . . of a . . . partisan character." Webster's so-called "taunts" had been so minor that, except for his own strategy, Douglas would never have mentioned them. Turning to Taylor's position, the Little Giant impaled the President's friends for "making the people . . . in each section" believe in '48 "that his opinions . . . harmonized with their own." How was it now? Why, "General Taylor . . . recommended non-action," which was "non-intervention, so far as . . . slavery is involved." Here Douglas argued loosely: "On this point . . . Taylor and . . . Cass occupy the same ground. In other respects . . . they differ . . . materially. . . . They agree . . . that no law should be passed upon the subject of slavery, and consequently *that the* PROVISO *should* NOT *be adopted.*"

Laboring to drive a wedge between the President and Seward, Douglas asked: "What becomes of the Senator's representations" alleging that Taylor favored the Proviso? Thus far, the Illinoisian gave the appearance of siding with Taylor and Cass against Seward, and with Cass against Webster. Later, however, he arraigned the Administration which, he held, would expose the West to "anarchy and violence." One wonders whether impartial listeners, not thoroughly indoctrinated in the niceties of debate, could make sense out of Douglas' comments.

Actually the Chicagoan's speech stands revealed when studied in full. Diametrically opposing Calhoun, Douglas also described Taylor's program as mistaken. "Anything is better than non-action; any form of government better than no government [as if that were the issue]; and any settlement preferable to no settlement." The question was "already settled . . . so far as slavery is concerned." Douglas echoed Webster, whom he had previously berated, when he found California "free by law and by fact" and destined to remain free. At long last Douglas paid tribute to Clay, whose "kindness, moderation, and firmness" he would have been more obvious in commending earlier. Clay "set the ball in motion. . . . The Union will not be put in peril; California will be admitted; governments for the territories must be established. . . . The controversy will end, and I trust forever."[2] Douglas' two-day oration thus terminated in agreement with Clay. Though he reached this conclusion in a roundabout manner, his aims and Clay's were never far apart. Nor were the Douglas-Webster "differences" much more than window dressing. Senator Douglas constantly kept his Democratic constituents in mind; hence his surface tangle with Webster and his reluctance to side more openly with Clay. But the Little Giant landed at the spot he had picked from the very outset—nominally on Clay's right hand but really in his very lap, sharing control of the driver's reins.

3

Douglas did more than talk. He acted. Because of his important sponsorship of "squatter sovereignty" in the next decade, it is tempting to dwell on portions of his speech outlining that policy in 1850. Of greater immediate note was his alliance with Toombs and Stephens as well as Clay.

Nearly a month before, Douglas initiated a *rapprochement* between House Whigs and Democrats. On February 18, at the peak of the House crisis, Doty of Wisconsin had thrown Southerners into turmoil with his resolution to admit California unconditionally. Thereupon Douglas directed McClernand to seek an understanding with Southern dissidents. Meeting at Cobb's house, Stephens, Boyd, Toombs and Clingman joined hands with McClernand, Richardson and John K. Miller of the North in assenting to a Douglas-approved compromise. Under Douglas' watchful eye McClernand agreed to bring out of the House Committee on Territories bills for New Mexico and Utah territorial organization—conditioned on no congressional exclusion of slavery, California's admission free and slavery's retention in the District. McClernand made good his promise, relieving the tension in the lower chamber. And Douglas reported like bills from the Senate's territorial committee. This action, affecting both houses of Congress, was considered of paramount significance. Eventually it would form the nub of the Compromise of 1850.

With Douglas laboring to such effect, and with groundwork laid for the creation of a senatorial compromise committee, the Clay-Douglas-Cass strategists thought they discerned an omen in their favor as they studied reactions to Seward's address. Praise welled forth for Seward in the antislavery press. Religious papers, the *Independent* in particular, lauded his reference to the "higher law." Conservative Whig journals, however, and nearly all "regular" Democratic editors—not to mention the unanimous South—slapped the New Yorker hard. From a practical viewpoint, still more damaging to Seward was the attitude of some friends and ex-friends. Representative Elbridge G. Spaulding wrote Weed on March 11: "Seward made an eloquent and fearless speech to day in favor of human liberty." D. H. Abell believed Seward's speech contained "qualities far above the effort of Clay & Webster." But Abell and Spaulding were in a minority. Another Weed henchman observed that Seward "should have said nothing about God's laws." He "should have gone in 'neck & heels' for old Zachs Plan." One of Fillmore's correspondents described Seward's remarks as part of a "plot" to organize a "New Whig party upon the platform of antislavery." Weed himself indicated to Seward that he disapproved of the line he took. And one story has it that Zachary Taylor opposed Seward, when North Carolina's Mangum tramped irate into the White House to protest against the "higher law."

According to the "Recollections of an Old Stager," the President was "so excited that he stuttered" when Mangum confronted him—and immediately called Bullitt into conference at the Mansion. "Aleck, this is a nice mess Governor Seward has got us into," Rough and Ready is quoted as saying. "Mangum swears he'll turn Democrat if Seward is the mouthpiece of my administration. The speech must be disclaimed at once, authoritatively and decidedly. Don't be mealy-mouthed about it, but use no harsh language. We can't stand for a moment on such principles."[3] Perhaps the Old Stager's quotations ought not to be taken at face value. Other evidence, however, corroborates Taylor's being upset by Seward. Bullitt rushed to print an anti-Seward editorial, and four days after Seward's speech, the *Republic* shot its wad: "When a Senator . . . proclaims . . . that he holds a commission to legislate as the steward of ALMIGHTY GOD, we are prepared to hear any paradox maintained, however repugnant to the common sense of men who transact public business upon mortal credentials."

This sarcasm was but the beginning, for Bullitt continued: "How dangerous a thing it is for a politician to discard the authority of constitutional law!" When Seward "grows chilly in contemplating slavery in this country, he . . . displays a much greater degree of sensibility . . . than the Saviour of mankind . . . who spent his days upon earth when the world was full of slavery." Commercial men were "amongst Mr. SEWARD'S warm supporters." What were they to think when their own Senator "may have imagined himself to be LAZARUS . . . sent on furlough to the world to preach meekness . . . to the well-to-do"? Guilty of "fanatical declamation," Seward assumed "an independence of constitutional obligations which, if followed by others, must end in the annihilation of all government, all law, all rights. . . . The doctrine which holds the Constitution at naught is a law-breaking, Constitution-defying, disunion doctrine. It is in the teeth of Whig teachings, as understood and practised everywhere."

Appearing in a paper widely considered Taylor's own echo, this *Republic* editorial exerted a profound impression. Editors elsewhere drew deductions accordingly. In New York the Whig *Morning Express* condemned the doctrine of the higher law as "heterodox and dangerous." The *Journal of Commerce* criticized the *Independent* for supporting Seward. The New Orleans *Picayune* termed Seward an "unscrupulous demagogue," and its Washington writer announced the Senator's dismissal from grace as a *fait accompli*. In Indiana Editor Colfax was advised by pro-Taylor Caleb Smith that "Gov. S. will not have the influence at the White House . . . he had last year." According to John L. Schoolcraft "the President said he regretted Seward['s] speech was so ultra." Weed, in Albany, took the cue, calling attention to the merits of Taylor's Plan more emphatically than ever in the *Journal*.

At about this time, Seward opened himself up to shafts of ridicule by giving Old Zack a silver-toothed currycomb to be used on his ancient war horse, Old Whitey. The New York *Herald's* correspondent thought this absurd. "Mr. Seward has not the nerve to meet the . . . contempt . . . poured upon him," sneered the Albany *Atlas*. ". . . The morning insults of Mr. Foote are met by invitations to tea-parties in the evening. He fawns about the President and makes a present of a . . . curry-comb to 'Old Whitey.' "

4

Numerous political angles were involved in these assaults. The Vice President's clique hoped that, with Seward out of favor, Fillmore might win Taylor's confidence and patronage. One Fillmoreite wanted to "organize every where on the Taylor platform . . . call meetings & strip the mask" from Weed and Seward. In Rochester another stated: "Seward's friends . . . insist that the article in the *Republic* . . . was written without the approbation of the administration. But I infer from Weed's subdued tone that he don't think so." A vice-presidential crony announced that "Seward's speech is fatal to him with the president cabinet and Senate." The anti-Seward tempest coincided with the appearance of a pro-Fillmore newspaper in the New York capital. Successive issues lambasted Seward and Weed, showering plaudits on Webster, Clay, Fillmore and (in a curious way) on Taylor. Thus antislavery radicalism, in the person of Seward, seemed to be on the run in the Empire State, while Senator Daniel S. Dickinson's Hunker Democrats backed Douglas, Cass and Clay to the limit.

Slam-bang as the struggle was, the fight against Seward composed only part of the compromise leaders' grand strategy. Taylor's entire Cabinet was a target. The compromisers reasoned that, if the Cabinet resigned and Taylor took counsel from seven new advisers, the Administration might come to terms.

Taylor thoroughly understood his Cabinet's liabilities. Clayton, suffering from neuralgia, grieving over his dear young son and engrossed in negotiations with Britain, could not give adequate time to problems involving slavery and spoils. Meredith, growing in esteem, was still confronted with charges of inexperience, and Cooper, his factional foe, harassed him whenever possible. Ewing, though retaining the respect of many Whigs, was a favorite whipping boy of the Democrats, and, with Collamer, vulnerable to disappointed office seekers. Toombs and Stephens particularly resented Preston's siding with Northerners on antiextension.

From the first the Washington *Union's* booming criticism had been directed at the Cabinet rather than at Taylor personally. The technique of divide and conquer was apparent, however, and Old Zack never fell for it. He did not propose to let his enemies tell him what disposition to make of his associates. Believing wholeheartedly in his Plan, Taylor refused to abandon its backers unless they proved corrupt or negligent. There remained, nevertheless, a more insidious weapon for use against the Cabinet than any Clay or Ritchie had found. This was the stiletto available only to the Bullitts and Burnleys of the palace guard.

Ever since the spring of '49 Burnley and many of his associates had been dissatisfied with the Cabinet, complaining that the ministers were cold, blundering and unapproachable, and recommending that they be replaced. Apparently no large policy matter motivated Burnley's initial observations. Perhaps he merely resented the fact that he, an original Taylor adherent, found himself reduced to playing second fiddle. With the *Republic's* establishment in mid-'49, and Bullitt's assuming the editorship, the New Orleans journalist sympathized with Burnley. In addition to personalities, the Deep South residence of Bullitt and Burnley may have led them to react unfavorably to department heads from Northern and border states on the score of antiextensionism.

At the outset, the *Republic* had functioned smoothly insofar as outsiders could discern. Since Burnley was away much of the time, he avoided the chafing daily contact with the secretaries who irritated him. Meanwhile, Bullitt, on the spot, consulted regularly with the Cabinet regarding issues to be projected and adversaries to be assailed. Taylor editors throughout the country expected the *Republic* to do for them what Ritchie accomplished for the Democrats. To be effectual, Bullitt had to secure the confidence of a well-disposed Cabinet. This confidence he failed to get, the President and Meredith being exceptions to the chilly reception accorded him.[4] Hence, while Burnley stayed away, Bullitt grew increasingly wrathful, and his ire was bubbling over when the Thirty-first Congress convened.

Henry Clay's appearance in Washington evoked old memories for Bullitt. Most of his life, he had been a Clay booster; prior to 1845 he was undeviatingly, enthusiastically, even hotly pro-Clay. Now, notwithstanding his dislike of many features of Clay's leadership, Bullitt hated the Cabinet and Seward more than anything or anybody else. He made no secret of his admiration for Webster. And in March, April and early May, he often removed the stops of restraint, hammering on the theme that no real difference separated the President's Plan and Clay's. At other times, incredible inconsistencies cropped up in *Republic* editorials; some days they sounded as if their author changed his mind from hour to hour. Clearly "Aleck" was unhappy and upset. Still devoted to the President, he felt the secretaries were "betraying" Taylor and that Clay was right on the slavery issue. Publication of his March 15 editorial must have thrilled Bullitt to the marrow because, while wading into Seward, he inferentially attacked Seward's Cabinet supporters. With Taylor presumably back of him, and the "higher law" blasted, might he not soon blow the ministers sky-high?

5

For the time being no Cabinet crisis developed. If this disappointed Bullitt, no doubt he was temporarily content to see Seward pilloried. The course of events encouraged Clay and Douglas, who regarded the weakening of the Administration front as a portent in their favor. Still, they realized, the Calhounites also must be reckoned with. Nothing in the anti-Seward battering-ram met the threats of the South's extremists. But at this juncture destiny seemed to supervene. On the last day of March Calhoun breathed his last. He had been failing for weeks. Benton, the Jacksonian who distrusted him, charged he was faking[5]—like an old ham actor. But the death rattle could be muffled only by God. And the Carolinian was no more.

Calhoun's funeral took place in the Senate on Tuesday, April 2, with Taylor and his Cabinet in attendance. Neither Taylor, Fillmore nor Cobb could follow the Episcopal ritual. Yet the ceremonies were suitable. Mangum, Clay, Webster, Cass, Berrien and King, all old Senate associates, acted as Calhoun's pallbearers. Clay joined Butler, Webster, Rusk and Clemens in praising the nullifier soft and low, and his eulogy may have been significant. Stressing Calhoun's early nationalism, the Kentuckian extended the olive branch to Calhoun's followers at the departed leader's bier. If it was true (as many writers have suggested) that Calhoun's last speech did his cause little good,[6] certainly his disappearance from the scene could have led compromisers to take heart.

CHAPTER XXVI

TAYLOR *vs.* CLAY: THE ISSUE JOINED

1

IF SOME of the tears shed for Calhoun in public were belied by secret rejoicings, senators showed genuine shock when one of their number pulled a pistol on another fifteen days after Calhoun's funeral. One month before Calhoun's death, John Bell had offered resolutions of a limited-compromise nature which some people thought might be acceptable to Taylor. Now, in mid-April, the Senate "considered" Foote's motion to refer the Clay and Bell programs to a Select Committee of Thirteen. The debating then and thereafter proved intricate, with Benton intent on trying to keep California's admission paramount. April 17 found the Missourian seeking to impose restrictions on the committee, even before its creation was authorized. When Benton proposed fourteen amendments to Senator Foote's original motion, Clay amended Benton's amendment and called for a vote on elimination of restrictions. This was perhaps the most vital test in the first four months of 1850. The compromisers won, twenty-nine to twenty-two. And the die was cast for nonrestriction.

Benton had been halted before, but never permanently, and he had often parried with the Kentucky wizard. Rising to demand a separate vote on each of the amendments he had offered, Old Bullion accused his adversary of scheming to stifle normal debate. Clay refrained from interrupting. But Foote (who, with Douglas, had been seconding Clay) attacked Benton's assertion that Calhoun's "Southern Address" was "the root of . . . agitation"—and that "the country has been alarmed without reason." The South definitely *was* imperiled by Northern aggression, replied Foote, who had been at odds with Calhoun, but now with breathless inconsistency sprinted to the deceased's defense. "Who is the author of the Southern Address?" Foote asked. "He is . . . the late illustrious Senator from South Carolina . . . over whose untimely death every good man . . . is now lamenting." Yet, "in our presence here to-day," Calhoun's famous paper was "denounced . . . as . . . having supplied food

326

for . . . excitement" involving "our institutions" in danger. Men who sanctioned it "are charged with being agitators. And by whom? . . . By a gentleman long denominated . . . the father of the Senate. By a gentleman who, on a late occasion——"

At this moment, Foote, whose seat was on the outer circle, backed down the aisle in Fillmore's direction with a five-chambered pistol in his hand. The unarmed Benton, a split second before, had advanced toward Foote outside the bar. Then he followed him "into the aisle down which the Senator from Mississippi had retreated." In an instant Whigs and Democrats sprang to their feet. Amid shrill calls to order and outcries for the sergeant-at-arms Fillmore pounded his gavel repeatedly and joined in the babel of command. The six-footer Henry Dodge of Wisconsin momentarily detained Benton, who exclaimed: "I have no pistols! Let him fire! Stand out of the way! I disdain to carry arms! Stand out of the way, and let the assassin fire!"

Breaking away from Dodge, the Missourian again approached the pistol-wielder. Foote, now near the Vice President's dais, was surrounded by a number of senators—including Dickinson, who seized the weapon and quickly locked it in his desk. On Butler's advice the diminutive Foote returned to his chair. Clay tut-tutted, "I hope . . . order will be restored." "We are not going to get off in this way," Benton flung back. "A pistol has been brought here to assassinate me."

"I brought it here to defend myself," the Mississippian explained lamely.

Benton: "It is a false imputation. I carry nothing of the kind, and no assassin has a right to draw a pistol on me."

Several senators: "Order, order!"

The Vice President: "Senators will be seated. . . . Business cannot proceed until order is restored."

Hale: "I hope order will be kept in the galleries."

The Vice President: "There is too much noise in the galleries. Quiet and order must be restored."

Foote now asked to continue his remarks, but Benton insisted that the Senate take official "cognizance" of all that transpired. His adversary offered watery explanations, pleading self-defense and insisting that Benton's language and gestures had menaced him. Fillmore told Foote to suspend his comments. Dodge, Hale, Mangum and Dickinson spoke pointedly. The Senate set up an investigating committee. Then, at last, the chamber adjourned.

2

At only one other nadir in American history has anything more reprehensible than this taken place on the Senate floor. An immediate hubbub ensued in the press, and there were seethings in private letters of public men. Foote was condemned from pulpit and platform. Free-Soilers, looking on Benton as their spokesman, demanded Foote's expulsion from Congress. Although many Northerners agreed, Southerners pleaded that the explosive Mississippian merely sought to protect himself from a physically powerful person, infuriated and menacing attack. It was like the familiar argument of small boys: "Yuh started it!" "Nah, I didn't, neither!" As the *Picayune* testified, too frequently men's viewpoints harmonized with "previous . . . bias." Moderns would be surprised to find so many journalists excusing Foote, did they not know that Democratic leaders favored compromise (which Foote upheld), while Clay's Whig faction abhorred Benton's politics. Awaiting the Senate investigators' report, not a few readers agreed with the *Picayune* that "no extenuations . . . acquit either party of a grave crime against the former good order . . . of the Senate."

No record tells what vivid expressions Taylor uttered when he heard of the outrage. Since the President and Benton had drawn ever closer, the presumption is that Rough and Ready warmly sympathized with his friend. With Cass, Douglas and Webster refraining from criticism of Foote, clearly the compromisers were not appalled. And Clay, proposing that Benton and Foote should report to a local magistrate, suggested that in his opinion both men had disturbed the peace.

Harry of the West was determined to permit no altercation to interfere with his drive for mastery. On April 18 all fourteen of Benton's amendments were voted down. On the nineteenth the Select Committee being authorized, Clay won election as its chairman. He hand-picked his fellow committeemen—Cass, Dickinson and Jesse D. Bright (Northern Democrats), Webster, Phelps and Cooper (Northern Whigs), King, Downs and Mason (Southern Democrats), Mangum, Bell and Berrien (Southern Whigs). Three of these accompanied Calhoun's remains from Washington to Charleston.[1] Hence all could not immediately serve with Clay, around the table behind closed doors, where the real business of the Senate would be conducted after a two-week interlude.

Because of the speed with which senators acted after the Foote-Benton fracas, it might be assumed that the flash of steel expedited the committee plan that Foote originally proposed and Clay readily accepted. It is equally natural to suppose that every committeeman was compromise-minded. Both assumptions are far from the truth. The Select Committee probably would have come into being the day before, had not the Foote-Benton theatricals interposed. Neither Bell nor Berrien was precisely a Clay man. Although Phelps objected to his appointment, his request to be excused was overruled. Mason, too, was no compromiser—as would be demonstrated later. Few, if any, White House supporters or Southern die-hards took part in the committee's creation. Being in the minority, they abstained from voting for its members—a feature never adequately stressed.

Another indication of weakness was the inclusion of Bright, rather than Douglas, in the committee's personnel. Why was not Douglas one of the thirteen? When Clay invited him, he demurred. Similar as were their aims, the two leaders went right on disagreeing as to means of operation. Douglas still thought the compromise could win only if individual bills were voted on separately. Clay, just as intent on the over-all approach, gave in to the extent of omitting Douglas from the committee when the Illinoisian insisted he would thus be freer to reintroduce the measures after their defeat *en masse.* For the moment Clay had his way as to methods, but he and the Democrats did not dismiss the redemptive value of the Douglas loophole.

3

While Clay planned committee strategy, minor matters nominally took up the Senate's time. It was a period of grave unrest, a season of strife and of something close to war. With last-minute preparations made for the heralded Nashville Convention, the Texas-New Mexico border feud excited hot heads, and even cool ones. In Washington the House heard allegations involving three Cabinet members in a money scandal. Concurrently rumors of a Clayton-Bulwer treaty reached a public suspicious of John Bull. In the West, Indian depredations led pioneers to cry for aid, as militiamen and the small Regular Army tried to cope with murderers and thieves.

Reading the *Congressional Globe,* however, one might never suspect that the Senate heeded the lurid tidings. Gold coinage, patents, railroads and Supreme Court appeals elicited the halfhearted interest of statesmen. The dispatching of a naval expedition into Arctic waters to look for an Englishman, Sir John Franklin, occupied them on May 1. During long

week-end adjournments senators traipsed home to repair their fences.
From Taylor's angle the most provoking topic debated by those remaining behind was the patronage issue spearheaded by Bradbury of Maine.
James Bradbury's change about (*with* Taylor on extension, *against* him
on jobs) symbolized 1850's kaleidoscopic shifts as perfectly as anything
else. A little later on we shall learn more about Bradbury's charges and
the Bell-Smith replies. But now we see Senate absentees hurrying back
before the gavel falls—in anticipation of higher drama, to be furnished
by Henry Clay.

On Wednesday May 8 Clay obliged them. His committee's report,
whipped into shape by Clay himself at the National Hotel and Charles
B. Calvert's house near Bladensburg, consumed more than an hour in the
reading. Its nucleus comprised three bills, recommended by a majority
of the thirteen senators but lacking their unanimous approval. The first,
farthest-reaching, and most debatable measure covered California, New
Mexico, Utah, the Texas boundary problem and Texas reimbursement.
The second dealt with fugitive slaves. The third was concerned only with
the slave trade in the District. The report also contained other matter
touching controversial issues. (Slavery in the District should not be
abolished, the Committee advised, and the thirteen unanimously reaffirmed Texans' right to carve additional states from their land at some
future date.) It was, however, to his first bill that Clay directed a major
portion of his audience's attention. The novel feature of this resolution
lay in the use of legislative stickum to connect would-be solutions for so
many urgent problems. Individual sections were substantially the same
as separate proposals long since sponsored by Douglas. Thus Clay's work
was less origination than improvisation. He connected old bills, altered
some of them slightly and caused the enactment of one to hinge on the
enactment of all.

California's statehood, Clay insisted, was no more important than setting up territorial governments for Utah and New Mexico. "A spirit
of mutual concession enjoins that the . . . measures should be connected."
Clay did not discuss his principal motive, which (as a Douglas apostle
explained) was to keep Taylor Whigs from opposing an independent
territorial bill. Hoping that a New Mexico-Utah link with California
would induce Taylorites to accept the whole, he also hooked the proposed Texas-New Mexico boundary and the payment of a substantial sum
to Texas onto the territorial-statehood provisions. By uniting them "every
question of difficulty . . . which has arisen out of . . . acquisitions from
Mexico will, it is hoped, be adjusted." A great deal could be said for

the Clay-approved boundary, which gave to New Mexico Santa Fe and much of the disputed region to which Texas cherished the claim that Rusk upheld so vigorously. For this relinquishment Clay planned to pay Texas "a large pecuniary equivalent"—unspecified in amount, but probably between $6,000,000 and $10,000,000. Though logic lay in bracketing the boundary and monetary schemes, tying them to the state-hood-territorial arrangements seemed less sensible to many. Numerous Northern Whigs and Democrats opposed the first bill, just as Taylor did. Other senators insisted the Supreme Court alone was qualified to settle the boundary controversy. From the hour Clay read his report it was certain that it would meet opposition.

The fugitive-slave provision was less complicated. Unattached to other clauses, it amounted to Mason's earlier bill with two pertinent variations. One required slaveowners to carry a record "adjudicating the facts of elopement and slavery" and describing the escapee; the other specified trial by jury in the state from which the Negro fled. These changes, plus stringent enforcement, would—the committee's majority believed—offer a really "effectual remedy" for Southerners' loss of human property. Re-garding the slave trade in the District, the committee premised its bill on the assumption that local residents "are believed . . . desirous that it should be discontinued." Compared to the sharp teeth given the law for returning fugitives to bondage, elimination of the trade in Washing-ton was unspectacular and inconsequential.

4

Notwithstanding the importance of his words Clay did not tarry in the limelight. After presenting the majority program, he gave minority members a chance to register differences and volley them home. First on his feet, Phelps disclaimed responsibility for Clay's conclusions. Mason regretted "deeply" that "difficulties" he foresaw still remained. Berrien wanted California split into two states, at 35° 30'—not 36° 30'. With these exceptions Clay appeared to make headway. Webster, King, and Bell were mum. Cass, Dickinson, and Bright said little. Downs's devia-tion was not extreme, Cooper's tone harmonious. Mangum, moreover, went the limit in behalf of the Kentuckian: "I cherish a strong hope that . . . these bills . . . will become laws. . . . I am ready to give . . . will, heart, and might . . . to the consummation of this . . . glorious . . . object."

Immediately verbal duels developed. When Clemens announced his intention to oppose Clay, the venerable Kentucky Whig vaulted to offset him. Foote supported Clay. Florida's David L. Yulee objected. Borland backed Yulee. Then Houston was recognized. "I am for compromise with all my heart," he declaimed, "unless it is proposed to compromise our honor and safety. I am for the Union, and for honorable efforts which will tend to its preservation." Borland characterized the committee's nostrum as a mere "embodiment of the views" previously expressed by Clay. This Mangum denied. Cass spoke for compromise—Dickinson likewise—Bright did the same. Democrats all, these stalwarts of Clay met virtually every test. On the initial skirmish front the compromise platoons emerged triumphant.

But wars often are lost when battles are won, and the silence of most Taylor Whigs lent an unreal aspect to the scene. The only earnest of Northerners' jaw-jutting determination lay in the phrases of Phelps and Hale. Clemens had said that "concession to fanaticism never satisfied fanatics." Accepting the stormy Alabamian's thesis, Hale turned it the other way—describing Clay's measures as a wholesale concession to Southerners, and asking: "If they are not satisfied" with this, "what do they want?" During Polk's presidency, Hale recalled, the South urged California's forming a constitution, entering the Union, and avoiding agitation. Now not only did Southerners fight this, but Clay's first bill "turns the . . . territories into a slave pasture, and offers no obstruction to the spread of slavery. . . . Then comes the fugitive slave bill, and you propose to pass that." If Southern fanatics' "opposition to this report is not a mere feint . . . let them put this report down, and then let us go home and tell the country we have exhausted the cup of concession. . . . These gentlemen . . . never mean to be satisfied, and they never will be." Hale's reminder that immediate California statehood long bore the seal of Democratic approval, including the Washington *Union's,* was an especially telling thrust.

5

The principal events of the next three weeks were Clay's formal addresses of May 13 and 21, the Bullitt-Sargent withdrawal from the *Republic* and that paper's May 27 blast in reply to Clay's of the twenty-first. Five days following his report, the Kentuckian held the floor two and a half hours, defending here, expanding there and inviting support from every quarter. His speech contained little that was new. Only in mentioning Taylor did he strike a uniquely significant note. "I came to

Washington," Clay averred, "with the most anxious desire . . . to co-operate . . . in all cases in which I could conscientiously cooperate with the Executive branch." This wish "I still entertain." But "I came here also with a settled purpose to follow the dictates of my own judgment." Did the Committee of Thirteen's findings constitute such co-operation? Yes, Clay insisted, this was true—to the extent the President "recommends." Taylor urged California's admission. So did the Select Committee. "There the President's recommendation stops, and there we . . . act upon . . . other parts of the territory acquired from Mexico."[2] The fact that Clay did not berate Taylor might indicate that he was conciliatory, and eager to win White House favor.

Clay's conciliation, however, rested on his own original terms. The President was to give in to him, not the Senator to Taylor. Clay was less than frank when he argued that the two plans were reconcilable. And the "settled purpose" he avowed conflicted with the "anxious desire" he professed. Not once in twenty years had Clay followed anyone. He was accustomed to command or, at least, to persuade others that his way was best. Even before his last Senate election Taylor Whigs feared he would "play hell and break things." His motivation? That is problematical. Perhaps his chagrin at his '48 defeat encrusted prejudice against his rival, insuring the impossibility of his seeing eye to eye with Old Zack. Clay was devoted to the Union, just as Zachary Taylor was. This truth has caused Clay admirers to pooh-pooh the existence of animus in his heart. But even now he was guilty on one count—guilty of misrepresentation. Alleging that Taylor's Plan stopped abruptly with the admission of California, Clay neglected to add that the President desired statehood for New Mexico. Taylor's New Mexico proposal hinged on the California bill's success, and thus relegated New Mexico to a secondary spot on his agenda. Clay must have known this. Everyone else did. Therefore, Clay was less than candid in deliberately ignoring it.

One additional factor no doubt entered into Clay's calculations. The *Republic* went right on assuming no discrepancy between his plan and Taylor's. Would this not have given Clay hope that the President might swing away from his moorings? Superficially there was much to justify the theory. Yet Clay should have had his ear to the ground, picking up murmurs of discontent with the *Republic's* course under Bullitt. Nearly two months before, Seward, Schoolcraft, Abell and Mrs. Seward were convinced that the President and Cabinet sided with Seward—not Bullitt—in the controversy. The editor's antipathy toward the Cabinet and his sympathy for Clay contributed to this conclusion. Whether Taylor

actually directed Bullitt to denounce Seward rests on questionable evidence. Within a fortnight Seward's explanations thoroughly satisfied
the President.[3] Taylor's true position, throughout April, either escaped
Bullitt or was ignored by him. What he wrote about Clay and the
Cabinet, therefore, represented only his personal beliefs. Eventually Taylor reached the decision that the journalist was doing less good than
harm.

When Bullitt's farewell came on May 14, his leave-taking was extremely dignified. Ascribing their departure from the *Republic* to "personal differences" with "members of the Cabinet," Bullitt and Sargent
emphasized that "our confidence in President Taylor is unimpaired."
Praising Taylor's "unselfish patriotism," they commended their successor,
Allen A. Hall, as entitled to their readers' esteem. It is noteworthy that
Hall was not a Northerner. A Tennessee Whig, he brought to the sanctum a newspaper background of twenty years' duration, unconditioned
by intimate connections with most of the Cabinet or with Seward. Hall
may have grown close to Meredith since he served under him in the
Treasury. But his roots were with John Bell—as Southwestern as Zachary
Taylor's.

For several days, under Hall, the *Republic* marked time. But soon he
published a statement of policy epitomizing Taylor's resolute stand. The
President's January recommendation for California's admission as an
"independent measure" had been received, wrote Hall, "with favor by
a large proportion of the people, and is . . . still generally acceptable"
to them. "An impression seems to have got abroad" that Taylor "now
wavers . . . in his opinion." This was unfounded. He remained "firm,"
and convinced that his course was "the best practicable." Taylor had
never "modified that opinion." Short and plain as Hall's leader was, it
did the work of a dozen columns of theatrical prose in informing Clay
and the Democrats that the President would not be cajoled into turning
the tide in a compromise direction. Despite the handicaps under which
Taylor labored (his lack of spanking Whig majorities in Congress being
the greatest), his attitude in May was the same as in January—and indeed
as in November and August.

Was there shortsightedness in Taylor's consistency? Should the Chief
Executive have acknowledged an error and then swung along with Clay?
That depended on whether he really *was* mistaken, and, *if* mistaken, on
his perception of his fault. Clay and Douglas felt he was pigheaded.
But two prime facts are equally certain: (1) Confidence in his own pro-
gram motivated Old Zack; (2) the long range of history presents at least

Death of Zachary Taylor

This crude lithograph was perpetrated by Nathaniel Currier before James Merritt Ives became his partner. The standing figures represent: Richard Taylor (in fact, not present when his father died), Meredith, Ewing, Colonel Bliss, the Reverend Smith Pyne, Collamer, Fillmore, Preston, Clayton, Johnson and Crawford. Mrs. Taylor and Mrs. Bliss weep at the President's bedside.

as many arguments favoring Taylor's concept of statesmanship as that to which his opponents adhered. A Southern man with a Southern background, Southern interests and Southern friends, Taylor had no selfish economic or personal ax to grind in opposing slavery's extension. The day was to come when the Compromise of 1850 would *seem* to have remedied sectional hurts. But another dawn followed, when many men concluded that at least one compromise ingredient proved a principal cause of aggravated pain.

This may not constitute sufficient evidence that the attempt of Clay and Douglas to reach an adjustment was unworthy of the effort. But the Compromise ultimately failed, and therein lurks the possibility that Taylor's Plan may have been as expedient as (in his mind) it was patriotic. In the Clay-Douglas proposals Taylor discerned seeds of weakness and controversy. So he said, in substance: "Don't give in to threats of secession or civil war. Admitting California in accordance with a plan which many of you who now oppose me once supported, we can side-step the Wilmot Proviso. Above all we must not yield an inch to veiled or flagrant disunionism!" In the background the veto power loomed as a weapon the Executive could wield. If inconsistency affected the presidential position, it lay in the likelihood that a Whig (despite Whig theorizing on "executive tyranny") would negate a congressional compromise by placing the veto brand on it.

6

Hall's clinching editorial appeared on May 20. The next day Clay launched his great offensive. Nominally replying to Louisiana's Pierre Soulé, the Kentuckian directed his assault mainly against the President. He was "constrained" to perform "a very painful duty," Clay expatiated: "I mean the duty of contrasting the plan proposed by the Executive" with the Committee of Thirteen's alternative. "Here are five wounds . . . bleeding and threatening the well being, if not the existence of the body politic." The plan of the President would heal only one, leaving "the other four to bleed more profusely." Continuing, Clay said: "I have seen with profound . . . regret" Taylor's "persistence . . . in his own peculiar plan. . . . A week ago, I" expected "reciprocation." Yes, "entertaining that constitutional deference to the wisdom of Congress which he had professed," the President "ought . . . to permit us to consider what is best for our common country." But, instead of concurring with the committee, Taylor adhered to his own ideas. How reprehensible!

How woeful! Once again Clay insisted that Taylor made no provision for New Mexico. And, summing up, he graphically compared the two schemes in parallel columns of the *Globe*—in such a way as to make his own appear superior to the President's.

Never before had Clay assailed Zachary Taylor so openly. Previously his remarks had contained an element of surface deference, predicated on the hope that the White House would capitulate. Through Hall the Administration replied to the Senator with equal vigor. Clay did Taylor "great injustice," the *Republic* asserted on May 27. The alleged neglect of New Mexico simply did not accord with the facts. "Nothing . . . exists . . . to prevent New Mexico from following the example of California." She probably would "do so before the close of the present session of Congress, unless . . . deterred by the declaration of the Senator that he will not vote for her admission." How unfair to charge that the President "proposes" leaving New Mexico under military government, in disregard of American obligations in the Treaty of Guadalupe Hidalgo! *"With a view to the faithful execution of the treaty,"* Taylor had told California and New Mexico of his "desire that each . . . should . . . form . . . a . . . constitution"—submitting it to Congress and seeking admission as a state. This was the record as it affected the rawest of the "wounds."

Turning to the boundary, Hall cited Taylor's stand that the Supreme Court could decide that issue if both Texas and New Mexico were states. In the deplorable existing circumstances, Taylor could only admit that "it remains for Congress to devise some mode of adjustment." Was this submission of the question to Congress tantamount to leaving it "untouched"? No—and New Mexico's statehood would be followed by referring the boundary to the Court, whose adjudication could "heal that wound." Utah residents had already adopted a provisional government. On a temporary basis, they enjoyed self-government, were well armed and "abundantly able to protect themselves from . . . Indian tribes." Should they need additional security, Taylor "will no doubt take care" of that.

"Non-action by Congress . . . is an important feature in the PRESIDENT'S policy," the *Republic* continued, to the extent that he opposed "establishment of territorial governments." Taylor hoped to achieve "settlement of the slavery question" by ending "all agitation" and relieving Congress from "the necessity of legislating on that subject." Certainly "no bill . . . could pass Congress without bringing up the . . . proviso." Taylor did not want seeds of future trouble sown "broadcast over the . . . free States." His plan "can be attended with no such consequences." But "if the Compromise bill should pass, and the fugitive slave bill be lost, will not . . . Southern supporters of the former impute bad faith to its Northern supporters?" Then, might there not be "a startling addition to the "bleeding wounds . . . described by the Senator?" Hall was on less solid ground regarding Taylor's attitude toward the slave trade and fugitives bills. "Who has . . . a right to assume . . . that . . . the PRESIDENT . . . is opposed" to adopting those measures? "Could they not . . . go hand in hand" with Taylor's policy? These "wounds" he "did not open . . . nor has he offered the slightest impediment to their being healed up."

"We are . . . unable," the *Republic* continued, "to see . . . superior remedial potency in the compromise plan." Such superiority, if it existed, was "not so manifest as to justify . . . *requiring* the PRESIDENT to . . . defeat the principle" he believed best. Originally Taylor's Plan had been "almost universally hailed . . . by patriotic men of all parties. . . . It is . . . a national misfortune" that anything disturbed this unity of sentiment. "It is not our purpose" to reproach anyone, least of all the "distinguished" Clay. The Kentuckian "obeyed the law of his nature, and yielded to the . . . coercion of circumstance." In leaving the tranquil shades of Ashland, Clay "came to lead, not to follow." He came to originate measures, not to adopt other men's. He returned to Washington with the "ambition of appropriating to himself the glory of a third compromise." Hall considered such ambition "both natural and laudable." But if the assumption was right, it accounted, "in some degree at least," for the absence of that "spirit of . . . mutual confidence . . . which ought to animate the departments of the Government," to which the Senator had referred.[4]

7

In the main the *Republic* leader was strong, accurate and convincing. At last Taylor had an editor whose loyalty was unconditional. There had been a "yes—but" hedge in almost everything Bullitt printed, creating an impossible situation—a political *impasse*. Most Presidents would have broken the log jam months sooner than Zachary Taylor, who probably permitted Bullitt to continue too long and with too much freedom.

The most telling portion of Hall's editorial concerned the first of Clay's bills and the President's alternative. Since this was the heart of the controversy, perhaps little need be said of the remainder. However, it is most unlikely that Taylor's view of Clay's second bill tallied with Hall's interpretation. Perhaps the new editor lacked time to acquaint himself fully with all the President's opinions; though absolute proof is lacking, this may well be the correct appraisal. Certainly it detracted little from the ringing presentation of New Mexico statehood. Though some might think statehood impractical because of the nature of New Mexico's population, it was untrue that Taylor ignored the issue—and Hall, in his leader, drove the point home.

Hall also argued that the boundary (and, by inference, Texas' indemnification) hinged on New Mexico's statehood plan. This paralleled Taylor's special message, demonstrating that more than nonaction was involved in White House policy. When he came to Clay's motivation, Hall might have been cruel, careless or brash. But, cautiously, he merely *suggested* that Clay, intent on his own way, loved to lead and courted the spectacular. Had this been the first occasion when personalities impinged on measures, the Republic might have been justly criticized for resorting to cheap tactics. Yet, considering the low punches aimed at Taylor, Hall was justified in retaliating with so mild an *ad hominem* thrust.

Because of Douglas-Cass Democrats' prominence among Senate compromisers it may seem astounding that Taylor's paper failed to mention them in its analysis. The explanation unquestionably lies in the peculiar challenge of that May and June. Douglas and Cass then stayed in the wings, while Clay stalked on the stage. From the start the compromisers commanded a Democratic majority, but badly needed new accessions. Pessimistic respecting Southern extremists, their strategy centered on Taylorites—most of them Whigs. The *Republic* sensibly met the issue even as Clay presented it, temporarily ignoring the Democrats. The hour might arrive when Taylor, past challenging Clay for Whig leadership, could focus attention on a breakdown of Senate Democratic votes. Up to now this angle was blurred by Douglas' record through the spring. Instructions from the Illinois Legislature had compelled the Little Giant to side with Benton and the Whigs in test after test, notwithstanding his speeches and maneuvers. This was true of James Shields also, and Cass had trouble on the same account. Thus prudence may have contributed to Hall's shying away from a premature showdown with the Democracy.

So on Whig terrain the warfare raged, featuring Clay-Taylor combat. For the first time the issue was joined. Previously the President had hoped that Clay would see merit in his Plan, while Clay vainly sought to induce Taylor and pro-Administration senators to come round to his way of thinking. Valuable to the President was the aid of nearly every Northern Whig senator. But the top trump was the veto power. So long as Zachary Taylor retained it, Clay was helpless. And he knew it, now that the *Republic* had spoken. With Northern Whigs tightly controlled by Taylor, and more and more Democrats joining Benton, only some disparate occurrence (a depression, scandal or Taylor's death) could offset the President's advantage and set Clay right side up again.

CHAPTER XXVII

THE GALPHIN CLAIM

1

FEW peacetime American crises have been more acute than 1850's. It was a period of turmoil—of broken friendships, shattered alliances, parties split and factions chipped into cracked schismatic remnants. Members of Congress swung this way and that, from long-loved loyalties to new, untried ones. Indeed, they seemed like marionettes jerked by a master puppeteer!

Actually it was no mere puppet show in Washington that steamy summer. National leaders' motivations as various as colors in an autumn landscape, they responded now to duty's clear call, now to partisan appeals, now to sectional needs and interests, now to passion, now to reason. It is doubtful that unalloyed purity of purpose was present in the performance given by every actor on that stage. The quality known as human nature shaded efforts to be objective. Clay's feeling toward Taylor, Taylor's feeling toward Clay, the seedier aspects of political expediency, fear-respect of voters back home, instinctive but blind devotion to a captain, personal grievances and grudges made the tragicomedy complex. Even today one must probe historians' backgrounds to determine whether modern interpreters of that pre-Civil War climax approximate judicial viewpoints. If great-grandsons of men alarmed by mid-century chaos can only *approach* the truth today, most commentators of 1850 were farther still from fair appraisals.

Democratic papers, like the Boston *Post,* condemned both abolitionists and Whigs for the "unholy sectional crusade." "Northern Whig members . . . are . . . perfectly reckless," the Baltimore *Sun's* correspondent asserted. The Richmond *Enquirer* feared "the compromise will be defeated in the Senate. . . . No one can predict . . . the result, short of . . . disunion itself."

The Philadelphia *Pennsylvanian* saw "two influences" at work to defeat the Clay committee—"abolition and free-soil leaders . . . *and the . . . Taylor administration.*" It was scarcely surprising to find Ritchie proclaiming "the whig party . . . disbanded and dissolved." But his admission that the Democracy was "beset by dangers . . . within its own ranks"—like those which "caused the . . . whig . . . division"—provided proof positive that Democrats, too, were harassing one another.

"We are not so secure from civil war . . . as we imagine," the Philadelphia *Bulletin's* reporter warned. There was talk of legislators' recessing and going home to sample sentiment. In June letters "from distinguished persons in the North" urged "immediate adjournment." A dispatch to the Charleston *Mercury* declared that "so far as results are concerned," not "a particle of difference" separated "the schemes of Mr. Clay, President Taylor, and Mr. Wilmot." Such comment showed "the excesses to which passion is running," barked Ritchie, "and how much 'madness rules the hour.' "[1] Thus regular Democrats continued to center their fire on Taylor and the Cabinet.

2

A revealing commentary on Taylor's reaction to the criticism was contained in a letter to Crittenden from Brown. The evening of April 18 found Taylor conversing "several hours" with Brown. "The President . . . disclosed . . . his feelings," speaking as a proud, brave and deeply injured man alone can speak of "unmerited wrong and unprovoked persecution." Brown listened "till my heart was sad and my eyes filled with tears." But "General Taylor is an unconquerable man. . . . He exclaimed that he always kept his flag flying in front of his tent and would never strike it." If "his station prevented him from righting his wrongs with his own hand," it "did not prevent him from having his character rightly defended and . . . *he meant to do it."* Slavery and territorial questions were "well considered" by the President. "Unobtrusive as he has always shown himself . . . , he refrained from disclosing his opinions" until forced to do so by "the strong desire of the Congress and the Country." Taylor's "plan for adjusting the difficulties . . . met with great favor every where." It could have worked. Democrats knew "it would greatly enhance the fame of the administration." Hence Democratic encouragement of Clay and supercilious sneering at Taylor.

"There has been from the Locofocos a systematic and unscrupulous attack on the President," Brown continued. Moreover Clay and Webster, instead of sustaining the Whig party, tried to reweave "the broken web of their own political fortunes." Democrats with "hypocritical cunning are stimulating them to assault the Administration—making each of the two believe" he "could reach the Presidency" in '53. The Cabinet was not perfect, Brown acknowledged. Although every member "discharged his duty with ability and fidelity," the secretaries were deficient in qualities that made an Administration popular. "In a praiseworthy effort to attain great reputation as a *working Cabinet,* they secluded themselves too much." Not meaning to be offensive or impolite, they created that impression and had been struck by a volume of "defamatory remarks." Taylor was "not subjected to . . . these accusations. He was accessible . . . and acceptable to all." He "retained the unbroken confidence" of Whigs until Congress met, when Clay and Webster began manning the Democratic guns.

No one was better fitted than Brown to reflect Taylor's reactions to the Washington scene. In May he confided that the capital was in a hum of wonder, speculation and conjecture. "Ritchie is in an agony. . . . Congress is a riddle. . . . Whig organization no where—Democratic harmony equally hard to find. . . . Old Zack is the only one who stands unmoved like 'the red moon on a summers night, unshaken . . . amidst the hurrying clouds.' " On May 23 the Commissioner wrote: "Reports this morning are . . . decidedly unfavorable to the passage of the bills. . . . True to his hates," Clay "has flung down . . . defiance to the friends of General Taylor. . . . I am glad . . . he has at last stept out with his armor on." An *avowed* enemy could be met. "Remember the Union and Old Zack and his need of friends to speak for him."

Taylor's supporters now were more numerous and ardent than is generally remembered. "Hurrah for old Zack, and Dam his enemies," wrote a Missouri Whig.[2] "The difficulties . . . surrounding . . . General Taylor . . . only . . . increase my . . . zeal for him," said Crittenden. His "resolute integrity and patriotism will bear him through . . . the storm . . . triumphantly." Weed agreed that "Gen. Taylor, with good Mates and a hearty Crew can take the ship through . . . in safety." "Old Zack is on . . . top . . . & can keep there," a Bostonian predicted. "Our President is . . . gaining rapidly with the Masses," another said. Taylor "is undoubtedly right, honest & patriotic," a Fillmore follower admitted. Ohio's Corwin, long a Clay adherent, described Clay's project as "impracticable"—and Taylor's as "the only permanent cure." On June 25 Weed wrote: "Old Zack's stock is looking up." Months before, Letcher foresaw that "the occasion . . . will require . . . the most uncompromising decision. . . . I can almost hear the old Hoss say . . . 'Posts all . . . of you. I shall quell the Rebellion.' "[3]

3

These and similar comments contained no quaver of doubt as to Taylor's rectitude. Meanwhile he won additional support. A meeting at Cazenovia, New York, praised the President as incorruptible, wise, brave and firm. Salem, Massachusetts, "friends of the Administration" passed "resolutions of approbation." The Baltimore *Patriot* admonished Whigs to abandon "disputes about means. Let us look only to the end—and . . . give . . . the Administration . . . earnest . . . support." The Rochester *Democrat* accused the compromisers of inconsistency and insincerity: The Washington *Union* promised the compromise would open New Mexico and Utah to slavery, but Northern papers boasted that it would carve *"free territory enough out of Texas . . . for three states . . . and . . . make Utah and New Mexico free."* Thus "opposite effects" were "claimed," depending on the audience.

While meetings upheld or upbraided Taylor, Greeley's *Tribune* (reputedly forthright) inveighed on both sides of the issue. "The President is daily gaining ground in the confidence and affection of . . . the people," it proclaimed. "They knew him before as brave and honest; they believe him now to be capable and wise." Yet Greeley still stuck to Clay. When attacking compromisers he concentrated on Webster. Talking out of both corners of his mouth, he failed to provide guidance for the crisis. And men turned elsewhere, while Greeley wobbled. The New York *Courier* professed surprise that several city presses offered "grave advice to the Whig party" to recognize Taylor as its leader! Why, whoever thought of anyone else? His "strength is greater in this State" than in 1848. When the *Democratic Review* snapped that Taylor had "an innate consciousness of incompetency," the New York *Commercial* answered: "Emergencies, sudden and threatening, have overtaken the Government . . . and he has met them with prudence and overcome" them "with vigor." When the Richmond *Whig* denounced Clay's strictures against the President, the Louisville *Courier* approved the editorial. Earlier the Staunton *Spectator* insisted: "No President . . . has ever met" so many "serious issues in so short a period . . . involving matters of such momentous importance." He "met them . . . as a patriot, capable of discerning the *right,* and firm in maintaining it."[4]

Nevertheless, individual Whigs and some newspapers shared the regret "that there is not more power in the administration." Despite Taylor's disposition "to do good," a Hoosier wrote Judge McLean, he could not "accomplish anything" positive. "Besides . . . unscrupulous war . . . from the locofoco party, he is the object of . . . vindictive assaults from his own." When Burnley growled, Crittenden reproved him: "We must support old Zack—He deserves it. . . . We must fight."

While Taylorites grew more determined, Clay made no appreciable gains—and, if anything, lost ground. On June 4 Chase observed: "Clay has not been very successful in hastening any question upon his bill. . . . The Nashville Convention . . . will probably take sides with . . . opponents of the Compromise." If so, "Clay himself will be inclined to give it up." Martin Van Buren, Jr., wrote his father: "All things are working together" to enable Benton to "table . . . the Compromise" and carry California's admission. More and more Northerners appeared to agree with a Southerner's statement that Taylor's policy "is the wisest and truest; it will alone relieve the country," admitting California and letting "the people . . . settle the rest."

"What a singular political conjunction is that of Cass, Clay & Webster," Chase exclaimed. "What a . . . team they make with Foote for a driver!" The compromise "patchwork" appealed to few. "The break between Clay and the Administration seems . . . complete. . . . His course reminds everybody of his action when Tyler came in. But . . . Clay now heads a faction—then he led a Party. The difference is great." Weed's paper echoed this: "The experiment . . . practised upon . . . Tyler will signally fail with . . . Taylor. No denunciation . . . will change his purpose." In late June a Clay admirer reported to New Yorkers that compromise prospects looked increasingly doubtful. "I heard Mr. Clay remark . . . that he was not without hopes . . . but had never been . . . very sanguine." Webb's *Courier* declared: "The Whigs . . . cannot honorably or safely fail to sustain . . . Gen. Taylor." As for Taylor himself a story depicted him receiving three senators at the White House and listening attentively "while they told him all they feared." Appearing anxious, he "held his face . . . buried between his hands." Finally the President "rose, strode around the room . . . and . . . said, in his peculiarly mild but firm voice, 'Gentlemen, I was placed here to support the Constitution. I have sworn to do it; I can do it; and I *will* do it.' " If Taylor's views respecting the Union failed to square with Clay's and the Democrats', no one doubted where he stood or questioned his inflexible purpose. On the slavery-containment question Old Rough and Ready was gaining strength as June and July ushered in one of Washington's hot, unendurable summers.[5]

4

On another front Taylor did not fare so well, an unexpected element of national politics magnifying his worries and eventually all but dissolving his Cabinet. The President took pride in his personal integrity as much as in patriotic enterprise, and his fondest hope was that his Administration would enjoy equally good repute. Therefore he was amazed and hurt when a most unusual "scandal" found its way to the White House threshold. Involving three Cabinet members, this scandal gave Taylor's foes ammunition to direct deadly barrages of criticism at an overwrought Executive. Prior to 1849 Taylor may never have heard of the Galphin Claim. In the spring of 1850, however, he probably thought of nothing else more often—save the Union's fate, with which the claim became so strangely intertwined. The press featured charges and revelations of "Galphinism" day after day during April, May and June. Readers delved into the claim's origins, which developed into a favorite topic in Washington and over the country.

The Galphin story extended back three quarters of a century. Before the Revolution, Creek and Cherokee Indians had ceded large tracts in Georgia to white intruders, provided bills they owed colonial traders would be paid out of the proceeds. The cession being ratified by the crown, certificates were issued to various traders—George Galphin's amounting to £9,791, 15s, 5d. Galphin had no chance to collect before the Revolution broke. Afterward London met other claims. But Galphin, having sided with the colonies, was denied payment by the British. Accordingly he and his heirs had attempted to obtain principal and interest from Georgia for more than forty years. Though from time to time Georgia's senate and house acknowledged the justice of the claim, the paucity of state funds prevented reimbursement. In 1835 someone inserted into an Indian treaty a clause binding Washington to make good the Galphin Claim. How this was done remains mysterious, but in any event the clause was struck out. Two years later Governor William Schley informed President Jackson: "The claim . . . has always been considered just by Georgia, but . . . it arose under a treaty stipulation, the fulfillment of which devolved . . . not on Georgia, but on the Government of the United States, which . . . succeeded . . . that of . . . Britain."

Thus "Who is to pay?" had remained the question in Milledgeville and Washington. In '46 and '47 the cause made progress in Congress. And in '48 the Galphin bill, passing the Senate without debate, went to the House and on August 12 coasted to victory without dissent. Although Secretary of the Treasury Walker paid the principal of $43,518.97, he did not write a draft for the interest. And so the problem of the larger sum—nearly five times the principal—was left for Meredith to solve.

In May '49 one Joseph Bryan, acting as Milledge Galphin's "attorney," had submitted an elaborate brief, for payment of interest, to Meredith. The latter, promptly referring it to Comptroller Elisha Whittlesey, requested study and recommendation. Whittlesey, a Whig appointed by Taylor, advised against allowing interest. (One of Walker's Democratic comptrollers originally took a similar position. Changing his mind, however, he deemed an interest payment proper, but only for an eleven-year period, since the Galphins first memorialized the United States in '38.) Perhaps because of the sum involved, as well as his own doubts in the matter, Meredith in September asked Attorney General Johnson for an opinion. Johnson obliged the following February, taking his time as lawyers do; he held the interest payment just, not merely for eleven years but for over seventy-three.

On receipt of Johnson's opinion, Meredith paid out $191,352.89, bringing the principal-and-interest total to nearly $235,000. No inconsiderable fortune, this probably would have caused commotion in legal circles and the press, even without its political sequel. As matters eventuated, one aspect of the claim turned out to be nitroglycerin. Secretary of War Crawford had been the Galphins' counsel and agent sixteen years. Employed on a contingent basis, he had pocketed half the principal—and now would receive half the interest as an additional reward for his services![6]

5

What a ruckus the Democrats raised on discovering three Cabinet members in a Whig "treasury raid"! What a picture the word artists painted! Had not the Secretary of the Treasury, advised by the Attorney General, dipped into the nation's funds to give the Secretary of War almost $100,000? Would the ministers deny the facts? Democratic papers wanted to know. In New York the Whig *Express* also said things that made Taylorites wince. No defense seemed quite adequate, for a claim of this size should have been scrutinized in advance in Cabinet council—on the theory that smart politicians avoid the substance *and appearance* of wrongdoing. If Meredith at a Cabinet meeting had mentioned the claim as a matter of routine, Crawford could scarcely have remained silent regarding his dual status. Political and legal implications could then have been aired, and Taylor would have had a full opportunity to listen to the pros and cons.

Unfortunately no thorough Cabinet discussion took place until after the "exposure." Meredith and Johnson disclaimed knowledge of Crawford's Galphin connection. In other words there was no collusion. Crawford later declared he had taken the problem to the President, carefully explaining that the claim had nothing to do with the War Department. According to Crawford's recollection Taylor replied that acceptance of office curtailed none of his "preexisting individual rights." A practiced politician in the Mansion might not have been so generous, and an authoritative student has written: "It is possible . . . that Crawford did not go . . . fully into . . . details" in his talk with Taylor. Whether or not he was at fault otherwise, Crawford apparently gave Taylor the impression that the claim still pended before Congress. Crawford later testified that, in a second interview, the President said he would have reacted the same way had he understood the situation more accurately. This was magnanimity plus. According to Ewing, the other Cabinet members urged Taylor to drop Crawford—but Taylor refused the easy way out.

Some peculiar ramifications of the Galphin issue have generally been minimized. Curiously Crawford was the only secretary agreeing with Stephens and Toombs (and differing with Taylor) on slavery extension. It was ironic, too, that his fellow Georgians had backed Crawford for the Cabinet in the first place, knowing all about his Galphin agency. (Toombs sponsored many Galphin memorials, and Stephens delivered the check for the principal to Crawford in Augusta.) Thus, indirectly responsible for a scandal jeopardizing the entire Cabinet, they now defended the claim in the House. A writer with a talent for histrionics might expand on such a theme. By ignoring Toombs and Stephens and picking Butler King for his Cabinet, Taylor would have ducked this blow. Of such conditions and decisions the chances of politics are composed.

It is to Crawford's credit that he requested an investigation, placing his fate in the hands of the House. Armistead Burt, Calhoun's nephew by marriage, headed the nine-man committee named by Speaker Cobb. The other Democrats were Winfield S. Featherston, Mississippi; David T. Disney, Ohio; Job Mann, Pennsylvania, and Joseph W. Jackson,

Georgia. The Whigs were Daniel Breck, Kentucky; Joseph Grinnell, Massachusetts; James G. King, New Jersey, and Charles M. Conrad, Louisiana. All nine committeemen agreed that legislation had required Walker to pay the principal. Democrats asserted and Whigs denied that interest should have been withheld, and that the claim itself "was not a just demand against the United States." Aside from these conclusions, the committee split three ways in presenting "arguments" to the House. The Whigs, maintaining that the "Government was under an equitable obligation" to meet the claim, insisted that both principal and interest "have been paid in conformity to law and precedent." Burt and Jackson were content to repeat that payment of interest was not justified, while the remaining Democrats recommended additional resolutions. Of these the most important were:

Resolved, That Congress should pass a law prohibiting the payment of interest in any case by any officer of the Government, unless expressly directed by law, [and]

Resolved, That Congress should pass a law prohibiting any member of the Cabinet from deciding on any claim or demand . . . in which any other member of the same Cabinet shall be interested.

On May 17, when the report, resolutions, and arguments were ordered printed, Representative James Brooks broke into the discussion with a vitriolic speech. Brooks attacked Crawford, Meredith, Johnson and even George Galphin's loyalty to the colonies' cause. His summation underscored "two very important questions"—whether "the Secretary of War should be interesting himself in claims . . . and . . . whether the Secretary of the Treasury should pay . . . interest, when Congress is in session, and . . . he has been" empowered only to "examine" and "adjust." Superficially the New Yorker seemed interested in defending Taylor. The President could not find time to study every aspect "of such a claim." The "fame" of Taylor—"that great and good man"—soared above smear. Critics "might as well think of blotting out Orion" as making mud stick to Old Zack.

Dramatic! Touching! But Brooks's honey failed to sweeten his vinegar. Favoring the compromise and opposing Taylor's Plan, he was at heart a Clay adherent. Congressional Democrats must have been delighted when a Whig led the chorus of Galphin criticism. There was cause for *both* Clay Whigs *and* Democrats to cheer Brooks's strictures to the echo.

6

More than a score of representatives spoke on the Galphin issue. Toombs replied to Brooks by defending the claim's integrity, the arrangements for its payment and especially Crawford's conduct. To Brooks's support rushed Harmon S. Conger, another Clay Whig, who attacked the Democrat Walker as well as Crawford, Meredith, and, "above all," Johnson. On July 1, Toombs, Conger, and Brooks spoke again. Breck, deprecating the "hue and cry," took the ground that the secretaries merely executed the '48 law and were sustained by equity and precedents. Toombs had offered an amendment to the Democratic committeemen's resolutions:

Resolved, That there is no evidence submitted by the committee to whom was referred the letter of George W. Crawford, asking "an investigation" . . . which impugns his personal or official conduct in relation to the settlement of the claim.

Now Robert C. Schenck, who disapproved of Crawford, proposed a substitute.

Resolved, That while this House . . . does not find cause to impute to the Secretary of War any corrupt "conduct" or fraudulent practice . . . yet it does not approve his "relation" to . . . [the] claim in . . . that he continued to be interested in the prosecution of it while it was to be examined, adjudicated, and paid, by one of the departments . . . he himself . . . holding office as the head of one of those departments.

Schenck also declared: "Whether the Galphin Claim was originally valid . . . or whether . . . the principal should have been settled but not the interest . . . have nothing to do with the true issue before us, or at . . . best are only collateral." Crawford demanded "an investigation into his 'conduct and relation to' the Galphin claim—that is all!"

After Stephens supported Toombs, and Featherston and Disney attacked Taylor and the Cabinet, Schenck gave evidence that he did not even agree with himself. Having offered a substitute for Toombs's amendment, he now said this resolution should stand as a substitute for the majority report—while in its stead he sponsored the following to terminate the Toombs trailer:

Provided, however, That this House is not understood as approving his [Crawford's] relation to that claim, in continuing to be interested in the prosecution of it when it was to be examined, adjusted, and paid by one of the departments of the Government, he himself being at the same time at the head of another of those departments; but the House considers that such connection and interest of a member of the Cabinet . . . would be dangerous as a precedent, and ought not to be sanctioned.

On July 3 Mississippi's Jacob Thompson enlivened the debate with his amendment, to be added to Schenck's amendment:

And consequently that the House also totally dissents from the correctness of the opinion expressed by the President . . . to the Secretary of War, "that his . . . being at the head of the War Department, and the agent of the claimants, did not take from him any rights he may have had as such agent, or would have justified him in having the examination and decision of the claims by the Secretary of the Treasury suspended."

Resolved, further, That this House decidedly disapproves of, and dissents from, the opinion given by the Attorney General in favor of an allowance of interest on said claim, and from the action of the Secretary of the Treasury in payment of the same claim.

Thompson, a leader of the South's Democracy, thus showed the lengths to which opponents would go to embarrass President Taylor.

As a further part of the parliamentary jockeying Schenck modified his substitute for Toombs's amendment so as to include it within his own amendment. Then David K. Cartter of Ohio lashed out in a speech as brutal as Brooks's. There was no distinction between Crawford's culpability and that of "his official associates." All, all were guilty, Cartter asserted. "If it was legally right for them to pay it, it was legally right for him to receive it."

Cartter did not have the last word. "There is no testimony," John W. Houston of Delaware replied, ". . . that . . . a majority of the . . . Cabinet knew anything of this claim or of its settlement." No representative really "believes . . . there is . . . anything to warrant the slightest presumption of fraud, corruption, or unfairness." How ridiculous to assume with the Democrats that "it was a just claim against nobody"! Had not Congress recognized its worth? Did not Polk approve it, and Walker pay the principal? Walker himself testified that, with an opinion like Johnson's before him, he would have paid the interest, too. Said Houston: "I cannot conceive how this claim can be" due, "without carrying the legal incident of interest with it." Indiscriminate and unjustified censure of the whole Administration smelled of partisanship.

Time and impartial history would vindicate the reputation of "these gentlemen."

New Jersey's James King was another Whig whose speech in defense proved effective. Three other Whigs followed. On July 6 a fourth, Charles E. Clarke of New York, drove his points home with the most conviction. After praising George Galphin's "efficient service" to the Revolutionary cause, Clarke tore into Burt. He recalled a letter Milledge Galphin received in '48: "Dear Sir: I have the pleasure to say that the bill in which you are interested has just been signed by the Speaker . . . and will be approved by the President. With great respect . . . ARMISTEAD BURT." Though the measure's passage had once "pleased" Burt, he now branded the bill unwarranted—when his "single objection would have defeated it." How odd that Crawford "entirely . . . escapes" Burt's rebuke, when the Carolinian strongly criticized Meredith! Perhaps it was "not . . . disastrous" to Burt to assail a Northerner, while his "southern friend . . . gets the money" without even Burt's reprimand! Aware that Brooks was no less vulnerable than Burt, Clarke ridiculed the self-righteous journalist who "calls upon his *Whig friends to run for their lives,* whilst he . . . sets fire to the funeral pile." When "a bold effort is made to cast a stigma on an upright . . . Administration, I deem it my duty to repel the effort." Clarke saw "no reason to flee." He felt "not the slightest disposition to be one of the officiating priests . . . to quiet the clamors of ignorance and party spirit, or the *vengeance of individual enemies.*"

Clarke drew on the opinions of three attorneys general to fortify the claim. He also stressed the Senate Judiciary Committee's finding that the United States was "justly liable to pay." Not only this, but the act itself made "the Secretary of the Treasury . . . bound to *examine, adjust, and pay*" the claim. How inconsistent of its opponents to "manifest . . . ignorance" of this premise, when several of them had failed to exercise "their great reasoning power" against the committee's report and the '48 law while the opportunity was theirs. Thus they locked the stable door only "after the steed was stolen."

Clarke offered no apology for Crawford, who, "having so deep an interest in so large a claim," should never have entered the Cabinet. But he also blamed Burt for neglecting to probe "the conduct of the Secretary of War, at whose request this investigation was begun." The Democrats' "enlargement of jurisdiction" was unprecedented, having "taken leave to criticise" persons "not on trial, and to pass . . . unfounded . . . judgment" on them. "The worst . . . feature in the whole transaction is the effort to interpose our good, honest, patriotic President as a shield between the Secretary of War and this House. The rules of this House will not permit me to characterize this . . . with the name it deserves."

7

When Clarke concluded, Burt replied ineffectually. Then the House voted on the resolutions, amendments, and substitutes—the outcome containing elements of victory, as well as setbacks, for the Administration. Schenck's amendment to Toombs's amendment passed, but the two washed out together on the following test. Things looked bleak for Taylor when Thompson's amendment to Schenck's substitute squeaked by, but it too disappeared from the agenda with the amended substitute's rejection. The three original resolutions, however (those on which the five Democrats agreed), passed the House by king-size majorities. Thus the representatives formally found that the claim was not a just demand against the United States; that Walker did right in paying the principal and that Meredith acted without authorization. The members did not censure Taylor, Meredith, Johnson or even Crawford.[7]

Concerned as we are chiefly with Taylor, we lack a foolproof way of determining which strains on his body and mind stemmed from the Galphin scandal, and which originated in the sectional struggle or the Clayton-Bulwer trials. The President endured great stress in April, May, June—and on into July. The pressures on him were tremendous. Superior experience in partisan politics might have supplied immunity, which his Army background failed to provide. His friends noticed a deterioration in Taylor's appearance. We may surmise that, without the claim to badger him, Taylor might have faced the summer with considerably less distress.

Brown told Crittenden in early May that Taylor showed signs of fatigue. Burnley thought him "dejected & haggard." Brown "found him looking badly—as if he did not sleep well and was unhappy." Some time before, "the hero-President" had confided that "he longed to return . . . to his quiet home"—being "sorely tired of . . . harassing responsibilities of . . . high office." Brown, himself homesick for Kentucky, went to the White House to "apprise" Taylor of "my intended resignation." But "I could not add to his troubles by intruding my own affairs . . . and so I left without saying a word." Burnley's "constrained & rather embarrassing . . . interview" suggests that he too took pity on Old Zack's distraught feelings. Meredith begged Brown not to mention resignation; "he knew . . . my society was a great relief to . . . Gen. Taylor & that he required just such a friend" when "deserted by others who had his affection & confidence."

Brown apparently did not share Bullitt's uncontrolled animosity. "I despise the Cabinet!" Bullitt cried. ". . . They are . . . ignorant, cold, contriving, selfish and treacherous . . . monsters," who "sit like foul toads upon the Presidents shoulder spitting poison into his ear. . . . You know how he has treated them," and how they repaid this trust. "I held still until I saw an effort made to saddle the President with the Galphin affair. This was so . . . gratuitous an act that my disgust boiled over.— That a Cabinet Minister should be a claim agent . . . needed only to be stated to be condemned. And yet these Cabinet humbugs . . . must . . . make gum-elastic" of the President's character "to stretch it over acts which will not bear the light."[8]

It might have been more manly of Bullitt to admit that he himself shared responsibility for Taylor's woes, because of his conduct of the *Republic*. At all events the President's decline coincided with both the Galphin exposé and Bullitt's dismissal. The wonder is that more people did not comment on Taylor's haggardness. He pulled himself together in late June—Seward writing, "The President . . . is in fine spirits"—and an observer noting his "smiling countenance" and "light heart." The acute Fredrika Bremer said nothing about fatigue or disease—only that "he is kind and agreeable . . . and was simply, almost negligently, dressed."

8

While some associates noticed the wear and tear on Taylor, he continued to apply himself unstintedly to his work and social duties. His messages to Congress had related not only to California, New Mexico, removals and the Clayton-Bulwer Treaty but to various secondary matters, which added to the load he bore.

Taylor's hope of rescuing Sir John Franklin from Arctic wastes went unrealized in 1849 due to the lack of "vessels suitable to encounter the perils of a proper exploration . . . and the want of an appropriation." Congress being in session, the "propriety . . . of an appropriation for fitting out an expedition . . . is respectfully submitted to your consideration," Taylor wrote in January. The legislators failed to act, but the President must have been pleased in May when crews sailed out, financed by the wealthy Henry Grinnell. Special messages regarding Indians, appropriations, Nicaragua, a claims convention with Brazil and Mann's Hungarian mission followed. A convention with New Granada, Canadian reciprocity and peace with Florida's Seminoles competed with more important business. Of infinitely greater significance were Taylor's messages of February 13 (submitting California's constitution), March 26 (Butler King's report), April 22 (the Clayton-Bulwer Treaty), May 22 (California correspondence), June 3 and 10 (Cuba filibustering) and June 17 and July 1 (orders and instructions regarding New Mexico).[9] In May, June and the first two days of July, the special messages numbered seventeen.

If these figures seem small by modern standards, it should be recalled that Taylor's secretarial help was limited. The little State Department staff, often hard pressed, assisted on international matters. Treasury and Interior clerks were drafted now and again. But Taylor wrote personal letters in his own hand, and nearly all routine replies to the multiplicity of inquiries and invitations were penned by one man, Bliss. Twice or thrice the number of letters, Bliss-composed and Taylor-signed, than are known to exist probably have been cached away in dust-laden attic trunks. Enough have been unearthed to establish "Perfect" Bliss as a valuable factor in White House procedures.

Ceremonies public and social have always been an integral ingredient of Presidents' way of life. Taylor had previously attended two congressional funerals; in May, the obsequies of Franklin H. Elmore (who succeeded Calhoun in the Senate) brought him to the Capitol. As flowers of springtime festooned Washington, the President attended weddings. Among others he honored the nuptials of Ellen Ewing and William T. Sherman. The reception in the Blair house found Clay, Webster, Clayton and Benton among Secretary Ewing's guests. "You labored very hard dear Mother & managed everything so beautifully" that the wedding "went off elegantly," Ellen wrote on her honeymoon. "Did you know . . . I . . . kissed the President? I did not know what I was doing until I had kissed him." Thus ecstatic young ladies, as well as cold corpses, received tributes from Old Zack. Few onlookers suspected the conflicts hidden beneath his placid face. Taylor's gracious reception of William Allen Butler and his bride was frequently duplicated. With cordiality, he welcomed visitors by the hundreds to the White House grounds on Saturdays, when the Marine Band played. Whether attending divine services, or witnessing tests of a "cast-iron bridge across Rock Creek" or exchanging "salutations" with Clay during a band concert, Taylor also found time to accept gifts—such as George Washington's writing case from Custis.

The Washington scene was enlivened by such diverse personalities as the actress Charlotte Cushman, the authors Grace Greenwood and Mrs. E. D. E. N. Southworth, the clown Dan Rice and the poet John Howard Payne.[10] At Cabinet members' parties women with fair and plain faces "jostled . . . in promiscuous confusion." When officials' wives were not holding "at-homes," they scattered calling cards with abandon. Forty-eight callers in one afternoon! "I had a terrible day," Mrs. Ewing groaned. Forgetting the time of Mrs. Winthrop's reception, one social-ite "was about sending" in her card when a servant came to her carriage and asked if she would not join the company. "I was obliged to go in" and found her sister looked "younger and much handsomer than Mrs. W———." Such comment, ironically, was a hostess' penalty for being on hand in her own parlor!

9

As Washingtonians settled down to the humidity and languor of summer, Zachary Taylor concerned himself with twists of politics as well as trivia. No mere figurehead, he kept his finger on the pulse of government. And few were better fitted to realize that the rose-vines "clustering across the . . . wall" which divided Seward's house from Crawford's symbolized more than a floral effect. There were thorns in those roses. Pricked to the bleeding point by the Galphin scandal, adhering to his antiextension position, Taylor began heeding recommendations to consider new Cabinet timber.

Weed has testified on this, and, though his witness value is debatable, he was not alone in advocating change. Allison wrote his brother-in-law: "Part of your Cabinet does not possess the confidence of the whigs in Kentucky. . . . Knowing the purity of your intentions I trust your course may . . . unite, not divide the whig party. . . . It is a growing idea . . . that your plan of compromise" will be the republic's anchor. "You do not" lose in popularity. Frequently, said Allison, "as much strength of mind . . . is . . . displayed" in supplanting as in retaining advisers. When "Jackson changed his Cabinet I well recollect thinking he was broken down." Instead, "he acquired more . . . popularity."[11]

Convinced of his rectitude in opposing extension, opposed to compromise, and resenting Southern threats, Taylor almost surely was thinking in terms of a Cabinet shake-up. The secretaries' strength belonged to the past. His own endured in the living present. Why might not Taylor gain immeasurably by following Old Hickory's example? Confronted from the first by a hostile Senate and by foemen in command of the House, he now was challenged—but not defeated—by opponents whose votes were chiefly Democratic, but whose arguments Clay declaimed. How better to meet all issues at once than to drop weak advisers, while pronouncing stern principles?

CHAPTER XXVIII

The Clayton-Bulwer Treaty

1

WHILE the Galphin Claim vied with slavery's containment for the President's attention, Zachary Taylor gingerly fingered his thorniest international issue. Bulwer's arrival on American soil had signaled the start of conversations leading to an important treaty. Though appointed to the Washington mission early in 1849, this seasoned diplomat remained in England until after Palmerston's exploratory talks with Bancroft, Rives and Lawrence. Early in '50 Bulwer began his discussions with Secretary Clayton, and no other phase of foreign affairs was so consequential as their give-and-take.

If Clayton did not change for the worse during his Cabinet service, his critics still accused him of breaking promises and of losing influence on the Hill. His patronage burden had decreased, however, and now he could devote most of his attention, uninterruptedly, to departmental business. Bulwer had more to recommend him for negotiations of this kind. A product of Harrow, Cambridge, Parliament and diplomatic triumphs in Europe, Bulwer was a clever writer and also a gambler who delighted in the spin of the wheel and the cut of the cards. As Britain's representative in Spain, he ran into trouble, due to Palmerston's intrigues. Yet, even when caught in the act of interfering with internal Spanish politics, he continued to rate ace-high in London and drew no rebuke on reaching home.

Bulwer's disposition and manner made him a universal favorite. "Sauntering through society with an air of languor, he veiled the keenest observation under an aspect of indifference." Whenever he was in reality cautious, he was seemingly negligent. His apparent casualness in relating an anecdote "gave it a peculiarly poignant effect," and his popularity was mainly attributable to mastery of subtle conversational arts. Fused with his suave personality, the fact that Bulwer was a knight commander of the Bath, brother of a famous novelist and the Iron Duke's nephew by marriage gave him unusual prestige. Sir Henry's natural and acquired graces, bargaining finesse and literary skill all enter into consideration of what he contributed diplomatically.

2

At the outset Clayton and Bulwer sought a tentative agreement before referring their preliminary *projet* to their superiors for critical
review. There was much to recommend this procedure. Lacking the advantage of a transatlantic cable, Bulwer would need six weeks to obtain
replies to dispatches sent his chief. Though Clayton could have consulted Taylor regarding the initial discussions, the President preferred
temporarily to grant him as much leeway as the British envoy's. The
result was that, in about a month, meeting informally in each other's
quarters, the two worked out a draft which met Palmerston's eyes not
long after Taylor first studied it.

This paper, sent Palmerston on February 3, pledged both nations not
to seek exclusive control over the canal. Neither country would "occupy . . . or colonize . . . Nicaragua, Costa Rica, the Mosquito Coast
or any part of Central America." Neither would assume or exercise
dominion, or use alliances or influence, for the purpose of acquiring or
holding advantages not offered to the other. Should an Anglo-American war occur in the future, American and British vessels "shall . . .
be exempted" from capture in the canal by either belligerent. "Persons
employed in making the . . . Canal . . . and their Property" would be
protected from unjust detention, confiscation and violence. Free ports
were to be established at each end, and governments which claimed
jurisdiction would aid in the canal's construction. It was specified that
the contracting parties would guarantee the canal's neutrality and secure
capital investments. Provision was made for "every Nation, State or
People" to contribute to the plan, and the negotiators adhered to the
principle that other approved trans-isthmian works would receive "protection" and "encouragement."

The *projet,* however, did not even mention Britain's controversial
Mosquito protectorate. This omission represented a conscious effort
to avoid entangling the canal in a basic disagreement. In his explanation to Palmerston, Bulwer stressed his determination not to yield in
this regard.[1] Clayton felt that the verb "occupy" and other language
achieved the same objective as a denial of Mosquito claims, in which
Britain would not join. Clayton's interpretation was destined to be debated by three generations of statesmen. In it lay many of the strengths
and weaknesses of the Clayton-Bulwer Treaty.

3

While Bulwer awaited word from Palmerston and Taylor scrutinized the *projet,* Sir Henry replied to Clayton's inquiry respecting Britain's Tigre seizure. Hot then, this aroused suspicions of English motives in America. In lieu of official instructions, Bulwer stated his "conviction" that seeking "colonies or conquests in . . . Central America" did not accord with British policy. "The object of H.M.'s Govt. was never to take permanent possession of Tigre"—occupation stemming from Britain's placing a lien on unmet claims. Thus Bulwer put his best foot forward. And on this phase Clayton was satisfied.

Bulwer was sick part of the time between February 7 and 14. About the twelfth he heard unofficially that all was not going well in connection with Taylor's reception of the *projet.* Careful not to show how much of the whole story he knew, the envoy wrote Clayton: "If your Cabinet" entertained "any doubts," it would be "desirable" to know what they were, that means might be devised for meeting them. Almost certainly word had reached him that his country's Mosquito protectorate was the root of White House disagreement. Reviewing Britain's position, Bulwer said: "We, in consequence of old engagements, took part with the Mosquito people against the Nicaraguans." This was not being "hostile to you." But if "you" support Nicaragua's claim, "you commit . . . an act of hostility towards us." Thanking Clayton for withholding Squier's treaty from Congress, he would prefer its submission to any bid for transferring Mosquito soil to Nicaragua. Why seek a quarrel? Sir Henry asked. Surely not for the canal's sake! "We will do everything to favour it." But "taking a possession from a people . . . for centuries under our protection" and handing it over "to another people . . . recently taken under your protection" was unwarrantable! Superficially a loose and personalized minor document, Bulwer's communication testifies to the deftness of a master hand.

Clayton now could no longer soft-pedal the Mosquito issue. On February 15 he supported Taylor's position that the United States could not relinquish her Nicaragua alliance unless England abandoned the Mosquito protectorate. Indian titles were only titles "by occupancy" and could be extinguished at will. This principle, deriving from "English precedents," applied to Mosquitos as much as to Shawnees, Blackfeet or Flatheads. Fewer than 500 Indians lived between Bluefields and the San Juan. Sensible nations should not expend lives and treasure over degraded, syphilitic Indians, who could be well cared for if let alone. With only "one spot yet discovered" for a canal, Britain took possession of the indispensable outlet. "We examined the title and found . . . you had . . . none"—then turned to Nicaragua, "the rightful authority," for permission to dig. Although Nicaragua granted permission, the United States offered all nations "equal advantages with ourselves," leaving "it open for the benefit of the human family."

"You seem to think . . . that you" alone must "make a sacrifice," Clayton continued. How mistaken! No Central American country would refuse to join the United States "tomorrow." Nevertheless, "we offer to agree" not to occupy any of them, "if you will only consent to give up your alliance with your Mosquito King." The end product of England's current Mosquito attitude would be American vindication of Nicaragua sovereignty "in the least offensive way." But if "you . . . extinguish the Indian title . . . or . . . abandon the protectorate" south of the Belize River, "we will agree with you not to colonize, fortify, occupy or exercise dominion over any part . . . of the Central American States or to make any . . . contract with them." Clayton added that President Taylor "thinks we make, by far, the greatest concessions." The Secretary then laid down an ultimatum: "If you . . . interfere to assist the Mosquitos, we . . . shall interpose in behalf of Nicaragua. Such are the President's instructions to me." In other words, Taylor felt compelled to send Squier's treaty to the Senate.[2]

4

This Taylor did on March 19, with the remark that "nothing narrow, selfish, illiberal, or exclusive" conditioned the American viewpoint. "British pretension to . . . San Juan in right of the Mosquito King" was "without just foundation," and "I shall ratify this treaty in case the Senate shall advise that course." Submission of the pact offended Bulwer. Indeed, in the month between the conversation at Clayton's house and the Squier treaty's submission, each side had hoped the other would give way on fundamentals. When Palmerston's instructions finally reached his envoy, however, they consisted largely of approval of the February 3 *projet*—which Taylor found inadequate. Bulwer discussed alternative propositions in dispatches dated February 18, including the possibility that Britain could reconcile American objections by accepting the *projet* and then interpreting its Mosquito application. However, Bulwer did not feel authorized to advance beyond his previous position. Hence Taylor considered himself obligated to turn over to the Senate the Squier treaty.

Bulwer then could have ended negotiations. Still, impressed by Central Americans' readiness to be annexed to the United States, he sought a new approach on the theory that Britain would never have a better opportunity. Why not capitalize on Clayton's *projet*, recognizing his reliance on the word "occupy," and trusting in the English definition to result in a triumph for London? Thus Bulwer, on March 27, told Clayton that he now held full power to conclude a convention. Incorporated in Palmerston's authorization, as the Secretary understood it, was the assurance that Britain would clarify her stand on the Mosquito Coast. Renewing Palmerston's promise to Lawrence, Bulwer was to affirm at the time of signing that Britain did not intend to use "the protection" to do "the things . . . disclaimed in the letter to Mr. Lawrence." In that document, as Clayton reminded Bulwer, the Foreign Secretary disavowed the purpose of occupying or colonizing "any part of Central America"—claiming no dominion in Mosquito and joining in assurances not to settle or fortify adjacent territory.

Reiterating the precise language several times, Clayton said: "The President . . . instructs me to declare" that nothing in an Anglo-American treaty "shall be construed to be an admission . . . of any right or title . . . in the Mosquito King" to any part of Central America. Palmerston's remarks in November "and the allusion to the Protectorate in your note" led the President to consider it his duty to restate Washington's position. With this understanding, Clayton concluded, Taylor "has directed me" to sign the proposed convention. "Happiest results may be anticipated" from an "alliance for the purpose of diffusing the blessings of commerce and civilization."

5

Though Bulwer objected to part of Clayton's note, he did not mention the basic conflict regarding the Mosquitos—differing with the United States only as to Squier's treaty. Sponsorship of Squier's pact seemed "unnecessary and unprovoked," Sir Henry wrote, when "we are endeavouring to arrange" matters "to your satisfaction." He asked that his note be considered "private" and requested Clayton to "think over the matter before we come . . . to a final decision." At the same time he expressed the "pain and surprise with which I find myself under the necessity of declaring" this opinion.

The jockeying continued. Taylor could not "conceive how . . . the simple fact" that the Administration recognized Nicaragua's sovereignty could "be offensive" to the British. Crampton had been duly informed. "We have never sought to conceal it." "The statement to which you object" was called for because of Bulwer's own mention of the Mosquito protectorate in one of his notes. As Clayton explained, the President had "carefully read over the projet" of the proposed Clayton-Bulwer Treaty. He "maintains . . . there is not a syllable in it inconsistent" with his recognition of the Nicaragua title, "& that if he refuses to recognize that title he breaks faith & forfeits the right acquired by the Nicaragua treaty & the contract to cut the Canal." If Bulwer sought to "compel us" to deny the title, "we may as well abandon the negotiation." Still, "I shall never think . . . that you have intended anything but in a friendly spirit." Clayton did not close without a fervent appeal to Sir Henry's common sense. After Britain asserted her Mosquito protectorate, the United States referred to the Nicaragua alliance. Yet one was only a "shadow"—the other "another shadow." Should a "substantial object be abandoned for the sake of shadows? "Is it not wise to agree upon everything upon which we can agree & then agree to disagree about other matters?" Clayton asserted: "Rely on it, I send you the Prest's ultimatum."

Clayton's note reached Bulwer that same Monday night. On the morrow, the plenipotentiary observed that "you . . . omitted some of the main points," and that "not a word was said respecting the Mosquito and Nicaragua dispute" in the initial talks. Although "you informed me" that the *projet* failed to satisfy some of the Cabinet, this had occurred a week after it was dispatched overseas—Clayton's colleagues fearing that Britain might do "covertly" what she stated she would not do "openly."

Bulwer hinted at the displeasure this development caused him. He objected strenuously to the presentation of "Mr. Squier's Treaty . . . to Congress" when he had understood this would not be done. "You stated that . . . you" submitted it "because you . . . conceived that our project would not be agreed to by my Government"—and because Palmerston's Tigre letter to Lawrence displeased the President. Yet in both London and Washington, Bulwer went on, the British authorities had previously been given to understand that the Squier convention would be altered to conform with the Clayton-Bulwer plan. Due to these assurances "I have acted . . . upon the supposition that we" would settle the canal question without bickering about Nicaragua and Mosquito. Bulwer "never dreamt until I received your note last Sunday" that Clayton would not only dispute the British claim, but also promote "a treaty with the Nicaraguans . . . recognizing their claim in opposition."

The Taylor-Clayton attitude might "be deemed . . . cause for an increase in our Naval Armaments," Sir Henry threatened. It was one thing to "state civilly . . . that it is not understood by you in our Treaty that you recognize thereby the title of the Mosquitos." But how different when ultimatums should justify expansion of Queen Victoria's navy! In his conclusion Bulwer left the diplomatic door slightly open. Much might be accomplished, he said, if—instead of recognizing Nicaragua's claim—"you state that you will do your utmost to obtain" a settlement of differences between her and Britain. But "I defy . . . you" to get English capital for the canal, "if you . . . recognise a title in Nicaragua" over land which London thought belonged to the Mosquitos.

"I will call upon you either this afternoon or tomorrow morning," Bulwer wrote on that ninth April day. And Clayton and Taylor waited to see what would come after this sharp retort.

6

There exists no transcript recording in detail the events occurring in the next week. Most of what was done was muffled. Negotiators moved on tiptoe. Finally, on April 19, Clayton and Bulwer affixed their names to the long-sought treaty, which Taylor sent to the Senate on April 22. The controversial first article follows:

The Governments of the United States and Great Britain hereby declare that neither . . . will . . . obtain or maintain . . . exclusive control over the . . . ship-canal; agreeing that neither will . . . erect or maintain . . . fortifications commanding the same, or in the vicinity thereof, or occupy, or fortify, or colonize, or assume or exercise any dominion over Nicaragua, Costa Rica, the Mosquito coast, or any part of Central America; nor will . . . make use of any protection which either affords or may afford, or any alliance which either has or may have to or with any State or people for the purpose of erecting or maintaining any such fortifications, or of occupying, fortifying, or colonizing Nicaragua, Costa Rica, the Mosquito coast, or any part of Central America, or of assuming or exercising dominion over the same; nor will the United States or Great Britain take advantage of any intimacy, or use any alliance, connection, or influence that either may possess, with any State or Government through whose territory the said canal may pass, for the purpose of acquiring or holding, directly or indirectly, for the citizens or subjects of the one any rights or advantages in regard to commerce or navigation through the said canal which shall not be offered on the same terms to the citizens or subjects of the other.

If the remaining articles did not differ importantly from those sketched in February, the first and vital one had been altered, notably by the interpolation of "any *protection* which either affords or may afford" nearly halfway down the list of provisions. In the main the treaty was more specific.[3] But, as Taylor remarked in a special message, it accorded with "the general views" he "expressed . . . to Congress in December last."

Its object, Taylor said, "is to establish a commercial alliance with all great maritime states" to protect a "canal through Nicaragua." It would also safeguard "every other interoceanic communication . . . adopted to shorten the transit" to California. "I found Great Britain in possession of nearly half of Central America, as the ally and protector of the Mosquito King. It has been my" purpose to secure the passage to the United States and, concurrently, to "maintain" the Central American republics' independence. Should the Senate confirm both this and the Nicaragua treaty, amendments might "be necessary" in order for them to conform with each other. "This is a task of no great difficulty." France and Russia "stand ready to accede," and no state would reject "so honorable" an arrangement.

With Taylor's straightforward recommendations Bulwer appeared in wholehearted accord. Squier's treaty still bothered Sir Henry. But such was his confidence in the Senate's "judgment," and the President's "superintending wisdom," that "I do not . . . fear" ratification of anything "in any other Treaty contrary to . . . our engagements." The transaction reflected "unselfish zeal," creditable to "our respective countries." Equally encouraging to Taylor was the fact that Clayton had taken leading senators into his confidence, ascertaining the treaty features they were willing to support. The Administration and Congress remained so far apart on domestic issues that bipartisan assurances were needed in an hour when anti-Taylor newspapers lashed out at the negotiators.

The usual delay followed, while Bulwer awaited word from London. "Use . . . your good offices," Clayton urged Lawrence, "to persuade Lord Palmerston" not to censure Bulwer "for consenting to so much." The Secretary felt justified in boasting that Britain's Mosquito protectorate "stands" only "the shadow of a name." The stage thus seemed set for attaching the ribbons and seals of protocol, when on June 29 Bulwer informed Clayton that Britain did "not understand the engagements . . . to apply to Her Majesty's settlement at Honduras or to its Dependencies." This massive condition proved nearly fatal. After five days' labor on a reply Clayton acknowledged that the treaty did not embrace British Honduras; however, he declined to affirm or deny the British title—either there or in the alleged dependencies.[4]

Regarding the next move Clayton and Bulwer always violently disagreed. Bulwer said he submitted a counter-declaration, dated July 4 and interpreting the Secretary's stand as follows: "You do not deem yourself called upon to mark out . . . the exact limits of Her Majesty's Settlement at Honduras, nor of the . . . Central American States, nor to define the dependencies"—and "you fully recognize that . . . Her Majesty's title . . . will remain" what it was before the treaty. Clayton, however, would contend that (although Bulwer talked in this vein) the American refused to receive the counterdeclaration. Indeed Clayton made a memorandum: "After signing my note . . . I delivered it to Sir Henry & we immediately proceeded . . . to exchange . . . ratifications." On July 5 Taylor proclaimed the treaty.[5]

7

Taylor did not survive to witness the treaty's far-reaching influence on Anglo-American relations and hemispheric history. If alive in '55, he might have been profoundly shocked; in '60, pleasurably surprised; in '85 saddened beyond disappointment; in 1950, gratified. No other American treaty has been more thoroughly drubbed and damned. Though Senate Democrats joined Whigs in ratifying the convention, Stephen A. Douglas and his friends soon made a political football of it. Clayton had been duped, they charged; the United States sacrificed more than she gained; the treaty negatived the Monroe Doctrine in part, and the first article was especially obnoxious—as vicious as it was vague.

In 1853, in the Senate, Clayton would parry the partisan assaults, reminding the treaty's most violent critics of their ratification votes. The principal bone of contention became England's interpretation, especially her avowal that the Bay Islands were "dependencies" of Belize, and that the Mosquito protectorate remained valid. Clayton denied these allegations, insisting that the treaty was sound—provided men interpreted it fairly. In buttressing his arguments he implied accusingly that

Bulwer's July 4 counterdeclaration had been secretly inserted in United States archives after Zachary Taylor's death. On Sir Henry's controversial note the British Honduras and Bay Islands portions of England's position largely hinged. Reverdy Johnson and Clayton's clerk substantiated Clayton's memorandum and memory. Bulwer, however, asserted that Clayton *had* incorporated the paper in the official correspondence. A search revealed that it *was* in the archives, lacking American endorsement—but it could have been added later. Published in the British *Parliamentary Papers,* it provided reason in English eyes for the Bay Islands' seizure and occupation.[6] Several eminent American historians, straining for objectivity, incline to Bulwer's side in the matter. Clayton, however, never gave in and convinced many people that he spoke the truth.

Even if the counterdeclaration had not haunted the diplomats, the treaty's ambiguity made misunderstandings likely. As the *Times* of London put it, the negotiations were a struggle "for generalship in the use of terms." This struggle, Clayton's critics insisted, he had lost— and thereby jeopardized American interests. Because of his assailants' fury, plus subsequent British moves, many Americans long regarded the treaty as a colossal blunder.

It is germane, however, to inquire whether alternatives would not have produced greater damage and much less good than followed in the treaty's aftermath. Failure to establish some *modus vivendi* affecting Central American affairs might have led to an Anglo-American war. Washington's primary interest lay in obtaining isthmian security through a joint protection commitment. The canal was uppermost in Clayton's mind, and by his interpretation he got what he wanted. True, he and Taylor would have preferred renunciation of the British protectorate lodged specifically in the terms. But this could never have been gained at a time when London's position in the isthmian region was considerably stronger than Washington's. If Clayton's interpretation was correct, the United States won on many counts—and lost on none of consequence.

8

Thus neutralization and security were real achievements under 1850 conditions. If the words "protection," "occupy," "dependencies" spelled wrangling and rebuffs, without the treaty to serve as a landmark would not even more disputes have plagued the English-speaking powers? Moreover the positive advantages in the treaty should be obvious. As

Richard W. Van Alstyne has written, the United States obtained "assurances of security and co-operation" respecting an isthmian canal—blunting "the edge of a dangerous . . . distrust," and creating "a permanent partnership to the end that lasting political peace and stability were to be sought in Central America through joint, rather than single, action."

Taylor's government also secured "treaty rights which it did not possess before"—the right to "an equal share" in the Mosquito question's settlement, "and the right to agree to any future fixing" of the Belize or Bay Islands status. "The latter two places were left . . . as they were, self-governing settlements of British subjects on land claimed by Central American republics." If some contemporary politicians would have vociferously disagreed with Van Alstyne's reference to the "blunting" of "distrust," within ten years even James Buchanan approved the treaty's implementation. It *needed* implementing, for it was not perfect—and Britain's Bay Islands occupation, William Walker's Nicaragua filibuster and other aggressions hurt it. Eventually, however, London agreed to dispose of the Mosquito and Bay Islands controversies in accordance with American wishes. And related features were likewise resolved to mutual satisfaction.

The Nicaragua canal was never built. Though revived periodically, the plan remained important because of later digging in Panama. The neutral status of the Central American region proved harassing to the United States until the Second Hay-Pauncefote Treaty superseded Bulwer's and Clayton's. Now, at last, the republic loomed as the dominant Caribbean power, which it was not in Taylor's day. Britain got all it wanted—a pledge of equality for her ships. Under Theodore Roosevelt's sponsorship the Panama Canal achieved Zachary Taylor's general waterway objective. Meanwhile nothing fundamental nullified Taylor's aims. Once implemented, the Clayton-Bulwer Treaty provided a splendid illustration of the security America needed.[7] Difficult to launch, subject to dispute, tossed in tempests of partisan debate, it proved seaworthy despite the fact that it never was truly popular.

CHAPTER XXIX

LÓPEZ AND LISBON

1

DEMOCRATIC objections to the treaty, in the course of the 1850s, were related to the Manifest Destiny doctrine, which many Southerners favored as a means of extending their slavery system. If Northerners dipped into Oriental trade and planned development of Pacific ports, why must the South remain quiescent? To domination of Central America and occupation of all Mexico, adventurers linked filibustering expeditions designed to expand the federal domain while opening up new lands for slavery. In '50 General Narciso López again brought the Cuban pot to a boil. Presuming that the Cuban people yearned for revolt against Madrid, he improved on his program of the previous summer when President Taylor checkmated him. Recruiting American "liberators," procuring money, and establishing a New Orleans base, López also sought to circumvent the 1818 neutrality law, which the President had invoked. Believing the law would be inoperative if filibusters attacked Cuba only *indirectly* from American shores, López hoped to guide his followers to a Caribbean rendezvous and thence dog-leg to Cuba without incurring Taylor's wrath.

At first everything seemed rosy to López. American backers encouraged him. Among his expedition's officers was Theodore O'Hara, poet, journalist and the son of Taylor's Kentucky schoolmaster. Louisiana's Chatham R. Wheat was another prominent veteran of Mexico. Mississippi Governor John A. Quitman, Ex-Senator John Henderson and other men of comparable dynamism contributed cash or influence. The New Orleans *Delta's* editor arranged for a supply of weapons from stores belonging to Southern states. A steamship and two sailing vessels composed López' flotilla, and a large and determined band embarked at the New Orleans water front, nominally bound for Panama. The steamer *Creole* and the *Susan Loud* on May 14 found the *Georgiana* anchored off Contoy, near Yucatan. Cheers heralded the reunion, but forty-nine men deserted prior to López' departure from Contoy, and Spanish warships seized fifty-two, headed for Cuba on the slow *Susan Loud* and *Georgiana.* Thus dawn of Sunday May 19 found López at Cárdenas with only the *Creole* and 470 men.[1]

Cárdenas, an attractive little city eighty miles east of Havana, had a garrison of forty soldiers who sharply resisted López' landing before surrendering unconditionally. For the American rank and file there was nothing constructive to do in Cárdenas. Such residents as did not fly to the hills, or hunt a refuge in harbor craft, made food and drink disarmingly available. But the town provided no evidence of enthusiasm for liberation, on which General López had counted. If a beachhead had been gained with relatively little loss of life, the limited triumph proved abortive. For soon word came that Spanish reinforcements were on their way to humble the interlopers and send them sprawling into the sea. López now showed commendable caution, directing the supplies' return to the *Creole* and assigning a rear guard of Kentuckians to cover their comrades' withdrawal in the event of an attack. When this charge occurred in late afternoon, most of the Americans had re-embarked—the Kentucky men killing thirty or forty lancers and holding their position until all was ready for departure about nine o'clock that night.

To make the episode more bizarre, the *Creole* then grounded in Cárdenas harbor, and provisions, weapons and ammunition went overboard to lighten it. With some seventy Americans killed or wounded, nothing of a permanent nature gained and everything fundamental lost, the expedition was a total failure. López, still dreaming, wished to land at Mantua for another fling at liberation. Officers and men, however, overruled him; whereupon the *Creole's* prow turned toward Key West, as the Spanish ship *Pizarro* pursued her. Arriving safely, López and his men thus came to the end of the expedition, leaving President Taylor entangled in its diplomatic and legal involvements.

2

The Administration faced three issues—maintenance of cordial relations between Madrid and Washington, the fate of fifty-two captured Americans and federal prosecution of the filibusters. Since there was no burning question of American invaders still at large in Cuba, Taylor could have courted cheap popularity in the South by soft-pedaling the prosecution. Instead, through Secretary Ewing, he directed the New Orleans district attorney to spare no effort in obtaining justice. "All leaders engaged in . . . the late expedition . . . worked great mischief," Ewing wrote Logan Hunton. ". . . Theirs . . . is no common crime—and more than ordinary care should be taken to punish it and . . . prevent its re-currence."[2]

Louisiana public and press opinion prevented fulfillment of Taylor's hopes. Of the many New Orleans newspapers only one was consistently anti-López. Even the *Picayune* lauded López and attacked the Adminis-tration. Moreover it was widely believed that Hunton knew what was going on long before the *Creole* sailed, and by his silence and inactivity really permitted her to leave. All this anticipated the feeling reflected when the trials commenced. With Quitman and Henderson lionized, and a drink named in López' honor, witnesses hampered investigations, refusing to answer questions on the ground of self-incrimination. Hen-derson, selected for trial, went free when three juries failed to convict. The prosecution of his friends was dropped, and efforts in New York and Ohio met with no greater success. After Taylor's death López (in Cuba once more) would be garroted at Havana.[3] But while he lived, the South revered him and assailed Taylor's "interference."

As Southern journalists charged the President with aiding Spanish tyranny, Europeans asked what sort of government could not keep its people from assaulting neighbors. British criticism scorched like Spain's. The *Times* of London was caustic, and Sir Henry Bulwer nodded assent, questioning Hunton's reliability and dubbing the Administration weak. In Washington, Calderón de la Barca insisted—as Madrid did—on punishment for filibusters, but became satisfied that Taylor and the Cabinet would live up to the letter and spirit of neutrality. In Madrid, Barringer made policy plain—and Taylor's prosecution troubles caused no foreign repercussions. The Contoy prisoners, according to Spain, had been captured in a preliminary stage of an invasion. The picture of these freemen in irons distressed Americans who disapproved of López. A popular defense was that they had hoped to go to California via Chagres, and perhaps were trying to come back from Contoy. Credit-ably Taylor and Clayton did not dwell on this supposition. Instead Clay-ton, with the President's support but the Cabinet's disapproval, argued that "intention to commit a crime did not constitute a crime"; hence Spain had no more right to arrest violators of an American law in neutral waters than at home. A Spanish court found forty-nine not guilty. And, as a result of Clayton's strategy, all were free later in the year.

An impartial historian has called this a "notable diplomatic victory." Actually it was more than that. Release of the Contoy men should be regarded not as a separate triumph, but as part of the total effect of Tay-lor's program. Fighting for Americans' lives when imperiled, Taylor

had been equally determined to safeguard Spanish interests when warranted. As Webster pointed out in the Senate, Washington repeatedly
promised Madrid the United States' good offices to maintain her possession of Cuba; among factors minimized by López' backers was the possibility that Spain might sell the island to Great Britain.[4] To the President's and Clayton's credit they did not retreat on fundamentals and still
upheld their country's honor.

3

Aside from López and the canal the most acute foreign problem tasking Taylor in '50 concerned the Portuguese claims. Ratification of a
commercial treaty with Hawaii, talk about a mission to Japan, Austria's
complaints regarding Mann, negotiations on the African slave trade,
and attempts to reconcile a Haiti-San Domingo feud[5] did not loom so
large as the Lisbon question. Concerned as he was respecting the indemnities, Taylor never wrote his special message on the subject. Instead
he hoped that Chargé Clay might sway the Portuguese to Washington's
viewpoint. Hedging on the *General Armstrong* case was thus a grievous
disappointment, and in March Clayton told Clay to impress on Tojal
that his country was demanding settlement for the last time. If Portugal
gave no definite assurance that the claims would be paid, Clay was to
demand his passports and board a war vessel in Lisbon harbor—his mission being at an end.

Tojal seemed to understand the situation's gravity. Nevertheless he
took the position that a third party might arbitrate the *Armstrong* case,
while Lisbon merchants could pass on the *Miles*. Refusing to meet the
Shepherd claim or to pay for *Magoun* and *Colonel Blum* damages, Tojal's assurance of reimbursement for the loss of the *Bolton's* boats was
so much chicken feed compared to the sums which Taylor sought. Clay
rejecting this proposal, Tojal in June tardily substituted a plan for submitting *all* claims to arbitration. This represented a tactical gain for
Washington and suggested that Clay's stand was well taken. However,
acting under Clayton's instructions, Clay could not accede to the alternative, even when Portugal in July agreed to pay all claims save that of the
Armstrong. Here the lack of speedy communication proved decisive;
although Portugal's final offer must have tantalized Clay, he abided by
instructions and requested his passports. Had Taylor lived into the
autumn, the last Tojal proposal might well have flowered into a satisfactory compromise. In June-July of '50, however, the controversy raged
unchecked.[6]

CHAPTER XXX

THE FLAMING CRISIS OF 1850

1

THAT same June the Nashville Convention met. But, long before it was called to order, charges and countercharges flew in preliminaries throughout the South. Mississippi had issued the original call. Still, Calhoun's role in '49 convinced many an observer that secession would be high on the agenda. Delaware, Kentucky, Louisiana, Maryland, Missouri and North Carolina sent no delegates. Only one came from Texas, two from Arkansas, and not a few registering on Cherry Street were conservative, compared to Rhett or Yancey. Judge Sharkey took a far from radical position; a Whig, he presided over the convention. But Democrats dominated the proceedings, and both address and resolutions bore the stamp of men convinced the South should serve notice it never would brook interference with Southern rights.

Because this gathering did nothing so drastic as those of '60 and '61, there has been a tendency to minimize the men participating in its sessions. They included such notable figures as Langdon Cheves and Beverley Tucker; Reuben Chapman and Benjamin Fitzpatrick, former governors of Alabama; Georgia's brilliant Walter T. Colquitt, the preacher-lawyer from Columbus; Texas' Ex-Governor J. Pinckney Henderson, who fought under Taylor in Mexico; and those prominent South Carolinians, Francis W. Pickens and James H. Hammond. Joseph W. Matthews of Mississippi and Aaron V. Brown of Tennessee also lent prestige to the convention.[1] Nearly 180 strong, hailing from nine Southern states, the delegates could not be accommodated in Odd Fellows' Hall and on June 4 moved to McKendree Methodist Church. There, in seats designed for God's worship, they settled down to transact their business.

Amid fiery speeches, a seventeen-man committee was created to pass on resolutions. Fifteen delegates offered proposals, and the gifted John A. Campbell's were selected with minor changes. With them, back to the convention floor, went the draft of an official address written by the fiery Rhett. Monday June 10 saw both introduced—the latter as amended by Polk's old law partner, Gideon Pillow. Four days earlier a Tennessee correspondent had reported to James Buchanan that the delegates expected to make 36° 30′ their ultimatum. Tennesseans feared "the real design" was to defeat Clay's bill in Congress by backing the Missouri Compromise extension, which in turn would fail of passage—with "the question left for agitation. This seemed . . . the point of difference between Tenn and the other states when I left." Cave Johnson was proved incorrect in that Tennessee supported 36° 30′ on the floor. Although a committee minority report was signed by two Tennessee delegates (plus one each from Alabama, Arkansas and Florida), the conservative Volunteer State sustained the committee's measure and also failed to join eight delegates in opposing Rhett's radical address. Thereby Tennessee's "moderates" sided with the hotspurs against Clay's Compromise.

Where, essentially, lay the difference between the address and the resolutions? The former asserted that the only adjustment acceptable to the South was "extension of the Missouri Compromise," with recognition of Southerners' right to take their slaves into "territory south of . . . 36° 30′." The resolutions did the very same thing. But, instead of adopting a "mode of resistance" to Northerners' aggression, the delegates assumed that—since Congress had not acted—they did not "feel at liberty to discuss . . . methods suitable for . . . resistance to measures not yet adopted." With this as their premise, they deferred final action to a second convention session scheduled to be held at Nashville six weeks after Congress' adjournment.[2]

Numerous writers have assumed that, because it devised no "mode of resistance," the convention was of minor significance. It is easy enough to point out that no overt anti-Union act originated in Nashville in '50. No explosion occurred in McKendree Church. No bugle call. No rat-a-tat. But conditions governing the postponement hinged on the possibility that Washington would relieve the situation along lines acceptable to the South. The November Nashville proceedings might have been entirely different, and indeed threatening, if one man's death had not reversed the national picture. In June-July, with Taylor in the White House and congressional debates still surging, there was evidence of great excitement in some portions of the South, despite the *National Era's* statement that the convention aroused "little interest." That many delegates and their friends ardently wished to threaten secession is scarcely beyond the limits of doubt. And everything said by the Davises and Yanceys, Rhetts, Pillows and Cobbs in the following weeks was affected by events on Nashville's Church Street.[3]

2

Concurrent with the Nashville Convention critical New Mexico-Texas developments sorely tried the President's patience. Taylor's old Florida subordinate, Brevet Colonel John Munroe, had become New Mexico's military governor in October '49. A doughty Scot, now fiftyish, with a long, lean face and penetrating eyes, Munroe was a West Pointer who served gallantly at Buena Vista. Just as his predecessor, Colonel Washington, had been confronted by Spruce M. Baird, Munroe faced another Austin agent in the person of Robert S. Neighbors. Complementing rather than supplanting Baird, Neighbors appeared as a Texas commissioner. The fact that Governor Bell appointed him spelled serious business at Santa Fe, for Bell's attitude toward New Mexico had been consistently aggressive. Neighbors was empowered to organize the New Mexican counties claimed by Texas, to hold elections for county officers, and to publish an address of Bell's wherein he asserted Texan "rights." Like Munroe, Neighbors was a man of mettle. Well acquainted with the region, he was strong-willed and energetic. Neither Texan nor national authorities could have done better than to select such sturdy spokesmen to represent them.

Beginning his organizational work at El Paso in February and March, Neighbors met no opposition there from Major Jefferson Van Horne. On March 23 he reported to Bell that El Paso County was properly organized, with elected officials performing their duties. Santa Fe, however, was another story. Superior Court Judge Joab Houghton, in a proclamation, advised the people to resist Neighbors' attempts to usurp "our land and boundaries." Each county should quickly hold meetings, Houghton urged, to draw up resolutions on the Texas claims. If voters followed Houghton's plan, he argued, the "mission of the Commissioner of Texas will be as useless as that of Judge Baird."[4]

When Neighbors reached Santa Fe in April, citizens received him courteously but gave no indication of encouraging his project. Houghton threatened to imprison anyone enforcing Texas laws. Munroe voiced approval of the status quo. And Neighbors learned he would not be allowed to print Bell's address in the local newspaper. Then George McCall appeared on the scene with word from Washington that President Taylor favored statehood for New Mexico; if the people wanted it, Monroe's command was "to advance their wishes." Notices were promptly posted, scheduling a meeting to be held "for the purpose of . . . requesting the governor" to call a constitutional convention. Over Neighbors' protest, the meeting took place. Governor Munroe then issued his call. And, from May 15 to 25, delegates approved a statehood plan and created a constitution excluding slavery, which the people endorsed in June by an overwhelming count. A petition seeking admission to the Union immediately went off to Congress. A subsequent election saw Henry Connelly selected for the state governorship, but, pending action in the federal capital, power lodged in Munroe's hands. Texas, however, angrily rejected every Santa Fe transaction. Soon news of repercussions at Austin was carried by couriers east and west.

The moment Munroe called the convention, Neighbors hastened back to Bell, who received a bluntly worded report on the failure of a mission. Months before, Bell recommended that he be authorized to send to Santa Fe (if the necessity existed) "a military force *sufficient* to enable . . . civil authorities" to execute Texas laws "without . . . regard to the military power of the United States." Texas legislators then declined to give Bell such extraordinary discretion. In June, however, no doubt existed as to where Texan sentiment lay. The popular and pugnacious Bell, with mass opinion arrayed on his side, arranged for a special legislative session (to be held at Austin in August) and planned a program of drastic action, which he expected to be approved.[5]

3

It would be hard to exaggerate the intensity of Texas feeling. As the *State Gazette* pointed out, the people called Munroe's last move an "outrage." An Austin mass meeting favored force. Crowds in other Texas communities mingled protests of Munroe's decision with secession cries and repeated demands for an armed expedition to Santa Fe. Fury mounted when New Mexico's constitution appeared in full in the public prints. Neighbors, on leaving Santa Fe, had not learned its precise provisions. Now knowledge that New Mexico sought to take all the disputed soil, plus land generally considered Texan, led to a mammoth gathering in early July at San Jacinto—and to resolutions approving enforcement of state jurisdiction. Word eventually reached Washington that Texas leaders intended dispatching state troops to Santa Fe before the coming of cold weather.

Meanwhile Bell advised the Texas congressmen that insults perpetrated by the military at Santa Fe had grown intolerable, and that, with legislative consent, he proposed to take forthright action. In a hot letter to Taylor, containing no very respectful terms, the Governor *demanded* to be informed whether Munroe's position was authorized and his proclamation approved. Corresponding with political leaders in Texas and throughout the South, Bell received encouraging responses to his belligerent ideas. From Charleston to New Orleans the plight of Texas was seized upon as furnishing the opportunity advanced secessionists long desired—a showdown between a state and Washington, with justice (as they saw it) on the former's side. What pleased them most was that Bell's letter amounted to a summary injunction on Taylor to explain himself. And all the time Bowie knives were figuratively flashing, while marksmen brandished Colt revolvers.

Long before Bell's letter reached the White House, President Taylor submitted to Congress a special message on New Mexico. This was in reply to a request that he "inform the Senate" whether orders had been sent military officers "to hold" Santa Fe against Texas' authority, or to embarrass or prevent "the exercise of her jurisdiction." No such orders "have been given" since "my last communication to the Senate on that subject," said Taylor, recalling that his former message referred to the boundary dispute. New information, he continued, revealed that "a certain Robert S. Neighbors, styling himself commissioner of . . . Texas, had proceeded to Santa Fe with a view of organizing counties." The region having been "acquired by the United States" from Mexico, and having since been held by the United States, "in my opinion" it "ought so to remain" until determination of the boundary question. Taylor added that he saw "no reason for seriously apprehending" that Texas would "interfere" with federal possession.

The President's position was hardly startling (but, for June 17, adequate) since news had not come of Bell's reaction to Commissioner Neighbors' report. Many Americans agreed that the boundary issue was not one for either Taylor or Bell to settle. Crawford's order to McCall had accompanied the earlier message to the Hill. Therefore, Old Zack did not mention it now, and even it contained no instructions respecting boundary definitions.[6] What *was* involved was New Mexicans' right to prefer statehood if they wished, and Munroe could help them achieve this objective. In his mid-June message, Taylor implied adherence to this long-held principle. Absence of explicit implementation doubtless stemmed from the fact that the crisis had not fully developed.

4

The crisis did not wait for long. According to one Washington journalist, writing on June 29, "there will be . . . startling intelligence . . . in less than six weeks. . . . Texas will" probably send "2,500 men" to New Mexico. Colonel Munroe's United States troops "number about five or six hundred," and six hundred more would join them. Texans in Washington believed their state would "arrest" the United States officers and "bring them to trial for obstructing . . . her laws." The *National Intelligencer* hoped "the worthy correspondent" was "prematurely alarmed for the safety of . . . the detachment . . . whose duty it will be to defend" Santa Fe. But Representative Stephens, on July 3, strenuously objected to the editor's language and assailed Taylor and Munroe: "The first Federal gun . . . fired against the people of Texas, without . . . authority of law, will . . . signal . . . freemen from the Delaware to the Rio Grande to rally to the rescue." The correspondent had asserted that "the sympathies of the whole South" supported Texas. But, said Stephens, more than sympathy ranged itself on Texas' side. "The cause of Texas . . . will be the cause of the entire South," he declared. ". . . When the 'Rubicon' is passed, the days of this Republic will be numbered."

The *Intelligencer* was "sorry to see" Stephens "indulging in such bloody visions." Other editors and statesmen shared the Washington paper's regret. In New York the *Journal of Commerce* continued to print warning accounts. "Rumors from Texas are alarming," its capital newsgatherer wrote July 5. They "justify" previous apprehensions. "I am . . . satisfied in regard to the President's intentions." Taylor's "last message . . . left his policy in doubt." But "if orders have not been, they will be sent" to Munroe to maintain national authority "in opposition to . . . military force which Texas may send into New Mexico. This was . . . defended as the policy of the President to day, by Mr. Bell" in the Senate. "The President is . . . right in this course. . . . Still, it will afford a pretext for . . . Southern malcontents to commence war upon the authority of the Union." From the tone of Neighbors' report and Judge Houghton's proclamation the New York *Express* concluded that "they are . . . impatient . . . to submit their 'claims' to the . . . arbitrament of arms. . . . We do not see . . . anything . . . likely to prevent so calamitous an issue. . . . We fear there would be other parties to the fray than Texans and New Mexicans, before it ceases."

The specter of fratricidal conflict haunted editorial sanctums. On July 2 the Hartford *Courant* said: "Should Texas . . . endeavor to establish her authority over the Santa Fe country by force, it . . . will lead to . . . civil war and, perhaps, disunion. We trust . . . that we have, in our President, a man" who would never allow a state to back boundary claims with guns when "there is a competent tribunal" to judge them. The Richmond *Republican,* on July 9, voiced conservative Southern opinion: "We await . . . intelligence from New Mexico with deep and painful solicitude. Of all . . . questions . . . exciting the public mind, this . . . cannot be delayed without the hazard of a collision . . . and perhaps involve the whole Union in the dire calamity of civil war." These papers are cited because they were typical of run-of-the-mill presses, reflecting the sentiment building up with regard to state rights, the Union and war. They were far more representative than Rhett's *Mercury* or Garrison's *Liberator,* whose proprietors screamed their heads off in projecting rival extremisms. Also their opinions were more in focus than the contradictory ones presented by the New York *Express* or *Tribune.*

By July 9 opinion was solidifying so fast that even the *Express* correspondent's conclusion hit near the truth: The President "has not sent any order to Col. Munroe . . . to resist Texas. . . . What may be done, hereafter, I cannot say. In case Texas invades New Mexico," then it was the government's "solemn duty" to preserve "things as they are." That "the President will issue an order, what Whig ought to doubt?" Similarly Greeley's *Tribune* swiftly veered to Taylor's support. On various occasions during the spring the gentleman with the chin-fringe whiskers avowed wide-eyed disbelief that Taylor was the antiextension champion. Nevertheless, on July 9, the *Tribune* admitted that the Administration took "the only right course."[7] Coming from Greeley, who worked and schemed against Taylor in '48 and fought him tooth and claw since his inauguration, such an admission was wonderful.

5

With the serious impasse thoroughly recognized, with Bell bellicose, his state up in arms and Southern camps training with Texas, the crisis was indeed a flaming one. Who in all the sweep of history, even on Carolina's rice plantations or in Charleston's sheltered gardens, could be more flamboyantly state-proud than Texas' rootin'-shootin' sons? Irked at Taylor because of defects in federal Indian defenses, leathery Texans felt he carried a chip on his shoulder due to old disciplinary problems with Texas soldiers. In an impassioned Senate speech Houston charged that Texans were "traduced" and "defamed" by "the present Executive" during the Mexican War. Who could expect open-mindedness of Taylor when he had been "unwarrantably" hostile? Fortunately Allen Hall rose in rebuttal. In the *Republic* Hall quoted in detail the wartime letter forming the basis of the Houston allegations; then he charged the Raven with "monstrous perversion of the language and meaning" of Rough and Ready.

Though Hall's reply to Houston was effective, it could not entirely erase the intensity of feeling in Texans' minds and Texans' hearts. Moreover Southern congressmen generally were so irate regarding Taylor's stand on containment that Texas' cause became their cause. Democrats, ranging from Soulé to Foote, offered amendments and resolutions to bolster Texas in the struggle. Cass's contribution to Taylor's discomfiture lay in directing the Committee on Military Affairs to consider prohibiting soldiers from exercising civil authority. Had the boundary business been uncomplicated by other major issues, it might have amounted only to an unpleasant speck on the landscape. But, with the compromise debate extending the session beyond all precedent, the crisis baffled senators and representatives—who were as distraught as Texas citizens.

For all the speeches and maneuverings of Clay, Cass, Foote, Webster and Douglas, their compromise was no nearer realization in July than in February. Southern die-hards, like Davis and Clemens, opposed concessions as determinedly as before. But the Southern Whig in the Executive Mansion constituted a more serious threat to the middle-roaders' aims. Taylor was not against *a solution;* he was against *this particular solution.* As thoroughly devoted to the Union as any man in Washington the President considered Clay-Douglas concessions a mere patchwork—salve on a cancer. Adhering to his plan of statehood for California and New Mexico, Taylor retained the allegiance of every Northern Whig senator with two exceptions, and also won over some Northern Democrats who formerly leaned the other way. Even Cass deemed the compromise incapable of passage in its omnibus form, because Democrats like Walker and Felch were switching to the Administration.[8] Never before had Taylor been so powerful, where antiextensionism was concerned, as at the outset of July.

6

The Texas and Washington situations being so strained, small wonder it was that Southern congressmen caucused desperately on learning that New Mexico's constitution had passed through Missouri and would soon reach the capital. Back in May many of them had dramatized their section's opposition to middle-ground newspapers by establishing an ultra press in Washington. This extremist paper now appeared regularly, embarrassing Ritchie, Douglas and Clay, and expanding fissures in the Democracy into chasms difficult to bridge. Since the compromisers chiefly relied on the Democrats, Whiggery's fate concerned them less. Nevertheless it was also ominous when Toombs-Stephens Whigs started to chop the last cables of their partisan moorings.

This they did July 1, appointing a committee of three to remonstrate with the President respecting his past attitude and rumored intentions for the future. When Charles M. Conrad, Humphrey Marshall and Robert Toombs called on Taylor, he told each in turn that he would not yield his position on New Mexico. According to a Southern historian even those regretting Old Zack's "obstinacy" felt he acted (as he "always" did) under honest convictions of duty. Conrad, Marshall and Toombs quickly concluded that there was "no longer any hope." At about the same time Crawford told Taylor he "could not sign" a contemplated order to Munroe to resist attempts of Texas "to exercise jurisdiction in New Mexico." Whereupon Taylor coolly remarked that "he would sign it himself."

At this point the record becomes clouded by controversial assertions. The Philadelphia *Bulletin's* correspondent charged that, when Taylor was ill, "southern ultraists . . . invaded . . . his sick chamber" to warn that—unless he protected the South—"they would vote a resolution of censure in the Galphin business." On July 5 "Stephens and Toombs" delivered a "similar . . . threat." When Stephens issued a denial, the newsman repeated that the Georgians addressed "improper language" to Taylor "in connection with . . . slavery . . . and the Galphin affair." Though shifting the episode's date from July 5 to July 3, the journalist stuck to his basic assertions. It would be easy to confuse the *Bulletin's* report with Weed-Hamlin testimony concerning Taylor's February run-in with the Southern malcontents. A quarter century later, Stephens and Toombs scouted Weed's version—which was corroborated by Hamlin, Alfred Pleasanton and a contemporary news report. Stephens then as-

serted that "no such interview" ever occurred, an infinitely stronger statement than the same man's '50 allegation. Moreover, in '76, Toombs
testified: "I never did call on General Taylor with . . . anybody . . . on
the subject of vetoing the bill for . . . admission of California."

Despite what appear to be categorical denials, covering both February
and July, it is more significant that Toombs said: "Both of us had frequent interviews separately and together with General Taylor, and urged
upon him . . . abandonment of his policy and . . . adoption of the compromise measures." Toombs acknowledged that "some of these interviews were earnest and decided on both sides," and in '50 Stephens was
explicit only in denying threats during Taylor's illness.[9] These patterns
in the mosaic of truth parallel available positive evidence, pointing the
conclusion that in both months Taylor received Toombs alone or the two
Georgians together, interpreting what he heard as threats. It is logical
to suppose that the final interview occurred July 3, and that Stephens did
not *then* accompany Toombs. That such a meeting definitely took place
is clearly admitted by Toombs himself, and witnessed by Northerners
and Southerners. This is the fundamental fact emerging from the maze
of testimony.

7

Thus the atmosphere of crisis was very real and replete with drama,
produced by domestic and foreign challenges as alarming as anything
Zachary Taylor ever faced on the battlefield. In a matter of weeks Taylor initiated prosecution of filibusters, sought to pacify Spanish officials,
adhered to his policy on Portuguese claims, received reports on the Nashville Convention and turned down Southern Whig demands to curtail
his program for slavery's containment.

Clayton's important declaration and Bulwer's version of his reply also
marked that hectic period, the President finally proclaiming the treaty
on July 5, as the Democratic press carried on its wild attacks. In Congress the Galphin debate was raging, and David L. Yulee of Florida
loudly protested the Cuban policy. Bradbury and Douglas continued to
assault the patronage program, pointing out that in Taylor's first year
6,210 removals and resignations had occurred—more than in a similar
period under any predecessor. Smith, Bell, Webster and Dawson replied
that the Whigs deserved half the spoils. But their arguments scarcely
dented the stout Democratic armor. With minor exceptions the Senate

still refused to confirm Taylor appointees, while the House abstained from passing an appropriation bill.

As if Taylor did not have enough worries, his Cabinet's position was precarious. At least twice Secretary Clayton had undertaken to resign, but Taylor had stood loyally by him as well as all the other ministers. Now Crawford had become a terrific liability, and Meredith and Johnson bore the Galphin brand. At last Taylor seriously considered substituting a completely new Cabinet for incumbent department heads. There is evidence that he thought of Winthrop, Fish, John Davis and Stanly for places in his official family. (Ewing and Preston might have remained.) Though such a move might have been interpreted as a victory for Taylor's critics, actually he would have gained in strength with advisers at his side immune to "Galphinism!" charges.

While Taylor mulled over Cabinet shifts, Stephens—in the latter's own words—earnestly "urged him to change his policy" respecting the dispatch of more troops to New Mexico and opposition to Texas' claims. Toombs and Stephens also "went to see Preston." The Secretary "was not at home." However, the Virginian chanced to meet the two Georgians "in front of the Treasury Building"—and, says Stephens, "I told Preston that if troops were ordered to Santa Fe, the President would be impeached. 'Who will impeach him?' asked he. 'I will if nobody else does.' "[10] Threats of impeachment, like votes of censure, are thus embodied in the record. Lacking a majority in either house of Congress, harassed by domestic and foreign trials, Zachary Taylor in early July enjoyed as little presidential placidity as any White House occupant.

Despite all the pressures brought to bear on him Taylor was consistent and courageous to the last. Maximum insight into his character can be derived most readily from a vital message to Congress which he ordered prepared on Texas and New Mexico. This message never was printed. The original draft has not come to light. Its very existence might be discounted except for testimony that Clayton or Ewing wrote it at the President's direction, and that he had every intention of signing it when he fell sick. Plans for the message negated compromisers' hopes that Zachary Taylor would bow to their will. Instead of backing down the President intended to meet Texan aggressiveness head-on. If Taylor was correct in opposing the compromise, then he was eternally right in refusing to be swayed by Bell in Austin or by Southern malcontents in Washington. Such Texas leaders as Houston, Rusk and Bell—plus rump-faction Whigs and the radical *Southern Press*—finally learned how drastic their differences with the President actually were. The next move was up to them. Would Texas legislators endorse Bell's militancy? Would militiamen leave their homes for the purpose of routing John Munroe? Might Southern sympathizers join in the slaughter of brother and brother? Taylor was willing to risk all this to uphold his conception of the Union.

Because of the forthcoming White House tragedy such questions superficially appear academic. Nevertheless, much evidence points to resoundingly affirmative answers, thus bringing the likelihood of civil war into the 1850 focus. Especially challenging is the probability that the President would call Texas' bluff; that the Union under Taylor would provide more support for Munroe than the South could furnish Bell and that the upshot might well have been a serious military and psychological setback for the Southern extremists.

8

Such historical might-have-beens rest in part on speculation. One cannot document a series of events which, because of Taylor's death, could never occur in the same sequence as if he had survived. Still, Taylor's character being what it was, it is inconceivable that he would have completely reversed himself. Something had to give way somewhere. If Taylor remained adamant, Texas must have made concessions. Or else a stalemate would have developed until the President was removed from office, or angry men took to the sword. Taylor told Pleasanton and others that he himself would lead federal forces into battle if Texas attacked the United States flag!

Congressional probabilities are easier to analyze. Impeachment certainly was in the wind. But the likelihood of Taylor's conviction remained remote because of his support in Congress and the North. After all, Andrew Jackson had been censured. But the censure of Taylor in the House—a move less difficult than conviction—was killed after a two-day lifetime. Taylor's chief strength lay in the Senate, where not even the wiles of Clay (combined with the Cass-Douglas votes) could have unseated him in favor of the pro-Compromise Millard Fillmore. As to the Compromise, it was doomed as long as Zachary Taylor lived. Even after Taylor's death it failed in its omnibus form, despite Fillmore's swinging the power of patronage in its favor. What was the prospect of piecemeal passage with Taylor in the Mansion? Conceivable, but highly doubtful! And if indeed the bills had passed, their sponsors lacked the two-thirds majority requisite to override Taylor's veto. What,

one might ask, had become of Whig "weak executive" theories—or of
Taylor's views on the use of the veto expressed in the First Allison Letter? Any "weak executive" notions he had long since discarded. And,
in Taylor's eyes, his promise to confine the veto to constitutional grounds
accorded with his position on Texas.

So Taylor was a "strong executive," in the Jacksonian sense, when illness came to carry him off. Moreover, the prospect was then developing
that in '52 he would head a predominately Northern party, composed
chiefly of Whig stalwarts but incorporating many antislavery Democrats.
The shaping of new partisan alignments was reflected on the Senate
floor, where Taylor's main spokesman was Benton. Bradbury, Hamlin,
Felch, Walker and Chase—in various ways—typified the times. Even
Douglas was burdened by instructions from the Illinois Legislature not
to oppose the Proviso. In the vanguard of the procession rode Seward,
who (it was thought) aimed at 1856, leaving '52 to Taylor. The Massachusetts press and public seemed pleasantly surprised at Taylor's stand.
Greeley now appeared pro-Taylor. And where would Hale, Wilson,
Mann, the Van Buren faction, Adams, Wilmot, Julian and Giddings
logically repair except to the Southern planter's banner?

Back in the '48 campaign Clayton advocated abandoning the Whig
label and substituting "Taylor Republicanism" in its place.[11] Old-line
Whigs had been vanquished so often—their issues discredited time and
again—that some new approach seemed imperative. There was no fundamental problem to deter Taylor in this regard. Northern Whigs in
the House and Senate outnumbered Southern Whigs overwhelmingly,
feeling much as the President did on the burning slavery topic. Little
could be lost, and much gained, by attracting to the Whig nucleus Northern Democrats who shared their basic containment opinions.

There is a reasonable possibility that, with the Compromise a failure
and the Texas furor silenced or squelched, Taylor would have emerged
triumphant from a '52 campaign, running as a candidate for re-election.
In that case it is hard to imagine Taylor in Franklin Pierce's shoes approving the Kansas-Nebraska Bill. It is equally difficult to conceive of Know-
Nothings dominating Whigs, with Old Zack in the driver's seat. Would
Taylor's Supreme Court appointments from '51 to '57 have affected the
Dred Scott line-up? By one vote, perhaps, though Roger Taney still
would have retained control. Even the Democratic split at Charleston
might have been altered, indirectly, by the presence for eight years of a
slaveholding Unionist in the White House! Such speculations have been
put in this book, after careful deliberation, in the belief that scholars

and the public prefer an expression of opinion to leaving the hot topic up in the air. In this connection it might be asked: "What worth has biography or history if specialists in a man or a period refuse to grapple with imponderables in one one-thousandth of a manuscript?" This applies especially in the case of a President who died at the peak of a crisis, when coming events of enormous magnitude cast their lengthened shadows before.

CHAPTER XXXI

DEATH OF ZACHARY TAYLOR

1

TO MODERN minds it is almost incredible that men opposed to slavery's spread should have invested heavily in additional lands and slaves. This, however, was what some did. Taylor's cotton crop again destroyed by the raging Mississippi, he agreed with his son that Taylor money be used to buy Fashion, a sugar estate in Saint Charles Parish, Louisiana. There was no inconsistency in this, for the President believed wholeheartedly in retaining slavery where it then existed. Only extension of the institution met with Taylor's disapproval. On June 12 Taylor thanked Richard for "informing me . . . you" purchased "a plantation & a number of servants." He wanted to "know the precise state of our affairs. . . . Our Merchants, I presume will meet the twenty one thousand . . . to be paid down, & the twenty thousand due Mr, Jos, Fowler." In April, "27,000$ . . . principal & interest . . . will fall due." This was "a pretty considerable sum"—since "we shall make nothing" at Cypress Grove "& a small crop" at Fashion. The amount payable in '52 would be larger, but "I hope . . . a fair crop . . . will pay the greater portion."

"I was gratified to hear," the planter President continued, that "you . . . determined to take the genl, supervision. . . . Everything will go on" well "in that case." Leave enough hands at Cypress Grove "to take care of the establishment & . . . carry on the lumber business." The house there should be "kept in order," so as "to make you comfortable when you visit." As for the sugar business, "many excellent planters" thought "85 or 90 good hands . . . are as many as can be worked to advantage." They could "make from 6 to 800 hogshead," which "ought" to yield "20,000 . . . dollars annually" after paying expenses. This was a princely income to anticipate from a $115,000 investment. That Taylor was not absurdly bullish, however, is indicated by the records of neighboring Louisiana sugar barons. In this era sugar paid very well. And what Taylor hoped Dick would get from Fashion, plus his own $25,000 salary as President, gave the family a bright outlook. The fact that he kept Cypress Grove is perhaps revealing, since he would have needed the small sum for its sale if he had been financially strapped.

Similarly the President retained his Louisville real estate and nearly all his bank stocks, and bought additional stocks. Indeed Taylor's financial picture was in many ways better than ever before.

In this letter to his son the President regretted that on nonbusiness matters "I have . . . little to communicate of interest." Taylor's eldest daughter Ann was at the White House and "will continue here" during the rest of June. His grandson John Wood also had "been with us . . . about two weeks." Promising, "modest & discreet," John would soon return to Annapolis. John's brother Bob "left . . . yesterday for West Point, which . . . he enters as a Cadet." Mrs. Taylor's health remained "about as usual." If Taylor mentioned no aches or pains of his own, this was not surprising. Possibly he did not now feel or show the wear and tear of high office, which had shocked Brown and Burnley in May. With Bliss's help the Taylor ladies were completing arrangements to visit Old Point Comfort,[1] starting the second week in July. It was thought the outing might provide a bracing change for the delicate Mrs. Taylor, who rarely left the Mansion except for divine services.

The capital had grown hot and humid. Sunday June 30 was "warm" and "oppressive." Horses, on the Avenue, looked "very frothy." The "churches were well attended," likewise the "bar-rooms." Remarks in private letters suggest the discomfort of the following fortnight. "Here I am in my shirt & pants—doors open, windows up endeavoring to keep cool; but . . . all in vain." The "heat is absolutely overpowering."

Asiatic cholera was still abroad in the land. Victims had fallen by hundreds and thousands. All the way from New Orleans and Saint Louis into Northern and Eastern states the clammy hand of death extended, and the scythe did its grisly work. There is no proof that this scourge invaded Washington in 1850. However, rumors went the rounds—whispers that cholera indeed had come. Some men talked of adjourning Congress. The army of office seekers diminished perceptibly, and a few husbands and fathers moved their families out of town. Society switched from lavish dinner parties to high-pitched prattle over cups of tea. Still, there is little indication that many members of the Washington community took the rumors seriously. Diarrhea and acute indigestion (then known as "cholera morbus," but having no connection with Asiatic cholera) were the prevailing troubles of the day. Washington's primitive water supply and arrangements for sewage disposal invited the worst from flies and insects. Though the death rate did not rise sharply, many prominent people lay sick. Clayton, Seward, Crawford, Bliss, Duer, Dick Thompson's daughter Kate, John C. Clark,

Joshua Giddings and Senator Bell took to their beds or abstained from activity in a two-week span.

Near the onset of this siege the *Republic* warned its readers: "Drink no . . . liquors. Do not unnecessarily heat yourselves, but, when heated, drink cold water in moderation. Eat no fresh meats, unless very good. Have your vegetables well cooked, and do not use milk at the same meal. Defer anxious thoughts to a cooler season. Do not . . . forego . . . repose. . . . Ice-water, in small quantities, is an excellent tonic; but some persons flood the stomach . . . till . . . internal chemistry . . . can no longer . . . overcome its effects." Since the article appeared in Taylor's own paper, it is interesting to wonder whether he was in the act of reaching for his copy when Marshall or Conrad or Stephens or Toombs called at his office and interrupted him.

2

The popular assumption long has been that Taylor enjoyed robust health when Thursday July 4 dawned. This probably was not true, his susceptibility to intestinal disorders having previously asserted itself, and the Burnley-Brown remarks suggesting that in May he was terribly tired. A contemporary stated specifically that July 3 found Taylor slightly under par. If that was the date when Toombs initiated his volcanic interview, the President coped with the Georgia leader under a physical disadvantage. On Independence Day he may have munched green apples immediately before or after attending a Sunday-school recital. In the afternoon he spent over two hours under a "hot sun" at the base of the Washington Monument, while Senator Foote and others orated.[2] The Monument formalities over, Taylor took "considerable exercise" in walking about the Potomac flats, the sun beating on his head which was probably bare most of the time. Arriving home, he was "very hungry." And then he indulged his appetite, consuming raw fruit or vegetables or both, and washing them down with frigid liquids. Exactly what did he eat and drink? Accounts differ. "Cucumbers, cherries, and cabbage." "A glass of milk." "Bread and milk and cherries." "Cherries and wild berries." "Copious draughts of iced milk and water." "Cucumbers and cherries . . . with mush and milk." The cherries-and-milk version has become part of White House legendary lore; one of the few things people "know" about Taylor's Presidency is that, on the Fourth of July, milk and cherries made him ill.

Ill he became. But precisely *when,* it is sheer guesswork to determine. One writer has it that during the night Taylor was slightly nauseated—"but this did not alarm him, or his family, as he was . . . subject to such attacks. No one thought of calling . . . a Physician." According to a second source, Dr. Alexander S. Wotherspoon was with the President at dinnertime, warned him against a second serving of cherries, and then "prescribed the usual remedies" when Taylor "in an hour" developed cramps, which "took the form of . . . cholera morbus." The two accounts agree that Taylor refused to swallow any medicine. One has it that "towards midnight" Thursday the attack "threatened desperate results"—Taylor continuing in this condition, "without much change, until the evening of the 6th." The other reporter insisted that "on Friday . . . the Cholera morbus continued not alarming"—Taylor resting "on a sofa," while "no Physician was sent for." Taylor, a hearty trencherman, is said to have had the digestion of "an ostrich." He tempted fate too far at a time when younger men, youths and children were confined to beds with bowel and stomach pains. As Giddings wrote, "almost every one has had or now has the diarrea. . . . I went to a little free soil party and we ate Ice Cream and raspberries. . . . Before the next morning more than half our number were taken with diarrea. . . . No one can stand fruits or cucumbers." "I am rather feeble," Julian recorded, but "about as well . . . as any body. . . . All seem to be complaining."

In diagnosing Taylor's case Asiatic cholera can be dismissed. Typhoid fever is out of the question; his symptoms simply were not those of typhoid. His ailment was acute gastroenteritis, the inflammation of the lining membrane of his stomach and intestines—the epidemic feature due to the milk or water supply. Here was a man in his middle sixties who had led a hard life and nearly died the year before. In less than the best of health, he sat two hours in the broiling sun, walked about beneath its rays, ate raw stuff and drank cold liquids. This, plus symptoms that developed, spelled "cholera morbus" to his doctors.

On Friday Taylor still could transact some of his presidential business. He wrote a correspondent that he hoped to visit the Syracuse fair, and thanked the donor of "two delicious salmon which . . . arrived most opportunely." The President also affixed his signature to the Clayton-Bulwer documents—his last political act of consequence.[3] On Saturday, said the New York *Express,* his worried family sent for Wotherspoon at three o'clock in the afternoon. The military surgeon "came immediately," administering calomel and opium. The drugs "had a good effect," and "no necessity was felt" for Wotherspoon's continued presence. The

Philadelphia *Bulletin,* assuming that Wotherspoon's visits began Thursday, said that Saturday "it was deemed advisable to call in other physicians." Dr. Richard H. Coolidge of the Army joined Wotherspoon on
the case, as did Dr. James C. Hall, a civilian with a large Washington
practice. The *Express* declared that Hall did not enter the picture until
early Monday, Coolidge arriving "subsequently," and Robert C. Wood
coming from Baltimore Monday morning "in the nine o'clock cars."
Regardless of minor discrepancies it is known that these four physicians
were in attendance Monday and Tuesday.

On Sunday "the symptoms varied," according to "one of the physicians." Signs of intermittent fever. More medicine. No "alarm," but
some "anxiety." Very thirsty, Taylor "ate ice constantly." Then his
stomach rejected the fluid. The patient's mind "was clear . . . but he
said, *'in two days I shall be a dead man.'* He began to be very despond-
ing." The realization that Taylor might die became fully appreciated at
length. But much that was printed borders on the meaningless unless
grains of truth can be extracted from the chaff. Item: "The disease . . .
made rapid encroachments . . . but . . . visible stages of the cholera
morbus were . . . checked. However, fever ensued, and from a remittent
character, it took the form of typhoid." Item: "Dr. Wood said it was
very like" Taylor's "attack at Erie," but Wood "was not frightened by
the symptoms. . . . More calomel was given, and more quinine. . . . The
violent passages had stopped. The disease seemed alleviated." Item:
"Toward the evening of the 8th, the chronic type of dysentery . . . disappeared." More vomiting followed. Taylor's condition being "critical," only physicians entered the sick chamber. The President's family
occupied an adjoining room—"overwhelmed with grief, and refusing
. . . repose." Bulletins informed "the masses" of "changes observable
in the patient," but hope vanished by eleven o'clock. From then until
daylight "anxiety prevailed." Item (July 8, 11:00 P.M.): "The President is laboring under a bilious remittent fever, following . . . severe
cholera morbus; and is considered . . . seriously ill."

3

Throughout Tuesday July 9, when contradictory reports began to dis-
seminate among distraught crowds, conciseness and brevity (if not complete accuracy) marked telegraph dispatches sent across the land. At
five o'clock in the morning, said one, the President showed improve-

ment. At ten o'clock hope soared: He had "rallied." Yet at nine: Taylor "passed a very bad night. . . . This forenoon he has not improved." Two hours later: "The President has suffered much from restlessness and pain. . . . All say he is dangerously ill." A rumor described Taylor as rallying. Another announced that he was dead. Near midday Daniel Webster was told hopes were "favorable." But at one o'clock, though the fever abated, "his case is considered more and more critical."[4]

On Capitol Hill, while the President suffered, his Administration had been warmly assailed and upheld. On Saturday the House, in the Galphin showdown, heard the masterful Clarke defense. But it was also then that ninety-one congressmen passed Thompson's amendment to *"censure the President"* for his "connection" with the claim. Toombs, Stephens and a Georgia Whig friend joined the majority on the test, instead of helping defeat the attempt by eighty-nine to eighty-eight. This, a Louisiana bystander observed, was "a sickening exhibition." Taylor was faithful to their comrade, Crawford, yet men responsible for Crawford's appointment stabbed the President in the back. The vote, commented the *Express,* was "personal, partizan, spiteful and . . . malicious. It was uncalled for"—since Old Zack "made no communication to Congress upon the subject of the Galphin claim," and only gave Crawford his "private . . . opinion" regarding Crawford's agency. On Monday the entire Schenck substitute (censure included) was overwhelmingly defeated. And so the black mark stained the record less than forty-eight humid hours. However, the Galphin debate still raged Tuesday afternoon, when Congress adjourned. (Notwithstanding Toombs-Stephens denials that Taylor was "threatened" while mortally ill, their votes—if reported to him—could scarcely have aided his peace of mind!)

The Senate crisis was less dramatic. Before and after the Fourth of July Tennessee's Bell and Connecticut's Smith buttressed Taylor's extension stand. Ironically South Carolina's Butler was again projecting the state-rights line, when Senate business hummed to a halt shortly after Tuesday noon. "A messenger called Mr. Fillmore from his chair," communicating "intelligence of most sad import"—then "tripped about" to Webster, Clay and Cass, "stooping to their ears" and telling it to them. Senators then, wheeling round their chairs, bent over "in groups of three and four"—passing along the news to their colleagues. Webster, at length, approached the Carolinian and, whispering, interrupted him. Butler "dropped at once in a seat." Whereupon Webster formally announced "the appalling news . . . that in a few hours the President would be no more." Webster's voice and manner were "full of emotion."

Tears "stood in many eyes." The Senate immediately adjourned, and the House followed suit.[5]

4

As chambers emptied and voices hushed and statesmen deserted the Capitol, attention centered on the White House. The Cabinet assembled. Fillmore appeared. Ann Wood and the Joe Taylors were on hand. Outside the Mansion plain people gathered; no order or edict commanded their presence—it was just that they loved the doughty old man, and, as always, he drew them to him.

All the day long the rumors seeped out. At two o'clock, Taylor was "sinking fast." At three he was "just alive." At four his condition changed "for the better" and the "pain disappeared." Bells rang in steeples, bonfires blazed and crowds rejoiced when the story spread that the patient had begun to recover. This gladness, however, was short-lived. Clergymen came. Physicians reassembled. "The strongest blisters had no power." At five: "No improvement; the White House gates shut." At six inquirers clustered on the portico, straggled into the vestibule, fanned out into the parlors. Before seven o'clock the Reverend Smith Pyne offered religious consolation. Off and on Taylor vomited. His pulse fell. Green matter came from his stomach. Forty grains of quinine had been given him, which apparently did no good. Nor did calomel, bleeding or blisters.

At seven a "pall of gloom . . . shrouded all faces." The "stream" of humanity was "greater than ever." In and out men padded and paused, muffled, deferential and futile. Upstairs Mrs. Taylor was prostrated—Betty "overwhelmed with grief"—Colonel Bliss "much dejected." Fillmore, the Cabinet, Mayor Walter Lennox, Marshal Wallach, Jefferson Davis, Joseph Taylor, Mrs. John Bell, the David Hunters, even the diplomats were reported in the sickroom. Ten o'clock! Another bulletin! The doctors said Taylor was sinking fast. "It is impossible for him to recover."

In his final hours could Taylor speak clearly? At one point he is said to have asked how long he might survive. Wotherspoon answered: "I hope . . . for many years—but . . . I fear not many hours."

"I know it," Rough and Ready responded.

Was he comfortable?

"Very," Taylor murmured, "but the storm, in passing, has swept away the trunk. . . . I am about to die—I expect the summons soon—I have endeavored to discharge all my official duties faithfully—I regret nothing, but am sorry that I am about to leave my friends."

These were "his last audible words." When Wotherspoon administered a stimulant, "it was powerless in reviving the functions." At half past ten Zachary Taylor was "not expected to live 15 minutes." In less than the allotted time the President passed to eternity.

His beloved Peggy's "abandonment" was "heart-piercing." Ann and Betty, his devoted daughters, wept. His three sons-in-law—Wood, Davis, Bliss (all old comrades of his military service)—turned to comfort the womenfolk.

White House clocks pointed to ten thirty-five.

It was Tuesday night, July 9, 1850.[6]

5

Most of our White House occupants have been carried out to vault or grave with little pomp or circumstance. As the first President to die in office at the zenith of a crisis and when Congress was in session, Taylor was honored by sable pageantry on an unprecedented scale. But what of the interlude, while his remains were entrusted to Undertaker Samuel Kirby? Wednesday was "calm" and "Sabbath-like" in Washington. "A spirit of sadness rests upon every one. . . . Little business was transacted. . . . Salutations were not cheerful." In the omnibus "to Georgetown and back again, not a single conversation arose." Flags hung at half-mast. "The appalling calamity . . . seems to benumb the faculties of all."

Someone scanned the heavens for portents. "Reader, do you believe in omens?" At half past four Wednesday morning "dense clouds" enveloped the western sky—and a gentle rain came down. A single "peal of thunder" echoed like a clap of artillery. Then behold the sun, and a "brilliant" rainbow—one arm seeming to rest on the White House, the other "lost in the . . . broad Potomac." A "great man" had fallen. "Earth . . . lost him, and Nature wept . . . and the artillery of Heaven welcomed his spirit to a brighter world!" The "bow of promise was hung out" to show that "hope should . . . end in fruition" and "the country should be saved."

Meanwhile the country's Thirteenth President did not sleep "one moment" that night. Shortly after Taylor's death the Cabinet had addressed his successor: "SIR: The . . . painful duty devolves on us to announce to you that Zachary Taylor . . . is no more. . . . We have the honor to be, very respectfully, your obedient servants. . . ." Fillmore answered: "GENTLEMEN: . . . I have no language to express the emotions of

my heart. . . . I am overwhelmed with grief. I shall . . . communicate
the sad intelligence to Congress, and . . . appoint a time . . . for taking
the oath. . . . Respectfully yours, MIILLARD FILLMORE." What were
the new Chief Magistrate's thoughts as he tossed while slumber eluded
him? Of boyhood hardships in upstate New York? Of practicing law?
Of taking part in the shrill intolerance of Anti-Masonry? Of Seward
and Weed and their split with him? Of Taylor living and Taylor dead?
Of Fillmore's, and the nation's, future? His brain may well have been
whirling as he listened to rain on the roof and awaited the dawn at
Willard's.

He seemed bland and placid as ever when the swearing-in occurred.
The time was noon of July 10; the place, the House of Representatives.
Every part of the chamber was "crowded" with history-minded spectators. Fillmore did not make a speech. But in his communication to
Congress, relative to Taylor's passing, he described his late chief as "a
great man"[7]—setting the style for many a eulogy featured in the American press.

In New York, Brooks's paper pictured Taylor as modest, brave, simple, truthful, magnanimous and bold. "He knew no one section of
country distinguished from the rest,—no one institution having peculiar
claims over another,—no class of people above or below the whole mass
of his fellow citizens." Greeley's *Tribune* said that Taylor "endeared
himself" to the people "to a degree . . . few public men . . . attain." His
goodness, sincerity, common sense, and firmness united in causing this.
And his "patriotism . . : threw an almost chivalrous halo over the sturdy
elements of his nature." In Hartford the *Courant* declared: "The death
of no" other "individual could . . . prove such a serious loss to our
country at the present emergency." Old Zack's popularity, decision and
energy could have accomplished everything "required in the existing
crisis." In Philadelphia his loss seemed "a national one," and "not a
few" people were apprehensive lest it be followed by "future . . . disaster."

Down in Nashville the *Republican Banner* deplored Taylor's death
as "a terrible calamity." His "patriotism . . . was a guaranty . . . that
. . . interests of the *whole* country would be maintained with . . . watchful care." The Richmond *Whig* discerned in Taylor "a striking resemblance to the Father of his Country, and . . . the late Chief Justice
Marshall." Rough and Ready was *"the man, emphatically, of his time."*
According to the Richmond *Republican,* the deceased President "combined . . . greatness and simplicity; self-respect and humility"—com-

manding "the world's admiration" and winning "a people's LOVE!" If
the Almighty's "warning . . . be not heeded," Taylor's death "may be
the precursor of the dissolution of the Republic!" The Augusta *Chronicle* was more restrained: "Few men of any age . . . were more successful"
in gaining public confidence. People "may differ" as to his measures'
expediency, but "none will doubt . . . he was influenced alone by considerations of duty, and . . . patriotism." The New Orleans *Picayune*
saw Taylor's name inscribed "among the most illustrious . . . men who
. . . served their country faithfully . . . and deserved . . . everlasting
remembrance."

If Northern Whig praise was the most ecstatic, Southern Whigs and
rival Democrats struck few sour notes. Some kept silent. Most had a
good word—though some eliminated references to New Mexico, to
dwell on Taylor's *military* fame. Confidential communications contain
such remarks as Francis Blair's that Taylor's death had made Clay happy.
Chase opined that, while "multitudes mourn . . . the Old General . . .
sincerely—other multitudes secretly rejoice." Still, such reactions were
not typical of majority emotional sentiment. No hypocrisy impinged on
most Americans' sorrow. At the Eckhart Mines, above Cumberland,
Maryland, the Eckhart Light Artillery fired minute guns in Taylor's
memory. In Richmond it was "one gun . . . every seven minutes" until
a hundred had been heard. In New York City "the decease of the President seems to be viewed as a . . . national calamity." Boston "is in
mourning. . . . Bells are tolling, and . . . shops . . . dressed in black."
Philadelphians paid tribute to the "glorious memory" of the "hero, sage,
and patriot." At Harrisburg, Governor Johnston presided at a meeting
of reverent farewell. Cincinnati was "filled with gloom." "Public
calamity" and "sad disaster" were expressions typical of the hour.

In New Orleans "bells have been tolled, minute guns fired, and flags
hoisted at half mast. . . . Great solemnity prevails." In Charleston the
news produced "a deep sensation amongst our citizens." At Tammany
Hall New York's Hunker Democrats heard "with deep and sincere regret . . . of the decease of . . . Zachary Taylor."[8] "As the stage stopped
at Oriskany Falls," wrote a correspondent of Weed's, ". . . the appalling
words fell upon my ear 'Genl. Taylor is *dead.*' . . . On reaching Clinton
men . . . gathered in groups, reading Black draped extras—from thence
to Utica there was no Conversation—— My own meditations were sad
enough." A Fillmoreite reported that the President's death "shrouds
the minds of all." Across the Canadian border, in Kingston, newspaper
printers reversed their rules. And it was announced that the steamship

Cambria, leaving Boston harbor Wednesday, "will be the first" to inform Europe. "The intelligence . . . will create a sensation there."

6

Nowhere, naturally, was the atmosphere of grief less relieved than in the White House. Mrs. Taylor was not equal to standing or sitting without support. Thrice the ice was taken from Taylor's body, which Kirby laid out periodically to enable the widow to view the remains. "These visits were most heart rending." Nor was Mrs. Taylor alone in her suffering, for Betty—"moaning sadly," confided: "We had thought of our mother's dying, for she is . . . seldom well; but our father . . . we never expected to die!" Mrs. Taylor would not permit her husband's corpse to be embalmed. Giuseppe Fagnani, an Italian artist, sketched Taylor's head and face; "no cast was taken" for fear that the "skin should be disfigured." Friday, Taylor's wife and daughters looked on his "loved features" for the last time. The body being removed to the East Room, the public was admitted—and shoved and pushed. Men and boys clutched at canopy and coffin in "their indecent haste" to gape, until Kirby and his associates threatened to "call . . . the Police." Eventually a sort of order was restored. "I pressed forward," wrote an eyewitness, "and oh! most touching was the lovely expression of the Hero's face! There was enough color . . . to look as if alive, and sweetly sleeping." The body lay in a leaden coffin, enclosed in one of mahogany, with silver decorations on it and "magnificent flowers" placed "in profusion." People lingered, filed slowly by, then left with "a leaf, a flower, a withered branch . . . consecrated by . . . having once rested on the bier of ZACHARY TAYLOR."

If sob-sister whimperings detract from these descriptions, the splendor of the funeral on Saturday supplants mere sentimentality with majesty and grandeur. Virtually all persons of prominence were present in the East Room on July 13. Before and after the stroke of noon they ascended the White House steps. Senate and House arrived *en masse.* Bulwer, Crawford, Stephens, Toombs, Seward, Jesup, Benton and Custis—intimate associate and sworn foe—attended Taylor's obsequies. In the center of the room the mortal tenement of Taylor lay. At the foot of the bier sat Fillmore and the Cabinet; at its head, Pyne and the Senate's chaplain. To the right, Winfield Scott and officers of all branches; alongside them, the Diplomatic Corps. To the left, the pallbearers, including Clay and Webster. Near them, Taylor's brother with Wood, Bliss, the grandsons, and Jefferson Davis. Rarely, if ever, in

White House history had so many distinguished leaders gathered at one time within its walls.

"All being seated . . . a choir . . . sang . . . the anthem: 'I heard a voice from Heaven saying . . . Henceforth blessed are the dead which die in the Lord.' " Zachary Taylor, like several other Presidents, was not a member of a Christian church. However, since he "most usually worshipped" with the Episcopalians, appropriately the Episcopal ritual was impressively intoned. Following the responses, Doctor Pyne read the beautiful "Now is Christ risen . . ." from the fifteenth chapter of First Corinthians. Then, in a sermon underscoring Taylor's "integrity" and "conscientiousness," Pyne dwelt on his preference for "convictions of right to any transient popularity." This, Pyne stressed, secured Taylor's "hold . . . on the confidence and . . . affection of the People." After the benediction, the Marines carried the coffin from the Mansion while Emilie and Virginia Eberbach (children whose singing pleased Taylor when living) "mingled . . . sweet voices" with the "measured tread."

The White House ceremony ending shortly after one o'clock, the procession began to move up the Avenue and out toward the Congressional Burying Ground. Solemn "sounds of martial music" and "dirges filled the air." The catafalque "was drawn by eight white horses, splendidly coparisoned"—conducted by white-turbaned grooms. From various cities of the East soldiers had come—prominent among them the militia of Maryland. Regular troops also marched in slow time, or took stations to fire salutes with their spit-and-polish brass.

Closing the Army's part of the procession rode General Scott, a "commanding figure" with a "towering plume of yellow feathers." Then came Mayor Lennox of Washington, congressional and local officials, Doctor Pyne and his fellow ministers—preceding Taylor's moving bier. "The car, large and elevated, covered with black" and festooned with white silk, was "surmounted by a canopy" and by an American eagle half hidden in crape. Near by were the pallbearers—Clay, Cass, Berrien, Winthrop, James McDowell of Virginia, Hugh White of New York, Custis, Jesup, Judge William Cranch, Commodore Henry E. Ballard, Benton, Webster, Smith, Linn Boyd, Congressmen Vinton and Isaac Holmes, Robert J. Walker, Joseph Gales, and Generals George Gibson and Archibald Henderson. There were more than a hundred carriages, Joe Taylor riding with Bliss and Wood, Preston with Crawford and Taylor's grandsons in Secretary Preston's vehicle. But no human, living or dead, attracted more attention from the crowds than Taylor's four-footed friend—Old Whitey. "All eyes" were on the "far-famed" horse, with holsters and inverted spurs on the saddle. Whitey pawed the ground and tossed his head "at every boom of the cannon"—advancing, "as it seemed, with a military air. . . . Poor fellow! he stepped proudly."

"The Procession" extended "nearly two miles." All the way along, carriage occupants, horsemen, children, groups of adults patiently awaited (many for hours) "the coming of the mourning train." From the Treasury (jam-packed early) to "the open windows of houses," clustering heads peered out on the scene. The very roofs seemed "tiled" with humanity—100,000 spectators, no less, reputedly being in Washington that day.

At the cemetery, the coffin, preceded by clergymen and attended by pallbearers, passed through the gate to the graveled walk fronting the receiving vault. While sentries kept the crowds at a distance, the coffin was set down, and the minister proclaimed the assurance of immortality, as all that was mortal of Zachary Taylor was committed to the vault and darkness. The infantry—Taylor's old arm—volleyed thrice. Artillerists also fired three rounds. "And," declared the Washington *Union* (which fought his every move as President) the valiant "warrior was left sleeping" the "sleep that knows no waking."[9]

7

Fillmore thoughtfully offered to postpone his occupancy of the White House in order to suit Mrs. Taylor's convenience and out of respect for her feelings. She, however, had no wish to linger, and, the evening of her husband's funeral, moved to Meredith's residence. On July 18 she left the capital. (She never returned, and never mentioned the Mansion for the duration of her days.) On July 24, Wood advised Meredith: "Mrs. Taylor and all the family are well, and as composed as could be expected." After three months in Baltimore, the former First Lady with Betty and Ann joined Dick in New Orleans in November.

There Taylor's estate was divided among the widow, son and surviving daughters. Three testamentary papers were found to have no legal validity, for in each the property's disposition was contingent on Taylor's falling in battle or dying during a military campaign. Bliss, the administrator, and all the family joined nevertheless in carrying out Zachary Taylor's basic intent. Negroes, lands, stocks and cash were apportioned as equally as possible in monetary value to the children. Mrs. Taylor wanted little. She received Taylor's substantial income-producing Louisville warehouses, the small lot in the same city, 105 shares of Bank of Louisville stock, and $1,716 from the sale of furniture in Washington. Five servants also went to her; these, with her income from stock and rentals, were all she required in the little cottage at East Pascagoula where she died two years after her husband. Since the Blisses lived with Mrs. Taylor during the balance of her life, they no doubt provided her with everything her own funds could not supply. Richard and Ann also stood ready to contribute to her comfort.

Mrs. Wood's share included twenty-three slaves valued at $9,225; stock in the Western Bank of Baltimore, $2,000; forty-five shares in the Bank of Louisville, $4,500; $9,810 in cash, and half of Cypress Grove, $10,000. Mrs. Bliss's share consisted of twenty-six slaves ($11,100); fifty shares in the Bank of Louisville, $5,000; thirty shares in the Northern Bank of Kentucky, $3,000; $8,310 in cash, and half of Cypress Grove, $10,000. The small difference in the daughters' inheritance stemmed from their father's wish that the Negress Mary and her offspring should go to Betty Bliss. Dick's share was eighty-three slaves ($43,825); he had received $7,500 less than each of his sisters during Zachary's lifetime. Fashion Plantation did not enter into the estate partition. With its sixty-four Negroes it stood in Dick's name, Ann and Betty specifically surrendering their claims to Fashion despite the "understanding" that "father was to have an interest . . . if he should choose."

On account of Fashion's total omission, the failure to evaluate the widow's property and changes in real-estate prices in the future, one cannot state to the last penny what Taylor's financial worth was when he died. His children divided $116,770.02 on December 9, 1850. Since this was exclusive of Mrs. Taylor's portion, we may start conservatively with over $130,000, even when the Cypress Grove appraisal is trimmed. Moreover, Dick had used Taylor capital to make a down payment of $19,500 on Fashion and its slaves the preceding spring. Though the total Fashion investment would amount to $115,000, most of this remained to be paid; hence this figure cannot be added arbitrarily to what the partition papers show. Maunsel White & Company estimated Taylor's property (no doubt including the Fashion investment) in the neighborhood of $200,000 even. This seems somewhat high. But White's word was good, and he may have known facts now unavailable.[10] In round numbers, then, it can be concluded that Taylor in '50 had something between $150,000 and $200,000.

8

Meanwhile Taylor's family determined on sending his remains to Kentucky for burial. Selection of the family cemetery, in Jefferson County, was appropriate. Though at various times a resident of more than a dozen states and territories, Taylor was a Kentuckian at heart—typical of the sturdy sons of Revolutionary stalwarts who came out from the Old Dominion to settle Louisville's eastern periphery. There he had lived as infant, boy and man. There a bride—later children—blessed his life. There he returned from the War of 1812. There he spent lengthy Army leaves. There he owned property. And there, too, he erected a stone wall around the graveyard where his parents, brothers and sisters lay. His widow did what Taylor would have wanted when she approved arrangements for Bliss and Joe Taylor to accompany his body over the mountains and down the Ohio to the family cemetery in the land he loved.

In Washington on October 25, under District officials' supervision, coffin and corpse went aboard a car furnished by the Baltimore & Susquehanna Railroad. With the dead man's son-in-law and brother in attendance, they proceeded by train through Baltimore and Harrisburg to Pittsburgh, where the river trip began. At Cincinnati Judge McLean joined the escort. And there a telegram was sent informing Kentuckians that the steamboat *Navigator* had departed Thursday October 31 and would reach Louisville about nine o'clock Friday. On November 1, when the *Navigator* arrived, all Louisville paid final tribute. The military, fire companies, mayor, council "and the citizens" marched down Sixth Street to Main, up Main to Fifth, down Fifth to Water, then to the wharf, where Mayor John M. Delph and his fellow officials formally received the coffin. John J. Crittenden was present, the man who contributed so greatly to Taylor's nomination and election. Addressing his remarks to Taylor's kinsmen, Crittenden declared that Kentuckians "felt a just pride that the family . . . selected the soil of this commonwealth as that in which the ashes of the deceased should repose." The departed patriot's grave, he was certain, "would be hallowed by a reverence only equalled by the affectionate regard with which . . . Taylor" was held when living.

The coffin then was lifted to the hearse. And, "the immense crowds that lined the streets" attesting "emotions felt by all classes," the military preceded and civilians followed the honored dead across Beargrass bridge and out into the countryside. "The body was attended by a large number of persons in vehicles and on horse-back" to the unostentatious vault, so near the President's boyhood home.[11] At last the warrior came back to his own. Earth's wanderer returned to his people.

CHAPTER XXXII

HIS PLACE IN HISTORY

1

IN THE sixteen weeks between Zachary Taylor's White House funeral and Kentucky burial the state of the Union changed almost completely from one of crisis to one of calm. Considering the rate at which events had been speeding toward a sectional showdown, the trend was halted and reversed with spectacular suddenness. The very day of the service in the Mansion Senator Chase wrote confidentially: "The general opinion is that . . . Fillmore . . . will be controlled by the Clay & Webster influence." "It is thought," said Francis Blair, that Clay, Fillmore and Webster "have patched up a coalition." Hannibal Hamlin, presuming that Webster would head the State Department, predicted: "The Omnibus will go down in the Senate. . . . We shall . . . kill it by a . . . 3 to 12" majority. Then the measures, taken up separately, "will pass in some shape." These prophecies were representative enough to show that what would soon become fact was foreseen by many at the capital.

On assuming the Presidency Millard Fillmore did not announce his Cabinet at once. Since he had favored the Compromise before Taylor's death, few were surprised when he picked Daniel Webster to be the first among his ministers. Other conservatives carefully considered were North Carolina's William A. Graham, Louisiana's Charles M. Conrad, Pennsylvania's Thomas M. T. McKennan and Missouri's Edward Bates. The extreme Southern element wanted Toombs in the War Department. Ewing and Meredith were backed for retention, and Vinton and Winthrop figured in the speculation, on the theory that one or two Taylor Whigs were needed. Fillmore and his advisers, however, had more dramatic tactics in mind, with many of their maneuvers revolving around Corwin and Crittenden. Corwin hesitated and even declined before agreeing to take the Treasury. (It was a fatal decision: he never climbed back to Senate heights or regained his former influence.) Corwin's transfer to the Cabinet constituted Fillmore's initial triumph, symbolizing the passivity—and resignation to defeat—of some Taylorites, now that Taylor was gone. Crittenden also accepted a portfolio, which would seem

401

curious except for the fact that Taylor's death released him from charges of "Bargain!"—such as might have occurred the year before. Now Clay acquiesced in the naming of Crittenden,[1] who with Corwin served Fillmore's purpose as a symbol of Compromise unity.

When Fillmore submitted his nominations to the Senate, they were unanimously confirmed. The slate consisted of Webster, Corwin, Bates, Graham, Crittenden, James A. Pearce and Nathan K. Hall (the President's Buffalo law partner). When Bates and Pearce later resisted the pressure, Conrad became Secretary of War, and McKennan (soon succeeded by Alexander H. H. Stuart) accepted the Interior temporarily. In August the Fillmore Cabinet contained four Northerners and three Southerners. In September the balance was reversed. But the important point remained that compromisers had mounted to the saddle—while Corwin and Crittenden strung along, at least to the extent of riding with them.

2

The Fillmore Cabinet's personnel suggested strongly that the Compromise could eventually pass piecemeal. Administration prestige and patronage now tipped the scales in its favor, instead of against it, as under Taylor. Congressmen (especially Northern Whigs), with votes to block it, began shifting to Fillmore even before the Cabinet's confirmation—and then fell over one another the moment that the die was cast. The whole New York City delegation "is said" to have "caved in," Charles E. Clarke reported to Weed. Clarke told of one who "laughs over his shame & admits it," naming upstaters as fellow converts to the Fillmore dispensation. Fillmore's lobbyists "are here every day in the Ho of Reprs & busy." Those "straws indicate the way of the wind."

As the trend continued, Henry Clay became prematurely sanguine. The Senate test was made by Clay himself, who, defeating a series of Benton's thrusts and Seward's New Mexican statehood efforts, on July 31 brought his bill to a vote. As Douglas had predicted, the Omnibus failed. First, a thirty-three to twenty-two vote struck out New Mexico's territorial provision. Next, the Texas boundary arrangement was eliminated, twenty-nine to twenty-eight. Statehood for California likewise went by the board, thirty-four to twenty-five. All that remained of Clay's basic first section was the Utah territorial portion, which passed on August 1.

Deeply disappointed, Clay was also physically exhausted. He promptly retreated to Rhode Island, where he hoped Newport's salt air would restore his strength. And the man who at last openly took charge was Douglas, who had always argued that the only way to achieve their objectives was to bring up the bills one at a time. As early as August 3, Douglas was confident. "I trust you will hear" of the California measure's "passage . . . before you receive this," he advised friends. Then would come "a Bill for the Texas Boundary which . . . Pearce . . . & myself are now preparing. . . . We shall . . . pass . . . the Bill for New Mexico . . . just as I reported it four months ago. Thus will all the Bills pass the Senate & I believe the House also. . . . They will be collectively . . . Clay's Compromise & separately the Bills reported by the committee on Territories four months ago."[2]

On Friday August 9 the boundary measure met with the approval of the Senate—thirty for, only twenty against—Texas receiving over 33,000 square miles above what Clay's committee planned. (Speculators in Texan securities rejoiced, for $10,000,000 were to go to Austin.) The following Tuesday thirty-four senators favored California's statehood, with only eighteen opposed. Thursday saw New Mexico's territorial bill winning lopsidedly, twenty-seven to ten. August 26, after a week of debate, the fugitive-slave bill scurried through—with harsher provisions than Webster had sought. Then came the District of Columbia bill, with a division of thirty-three to nineteen. Thus, every fundamental aim of Douglas, Clay and Millard Fillmore was realized in the upper chamber—the most important in less than four weeks.

Off at a fast clip the House of Representatives imitated the Senate's example. With Linn Boyd their nominal sponsor, but Douglas actually the guiding genius, the boundary and New Mexico measures were combined. After a week's debate the Douglas-captained majority came out triumphant by eleven votes. The California statehood and Utah territorial bills galloped through, the fugitive-slave bill hard after. The Senate ratifying the union of the Texas and New Mexico measures, the House overwhelmingly approved the District of Columbia provisions. Fillmore's signature made the component parts of the Compromise the law of the land. And, September 30, Congress adjourned, after functioning 302 days, the longest session then on record.

The week end beginning September 7 was a wild one at the capital. With victory in sight the compromisers drank like mad—even on the Sabbath. Webster, serenaded on Saturday night, was supported on each side by friends. "Now is the summer—no!" he exclaimed. "Now is the winter of our discontent made glorious summer by this sun of York!"

Sunday morning found Douglas prostrated. Other senators lay low,[3] after the costly wines had sparkled and the liquors freely flowed. Kicking up their heels, the compromisers had cavorted in bonfires' red glare. Having "saved the Union," they crowed. Sectional trials and slavery tribulations were over forever—so they supposed.

3

If the "morning after" proved painful, it was only so in the physical sense, for Douglas and his lieutenants thought they had scored a legislative triumph. This was balm for their bleary eyes, an ice bag for their aching heads. The real "morning after" would not torment them till years slid by in the haze of a roseate illusion which the Compromise induced. It may have been a quirk of fate that the man who achieved the Compromise subsequently reopened the conflict with his Kansas-Nebraska Act. Although the crisis subsided perceptibly at 1850's end, the Compromise contained the prickles and one sharp thorn of future irritation.

In the North the Fugitive Slave Law met with opposition from the first. Federal commissioners received five dollars for each Negro discharged, but double that sum for arrest warrants issued; this was a most unpopular feature. Alleged fugitives were denied *habeas corpus* and trial by jury, nor could they testify in their own defense. From New England out to Chicago friends of the colored people held mass meetings, protesting vigorously against the law. Negroes themselves were scared to death. And Fillmore's rigid enforcement "produced an era of slave hunting and kidnapping"—driving runaways into Canada, creating vigilance committees, increasing underground railroad operations and stimulating Mrs. Stowe to write *Uncle Tom's Cabin.*

That being true, how can it be said that "the state of the Union changed almost completely from one of crisis to one of calm"? This was the reason for the word "almost"—but possibly the qualification need not be made with respect to the masses of Americans. Newspapers and letters of the times reveal that the initial majority reaction to the Compromise was one of relief. Southerners generally were pleased with the fugitive-slave, Texas-boundary and territorial features. Similarly most Northerners seemed gratified that California was admitted and the Union preserved without immediate danger of war. Opposition to harsh provisions covering the capture and return of fugitives increased tremendously in the next decade; it would be a mistake to exaggerate the extent of its growth that autumn.

In Texas and New Mexico the effect of the Compromise was instantaneous. Though Fillmore asserted the right to prevent Santa Fe's seizure by the Texans, Bell and his legislators cooled off when they saw most of their dreams fulfilled. The special session at Austin adjourning, the Santa Fe crisis dissolved with it. The Nashville Convention met again in November but did nothing meaningful and quickly broke up. In South Carolina, and scattered elsewhere, some vocal die-hards remained. But Georgia moderates won two clear-cut tests, and Mississippi in '51 preferred Foote to Davis for the governorship. The Nashville debacle was one with this trend, the Compromise and Taylor's death creating the contrast between the two gatherings there.

4

The importance of Taylor's blocking the Compromise, his death, and Fillmore's approval of the Compromise have been appreciated by outstanding writers. McMaster, Channing, Garrison, Macy and Rhodes realized how diametrically opposed were the two Presidents' policies. Some important younger historians—Nevins, Craven, Morison, Commager[4]—also stress the dramatic shift. Many general histories, however, miss the significance of Taylor's stand. Especially disappointing are the books of the Beards, who discuss the Senate speeches as if Taylor were not in the picture, instead of underscoring his influence on the Great Debate's form and length, and on the fate of the Compromise.[5] Many studies of Taylor's contemporaries such as Beveridge's Lincoln volumes fail to acknowledge his impact.[6]

The above criticism has nothing to do with the abstract "right" of Taylor's stand. Opinions of "wrong" and "right" depend on the individual's concept of the Union, state rights, agitation, loyalty to section and to class, slavery, the extension of slavery and probabilities of civil war in '50 rather than '61. All these are debatable. But the fact that Taylor was a powerful influence in '50 is a historic truth. For Old Zack profoundly affected the march of events during his lifetime. And his death resulted in as wholesale a transformation of policy and the nation's political temper as ever occurred in similar circumstances.[7] Thus the placing of Taylor's name alongside Fillmore's on a roster of "below-average" Presidents by a cross-section of fifty-four historians is meaningless when one learns that thirty-two gave them the very same rating. This makes no sense whatever. The foremost issues confronting Presidents from Taylor to Lincoln were the Union and related slavery extension. Since Taylor and Fillmore were utterly at odds, they could not have been equally right—or, conversely, equally wrong—as twenty-two pollees[8] understood. This, in turn, logically made one superior to the other as President.

It has become depressingly fashionable to perpetuate misconceptions respecting the Presidency in '50; to do as little spadework as possible, and to rehash three or four Senate speeches without relating them to the aggregate of events in that critical year. Such a charge does not apply to a few conscientious scholars noted for their digging ability. It certainly applies to flashy fellows who follow pseudopsychological styles, forever striving for sensationalism in half-baked historical pastiches. Many errors respecting Taylor spring from the fact that no one has written a comprehensive history of the Compromise.[9] There are useful monographs, of course—the best being a brief article by the late Frank H. Hodder, who (with George Fort Milton) stressed Stephen Douglas' major role. Hodder also succinctly declared: "The Compromise was more largely a Democratic measure than a Whig measure and more largely a southern measure than a northern one."

In an analysis of Senate votes in August it is significant that Clarke, Greene, John Davis, Phelps, Smith and Wales supported the Texas boundary bill; also Dayton and Miller were absent. Had they voted the other way, as would have been the case under Taylor, the legislation would have been defeated. Likewise enough representatives switched over and backed the key bill in the House to provide the margin there. Patronage plus special messages, dispatched by Fillmore to the Hill, gave Douglas extra ammunition. Still the pro-Compromise nucleus and most of its leaders were Democratic. The victory at base was a Democratic victory. And factors contributing to the Whig party's death are traceable to Douglas' success.

With Taylor's importance in the setting established, it would be easy to make much of a Clay biographer's assertion that the Compromise settled nothing. Between '50 and '60 the Fugitive Slave Law was not the only cause of friction. Douglas believed the Compromise endorsed the people's "right . . . to form and regulate their own internal concerns and domestic institutions in their own way." But Toombs and other Southerners saw in it "the principle of noninterference with slavery by Congress," and the "right . . . to hold slaves in a common Territory." This was a "fundamental . . . discrepancy"—a "portent of further disagreement." The Compromise fuse was long and winding. But, eventually, the bomb exploded in Douglas'—and Toombs's—face.

Was Zachary Taylor's alternative better? How expedient was the "President's Plan"? The late Herbert D. Foster outlined, as tellingly as anyone else, economic and social developments of the decade between '50 and '60. In every aspect detailed by Foster the North gained appreciably over the South. In population, industrialization and especially its railway network the North acquired an enormous military-potential advantage. Predicated on this alone—the differences obtaining in '50 and in '61—it was fortunate for the Union cause that President Taylor died when he did.

Yet that is hardly the whole story. Industrial, man-power and communication phases of changes made in eleven years were no more important than political and psychological aspects. In 1850 the country still had two *national* political parties with considerable popular backing. Just as Whiggery had not died, the Democrats had not split, and the *sectional* Republican party—later anathema to the South—was not even in existence. Later many Southerners concluded (some very reluctantly) that they could trust neither Republicans nor the Northern Democratic wing. In 1850, this line of thinking had by no means stiffened. Although blood might have been shed by Southerners (supporting Texas militiamen) and Northerners (spearheaded by Munroe), the spark of wholesale civil war would have been dampened by conservative convictions of millions in both sections. Despite South Carolina's ardor and Governor Bell's militancy, Taylor had an excellent chance of quelling Texan aggressiveness with far less slaughter than that of the 'sixties. This cannot be *proved,* one way or the other. Admittedly, a rebuttalist may argue that in '50 a unified South could have defeated a unified North. But had the South already achieved the degree of sectional solidarity existing ten years afterward? Unless this is answered affirmatively, from the Union viewpoint it was tragic that Taylor did not live to assert his Unionism—thereby possibly preventing a brothers' war of gigantic proportions.

Hindsight teaches that the Compromise failed to attain the goal which its sponsors eloquently claimed for it. The Compromise did not prevent civil war. It merely postponed the resort to arms, and perhaps made it inevitable. Taylor was convinced the Compromise was faulty. Lacking the congressional backing possessed by Jackson in '32, and by Lincoln in '61, he took a position comparable to theirs—and carried his unfulfilled measures to his grave. A historian has asked "How can we know . . . ?" with reference to Taylor's White House rating; "he was president such a short time." We *cannot* know. We can only estimate, grappling with ponderables *and* imponderables. Another scholar based his conclusions, respecting various administrations, on: "To what extent did each . . . advance the common interest of its day?" He considered Taylor "average"—Polk and Fillmore "below average"[10]—presumably identifying "common interest" with the Union's defense and preservation. With this conclusion the present writer agrees, except that on such a premise he would place Taylor higher than "average." (But if territorial expansion should be taken as the test, he would list President Polk as "great"—and rank Taylor at the very bottom.) When greatness and failure are calmly measured, not only individuals' weaknesses and strengths but conditions surrounding them and major issues confronting them must enter into the reckoning.

5

If Taylor may have been more farseeing than many of his contemporaries, why has his impact on American politics been ignored or played down in so many books?

Five factors contribute to the warp and twist. One is the paucity of Taylor's private papers, particularly for the presidential period. Most were destroyed when Civil War soldiers burned his son's Louisiana house. Others are fugitive. There is no big collection comparable to the Polk, Fillmore, Buchanan or Lincoln manuscripts. And taking the trouble to piece out the truth lacked appeal for impatient writers, eager to break quickly into print. With occasional exceptions they have been unwilling to study with care the *Congressional Globe* and kindred sources demonstrating the extent of Taylor's influence. Nowhere is a public man's character illumined more perfectly than in correspondence. Since for Taylor this source is largely lacking, it is essential to search for substitutes in the writings of men he knew and in contemporary newspapers. Though more difficult, this now has been done. And Old Zack's influence, so obvious in war, stands re-created in peace as well.

Another cause for misjudging Taylor lies in the supposedly baffling contrast between what his background indicated he would do and what he actually did. The exclusively military nature of his pre-presidential duties was often stressed in '48. But, respecting his White House service, writers are prone to emphasize Taylor's ownership of slaves—speculating why an investor in such property proved so stanch a Unionist. Really there is no mystery at all. Young and old, Taylor was nationally minded; private economic interests never oversloughed his devotion to the Union. It was as a patriotic soldier (not primarily as a planter) that he developed his policies as President. His roots were in the Richard Taylor-George Rogers Clark Kentucky environment, and so such a stand was not surprising.

A third aspect of Zachary Taylor's significant political foray, confusing to some interpreters, is the contradictory support given him in '48—with special reference to Southern backers' turnabout in '50. If Taylor's acts as President shocked Stephens and Toombs, why did they err at the outset in analyzing their man? The answer is that the candidate kept discreetly silent much of the time. If he had broadcast what he thought and felt about every issue disturbing the nation, he could not have been elected. During '48 he probably gave private antiextension assurances to Truman Smith and other Northerners.[11] At about the same time that antislavery Whigs began warming up to Taylor, Calhounites decided against supporting him.[12] Stephens and Toombs campaigned as ardently for the General as Seward and Corwin. But he probably did not make confidential pledges to them, and they acted on assumptions which Calhoun had discarded. The statement that Taylor favored extension, reversing himself when Seward became the Administration's "directing spirit,"[13] rests on flimsy guesswork. The simple truth is that Calhoun and Seward correctly estimated Taylor's attitude, while Toombs and Stephens missed it completely. Not until King went to California, and Taylor delivered his Mercer speech, did the Georgians see the light!

The fourth factor, not firmly grasped, is the origin of the President's Plan. No makeshift of the moment, this was virtually identical with Preston's proposal which so many Southerners endorsed. As Hamlin pointed out, Taylor adopted ideas and language of congressmen now fighting precisely what they had previously favored. Thus Taylor's Plan cannot be attributed to Seward's becoming "the directing spirit"!

The fifth misinterpretation of Taylor hinges on the first and second. He was *more* than a successful soldier. Rough and ready in battle, he exemplified in peace an attractive mingling of Virginia gentility and frontier earthiness. Stormy when aroused to anger, he was calm, considerate, modest, patient in the majority of his contacts. At times he failed to assert himself. And his most damaging tactical error lay in his reluctance to dismiss his ministers. But, just as he developed as a soldier, he improved as a political leader, gaining confidence from day to day. With the Compromise blocked, a new Cabinet installed and threatening Texans met or mastered, Taylor's following no doubt would have grown between '50 and '53. At the start self-depreciation was his gravest executive drawback. But his grip grew firmer, and assurance burgeoned, during his sixteen months in office.

6

Thomas H. Benton wrote of Taylor: "His death was a public calamity. No man could have been more devoted to the Union, or more opposed to the slavery agitation; and his position as a Southern man . . . would have given him a power in the settlement of those questions which no President without these qualifications could have possessed." Theodore Roosevelt wrote that Taylor "was an able and gallant soldier, a loyal and upright public servant, and a most kindly, honest, and truthful man. His death was a greater loss to the country than perhaps the people ever knew." Said James G. Blaine: Taylor's death "gave the opportunity for the success of the Compromise measures. Had . . . Taylor lived, their defeat was assured. As a Southern man, coming from a Gulf State, personally interested in the institution of slavery, he had a vantage ground which a Northern President could never attain. He had, moreover, the courage and . . . intelligence to uphold his principles, even in a controversy with . . . Clay."

If it be argued that their politics prejudiced Roosevelt and Blaine, we find a Clay biographer calling the "so-called compromises" merely "expedients which proved abortive." Also, a friendly Cass biographer—noting Taylor's "obstinate opposition"—attributed it "partly" to his "loyal heart" ("stirred to resentment by . . . treasonable threats"), and "partly" to his approving "from the first" California's admission as a state. Fillmore "became president," wrote the crisp A. C. McLaughlin, "and the weight of executive influence was thrown in favor of the compromise." An eminent authority, St. George L. Sioussat, concluded one of his path-marking monographs: "It is hardly possible . . . to avoid the impression that the . . . death of General Taylor was an event of greater significance than has sometimes been realized. . . . The history of the compromise of 1850 is still worthy of investigation."[14]

7

In Boston, on July 13, "Theodore Parker . . . preached so disgustingly of General Taylor . . . that decent people left the Church." In Salt

Lake City Brigham Young exclaimed: "Zachary Taylor is dead and gone to hell, and I am glad of it!" In Washington Clay failed to eulogize Taylor and (said Blair) seemed very happy. Coldly Clay predicted with no trace of sorrow: "I think the event . . . will favor the passage of the Compromise bill." In contrast, Robert Winthrop said: "The roll of our Chief Magistrates . . . presents the name of no man who has enjoyed a higher reputation with his contemporaries, or . . . will enjoy a higher reputation with posterity than ZACHARY TAYLOR, for some of the . . . noblest qualities which adorn our nature." Taylor combined gentleness with firmness, declared Edward D. Baker. "The achievements of Buena Vista . . . are deeds that will never die—it was the great event of the age." In the Presidency "honest and unostentatious" Taylor "exhibited the same . . . decision"—approaching "difficult questions with . . . singleness of purpose." When "impartial history shall record the events of his Administration, they will be found worthy of his past life, and a firm foundation for his future renown."

Jefferson Davis was already on record respecting Taylor, the soldier and the man. In 1847 he wrote that—brilliant as were Taylor's victories, attracting admiration and gratitude—"those who . . . know . . . him best will equally . . . honor him for the purity, the generosity, and . . . magnanimity of his private character. His colossal greatness is presented in the garb of the strictest republican simplicity." To this, no doubt, was due men's feeling that "we are learning to regard him with a filial affection." In 1848 Davis added that Taylor's life—"wholly devoted to his country"—had become "a pyramid," beautiful in simplicity, sublime in grandeur. His obelisk should resemble the Bunker Hill Monument— "its head amid the clouds," despising "assaults of . . . creeping things that crawl around its base."

Later Davis comments were also laudatory. But, in the light of subsequent events, no other statement could be so pertinent as Abraham Lincoln's in Chicago. Lincoln did not believe that *"all"* patriotism and wisdom died with Taylor. But *"wisdom* and *patriotism,"* he said, "are . . . worthless" unless "sustained" by the people's confidence. In his death "we have lost a degree of that confidence . . . which will not soon . . . pertain to any successor. . . . I fear the one *great* question of the day, is not now so likely to be partially acquiesced in by the different sections of the Union, as it would have been, could Gen. Taylor have been spared to us." The Presidency "is no bed of roses." Taylor, "like others, found thorns within it." Still Lincoln believed that—when Taylor's "conduct . . . shall . . . be viewed in the calm light of history"—he "will be found to have *deserved* as little" censure as any man succeeding him.

The final witness called before the bar is an Englishman, Sir Henry Lytton Bulwer. Shrewd observer and skilled reporter, Bulwer wrote to Palmerston:

"General Taylor . . . was chosen by the People not because he belonged to a party, but because he had distinguished himself as an individual; or rather as a soldier. This fact constituted the principal . . . difficulty of his position. Disliked by the Whig leaders because he had superseded their pretentions to power he had to govern with the Whig party, which, however influential and respectable, does not even when united form the strongest party in this Country. A majority in the two houses was opposed to his administration and a party attack in which his own name was comprehended disturbed the . . . last conscious hours of his existence. His general abilities were good, his experience in public life and political affairs small; his mind not uncultivated; he seems to have possessed some military genius, and to have been uniformly fortunate in war. Firmness, which his opponents called obstinacy, was his predominant characteristic. His intentions were always good; his word could always be relied upon; his manners were downright, simple, straightforward; his name was popular throughout the Union, and he died almost universally respected and lamented."[15]

Such was the native son of Virginia—the boy and youth of pioneer Kentucky, the cotton planter of Mississippi, the resident of Louisiana, the hero of Buena Vista—who marched on from four wars to become America's Soldier-President.

THE END

NOTES, BIBLIOGRAPHY, PERSONAL ACKNOWLEDGMENTS
AND INDEX

NOTES

[In order to provide more space for the story proper, it has been necessary to abbreviate the notes in four minor respects. First, in the case of many printed sources, the author cites a shortened title (followed by three dots) in lieu of the complete title, but only when the bibliographical identity of the work in question is entirely clear. Secondly, some long newspaper titles, such as the *Baltimore Patriot and Commercial Gazette*, have been cut and cited without the dots. Thirdly, in the case of the *Congressional Globe* and its *Appendix*, "Thirty-first Congress, First Session" may be assumed in instances where the Congress and session are not given. Finally, the following key is provided for the location of certain manuscript sources—LC denoting Division of Manuscripts, Library of Congress, Washington. APPLETON: Appleton-Sumner Correspondence, Boston Public Library. ARCHIVES: National Archives, Washington. BUFFALO: Millard Fillmore Papers, Buffalo Historical Society. CINCINNATI: Thomas B. Stevenson Papers, Historical and Philosophical Society of Ohio, Cincinnati. CLEMENTS: Lewis Cass Papers, William L. Clements Library, University of Michigan, Ann Arbor. CONCORD: New Hampshire Historical Society, Concord. FILSON: Filson Club, Louisville. GREELEY: Horace Greeley Papers, New-York Historical Society, New York City. HAMILTON COLLECTION: Zachary Taylor and Miscellaneous Papers, collection of Holman Hamilton, Fort Wayne, Indiana. HUNTINGTON: Henry E. Huntington Library, San Marino, California. ILLINOIS: Patton Papers, Illinois State Historical Library, Springfield. INDIANA: Indiana State Library, Indianapolis. KENTUCKY: Kentucky Historical Society, Frankfort. LINCOLN: Lincoln National Life Foundation, Fort Wayne, Indiana. LONDON: Foreign Office Papers, Public Record Office, London. MASSACHUSETTS: Massachusetts Historical Society, Boston. MINNESOTA: Alexander Ramsey Papers, Minnesota Historical Society, Saint Paul. MISSISSIPPI: Mississippi Department of Archives and History, Jackson. PENNSYLVANIA: William M. Meredith Papers, Historical Society of Pennsylvania, Philadelphia. ROCHESTER: University of Rochester. SEA COLLECTION: Collection of the late Andrew M. Sea, Jr., Louisville. STAUFFER COLLECTION: Zachary Taylor Papers, collection of the late Mrs. Walter R. Stauffer, New Orleans. WOOD COLLECTION: Zachary Taylor Papers, collection of Trist Wood, New Orleans.]

CHAPTER I

[1] Evidence of Taylor's wartime popularity is found in Holman Hamilton, *Zachary Taylor: Soldier of the Republic* (1941), 196-199, 217, 247-254. Accurate and readable treatments of the European uprisings abound. An illuminating contemporary summary is "Europe in 1848," *Whig Almanac . . . for 1849*, 15-21. See also Walter P. Hall and William S. Davis, *The Course of Europe Since Waterloo* (1941), 93-137; Carlton J. H. Hayes, *A Political and Cultural History of Modern Europe* (1939), II, 79-100; J. Salwyn Schapiro, *Modern and Contemporary European History* (1922), 102-103,

128-138, 205-207; Arnold Whitridge, *Men in Crisis* . . . (1949), *passim;* Sir J. A. R. Marriott, *A History of Europe from 1815 to 1923* (1931), 115-116, 133-135, 145-147.

[2] A somewhat satisfactory overview of the era is Carl R. Fish, *The Rise of the Common Man, 1830-1850* (1944), particularly 256-275, 313-338. Although California was *de facto* part of the United States, it was not formally annexed until 1848. Wisconsin entered the Union as a state in '48. This account is written from the late 1847 standpoint.

[3] Morris H. Hansen (compiler), *Statistical Abstract* . . . (1946), 4; Milo M. Quaife (editor), *The Diary of James K. Polk* . . . (1910), III, 469; Samuel F. Bemis (editor), *The American Secretaries of State* . . . (1927-1929), V, 62, 220-222, 305, 321, 328-329, 335, 415; George Bancroft to Lewis Cass, October 20, 1848, CLEMENTS; Fish, *op. cit., passim;* Alice F. Tyler, *Freedom's Ferment* . . . (1944), *passim.*

[4] Roy P. Basler (editor), *Abraham Lincoln: His Speeches and Writings* (1946), 335. The influence of Gamaliel Bailey and several other abolition leaders was unduly minimized by nineteenth-century historians, because of the emphasis placed on Garrison. *Uncle Tom's Cabin* first appeared, in serial form, in Bailey's *National Era.*

[5] So colorful and vocal were ante-bellum radicals that it is easy to overlook the comparatively quiet moderates. *Cf.* James T. Adams, *America's Tragedy* (1934), 59; Lillian A. Kibler, *Benjamin F. Perry* . . . (1946), *passim.*

[6] Jefferson County Tax Books, 1812, 1814, KENTUCKY; Notary Record Book B, Feliciana (now West Feliciana) Parish, Saint Francisville, Louisiana, 587-588; Deed Book G, Wilkinson County, Woodville, Mississippi, 114-115; Deed Book 55, Jefferson County, Louisville, Kentucky, 567-569; Auditor's Records, Jefferson County, Mississippi, Personal Assessment Roll for 1846, 1848, MISSISSIPPI; *20 Kentucky Reports* (4 T. B. Monroe), 267-268; *34 Kentucky Reports* (4 J. G. Dana), 198-206; Taylor Family Records, collection of the late Mrs. Jouett Taylor Cannon, FILSON.

[7] Notary Record Book H, West Feliciana Parish, Saint Francisville, Louisiana, 586-588; copy of deed, May 3, 1844, STAUFFER COLLECTION; *Agriculture of the United States in 1860* . . . (1864), 248; Zachary Taylor to Maunsel White, October 13, 1846, White Papers, Southern Historical Collection, University of North Carolina, Chapel Hill; Avery Craven, *The Coming of the Civil War* (1942), 151-174; Adams, *op. cit.,* 92-93; Hansen (compiler), *op. cit.,* 6.

[8] There is an interesting contrast, regarding the progressive or laggard nature of the South and Southerners, in *The Commercial Review of the South and West* (New Orleans), VIII, 45-57, 589. *The Commercial Review,* IV, 556, contains a colorful contemporary picture of New Orleans. See also Allan Nevins, *Ordeal of the Union* (1947), I, 47-48.

[9] Because of changes in the river's course, Rodney is now several miles inland and virtually deserted. In Taylor's day, it was a thriving community. There is a reference to Taylor's buying "comforts and conveniences" for his Negroes in Rodney, in the Maysville (Kentucky) *Eagle,* May 27, 1847.

[10] An exception might be made of John Tyler. But Tyler had held high civil offices, as had the far-from-obscure James K. Polk. Grover Cleveland was the only other elected President as unknown as Taylor four years before his inauguration.

CHAPTER II

[1] Maysville (Kentucky) *Eagle,* May 8, July 11, 1847; Louisville *Weekly Courier,* June 17, 1848; Buffalo *Courier,* April 21, 1849; Lady Emmeline Stuart-Wortley, *Travels in the United States . . .* (1851), 86; Miss Mary K. Jones to Trist Wood, May 13, 1892, WOOD COLLECTION. Taylor's recorded illnesses, up to this time, were almost always described as "fever." On several occasions, he may have suffered from malaria. His only ailments in Mexico were "fever" and a leg infection.

[2] Holman Hamilton, *Zachary Taylor: Soldier of the Republic* (1941), 230; East Pascagoula, Mississippi, correspondence of the Mobile *Herald,* dated August 19, 1848, clipping in George W. Julian's "Political Memorandum Book for 1848," Julian Papers, INDIANA; *Cist's Weekly Advertiser* (Cincinnati), January 31, New Orleans *Delta,* May 7, *The Battery* (Washington), October 26, 1848; Maysville *Eagle,* June 10, July 10, 1847; Buffalo *Express,* September 12, 1849; Buffalo *Courier,* January 10, 1850; Oran Perry (editor), *Indiana in the Mexican War* (1908), 82; George W. Julian, *Political Recollections . . .* (1884), 82; Nathan Sargent to John J. Crittenden, July 15, 1849, Crittenden Papers, LC; statement of the late Mrs. Arabella Taylor Clarke to the author, 1935. Mrs. Clarke was the niece of President Taylor, who knew her as "Little Belle."

[3] Benjamin Alvord to Marcus C. M. Hammond, April 21, 1848, James H. Hammond Papers, Taylor to Thomas S. Jesup, April 20, 1820, copy, Taylor Papers, LC; *Cist's Weekly Advertiser* (Cincinnati), January 31, 1848; Stuart-Wortley, *op. cit.,* 86; George F. Train, *My Life in Many States . . .* (1902), 81; Taylor to Thomas Lawson, undated, HAMILTON COLLECTION; Maunsel White to W. V. Graves, February 17, 1848, copy, White Papers, collection of Carl White, Jr., Tulsa, Oklahoma. What decline there was in Taylor's pre-presidential popularity occurred between January and April, 1848. McGehee was also a railroad and textile pioneer; he figures prominently in Stark Young, *So Red the Rose* (1934), *passim.* White is vividly portrayed in Harnett T. Kane, *Deep Delta Country* (1944), 48-51; he was Andrew Jackson's factor, as well as Zachary Taylor's. William Taylor's plantation diary for 1837-1842 was acquired in 1948 by the Department of Archives, Louisiana State University, Baton Rouge.

[4] New York *Times,* October 20, 1906; *The Literary Digest,* LXXXVI, Number 5, 40, 42; New York *Sun,* June 5, 1893; Louisville *Weekly Courier,* October 7, 1848; Taylor to Jesup, September 18, 1820, copy, Taylor Papers, LC; White to Mrs. Zachary Taylor, May 4, 1849, copy, White Papers, White Collection, Tulsa; statement of the late Mrs. Clarke to the author. Mrs. Margaret Mackall Smith Taylor was the daughter of Walter and Ann Mackall Smith of Calvert County, Maryland. *Cf.* Christopher Johnson, "Smith Family of Calvert County," *Maryland Historical Magazine,* III, 66-71, 73, IV, 65-66; Ben: Perley Poore, *Perley's Reminiscences . . .* (1886), I, 353; *Shelby News* (Shelbyville, Kentucky), March 7, 1849; S. Somervell Mackall, *Early Days of Washington* (1934), 130-132, 139-140.

[5] *The Autograph* (New York), I, 127-128, 181; Louisville *Weekly Courier,* October 7, 1848; Señora Calderón de la Barca to William H. Prescott, July 17, 1849, Prescott Papers, MASSACHUSETTS; [William T. Sherman], *Memoirs*

of Gen. W. T. Sherman (1892), I, 121; George Sykes to Miss Mary Elizabeth Taylor, undated card, Passport Number 30,269 (issued to Richard Taylor by Hamilton Fish), Zachary Taylor to James Taylor, May 24, 1846, copy, STAUFFER COLLECTION; George W. Cullum, *Biographical Register of the Officers and Graduates of . . . West Point* (1879), 542-545; James G. Wilson and John Fiske (editors), *Appleton's Cyclopaedia of American Biography* (1888-1889), I, 294; Washington *National Intelligencer,* April 27, 1847; Jackson B. Davis, "The Life of Richard Taylor," *Louisiana Historical Quarterly,* XXIV, 50-51; William H. Samson (editor), *Letters of Zachary Taylor . . .* (1908), 9, 25, 34, 152; Taylor to Robert C. Wood, July 31, 1846, Taylor Papers, collection of Miss Lola M. Wood, Maddox, Saint Mary's County, Maryland; Dabney H. Maury, "Reminiscences of General [Richard] Taylor," *Appleton's Journal,* New Series, VI, 568; Taylor to [James G.] Carter, September 28, 1840, HAMILTON COLLECTION. Maury tells several amusing Dick Taylor anecdotes, one involving his friend, the Prince of Wales, later King Edward VII.

[6] A sample of Richard Taylor's storytelling gifts is found in his letter to William A. Seaver, January 8, 1879: "[Thomas Henry] Huxley, with others, was standing at the window of the 'Atheneum' on a day when a rain storm had driven the cabs from Pall Mall. Three men, desiring to leave, could get but one cab, which they entered. Whereupon a companion called Huxley's attention to the circumstance, observing that three men in one cab was quite like the Trinity. 'Not so,' replied Huxley. 'To reassemble the Trinity you must have one man in three cabs.' " HAMILTON COLLECTION.

[7] Samson, *op. cit.,* 115-116, 138, 145; Taylor to Wood, July 31, 1846, Taylor Papers, Wood Collection, Maddox, Maryland; *The Autograph* (New York), I, 129; statement of the late Mrs. Clarke to the author; information supplied by Trist Wood, New Orleans; "General Taylor's Residence at Baton Rouge," *Harper's New Monthly Magazine,* IX, 763-765; *Cist's Weekly Advertiser* (Cincinnati), February 8, 1848.

CHAPTER III

[1] William E. Railey, *History of Woodford County [Kentucky]* (1938), 146, 190; Deed Book K, 341, Deed Book 2, 179-180, Woodford County, Versailles, Kentucky; Taylor to Jesup, December 4, 1832, copy, Taylor Papers, LC; information provided by Miss Mabel C. Walker, Versailles, based in part on Thornton Family Bible.

[2] Data contained in Ringgold Family Bible and other documents, furnished by Miss Minnie Ker Ringgold, Shreveport, and Mrs. Emmette A. Tomb, Alexandria, Louisiana; the late Gilbert W. Mead to the author, May 5, 1947; Stephen F. Tillman, *Tilghman-Tillman Family . . .* (1946), 23; Maysville *Eagle,* May 27, 1847; John S. Bassett, *The Southern Plantation Overseer . . .* (1925), 3-10, 39-220, 260-276.

[3] *The Commercial Review* (New Orleans), VI, 128; *The Commercial Review of the South and West* (New Orleans), VI, 443; Thomas P. Martin, "Cotton and Wheat . . . ," *Journal of Southern History,* I, 296-298; Zachary Taylor to Joseph P. Taylor, June 17, 1843, Taylor Papers, LC; Stuart-Wortley, *op. cit.,* 117-118; [Victoria Stuart-Wortley], *A Young Traveller's Journal . . .* (1852), 127; New Orleans *Crescent,* March 29, 1848; interview with the late Judge Jeff Truly, Fayette, Mississippi; Taylor to Thomas W. Ring-

gold, May 13, 1846, photostat supplied by James H. Drake, New York City; *Cist's Weekly Advertiser* (Cincinnati), January 31, 1848.

[4] *Local Laws of the State of Indiana* . . . (1848), 171; "Partition between the Heirs of Genl Zachary Taylor," copy notarized by Adolphe Mazureau, William W. S. Bliss to Richard Taylor, August 8, 1850, STAUFFER COLLECTION; Deed Book 81, 315-316, Deed Book 79, 507-508, Deed Book 10, 333-334, Deed Book M, 393-394, Deed Book K, 329-334, Deed Book R, 220-221, Deed Book 52, 178-180, Jefferson County, Louisville, Kentucky; Notary Record Book K, 322-323, West Feliciana Parish, Saint Francisville, Louisiana; Buffalo *Republic*, August 14, 1848; Deed Book G, 463 *et seq.*, Jefferson County, Fayette, Mississippi; Schedule 4, "Productions of Agriculture," Jefferson County, Mississippi, Seventh Census, 747-748, MISSISSIPPI.

[5] John S. Allison to Taylor, July 18, 1849, Zachary Taylor to Richard Taylor, June 12, 1850, Taylor to H. R. W. Hill, May 9, 1850, draft, STAUFFER COLLECTION; Taylor to Wood, July 2, 1843, Taylor Papers, Wood Collection, Maddox, Maryland; Taylor to Ringgold, June 9, 1846, Taylor Papers, New-York Historical Society, New York City; Zachary Taylor to Joseph P. Taylor, May 9, 1847, Taylor Papers, LC; Schedule 4, "Productions of Agriculture," Jefferson County, Mississippi, Seventh Census, 747-748, MISSISSIPPI; Taylor to Ringgold, September 15, 1845, copy, Taylor Papers, LC; Taylor to Ringgold, November 13, 1845, Philadelphia *Platform*, quoted in Louisville *Weekly Courier*, October 28, 1848.

[6] Taylor to Jefferson Davis, July 27, 1847, Zachary Taylor to Joseph P. Taylor, January 19, March 10, May 15, 1848, Taylor to Ringgold, September 15, 1845, copy, Taylor Papers, LC; Taylor to Ringgold, September 15, 1847, *Massachusetts Historical Society Proceedings*, LXII, 142-143; Zachary Taylor to Richard Taylor, June 12, 1850, STAUFFER COLLECTION; [Victoria Stuart-Wortley], *op. cit.*, 126, 129; *Mississippi Free Trader* (Natchez), March 23, 1848; Zachary Taylor to Hancock Taylor, August —, 1838, copy, Taylor Papers, collection of Dr. R. Alexander Bate, Louisville.

CHAPTER IV

[1] Zachary Taylor to J. Trumbull Van Alen, July 17, 1846, collection of Foreman M. Lebold, Chicago; New York *Evening Mirror*, June 18, 20, 1846; *Niles' National Register* (Baltimore), LXX, 21; *The Battery* (Washington), August 24, 1848; Taylor to Nathaniel Young, July 18, 1846, Taylor Papers, Historical Society of Delaware, Wilmington; William H. Samson (editor), *Letters of Zachary Taylor* . . . (1908), 14, 21-22, 32, 67, 76 (italics author's), 134; Taylor to Crittenden, September 1, 1846, Crittenden Papers, LC.

[2] *General Taylor's Letters: Letters of Gen. Taylor to Gen. Gaines* . . . (1847?), 1-4; Zachary Taylor to Joseph P. Taylor, May 29, 1847, Taylor Papers, LC; Samson (editor), *op. cit.*, 90, 103, 114, 130, 147; Allan Nevins (editor), *The Diary of Philip Hone* . . . (1927), II, 795, 798; *The Taylor Text-book* . . . (1848), 9, 11.

[3] Taylor to Crittenden, May 15, 1847, Crittenden Papers, Thurlow Weed to Joseph P. Taylor, April 3, 1847, Weed Papers, LC; Samson (editor), *op. cit.*, 109, 122, 125, 134-135, 143; Theodore C. Blegen, "James Wickes Taylor . . . ," *Minnesota History Bulletin*, I, 154-157; *Niles' National Register* (Baltimore), LXXIII, 63, 288; *The Battery* (Washington), August 24, 1848;

William H. Seward to Weed, August 27, 1847, Weed Papers, ROCHESTER.

⁴ Taylor to Jefferson Davis, July 27, August 16, 1847, Taylor Papers, LC; Samson (editor), *op. cit.*, 81, 87, 100, 134-135, 142, 173-186.

⁵ "I have not for a moment lost sight óf what was due to him [Polk] as a gentleman, or to the distinguished position he occupied" (*ibid.*, 184). Taylor customarily omitted Polk's name when he berated Marcy, Cass, Scott, Jesup and others.

⁶ Zachary Taylor to Joseph P. Taylor, March 27, April 22, 25, May 15, 29, June 4, 1847, Taylor Papers, LC; Samson (editor), *op. cit.*, 7, 9-10, 15, 21, 35, 48, 78, 90, 92, 95, 103, 114, 118-119, 136, 143, 168; Taylor to Robert C. Wood, March 1, 1847, HAMILTON COLLECTION.

⁷ Taylor to Crittenden, May 15, Crittenden Papers, Zachary Taylor to Joseph P. Taylor, January 19, 1847, Taylor Papers, LC; Samson (editor), *op. cit.*, 16-17, 110, 113, 135, 137, 139, 143, 156.

CHAPTER V

¹ Samuel E. Morison and Henry S. Commager, *The Growth of the American Republic* (1942), I, 553-555; Marquis James, *Andrew Jackson: Portrait of a President* (1937), 46, 51, 67, 163, 428-433; Arthur M. Schlesinger, Jr., *The Age of Jackson* (1945), *passim*; E. Malcolm Carroll, *Origins of the Whig Party* (1925), *passim*; Henry R. Mueller, *The Whig Party in Pennsylvania* (1922), 236-246; Bernard Mayo, *Henry Clay* . . . (1937), 270, 343, 403; Glyndon G. Van Deusen, *The Life of Henry Clay* (1937), 29, 37, 246-306, 330-333, 343-356, 387-388; Gerald W. Johnson, *America's Silver Age* . . . (1939), 4-5; George W. Julian, *Political Recollections* . . . (1884), 83, 85; [Horace Greeley], *The Autobiography of Horace Greeley* . . . (1872), 250; George Bancroft, "A Few Words About Henry Clay," *Century Magazine*, XXX, 479; George R. Poage, *Henry Clay and the Whig Party* (1936), 49-106, 152, 155; Joseph M. Rogers, *The True Henry Clay* (1905), 198-200; Carl Schurz, *Life of Henry Clay* (1887), II, 168-169; Calvin Colton (editor), *Works of Henry Clay* . . . (1897), III, 19.

² William Burnet to John McLean, February 23, David B. Ogden to McLean, January 25, 1848, Silas Read to McLean, October 26, 1846, McLean Papers, John L. Helm to John J. Crittenden, January 11, 1848, Crittenden Papers, LC; Schurz, *op. cit.*, II, 292, 408; Claude M. Fuess, *Daniel Webster* (1930), *passim*; [Greeley], *op. cit.*, 250-251; Theodore L. Cuyler, *Recollections of a Long Life* (1902), 126; Allan Nevins (editor), *The Diary of John Quincy Adams* . . . (1928), 531; Charles F. Adams, Jr., *Charles Francis Adams* (1900), 85; Charles W. Elliott, *Winfield Scott* . . . (1937), 373-376, 378-380, 427-431; Washington *National Intelligencer*, December 17, 1844.

³ Francis P. Weisenburger, *The Life of John McLean* (1937), *passim*; Edgar A. Holt, "Party Politics in Ohio, 1840-1850," *Ohio Archaeological* . . . *Society Publications*, XXXVIII, 168-169; Harriet A. Weed (editor), *Autobiography of Thurlow Weed* (1883), 182; Poage, *op. cit.*, 153-155; Washington *Republic*, May 27, 1851; Mrs. Chapman Coleman, *The Life of John J. Crittenden* (1871), *passim*; Allen E. Ragan, "John J. Crittenden, 1787-1863," *Filson Club History Quarterly*, XVIII, 3-13; George W. Williams to Crittenden, January 7, G. B. Kinkead to Crittenden, January 2, 1847, Crittenden Papers, LC; Gideon Welles, Unpublished Diary, entry for February

20, 1849, HUNTINGTON; Joseph P. Comegys, *Memoir of John M. Clayton*
(1882), 16, 45-47, 139-141; Samuel F. Bemis (editor), *The American Secretaries of State . . .* (1927-1929), VI, 3-10.

⁴ Van Deusen, *Thurlow Weed . . .* (1947), 81, 87, 100-104, 108-111,
114-118, 142-146, 157-160, 240-241; Richard L. Watson, Jr., "Thurlow
Weed, Political Boss," *New York History*, XXII, 411-425; Thurlow Weed
Barnes, *Memoir of Thurlow Weed* (1884), 174; Frederick W. Seward, *Seward
at Washington . . . 1846-1861* (1891), 105; Frederic Bancroft, *The Life of
William Henry Seward* (1900), I, 5, 13; John S. Jenkins, *Lives of the Governors . . .* (1852), 684-688; DeAlva S. Alexander, *A Political History of
the State of New York* (1906-1909), II, 142-143; Jeter A. Isely, *Horace
Greeley and the Republican Party, 1853-1861* (1947), 10-11, 19-30, 68-75.
Albany *Evening Journal* editorials show that Weed's support of Taylor was
guarded. However, their tone was usually pro-Taylor. Cf. *Journal,* May 25,
28, June 18, 1846.

⁵ Gideon Welles, Unpublished Diary, undated entry for autumn of 1848,
HUNTINGTON; Thomas Dowling to Caleb B. Smith, December 8, 1848, Smith
Papers, Orlando Brown to Crittenden, July 24, 1849, Crittenden Papers, LC;
Allen Johnson and Dumas Malone (editors), *Dictionary of American Biography* (1928-1936), XI, 193; XVII, 350; XVIII, 569-570; Washington
Hunt to Weed, January 24, February 16, August 22, December 5, 1847,
Weed Papers, ROCHESTER; Albert J. Beveridge, *Abraham Lincoln, 1809-1858*
(1928), I, 433, 441; Myrta L. Avary (editor), *Recollections of Alexander
H. Stephens . . .* (1910), 21-22; Poage, *op. cit.,* 157-158; Alice E. Trabue,
A Corner in Celebrities (1923), 20, 29-30, 50-51; Brown Papers, *passim,*
KENTUCKY and FILSON; G. W. Griffin, *Memoir of Col. Chas. S. Todd*
(1873), *passim.*

⁶ Martha A. Burnley, "Albert Triplett Burnley," *Texas State Historical
Association Quarterly*, XIV, 150-152; manuscript sketch of Burnley, Brown
Papers, KENTUCKY; New Orleans *Times-Picayune,* January 25, 1937; *New
Orleans Annual and Commercial Register for 1846,* 127; Thomas E. Dabney,
One Hundred Great Years . . . (1944), 57; Fayette Copeland, *Kendall of the
Picayune* (1943), *passim;* information supplied by Neville S. Bullitt, Louisville; Trabue, *op. cit.,* 11-12; James Y. Love to Logan Hunton, December
24, 1871, SEA COLLECTION; James G. Wilson and John Fiske (editors),
Appleton's Cyclopaedia of American Biography (1888-1889), III, 327; J.
Thomas Scharf, *History of Saint Louis City and County* (1883), II, 1501;
W. V. N. Bay, *The Bench and Bar of Missouri* (1878), 322; Joshua W.
Caldwell, *Sketches of the Bench and Bar of Tennessee* (1898), 241-245; *A
Biographical Congressional Directory . . . 1774-1903* (1903), 741; *Niles'
National Register* (Baltimore), LXX, 372, 400.

CHAPTER VI

¹ Balie Peyton to John J. Crittenden, January 25, John L. Helm to Crittenden, January 11, Zachary Taylor to Crittenden, March 25, 1848, Crittenden
Papers, David B. Ogden to John McLean, January 15, 1848, Zachary Taylor
to Joseph P. Taylor, March 10, 1848, Taylor Papers, LC; Thomas Dowling
to Richard W. Thompson, January 27, 1848, Thompson Papers, LINCOLN;
Frederick W. Seward, *Seward at Washington . . . 1846-1861* (1891), 62;

The Battery (Washington), August 24, 1848; Taylor to Orlando Brown, March 15, 1848, Brown Papers, KENTUCKY; George R. Poage, *Henry Clay and the Whig Party* (1936), 168-169.

[2] New York *Herald,* December 25, 1847; Seward, *op. cit.,* 62-63; Caleb B. Smith to Allen Hamilton, February 16, 1848, Hamilton Papers, INDIANA; William Burnet to McLean, February 23, H. E. Spencer to McLean, February 24, 1848, McLean Papers, Robert P. Letcher to Crittenden, January —, January 20, February—, Richard Hawes to Mrs. Crittenden, February 23, Crittenden Papers, Thomas B. Stevenson to Henry Clay, May 22, 1848, Clay Papers, LC; Edgar A. Holt, "Party Politics in Ohio, 1840-1850," *Ohio Archaeological . . . Society Publications,* XXXVIII, 178, 261-262, 272; *Ohio State Journal* (Columbus), January 20, 21, 22, 1848.

[3] John W. Russell to Crittenden, March 1, 1848, Crittenden Papers, James B. Mower to McLean, February 15, 1848, McLean Papers, LC; Lexington *Observer and Reporter,* April 8, New York *Tribune,* February 23, April 14, 1848; Seth C. Hawley to James Bowen, November 4, George W. Patterson to Thurlow Weed, November 26, 1847, Weed Papers, ROCHESTER; Poage, *op. cit.,* 163; Glyndon G. Van Deusen, *Thurlow Weed . . .* (1947), 159. For James G. Bennett's peculiar support of Taylor, *cf.* New York *Herald,* February 14, April 15, 29, May 22, 1848. John M. Morehead, a Clay man, was an exception to the North Carolina delegate trend.

[4] Taylor to Brown, December 18, 1847, March 15, 1848, Brown Papers, KENTUCKY; Taylor to Crittenden, January 3, February 13, March 25, Peyton to Crittenden, January 25, 1848, Crittenden Papers, Zachary Taylor to Joseph P. Taylor, January 19, March 10, 1848, Taylor Papers, LC; New Orleans *Picayune,* January 8-15, 1848; *Semi-Weekly Natchez Courier,* December 14, 21, 1847, January 14, 18, 28, February 22, 29, 1848.

[5] Alexander H. H. Stuart to Thompson, February 9, 1848, Thompson Papers, LINCOLN; Thomas Metcalfe to Crittenden, February 17, John W. Russell to Crittenden, March 1, Albert T. Burnley to Crittenden, April 4, 1848, Crittenden Papers, Mower to McLean, March 20, April 3, Salmon P. Chase to McLean, February 12, 1848, McLean Papers, LC; Washington Hunt to Weed, March 19, April 7, 1848, Weed Papers, ROCHESTER; John G. Nicolay and John Hay (editors), *Complete Works of Abraham Lincoln* (1905), II, 17; Ulrich B. Phillips (editor), "The Correspondence of Robert Toombs, Alexander H. Stephens, and Howell Cobb," *Annual Report of the American Historical Association for the Year 1911* (1913), II, 104; Smith to Hamilton, March 26, 1848, Hamilton Papers, INDIANA.

[6] Allan Nevins (editor), *The Diary of Philip Hone . . .* (1927), II, 837; Burnley to Crittenden, April 4, 1848, Crittenden Papers, James E. Harvey to McLean, April 27, Mower to McLean, April 10, 17, Ogden to McLean, January 25, Elisha Whittlesey to McLean, April 12, 1848, McLean Papers, LC; John Bell to William B. Campbell, April 13, 1848, Campbell Papers, Duke University, Durham, North Carolina; Holt, *loc. cit.,* XXXVIII, 270; Weed to Patterson, April 9, Patterson Papers, Seward to Weed, April 11, 1848, Weed Papers, ROCHESTER.

[7] Harvey to McLean, April 27, May 10, John Teesdale to McLean, April 15, Mower to McLean, April 19, 20, Whittlesey to McLean, April 12, May 11, Hugh White to McLean, May 6, Dowling to McLean, April 26, 1848, McLean Papers, LC; Joseph P. Taylor to Weed, April 28, Hunt to Weed, April 17, May 31, 1848, Weed Papers, ROCHESTER; Godlove S. Orth to Schuyler

Colfax, April 29, 1848, Orth Papers, INDIANA; Holt, *loc. cit.*, XXXVIII, 272, 279.

[8] Mower to McLean, January 29, February 7, 25, April 24, Dowling to McLean, February 26, Chase to McLean, February 12, John C. Vaughan to McLean, February 11, Burnet to McLean, February 23, Whittlesey to Mc-Lean, April 12, Harvey to McLean, April 27, Ogden to McLean, January 25, 1848, McLean Papers, LC; Sam Partridge to Weed, May 27, 1848, Weed Papers, ROCHESTER; George F. Hoar, *Autobiography of Seventy Years* (1903), I, 151; Thurlow Weed Barnes, *Memoir of Thurlow Weed* (1884), 168-169.

[9] Seward, *op. cit.*, 62; Burnet to McLean, February 23, Dowling to Mc-Lean, February 26, Mower to McLean, January 29, February 15, April 19, White to McLean, May 6, 1848, McLean Papers, LC; *The Battery* (Washington), July 6, 1848; Weed to Patterson, April 9, 1848, Patterson Papers, Hunt to Weed, April 17, 1848, Weed Papers, ROCHESTER; New Orleans *Picayune*, April 25, 1848.

CHAPTER VII

[1] *Louisville City Directory, 1838-39*, 3; [Louisville] *City Directory for 1841*, 47; *New Orleans Annual and Commercial Register for 1846*, 25; Richard T. Allison to John C. Bullitt, September 3, 1844, June 13, 1845, Logan McKnight to Bullitt, May 18, 1846, collection of William Marshall Bullitt, Louisville; Zachary Taylor testamentary paper, November 20, 1837, John S. Allison to Taylor, July 18, 1849, STAUFFER COLLECTION; Zachary Taylor to John G. Taylor, March 2, 1829, copy, collection of Dr. R. Alexander Bate, Louisville; Francis B. Heitman, *Historical Register of the United States Army* . . . (1890), 86; Baltimore *Sun*, April 11, 1909; James Y. Love to Logan Hunton, December 24, 1871, SEA COLLECTION. Much of the information in this part of the chapter was supplied by the late Mrs. Walter R. Stauffer and by Trist Wood, New Orleans.

[2] Allen E. Ragan, "John J. Crittenden, 1787-1863," *Filson Club History Quarterly*, XVIII, 15; Rudolph Von Abele, *Alexander H. Stephens* . . . (1946), 112-113; John G. Nicolay and John Hay (editors), *Complete Works of Abraham Lincoln* (1905), II, 55-56; Albert J. Beveridge, *Abraham Lincoln, 1809-1858* (1928), I, 450*n.*; Logan Hunton to Balie Peyton and others, April 20, 1848, SEA COLLECTION; William H. Seward draft, designated by the number 749, Washington Hunt to Thurlow Weed, February 15, April 17, James Bowen to Weed, April 26, 1848 (italics Bowen's), Weed Papers, Weed to George W. Patterson, April 9, 1848, Patterson Papers, ROCHESTER; James E. Harvey to John McLean, April 27, 1848, McLean Papers, LC. Contrary to Nicolay and Hay, internal evidence shows Lincoln's advice to be of preconvention vintage. Stephens claimed the authorship of the Second Allison Letter, not the First, for the Crittenden-Toombs-Stephens triumverate. *Cf.* Mrs. Chapman Coleman, *The Life of John J. Crittenden* (1871), I, 294, in which Stephens states that—following a conference with the Georgians—Crittenden drafted the *Second* Allison Letter "in substance." This version was kept intact in Myrta L. Avary (editor), *Recollections of Alexander H. Stephens* . . . (1910), 34. Later writers have not been so careful.

[3] Love to Hunton, December 24, 1871, Hunton to Peyton and others, April

20, 1848, Taylor to John S. Allison, April 22, 1848, SEA COLLECTION. A photostatic copy of the First Allison Letter is in the author's files, together with copies of the Hunton-Love-Peyton correspondence.

⁴ Hunt to Weed, May 19, 1848, Weed Papers, ROCHESTER; Hugh White to McLean, May 6, Thomas Dowling to McLean, May 4, 12, Harvey to McLean, May 10, Elisha Whittlesey to McLean, May 11, James B. Mower to McLean, May 22, Caleb B. Smith to McLean, May 28, 1848, McLean Papers, LC; Love to Hunton, December 24, 1871, SEA COLLECTION; Washington *Union,* May 4, 1848.

⁵ *Semi-Weekly Natchez Courier,* April 25, Buffalo *Republic,* May 26, New Orleans *Crescent,* May 10, *Indiana State Journal* (Indianapolis), April 17, May 1, 1848; Mower to McLean, May 22, June 5, Dowling to McLean, May 4, 1848, McLean Papers, LC; McLean to Seward, April 20, Philo C. Fuller to Weed, May 20, 1848, Weed Papers, ROCHESTER.

⁶ Charles S. Todd to Isaac S. Todd, April 15, 22, May 8, 29, Todd to Mrs. Todd, April 5, 1848, Todd Papers, Orlando Brown and others "To the Friends of General Taylor in Kentucky," April 21, 1848, Brown Papers, FILSON; Richard H. Shryock, *Georgia and the Union in 1850* (1926), 162-163; *Semi-Weekly Natchez Courier,* March 10, Buffalo *Republic,* May 27, 1848; Albert T. Burnley to Crittenden, April 4, 1848, Crittenden Papers, LC; Seward to Weed, May 22, Trumbull Cary to Weed, May 19, 1848, Weed Papers, ROCHESTER; Avary (editor), *op. cit.,* 22-24; New York *Journal of Commerce,* April 28, 1848.

CHAPTER VIII

¹ William H. Samson (editor), *Letters of Zachary Taylor . . .* (1908), 143, 153-154; Alexander K. McClure, *Our Presidents . . .* (1905), 110; James E. Harvey to John McLean, April 27, Caleb B. Smith to McLean, May 1, 28, Elisha Whittlesey to McLean, May 11, 1848, McLean Papers, LC. Abraham Lincoln's ideas paralleled Taylor's. *Cf.* John G. Nicolay and John Hay (editors), *Complete Works of Abraham Lincoln* (1905), II, 17.

² *The Battery* (Washington), July 6, 1848, January 25, 1849; James Harlan to Henry Clay, June 2, Leslie Combs to Clay, June 10, 1848, Clay Papers, LC; Washington Hunt to Thurlow Weed, June 4, 1848, Weed Papers, ROCHESTER; *Niles' National Register* (Philadelphia), LXXIV, 349; Philadelphia *Public Ledger,* June 5, 9, Philadelphia *North American,* June 8, Buffalo *Commercial Advertiser,* June 13, New Orleans *Crescent,* June 12, 1848; Joseph Jackson, *Encyclopedia of Philadelphia* (1931-1933), III, 915; *National Cyclopaedia of American Biography* (1898-1949), IX, 498-499; Allen Johnson and Dumas Malone (editors), *Dictionary of American Biography* (1928-1936), I, 342-343, II, 277-278, IX, 54-56; Samson (editor), *op. cit.,* 162; information supplied by Neville S. Bullitt, Louisville. George Street is now Sansom Street.

³ Harriet A. Weed (editor), *Autobiography of Thurlow Weed* (1883), 577; Zachary Taylor to Joseph P. Taylor, July 7, 1848, Taylor Papers, LC; J. H. Boyd to Millard Fillmore, December 12, 1848, BUFFALO; Thurlow Weed Barnes, *Memoir of Thurlow Weed* (1884), 168-169; William H. Seward to Weed, May 27, 1848, Weed Papers, ROCHESTER; Carl Schurz, *Henry Clay* (1899), II, 305-306; Clay to Thomas B. Stevenson, August 5, 1848, copy, CINCINNATI; Philadelphia *Public Ledger,* June 8-10, 1848; *The Battery*

(Washington), January 25, 1849; Washington *National Intelligencer*, June 10, 1848. The author has employed the terms "chairman" and "vice-chairmen," instead of "president" and "vice-presidents," to avoid confusion with candidates for the country's two highest offices.

[4] Taylor to Balie Peyton, May 20, 1848, copy, collection of William Marshall Bullitt, Louisville; Philadelphia *Public Ledger*, June 9, Washington *National Intelligencer*, June 10, 1848; Washington *Republic*, June 13, 1849; *The Battery* (Washington), January 25, 1849; Joshua W. Caldwell, *Sketches of the Bench and Bar of Tennessee* (1898), 240-241; Johnson and Malone (editors), *op. cit.*, X, 343-344; Clay to Stevenson, June 14, 1848, copy, CINCINNATI; J. L. Lawrence to Clay, June 9, Horace Greeley to Clay, June 21, 1848, Clay Papers, LC.

[5] *The Battery* (Washington), January 25, 1849; Philadelphia *Public Ledger*, Buffalo *Republic*, June 10, 1848; George F. Hoar, *Autobiography of Seventy Years* (1903), I, 146; Johnson and Malone (editors), *op. cit.*, XV, 416-417; John Nichols, "Kenneth Rayner and the Presidency," Raleigh *News and Observer* undated clipping, supplied by J. G. de Roulhac Hamilton, Chapel Hill, North Carolina. Weed's version of what occurred appears in Weed (editor), *op. cit.*, 575-578.

[6] William E. Griffis, *Millard Fillmore* . . . (1915), 20-21; Johnson and Malone (editors), *op. cit.*, VI, 380; Fillmore to Weed, June 28, 1842, Seward to Weed, March 29, May 27, June 10, Hunt to Weed, February 15, George W. Patterson to Weed, March 20, 1848, Weed Papers, ROCHESTER; Poughkeepsie *Eagle*, June 18, 1842; Glyndon G. Van Deusen, *The Life of Henry Clay* (1937), 366; Frank H. Severance (editor), "Millard Fillmore Papers," *Publications of the Buffalo Historical Society*, XI, 183-187, 191-192, 195; James B. Mower to McLean, January 29, 1848, McLean Papers, LC.

[7] Weed (editor), *op. cit.*, 585; George H. Haynes, *Charles Sumner* (1909), 117n.; Edward L. Pierce, *Memoir and Letters of Charles Sumner* (1893-1894), III, 162; Nathan Appleton to Sumner, September 4, 1848, copy, APPLETON; Johnson and Malone (editors), *op. cit.*, VI, 237-238; Lloyd Lewis, *Sherman: Fighting Prophet* (1932), 14, 82; *The Battery* (Washington), January 25, 1849; *The Campaign* (Washington), May 31, 1848; Philadelphia *Public Ledger*, Philadelphia *Pennsylvanian*, June 10, Buffalo *Commercial Advertiser*, June 12, New York *Tribune*, June 14, 1848; Springfield *Republican*, October 14, 1933; William Bebb to John J. Crittenden, November 24, 1848, Crittenden Papers, LC; Henry Wilson, *History of the Rise and Fall* . . . (1872-1877), II, 137, *et seq.*; McClure, *op. cit.*, 105.

CHAPTER IX

[1] *The Campaign* (Washington), June 7, 1848; Andrew C. McLaughlin, *Lewis Cass* (1899), 240-244; Wilfred E. Binkley, *American Political Parties* . . . (1943), 185; *Niles' National Register* (Philadelphia), LXXIV, 19; *Massachusetts Historical Society Proceedings*, LX, 118-119; H. D. A. Donovan, *The Barnburners* (1925), *passim*; Holmes Alexander, *The American Tallyrand* . . . (1935), 403-405; Edward Stanwood, *A History of the Presidency from 1788 to 1897* (1898), 223; *Whig Almanac* . . . *for 1846*, 62; William J. Brown to Lewis Cass, September 25, 1848, CLEMENTS.

[2] Albert B. Moore, *History of Alabama* . . . (1928), I, 260-265; Allen

Johnson and Dumas Malone (editors), *Dictionary of American Biography* (1928-1936), IV, 20-21; J. W. Du Bose, *William Lowndes Yancey* (1892), 217-229; McLaughlin, *op. cit.*, 244-245; Lucian L. Knight, *Reminiscences of Famous Georgians* (1907-1908), II, 254-256; Stephen A. Douglas to Cass, June 13, 1848, CLEMENTS; Chauncey S. Boucher, "Sectionalism, Representation and the Electoral Question . . . ," *Washington University Studies*, IV, Part II, 13, 16; Lillian A. Kibler, *Benjamin F. Perry* . . . (1946), 18, 144, 226-229; John C. Calhoun to Franklin H. Elmore, December 22, 1847, Elmore Papers, LC; Stanwood, *op. cit.*, 16, 223-225; Rita K. Carey, "Samuel Jarvis Peters," *Louisiana Historical Quarterly*, XXX, 466-467; *DeBow's Review* (New Orleans), XIV, 85, XXV, 480-482; *Whig Almanac . . . for 1846*, 62.

[3] Douglas to Cass, June 13, Thomas H. Benton to Cass, July 10, 1848, CLEMENTS; Stanwood, *op. cit.*, 148, 163, 185, 203, 223; Richard H. Shryock, *Georgia and the Union in 1850* (1926), 104, 110, 163, 167, 173-176; John M. Berrien to John S. Pendleton, September 6, 1848, Berrien Papers, Albert T. Burnley to John J. Crittenden, April 4, Pendleton to Crittenden, September 14, 1848, Crittenden Papers, LC; Johnson and Malone (editors), *op. cit.*, XV, 635-637; Washington *National Intelligencer*, April 27, 1847; New Orleans *Crescent*, October 7, 1848; *The Battery* (Washington), August 24, 1848 (italics in newspaper account); *Niles' National Register* (Philadelphia), LXXIV, 95; Louisville *Weekly Courier*, July 1, 1848; Henry T. Shanks, *The Secession Movement in Virginia, 1847-1861* (1934), 14-16; Arthur C. Cole, *Whig Party in the South* (1913), 133; Mrs. Chapman Coleman, *The Life of John J. Crittenden* (1871), I, 303-313; Albert J. Beveridge, *Abraham Lincoln, 1809-1858* (1928), I, 447; *Whig Almanac . . . for 1849*, 56-57, 59-60, 62.

[4] Louisville *Weekly Courier*, June 24, July 1, September 30, 1848; Zachary Taylor to Joseph P. Taylor, July 7, 1848, Taylor Papers, LC; William H. Samson (editor), *Letters of Zachary Taylor* . . . (1908), 159, 161; *Niles' National Register* (Baltimore and Philadelphia), LXXIII, 293, LXXIV, 19; William H. Hull to Howell Cobb, July 22, 1848, Cole, *op. cit.*, 132; McLaughlin, *op. cit.*, *passim*; *The Campaign* (Washington), June 7, 1848.

[5] Lexington *Atlas*, June 17, New Orleans *Picayune*, June 13, 24, New Orleans *Weekly Delta*, June 12, 19, 26, New Orleans *Weekly Picayune*, July 10, Buffalo *Express*, July 19, August 19, *Semi-Weekly Natchez Courier*, *passim*, New Orleans *Crescent*, November 7, 1848; James K. Greer, "Louisiana Politics, 1845-1861," *Louisiana Historical Quarterly*, XII, 560-563; Philip M. Hamer, *The Secession Movement in South Carolina, 1847-1852* (1918), 19; Ben: Perley Poore, *Perley's Reminiscences* . . . (1886), I, 345; *Whig Almanac . . . for 1848*, 50; Cleo Hearon, "Mississippi and the Compromise of 1850," *Mississippi Historical Society Publications*, XIV, 30-31; Shryock, *op. cit.*, 167, 169, 174-175.

[6] Cole, *op. cit.*, 136; *Whig Almanac . . . for 1849*, 56-57; Hamer, *op. cit.*, 20; Charleston *Mercury*, July 21, August 21, Charleston *Courier*, August 22, 1848; Charles M. Wiltse to the author, September 19, 1947; Gideon Welles, Unpublished Diary, undated entry between September 19 and 30, 1848, HUNTINGTON.

[7] Johnson and Malone (editors), *op. cit.*, XV, 476; Hamer, *op. cit.*, 21; Balie Peyton to Crittenden, August 29, 1848, Crittenden Papers, LC; Hilary A. Herbert, "Alabama in Federal Politics," in *Memorial Record of Alabama*

(1893), I, 36-37; *Semi-Weekly Natchez Courier*, October 3, 1848; Samuel
J. Peters to Thurlow Weed, July 2, 1848, Weed Papers, ROCHESTER; Shryock,
op. cit., 171-174; Stanwood, *op. cit.*, 223, 243.

CHAPTER X

[1] *Whig Almanac . . . for 1846*, 62; Edward Stanwood, *A History of the
Presidency from 1788 to 1897* (1898), 163, 223; Buffalo *Republic*, June 29,
1848; Horace Greeley to Henry Clay, June 21, John M. Botts to Clay, July
3, August 23, Nicholas Dean to Clay, September 5, October 5, Dudley Selden
to Clay, October 9, 1848, Clay Papers, LC; Erastus D. Culver to Thurlow
Weed, June 11, D. S. Crandall to Weed, June 19, George W. Patterson to
Weed, August 24, 1848, Weed Papers, ROCHESTER; Allan Nevins (editor),
The Diary of Philip Hone . . . (1927), II, 851; *Niles' National Register*
(Philadelphia), LXXIV, 165.

[2] Buffalo *Republic*, May 31, June 3, 7, 16, July 24, Buffalo *Commercial
Advertiser*, June 16, 1848; Erwin H. Price, "The Election of 1848 in Ohio,"
Edgar A. Holt, "Party Politics in Ohio, 1840-1850," *Ohio Archaeological . . .
Society Publications*, XXXVI, 243-246, 293-298, XXXVIII, 102, 137, 139,
162-167, 261, 272, 281, 284-285, 292-293, 308-309; Washington Hunt to
Weed, June 27, A. C. Brown to Weed, June 15, G. M. Buckley to Weed,
June 21, 1848, Weed Papers, ROCHESTER; Thomas B. Stevenson to John J.
Crittenden, September 7, 1848, Crittenden Papers, LC.

[3] *Ohio State Journal* (Columbus), August 8, Buffalo *Commercial Adver-
tiser*, June 27, Louisville *Weekly Courier*, July 22, 1848; Washington *Union*,
March 22, 1850; Philadelphia *Sunday Dispatch*, September 12, 1847; William
Allen to Lewis Cass, September 9, James K. Polk to Cass, August 24, 1848,
CLEMENTS; Thomas Corwin to Stevenson, June 13, 15, 1848, CINCINNATI;
Richard N. Current, *Old Thad Stevens . . .* (1942), 79-84; Alexander K.
McClure, *Old Time Notes of Pennsylvania* (1905), I, 89-90; *Niles' National
Register* (Baltimore and Philadelphia), LXXI, 112, LXXIV, 19, 367; Sister
M. Theophane Geary, *A History of Third Parties . . .* (1938), 123, 136-137;
Whig Almanac . . . for 1851, 56; Henry R. Mueller, *The Whig Party in
Pennsylvania* (1922), 155; Lee F. Crippen, *Simon Cameron: Ante-Bellum
Years* (1942), 99-100; Alexander Ramsey to Weed, November 2, 1848, Weed
Papers, ROCHESTER. For a Democrat's optimism respecting Pennsylvania, *cf.*
Cameron to Cass, July 12, 1848, CLEMENTS.

[4] George F. Hoar, *Autobiography of Seventy Years* (1903), I, 146-150;
Albert J. Beveridge, *Abraham Lincoln, 1809-1858* (1928), I, 466-468; Buf-
falo *Republic*, November 13, 1848; Edward L. Pierce, *Memoir and Letters of
Charles Sumner* (1893-1894), III, 179-180; Nathan Appleton to Sumner,
July 6, August 17, September 4, Sumner to Appleton, August 31, 1848,
copies, APPLETON; Robert C. Winthrop, Jr., *A Memoir of Robert C. Win-
throp* (1897), 85; Philip Greely, Jr., to Weed, September 8, 1848, Weed
Papers, ROCHESTER; Stanwood, *op. cit.*, 148, 163, 185, 203, 223.

[5] Nels Anderson, *Desert Saints . . .* (1942), 78; Theodore C. Smith, *The
Liberty and Free Soil Parties in the Northwest* (1897), 58-59, 75, 123, 154-
159, 191, 198, 305; *Whig Almanac . . . for 1848*, 14-15, 50; *Niles' National
Register* (Philadelphia), LXXIV, 38, 95, 165, 333, 347; *Whig Almanac . . .
for 1849*, 53, 61-64; Roy F. Nichols, *Franklin Pierce . . .* (1931), 174-179;
Gideon Welles, Unpublished Diary, undated entry, HUNTINGTON; Beveridge,

op. cit., I, 471; [Roger S. Baldwin], *Speech of Hon. R. S. Baldwin* . . . (1848), 1.

⁶ New York *Tribune*, September 13-15, 18, November 16, Buffalo *Republic*, June 27, 1848; *Niles' National Register* (Philadelphia), LXXIV, 95; Crippen, *op. cit.*, 99-100; Patterson to Weed, August 24, William H. Seward to Weed, August 26, James A. Hamilton to Weed, September 8, 1848, Weed Papers, ROCHESTER; William A. Butler, *A Retrospect of Forty Years* (1911), 191-192.

⁷ *Niles' National Register* (Philadelphia), LXXIV, 165; Joshua L. Brown to Weed, August 29, William L. Perkins to Weed, September 1, 1848, Weed Papers, ROCHESTER; Crittenden to Waddy Thompson, October 2, 1848, HAMILTON COLLECTION; Buffalo *Republic*, August 29, 30, 1848; George M. McConnel, *Presidential Campaigns* . . . (1908), 93-95.

CHAPTER XI

¹ New Orleans *Picayune*, July 2, 4, *Semi-Weekly Natchez Courier*, July 7, *Mississippi Free Trader* (Natchez), August 23, Buffalo *Republic*, August 22, *Indiana State Journal* (Indianapolis), November 27, 1848; Seth C. Hawley to Thurlow Weed, July 5, Edward Dodd to Weed, August 3, 1848, Weed Papers, ROCHESTER; *Niles' National Register* (Philadelphia), LXXIV, 69; Ben: Perley Poore, *Perley's Reminiscences* . . . (1886), I, 345-346; Zachary Taylor to Edward Kent, July 27, 1848, Taylor Papers, HUNTINGTON.

² Charles W. Upham, *Eulogy . . . of Zachary Taylor* (1850), 55; Francis B. Heitman, *Historical Register of the United States Army* . . . (1890), 249; Allen Johnson and Dumas Malone (editors), *Dictionary of American Biography* (1928-1936), VII, 158-159, XI, 285-286; Louisville *Weekly Courier*, September 30, *Indiana State Journal* (Indianapolis), August 28, New Orleans *Crescent*, October 14, 1848; Taylor to J. H. Clay Mudd, July 23, 1848, HAMILTON COLLECTION; Taylor to William Holdredge, July 29, 1848, copy, Hayes Memorial Library, Fremont, Ohio; *Niles' National Register* (Philadelphia), LXXIV, 165; Dodd to Weed, August 18, 1848, Weed Papers, ROCHESTER; Millard Fillmore to Solomon G. Haven, August 19, 1848, Fillmore Papers, LC.

³ East Pascagoula, Mississippi, correspondence of Mobile *Herald* dated August 19, 1848, clipping in George W. Julian's "Political Memorandum Book for 1848," Julian Papers, INDIANA; New Orleans *Picayune*, September 7, 1848; Harriet A. Weed (editor), *Autobiography of Thurlow Weed* (1883), 578-579, 582-583; clipping of sketch from Mobile *Register*, Taylor scrapbook of Mrs. Eleanor Custis Lewis (Nelly Custis), WOOD COLLECTION; Myrta L. Avary (editor), *Recollections of Alexander H. Stephens* . . . (1910), 34; James Y. Love to Logan Hunton, December 24, 1871, SEA COLLECTION; *Niles' National Register* (Philadelphia), LXXIV, 200-201; Truman Smith to John J. Crittenden, September 23, 1848, Crittenden Papers, LC; John Y. Mason to Lewis Cass, September 25, 1848, CLEMENTS; data supplied by Mrs. Elleine H. Stones, Detroit Public Library; *Whig Almanac . . . for 1850*, 56; Theodore C. Smith, *The Liberty and Free Soil Parties in the Northwest* (1897), 153.

⁴ Albert J. Beveridge, *Abraham Lincoln, 1809-1858* (1928), I, 470; *Whig Almanac . . . for 1849*, 54; *Whig Almanac . . . for 1850*, 56; Charles Sumner to Nathan Appleton, August 31, 1848, copy, APPLETON; Gideon Welles,

Unpublished Diary, entry for September 19, 1848, HUNTINGTON; Calvin Fletcher, Unpublished Diary, entry for August 7, 1848, Indiana Historical Society, Indianapolis; New Orleans *Crescent,* October 27, 1848; William H. Seward to Weed, October 9, 1848, Weed Papers, ROCHESTER; Lyon G. Tyler, *The Letters and Times of the Tylers* (1884-1896), II, 460-461.

⁵ George M. Dallas to Cass, October 21, Mason to Cass, William J. Brown to Cass, September 25, William B. Lawrence to Henry Ledyard, October 14, Cass to Samuel Beardsley, October 6, 1848, CLEMENTS; Philo S. Shelton to Weed, October 10, Simeon Draper to Weed, October 17, Hawley to Alvah Hunt, November 2, A. B. Dickinson to Weed, October 17, 1848, Weed Papers, ROCHESTER; Buffalo *Republic,* November 4, New York *Tribune,* September 22, New Orleans *Crescent,* October 7, Louisville *Weekly Courier,* October 7, 1848; Milo M. Quaife (editor), *The Diary of James K. Polk . . .* (1910), IV, 166; Horace Greeley to Weed, September 22, October 28, 1848, GREELEY; Allan Nevins (editor), *The Diary of Philip Hone . . .* (1927), II, 855; Henry Clay to Thomas B. Stevenson, September 4, 12, 1848, copies, CINCINNATI.

⁶ Thomas Ewing to Taylor, July 22, 1848, copy, Ewing Papers, Ewing to Crittenden, October 6, 1848, Stevenson to Crittenden, September 7, 1849, Crittenden Papers, LC; Thomas Corwin to Stevenson, September 17, Clay to Stevenson, October 9, 1848, copy, CINCINNATI; Edgar A. Holt, "Party Politics in Ohio, 1840-1850," Erwin H. Price, "The Election of 1848 in Ohio," *Ohio Archaeological . . . Society Publications,* XXXVIII, 304, 306, 309, XXXVI, 297; Dickinson to Weed, October 29, 1848, Weed Papers, ROCHESTER; Greeley to Weed, October 28, 1848, GREELEY; Smith, *op. cit.,* 150-151, 304-305.

⁷ Louisville *Weekly Courier,* September 30, Charleston *Courier,* October 9, 10, 14, 1848; Susan D. Smedes, *Memorials of a Southern Planter* (1899), 130-132; Cass to Beardsley, October 6, 1848, CLEMENTS; Samuel J. Peters to Weed, July 2, 1848, Weed Papers, ROCHESTER; Philip M. Hamer, *The Secession Movement in South Carolina, 1847-1852* (1918), 21; *The Magazine of History* (New York), III, 393; Taylor to Lyman C. Draper, October 30, 1848, Draper Papers, Wisconsin State Historical Society, Madison; Gideon Welles, Unpublished Diary, entry for October 14 or 16, 1848, HUNTINGTON; Frederick W. Seward, *Seward at Washington . . . 1846-1861* (1891), 76; Poore, *op. cit.,* I, 346-347; *The Autograph* (New York), I, 22-24; Arthur Voss, "Backgrounds of Lowell's Satire in 'The Biglow Papers,'" *New England Quarterly,* XXIII, 54-57.

⁸ Weed to Greeley, October 3, 1848, Weed Papers, ROCHESTER; George Bancroft to Cass, October 20, 1848, CLEMENTS; Gideon Welles, Unpublished Diary, undated October entry, entry for November 8, 1848, HUNTINGTON; New Orleans *Crescent,* September 30, October 27, 30, New Orleans *Picayune,* September 24, October 26, 29, Louisville *Weekly Courier,* December 2, Buffalo *Republic,* September 24, 1848; John Delap to Taylor, February 22, 1849, PENNSYLVANIA.

⁹ Philip Greely, Jr., to Weed, October 28, 1850, Weed Papers, ROCHESTER; Smith, *op. cit.,* 148, 154; *The Battery* (Washington), July 20, August 10, September 14, October 19, *The Campaign* (Washington), October 18, Buffalo *Commercial Advertiser,* June 13, New Orleans *Crescent,* October 28, November 6, Louisville *Weekly Courier,* October 28, 1848; Daniel S. Dickinson to Cass, July 10, 1848, CLEMENTS.

[10] William L. Marcy to Cass, October 26, 1848, CLEMENTS; Washington *Union*, November 5, Louisville *Weekly Courier*, December 2, 1848; *Whig Almanac . . . for 1849*, 55, 58-60, 64; *Whig Almanac . . . for 1850*, 56; Edward Stanwood, *A History of the Presidency from 1788 to 1897* (1898), 223, 243; Weed (editor), *op. cit.*, 583; *Niles' National Register* (Philadelphia), LXXV, 52; Greely to Weed, October 20, 1848, Weed Papers, ROCHESTER; *Whig Almanac . . . for 1851*, 56.

CHAPTER XII

[1] Lewis Scrapbook, WOOD COLLECTION; *St. Joseph Valley Register* (South Bend), November 16, Louisville *Weekly Courier*, November 25, 1848; John Delap to Zachary Taylor, February 22, 1849, PENNSYLVANIA; Gideon Welles, Unpublished Diary, entry for November 8, 1848, undated entry for late 1848 or early 1849, HUNTINGTON; Milo M. Quaife (editor), *The Diary of James K. Polk . . .* (1910), IV, 184; Polk to Lewis Cass, November 14, Cass to Samuel Beardsley, December 12, 1848, CLEMENTS; M. A. DeWolfe Howe, *The Life and Letters of George Bancroft* (1908), 132; Susan D. Smedes, *Memorials of a Southern Planter* (1899), 132; William Ballard Preston to William Campbell Preston, December 7, 1848, collection of Preston Davie, New York City.

[2] Marriage License Book 2, 101, East Baton Rouge Parish, Baton Rouge, Louisiana; New Orleans *Crescent*, November 29, Louisville *Weekly Courier*, November 25, 1848, *Mississippi Free Trader* (Natchez), December 13, 20, 1848, January 24, 1849; William H. Samson (editor), *Letters of Zachary Taylor . . .* (1908), 169; *American Book-Prices Current* (1906, 1913, 1915); Taylor to George Lunt, November 17, 1848, LINCOLN; Alexander H. Stephens to John J. Crittenden, December 6, 1848, Crittenden Papers, LC; Simeon Draper to Thurlow Weed, February 6, 1849, Weed Papers, ROCHESTER.

[3] Robert Toombs to Crittenden, December 3, Balie Peyton to Crittenden, August 29, Taylor to Crittenden, July 1, John M. Clayton to Crittenden, August 11, December 13, Stephens to Crittenden, December 6, Albert T. Burnley to Crittenden, July 17, 1848, January 12, 1849, Richard Hawes to Crittenden, May 2, 1850, Crittenden Papers, Henry D. Gilpin to Martin Van Buren, June 13, 1849, Van Buren Papers, LC; Philo Shelton to Weed, November 27, 1848, Weed Papers, ROCHESTER; Washington *Union*, April 4, 1850; Claude M. Fuess, *Daniel Webster* (1930), II, 184-186, 190-193; Charles C. Binney, *The Life of Horace Binney* (1903), 2, 57-134, 202, 214-232; *Mississippi Free Trader* (Natchez), January 24, Cincinnati *Enquirer*, March 3, 1849.

[4] Allen Johnson and Dumas Malone (editors), *Dictionary of American Biography* (1928-1936), VI, 199-200; James G. Blaine, *Twenty Years of Congress* (1884-1886), I, 70; Clayton to Crittenden, December 13, Stephens to Crittenden, December 6, Crittenden Papers, Crittenden to Clayton, December 19, 1848, Clayton Papers, LC; Philip Greely, Jr., to Weed, November 28, William H. Seward to Weed, December 11, 14, 1848, Weed Papers, ROCHESTER; Bradley B. Meeker to Charles S. Todd, November 20, 1848, Todd Papers, FILSON; Clayton to Joseph P. Comegys, June 10, 17, 1848, Clayton Papers, collection of the Honorable C. Douglass Buck, New Castle County, Delaware; Washington *National Intelligencer*, February 23, 1849; Gideon Welles, Unpublished Diary, entry for February 26, 1849, HUNTINGTON.

[5] J. Madison Cutts to Todd, December 6, J. S. Havilland to Todd, December 10, 1848, Todd to Isaac S. Todd, February 3, 1849, Todd Papers, FILSON; Seward to Weed, November 29, 1848, Weed Papers, ROCHESTER; *St. Joseph Valley Register* (South Bend), December 21, 1848; Caleb B. Smith to Allen Hamilton, December 20, 1848, Hamilton Papers, INDIANA; Toombs to Crittenden, January 9, Ewing memorial signed by Ohio legislators, February 6, 1849, Stephens to Crittenden, December 6, 1848, Crittenden Papers, Crittenden to Clayton, February 17, 1849, Clayton Papers, LC; Gideon Welles, Unpublished Diary, undated entry for late 1848 or early 1849, HUNTINGTON.

[6] Taylor to Crittenden, May 15, 1847, Crittenden Papers, LC; Taylor to Truman Smith, December 6, copy, Weed to Fitz Henry Warren, December 19, Seward to Weed, December 11, 19, Shelton to Weed, November 27, Greely to Weed, November 28, 1848, Weed Papers, ROCHESTER; Binney, *op. cit.*, 232; Cutts to Todd, December 6, 1848, Todd Papers, FILSON; William B. Preston to William C. Preston, December 7, 1848, Davie Collection, New York City.

[7] W. A. Croffut (editor), *Fifty Years in Camp and Field* . . . (1909), 348; [Enoch R. or Solomon H.] Mudge to Charles A. Stetson, January 3, 1849, unsigned copy, Weed Papers, ROCHESTER; Burnley to Crittenden, January 12, 1849, Crittenden Papers, LC; Samson (editor), *op. cit.*, 168-169; Glyndon G. Van Deusen, *The Life of Henry Clay* (1937), 394; George R. Poage, *Henry Clay and the Whig Party* (1936), 190-192; J. S. Chambers, *The Conquest of Cholera* (1938), 204; Louisville *Weekly Courier*, January 27, 1849.

[8] Dorothy B. Goebel, *William Henry Harrison* . . . (1926), 366-368, 375; Freeman Cleaves, *Old Tippecanoe* . . . (1939), 339-340; Henry Clay to W. H. Harrison, March 15, 1841, Harrison Papers, Clay to Robert P. Letcher, December 13, 1840, Peyton to Crittenden, August 29, 1848, John P. Gaines to Crittenden, January 18, Burnley to Crittenden, January 12, 1849, Crittenden Papers, Clay to Nicholas Dean, August 24, [George D. Prentice?] to Clay, September 13, 1848, Henry Clay Papers, Clay to David Graham, June 16, 1848, newspaper clipping, Thomas J. Clay Papers, Crittenden to Clayton, January 7, 1849, Clayton Papers, LC; Oliver P. Chitwood, *John Tyler* . . . (1939), 209-211, 213-224; Hugh R. Fraser, *Democracy in the Making* . . . (1938), 170-177; Clay to Thomas B. Stevenson, June 14, August 5, September 4, October 9, 29, 1848, copies, CINCINNATI; Clay to William R. Hervey, December 19, 1848, HAMILTON COLLECTION; New York *Times*, May 3, 1860; Clay to Horace Greeley, September 21, 1848, Rufus W. Griswold Papers, Boston Public Library; *Journal of the Senate of the Commonwealth of Kentucky* . . . (1849), 170.

[9] John W. Caughey, *California* (1947), 292-296; Clayton to Crittenden, December 13, 1848, Toombs to Crittenden, January 22, 1849, Crittenden Papers, Crittenden to Clayton, December 19, 1848, Clayton Papers, Francis P. Blair to Martin Van Buren, February 17, 1849, Van Buren Papers, LC; *Congressional Globe*, Thirtieth Congress, Second Session, 319, 477-480, 607-608; Washington *Republic*, April 22, June 26, 1850; Quaife (editor), *op. cit.*, IV, 286, 293; Joseph H. Parks, "John Bell and the Compromise of 1850," *Journal of Southern History*, IX, 330-331; Polk to Cass, December 15, 1848, CLEMENTS; Robert P. Brooks, "Howell Cobb and the Crisis of 1850," *Mississippi Valley Historical Review*, IV, 281-284.

[10] Louisville *Weekly Courier*, February 10, 17, Natchez *Weekly Courier*,

January 31, February 7, *Mississippi Free Trader* (Natchez), February 7, 14, 1849; Ben: Perley Poore, *Perley's Reminiscences* . . . (1886), I, 353; Taylor to Roger Jones, December 21, 1848, War Department Records, ARCHIVES. For a colorful, amusing and at least partly apocryphal account of Taylor's boarding the wrong boat at Vicksburg, *cf.* J. C. Rockwell, "The Kidnapping of the Late President," *The Green Bag* (Boston, 1902), 214.

[11] *Kentucky Yeoman* (Frankfort), February 15, Louisville *Weekly Courier*, February 17, Cincinnati *Enquirer*, February 20, 22, Washington *National Intelligencer*, February 23, Frankfort *Commonwealth*, February 16, 1849; Warner L. Underwood, Diary, entry for February 14, 1849, Western Kentucky State College, Bowling Green; William W. Woollen, *Biographical* . . . *Sketches of Early Indiana* (1883), 405; Lewis Scrapbook, WOOD COLLECTION; Jefferson Davis to Crittenden, January 30, Toombs to Crittenden, January 22, 1849, Stephens to Crittenden, December 5, 1848, Crittenden Papers, Crittenden to Clayton, February 17, 1849, Clayton Papers, LC.

[12] Cincinnati *Enquirer*, February 17, 20, Washington *Union*, February 22, Wheeling *Gazette*, February 13, 14, 19, 20, Washington *National Intelligencer*, February 23, 24, 26, 1849; Lewis Scrapbook, WOOD COLLECTION; James C. Hall to Clayton, February 16, 1849, Clayton Papers, LC; James Hadden, *History of Uniontown* . . . *Pennsylvania* (1913), 772-773; Earle R. Forrest, *History of Washington County, Pennsylvania* (1926), I, 943; Thomas B. Searight, *The Old Pike* . . . (1894), 174; Wilhelmine M. Easby-Smith, *Personal Recollections* . . . (1913), 9-10.

CHAPTER XIII

[1] Washington *Union*, February 25, Cincinnati *Enquirer*, March 3, Washington *National Intelligencer*, February 27, March 1, 2, 1849; Francis P. Blair to Martin Van Buren, February 24, 1849, Van Buren Papers, LC; Milo M. Quaife (editor), *The Diary of James K. Polk* . . . (1910), IV, 352-353, 355, 358-359; Frederick W. Seward, *Seward at Washington* . . . *1846-1861* (1891), 100, 102; Allan Nevins (editor), *The Diary of Philip Hone* . . . (1927), II, 865; Lewis Scrapbook, WOOD COLLECTION; Lewis Cass to Aaron Hobart, November 28, 1848, CLEMENTS.

[2] Allen Johnson and Dumas Malone (editors), *Dictionary of American Biography* (1928-1936), XI, 193, XVIII, 6; John J. Crittenden to John M. Clayton, February 17, Clayton Papers, Henry Clay to James Harlan, March 13, Henry Clay Papers, Clayton to Crittenden, March 16, Crittenden Papers, S. R. Williams to Robert J. Breckinridge, February 20, 1849, Breckinridge Papers, LC; Charles F. Adams (editor), *Memoirs of John Quincy Adams* . . . (1874-1877), VIII, 336; Andrew Stewart to Zachary Taylor, August 8, 1849, STAUFFER COLLECTION; Cincinnati *Enquirer*, March 3, 1849; Henry R. Mueller, *The Whig Party in Pennsylvania* (1922), 161; Clayton to William M. Meredith, February 28, 1849, PENNSYLVANIA.

[3] Charleston *Courier*, March 8, Washington *Republic*, June 15, Washington *National Intelligencer*, March 3, 24, 1849; Robert Toombs to Crittenden, January 9, Crittenden Papers, Blair to Van Buren, March 1, 1849, Van Buren Papers, LC; Ben: Perley Poore, *Perley's Reminiscences* . . . (1886), I, 350-352; William H. Seward to Thurlow Weed, March 1, 4, 1849, Weed Papers, ROCHESTER; William R. Lawrence (editor), *Extracts from the Diary* . . .

of . . . Amos Lawrence (1855), 266-267; James G. Blaine, *Twenty Years of Congress* (1884-1886), I, 87.

[4] *Congressional Globe,* Thirtieth Congress, Second Session, 190-192, 573, 607-608, 666-698; *Congressional Globe Appendix,* Thirtieth Congress, Second Session, 253-255; Arthur C. Cole, *Whig Party in the South* (1913), 144; Washington *National Intelligencer,* March 5, 30, 1849; Quaife (editor), *op. cit.,* IV, 363-370; [Mary Mann], *Life of Horace Mann* (1891), 277; *Niles' National Register* (Philadelphia), LXXV, 219; George H. Haynes, "'President of the United States for a Single Day,'" *American Historical Review,* XXX, 308-310.

[5] Washington *National Intelligencer,* March 5, 6, Washington *Union,* March 6, 1849; John Pegram to Miss Mary E. Pegram, January 24, Pegram to Mrs. Virginia Pegram, February 23, 1849, Pegram-Johnson Papers, Brock Collection, HUNTINGTON; Seward, *op. cit.,* 102, 104; Grace Julian Clarke, *George W. Julian* (1923), 87; Quaife (editor), *op. cit.,* IV, 374-375; Poore, *op. cit.,* I, 353-354; *Congressional Globe,* Thirtieth Congress, Second Session, 690-691; William E. Griffis, *Millard Fillmore . . .* (1915), 46-47; New Orleans *Crescent,* May 12, 1848.

[6] James D. Richardson (editor), *A Compilation of the Messages . . . of the Presidents . . .* (1899), V, 4-6; Washington *National Intelligencer,* February 20, March 5, 6, 8, April 4, Washington *Union,* March 6, Washington *Whig,* February 8, *Mississippi Free Trader* (Natchez), January 31, 1849; Seward to Weed, March 1, 1849, Weed Papers, ROCHESTER; Quaife (editor), *op. cit.,* IV, 375-376; Poore, *op. cit.,* I, 354; Polk to Cass, November 26, 1848, CLEMENTS; Douglas S. Freeman, *R. E. Lee* (1934-1935), I, 304; Allen T. Rice (editor), *Reminiscences of Abraham Lincoln . . .* (1886), 19; Nevins (editor), *op. cit.,* II, 865-866.

[7] Laura C. Holloway, *The Ladies of the White House* (1882), 447-448; Washington *National Intelligencer,* March 6, April 4, 1849; Esther Singleton, *The Story of the White House* (1907), II, 5; Rice (editor), *op. cit.,* 19-20; Quaife (editor), *op. cit.,* IV, 376-377; Jefferson Davis to Crittenden, January 30, 1849, Crittenden Papers, LC.

CHAPTER XIV

[1] Samuel F. Bemis (editor), *The American Secretaries of State . . .* (1927-1929), VI, 4-9, 11; Charles F. Adams (editor), *Memoirs of John Quincy Adams . . .* (1874-1877), VIII, 213; Allen Johnson and Dumas Malone (editors), *Dictionary of American Biography* (1928-1936), IV, 185, VI, 408-409; Joseph P. Comegys, *Memoir of John M. Clayton* (1882), 22-23, 139-141, 287-288; Clayton to Comegys, June 10, 17, 1848, Clayton Papers, collection of the Honorable C. Douglass Buck, New Castle County, Delaware; Washington *National Intelligencer,* February 23, 1849; Clayton to John J. Crittenden, April 8, Robert Toombs to Mrs. Chapman Coleman, June 22, 1849, Crittenden Papers, LC; William H. Seward to Thurlow Weed, March 10, July 25, 1848, March 20, 1849, Weed Papers, ROCHESTER; Frederick W. Seward, *Seward at Washington . . . 1846-1861* (1891), 519; Gideon Welles, Unpublished Diary, entry for June 12, 1849, HUNTINGTON.

[2] Philadelphia *North American,* August 17, 21, 1873, February 4, 1912; Johnson and Malone (editors), *op. cit.,* XII, 548-549; William M. Meredith to D. P. Brown, August 3, 1857, William Meredith to William M. Meredith,

March 2, 8, John M. Read to Meredith, March 2, W. H. Winden to Meredith, March 1, David B. Ogden to Meredith, March 6, 1849, Robert P. Letcher to Meredith, February 9, 1850, PENNSYLVANIA; New York *Sun,* June 5, 1893; Lewis C. Levin to William D. Lewis, May 8, 1849, Levin Papers, HUNTINGTON; Henry R. Mueller, *The Whig Party in Pennsylvania* (1922), 161-163, 176-178; Washington *Union,* March 7, Boston *Atlas,* March 12, 1849; Letcher to Orlando Brown, February 7, 1850, Brown Papers, KENTUCKY.

³ Lloyd Lewis, *Sherman: Fighting Prophet* (1932), 5-19, 22-26, 32-34, 38-42, 59-60, 68-73; Johnson and Malone (editors), *op. cit.,* VI, 237-238; Harriet Martineau, *Retrospect of Western Travel* (1838), I, 179; Anna McAllister, *Ellen Ewing . . .* (1936), 5-16, 23-25, 28-31, 37, 40-41, 57; Erwin H. Price, "The Election of 1848 in Ohio," *Ohio Archaeological . . . Society Publications,* XXXVI, 295; William Bebb to Crittenden, November 24, 1848, Crittenden Papers, LC; Washington *Union,* March 2, 1849; Gideon Welles, Unpublished Diary, entry for February 26, 1849, HUNTINGTON; Mrs. Thomas Ewing to Mrs. William T. Sherman, May 20, 28, 1850, collection of Miss Eleanor S. Ewing, Landover, Maryland; James G. Blaine, *Twenty Years of Congress* (1884-1886), I, 87.

⁴ Johnson and Malone (editors), *op. cit.,* IV, 520, XV, 206-207; Robert Toombs to Crittenden, January 9, Crittenden Papers, Blair to Van Buren, March 1, 1849, Van Buren Papers, LC; Washington *Union,* March 13, 1849; Lucian L. Knight, *Reminiscences of Famous Georgians* (1907-1908), II, 111-125; William P. Brandon, "The Galphin Claim," *Georgia Historical Quarterly,* XV, 113-126; Myrta L. Avary (editor), *Recollections of Alexander H. Stephens . . .* (1910), 24-25; D. H. Abell to Weed, June 20, 1850, Weed Papers, ROCHESTER.

⁵ Gideon Welles, Unpublished Diary, entries for April 19, June 2, 8, undated entry for late March or early April, 1849, HUNTINGTON; Johnson and Malone (editors), *op. cit.,* IV, 300; anonymous to Millard Fillmore, [July, 1850], BUFFALO; Blaine, *op. cit.,* I, 87; Zachary Taylor to Jefferson Davis, September 11, 1849, collection of Henry N. Flynt, New York City; Bernard C. Steiner, *Life of Reverdy Johnson* (1914), 1-11, 15-16, 18-22; *Mississippi Free Trader* (Natchez), March 21, 1849; Mrs. Sherman to Mrs. Ewing, May 9, 1850, Ewing Collection, Landover, Maryland; S. Somervell Mackall, *Early Days of Washington* (1934), 130-132, 139-140.

⁶ Nashville *Republican Banner,* March 5, New York *Herald,* March 5, 6, Memphis *Appeal,* March 6, Baltimore *Patriot,* March 7, *Kentucky Yeoman* (Frankfort), Philadelphia *North American,* March 8, New York *Courier and Enquirer,* March 9, Cincinnati *Enquirer,* New York *Weekly Tribune,* March 10, Richmond *Republican,* March 13, *New Hampshire Patriot* (Concord), March 15, Louisville *Courier,* March 20, 1849.

⁷ Schuyler Colfax to Caleb B. Smith, April 2, Smith Papers, Blair to Van Buren, March 1, 5, Van Buren Papers, Albert T. Burnley to Crittenden, July 22, 1849, Crittenden Papers, LC; John F. Crampton to Viscount Palmerston, March 18, 1849, LONDON; Gideon Welles, Unpublished Diary, entries for April 19, June 2, 8, 12, also undated entry for early March, 1849, HUNTINGTON; New Orleans *Picayune,* March 11, 1849; Lyon G. Tyler, *The Letters and Times of the Tylers* (1884-1896), II, 462; Seward to Weed, February 27, 1849, Weed Papers, ROCHESTER.

⁸ Harry J. Carman and Reinhard H. Luthin, "The Seward-Fillmore Feud and the Crisis of 1850," *New York History,* XXIV, 163-168; Boston *Atlas,*

December 13, 1848; Washington *National Intelligencer,* March 30, 1849; Charles A. Stetson to Weed, January 14, [Enoch R. or Solomon H.] Mudge to Charles A. Stetson, January 3, 1849, copy, Seward to Weed, November 21, 1848, February 27, March 8, 25, 28, 30, 1849, Weed Papers, Seward to George W. Patterson, March 29, 1849, Patterson Papers, ROCHESTER; Seward, *op. cit.,* 87-88; Frank H. Severance (editor), "Millard Fillmore Papers," *Buffalo Historical Society Publications,* X, xxxvi; statement of B. F. Fox, BUFFALO; New York *Express,* July 12, 1850; Harriet A. Weed (editor), *Autobiography of Thurlow Weed* (1883), 586-587.

⁹ Burnley to Crittenden, January 12, July 22, 1849, Crittenden Papers, LC; William E. Smith, *The Francis Preston Blair Family in Politics* (1933), I, 76-81; Charles H. Ambler, *Thomas Ritchie . . .* (1913), 264-265, 296;˙ Martha A. Burnley, "Albert Triplett Burnley," *Texas State Historical Association Quarterly,* XIV, 150-152; biographical sketch of Burnley, Brown Papers, KENTUCKY; information supplied by Neville S. Bullitt, Louisville; New Orleans *Times-Picayune,* January 25, 1937; Buffalo *Courier,* September 17, 1849; Johnson and Malone (editors), *op. cit.,* XVI, 362-363.

¹⁰ Buffalo *Courier,* January 21, 1850; Mrs. Ewing to Miss Ellen Ewing, August 28, 1849, Ewing Collection, Landover, Maryland; Washington *Union,* July 7, 1849; Taylor to Davis, September 11, 1849, Flynt Collection, New York City; Holman Hamilton, *Zachary Taylor: Soldier of the Republic* (1941), 101, 104-105, 209-210, 237-238, 244; Brown to Crittenden, July 10, Burnley to Crittenden, July 22, John S. Pendleton to Crittenden, October 12, 1849, Crittenden Papers, LC; statements of Mrs. John Van Brunt, Kansas City, Missouri, Mrs. James T. Kerr, Washington, Mrs. Gerald W. Bennett, Colorado Springs, and the late Mrs. Arabella Taylor Clarke, Winchester, Virginia, to the author; New York *Sun,* June 5, 1893. Mrs. Van Brunt's grandmother was Mrs. Elizabeth Lee Taylor, the President's eldest sister. Mrs. Clarke's father was Joseph P. Taylor. Mrs. Kerr's father was Joseph H. Eaton. Mrs. Bennett's great-grandfather was Jefferson Davis.

CHAPTER XV

¹ Milo M. Quaife (editor), *The Diary of James K. Polk . . .* (1910), IV, 296, 375-376; Washington *National Intelligencer,* March 30, Washington *Union,* March 13, Charleston *Courier,* April 11, 1849; Arthur C. Cole, *Whig Party in the South* (1913), 147; Cardinal Goodwin, *The Establishment of State Government in California . . .* (1914), 51-53, 55, 58-59; Allen Johnson and Dumas Malone (editors), *Dictionary of American Biography* (1928-1936), XII, 314.

² James D. Richardson (editor), *A Compilation of the Messages . . . of the Presidents . . .* (1899), IV, 636; Robert G. Cleland, *A History of California: The American Period* (1922), 230; John W. Caughey, *California* (1947), 292-296; Goodwin, *op. cit.,* 49-50, 56, 59, 71-74; Hubert H. Bancroft, *History of California* (1884-1890), VI, 158-159; Johnson and Malone (editors), *op. cit.,* XII, 373-374; Frank Soulé, John H. Gihon and James Nisbet, *The Annals of San Francisco* (1855), 208; Raphael P. Thian (compiler), *Notes Illustrating the Military Geography . . .* (1881), 25; Order Number 13, Headquarters, Military Department 10, April 13, 1849, Adjutant General's Office, Documents File, War Department Papers, ARCHIVES.

³ *House Executive Document 17,* Thirty-first Congress, First Session, 9-11;

John J. Crittenden to John M. Clayton, April 11, T. Butler King to Clayton, June 20, Clayton Papers, Clayton to Crittenden, April 18, 1849, Crittenden Papers, LC; Goodwin, *op. cit.*, 76-79, 81-88; J. Ross Browne, *Report of the Debates in the Convention of California* (1849), 3-5, 7-8, 19-22, 29, 478-479; P. F. Smith to Zachary Taylor, September —, 1849, STAUFFER COLLECTION; Bancroft, *op. cit.*, VI, 286; Johnson and Malone (editors), *op. cit.*, VIII, 64-65, X, 403, XV, 608-609, XVII, 331-332; Caroline C. Lovell, *The Golden Isles of Georgia* (1939), 145-146, 248-254.

[4] Holman Hamilton, *Zachary Taylor: Soldier of the Republic* (1941), 232, 234, 239; *House Executive Document 17*, Thirty-first Congress, First Session, 261, 271-272; William C. Binkley, "The Question of Texan Jurisdiction . . . ," *Southwestern Historical Quarterly*, XXIV, 1-16; *House Executive Document 70*, Thirtieth Congress, First Session, 4; *Congressional Globe*, Thirtieth Congress, Second Session, 33; *Niles' National Register* (Philadelphia), LXXIV, 211; Spruce M. Baird to John M. Washington, November 22, Baird to Washington D. Miller, November 10, December 10, Washington to Baird, November 22, 23, 1848, Texas State Library, Austin.

[5] Binkley, *loc. cit.*, XXIV, 16, 21; Annie H. Abel (editor), *Official Correspondence of James S. Calhoun* (1915), 70; *House Executive Document 17*, Thirty-first Congress, First Session, 93-104, 280-281; Johnson and Malone (editors), *op. cit.*, II, 160-161; Allan Nevins, *Ordeal of the Union* (1947), I, 329; Dale L. Morgan, "The State of Deseret," *Utah Historical Quarterly*, VIII, 72-91; Richardson (editor), *op. cit.*, V, 23.

[6] *Register of All Officers . . . on the Thirtieth September, 1849 . . .* (1849), *1-*2, 14-16, 242; *Senate Executive Document 1*, Thirty-first Congress, First Session, 93-94, 117, 119-122, 125-126, 132-133, 136, 774, 790; *House Executive Document 4*, Thirty-first Congress, First Session, 1, 5, 15-17, 19-20; John Davis to Meredith, August 13, Meredith to Davis, October 15, 1849, copy, PENNSYLVANIA; Orlando Brown to Crittenden, August 29, 1849, Crittenden Papers, LC; Washington *Union*, March 22, 1850. A Third Seminole War did break out in the mid-1850s; it would have been the Fourth Seminole War, if the troubles of 1849 had developed into full-scale combat.

[7] *Senate Executive Document 1*, Thirty-first Congress, First Session, 108-115, 138-142, 149-152; Henry L. Kinney to Taylor, August 25, 1849, STAUFFER COLLECTION; Washington *Union*, September 11, 25, 1849.

CHAPTER XVI

[1] Allen Johnson and Dumas Malone (editors), *Dictionary of American Biography* (1928-1936), II, 223; Francis B. Heitman, *Historical Register of the United States Army . . .* (1890), 530; *Register of All Officers . . . on the Thirtieth September, 1849 . . .* (1849), 1-2; John M. Clayton to John J. Crittenden, March 16, April 8, 18, 1849, Crittenden Papers, LC; Guillaume Tell Poussin to James Buchanan, February 7, with enclosures, Poussin to Clayton, March 10, 30, April —, 1849, Notes from French Legation, XIV, Clayton to Poussin, March 10, 28, April 10, 21, 1849, Notes to French Legation, VI, State Department Papers, ARCHIVES.

[2] Clayton to Richard Rush, June 5, 1849, Instructions, France, XV, Poussin to Clayton, May 12, 30, Alexis de Tocqueville to Clayton, October 11, 1849, Notes from French Legation, XIV, Clayton to Poussin, May 28, September 14, 1849, Notes to French Legation, VI, Tocqueville to Rush, August 9,

copy, Rush to Clayton, August 13, William C. Rives to Clayton, October 10, 1849, Dispatches, France, XXXI, XXXII, State Department Papers, Archives; Washington *Union*, September 23, 1849; Washington *Republic*, March 19, 1850; Robert P. Letcher to Crittenden, November 8, Crittenden Papers, Rives to Clayton, November 8, Clayton to Tocqueville, November 10, 1849, draft, Clayton Papers, LC; James D. Richardson (editor), *A Compilation of the Messages . . . of the Presidents . . .* (1899), V, 10.

³ George W. Hopkins to Clayton, March 11, 18, June 29, July 19, 25, October 18, James B. Clay to Clayton, October 19, 20, November 8, 17, 1849, with enclosures, Dispatches, Portugal, XV, Clayton to Hopkins, April 20, 1849, Instructions, Portugal, XIV, State Department Papers, Archives; Johnson and Malone (editors), *op. cit.*, XV, 480-481; Richardson (editor), *op. cit.*, V, 13.

⁴ Steen Bille to Clayton, April 2, 9, 1849, Notes from Danish Legation, II, Clayton to Baron Friedrich Ludwig von Roenne, April 10, 29, May 5, 1849, Notes to German Legation, VI, Roenne to Clayton, April 14, May 1, 1849, Notes from German Legation, II, State Department Papers, Archives; Richardson (editor), *op. cit.*, V, 10-11; Washington *Union*, June 13, 26, Washington *National Intelligencer* June 21, Charleston *Courier*, April 3, 1849; *Senate Executive Document 1*, Thirty-first Congress, First Session, 18-48; John F. Crampton to Viscount Palmerston, April 2, March 18, 1849, London; Philo Shelton to Thurlow Weed, July 23, 1849, Weed Papers, Rochester.

⁵ Clayton to E. George Squier, May 1, 1849, Instructions, Central America, XV, Clayton to George Bancroft, May 2, April 30, Clayton to Abbott Lawrence, October 20, 1849, instructions, Great Britain, XV, XVI, Elijah Hise to Buchanan, December 20, 1848, Dispatches, Guatemala (Central America), I, Bancroft to Clayton, June 29, August —, 1849, Dispatches, Great Britain, LIX, State Department Papers, Archives; Crampton to Palmerston, October 1, 1849, London; Johnson and Malone (editors), *op. cit.*, IX, 69, XVII, 488-489; Washington *Union*, April 5, 1849.

⁶ Hise to Clayton, May 25, September 15, Squier to Clayton, September 10, 1849, Dispatches, Guatemala (Central America), I, II, Buchanan to Hise, June 3, 1848, Instructions, Central America, XV, Bancroft to Clayton, June 29, August —, Lawrence to Clayton, October 11, November 9, 1849, Dispatches, Great Britain, LIX, LX, Clayton to Rives, August 16, 1849, Instructions, France, XV, Rives to Clayton, September 25, 1849, Dispatches, France, XXXII, Clayton to Lawrence, October 20, 1849, Instructions, Great Britain, XVI, State Department Papers, Archives.

⁷ Lawrence to Clayton, November 14, with enclosures, November 23, 29, December 28, 1849, January 25, 1850, Dispatches, Great Britain, LX, Squier to Clayton, August 20, October 10, 25, 1849, Dispatches, Guatemala (Central America), II, State Department Papers, Archives; Crampton to Palmerston, October 1, 1849, London.

⁸ *Senate Executive Document 43*, Thirty-first Congress, First Session, 3-7, 13; Johnson and Malone (editors), *op. cit.*, XII, 239-240; *Senate Document 279*, Sixty-first Congress, Second Session, 2-27; Chevalier Johann Georg von Hülsemann to Daniel Webster, July 27, 1850, Notes from Austrian Legation, II, State Department Papers, Archives; Merle E. Curti, *Austria and the United States, 1848-1852* (1926), *passim*.

⁹ Buchanan to Clayton, April 12, Crittenden to Clayton, July 20, Clayton Papers, Clayton to Crittenden, April 18, 1849, Crittenden Papers, Zachary

Taylor to Thomas S. Jesup, January 20, 1824, copy, Taylor Papers, LC; *The Commercial Review of the South and West* (New Orleans), VI, 9; Robert G. Caldwell, *The Lopez Expeditions . . .* (1915), 43-50; Douglas S. Freeman, *R. E. Lee* (1934-1935), I, 306-308; Clayton to Daniel M. Barringer, August 2, 1849, Instructions, Spain, XIV, State Department Papers, ARCHIVES; *Senate Executive Document 57*, Thirty-first Congress, First Session, 4-8, 67-69.

CHAPTER XVII

[1] *Congressional Globe Appendix*, 47-51; James D. Richardson (editor), *A Compilation of the Messages . . . of the Presidents . . .* (1899), V, 6; Gideon Welles, Unpublished Diary, entries for April 19, May 10, 26, June 8, July 3, 24, 1849, HUNTINGTON; Thurlow Weed Barnes, *Memoir of Thurlow Weed* (1884), 175; Washington *Union*, July 3, 1849; Orlando Brown to John J. Crittenden, July 24, 1849, Crittenden Papers, Zachary Taylor to Ethan A. Hitchcock, May 19, July 28, 1841, Taylor Papers, LC; Carl R. Fish, "Removals of Officials by the Presidents of the United States," *Annual Report of the American Historical Association for the Year 1899* (1900), I, 69-78, 84-85; Oliver P. Chitwood, *John Tyler . . .* (1939), 368, 371-372; incomplete letter to Thurlow Weed, possibly dictated by Philip Greely, Jr., November 17, 1849, Weed Papers, ROCHESTER.

[2] *Journal of the Executive Proceedings of the Senate . . .* (1887), VIII, 60, 73, 76-78, 80, 83-88, 93-95; *National Cyclopaedia . . .* (1898-1949), XIII, 319; Charleston *Courier*, June 11, 15, Washington *Whig*, March 16-21, Washington *Union*, March 16-19, 21, 1849; Crittenden to John M. Clayton, April 6, 11, June 8, Clayton Papers, Clayton to Crittenden, April 18, May 7, 1849, Crittenden Papers, LC; Claude M. Fuess, *Daniel Webster* (1930), II, 195-196; *A Register of All Officers . . . on the Thirtieth September, 1851 . . .* (1851), 9; Allen Johnson and Dumas Malone (editors), *Dictionary of American Biography* (1928-1936), IV, 200-201, VI, 200, XIV, 443, XVII, 244-245; Gideon Welles, Unpublished Diary, entry for May 1, 1849, HUNTINGTON; Willie P. Mangum to William M. Meredith, April 2, 1849, PENNSYLVANIA; Usher F. Linder, *Reminiscences of the Early Bench and Bar of Illinois* (1879), 239.

[3] Washington *Whig*, April 5, 6, 9, 17, 20, May 2, 15, 19, June 1, 8, Washington *Union*, March 14, 16, April 19, July 3, Charleston *Courier*, April 24, Washington *National Intelligencer*, November 1, Washington *Republic*, June 29, July 13, 1849, March 12, 1850; Meredith to Nathaniel Young, April 20, 1849, copy, PENNSYLVANIA; Johnson and Malone (editors), *op. cit.*, VI, 227-228; Lewis C. Levin to William D. Lewis, April 15, 16, 27, 29, May 2, 1849, Levin Papers, HUNTINGTON; John H. Lathrop to Weed, October 24, 1849, Weed Papers, ROCHESTER.

[4] Caroline C. Marsh, *Life and Letters of George Perkins Marsh* (1888), 52-114, 136-137; Washington *Whig*, April 17, May 16, June 13, 18, Washington *Republic*, June 11, 14, August 24, Charleston *Courier*, June 6, 10, 11, 15, Washington *National Intelligencer*, September 21, November 28, 1849; John Henderson to William C. Rives, February 16, Rives Papers, Clayton to Crittenden, May 31, Crittenden Papers, Rives to Clayton, March 31, Clayton to Taylor, August 16, Crittenden to Clayton, September 3, 1849, Clayton Papers, LC; Holman Hamilton, *Zachary Taylor: Soldier of the Republic* (1941), 209-210; Taylor to J. Trumbull Van Alen, July 17, 1846, Lebold

Collection, Chicago; William H. Samson (editor), *Letters of Zachary Taylor* . . . (1908), 150-151, 156; Gideon Welles, Unpublished Diary, entry for May 1, undated entry for late March or early April, 1849, HUNTINGTON; Johnson and Malone (editors), *op. cit.*, I, 648, IV, 179, VI, 494, 537-538, XV, 635-637; Marquis James, *Andrew Jackson: Portrait of a President* (1937), 193-194, 444; Fish, *loc. cit.*, 78, 84-85; Fish, *The Civil Service and the Patronage* (1920), 163; *National Cyclopaedia* . . . (1898-1949), IV, 534; Albert J. Beveridge, *Abraham Lincoln, 1809-1858* (1928), I, 493. It is only fair to recall that Beveridge died before completing his book. Indelicate as it may seem to criticize his unfinished work, Beveridge's volumes are so widely read that the public should be placed on guard against certain of what may have been tentative conclusions.

[5] Roy P. Basler (editor), *Abraham Lincoln: His Speeches and Writings* (1946), 256; John G. Nicolay and John Hay (editors), *Complete Works of Abraham Lincoln* (1905), 111, 114-115, 118-119, 125, 127; Paul I. Miller (editor), "Lincoln and the Governorship of Oregon," *Mississippi Valley Historical Review*, XXIII, 391-394; Beveridge, *op. cit.*, I, 490 (italics author's), 492-493; Thomas Ewing, "Lincoln and the General Land Office, 1849," *Journal of the Illinois State Historical Society*, XXV, 139-153; Washington *Republic*, June 22, *Illinois State Register* (Springfield), June 14, 1849.

[6] Winfield S. Nevins, "Nathaniel Hawthorne's Removal . . . ," *Historical Collections of the Essex Institute*, LIII, 97, 99, 102-122, 125-131; Robert Cantwell, *Nathaniel Hawthorne: The American Years* (1948), 397, 417-427; Randall Stewart, *Nathaniel Hawthorne: A Biography* (1948), 53, 57-58, 87-88, 92-93; Nathaniel Hawthorne, *The Scarlet Letter* (Old Manse Edition, 1900), 3-4, 14, 35, 48; Washington *Whig*, June 8, Washington *Union*, June 13, 14, Philadelphia *Bulletin*, June 15, 1849; Lloyd Morris, *The Rebellious Puritan* . . . (1927), 211-212; Meredith to Daniel Webster, June 20, copy, Webster to Meredith, June 23, Edward Everett to Meredith, June 27, 1849, PENNSYLVANIA; Johnson and Malone (editors), *op. cit.*, VIII, 426-427.

[7] John D. Defrees to Caleb B. Smith, March 22, Schuyler Colfax to Smith, April 2, Smith Papers, Crittenden to Clayton, April 6, 11, June 29, Charles A. Davis to Clayton, May 16, William H. Seward to Clayton, April 4, Washington Hunt to Clayton, April 8, 1849, Clayton Papers, LC; Robert P. Letcher to Orlando Brown, June 16, 28, 1849, Brown Papers, KENTUCKY; Gilbert C. Russell to Meredith, September 4, 1849, PENNSYLVANIA; St. George L. Sioussat, "Tennessee, the Compromise of 1850, and the Nashville Convention," *Mississippi Valley Historical Review*, II, 314n.; Lewis Benedict, Jr., to Weed, May 9, O. Boardman to Weed, May 14, Charles [A. Stetson] to Weed, July 7, E. J. Fowle to Weed, August 19, 1849, Weed Papers, ROCHESTER.

[8] Washington *Union*, February 24, April 10, 12, May 17, June 13, 21, New York *Tribune*, April 13, Buffalo *Courier*, April 12, 1849; New York *Express*, January 19, 1850; Brantz Mayer to Charles S. Todd, September 8, 1849, Todd Papers, FILSON; Nicolay and Hay (editors), *op. cit.*, II, 132-133; John S. Pendleton to Crittenden, October 12, Charles D. Drake to Crittenden, April 2, Crittenden Papers, Henry D. Gilpin to Martin Van Buren, June 13, Van Buren Papers, Crittenden to Clayton, April 6, 1849, Clayton Papers, LC.

[9] Baltimore *Sun*, May 16, Washington *Republic*, June 15, July 17, Washington *Union*, June 13, 17, 29, 30, 1849; James K. Polk to Lewis Cass, November 14, 1848, CLEMENTS; Nathan Sargent to Crittenden, July 15, 1849,

Crittenden Papers, LC; Nicolay and Hay (editors), *op. cit.*, II, 131-132; Gilbert A. Tracy (editor), *Uncollected Letters of Abraham Lincoln* (1917), 39-40.

CHAPTER XVIII

[1] Gideon Welles, Unpublished Diary, entries for April 6, 9, 1849, HUNTINGTON; Charleston *Courier*, March 16, 24, *Mississippi Free Trader* (Natchez), March 21, 1849; Anna McAllister, *Ellen Ewing* . . . (1936), 60; Lewis Scrapbook, WOOD COLLECTION; Salmon P. Chase to Mrs. Chase, March 8, 1849, Chase Papers, LC; New York *Sun*, June 5, 1893; William Q. Force, *Picture of Washington* . . . (1848), 69-71; George Watterston, *New Guide to Washington* (1847-8), 58-59; Claude G. Bowers, *The Party Battles of the Jackson Period* (1922), 47-48; Ben: Perley Poore, *Perley's Reminiscences* . . . (1886), I, 358; original invitations in WOOD COLLECTION and PENNSYLVANIA; Lila G. A. Woolfall, *Presiding Ladies of the White House* (1903), 124-125; Katharine Anthony, *Dolly Madison* . . . (1949), 225.

[2] Poore, *op. cit.*, I, 357; Force, *op. cit.*, 78; Watterston, *op. cit.*, 61-63; Anthony, *op. cit.*, 225; Wilhelmus B. Bryan, *A History of the National Capital* (1914-1916), II, 6-8, 227, 251-252, 323-324; Washington *National Intelligencer*, March 10, 12, 13, 16, 19, 20, 21, 28, April 5, 12, July 6, 10, 16, 1849, January 12, 1850; Charleston *Courier*, March 13, April 9, Washington *Union*, March 11, April 26, 27, July 7, 10, 17, Washington *Whig*, April 24, Washington *Republic*, June 19, 21, 26, 27, 1849; Buffalo *Courier*, January 21, 1850; Marian Gouverneur *As I Remember* (1911), 170; Rufus R. Wilson, *Washington, the Capital City* (1901), II, 66; Samuel C. Busey, *Personal Reminiscences* . . . (1895), 64-65; *Niles' National Register* (Philadelphia), LXXV, 193; John F. Crampton to Viscount Palmerston, April 15, 1849, LONDON; John M. Clayton to John J. Crittenden, April 18, 1849, Crittenden Papers, LC; Elizabeth L. Dean, *Dolly Madison* . . . (1928), 241-243. Irving Brant, *James Madison: Father of the Constitution, 1787-1800* (1950), 401-403, stresses the spelling of "Dolley."

[3] J. S. Chambers, *The Conquest of Cholera* (1938), 197-204, 211, 219, 225-238; Washington *National Intelligencer*, July 4, August 14, 16, 17, 23, Washington *Republic*, August 6, 10, 11, 13-15, 18, 20, 21, 23, 30, September 1, New Orleans *Courier*, August 22, September 4, Washington *Union*, August 16, Pittsburgh *Gazette*, August 28, 29, 31, 1849; Jacob Ezekiel to Zachary Taylor, August 5, 1849, STAUFFER COLLECTION; Crittenden to Clayton, August 3, 1849, Clayton Papers, LC; William F. Worner, "Visit of Zachary Taylor to Lancaster . . . ," *Papers Read Before the Lancaster County Historical Society*, XXVII, 171-174; James D. Richardson (editor), *A Compilation of the Messages . . . of the Presidents* . . . (1899), V, 7-8; Robert G. Caldwell, *The Lopez Expeditions* . . . (1915), 54-55; Taylor to Jefferson Davis, September 11, 1849, Flynt Collection, New York City.

[4] Clayton to Taylor, August 13, Robert C. Wood to Clayton, August 29, 1849, Clayton Papers, LC; Washington *National Intelligencer*, August 24, 25, Buffalo *Express*, September 3, 11, *Lawrence Journal* (New Castle), August 25, New York *Tribune*, September 10, Erie *Gazette*, August 30, Erie *Weekly Observer*, September 8, New York *Courier & Enquirer*, September 3, Washington *Republic*, September 7, Buffalo *Courier*, August 29-September 1, Lower Sandusky *Freeman*, September 1, 1849; James F. Rhodes, *History of*

the United States . . . (1893-1906), I, 109; Lewis Scrapbook, WOOD COLLECTION; Taylor to Davis, September 11, 1849, Flynt Collection, New York City; George W. Patterson to Thurlow Weed, August 25, 1849, Weed Papers, ROCHESTER.

[5] Washington *Republic,* September 6, 8, 10, 11, 14, Buffalo *Express,* September 3, 7, 8, Buffalo *Courier,* September 3, 4, 6, Buffalo *Commercial Advertiser,* September 3, 4, 6, 7, Washington *National Intelligencer,* September 10, 14, Charleston *Courier,* September 10, 1849; *The Commercial Advertiser Directory* . . . (1849), 59; Taylor to Davis, September 11, 1849, Flynt Collection, New York City; Alexander C. Bullitt to Orlando Brown, September 5, 1849, Brown Papers, KENTUCKY; Gouverneur, *op. cit.,* 152; Lewis Scrapbook, WOOD COLLECTION. Mrs. Dudley lived at 59 North Pearl Street, Albany.

[6] Buffalo *Courier,* September 8, 15, October 2, Washington *Union,* August 26, 29, Washington *Republic,* August 30, Buffalo *Express,* September 8, Washington *National Intelligencer,* September 19, 1849; Simeon Draper to Weed, September 8, E. G. Spaulding to Weed, September 4, 1849, Weed Papers, ROCHESTER; Abbott Lawrence to Taylor, September 11, 1849, STAUFFER COLLECTION.

CHAPTER XIX

[1] Arthur C. Cole, *Whig Party in the South* (1913), 145-146; Albert B. Moore, *History of Alabama* . . . (1928), I, 264-265; Henry W. Hilliard to Zachary Taylor, August 15, 1849, STAUFFER COLLECTION; Thomas B. Stevenson to Orlando Brown, August 9, 1849, Brown Papers, KENTUCKY; Richard H. Shryock, *Georgia and the Union in 1850* (1926), 182-184, 199-200, 208-210, 219-220, 237-238; Ulrich B. Phillips, *The Life of Robert Toombs* (1913), 64-66; Allen Johnson and Dumas Malone (editors), *Dictionary of American Biography* (1928-1936), IV, 220-221; *Mississippi Free Trader* (Natchez), December 8, 1849.

[2] J. Franklin Jameson (editor), "Correspondence of John C. Calhoun," *Annual Report of the American Historical Association for the Year 1899* (1900), II, 765, 766, 769-771, 1198, 1205-1208; Washington *National Intelligencer,* June 6, 1850; *National Era* (Washington), June 12, 1851; Cleo Hearon, "Mississippi and the Compromise of 1850," *Publications of the Mississippi Historical Society,* XIV, 46-47, 50-63, 67-68.

[3] *The Liberator* (Boston), March 16, June 15, August 17, October 19, *National Era* (Washington), March 22, April 19, May 3, August 30, September 6, Charleston *Courier,* April 9, 1849; Edgar A. Holt, "Party Politics in Ohio, 1840-1850," *Ohio Archaeological* . . . *Society Publications,* XXXVIII, 342, 358-366; George W. Julian, *Political Recollections* . . . (1884), 65, 71-72; Theodore C. Smith, *The Liberty and Free Soil Parties in the Northwest* (1897), 177-179, 187-191, 194-196, 199-203, 209-213, 221; *Whig Almanac* . . . *for 1850,* 17.

[4] James B. Mower to John McLean, August 13, McLean Papers, Henry Clay to James Harlan, March 13, Clay to Nicholas Dean, June 21, Taylor to Clay, May 28, Stevenson to Clay, April 30, Clay Papers, Caleb Atwater to Willie P. Mangum, August 24, 1849, Mangum Papers, Brown to John J. Crittenden, April 19, 1850, Crittenden Papers, LC; *The Flying Quill* (Boston), June, 1948; Claude M. Fuess, *Daniel Webster* (1930), II, 195-196; William

H. Seward to Thurlow Weed, October 18, Seward to Taylor, October 18, 1849, Weed Papers, ROCHESTER; William M. Watts to William M. Meredith, April 2, Charlton Potts to Meredith, May 17, S. D. Meredith to Meredith, August 27, Charles B. Penrose to Meredith, October 9, H. M. Watts to Meredith, October 20, 1849, PENNSYLVANIA; Lewis C. Levin to William D. Lewis, May 2, 1849, Levin Papers, HUNTINGTON; Stevenson to Brown, June 2, 1849, Brown Papers, KENTUCKY; Phillips, *op. cit.*, 64-67; J. E. Caldwell to Millard Fillmore, November 12, 1849, BUFFALO; Clay to Stevenson, April 21, June 18, copies, Thomas Corwin to Stevenson, August 3, December 13, 1849, CINCINNATI; Brantz Mayer to Charles S. Todd, September 8, 1849, Todd Papers, FILSON.

[5] Frederick W. Seward, *Seward at Washington . . . 1846-1861* (1891), 111; Washington *National Intelligencer*, October 19, Washington *Union*, June 13, New York *Herald*, August 16, October 14, November 9, December 2, 6, 24, Buffalo *Courier*, September 12, 14, 1849, February 2, 1850; Myrta L. Avary (editor), *Recollections of Alexander H. Stephens . . .* (1910), 22-26; George E. Pomeroy to Weed, January 29, 1850, Weed Papers, ROCHESTER; J. Madison Cutts to Todd, November 22, 1849, Todd Papers, FILSON; Crittenden to John M. Clayton, September 1, Clayton Papers, Truman Smith to Crittenden, September 10, Crittenden Papers, Stevenson to Clay, April 30, Clay to Dean, June 21, Clay to James B. Clay, October 15, 1849, Clay Papers, LC; Andrew C. McLaughlin and Albert B. Hart (editors), *Cyclopedia of American Government* (1914), I, 389-390; Lexington *Observer and Reporter*, December 10, 20, 27, 1848, January 24, February 3, 1849; *Kentucky Yeoman* (Frankfort), January 25, Charleston *Courier*, September 19, Washington *Republic*, October 12, Baltimore *Sun*, November 10, 1849; New York *Express*, July 12, 1850; Taylor to Jefferson Davis, September 11, 1849, Flynt Collection, New York City; Holman Hamilton, *Zachary Taylor: Soldier of the Republic* (1941), 40, 82.

[6] Washington *Union*, October 11, Charleston *Courier*, October 10, Baltimore *Sun*, October 11-13, Baltimore *Clipper*, October 11, 12, Baltimore *American*, October 11, 13, Washington *Republic*, October 11-13, Washington *National Intelligencer*, October 13, 22, 1849; Francis P. Blair to Martin Van Buren, Jr., October 16, 1849, Van Buren Papers, LC; *The Collector* (New York), September, 1938; Taylor to "Coleman & Stetson," October 22, 1849, HAMILTON COLLECTION; *House Executive Document 17*, Thirty-first Congress, First Session, 280-281; James D. Richardson (editor), *A Compilation of the Messages . . . of the Presidents . . .* (1899), V, 9-42.

[7] Washington *Republic*, September 17, November 7, 12, 27, December 1, Washington *National Intelligencer*, November 17, 22, 26-28, Washington *Union*, April 29, Baltimore *Sun*, September 18, October 25, November 7, 1849; Ben: Perley Poore, *Perley's Reminiscences . . .* (1886), I, 358; Lewis Scrapbook, WOOD COLLECTION. The dinner hour at the Mansion was six o'clock. The Bentons dined at five, W. W. Corcoran at six.

CHAPTER XX

[1] Robert C. Winthrop, Jr., *A Memoir of Robert C. Winthrop* (1897), 43; Myrta L. Avary (editor), *Recollections of Alexander H. Stephens . . .* (1910), 17, 25-27; Allen Johnson and Dumas Malone (editors), *Dictionary of American Biography* (1928-1936), IV, 241-242, XIII, 157, XVII, 515, 569-570,

XVIII, 590, XIX, 284-285, XX, 416; Ulrich B. Phillips, *The Life of Robert Toombs* (1913), 64-72; William H. Seward to Thurlow Weed, December 7, 1849, Weed Papers, ROCHESTER; Madelene V. Dahlgren, "Samuel Finley Vinton," *Ohio Archaeological . . . Society Publications*, IV, 231-262; *Congressional Globe*, 117; Jennie C. Morton, "Governor Charles S. Morehead, Sketch of His Life," *Register of the Kentucky State Historical Society*, IV, 7-18; Morehead to John J. Crittenden, December 25, 1849, Crittenden Papers, LC; Charles F. Adams (editor), *Memoirs of John Quincy Adams . . .* (1874-1877), XI, 19; Robert P. Brooks, "Howell Cobb and the Crisis of 1850," *Mississippi Valley Historical Review*, IV, 279-284; Rudolph Von Abele, *Alexander H. Stephens . . .* (1946), 8, 138, 183.

    [2] Johnson and Malone (editors), *op. cit.*, II, 527-528, III, 100-101, VII, 549-550, X, 117-118, XI, 587-588, XII, 30-31, XVII, 523-524, XVIII, 153-155; *National Cyclopaedia of American Biography* (1909), XI, 562; Oliver H. Smith, *Early Indiana Trials and Sketches* (1858), 366; Salmon P. Chase to E. S. Hamlin, January 12, 1850, Chase Papers, LC; Cleveland *Weekly Plain Dealer*, January 23, 1850; Mount Vernon (Ohio) *Democratic Banner*, February 5, 1850; *The Biographical Cyclopaedia . . . of the State of Ohio* (1883-1895), I, 142-143; Robert D. Holt, "The Political Career of William A. Richardson," *Illinois State Historical Society Journal*, XXVI, 229-232; Albert J. Beveridge, *Abraham Lincoln, 1809-1858* (1928), I, 179, II, 117, 365; George W. Julian, *Political Recollections . . .* (1884), 73.

    [3] *Congressional Globe*, 2-12, 15-22; Morehead to Crittenden, December 25, 1849, Crittenden Papers, LC; Johnson and Malone (editors), *op. cit.*, IX, 165.

    [4] Charleston *Courier*, December 17, 1849; *Congressional Globe*, 22-39, 41-44, 46-48, 51, 61-67.

CHAPTER XXI

    [1] Orlando Brown to John J. Crittenden, January 11, Charles S. Morehead to Crittenden, March 30, Robert Toombs to Crittenden, April 23, 1850, Crittenden Papers, LC; Charleston *Courier*, December 11, 17, 1849; J. Franklin Jameson (editor), "Correspondence of John C. Calhoun," *Annual Report of the American Historical Association for the Year 1899* (1900), II, 776, 780; *Congressional Globe*, 97-98, 119-120; New York *Daily Tribune*, January 3, 9, New York *Herald*, January 3, 1850; Cleo Hearon, "Mississippi and the Compromise of 1850," *Publications of the Mississippi Historical Society*, XIV, 63-68, 117; Dallas T. Herndon, "The Nashville Convention of 1850," *Alabama Historical Society Transactions*, V, 212-216; William H. Seward to Thurlow Weed, November 20, December 3, 1849, Weed Papers, ROCHESTER.

    [2] Charleston *Courier*, December 11, 17, 1849; Robert P. Letcher to Crittenden, November 8, 21, 1849, Brown to Crittenden, January 11, 1850, Crittenden Papers, LC; Jameson (editor), *op. cit.*, II, 776; Nathan K. Hall to Millard Fillmore, December 13, John S. Williams to Fillmore, November 20, 1849, Elijah Dixon to Fillmore, May 5, 1850, BUFFALO; [William T. Sherman], *Memoirs of Gen. W. T. Sherman* (1892), I, 111; Seward to Weed, November 30, 1849, Weed Papers, ROCHESTER; unsigned, undated George P. Fisher manuscript, PENNSYLVANIA; L. A. Gobright, *Recollection of Men and Things . . .* (1869), 99.

    [3] James D. Richardson (editor), *A Compilation of the Messages . . . of the Presidents . . .* (1899), V, 9-24 (italics author's).

⁴ Baltimore *Sun*, Philadelphia *Inquirer*, Washington *Union*, Washington
National Intelligencer, New York *Tribune*, New York *Herald*, December 25,
Ohio State Journal (Columbus), December 26, Hartford *Courant*, Boston
Courier, Boston *Atlas*, *Illinois State Journal* (Springfield), Louisville *Journal*,
New Orleans *Picayune*, Philadelphia *Pennsylvanian*, Boston *Post*, December
27, Augusta *Chronicle*, Charleston *Mercury*, *The Liberator* (Boston), Decem-
ber 28, *Indiana State Sentinel* (Indianapolis), New York *Courier and En-
quirer* quoted in Washington *Republic*, December 29, *Indiana State Journal*
(Indianapolis), December 31, 1849, Richmond *Enquirer*, January 1, *New
Hampshire Patriot* (Concord), *National Era* (Washington), January 3, Knoxville *Whig*, January 5, 1850.

⁵ *Congressional Globe*, 73-75; Charleston *Courier*, December 31, 1849;
Washington *National Intelligencer*, December 19, 21, 25, 1849, January 2,
March 19, 1850; Washington *Republic*, December 24, 25, 31, 1849, January
2, 15, 16, 28, 1850; Washington *Union*, December 29, 1849; Buffalo *Courier*,
December 31, 1849; Henry D. Gilpin to Martin Van Buren, January 27,
1850, Van Buren Papers, LC; statement of the late Mrs. Arabella Taylor
Clarke to the author; Leslie Stephen and Sidney Lee (editors), *Dictionary of
National Biography* (1885-1901), XXXIV, 387; John F. Maguire, *Father
Mathew . . .* (1864), 486-487; Frederick W. Seward, *Seward at Washing-
ton . . . 1846-1861* (1891), 116.

⁶ *Congressional Globe*, 74-75, 87, 90-91, 94-100, 106-107, 117-126, 130-
141, 156-157, 161-162, 174-175, 186-187, 195; Washington *Union*, March
22, Buffalo *Courier*, February 1, 1850; Allen Johnson and Dumas Malone
(editors), *Dictionary of American Biography* (1928-1936), IV, 191-192;
Congressional Globe Appendix, 52-54; Richardson (editor), *op. cit.*, V, 27-
30.

⁷ Philadelphia *Pennsylvanian*, New York *Evening Post*, January 22, Washington *National Intelligencer*, January 23, Richmond *Enquirer*, January 24,
Charleston *Mercury*, January 25, Nashville *Union*, January 30, *New Hampshire Patriot* (Concord), January 31, 1850; Arthur C. Cole, *The Whig Party
in the South* (1913), 156; Saint Louis *Republican*, quoted in Washington
Republic, February 20, 1850.

⁸ Washington *Republic*, January 11, 28, February 5, 1850. For exceptions,
cf. ibid., January 15, 29, 1850.

CHAPTER XXII

¹ *Congressional Globe*, 165-167, 176-180, 200-209, 233-236; *Congressional Globe Appendix*, 58-83, 91-97; *The United States Magazine . . .* , I,
89; Francis P. Blair to Martin Van Buren, December 30, 1848, January 27,
1849, Van Buren Papers, LC; Oliver Dyer, *Great Senators . . .* (1889), 196-
214; information furnished by William N. Chambers, Saint Louis; Washington *Union*, April 11, 1858; James D. Lynch, *The Bench and Bar of
Mississippi* (1881), 286-288; Clayton Rand, *Men of Spine in Mississippi*
(1940), 161; Dunbar Rowland, "Political and Parliamentary Orators of
Mississippi," *Mississippi Historical Society Publications*, IV, 369-372.

² George W. Bungay, *Off-hand Takings . . .* (1854), 92-93; Dyer, *op. cit.*,
45-47; Clarence E. Carter (editor), *The Territorial Papers . . .* (1934——),
X, XI, XII, *passim*; Allen Johnson and Dumas Malone (editors), *Dictionary
of American Biography* (1928-1936), III, 562-564, IV, 173-179; George

F. Milton, *The Eve of Conflict* . . . (1934), 2-3, 15-32; Washington *Republic*, January 28, 29, 1850; George Bancroft, "A Few Words about Henry Clay," *Century Magazine*, XXX, 479, 481; "Henry Clay as an Orator," *Putnam's Monthly Magazine*, III, 500-502; Gerald W. Johnson, *America's Silver Age* . . . (1939), 4-5, 28-29, 34-37; Harriet Martineau, *Retrospect of Western Travel* (1838), I, 173-174, 178-179; Alexander Mackay, *The Western World* . . . (1849), I, 192; *Congressional Globe*, 244-247.

[3] New York *Express*, January 31, Baltimore *Sun*, February 6, New York *Herald*, New York *Tribune*, Philadelphia *Inquirer*, February 7, 1850; *Congressional Globe*, 244-252; Henry Clay to Mrs. Clay, January 11, 21, February 7, 19, 1850, Thomas J. Clay Papers, LC; Carl Schurz, *Life of Henry Clay* (1887), II, 334-335; Calvin Colton (editor), *Works of Henry Clay* . . . (1897), III, 130.

[4] *Congressional Globe Appendix*, 115-127; Baltimore *Sun*, February 6, Richmond *Whig*, February 26, 1850; Schurz, *op. cit.*, I, 11; James F. Rhodes, *History of the United States* . . . (1893-1906), I, 120; Nicholas Dean to James B. Clay, February 28, 1850, Henry Clay Papers, LC; John B. McMaster, *A History of the People of the United States* . . . (1913), VIII, 19; Lewis C. Levin Papers, HUNTINGTON, *passim*; PENNSYLVANIA, *passim*.

[5] Senator Clarke wrote that "from the North & West we can safely depend upon" John Davis, Phelps, Upham, Greene, Smith, Baldwin, Seward, Dayton, Miller, Corwin and himself (Whigs), Hamlin, Bradbury, Felch, Walker and Henry Dodge (Democrats), plus Hale and Chase. Wales was a Taylor supporter. Spruance wavered, but Clarke expected him to vote against the Compromise. (John H. Clarke to Meredith, June 1, 1850, PENNSYLVANIA.)

[6] Richard H. Shryock, *Georgia and the Union in 1850* (1926), 267-269. Shryock is one of the few writers who have grasped Berrien's emphasis on "economic pressure against the North." Robert P. Brooks is another.

[7] *Senate Miscellaneous Document 110*, Thirty-second Congress, First Session, 172; New York *Tribune*, January 8, 1849; Joseph H. Parks, *John Bell of Tennessee* (1950), 244-247, 253-257, Bell was slow, studious, judicious, earnest. Reversing himself on one or two matters during the debate, he had the moral courage or political naïveté to call attention to his self-reversal. It is dangerous to be dogmatic about Pearce. Bernard C. Steiner, "James Alfred Pearce," *Maryland Historical Magazine,* XVI-XIX, is not especially helpful except on Pearce's friendship for Corwin and his attitude toward Clay after Taylor's death (XVII, 346-350).

[8] Lewis Cass to Henry Ledyard, June 13, 1850, CLEMENTS; Clarke to Meredith, June 1, 1850, PENNSYLVANIA. Claudius B. Grant, "Life and Character of Alpheus Felch," *Michigan Pioneer* . . . *Society Collections*, XXVIII, 94-104, is disappointing.

[9] Like Clay, Calhoun and Webster, such twentieth-century figures as the elder Lodge, the elder LaFollette, the elder Long, Borah and Wheeler achieved most of their fame or notoriety as Administration opponents. In general, they were more widely known than pro-Administration senators.

CHAPTER XXIII

[1] Marquis James, *The Raven* . . . (1929), 20, 29-37, 48, 51-54, 59-60, 68-88, 98-104, 248-257, 266, 320, 359, 379; Ben: Perley Poore, *Perley's Reminiscences* . . . (1886), I, 369, 371; Boston *Atlas*, August 10, 1848;

Alexander Mackay, *The Western World* . . . (1849), I, 191; Francis B. Heit-man, *Historical Register of the United States Army* . . . (1890), 123, 351; Allen Johnson and Dumas Malone (editors), *Dictionary of American Biography* (1928-1936), IX, 263, 266; *Congressional Globe Appendix*, 97-102.

² Other Americans used the "house divided" idea or language prior to Lincoln's speech in 1858. Edmund Quincy did so in 1852. (Allan Nevins, *Ordeal of the Union* [1947], II, 78.) However, in 1843, Lincoln was one of three signing a Whig circular which contained the sentence: ". . . He whose wisdom surpasses that of all philosophers has declared that 'a house divided against itself cannot stand.' " (John G. Nicolay and John Hay [editors], *Complete Works of Abraham Lincoln* [1905], I, 255.)

³ *Congressional Globe Appendix*, 102, 149-157, 202-211; Stephen F. Miller, *The Bench and Bar of Georgia* (1858), 44-109; Lucian L. Knight, *Reminiscences of Famous Georgians* (1907-1908), II, 95; Claude G. Bowers, *The Party Battles of the Jackson Period* (1922), 60; Johnson and Malone (editors), *op. cit.*, II, 225; J. F. C. Fuller, *Decisive Battles* . . . (1940), 669; Holman Hamilton, *Zachary Taylor: Soldier of the Republic* (1941), 104-105, 108-109; Oliver Dyer, *Great Senators* . . . (1889), 123-125; Robert McElroy, *Jefferson Davis* . . . (1937), I, 70, 149; Douglas S. Freeman, *R. E. Lee* (1934-1935), I, 516-517; Albert J. Beveridge, *Abraham Lincoln, 1809-1858* (1928), I, 83. Vattel (1714-1767) was the author of *Droit des Gens*. Davis' phrase "the gathering storm" is one of several colorful Great Debate expressions, which other men later made famous. In this case, it was Winston S. Churchill in 1949.

⁴ For Bryan and Hoover comparisons, *cf.* William J. Bryan, *The First Battle* (1896), 205, and William Starr Myers (editor), *The State Papers* . . . *of Herbert Hoover* (1934), II, 418.

⁵ *Congressional Globe Appendix*, 149-157, 165-176, 310-318; Minnie M. Ruffin, "General Solomon Weathersbee Downs . . . ," *Louisiana Historical Quarterly*, XVII, 6-11, 20-22, 25-28; Lucius Q. C. Elmer, *The Constitution and Government of* . . . *New Jersey* . . . (1872), 434-435; William Nelson, *Nelson's Biographical Cyclopedia of New Jersey* (1913), I, 100 *et seq.*; information supplied by a Miller descendant through Elmer T. Hutchinson of Elizabeth; Erwin H. Price, "The Election of 1848 in Ohio," *Ohio Archaeological* . . . *Society Publications*, XXXVI, 265-266. Downs was thirty-three when William Weathersbee gave him legal recognition as a son. The contrast in duration of Senate service between 1850 and 1950 makes a revealing study; Miller, relatively, was an old-timer after nine years on the Hill.

⁶ Washington *National Intelligencer*, February 22, 23, 26, Richmond *Times*, February 22, 25, Richmond *Whig*, February 26, Richmond *Enquirer*, February 22, 26, Washington *Republic*, February 28, New Orleans *Picayune*, March 11, 1850; Richmond *Times-Dispatch*, September 30, 1934; John B. Mordecai, *A Brief History* . . . (1940), 9; Lyon G. Tyler, *The Letters and Times of the Tylers* (1884-1896), II, 462; Heitman, *op. cit.*, 102; Freeman, *op. cit.*, I, 534, 639; Beveridge, *op. cit.*, II, 76.

⁷ New Orleans *Weekly Picayune*, March 4, 11, Washington *Republic*, February 23, Washington *Union*, February 2, 3, 1850; Thomas B. Stevenson to Orlando Brown, January 17, 1850, Brown Papers, KENTUCKY; William H. Seward to Thurlow Weed, February 2, David H. Abell to Weed, February 1, 1850, Weed Papers, ROCHESTER; Jerome Fuller to Millard Fillmore, January 25, John L. Dox to Fillmore, February 2, 1850, BUFFALO; H. H. Sibley

to Alexander Ramsey, February 9, 1850, MINNESOTA; Brown to John J. Crittenden, February 1, 1850, Crittenden Papers, LC.

[8] *Congressional Globe,* 200-205, 257-261; James Buchanan to Cave Johnson, January 1, 1850, Buchanan Papers, Historical Society of Pennsylvania, Philadelphia; Edward Everett to Colonel [Thomas?] Aspinwall, February 5, 1850, copy, MASSACHUSETTS; Seward to Weed, February 2, 1850, Weed Papers, ROCHESTER; Baltimore *Sun,* New York *Daily Tribune,* March 16, New Orleans *Picayune,* March 11, 25, 1850; *Congressional Globe Appendix,* 225-228.

[9] Thurlow Weed Barnes, *Memoir of Thurlow Weed* (1884), 176-178; New York *Tribune,* February 25, 1850; Elmer, *op. cit.,* 435-438. There were *several* interviews involving Taylor, Toombs and Stephens.

CHAPTER XXIV

[1] J. Franklin Jameson (editor), "Correspondence of John C. Calhoun," *Annual Report of the American Historical Association for 1899* (1900), II, 781; information supplied by Charles M. Wiltse, Washington; Allen Johnson and Dumas Malone (editors), *Dictionary of American Biography* (1928-1936), XVI, 236-237; *Congressional Globe Appendix,* 233-239; Wiltse, *John C. Calhoun, Nationalist* (1944), 28, 135, 144, 266-267; Hermann von Holst, *John C. Calhoun* (1899), 366; James F. Rhodes, *History of the United States . . .* (1893-1906), I, 127.

[2] Vernon L. Parrington, *Main Currents . . .* (1927-1930), II, 69-82; Harriet Martineau, *Retrospect of Western Travel* (1838), I, 147; [Varina Davis], *Jefferson Davis . . . A Memoir* (1890), I, 210; Gerald W. Johnson, *America's Silver Age . . .* (1939), 46; *Congressional Globe,* 451-455, 476; Rhodes, *op. cit.,* I, 127; New York *Tribune,* March 5, 1850; Johnson and Malone (editors), *op. cit.,* III, 419, VIII, 196-198; Charles E. Hamlin, *The Life and Times of Hannibal Hamlin . . .* (1899), 18-181, 204-205, 212-213; *Congressional Globe Appendix,* 242-248, 277-290.

[3] Claude M. Fuess, *Daniel Webster* (1930), I, 14, 16, 334-337, 361, 385, II, 17, 73, 76, 89-93, 105-116, 129, 148-149; Edward Channing, *A History of the United States* (1926-1927), VI, 78-79; Lloyd Lewis, *Sherman: Fighting Prophet* (1932), 83. Webster's speech was printed in both the *Globe,* 476-484, and the *Appendix,* 269-276. The revised *Appendix* version is quoted here, giving Webster the privilege—accorded other senators—to dress up his language for the record. Taylor laughingly told Senator Miller that Webster "made a very smooth speech, but . . . lost one of the leaves, and had to make a supplement the next day" (Lucius Q. C. Elmer, *The Constitution and Government of . . . New Jersey . . .* [1872], 437).

[4] Louis McDuffee to John P. Hale, April 22, A. Merrill to Hale, March 18; James W. Stone to Hale, June 15, M. W. Tappan to Hale, April 16, 1850, Hale Papers, CONCORD: J. M. Wainwright to Webster, March 11, Linus Child to Webster, April 1, William Anderson to Webster, March 8, Daniel Lord to Webster, April 4, 1850, Webster Papers, LC.

[5] Samuel Longfellow (editor), *Life of Henry Wadsworth Longfellow . . .* (1891), II, 174, 208; Moorfield Storey, *Charles Sumner* (1900), 73; John B. McMaster, *A History of the People of the United States . . .* (1883-1913), VIII, 27; Allan Nevins, *Ordeal of the Union* (1947), I, 292; Bliss Perry,

John Greenleaf Whittier: A Sketch of His Life . . . with Selected Poems (1907), 89-91.

⁶ James W. Allen to Webster, March 26, Wainwright to Webster, March 11, Lord to Webster, April 4, James B. Thornton to Webster, March 28, William Jones to Webster, March 17, S. S. Wilde to Webster, April 9, Thomas Allen to Webster, March 26, 1850, Webster Papers, LC; R. B. Barker to Webster, April 13, anonymous to Webster, May 20, W. H. Winder to Webster, March 12, Joel R. Poinsett to Webster, April 10, Robert B. Minturn to Webster, April 4, Francis Lieber to Webster, May 4, Edward A. Newton to Webster, March 28, Daniel Dana to Webster, April 10, William N. Bond to Webster, March 15, 1850, Webster Papers, CONCORD.

⁷ Herbert D. Foster, "Webster's Seventh of March Speech and the Secession Movement, 1850," *American Historical Review*, XXVII, 265-267; Asa A. Tufts to John P. Hale, March 15, McDuffee to Hale, April 22, Merrill to Hale, March 18, W. Plummer, Jr., to Hale, March 22, E. B. Hillard to Hale, April 15, Stone to Hale, June 15, John B. Stevens to Hale, April 11, Benjamin Walter to Hale, June 24, 1850, Hale Papers, CONCORD.

⁸ Robert C. Winthrop to Edward Everett, March 3, April 7, 1850, Everett Papers, MASSACHUSETTS; Foster, *loc. cit.*, XXVII, 261-264; [Mary Mann], *Life of Horace Mann* (1891), 293-297; Robert C. Winthrop, Jr., *A Memoir of Robert C. Winthrop* (1897), 109-114; George T. Curtis, *Life of Daniel Webster* (1870), II, 397; Godfrey T. Anderson, "The Slavery Issue as a Factor in Massachusetts Politics from the Compromise of 1850 to the Outbreak of the Civil War" (unpublished University of Chicago doctoral dissertation); Henry Clay to Mrs. Clay, March 7, 1850, Thomas J. Clay Papers, LC.

CHAPTER XXV

¹ [Henry Adams], *The Education of Henry Adams* (1918), 104; Frederick W. Seward, *Seward at Washington . . . 1846-1861* (1891), 105, 125; Burton J. Hendrick, *Lincoln's War Cabinet* (1946), 8-9; Carl Sandburg, *Abraham Lincoln: The War Years* (1939), I, 142-143; Thornton K. Lothrop, *William Henry Seward* (1899), 16, 54; Frederic Bancroft, *The Life of William H. Seward* (1900), I, 183-185, 190; New York *Tribune*, March 16, 1850; Seward to Thurlow Weed, October 27, 1848, Weed Papers, ROCHESTER.

² *Congressional Globe Appendix*, 261-269, 292-297, 364-392, 435-443, 446-450, 468-480, 526-536.

³ *Congressional Globe*, 375-376, 592, 628-629; Alexander H. Stephens, *A Constitutional View . . .* (1868-1870), II, 201-205; George F. Milton, *The Eve of Conflict . . .* (1934), 58-59; Robert P. Brooks, "Howell Cobb and the Crisis of 1850," *Mississippi Valley Historical Review*, IV, 285; New York *Express*, April 13, New York *Herald*, March 13, *New Hampshire Patriot* (Concord), March 21, *Brownlow's Knoxville Whig*, April 13, 1850 (but also see laudatory editorials in such papers as New York *Tribune*, March 13, and Boston *Atlas*, March 15, 1850); Weed to Seward, March 17, Weed to Mrs. Seward, July 4, 1850, Seward Papers, Seward to Weed, March 15, 22, 31, E. G. Spaulding to Weed, March 11, D. H. Abell to Weed, probably March 18, J. C. Clark to Weed, March 17, 1850, Weed Papers, ROCHESTER: Gideon Hard to Millard Fillmore, April 4, 1850, BUFFALO; "Recollections of an Old

Stager," *Harper's New Monthly Magazine*, XLVII, 589. Brooks errs in stating that Doty introduced his resolution on February 28.

[4] Washington *Republic*, March 15, New York *Express*, April 13, 25, New Orleans *Picayune*, March 25, April 1, Washington *Union*, March 20, 22, 1850; Schuyler Colfax to Caleb B. Smith, April 23, 1850, Smith Papers, Humphrey Marshall to John J. Crittenden, March 10, Robert Toombs to Crittenden, April 23, 1850, Albert T. Burnley to Crittenden, July 22, 1849, May 15, 1850, Orlando Brown to Crittenden, July 10, 1849, John S. Pendleton to Crittenden, October 12, 1849, Robert P. Letcher to Crittenden, November 17, 1849, Charles S. Morehead to Crittenden, March 30, 1850, Richard Hawes to Crittenden, May 2, 1850, Crittenden Papers, Crittenden to John M. Clayton, August 15, 1849, Clayton Papers, LC; John L. Schoolcraft to Weed, March 15, E. G. Spaulding to Weed, March 25, 1850, Seward to Weed, December 9, 1849, Weed Papers, ROCHESTER; Hard to Fillmore, April 4, Alexander Mann to Fillmore, March 22, Jerome Fuller to Fillmore, March 20, 1850, BUFFALO; Charlton Potts to William M. Meredith, PENNSYLVANIA; Mrs. Chapman Coleman, *The Life of John J. Crittenden* (1871), I, 341.

[5] Spaulding to Weed, March 8, 1850, Weed Papers, ROCHESTER; Washington *Republic*, March 20, 22, 27, April 3, 6, May 4, 6, Washington *Union*, March 28, 1850; Alexander C. Bullitt to Orlando Brown, June 2, 1850, Brown Papers, KENTUCKY; Francis P. Blair to Martin Van Buren, March 24, Van Buren Papers, Salmon P. Chase to Mrs. Chase, March 31, 1850, Chase Papers, LC.

[6] Washington *Union*, April 3, Washington *Republic*, April 3, Washington *National Intelligencer*, April 2, 1850; Howell Cobb to Mrs. Cobb, April 21, 1850, Cobb Papers, Erwin Collection, Athens, Georgia, quoted in Milton, *op. cit.*, 66; *Congressional Globe*, 623-625. This seems to have been the general impression regarding Calhoun's speech, notwithstanding praise in Charleston *Mercury*, March 7, Baltimore *Sun*, March 5, and New York *Herald*, March 6, 1850. To balance this view, *cf.* Augusta *Chronicle*, March 9, Boston *Courier*, March 6, and Louisville *Journal*, March 13, 1850. Other pertinent comments are in Washington *Union*, March 6, Washington *Republic*, March 5, New York *Tribune*, March 5, Hartford *Courant*, March 9, 12, and Philadelphia *Inquirer*, March 7, 1850.

CHAPTER XXVI

[1] *Congressional Globe*, 436-439, 508-510, 704-714, 721-722, 747-748, 751-764, 769-775, 779-781. Foote's version is in Henry S. Foote, *Casket of Reminiscences* (1874), 338-339. The senators who went to South Carolina were Berrien, Clarke, Jefferson Davis, Dickinson, A. C. Dodge and Mason.

[2] Stephen A. Douglas to Charles H. Lanphier and George Walker, August 3, 1850, original in possession of Dr. Charles L. Patton, Springfield, Illinois; *Congressional Globe*, 780, 806, 815-818, 844-854, 864-874, 884-891, 931-939, 944-956; *Congressional Globe Appendix*, 536-543, 567-573; Henry Clay to Mrs. Clay, April 25, 1850, Thomas J. Clay Papers, LC; Katherine Scarborough, *Homes of the Cavaliers* (1930), 76-78; Allen Johnson and Dumas Malone (editors), *Dictionary of American Biography*, III, 427-428; New York *Express*, May 9, 1850; Thomas L. Harris to Lanphier, April 11, 1850, ILLINOIS.

[3] James D. Richardson (editor), *A Compilation of the Messages . . . of the*

Presidents ... (1899), V, 28-29; Washington *Republic,* April 24, 25, May 1, 9-11, 1850; John L. Schoolcraft to D. H. Abell, March 21, William H. Seward to Thurlow Weed, March 22, Schoolcraft to Weed, March 21, Orsamus B. Matteson to Weed, March 24, E. G. Spaulding to Weed, March 22, Abell to Weed, [March —], Weed Papers, Mrs. Seward to Mrs. Lazette Worden, March 19, 21, April 4, 27, 1850, Seward Papers, ROCHESTER.

   4 Washington *Republic,* May 14, 15, 20, 27, 1850; Joseph H. Parks, *John Bell of Tennessee* (1950), 73, 197, 233, 251-252, 265; *Congressional Globe Appendix,* 612-616.

CHAPTER XXVII

   1 Washington *Union,* April 28, May 14, 15, 16, 28; New York *Express,* June 4, 1850.

   2 Orlando Brown to John J. Crittenden, April 18, 19, May 23, 1850, Crittenden Papers, LC; D. D. Mitchell to Brown, May 28, 1850, Brown Papers, KENTUCKY.

   3 Mrs. Chapman Coleman, *The Life of John J. Crittenden* (1871), I, 372-374; Thurlow Weed to Francis Granger, February 3, 1850, GREELEY; Philip Greely, Jr., to Weed, June 27, Philo S. Shelton to Weed, June 28, 1850, Weed Papers, ROCHESTER; Jerome Fuller to Millard Fillmore, June 14, 1850, BUFFALO; Thomas Corwin to Crittenden, June 4 [7?], 1850, Crittenden Papers, LC; Weed to George Harrington, June 25, 1850, HUNTINGTON; Robert P. Letcher to Brown, undated, Brown Papers, KENTUCKY.

   4 New York *Express,* May 13, June 13, Washington *Republic,* April 20, 25, May 15, June 17, Washington *National Intelligencer,* May 13, 1850.

   5 E. W. Huntington to John McLean, June 15, McLean Papers, Crittenden to Albert T. Burnley, July 5, Crittenden Papers, Salmon P. Chase to Mrs. Chase, June 4, 9, Chase to E. S. Hamlin, May 27, Chase Papers, Martin Van Buren, Jr., to Martin Van Buren, May 27, 1850, Van Buren Papers, LC; Washington *Republic,* June 17, Washington *Union,* May 29, New York *Express,* June 26, 28, 1850; Lewis Scrapbook, WOOD COLLECTION.

   6 *Congressional Globe Appendix,* 546-548; William P. Brandon, "The Galphin Claim," *Georgia Historical Quarterly,* XV, 114-129; Ulrich B. Phillips, *The Life of Robert Toombs* (1913), 138-142; "Opinions of Attorneys General," Part II, 1838-1851, *House Executive Document 55,* Thirty-first Congress, Second Session, 2088-2091.

   7 Washington *Union,* March 29 *et seq.,* New York *Herald,* April 4, 9, May 17, 18, 19, 26, 1850; Brandon, *loc. cit.,* 123, 129-133; *Congressional Globe Appendix,* 546-556, 616-626, 823-832, 843-848, 886-889, 894-897, 930-935; *Congressional Globe,* 628, 633, 680, 682, 1019-1026, 1280, 1321-1328, 1331, 1340, 1344-1347, 1351-1354; Phillips, *op. cit.,* 141, 144; Robert Toombs to Crittenden, January 9, 1849, Crittenden Papers, LC.

   8 Brown to Crittenden, May 9, 1850, Burnley to Crittenden, May 8, 1850, Crittenden Papers, LC; Lady Emmeline Stuart-Wortley, *Travels in the United States* ... (1851), 86-87; Alexander C. Bullitt to Brown, June 2, 1850, Brown Papers, KENTUCKY.

   9 Frederick W. Seward, *Seward at Washington* ... *1846-1861* (1891), 141; New York *Express,* July 10, New York *Daily Tribune,* May 28, 1850; Adolph B. Benson (editor), *America of the Fifties* ... (1924), 171; James D. Rich-

ardson (editor), *A Compilation of the Messages . . . of the Presidents . . .* (1899), V, 25-49.

[10] Zachary Taylor to H. A. Coolidge, May 13, 1850, collection of John T. Winterich, Ossining, New York; Taylor to Benjamin Matthias and others, June 21, 1850, Historical Society of Pennsylvania, Philadelphia; *Congressional Globe*, 915, 1106-1107; Mrs. William T. Sherman to Mrs. Thomas Ewing, May 4, Mrs. Ewing to Mrs. Sherman, June 8, 1850, Ewing Collection, Landover, Maryland; William A. Butler, *A Retrospect of Forty Years* (1911), 230; Washington *Republic*, April 12, May 25, June 11, 20, July 1, 23, 1850; Washington *National Intelligencer*, April 1, 1850.

[11] Chase to Mrs. Chase, February 13, 1850, Chase Papers, LC; Mrs. Ewing to Mrs. Sherman, May 28, 1850; Ewing Collection, Landover, Maryland; Seward, *op. cit.*, 136; Harriet A. Weed (editor), *Autobiography of Thurlow Weed* (1883), 590-592; John S. Allison to Taylor, June 9, 1850, STAUFFER COLLECTION.

CHAPTER XXVIII

[1] London *Times*, February 5, Washington *Union*, March 1, 1849; Leslie Stephen and Sidney Lee (editors), *Dictionary of National Biography* (1885-1901), VII, 263-265; Sir Henry Lytton Bulwer to Viscount Palmerston, January 6, February 3, 1850, LONDON.

[2] Bulwer to John M. Clayton, February 7, 14, Clayton to Bulwer February 15, 1850, Clayton Papers, LC.

[3] James D. Richardson (editor), *A Compilation of the Messages . . . of the Presidents . . .* (1899), V, 33-40; Bulwer to Palmerston, February 18, 1850, LONDON; Bulwer to Clayton, March 27, 1850, Notes from British Legation, XXVII, State Department Papers, ARCHIVES; Clayton to Bulwer, April 6, draft, April 7, April 8, draft, Bulwer to Clayton, April 9, 1850, Clayton Papers, LC; William M. Malloy (compiler), "Treaties, Conventions, International Acts, Protocols and Agreements Between the United States of America and Other Powers, 1776-1909," *Senate Document 357*, Sixty-first Congress, Second Session, I, 659-663.

[4] Richardson (editor), *op. cit.*, V, 42-44; Bulwer to Clayton, April 19, June 29, 1850, Notes from British Legation, XXVII, State Department Papers, ARCHIVES; New York *Express*, May 1, New York *Herald*, April 8, 12, 16, 25, May 6, Washington *Union*, April 13, 24, 25, 28, May 3, 18, 1850; Clayton to Abbott Lawrence, April 22, 1850, draft, Clayton Papers, LC; *Senate Executive Document 12*, Thirty-second Congress, Second Session, 2-3.

[5] "Correspondence with the United States Respecting Central America," Great Britain, House of Commons, *Sessional Papers*, 1856, LX, 64-65; Clayton to William L. Marcy, May 21, 1856, draft, Clayton Papers, LC; Clayton memorandum, July 5, 1850, on reverse of Bulwer's June 29 declaration, Notes to British Legation, VII, State Department Papers, ARCHIVES; Malloy (compiler), *op. cit.*, I, 659. But see also Richard W. Van Alstyne, "British Diplomacy and the Clayton-Bulwer Treaty, 1850-60," *Journal of Modern History*, XI, 149-161, and "The Central American Policy of Lord Palmerston, 1846-1848," *Hispanic American Historical Review*, XVI, *passim*.

[6] *Congressional Globe*, Thirty-second Congress, Second Session, 391, 414-417, 941, Thirty-third Congress, First Session, 28, 107-110, 148, 160; *Congressional Globe Appendix*, Thirty-second Congress, Second Session, 245-280,

284-290, Thirty-third Congress, First Session, 61-72, 89-103; Clayton to Marcy, May 28, George P. Fisher to Clayton, May 21, 1856, Clayton Papers, LC; John Bigelow, *Breaches of Anglo-American Treaties* . . . (1917), 121-131; J. D. Ward, "Sir Henry Bulwer and the United States Archives," *Cambridge Historical Journal*, III, 304-313; *Senate Executive Document 13*, Thirty-third Congress, First Session, 14-19; Great Britain, House of Commons, *Sessional Papers*, 1856, XI, 64-65.

[7] London *Times*, January 19, 1856; Van Alstyne, *American Diplomacy in Action* (1947), 41-42, 148-159, 523-528, 602, 637, and "British Diplomacy . . . ," *Journal of Modern History*, XI, 161-183.

CHAPTER XXIX

[1] Robert G. Caldwell, *The Lopez Expeditions* . . . (1915), 28-42, 55-67, 79; Chester S. Urban, "New Orleans and the Cuban Question . . . ," *Louisiana Historical Quarterly*, XXII, 1095-1106, 1121-1126; Allen Johnson and Dumas Malone (editors), *Dictionary of American Biography* (1928-1936), XIV, 4-5; Edgar E. Hume, *Colonel Theodore O'Hara* . . . (1936), *passim*.

[2] Urban, *loc. cit.*, XXII, 1126; Caldwell, *op. cit.*, 67-74; Thomas Ewing to Logan Hunton, June 10, 1850, quoted in Caldwell, 77-78.

[3] Caldwell, *op. cit.*, 78-79, 112; Urban, *loc. cit.*, XXII, 1097, 1099, 1121, 1125-1131, 1134.

[4] London *Times*, June 8, 1850; Sir Henry Lytton Bulwer to Viscount Palmerston, May 16, June 3, 1850, LONDON; John M. Clayton to Daniel M. Barringer, August 2, 1849, June 10, July 1, 1850, Instructions, Spain, XIV, Barringer to Clayton, June 19, August 7, 1850, Dispatches, Spain, XXXVI, Angel Calderón de la Barca to Clayton, May 31, June 7, 14, July 2, 1850, Notes from Spanish Legation, XII, Clayton to Calderón, May 18, June 4, 1850, Notes to Spanish Legation, VI, State Department Papers, ARCHIVES; Caldwell, *op. cit.*, 77, 80-81; New Orleans *Bee*, May 14, June 3, 12, New Orleans *Weekly Delta*, June 3, New Orleans *Crescent*, June 1, 4, 1850; *Congressional Globe*, 1030-1035; Hunter Miller (editor), *Treaties and Other International Acts* . . . (1937), V, 591-628.

[5] Washington *National Intelligencer*, September 6, 1849; Aaron H. Palmer to Zachary Taylor, September 11, 1849, Taylor Papers, STAUFFER COLLECTION; Inazo Nitobe, "American-Japanese Intercourse Prior to the Advent of Perry," *Annual Report of the American Historical Association for the Year 1911* (1913), 139; Tyler Dennett, *Americans in Eastern Asia* (1922), 252-253; Clayton to Bulwer, April 24, 1850, draft, Clayton Papers, LC; Clayton to the Chevalier Sergio de Macedo, August 28, 1849, May 13, 1850, Notes to Brazilian Legation, VI, De Macedo to Clayton, April 25, 1850, Notes from Brazilian Legation, III, State Department Papers, ARCHIVES; James D. Richardson (editor), *A Compilation of the Messages . . . of the Presidents . . .* (1899), V, 41; Paul R. Frothingham, *Edward Everett* . . . (1925), 321-324, 359-361; Washington *Union*, April 4, 1850; Merle E. Curti, *Austria and the United States, 1848-1852* (1926), *passim*; Bulwer to Palmerston, June 3, Clayton to Bulwer, May 20, 1850, copy, LONDON.

[6] Clayton to James B. Clay, March 2, 8, 1850, Instructions, Portugal, XIV, James B. Clay to Clayton, January 8, 29, February 18, March 8, 18, April 22, 28, May 8, 18, 28, 30, June 8, 18, 28, July 8, 18, 1850, Dispatches Portugal, XV, State Department Papers, ARCHIVES; Henry Clay to James B.

Clay, December 4, 1849, January 2, 8, March 6, 13, 17, 25, 1850, James B. Clay to Henry Clay, February 2, 18, May 26, June 18, 1850, Thomas J. Clay Papers, LC.

CHAPTER XXX

[1] St. George L. Sioussat, "Tennessee, the Compromise of 1850, and the Nashville Convention," *Mississippi Valley Historical Review*, II, 330-332, 335; Dallas T. Herndon, "The Nashville Convention of 1850," *Alabama Historical Society Transactions*, V, 216-217; Richard H. Shryock, *Georgia and the Union in 1850* (1926), 269-275; Johnson and Malone (editors), *op. cit.*, IV, 20-21, VIII, 207-208, XIV, 559-561, XIX, 36-37; *A Biographical Congressional Directory* . . . (1903), 449, 466, 533, 574, 590, 743; Cleo Hearon, "Mississippi and the Compromise of 1850," *Mississippi Historical Society Publications*, XIV, 47, 63, 78-79, 82, 124; *McMakin's Model American Courier* (Philadelphia), July 6, 1850. The author of the *Courier* article was Joseph Holt Ingraham, a Mississippian.

[2] Nashville *Republican Banner*, June 5, 6, Washington *National Intelligencer*, June 8, July 13, 1850; Herndon, *loc. cit.*, V, 216-226; Hearon, *loc. cit.*, XIV, 126-127; Sioussat, *loc. cit.*, II, 336-337, 339; Cave Johnson to James Buchanan, June 6, 1850, Buchanan Papers, Historical Society of Pennsylvania, Philadelphia; *Congressional Globe Appendix*, 1052.

[3] Hearon, *loc. cit.*, XIV, 126-127, 148-158; Washington *National Intelligencer*, July 13, *National Era* (Washington), June 20, 1850; Sioussat, *loc. cit.*, II, 332, 337.

[4] Francis B. Heitman, *Historical Register and Dictionary of the United States Army* . . . (1890), 483; George W. Cullum, *Biographical Register of the Officers and Graduates* . . . *of West Point* (1879), 94; William C. Binkley, "The Question of Texan Jurisdiction . . . ," *Southwestern Historical Quarterly*, XXIV, 24-27; Johnson and Malone (editors), *op. cit.*, XIII, 407-408; Texas *Senate Journal*, Third Legislature, Second Session, *Appendix*, 1-6, 11-12; Washington *Union*, May 28, 1850; *House Executive Document 66*, Thirty-first Congress, First Session, 2.

[5] Binkley, *loc. cit.*, XXIV, 22-24, 27-35.

[6] *Texas State Gazette* (Austin), June 8, 15, July 13, August 24, 31, 1850; Binkley, *loc. cit.*, XXIV, 30-31, 33-34; New York *Express*, June 17, 1850; *House Executive Document 82*, Thirty-first Congress, First Session, 6-7; Texas *Senate Journal*, Third Legislature, Second Session, *Appendix*, 81-83; Allan Nevins, *Ordeal of the Union* (1947), I, 329; Richardson (editor), *op. cit.*, V, 47-48; *House Executive Document 17*, Thirty-first Congress, First Session, 280-281.

[7] Washington *National Intelligencer*, July 3, 4, Louisville *Journal*, July 13, New York *Express*, July 10, 11, Hartford *Courant*, July 2, Richmond *Republican*, July 9, New York *Tribune*, April 19, May 10, July 9, 1850.

[8] *Congressional Globe*, 1318-1321; Washington *Republic*, July 6, 1850; Lewis Cass to Henry Ledyard, June 13, 1850, CLEMENTS.

[9] Washington *Union*, May 14, 15, Philadelphia *Evening Bulletin*, July 11, Washington *National Intelligencer*, July 4, New York *Express*, July 18, New York *Tribune*, July 10, 1850; *American Historical Review*, VI, 249-252; New York *Herald*, August 8, 1876; Thurlow Weed Barnes, *Memoir of Thurlow Weed* (1884), 176-178, 180-181.

[10] *Congressional Globe*, 1032-1034, 1125-1126, 1130, 1254; *Congressional Globe Appendix*, 480-496, 1041-1049; Carl R. Fish, *The Civil Service and the Patronage* (1920), 163; Washington *Republic*, March 22, April 29, May 18, 20, June 1, 18, 21, New York *Express*, May 21, Washington *Union*, May 28, 1850; Samuel F. Bemis (editor), *The American Secretaries of State . . .* (1927-1929), VI, 71; Orlando Brown to J. J. Crittenden, May 18, 1850, Crittenden Papers, LC; Harriet A. Weed (editor), *Autobiography of Thurlow Weed* (1883), 590-592; Theodore Barnett to Caleb B. Smith, May 14, 1850, Smith Papers, LC; Myrta L. Avary (editor), *Reminiscences of Alexander H. Stephens . . .* (1910), 26-27.

[11] New York *Herald*, July 13, New York *Tribune*, July 9, 16, Richmond *Enquirer*, July 17, Barnes, *op. cit.*, 180-181; *Congressional Globe*, 1346-1347, 1351; Henry W. Hilliard, *Politics and Pen Pictures . . .* (1892), 231; Cass to Ledyard, June 13, 1850, CLEMENTS; New York *Herald-Tribune*, February 19, 1950; Henry A. Wise, *Seven Decades of the Union . . .* (1881), 241-242; Charles F. Adams, Jr., *Charles Francis Adams* (1900), 102-104; [Thomas H. Benton], *Thirty Years' View . . .* (1854-1856), II, 740, 765-766; William H. Seward to Weed, December 3, 1848, Weed Papers, ROCHESTER. Indications of Taylor's growing strength are evident in [Mary Mann], *Life of Horace Mann* (1891), 292, 305, 307, and in Salmon P. Chase to Mrs. Chase, June 1, 1850, Chase Papers, LC.

CHAPTER XXXI

[1] Zachary Taylor to Richard Taylor, June 12, William W. S. Bliss to Richard Taylor, August 8, 1850, STAUFFER COLLECTION; Conveyance Book A, 32-46, Saint Charles Parish, Hahnville, Louisiana; New York *Express*, July 15, 1850.

[2] Washington *Republic*, June 28, July 1, 2, New York *Express*, July 10, 11, 12, 16, 17, Washington *National Intelligencer*, July 6, 1850; Henry S. Foote, *Casket of Reminiscences* (1874), 167; Joshua R. Giddings to Miss Laura Giddings, July 14, George W. Julian to Mrs. Julian, July 9, Julian Papers, Richard W. Thompson to Harvey D. Scott, July 14, 1850, Thompson Papers, INDIANA; J. S. Chambers, *The Conquest of Cholera* (1938), 197-200, 203-206, 211-218, 224-238, 242-253; William H. Seward to Thurlow Weed, July 11, 1850, Weed Papers, ROCHESTER; *St. Joseph Valley Register* (South Bend), July 25, 1850. Clark and the Thompson girl died.

[3] Philadelphia *Bulletin*, July 11, New York *Express*, July 11, 12, Washington *National Intelligencer*, July 12, 1850; Foote, *op. cit.*, 167-168; Millard Fillmore to John Neafie, May 17, 1873, copy, BUFFALO; Giddings to Miss Giddings, July 14, Julian to Mrs. Julian, July 9, Julian Papers, INDIANA; analyses of two physicians, Dr. Allen Hamilton of La Jolla, California, and Dr. Paul L. Stier of Fort Wayne, Indiana; Zachary Taylor to H. S. Favor, July 5, 1850, HAMILTON COLLECTION; William M. Malloy (compiler), "Treaties, Conventions, International Acts, Protocols and Agreements Between the United States of America and Other Powers, 1776-1909," *Senate Document 357*, Sixty-first Congress, Second Session, I, 659.

[4] New York *Express*, July 10, 12, Philadelphia *Bulletin*, July 11, Washington *Republic*, Washington *National Intelligencer*, July 9, Louisville *Journal*, July 10, 1850; D. S. Lamb and others, *The History of the Medical Society of*

the District of Columbia, 1817-1909 (1909), 228; Lewis Scrapbook, WOOD COLLECTION.

[5] *Congressional Globe Appendix*, 829-832, 930-935, 1088-1106, 1173-1186; *Congressional Globe*, 1346-1347, 1351, 1360, 1362-1363; New York *Express*, July 9, 12, 13, 1850; Joseph H. Parks, *John Bell of Tennessee* (1950), 253-259.

[6] Philadelphia *Bulletin*, July 11, Louisville *Journal*, July 10, New York *Express*, July 10, 11, 1850; Lewis Scrapbook, WOOD COLLECTION.

[7] Washington *National Intelligencer*, July 11, *Indiana State Sentinel* (Indianapolis), August 1, New York *Tribune*, July 12, 15, New York *Herald*, July 14, Washington *Republic*, July 11, 16, Washington *Union*, July 16, New York *Express*, July 11, 13, 1850; statement of Mrs. S. G. Haven, BUFFALO; James D. Richardson (editor), *A Compilation of the Messages . . . of the Presidents . . .* (1899), V, 51; Frank H. Severance (editor), "Millard Fillmore Papers," *Publications of the Buffalo Historical Society*, X, xliii-xliv, 1-15; *Congressional Globe*, 1363-1366.

[8] New York *Express*, July 11-13, 16, New York *Tribune*, July 10, Hartford *Courant*, Philadelphia *Inquirer*, Richmond *Whig*, Richmond *Republican*, Augusta *Chronicle*, July 11, Nashville *Republican Banner*, New Orleans *Picayune*, July 15, Washington *Union*, July 16, 1850; Francis P. Blair to Martin Van Buren, July 15, Van Buren Papers, Salmon P. Chase to Mrs. Chase, July 13, Chase Papers, F. Ball to John McLean, July 10, W. G. Ewing to Caleb B. Smith, July 18, 1850, Smith Papers, LC.

[9] Alvah Hunt to Weed, July 28, 1850, Weed Papers, ROCHESTER; Leonard P. Rising to Fillmore, July 10, 1850, BUFFALO; New York *Express*, July 12, 13, 15, 16, 18, *St. Joseph Valley Register* (South Bend), July 25, Washington *National Intelligencer*, July 12, 15, Washington *Union*, July 16, 1850.

[10] Fillmore to Mrs. Zachary Taylor, July 10, 1850, draft, BUFFALO; New York *Express*, July 13, 16, Washington *National Intelligencer*, July 15, 1850; Frederick W. Seward, *Seward at Washington . . . 1846-1861* (1891), 147; statement of the late Mrs. Walter R. Stauffer to the author; Robert C. Wood to William M. Meredith, July 24, 1850, PENNSYLVANIA; William W. S. Bliss to Richard Taylor, August 8, with enclosures, October 18, 1850, January 10, 1853, "Agreement & Settlement between the Widow & Heirs of Genl Zachary Taylor" and "Partition between the Heirs of Genl Zachary Taylor," copies notarized by Adolphe Mazureau, STAUFFER COLLECTION; New Orleans *Picayune*, New Orleans *Commercial Bulletin*, August 17, 1852; New Orleans newspaper clipping, Lewis Scrapbook, WOOD COLLECTION. Mrs. Taylor died at East Pascagoula, Mississippi, August 14, 1852.

[11] Holman Hamilton, *Zachary Taylor: Soldier of the Republic* (1941), 25-33, 37, 47, 57-59, 64, 74-77, 81-82, 142; Zachary Taylor to Joseph P. Taylor, July 7, 1848, John S. Allison to Zachary Taylor, November 19, 1849, with enclosure, STAUFFER COLLECTION; Baltimore *Sun*, October 26, Louisville *Journal*, October 26, 31, November 1, 2, 1850.

CHAPTER XXXII

[1] Salmon P. Chase to Mrs. Chase, July 13, Chase Papers, Francis P. Blair to Martin Van Buren, July 15, Van Buren Papers, Theodore Barnett to Caleb B. Smith, July 15, Smith Papers, Henry Clay to Thomas H. Clay, August 6, 1850, Thomas J. Clay Papers, LC; Hannibal Hamlin to unknown, July 19,

1850, HUNTINGTON; Daniel Webster, memorandum to Millard Fillmore, [July, 1850], BUFFALO; New York *Express,* July 12, 16, 18, 23, 1850; Robert C. Winthrop, Jr., *A Memoir of Robert C. Winthrop* (1897), 128-133; Orsamus B. Matteson to Thurlow Weed, July 14, 1850, Weed Papers, ROCHESTER; Mrs. Chapman Coleman, *The Life of John J. Crittenden* (1871), I, 374-375.

² Washington *Union,* July 21, New York *Express,* July 23, 1850; Allen Johnson and Dumas Malone (editors), *Dictionary of American Biography* (1928-1936), XII, 89, XVIII, 160; Charles E. Clarke to Weed, July 29, 1850, Weed Papers, ROCHESTER; *Congressional Globe Appendix,* 1470-1485; *Congressional Globe,* 1504; Glyndon G. Van Deusen, *The Life of Henry Clay* (1937), 412-414; Stephen A. Douglas to Charles H. Lanphier and George Walker, August 3, 1850, original in possession of Dr. Charles L. Patton, Springfield, Illinois.

³ *Congressional Globe,* 1555, 1573, 1589, 1647, 1659-1660, 1682-1687, 1762-1765, 1769-1777, 1784, 1806-1807, 1829-1830, 1837, 2072, 2074; Ben: Perley Poore, *Perley's Reminiscences* . . . (1886), I, 384-385; Allan Nevins, *Ordeal of the Union* (1947), I, 343.

⁴ John B. McMaster, *A History of the People of the United States* . . . (1913), VIII, 19, 38, 40-41, 45-48; James T. Adams (editor), *Dictionary of American History* (1940), II, 354-355; St. George L. Sioussat, "Tennessee, the Compromise of 1850, and the Nashville Convention." *Mississippi Valley Historical Review,* II, 342-347; Richard H. Shryock, *Georgia and the Union in 1850* (1926), 319-337, 350-354; Cleo Hearon, "Mississippi and the Compromise of 1850," *Mississippi Historical Society Publications,* XIV, 201-216; Edward Channing, *A History of the United States* (1926-1927), VI, 76-78, 86; George P. Garrison, *Westward Extension, 1841-1850* (1906), 315-317, 329; Jesse Macy, *The Anti-Slavery Crusade* . . . (1919), 105-107; James F. Rhodes, *History of the United States* . . . (1893-1906), I, 175-181; Nevins, *op. cit.,* I, 335-336; Avery Craven, *The Coming of the Civil War* (1942), 259; Samuel E. Morison and Henry S. Commager, *The Growth of the American Republic* (1942), I, 603-607.

⁵ Charles A. Beard and Mary R. Beard, *The Rise of American Civilization* (1935), I, 713-717, *A Basic History of the United States* (1944), 251-252, 257; Charles A. Beard, *The Presidents in American History* (1935), 63-64.

⁶ Albert J. Beveridge, *Abraham Lincoln, 1809-1858* (1928), II, 71-135. Beveridge's failure is the more remarkable because of the space he devotes to the compromise debates. One of his most amazing omissions, considering Hamlin's later link with Lincoln, is that of Hamlin's reply to Calhoun.

⁷ The policy shift in the change-over from Harrison to Tyler has been repeatedly and properly stressed. However, it was neither so immediate nor so dramatic as that of 1850.

⁸ Arthur M. Schlesinger, *Paths to the Present* (1949), 95-99; Elizabeth F. Hoxie to the author, January 24, 1949. Fifty-five historians took part in the Schlesinger symposium; one did not vote on Taylor, due to the brevity of his presidential service.

⁹ This opinion is shared by Professors Wendell H. Stephenson, Tulane University; John D. Barnhart, Indiana University, and Robert R. Russel, Western Michigan College of Education, Kalamazoo.

¹⁰ Frank H. Hodder, "The Authorship of the Compromise of 1850," *Mississippi Valley Historical Review,* XXII, 534-535; *Congressional Globe,* 1555;

James D. Richardson (editor), *A Compilation of the Messages . . . of the Presidents . . .* (1899), V, 67-73; Carl Schurz, *Life of Henry Clay* (1887), II, 369, 371; George F. Milton, *The Eve of Conflict . . .* (1934), 78; Herbert D. Foster, "Webster's Seventh of March Speech and the Secession Movement, 1850," *American Historical Review*, XXVII, 268-269; Elizabeth F. Hoxie to the author, January 24, 1949.

[11] During the '48 campaign, Corwin sought to convince "the people of Ohio . . . that Gen. Taylor is a Wilmot provisoist, by intimations that he has in his possession a private letter to that effect. Thomas Ewing so declares & Mr. Corwin does not deny it." (George M. Swan to Van Buren, October 17, 1848, Van Buren Papers, LC.)

[12] John C. Calhoun to Henry Gourdin, January 8, Armistead Burt to Henry W. Conner, February 18, Calhoun to Conner, July 9, 1848, Conner Papers, Charleston Library Society; Ellwood Fisher to Calhoun, February 26, A. B. Longstreet to Calhoun, July 4, Calhoun to Eustis Prescott, Jr., July 15, R. K. Crallé to Calhoun, July 23, 1848, Calhoun Papers, Clemson College, South Carolina; John J. Crittenden to Waddy Thompson, October 2, 1848, HAMILTON COLLECTION; Philip M. Hamer, *The Secession Movement in South Carolina, 1847-1852* (1918), 19-21. Charles M. Wiltse, Washington, has been especially helpful on this problem.

[13] Rhodes, *op. cit.*, I, 102. A more accurate statement is: "Seward's influence with President Taylor was strong" (David S. Muzzey, *The United States of America* [1922-1924], 453-454).

[14] Thomas H. Benton, *Thirty Years' View . . .* (1854-1856), II, 765-766; Theodore Roosevelt, *Thomas Hart Benton* (1899), 299; James G. Blaine, *Twenty Years of Congress* (1884-1886), I, 95; Joseph M. Rogers, *The True Henry Clay* (1905), 355; Andrew C. McLaughlin, *Lewis Cass* (1899), 281-282; Sioussat, *loc. cit.*, II, 347.

[15] New York *Express*, July 18, 1850; M. R. Werner, *Brigham Young* (1925), 378-379; Blair to Van Buren, July 15, 1850, Van Buren Papers, LC; Calvin Colton (editor), *Works of Henry Clay . . .* (1897), IV, 610-611; *Congressional Globe*, 1367-1368; Dunbar Rowland (editor), *Jefferson Davis: Constitutionalist* (1923), I, 101, 190; Paul M. Angle (editor), *New Letters and Papers of Lincoln* (1930), 74-75; *American Historical Review*, XXXII, 553-554.

BIBLIOGRAPHY

[The author has excluded from this bibliography numerous books, articles and manuscript collections consulted in the course of his research, which failed to survive critical examination or added nothing to less limited citations. Only those published and unpublished sources, which materially strengthened the documentation, are listed below. Contributions of individuals and institutions appear in the section headed "Personal Acknowledgments."]

MANUSCRIPT SOURCES

Public Collections

Boston Public Library, Appleton-Sumner Correspondence and Rufus W. Griswold Papers.

Buffalo Historical Society, Millard Fillmore Papers.

Charleston Library Society, Henry W. Conner Papers.

William L. Clements Library, University of Michigan, Ann Arbor, Lewis Cass Papers.

Clemson College, South Carolina, John C. Calhoun Papers.

Duke University, Durham, North Carolina, Campbell Family Papers.

East Baton Rouge Parish, Baton Rouge, Louisiana, marriage records.

Feliciana (now West Feliciana) Parish, Saint Francisville, Louisiana, land records.

Filson Club Archives, Louisville, Papers of Orlando Brown, Mrs. Jouett Taylor Cannon and Charles S. Todd.

Hayes Memorial Library, Fremont, Ohio, miscellaneous manuscripts.

Historical and Philosophical Society of Ohio, Cincinnati, Thomas B. Stevenson Papers.

Historical Society of Delaware, Wilmington, Zachary Taylor Papers.

Historical Society of Pennsylvania, Philadelphia, Papers of James Buchanan, William M. Meredith, and Zachary Taylor.

Henry E. Huntington Library, San Marino, California, Gideon Welles's Unpublished Diary, and Papers of Hannibal Hamlin, Lewis C. Levin, Pegram-Johnson Family (Brock Collection), Zachary Taylor and Thurlow Weed.

Illinois State Historical Library, Springfield, Patton Papers.

Indiana Historical Society, Indianapolis, Calvin Fletcher's Unpublished Diary.

Indiana State Library, Indianapolis, Papers of Allen Hamilton, George W. Julian, Godlove S. Orth and Richard W. Thompson.

Jefferson County, Fayette, Mississippi, land records.

Jefferson County, Louisville, Kentucky, land records.

Kentucky Historical Society, Frankfort, Orlando Brown Papers, and Jefferson County, Kentucky, tax books.

Library of Congress, Washington, Papers of John M. Berrien, Robert J. Breckinridge, Salmon P. Chase, Henry Clay, Thomas J. Clay, John M. Clayton, John J. Crittenden, Franklin H. Elmore, Thomas Ewing, Millard Fillmore, James H. Hammond, William H. Harrison, John McLean, Willie P. Mangum, William C. Rives, Caleb B. Smith, Zachary Taylor, Martin Van Buren, Daniel Webster and Thurlow Weed.

Lincoln National Life Foundation, Fort Wayne, Indiana, Papers of Zachary Taylor and Richard W. Thompson.

Massachusetts Historical Society, Boston, Papers of Edward Everett and William H. Prescott.

Minnesota Historical Society, Saint Paul, Alexander Ramsey Papers.

Mississippi Department of Archives and History, Jackson, land and assessment records.

National Archives, Washington, State Department and War Department, official records.

New Hampshire Historical Society, Concord, Papers of John P. Hale and Daniel Webster.

New-York Historical Society, New York City, Horace Greeley Papers.

Public Record Office, London, Foreign Office Papers. (Microfilm at the Library of Congress.)

Saint Charles Parish, Hahnville, Louisiana, land records.

Texas State Library, Austin, official records.

University of Chicago, Godfrey T. Anderson, "The Slavery Issue as a Factor in Massachusetts Politics from the Compromise of 1850 to the Outbreak of the Civil War" (Unpublished University of Chicago doctoral dissertation).

University of North Carolina, Chapel Hill, Southern Historical Collection.

University of Rochester, Papers of George W. Patterson, William H. Seward and Thurlow Weed.

Western Kentucky State College, Bowling Green, Warner L. Underwood's Diary.

West Feliciana Parish, Saint Francisville, Louisiana, land records.

Wilkinson County, Woodville, Mississippi, land records.

Wisconsin State Historical Society, Madison, Lyman C. Draper Papers.

Woodford County, Versailles, Kentucky, land records.

PRIVATE COLLECTIONS

R. Alexander Bate, Louisville.
C. Douglass Buck, New Castle County, Delaware.
William Marshall Bullitt, Louisville.
Preston Davie, New York City.
Miss Eleanor S. Ewing, Landover, Maryland.
Henry N. Flynt, New York City.
Holman Hamilton, Fort Wayne, Indiana.
Foreman M. Lebold, Chicago.
Charles L. Patton, Springfield, Illinois.
Miss Minnie K. Ringgold, Shreveport, Louisiana.
The late Andrew M. Sea, Jr., Louisville.
The late Mrs. Walter R. Stauffer, New Orleans.
Mrs. Stanley Stillman, Jr., San Francisco.
Miss Mabel C. Walker, Versailles, Kentucky.
Carl White, Jr., Tulsa, Oklahoma.

John T. Winterich, Ossining, New York.
Miss Lola M. Wood, Maddox, Saint Mary's County, Maryland.
Trist Wood, New Orleans.

PRINTED SOURCES

NEWSPAPERS

Albany *Evening Journal,* 1846-1850.
Augusta *Chronicle and Sentinel,* 1849-1850.
Baltimore *American,* 1849.
Baltimore *Clipper,* 1849.
Baltimore *Patriot and Commercial Gazette,* 1849.
Baltimore *Sun,* 1848-1850.
The Battery (Washington), 1848-1849.
Boston *Daily Atlas,* 1848-1850.
Boston *Daily Courier,* 1849-1850.
Boston *Post,* 1849.
Brownlow's Knoxville Whig and Independent Journal, 1850.
Buffalo *Commercial Advertiser,* 1848-1849.
Buffalo *Daily Courier,* 1849-1850.
Buffalo *Express,* 1848-1849.
Buffalo *Republic,* 1848.
The Campaign (Washington), 1848.
Charleston *Courier,* 1848-1849.
Charleston *Mercury,* 1848-1850.
Cincinnati *Enquirer,* 1849.
Cist's Weekly Advertiser (Cincinnati), 1848.
Cleveland *Weekly Plain Dealer,* 1850.
Erie *Gazette,* 1849.
Erie *Weekly Observer,* 1849.
Frankfort *Daily Commonwealth,* 1849.
Hartford *Courant,* 1849-1850.
Illinois State Journal (Springfield), 1849.
Illinois State Register (Springfield), 1849.
Indiana State Journal (Indianapolis), 1848-1850.
Indiana State Sentinel (Indianapolis), 1848-1850.
Kentucky Yeoman (Frankfort), 1849.
Lawrence Journal (New Castle, Pennsylvania), 1849.
Lexington *Observer and Reporter,* 1848-1849.
Lexington *Tri-Weekly Atlas,* 1848.
The Liberator (Boston), 1848-1850.
Louisville *Daily Courier,* 1849.
Louisville *Daily Journal,* 1849-1850.
Louisville *Weekly Courier,* 1848-1849.
Lower Sandusky *Freeman,* 1849.
McMakin's Model American Courier (Philadelphia), 1850.
Maysville (Kentucky) *Eagle,* 1847.
Memphis *Tri-Weekly Appeal,* 1849.
Mississippi Free Trader (Natchez), 1848-1849.
Morning Courier and New York Enquirer (New York), 1848-1850.

Mount Vernon (Ohio) *Democratic Banner*, 1850.
Nashville *Union*, 1850.
Natchez *Weekly Courier*, 1849.
National Era (Washington), 1848-1851.
New Hampshire Patriot and State Gazette (Concord), 1849 1850.
New Orleans *Bee*, 1850.
New Orleans *Commercial Bulletin*, 1850.
New Orleans *Courier*, 1849.
New Orleans *Crescent*, 1848-1850.
New Orleans *Daily Picayune*, 1848-1850.
New Orleans *Delta*, 1848.
New Orleans *Times-Picayune*, January 25, 1937.
New Orleans *Weekly Delta*, 1848, 1850.
New Orleans *Weekly Picayune*, 1848-1850.
New York *Daily Tribune*, 1848-1850.
New York *Evening Mirror*, 1846.
New York *Evening Post*, 1848-1850.
New York *Herald*, 1847-1850; August 8, 1876.
New York *Herald-Tribune*, February 19, 1950.
New York *Journal of Commerce*, 1848.
New York *Morning Express*, 1849-1850.
New York *Sun*, June 5, 1893.
New York *Times*, May 3, 1860; October 20, 1906.
New York *Weekly Tribune*, 1849.
Ohio State Journal (Columbus), 1848-1849.
Pennsylvania Inquirer and Daily Courier (Philadelphia), 1849-1850.
Philadelphia *Evening Bulletin*, 1849-1850.
Philadelphia *North American*, February 4, 1912.
Philadelphia *North American and United States Gazette*, 1848-1850.
Philadelphia *Pennsylvanian*, 1848-1850.
Philadelphia *Public Ledger and Daily Transcript*, 1848-1850.
Philadelphia *Sunday Dispatch*, 1847.
Pittsburgh *Gazette*, 1849.
Poughkeepsie *Eagle*, June 18, 1842.
Republican Banner and Nashville Whig (Nashville), 1849-1850.
Richmond *Daily Republican*, 1849-1850.
Richmond *Daily Whig*, 1850.
Richmond *Enquirer*, 1850.
Richmond *Times*, 1850.
Richmond *Times-Dispatch*, September 30, 1934.
St. Joseph Valley Register (South Bend, Indiana), 1848, 1850.
Semi-Weekly Natchez Courier, 1848.
Shelby News (Shelbyville, Kentucky), 1849.
Springfield (Massachusetts) *Republican*, October 14, 1933.
Texas State Gazette (Austin), 1850.
The Times (London), 1849-1850.
Washington *National Intelligencer*, December 17, 1844; 1847-1850.
Washington *National Whig*, 1848-1849.
Washington *Republic*, 1849-1851.
Washington *Union*, 1848-1850.
Wheeling *Gazette*, 1849.

BOOKS, PERIODICALS AND PUBLISHED DOCUMENTS

Annie H. Abel (editor), *Official Correspondence of James S. Calhoun* (1915).

Charles F. Adams (editor), *Memoirs of John Quincy Adams . . . ,* 12 volumes (1874-1877).

Charles F. Adams, Jr., *Charles Francis Adams* (1900).

[Henry Adams], *The Education of Henry Adams* (1918).

James T. Adams, *America's Tragedy* (1934).

James T. Adams (editor), *Dictionary of American History,* 5 volumes (1940).

Agriculture of the United States in 1860, Compiled from the Original Returns of the Eighth Census . . . (1864).

DeAlva S. Alexander, *A Political History of the State of New York,* 3 volumes (1906-1909).

Holmes Alexander, *The American Tallyrand: The Career and Contemporaries of Martin Van Buren, Eighth President* (1935).

Charles H. Ambler, *Thomas Ritchie: A Study in Virginia Politics* (1913).

American Book-Prices Current (1906, 1913, 1915).

American Historical Review, VI, XXXII.

Nels Anderson, *Desert Saints: The Mormon Frontier in Utah* (1942).

Paul M. Angle (editor), *New Letters and Papers of Lincoln* (1930).

Katharine Anthony, *Dolly Madison: Her Life and Times* (1949).

The Autograph (New York), I.

Myrta L. Avary (editor), *Reminiscences of Alexander H. Stephens . . .* (1910).

[Roger S. Baldwin], *Speech of Hon. R. S. Baldwin, at a Whig Meeting Held at the Exchange Hall, in the City of New Haven, on the 8th of September, 1848* (1848).

Frederic Bancroft, *The Life of William H. Seward,* 2 volumes (1900).

George Bancroft, "A Few Words about Henry Clay," *Century Magazine,* XXX.

Hubert H. Bancroft, *History of California,* 7 volumes (1884-1890).

Thurlow Weed Barnes, *Memoir of Thurlow Weed* (1884).

Roy P. Basler (editor), *Abraham Lincoln: His Speeches and Writings* (1946).

John S. Bassett, *The Southern Plantation Overseer as Revealed in His Letters* (1925).

W. V. N. Bay, *The Bench and Bar of Missouri* (1878).

Charles A. Beard, *The Presidents in American History* (1935).

Charles A. Beard and Mary R. Beard, *A Basic History of the United States* (1944).

Charles A. Beard and Mary R. Beard, *The Rise of American Civilization,* 2 volumes bound together (1935).

Samuel F. Bemis (editor), *The American Secretaries of State and Their Diplomacy,* 10 volumes (1927-1929).

Adolph B. Benson (editor), *America of the Fifties: Letters of Fredrika Bremer* (1924).

[Thomas H. Benton], *Thirty Years' View . . . ,* 2 volumes (1854-1856).

Albert J. Leveridge, *Abraham Lincoln, 1809-1858,* 2 volumes (1928).

John Bigelow, *Breaches of Anglo-American Treaties: A Study in History and Diplomacy* (1917).

Wilfred H. Binkley, *American Political Parties: Their Natural History* (1943).

William C. Binkley, "The Question of Texan Jurisdiction in New Mexico under the United States, 1848-1850," *Southwestern Historical Quarterly,* XXIV.

Charles C. Binney, *The Life of Horace Binney* (1903).

A Biographical Congressional Directory, 1774 to 1903 (1903).

The Biographical Cyclopaedia . . . of the State of Ohio, 6 volumes (1883-1895).

James G. Blaine, *Twenty Years of Congress,* 2 volumes (1884-1886).

Theodore C. Blegen, "James Wickes Taylor: A Biographical Sketch," *Minnesota History Bulletin,* I.

Chauncey S. Boucher, "Sectionalism, Representation and the Electoral Question in Ante-Bellum South Carolina," *Washington University Studies,* IV.

Claude G. Bowers, *The Party Battles of the Jackson Period* (1922).

William P. Brandon, "The Galphin Claim," *Georgia Historical Quarterly,* XV.

Irving Brant, *James Madison: Father of the Constitution, 1787-1800* (1950).

Robert P. Brooks, "Howell Cobb and the Crisis of 1850," *Mississippi Valley Historical Review,* IV.

J. Ross Browne, *Report of the Debates in the Convention of California* (1849).

Wilhelmus B. Bryan, *A History of the National Capital,* 2 volumes (1914-1916).

William J. Bryan, *The First Battle* (1896).

George W. Bungay, *Off-hand Takings; or Crayon Sketches of the Noticeable Men of Our Age* (1854).

Martha A. Burnley, "Albert Triplett Burnley," *Texas State Historical Association Quarterly,* XIV.

Samuel C. Busey, *Personal Reminiscences and Recollections* (1895).

William A. Butler, *A Retrospect of Forty Years* (1911).

Joshua W. Caldwell, *Sketches of the Bench and Bar of Tennessee* (1898).

Robert G. Caldwell, *The Lopez Expeditions to Cuba, 1848-1851* (1915).

Robert Cantwell, *Nathaniel Hawthorne: The American Years* (1948).

Rita K. Carey, "Samuel Jarvis Peters," *Louisiana Historical Quarterly,* XXX.

Harry J. Carman and Reinhard H. Luthin, "The Seward-Fillmore Feud and the Crisis of 1850," *New York History,* XXIV.

E. Malcolm Carroll, *Origins of the Whig Party* (1925).

Clarence E. Carter (editor), *The Territorial Papers of the United States,* 16 volumes (1934——).

John W. Caughey, *California* (1947).

J. S. Chambers, *The Conquest of Cholera* (1938).

Edward Channing, *A History of the United States,* 6 volumes (1926-1927).

Oliver P. Chitwood, *John Tyler: Champion of the Old South* (1939).

Freeman Cleaves, *Old Tippecanoe: William Henry Harrison and His Time* (1939).

Robert G. Cleland, *A History of California: The American Period* (1922).

Margaret L. Coit, *John C. Calhoun: American Portrait* (1950).

Arthur C. Cole, *The Whig Party in the South* (1913).

Mrs. Chapman Coleman, *The Life of John J. Crittenden*, 2 volumes (1871).

The Collector (New York), September, 1938.

Calvin Colton (editor), *Works of Henry Clay . . .*, 7 volumes (1897).

Joseph P. Comegys, *Memoir of John M. Clayton* (1882).

The Commercial Advertiser Directory for the City of Buffalo (1849).

The Commercial Review (New Orleans). See *DeBow's Review*.

The Commercial Review of the South and West (New Orleans). See *DeBow's Review*.

Congressional Globe, Thirtieth Congress, Thirty-first Congress, and Thirty-second Congress.

Congressional Globe Appendix, Thirtieth and Thirty-first Congresses.

Fayette Copeland, *Kendall of the Picayune* (1943).

"Correspondence with the United States Respecting Central America," Great Britain, House of Commons, *Sessional Papers*, 1856, LX.

Avery Craven, *The Coming of the Civil War* (1942).

Lee F. Crippen, *Simon Cameron: Ante-Bellum Years* (1942).

W. A. Croffut (editor), *Fifty Years in Camp and Field, the Diary of Major-General Ethan Allen Hitchcock, U.S.A.* (1909).

George W. Cullum, *Biographical Register of the Officers and Graduates . . . of West Point* (1897).

Richard N. Current, *Old Thad Stevens: A Story of Ambition* (1942).

Merle E. Curti, *Austria and the United States, 1848-1852* (1926).

George T. Curtis, *Life of Daniel Webster*, 2 volumes (1870).

Theodore L. Cuyler, *Recollections of a Long Life* (1902).

Thomas E. Dabney, *One Hundred Great Years: The Story of the Times-Picayune from Its Founding to 1940* (1944).

Madelene V. Dahlgren, "Samuel Finley Vinton," *Ohio Archaeological and Historical Society Publications*, IV.

Jackson B. Davis, "The Life of Richard Taylor," *Louisiana Historical Quarterly*, XXIV.

[Varina Davis], *Jefferson Davis . . . A Memoir*, 2 volumes (1890).

Elizabeth L. Dean, *Dolly Madison, The Nation's Hostess* (1928).

DeBow's Review (New Orleans), IV, VI, VIII, XIV, XXV. This magazine was published under various names. Volumes IV, VI, and VIII are cited in the notes under *The Commercial Review* and *The Commercial Review of the South and West*, depending on the title of the issue in question.

Tyler Dennett, *Americans in Eastern Asia* (1922).

H. D. A. Donovan, *The Barnburners* (1925).

J. W. Du Bose, *William Lowndes Yancey* (1892).

Oliver Dyer, *Great Senators of the United States Forty Years Ago* (1889).

Wilhelmine M. Easby-Smith, *Personal Recollections of Early Washington and a Sketch of the Life of Captain William Easby* (1913).

Charles W. Elliott, *Winfield Scott: The Soldier and the Man* (1937).

Lucius Q. C. Elmer, *The Constitution and Government of . . . New Jersey . . . and Reminiscences of the Bench and Bar, During More Than Half a Century* (1872).

Thomas Ewing, "Lincoln and the General Land Office, 1849," *Journal of the Illinois State Historical Society*, XXV.

Carl R. Fish, *The Civil Service and the Patronage* (1920).

Carl R. Fish, "Removals of Officials by the Presidents of the United States," *Annual Report of the American Historical Association for the Year 1899* (1900), I.

Carl R. Fish, *The Rise of the Common Man, 1830-1850* (1944).

The Flying Quill (Boston), June, 1948.

Henry S. Foote, *Casket of Reminiscences* (1874).

William Q. Force, *Picture of Washington and Vicinity* (1848).

Earle R. Forrest, *History of Washington County, Pennsylvania*, 3 volumes (1926).

Herbert D. Foster, "Webster's Seventh of March Speech and the Secession Movement, 1850," *American Historical Review*, XXVII.

Hugh R. Fraser, *Democracy in the Making: The Jackson-Tyler Era* (1938).

Douglas S. Freeman, *R. E. Lee*, 4 volumes (1934-1935).

Paul R. Frothingham, *Edward Everett: Orator and Statesman* (1925).

Claude M. Fuess, *Daniel Webster*, 2 volumes (1930).

J. F. C. Fuller, *Decisive Battles: Their Influence upon History and Civilisation* (1940).

George P. Garrison, *Westward Extension, 1841-1850* (1906).

Sister M. Theophane Geary, *A History of Third Parties in Pennsylvania, 1840-1860* (1938).

General Taylor's Letters: Letters of Gen. Taylor to Gen. Gaines—Secretary Marcy's Reprimand of Gen. Taylor—and Gen. Taylor's Reply: with the Fable Alluded to Annexed (1847?).

"General Taylor's Residence at Baton Rouge," *Harpers New Monthly Magazine*, IX.

L. A. Gobright, *Recollection of Men and Things at Washington* (1869).

Dorothy B. Goebel, *William Henry Harrison: A Political Biography* (1926).

Cardinal Goodwin, *The Establishment of State Government in California, 1846-1850* (1914).

Marian Gouverneur, *As I Remember* (1911).

Claudius B. Grant, "Life and Character of Alpheus Felch," *Michigan Pioneer and Historical Society Collections*, XXVIII.

[Horace Greeley], *The Autobiography of Horace Greeley . . .* (1872).

James K. Greer, "Louisiana Politics, 1845-1861," *Louisiana Historical Quarterly*, XII.

G. W. Griffin, *Memoir of Col. Chas. S. Todd* (1873).

William E. Griffis, *Millard Fillmore . . .* (1915).

James Hadden, *History of Uniontown . . . Pennsylvania* (1913).

Walter P. Hall and William S. Davis, *The Course of Europe Since Waterloo* (1941).

Philip M. Hamer, *The Secession Movement in South Carolina, 1847-1852* (1918).

Holman Hamilton, *Zachary Taylor: Soldier of the Republic* (1941).

Charles E. Hamlin, *The Life and Times of Hannibal Hamlin . . .* (1899).

Morris H. Hansen (compiler), *Statistical Abstract of the United States* (1946).

Nathaniel Hawthorne, *The Scarlet Letter* (Old Manse Edition, 1900).

Carlton J. H. Hayes, *A Political and Cultural History of Modern Europe* (1939).

George H. Haynes, *Charles Sumner* (1909).

George H. Haynes, " 'President of the United States for a Single Day,' " *American Historical Review*, XXX.

Cleo Hearon, "Mississippi and the Compromise of 1850," *Mississippi Historical Society Publications*, XIV.

Francis B. Heitman, *Historical Register and Dictionary of the United States Army, from . . . September 29, 1789, to September 29, 1889* (1890).

Burton J. Hendrick, *Lincoln's War Cabinet* (1946).

"Henry Clay as an Orator," *Putnam's Monthly Magazine*, III.

Hilary A. Herbert, "Alabama in Federal Politics," in *Memorial Record of Alabama*, 2 volumes (1893).

Dallas T. Herndon, "The Nashville Convention of 1850," *Alabama Historical Society Transactions*, V.

Henry W. Hilliard, *Politics and Pen Pictures at Home and Abroad* (1892).

George F. Hoar, *Autobiography of Seventy Years*, 2 volumes (1903).

Frank H. Hodder, "The Authorship of the Compromise of 1850," *Mississippi Valley Historical Review*, XXII.

Laura C. Holloway, *The Ladies of the White House* (1882).

Hermann von Holst, *John C. Calhoun* (1899).

Edgar A. Holt, "Party Politics in Ohio, 1840-1850," *Ohio Archaeological and Historical Society Publications*, XXXVIII.

Robert D. Holt, "The Political Career of William A. Richardson," *Illinois State Historical Society Journal*, XXVI.

House Executive Document 4, 5, 17, 66, 82, Thirty-first Congress, First Session.

House Executive Document 70, Thirtieth Congress, First Session.

M. A. DeWolfe Howe, *The Life and Letters of George Bancroft* (1908).

Edgar E. Hume, *Colonel Theodore O'Hara, Author of the Bivouac of the Dead* (1936).

Jeter A. Isely, *Horace Greeley and the Republican Party, 1853-1861* (1947).

Joseph Jackson, *Encyclopedia of Philadelphia*, 4 volumes (1931-1933).

Marquis James, *Andrew Jackson: Portrait of a President* (1937).

Marquis James, *The Raven: A Biography of Sam Houston* (1929).

J. Franklin Jameson (editor), "Correspondence of John C. Calhoun," *Annual Report of the American Historical Association for the Year 1899* (1900), II.

John S. Jenkins, *Lives of the Governors of the State of New York* (1852).

Allen Johnson and Dumas Malone (editors), *Dictionary of American Biography*, 20 volumes (1928-1936).

Christopher Johnson, "Smith Family of Calvert County," *Maryland Historical Magazine*, III, IV.

Gerald W. Johnson, *America's Silver Age: The Statecraft of Clay-Webster-Calhoun* (1939).

Journal of the Executive Proceedings of the Senate of the United States of America . . . , VIII (1887).

Journal of the Senate of the Commonwealth of Kentucky . . . (1849).

George W. Julian, *Political Recollections, 1840 to 1872* (1884).

Harnett T. Kane, *Deep Delta Country* (1944).

20 Kentucky Reports (4 T. B. Monroe).

34 Kentucky Reports (4 J. G. Dana).

Lillian A. Kibler, *Benjamin F. Perry: South Carolina Unionist* (1946).

Lucian L. Knight, *Reminiscences of Famous Georgians,* 2 volumes (1907-1908).

D. S. Lamb and others, *The History of the Medical Society of the District of Columbia, 1817-1909* (1909).

William R. Lawrence (editor), *Extracts from the Diary and Correspondence of the Late Amos Lawrence* (1855).

Lloyd Lewis, *Sherman: Fighting Prophet* (1932).

Usher F. Linder, *Reminiscences of the Early Bench and Bar of Illinois* (1879).

The Literary Digest, LXXXVI.

Local Laws of the State of Indiana Passed at the Thirty-second Session of the General Assembly (1848).

Samuel Longfellow (editor), *Life of Henry Wadsworth Longfellow with Extracts from His Journals and Correspondence,* 3 volumes (1891).

Thornton K. Lothrop, *William Henry Seward* (1899).

Louisville City Directory, 1838-39.

[Louisville] *City Directory for 1841.*

Caroline C. Lovell, *The Golden Isles of Georgia* (1939).

James D. Lynch, *The Bench and Bar of Mississippi* (1881).

Anna McAllister, *Ellen Ewing, Wife of General Sherman* (1936).

Alexander K. McClure, *Old Time Notes of Pennsylvania,* 2 volumes (1905).

Alexander K. McClure, *Our Presidents and How We Make Them* (1905).

George M. McConnel, *Presidential Campaigns from Washington to Roosevelt* (1908).

Robert McElroy, *Jefferson Davis, the Unreal and the Real,* 2 volumes (1937).

S. Somervell Mackall, *Early Days of Washington* (1934).

Alexander Mackay, *The Western World; or, Travels in the United States in 1846-47 . . . ,* 3 volumes (1849).

Andrew C. McLaughlin, *Lewis Cass* (1899).

Andrew C. McLaughlin and Albert B. Hart (editors), *Cyclopedia of American Government,* 3 volumes (1914).

John B. McMaster, *A History of the People of the United States . . . ,* 8 volumes (1883-1913).

Jesse Macy, *The Anti-Slavery Crusade: A Chronicle of the Gathering Storm* (1919).

The Magazine of History (New York), III.

John F. Maguire, *Father Mathew: A Biography* (1864).

William M. Malloy (compiler), "Treaties, Conventions, International Acts, Protocols and Agreements Between the United States of America and Other Powers, 1776-1909," *Senate Document 357,* Sixty-first Congress, Second Session.

[Mary Mann], *Life of Horace Mann* (1891).

Sir J. A. R. Marriott, *A History of Europe from 1815 to 1923* (1931).

Caroline C. Marsh, *Life and Letters of George Perkins Marsh* (1888).

Thomas P. Martin, "Cotton and Wheat in Anglo-American Trade and Politics, 1846-1852," *Journal of Southern History,* I.

Harriet Martineau, *Retrospect of Western Travel,* 2 volumes (1838).

Massachusetts Historical Society Proceedings, LX, LXII.

Dabney H. Maury, "Reminiscences of General [Richard] Taylor," *Appleton's Journal*, New Series, VI.

Bernard Mayo, *Henry Clay: Spokesman of the New West* (1937).

Hunter Miller (editor), *Treaties and Other International Acts of the United States of America*, 7 volumes (1931——).

Paul I. Miller (editor), "Lincoln and the Governorship of Oregon," *Mississippi Valley Historical Review*, XXIII.

Stephen F. Miller, *The Bench and Bar of Georgia* (1858).

George F. Milton, *The Eve of Conflict: Stephen A. Douglas and the Needless War* (1934).

Albert B. Moore, *History of Alabama and Her People*, 3 volumes (1928).

John B. Mordecai, *A Brief History of the Richmond, Fredericksburg and Potomac Railroad* (1940).

Dale L. Morgan, "The State of Deseret," *Utah Historical Quarterly*, VIII.

Samuel E. Morison and Henry S. Commager, *The Growth of the American Republic*, 2 volumes (1942).

Lloyd Morris, *The Rebellious Puritan: Portrait of Mr. Hawthorne* (1927).

Jennie C. Morton, "Governor Charles S. Morehead, Sketch of His Life," *Register of the Kentucky State Historical Society*, IV.

Henry R. Mueller, *The Whig Party in Pennsylvania* (1922).

David S. Muzzey, *The United States of America*, 2 volumes (1922-1924).

William S. Myers (editor), *The State Papers and Other Public Writings of Herbert Hoover*, 2 volumes (1934).

The National Cyclopaedia of American Biography, 35 volumes (1898-1949).

William Nelson, *Nelson's Biographical Cyclopedia of New Jersey*, 2 volumes (1913).

Allan Nevins (editor), *The Diary of John Quincy Adams, 1794-1845* (1928).

Allan Nevins (editor), *The Diary of Philip Hone, 1828-1851*, 2 volumes (1927). Quoted by permission of the publishers, Dodd, Mead & Company.

Allan Nevins, *Ordeal of the Union*, 2 volumes (1947).

Winfield S. Nevins, "Nathaniel Hawthorne's Removal from the Salem Custom House," *Historical Collections of the Essex Institute*, LIII.

New Orleans Annual and Commercial Register for 1846.

Roy F. Nichols, *Franklin Pierce: Young Hickory of the Granite Hills* (1931).

John G. Nicolay and John Hay (editors), *Complete Works of Abraham Lincoln*, 12 volumes (1905).

Niles' National Register (Baltimore and Philadelphia), LXX, LXXI, LXXIII, LXXIV, LXXV.

Inazo Nitobe, "American-Japanese Intercourse Prior to the Advent of Perry," *Annual Report of the American Historical Association for the Year 1911* (1913).

"Opinions of Attorneys General," Part II, 1838-1851, *House Executive Document 55*, Thirty-first Congress, Second Session.

Joseph H. Parks, "John Bell and the Compromise of 1850," *Journal of Southern History*, IX.

Joseph H. Parks, *John Bell of Tennessee* (1950).

Vernon L. Parrington, *Main Currents in American Thought,* 3 volumes (1927-1930).

Bliss Perry, *John Greenleaf Whittier: A Sketch of His Life . . . with Selected Poems* (1907).

Oran Perry (editor), *Indiana in the Mexican War* (1908).

Ulrich B. Phillips (editor), "The Correspondence of Robert Toombs, Alexander H. Stephens, and Howell Cobb," *Annual Report of the American Historical Association for the Year 1911* (1913), II.

Ulrich B. Phillips, *The Life of Robert Toombs* (1913).

Edward L. Pierce, *Memoir and Letters of Charles Sumner,* 4 volumes (1893-1894).

George R. Poage, *Henry Clay and the Whig Party* (1936).

Ben: Perley Poore, *Perley's Reminiscences of Sixty Years in the National Metropolis,* 2 volumes (1886).

Erwin H. Price, "The Election of 1848 in Ohio," *Ohio Archaeological and Historical Society Publications,* XXXVI.

Milo M. Quaife (editor), *The Diary of James K. Polk During His Presidency, 1845 to 1849,* 4 volumes (1910).

Allen F. Ragan, "John J. Crittenden, 1787-1863," *Filson Club History Quarterly,* XVIII.

William E. Railey, *History of Woodford County [Kentucky]* (1938).

Clayton Rand, *Men of Spine in Mississippi* (1940).

"Recollections of an Old Stager," *Harper's New Monthly Magazine,* XLVII.

Register of All Officers and Agents, Civil, Military, and Naval in the Service of the United States on the Thirtieth September, 1849 . . . (1849).

Register of All Officers and Agents . . . on the Thirtieth September, 1851 . . . (1851).

James F. Rhodes, *History of the United States from the Compromise of 1850,* 7 volumes (1893-1906).

Allen T. Rice (editor), *Reminiscences of Abraham Lincoln by Distinguished Men of His Time* (1886).

James D. Richardson (editor), *A Compilation of the Messages and Papers of the Presidents, 1789-1897,* 10 volumes (1899).

J. C. Rockwell, "The Kidnapping of the Late President," *The Green Bag* (Boston), 1902.

Joseph M. Rogers, *The True Henry Clay* (1905).

Theodore Roosevelt, *Thomas Hart Benton* (1899).

Dunbar Rowland (editor), *Jefferson Davis: Constitutionalist,* 10 volumes (1923).

Dunbar Rowland, "Political and Parliamentary Orators of Mississippi," *Mississippi Historical Society Publications,* IV.

Minnie M. Ruffin, "General Solomon Weathersbee Downs . . . Democratic Leader of North Louisiana, 1840-1854," *Louisiana Historical Quarterly,* XVII.

William H. Samson (editor), *Letters of Zachary Taylor from the Battlefields of the Mexican War* (1908).

Carl Sandburg, *Abraham Lincoln: The War Years,* 4 volumes (1939).

Katherine Scarborough, *Homes of the Cavaliers* (1930).

J. Salwyn Schapiro, *Modern and Contemporary European History* (1922).

J. Thomas Scharf, *History of Saint Louis City and County,* 2 volumes (1883).

Arthur M. Schlesinger, *Paths to the Present* (1949).

Arthur M. Schlesinger, Jr., *The Age of Jackson* (1945).

Carl Schurz, *Life of Henry Clay*, 2 volumes (1887).

Thomas B. Searight, *The Old Pike: A History of the National Road* (1894).

Senate Document 279, Sixty-first Congress, Second Session.

Senate Executive Document 1, 43, 57, Thirty-first Congress, First Session.

Senate Executive Document 12, Thirty-second Congress, Second Session.

Senate Executive Document 13, Thirty-third Congress, First Session.

Senate Miscellaneous Document 110, Thirty-second Congress, First Session.

Frank H. Severance (editor), "Millard Fillmore Papers," *Publications of the Buffalo Historical Society*, X, XI.

Frederick W. Seward, *Seward at Washington as Senator and Secretary of State . . . 1846-1861* (1891).

Henry T. Shanks, *The Secession Movement in Virginia, 1847-1861* (1934).

[William T. Sherman], *Memoirs of Gen. W. T. Sherman*, 2 volumes (1892).

Richard H. Shryock, *Georgia and the Union in 1850* (1926).

Esther Singleton, *The Story of the White House*, 2 volumes (1907).

St. George L. Sioussat, "Tennessee, the Compromise of 1850, and the Nashville Convention," *Mississippi Valley Historical Review*, II.

Susan D. Smedes, *Memorials of a Southern Planter* (1899).

Oliver H. Smith, *Early Indiana Trials and Sketches* (1858).

Theodore C. Smith, *The Liberty and Free Soil Parties in the Northwest* (1897).

William E. Smith, *Francis Preston Blair Family in Politics*, 2 volumes (1933).

Frank Soulé, John H. Gihon and James Nisbet, *The Annals of San Francisco* (1855).

Edward Stanwood, *A History of the Presidency from 1788 to 1897* (1898).

Bernard C. Steiner, "James Alfred Pearce," *Maryland Historical Magazine*, XVI-XIX.

Bernard C. Steiner, *Life of Reverdy Johnson* (1914).

Leslie Stephen and Sidney Lee (editors), *Dictionary of National Biography*, 66 volumes (1885-1901).

Alexander H. Stephens, *A Constitutional View of the Late War Between the States . . .* , 2 volumes (1868-1870).

Randall Stewart, *Nathaniel Hawthorne: A Biography* (1948).

Moorfield Storey, *Charles Sumner* (1900).

Lady Emmeline Stuart-Wortley, *Travels in the United States . . . during 1849 and 1850* (1851).

[Victoria Stuart-Wortley], *A Young Traveller's Journal of a Tour in North and South America during the Year 1850* (1852).

The Taylor Text-book, or Rough and Ready Reckoner (1848).

Texas State Journal, Third Legislature, Second Session, *Appendix*.

Raphael P. Thian (compiler), *Notes Illustrating the Military Geography of the United States, 1813-1880* (1881).

Stephen F. Tillman, *Tilghman-Tillman Family, 1225-1945* (1946).

Alice E. Trabue, *A Corner in Celebrities* (1923).

Gilbert A. Tracy (editor), *Uncollected Letters of Abraham Lincoln* (1917).

George F. Train, *My Life in Many States and in Foreign Lands* (1902).

Alice F. Tyler, *Freedom's Ferment: Phases of American Social History to 1860* (1944).

Lyon G. Tyler, *The Letters and Times of the Tylers,* 3 volumes (1884-1896).

The United States Magazine and Democratic Review, I.

Charles W. Upham, *Eulogy on the Life and Character of Zachary Taylor* (1850).

Chester S. Urban, "New Orleans and the Cuban Question during the Lopez Expeditions of 1849-1851: A Local Study in 'Manifest Destiny,'" *Louisiana Historical Quarterly,* XXII.

Richard W. Van Alstyne, *American Diplomacy in Action* (1947).

Richard W. Van Alstyne, "British Diplomacy and the Clayton-Bulwer Treaty, 1850-1860," *Journal of Modern History,* XI.

Richard W. Van Alstyne, "The Central American Policy of Lord Palmerston, 1846-1848," *Hispanic American Historical Review,* XVI.

Glyndon G. Van Deusen, *The Life of Henry Clay* (1937).

Glyndon G. Van Deusen, *Thurlow Weed: Wizard of the Lobby* (1947).

Rudolph Von Abele, *Alexander H. Stephens: A Biography* (1946).

Arthur Voss, "Backgrounds of Lowell's Satire in 'The Biglow Papers,'" *New England Quarterly,* XXIII.

J. D. Ward, "Sir Henry Bulwer and the United States Archives," *Cambridge Historical Journal,* III.

Richard L. Watson, Jr., "Thurlow Weed, Political Boss," *New York History,* XXII.

George Watterston, *New Guide to Washington* (1847-8).

Harriet A. Weed (editor), *Autobiography of Thurlow Weed* (1883).

Francis P. Weisenburger, *The Life of John McLean* (1937).

M. R. Werner, *Brigham Young* (1925).

Whig Almanac and United States Register for 1846; . . . for 1848; . . . for 1849; . . . for 1850; . . . for 1851.

Arnold Whitridge, *Men in Crisis: The Revolutions of 1848* (1949).

Henry Wilson, *History of the Rise and Fall of the Slave Power in America,* 3 volumes (1872-1877).

James G. Wilson and John Fiske (editors), *Appleton's Cyclopaedia of American Biography,* 6 volumes (1888-1889).

Rufus R. Wilson, *Washington, the Capital City,* 2 volumes (1901).

Charles M. Wiltse, *John C. Calhoun, Nationalist* (1944).

Robert C. Winthrop, Jr., *A Memoir of Robert C. Winthrop* (1897).

Henry A. Wise, *Seven Decades of the Union . . .* (1881).

Lila G. A. Woolfall, *Presiding Ladies of the White House* (1903).

William W. Woollen, *Biographical and Historical Sketches of Early Indiana* (1883).

William F. Worner, "Visit of Zachary Taylor to Lancaster . . . ," *Papers Read Before the Lancaster County Historical Society,* XXVII.

Stark Young, *So Red the Rose* (1934).

PERSONAL ACKNOWLEDGMENTS

It was Nathaniel Hawthorne who said that "the knowledge communicated by the historian and biographer is analogous to that which we acquire of a country by the map—minute, perhaps, and accurate . . . but cold and naked." In our own time Professor Henri Peyre of Yale has remarked that "a grave blow was dealt to our culture when, approximately half a century ago, history ceased to be a part of literature." Peyre added, however, that "biographers stepped in where historians feared to tread and their art has become an important province of literature."

The question might be asked whether, during the last forty years, *many* biographers and historians have not made a successful effort to write entertainingly and even artistically about men and events in the realm of actuality. Some, to be sure, stray away from the facts—so absorbed do they become in their artistic end product. But Nevins, Freeman, Sandburg, James and numerous other contemporary Americans have managed to adhere resolutely to the truth, while attaining their other goal of fine literature. To what extent *Zachary Taylor: Soldier in the White House* may be bracketed with the works of these latter-day masters, it is for the reader and critic to determine. But it is the author's firm belief, based on examples all about him, that both history and biography can be made readable without sacrifice of truth. And it is his hope that this book will win a place in the *literature* of Americana. Despite conditions of documentation, despite the need of returning again and again to the manuscript sources, accuracy need not be sacrificed on the altar of literary merit—nor should an acceptable style be contingent on slovenly or superficial research. Historians and biographers to be remembered are those who combine good writing with sound searching. To strain toward an artistic end, while giving a warp or twist to truth, would defeat the objectives of both those who seek to make history readable and those intent on making history *history*.

As in the case of *Zachary Taylor: Soldier of the Republic*, this volume is the product of many minds. Friends in every part of the land have contributed facts, suggestions, clues. My most fundamental indebtedness, of course, is to my beloved wife. The number of times Suzanne Bowerfind Hamilton gave up things she wanted to do because of my historical work is altogether beyond the counting. Though history is not her primary interest, her sacrifices and her thoughtfulness helped see this volume through to publication. And so I thank her from a full heart for every aspect of her assistance. I am grateful, too, to my father and mother—Dr. and Mrs. Allen Hamilton—for their interest, long sustained; to my aunts, the Misses Jessie and Agnes Hamilton, who shared my plans and dreams at the very start, and to my little daughter Susan who time and again has looked up from her toys to say: "Daddy, *when* will you finish that book?" Among nonkinsmen I first thank two magnificent old-timers who have guided and counseled me. Trist Wood of New Orleans, Taylor's great-grandson, helped beyond measure in the prewar years before a series of accidents and illnesses waylaid him. Otto A. Rothert—"Uncle Otto" of Louisville—is the most unselfish man I have ever known; I count myself especially fortunate that I am one of the many authors he has aided. This book *might* have been penned without the encouragement of the Messrs. Wood and Rothert; however, it would have been a poorer book—and the writer would have been denied two of his most meaningful friendships.

Professor Allan Nevins of Columbia University, Marquis James of Rye, New York, Professors John D. Barnhart and Donald F. Carmony of Indiana University, Dr. Hambleton Tapp and Professor J. Merton England of the University of Kentucky, Watt P. Marchman, director of the Hayes Memorial Library, Fremont, Ohio, and Professor R. Gerald McMurtry of Lincoln Memorial University, Harrogate, Tennessee, have read and criticized many of the chapters. Dr. Charles M. Wiltse of Washington interrupted his own work on John C. Calhoun to devote a solid week to a careful analysis of the entire manuscript except one chapter. John V. Roberts served as "cliché-raker," bringing his critical faculties to bear. His father, Frank Roberts of Fort Wayne, my old friend and colleague of the *Journal-Gazette,* offered valuable suggestions from time to time. I deeply appreciate the contributions of each one of these gentlemen, at the same time hastening to absolve them from blame for any errors which may remain. I wish to express my gratitude also to Alva J. McAndless, president of the Lincoln National Life Insurance Company, and to Dr. Louis A. Warren, director of the Lincoln National Life Foundation, for generously permitting me to do much of my writing in the Foundation library. Through their courtesy I have had access to one of the finest collections of books and pamphlets on the Civil War and ante-bellum periods; more than that, I have benefited from Doctor Warren's sympathetic understanding of numerous problems confronting a biographer. To Executive Secretary Henry Allen Moe and the trustees of the John Simon Guggenheim Memorial Foundation I am indebted for the award of a Guggenheim Fellowship. Recognition from such a source warms the cockles of a student's heart.

In my home state of Indiana no one has given more freely of time and service than Miss Caroline Dunn of the Indiana Historical Society, Miss Margaret Donnell and Mrs. Hazel W. Hopper of the Indiana State Library and Albert F. Diserens of the Fort Wayne Public Library. Other helpful Hoosiers include: Howard H. Peckham, director of the Indiana Historical Bureau; President David Laurance Chambers, Editors Harrison Platt and Rosemary York of The Bobbs-Merrill Company, Indianapolis; Librarian Rex M. Potterf, Allan McMahan, J. Clifford Milnor, Park D. Williams, Robert E. Thompson, Robert Smith, Frederick A. Schminke, Mrs. Karl F. Schmidt, Mrs. Lydia Nord, Miss Margaret Moellering, Dr. Paul L. Stier, Patrick W. Murray, Miss Muriel J. Norton, Mrs. Ethel Youse, Miss Mary J. Armstrong, Clayton E. Kilpatrick, John T. Thackeray and especially Miss Ann Studer—all now or formerly of Fort Wayne; Mrs. Alberta Morlock, Carmel, Indiana; Mrs. T. E. Stanfield, South Bend; Mrs. Harry Temple Watts, Vincennes; the late William A. Kunkel, Jr., Bluffton; Cornelius O'Brien, Lawrenceburg and Aurora; Harold F. Brigham, Miss Gayle Thornbrough, Miss Dorothy Riker, Miss Mary V. Gorgas, Harold J. Sander, Miss Lila Brady, Mrs. Carl W. Johnson, Harold J. Burton and Walter Lange, who assisted me in Indianapolis; Professor Emeritus W. O. Lynch and E. L. Craig of Bloomington, and Dr. Thomas P. Martin, now of Bloomington but for many years the assistant chief of the Division of Manuscripts, Library of Congress.

Across the Ohio River, in Kentucky (which I like to call "my other state"), not only Mr. Rothert but Miss Ludie J. Kinkead, Miss Evelyn R. Dale, Miss Mary Verhoeff, Judge Richard H. Hill, Colonel Lucien Beckner,

Miss Mabel C. Weaks, John Frederick Dorman III and the late R. C. Ballard Thruston have welcomed me often to the Filson Club, Louisville. Miss Alice E. Trabue, William Marshall Bullitt, Neville S. Bullitt, Dr. R. Alexander Bate and Miss Edna J. Grauman of Louisville also contributed to the project—as did Bayless E. Hardin and his staff of the Kentucky Historical Society, Frankfort; Miss Mabel C. Walker and the Reverend Robert Stuart Sanders, Versailles; Charles K. O'Connell, Frankfort; Mrs. Mary T. Moore and Gayle R. Carver, Bowling Green, and three kind friends who have passed away: Mrs. Jouett Taylor Cannon, Frankfort, Andrew M. Sea, Jr., Louisville, and the Reverend Lucien V. Rule, Goshen. In Lexington, Dr. Lawrence S. Thompson, director of the University of Kentucky Libraries, and his head archivist, Dr. Jacqueline Bull, did their very-good best for me. C. Frank Dunn and Virginia Hayes were likewise helpful. And when I think of my happy associations with Dr. Tapp, Colonel J. Winston Coleman, Jr., Professor Thomas D. Clark and William H. Townsend of Lexington, my cup of gratitude is full to overflowing. The delightful hours spent with "Uncle Otto" and these other choice Kentucky spirits, in Colonel Coleman's library at Winburn Farm, are among the most memorable of my life.

In Illinois, many friends pitched in. My Chicago headquarters continues to be the Abraham Lincoln Book Shop on East Chestnut Street—where Ralph Geoffrey Newman sets the standards for the bibliophiles. Dr. Paul M. Angle, Professor and Mrs. Donald W. Riddle, Roy E. Basler, J. Monaghan, Harry E. Pratt, Foreman M. Lebold, Franklin J. Meine, Dr. Charles L. Patton, C. N. Owen, Miss Winifred Ver Nooy, Miss Margaret A. Flint and Mr. and Mrs. Wright Howes also have shown me courtesies. In Ohio, I have been aided by Erwin C. Zepp and John O. Marsh of the Ohio State Museum, Columbus; by Virginius C. Hall and Mrs. Alice P. Hook of the Ohio Historical and Philosophical Society, Cincinnati; by Miss Gertrude Hassler of the Western Reserve Historical Society, Cleveland, and by Charles I. Ball, Cleveland. In Philadelphia, I derived great benefit from the William M. Meredith and other collections at the Historical Society of Pennsylvania; first, Dr. Julian P. Boyd (now of Princeton University) and, later, R. N. Williams II were patient beyond belief in answering my endless inquiries. My list of co-operative Pennsylvanians ranges from James S. Crutchfield of Pittsburgh, John W. Starr, Jr., of Millersburg, Earle R. Forrest of Washington, H. T. Fowler of Erie and James Rawle of Bryn Mawr, to Harold Donaldson Eberlein, James L. Hook, the Reverend Hugh J. Nolan and Lawrence M. C. Smith of Philadelphia.

One of the high spots of my research was my visit to the University of Rochester, where I worked on the Weed and Seward Papers, and where Professor Glyndon G. Van Deusen, John R. Russell and Miss Margaret Butterfield made me glad that I had come. New Yorkers helpful in various ways include: Philip L. Alger, Schenectady; Robert W. Bingham, Alexander Galt and Miss Alice Pickup, Buffalo; Robert Cantwell, Riverdale; Edna L. Jacobsen and Thomas Mittler, Albany; Thomas Robson Hay, Locust Valley; George N. Malpass, East Rochester; the late William H. Seward III, Auburn; H. Armour Smith, Yonkers; M. A. Willsey, Cooperstown; the late Rufus Rockwell Wilson, Elmira; John T. Winterich, Ossining, and Dorothy C. Barck, Mary A. Benjamin, Preston Davie, James H. Drake, Emily Driscoll, Thomas Ewing III, Henry N. Flynt, Rodman Gilder, Carl Haverlin, Miss Ethelwyn Manning, Frederick Hill Meserve, W. John Niven, Jr., Paul North Rice, Nathaniel E. Stein and Arthur Swann of New York City. Over in New Jersey I was aided by Elmer T. Hutchinson of Elizabeth, Mrs. M. H. Greene and Mrs. Henry Lindenkohl of Newark and Lawrence B. Mason of Cranford; in Maryland, by Mrs. George E. Albee, Laurel, Miss Eleanor S. Ewing, Landover, James W. Foster and Miss Eleanora V. Lynn, Baltimore, Dr. Reginald B. Henry, Annapolis, the late Gilbert W. Mead, Chestertown, Mrs. Frank W. Mish, Jr., and Miss Josephine Sweeny, Hagerstown, and Miss Lola M. Wood, Maddox, Saint Mary's County; in West Virginia, by Elizabeth J. Meek, Wheeling; and in Delaware by Miss Gertrude Brincklé and by the Honorable Clayton Douglass Buck, former governor and United States senator.

In Boston it was Stephen T. Riley, librarian of the Massachusetts Historical Society, who came to my rescue time and again. Dr. Clarence S. Brigham, director of the American Antiquarian Society, Worcester, did me worlds of good on my visit there. I am also indebted to Miss Charlotte D. Conover of the New Hampshire Historical Society, Concord; to Howard Corning of the Essex Institute, Salem, Massachusetts; to Gordon T. Banks of Goodspeed's, Boston; to Zoltán Haraszti and Ellen M. Oldham of the Boston Public Library; to Professor Arthur M. Schlesinger and his secretary, Elizabeth F. Hoxie, Harvard University; to Arthur Meserve Wiggin, Brookline; to Professor Randall Stewart of Brown University, Providence, Rhode Island; to John Marshall Holcombe, Jr., of Hartford, Connecticut, and to Norman Holmes Pearson of Yale.

Skipping back to the Midwest, I should be remiss were I not to stress the kindness of the late Dr. Randolph G. Adams and his associate, Colton Storm, of the William L. Clements Library, Ann Arbor, Michigan; Thomas F. Thiele of Willow Run Village; Karl W. Detzer of Leland; Forest H. Sweet of Battle Creek; F. B. Voegele of Muskegon Heights, and Milo Milton Quaife, Mrs. Elleine H. Stones, Thomas I. Starr, Frank B. Howard and Weldon Petz of Detroit. Mrs. George C. Hume and Ralph A. Miller of Chilton, Wisconsin, Miss Bertha L. Heilbron of Saint Paul, Minnesota, and Allyn K. Ford of Minneapolis graciously brought documents to my attention. On the West Coast, I was assisted by Professor Kenneth M. Stampp, George P. Hammond and Frank S. Brezee of the University of California, Berkeley; Professor Brainerd Dyer of the University of California, Los Angeles, who released his priority rights to quotations from Gideon Welles's unpublished diary; Professor Richard W. Van Alstyne of the University of Southern California, who read Chapters XVI and XXVIII; Dr. Louis B. Wright (now director of the Folger Shakespeare Library, Washington), Herbert C. Schulz, Leslie E. Bliss, Norma Cuthbert, Mary Isabel Fry and Phyllis Rigney—all of the Henry E. Huntington Library, San Marino; Mrs. Stanley Stillman, Jr., and Harry B. Smith of San Francisco; Dr. Herbert S. Thompson of Berkeley, and Miss Alice V. Carey, Mrs. Zelma B. Locker and Mrs. Isabella C. Anthony of the La Jolla Public Library.

In the Deep South, I was "proudly friended." The late Mrs. Betty Taylor Stauffer, granddaughter of Old Rough and Ready, entertained me in New Orleans on my twenty-fourth birthday. "Yes, I shall be glad to help you," this spirited gentlewoman said, "even though you are a damyankee!" She gave me all the material she had. And there, in her parlor, after relishing more than one man's quota of crêpes Suzettes, I sat surrounded by Taylor busts and portraits while examining Taylor manuscripts. The charming Mrs. Lewis Hardie carried on after her mother's death. Only last summer she and Walter Stauffer shipped all their Taylor Papers to Indiana for my final perusal. I am indebted not only to them but also to Professor Wendell H. Stephenson of Tulane, to Miss Marguerite D. Renshaw of the Howard-Tilton Memorial Library, to John Hall Jacobs of the New Orleans Public Library, to Harnett T. Kane, Edward D. Seghers, Mrs. Dorothy H. Le Doux, Arthur Nuhrah and George Raffalovitch of New Orleans; to Miss Minnie Ker Ringgold of Shreveport, Mrs. Emmette A. Tomb, Alexandria, Dr. G. M. G. Stafford, Baton Rouge, and V. L. Bedsole and Guy R. Lyle of Louisiana State University, Baton Rouge.

Director William D. McCain and Miss Charlotte Capers of the Mississippi Department of Archives and History, Jackson, have been in my corner from first to last. I have not forgotten the kindnesses of the late Judge Jeff Truly of Fayette, Mississippi, or of Mrs. Mary Magruder McGehee and Maxwell Bramlette of Woodville. In Alabama (where I lived a year and a half) my friends include Professor Joseph H. Parks of Birmingham-Southern College, Birmingham; Professor Clanton W. Williams of the University of Alabama, and Horace S. Moses of the Mobile Public Library. Other residents of Southern states who proved particularly helpful were: Mrs. John Trotwood Moore, for many years Tennessee's state librarian and archivist; Professor William C. Binkley of Vanderbilt University; Miss Bettye E. Bell, Nashville Public Library; Mrs. Lilla M. Hawes of the Georgia Historical Society, Savannah; W. W. De Renne, University of Georgia, Athens; Professor J. Harold Easterby and Miss Mary V. Powers of the College of Charleston, South Carolina; Mrs. Alberta Johnson, librarian of the Florida Historical Society, Saint Augustine; Professor Alfred Jackson Hanna of Rollins College, Winter Park, Florida; Professor William E. Baringer of the Florida State College for Women, Tallahassee; Professor William B. Hamilton of Duke University, Durham, North Carolina; Professors Fletcher M. Green and J. G. de Roulhac Hamilton of the University of North Carolina, Chapel Hill; Christopher Crittenden and D. L. Corbitt of the North Carolina Department of Archives and History, Raleigh, and Harry Z. Tucker of Stokesdale, North Carolina.

This volume, like its predecessor, has benefited from remarks made to me in 1935 by the late Mrs. Arabella Taylor Clarke, who not only was Uncle Zack's White House guest but sat on the knee of Henry Clay, later danced with the Prince of Wales, borrowed change from Mrs. Robert E. Lee and knew Abraham and Mary Lincoln. When I met Mrs. Clarke, she was ninety-seven. I tested her mind on various matters, to which I had the documented answers, and it was as clear as a wedding bell. My interview with her in Winchester proved a memorable part of my Virginia research. Thomas B. Gentry (an old Army friend) of the Virginia Military Institute, Lexington; Professor Bernard Mayo of the University of Virginia, Charlottesville, Miss Lucy Powell of Warrenton and especially Milton C. Russell of the Virginia State Library, Richmond, have also aided me in the Old Dominion.

One of the most pleasant experiences a devotee of Clio's can enjoy is to come into contact with Elmer Ellis, genial dean of the University of Missouri. I am grateful for his interest in this book, and I also thank Mrs. John Van Brunt, Kansas City, Missouri; Mrs. Vernon Mason, Independence; Mrs. Brenda R. Gieseker, Missouri Historical Society, Saint Louis, and William N. Chambers, Washington University, for all that they have done for me. Professor Walter Prescott Webb, H. Bailey Carroll and Maxine Smith of the Texas State Historical Association, Austin; Edwin Worthley of Sherman, Texas; Grant Foreman of Muskogee, Oklahoma; Carl White, Jr., of Tulsa;

Dale L. Morgan of Salt Lake City, Utah, and Arthur J. O. Anderson of the Museum of New Mexico, Santa Fe, have also made contributions—as have Max Beloff of Oxford, England, the Honorable Claude G. Bowers of Santiago, Chile, Seth C. H. Taylor of Montreal, Canada, and Stuart Z. T. Wood of the Royal Canadian Mounted Police—a direct descendant of Zachary Taylor—who escorted King George VI and Queen Elizabeth on their tour of the Dominion in 1939.

Finally and enthusiastically I thank my benefactors in Washington, D. C., where so many manuscripts and books have been made available. The entire staff of the Library of Congress, from Dr. Luther H. Evans down, contributed directly or indirectly to the making of this biography. David C. Mearns, Solon J. Buck, St. George L. Sioussat, C. Percy Powell, Miss Elizabeth G. McPherson, Hirst D. Milhollen, Milton Kaplan, Miss Virginia Daiker, Donald G. Patterson, Vincent L. Eaton and Donald C. Holmes all lent a hand. Over in the National Archives, Mrs. Julia B. Carroll, Miss Josephine Cobb, Almon T. Wright, E. G. Campbell, Elizabeth B. Drewry and the late Miss Edna Vosper encouraged the author and provided him with records.

Among other helpful Washingtonians were Mrs. Ethel F. Armitage, David Rankin Barbee, the Reverend Lawrence C. Gorman, S. J., Robert Selph Henry, Roscoe R. Hill, Mrs. James T. Kerr, the late State Department Counselor R. Walton Moore, John Clagett Proctor, the late Professor Richard J. Purcell, the Reverend William C. Repetti, S. J., the Misses Clara and Rose Stutz, the late Colonel John R. M. Taylor and Colonel Stephen F. Tillman. Most helpful of them all was Miss Omo E. Greener of Washington and Alexandria, to whom the author has felt free to turn for all manner of verification.

In the long ago I thought of devoting part of this space to a summing-up of the more significant discoveries made in the course of my research. Some of these discoveries, such as the authorship of the two Allison letters, will at once be recognized as important by specialists in the period. Others—like Webster's lack of success in achieving his objective on the Seventh of March—may seem more surprising to the general reader than to scholars familiar with Hodder's monograph, which I have independently carried on to its logical conclusion. However, it at length seemed wise not to dwell here on the differences between that part of the traditional story which (under scrutiny) I accept, and those major corrections and changes which long-overlooked documents warrant. In the text I have sought to reweave old threads of truth with new threads of truth—discarding old patterns and creating a new one. With artistry as well as accuracy in mind, it seemed better to produce an acceptable narrative than to stop periodically and exclaim: "Harken ye, brethren! Behold the wonders of this new contribution or that!" At this point, too, I have enough confidence in scholarly Americans to feel that they will understand what has been done—without having it spelled out over and over. So, saying that, I present this volume to readers who, I trust, will share my enjoyment of a colorful, historic drama—and of a leading actor in it.

H. H.

Fort Wayne, Indiana,
March 31, 1951.

ADDITIONAL ACKNOWLEDGMENTS

Grateful acknowledgment is made to the following publishers and individuals for permission to reprint material of which they are the authorized publishers or owners, as follows:

To the American Historical Association: for quotations from *The Whig Party in the South* by A. C. Cole (1913).

To Appleton-Century-Crofts, Inc.: for quotations from *As I Remember* by Marian Gouverneur (1911).

To Dodd, Mead and Company: for quotations from *The Diary of Philip Hone* edited by Allan Nevins (1927).

To Doubleday & Company, Inc.: for quotations from *Reminiscences of Alexander H. Stephens* edited by Myrta L. Avery (1910).

To Claude M. Fuess: for a quotation from *Daniel Webster* by Claude M. Fuess (Little, Brown & Company, 1930).

To Harcourt, Brace and Company, Inc.: for quotations from *The Rebellious Puritan: Portrait of Mr. Hawthorne* by Lloyd Morris (1927) and from *Brigham Young* by M. R. Werner (1925).

To Harper & Brothers: for quotations from *Our Presidents and How We Make Them* by Alexander K. McClure (1905) and *America's Silver Age* by Gerald W. Johnson (1939).

To Harvard University Press: for quotations from *The Liberty and Free Soil Parties in the Northwest* by Theodore C. Smith (1897).

To the Henry E. Huntington Library: for excerpts from three letters: Thurlow Weed to George Harrington, June 25, 1850; Hannibal Hamlin to an unknown recipient, July 19, 1850; and Zachary Taylor to Edward Kent, July 27, 1848.

To Houghton Mifflin Company: for quotations from *Uncollected Letters of Abraham Lincoln* edited by Gilbert L. Tracy (1917); *Thomas Hart Benton* by Theodore Roosevelt (1899); *John Greenleaf Whittier* by Bliss Perry (1907); *The Eve of Conflict* by George F. Milton (1934); *Lewis Cass* by Andrew C. McLaughlin (1899); *Abraham Lincoln, 1809-1858* by Albert J. Beveridge (1928).

To the Mississippi Department of Archives and History: for quotations from *Jefferson Davis: Constitutionalist* by Dunbar Rowland (1923).

To Oxford University Press, Inc.: for quotations from *The Growth of the American Republic* by Samuel E. Morison and Henry S. Commager (1942).

To Princeton University Press: for quotations from *The Lopez Expeditions to Cuba* by Robert G. Caldwell (1915).

To Charles Scribner's Sons: for brief quotations from *Ordeal of the Union* by Allan Nevins (1947); *Autobiography of Seventy Years* by George F. Hoar (1903) and *Decisive Battles* by J. F. C. Fuller (1940).

To Stanford University Press: for quotations from *American Diplomacy in Action* by Richard W. Van Alstyne (1947).

INDEX

Abadie, Juan, 187.
Abell, D. H., 321, 333.
Adams, Abigail, 221.
Adams, C. F., 111, 125, 233, 384.
Adams, John Quincy, 52, 55, 57, 59, 162, 204.
Adams, Mrs. John Quincy, 223, 261.
Alabama, Whig legislators, 82; in 1848 election, 98, 99, 101, 127, 132, 133; mentioned, 63, 88, 90, 93, 100, 107, 108, 229, 230.
Albany, N. Y., 115, 128, 226, 227.
Albany *Atlas,* 323.
Albany *Evening Journal,* 61, 68, 125, 298, 322, 421.
Allen, Charles, 88, 95, 96, 246, 249.
Allen, William, 53.
Allison, Emily Taylor, 76.
Allison, John S., 28, 33, 34, 76, 77, 79, 355. *See also* Allison letters.
Allison, Richard T. (Dick), 208.
Allison letters, 75-83, 85, 86, 91, 118, 121-125, 131, 170.
American Board of Commissioners for Foreign Missions, 241.
American River, 176.
American Sunday School Union, 241.
Anderson, Godfrey T., 314.
Anderson, Samuel J., 207.
Anti-Catholicism, 15, 59, 111.
Anti-Masons, 15, 59, 394.
Antislavery reforms, 15-18, 32, 232, 262, 263.
Apache Indians, 185, 186.
Appleton, Nathan, 112.
Aquia Creek, 294, 297.
Archer, William S., 88, 105, 152.
Arkansas, 27, 82, 87, 91, 93, 100, 108, 127, 132, 133, 245, 372.
Arlington, 218, 223.
Ashmun, George, 65, 88, 136, 139, 167, 243, 247, 249, 250, 251, 314.
Atchison, David R., 153-154, 263.
Atlantic and Pacific Ship-Canal Company, 192, 193, 195, 198.
Attorney General, selection, 137, 138, 139, 151, 152.
Atwater, Caleb, 234.
Auburn, N. Y., 62.
Augusta, Ga., 19, 347.
Augusta *Chronicle,* 395.

Austin, Tex., 180, 181.
Austria, 187, 198-199, 371.

Badger, George E., 285, 319.
Bailey, Gamaliel, 16, 232, 259, 311, 416.
Baird, Spruce M., 181, 374.
Baker, Edward D., 137, 297, 411.
Baker family, 223.
Baldwin, Roger S., 114, 235, 285, 286.
Ballard, Henry E., 397.
Baltimore, Md., Democratic National Convention at, 87, 97, 98, 120; Taylor visits, 238-240, 241; mentioned, 147, 165, 168, 176, 224, 227, 234.
Baltimore, the, 294, 297.
Baltimore *American,* 298.
Baltimore & Susquehanna Railroad, 400.
Baltimore *Patriot,* 166, 343.
Baltimore *Sun,* 216, 239, 340.
Bancroft, George, 15, 69, 98, 194, 195, 196, 357.
Bancroft, Hubert Howe, 179.
Bank of Louisville, 34, 398, 399.
Baptists, 303.
Barbour family, 218.
Barnburner Democrats, 17, 98, 113, 120, 133, 233.
Barnum's City Hotel, Baltimore, 238.
Barringer, Daniel M., 200, 208, 370.
Bates, Edward, 401, 402.
Baton Rouge, La., Taylor cottage at, 25, 28-29, 144; mentioned, 20, 21, 24, 27, 32, 37, 51, 77, 78, 82, 117, 127, 136, 141, 143.
"Battle of the Chalk-Backs," 83-85.
Bay Islands, 365-366, 367.
Bayly, Thomas H., 249, 250.
Bay State, the, 226-227.
Beall, Benjamin L., 181-182.
Beard, Charles, 405.
Beard, Mary, 405.
Beaver, Pa., 225.
Bebb, William, 96, 110.
Bedford, Pa., 225.
Belgium, 206.
Belize, 193, 365, 367.
Bell, John, patronage, 381; and illness, 388; on extension, 391; mentioned, 77, 88, 94, 105, 150, 152, 205, 285, 326, 328, 329, 331, 334, 377.
Bell, Mrs. John, 150, 392.